Microsoft® Official Academic Course

Designing and Implementing a Server Infrastructure (70-413)

Patrick Regan

Garrett Stevens

WILEY

Credits

VP & PUBLISHER	Don Fowley
EXECUTIVE EDITOR	John Kane
EXECUTIVE MARKETING MANAGER	Chris Ruel
MICROSOFT PRODUCT MANAGER	Natasha Chornesky of Microsoft Learning
EDITORIAL PROGRAM ASSISTANT	Jessy Lentz
TECHNICAL EDITOR	Brian Svidergol
ASSOCIATE MARKETING MANAGER	Debbie Martin
SENIOR PRODUCTION & MANUFACTURING MANAGER	Janis Soo
PRODUCTION EDITOR	Joyce Poh
CREATIVE DIRECTOR	Harry Nolan
COVER DESIGNER	Georgina Smith
SENIOR PRODUCT DESIGNER	Thomas Kulesa
CONTENT EDITOR	Wendy Ashenberg

This book was set in Garamond by Aptara, Inc.

ISBN 978-1-118-78918-6

Printed in the United States of America

10 9 8 7 6 5 4 3 2 1

www.wiley.com/college/microsoft *or*
call the MOAC Toll-Free Number: 1+(888) 764-7001 (U.S. & Canada only)

Foreword from the Publisher

Wiley's publishing vision for the Microsoft Official Academic Course series is to provide students and instructors with the skills and knowledge they need to use Microsoft technology effectively in all aspects of their personal and professional lives. Quality instruction is required to help both educators and students get the most from Microsoft's software tools and to become more productive. Thus, our mission is to make our instructional programs trusted educational companions for life.

To accomplish this mission, Wiley and Microsoft have partnered to develop the highest-quality educational programs for information workers, IT professionals, and developers. Materials created by this partnership carry the brand name "Microsoft Official Academic Course," assuring instructors and students alike that the content of these textbooks is fully endorsed by Microsoft, and that they provide the highest-quality information and instruction on Microsoft products. The Microsoft Official Academic Course textbooks are "Official" in still one more way—they are the officially sanctioned courseware for Microsoft IT Academy members.

The Microsoft Official Academic Course series focuses on *workforce development*. These programs are aimed at those students seeking to enter the workforce, change jobs, or embark on new careers as information workers, IT professionals, and developers. Microsoft Official Academic Course programs address their needs by emphasizing authentic workplace scenarios with an abundance of projects, exercises, cases, and assessments.

The Microsoft Official Academic Courses are mapped to Microsoft's extensive research and job-task analysis, the same research and analysis used to create the Microsoft Certified Solutions Expert (MCSE) exam. The textbooks focus on real skills for real jobs. As students work through the projects and exercises in the textbooks and labs, they enhance their level of knowledge and their ability to apply the latest Microsoft technology to everyday tasks. These students also gain resume-building credentials that can assist them in finding a job, keeping their current job, or in furthering their education.

The concept of life-long learning is today an utmost necessity. Job roles, and even whole job categories, are changing so quickly that none of us can stay competitive and productive without continuously updating our skills and capabilities. The Microsoft Official Academic Course offerings, and their focus on Microsoft certification exam preparation, provide a means for people to acquire and effectively update their skills and knowledge. Wiley supports students in this endeavor through the development and distribution of these courses as Microsoft's official academic publisher.

Today educational publishing requires attention to providing quality print and robust electronic content. By integrating Microsoft Official Academic Course products, MOAC Labs Online, and Microsoft certifications, we are better able to deliver efficient learning solutions for students and teachers alike.

Joseph Heider

General Manager and Senior Vice President

Preface

Welcome to the Microsoft Official Academic Course (MOAC) program for becoming a Microsoft Certified Solutions Expert for Windows Server 2012. MOAC represents the collaboration between Microsoft Learning and John Wiley & Sons, Inc. Microsoft and Wiley teamed up to produce a series of textbooks that deliver compelling and innovative teaching solutions to instructors and superior learning experiences for students. Infused and informed by in-depth knowledge from the creators of Windows Server 2012, and crafted by a publisher known worldwide for the pedagogical quality of its products, these textbooks maximize skills transfer in minimum time. Students are challenged to reach their potential by using their new technical skills as highly productive members of the workforce.

Because this knowledgebase comes directly from Microsoft, architect of Windows Server 2012 and creator of the Microsoft Certified Solutions Associate exams, you are sure to receive the topical coverage that is most relevant to students' personal and professional success. Microsoft's direct participation not only assures you that MOAC textbook content is accurate and current; it also means that students will receive the best instruction possible to enable their success on certification exams and in the workplace.

■ The Microsoft Official Academic Course Program

The Microsoft Official Academic Course series is a complete program for instructors and institutions to prepare and deliver great courses on Microsoft software technologies. With MOAC, we recognize that because of the rapid pace of change in the technology and curriculum developed by Microsoft, there is an ongoing set of needs beyond classroom instruction tools for an instructor to be ready to teach the course. The MOAC program endeavors to provide solutions for all these needs in a systematic manner in order to ensure a successful and rewarding course experience for both instructor and student—including technical and curriculum training for instructor readiness with new software releases; the software itself for student use at home for building hands-on skills, assessment, and validation of skill development; and a great set of tools for delivering instruction in the classroom and lab. All are important to the smooth delivery of an interesting course on Microsoft software, and all are provided with the MOAC program. We think about the model below as a gauge for ensuring that we completely support you in your goal of teaching a great course. As you evaluate your instructional materials options, you may wish to use the model for comparison purposes with available products.

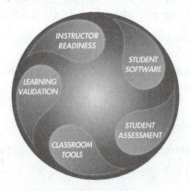

www.wiley.com/college/microsoft *or*
call the MOAC Toll-Free Number: 1+(888) 764-7001 (U.S. & Canada only)

■ Textbook Organization

This textbook is organized in twenty lessons, with each lesson corresponding to a particular exam objective for the 70-413 Designing and Implementing a Server Infrastructure exam. This MOAC textbook covers all the learning objectives for the 70-413 certification exam, which is the first of two exams needed in order to obtain a Microsoft Certified Solutions Expert (MCSE) certification. The exam objectives are highlighted throughout the textbook.

■ Pedagogical Features

Many pedagogical features have been developed specifically for Microsoft Official Academic Course programs.

Presenting the extensive procedural information and technical concepts woven throughout the textbook raises challenges for the student and instructor alike. The Illustrated Book Tour that follows provides a guide to the rich features contributing to Microsoft Official Academic Course program's pedagogical plan. Following is a list of key features in each lesson designed to prepare students for success on the certification exams and in the workplace:

- Each lesson begins with an overview of the skills covered in the lesson. More than a standard list of learning objectives, the overview correlates skills to the certification exam objective.

- Illustrations: Screen images provide visual feedback as students work through the exercises. The images reinforce key concepts, provide visual clues about the steps, and allow students to check their progress.

- Key Terms: Important technical vocabulary is listed at the beginning of the lesson. When these terms are used later in the lesson, they appear in bold italic type and are defined.

- Engaging point-of-use reader aids, located throughout the lessons, tell students why this topic is relevant (*The Bottom Line*), provide students with helpful hints (*Take Note*), or show cross-references to where content is covered in greater detail (*X Ref*). Reader aids also provide additional relevant or background information that adds value to the lesson.

- Certification Ready features throughout the text signal students where a specific certification objective is covered. They provide students with a chance to check their understanding of that particular exam objective and, if necessary, review the section of the lesson where it is covered.

- Using Windows PowerShell: *Windows PowerShell* is a Windows command-line shell that can be utilized with many Windows Server 2012 functions. The Using Windows PowerShell sidebar provides Windows PowerShell-based alternatives to graphical user interface (GUI) functions or procedures. These sidebars begin with a brief description of what the Windows PowerShell commands can do, and they contain any parameters needed to perform the task at hand. When needed, explanations are provided for the functions of individual parameters.

- Knowledge Assessments provide lesson-ending activities that test students' comprehension and retention of the material taught, presented using some of the question types that they'll see on the certification exam.

- An important supplement to this textbook is the accompanying lab work. Labs are available via a Lab Manual, and also by MOAC Labs Online. MOAC Labs Online provides students with the ability to work on the actual software simply by connecting through their Internet Explorer web browser. Either way, the labs use real-world scenarios to help students learn workplace skills associated with designing and implementing a Windows Server 2012 infrastructure in an enterprise environment.

▪ Lesson Features

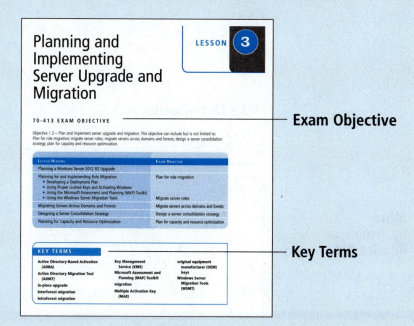

Exam Objective

Key Terms

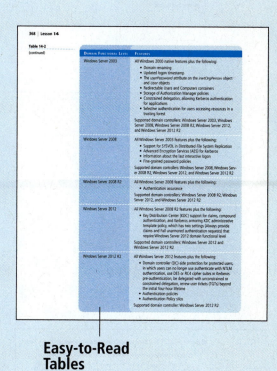

Easy-to-Read Tables

Bottom Line Reader Aid

Certification Ready Alert

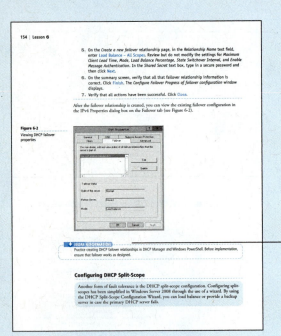

More Information Reader Aid

Take Note Reader Aid

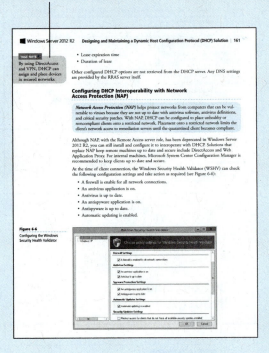

Warning Reader Aid

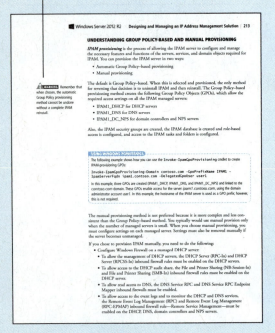

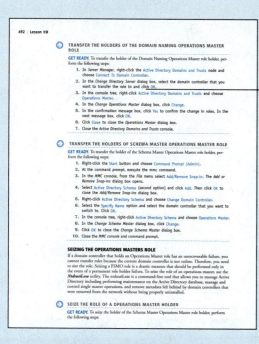

Step-by-Step Exercises

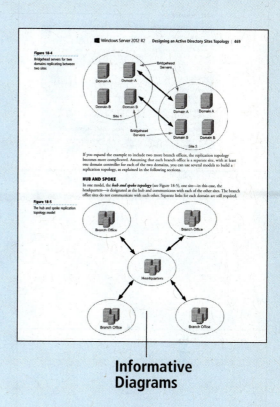

Informative Diagrams

Screen Images

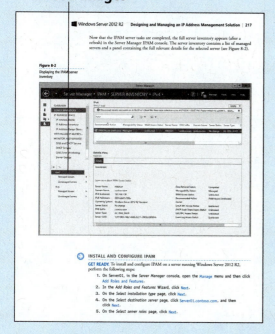

Windows Server 2012 R2   Designing and Managing an IP Address Management Solution | 227

6. On the *Manufacturer and Model* page, in the *Manufacturer* list, click Microsoft. In the *Model* list, click Microsoft Windows Server IP Address Management. Then click Next.

7. On the *Credentials* page, click Browse. In the *Select a Run As Account* dialog box, specify the service account. If the account is not created, click Create Run As Account to create a new Run As account. Click Next.

8. On the *Connection String* page, in the *Connection string* text box, type the fully qualified domain name (FQDN) of the IPAM server, and then click Next.

9. On the *Provider* page, in the *Configuration provider* list, select Microsoft IP Address Management Provider, and then click Test to run basic validation tests with the provider. If tests indicate that the provider works as expected with the IPAM server, click Next.

10. On the *Host Group* page, select one or more host groups for which you want integration between the IPAM server and the VMM server. Click Next.

11. On the *Summary* page, review and confirm the settings, and then click Finish.

12. Confirm that the IPAM server is listed under *Network Services*. Whenever you want to send or receive the latest settings to and from the IPAM server, you can right-click the listing for the IPAM server and then click Refresh.

SKILL SUMMARY ———————————————— **Skill Summary**

IN THIS LESSON YOU LEARNED:

- IP Address Management (IPAM), a feature within Windows Server 2012 and Windows Server 2012 R2, is used to plan, manage, track, and audit IP addresses.

- IPAM provisioning allows the IPAM server to configure and manage the necessary features and functions of the servers, services, and domain objects required for IPAM.

- Windows Server IPAM can manage only one Active Directory forest. You can deploy IPAM into one of three topologies: Centralized, Distributed, and Hybrid.

- Within IP address management are several sets of tasks that might require separate staff to carry them out. For this reason, IPAM relies on RBAC to provide the necessary delegate administrative features.

- After installing the IPAM feature and configuring the provisioning and discovery, you can choose to migrate all the IP address space data into the IPAM database.

- IPAM can monitor DHCP and DNS servers from any physical location in the organization, as well as simultaneously manage multiple DHCP servers or scopes that exist among multiple DHCP servers.

- You can integrate IPAM and Virtual Machine Manager (VMM) so that IP address settings associated with the logical networks and the virtual machine networks are stored in the IPAM server. You can then use the IPAM server to monitor the usage of VM networks that have been configured or changed in VMM.

228 | Lesson 8

■ Knowledge Assessment ———————————————— **Knowledge Assessment**

Multiple Choice

1. Which of the following GPOs is not created when you provision IPAM by using the automatic Group Policy method?
   a. IPAM1_DHCP
   b. IPAM1_DNS
   c. IPAM1_NPS
   d. IPAM1_DC_NPS

2. How many DNS servers can be managed from a single IPAM server?
   a. 25
   b. 500
   c. 250
   d. 50

3. How much RAM is required to install an IPAM server?
   a. 1 GB
   b. 2 GB
   c. 4 GB
   d. 8 GB

4. How many DHCP scopes can a single IPAM server support?
   a. 150
   b. 500
   c. 2,000
   d. 6,000

5. You are an administrator for a large organization. Which IPAM topology would you use if you deploy an IPAM to every site?
   a. Centralized
   b. Distributed
   c. Hybrid
   d. Isolated

6. You have IPAM loaded on a server running Windows Server 2012. Because the IPAM database has grown larger then you expected, you decided to migrate the database to a centralized SQL server. What should you do?
   a. Upgrade the server to Windows Server 2012 R2
   b. Export the database to a backup file, and import the database in the dedicated SQL server
   c. Run the Migrate utility to move the database to the SQL server
   d. Rerun the IPAM provisioning program

7. Which IPAM security group allows access to IP address tracking information but not full administration of an IPAM server? (Choose two answers)
   a. IPAM Audit administrators
   b. IPAM ASM Administrators
   c. IPAM Users
   d. IPAM Administrators

230 | Lesson 8

Matching and Identification

1. Identify which of the following are IPAM server tasks.
   _____ a) AuditTracking
   _____ b) IPAM discovery
   _____ c) DNSDataCollection
   _____ d) ServerConfiguration
   _____ e) GPOCollection
   _____ f) Audit
   _____ g) DHCPcpDataCollection
   _____ h) ForestCollection
   _____ i) ServerAvailability
   _____ j) EFS recovery
   _____ k) AddressExpiry

Build a List

1. Identify the correct order in which IPAM post configuration tasks are carried out. Not all steps will be used.
   _____ Select or add servers to manage.
   _____ Start Forest Discovery.
   _____ Provision the IPAM server.
   _____ Template.
   _____ Configure Server Discovery.
   _____ Start Server Discovery.
   _____ AD Discovery.
   _____ Connect to IPAM server.
   _____ Retrieve data from managed servers.

2. Identify in order the steps in which IP address management is carried out. Not all steps will be used.
   _____ Create IP addresses (static).
   _____ Create DHCP scopes.
   _____ Create IP address blocks.
   _____ Create DNS zones.
   _____ Collect all IP data from servers.
   _____ Create IP address ranges.

■ Business Case Scenarios ———————————————— **Business Case Scenarios**

Scenario 8-1: Planning IPAM Deployment

You are an administrator for Contoso Corporation. Contoso has a forest root domain called contoso.com with subdomains in three trees: Eu.Contoso.com, US.contoso.com, and adarium.com. The CTO has asked you to recommend an IPAM deployment option but wants each domain administrator to have full control of the infrastructure in his or her own domain. What do you recommend?

www.wiley.com/college/microsoft *or*
call the MOAC Toll-Free Number: 1+(888) 764-7001 (U.S. & Canada only)

Conventions and Features Used in This Book

This book uses particular fonts, symbols, and heading conventions to highlight important information or to call your attention to special steps. For more information about the features in each lesson, refer to the Illustrated Book Tour section.

CONVENTION	MEANING
↓ THE BOTTOM LINE	This feature provides a brief summary of the material to be covered in the section that follows.
CERTIFICATION READY	This feature signals the point in the text where a specific certification objective is covered. It provides you with a chance to check your understanding of that particular exam objective and, if necessary, review the section of the lesson where it is covered.
TAKE NOTE* ✚ MORE INFORMATION	Reader aids appear in shaded boxes found in your text. *Take Note* and *More Information* provide helpful hints related to particular tasks or topics.
USING WINDOWS POWERSHELL	The Using Windows PowerShell sidebar provides Windows PowerShell-based alternatives to graphical user interface (GUI) functions or procedures.
⚠ WARNING	*Warning* points out instances when error or misuse could cause damage to the computer or network.
X REF	These *X Ref* notes provide pointers to information discussed elsewhere in the textbook or describe interesting features of Windows Server that are not directly addressed in the current topic or exercise.
A *shared printer* can be used by many individuals on a network.	Key terms appear in bold italic.
cd\windows\system32\ ServerMigrationTools	Commands that are to be typed are shown in a special font.
Click Install Now.	Any button on the screen you are supposed to click on or select will appear in blue.

Instructor Support Program

The Microsoft Official Academic Course programs are accompanied by a rich array of resources that incorporate the extensive textbook visuals to form a pedagogically cohesive package. These resources provide all the materials instructors need to deploy and deliver their courses. Resource information available at www.wiley.com/college/microsoft includes:

- **DreamSpark Premium** is designed to provide the easiest and most inexpensive developer tools, products, and technologies available to faculty and students in labs, classrooms, and on student PCs. A free three-year membership is available to qualified MOAC adopters.

  Note: Windows Server 2012 R2 can be downloaded from DreamSpark Premium for use in this course.

  Instructor's Guide. The Instructor's Guide contains solutions to all the textbook exercises as well as chapter summaries and lecture notes. The Instructor's Guide and Syllabi for various term lengths are available from the Instructor's Book Companion site.

- **Test Bank.** The Test Bank contains hundreds of questions organized by lesson in multiple-choice, best answer, build list, and essay formats and is available to download from the Instructor's Book Companion site. A complete answer key is provided.

- **Lecture Slides.** A complete set of PowerPoint lecture slides is available on the Instructor's Book Companion site to enhance classroom presentations. Tailored to the text's topical coverage, these presentations are designed to convey key Windows Server 2012 concepts addressed in the text.

- **Available Textbook Figures.** All figures from the text are on the Instructor's Book Companion site. By using these visuals in class discussions, you can help focus students' attention on key elements of Windows Server and help them understand how to use it effectively in the workplace.

- **MOAC Labs Online.** MOAC Labs Online is a cloud-based environment that enables students to conduct exercises using real Microsoft products. These are not simulations but instead are live virtual machines where faculty and students can perform any activities they would on a local virtual machine. MOAC Labs Online relieves the need for local setup, configuration, and most troubleshooting tasks. This represents an opportunity to lower costs, eliminate the hassle of lab setup, and support and improve student access and portability. Contact your Wiley rep about including MOAC Labs Online with your course offering.

- **Lab Answer Keys.** Answer keys for review questions found in the lab manuals and MOAC Labs Online are available on the Instructor's Book Companion site.

- **Lab Worksheets.** The review questions found in the lab manuals and MOAC Labs Online are gathered in Microsoft Word documents for students to use. These are available on the Instructor's Book Companion site.

- **Sharing with Fellow Faculty Members.** When it comes to improving the classroom experience, there is no better source of ideas and inspiration than your colleagues teaching the same material. The Wiley Faculty Network connects teachers with technology, facilitates the exchange of best practices, and helps to enhance instructional efficiency and effectiveness. Faculty Network activities include technology training and tutorials, virtual seminars, peer-to-peer exchanges of experiences and ideas, personal consulting, and sharing of resources. For details visit www.WhereFacultyConnect.com.

Wiley Faculty Network

www.wiley.com/college/microsoft *or*

DREAMSPARK PREMIUM—FREE 3-YEAR MEMBERSHIP AVAILABLE TO QUALIFIED ADOPTERS!

DreamSpark Premium is designed to provide the easiest and most inexpensive way for schools to make the latest Microsoft developer tools, products, and technologies available in labs, classrooms, and on student PCs. DreamSpark Premium is an annual membership program for departments teaching Science, Technology, Engineering, and Mathematics (STEM) courses. The membership provides a complete solution to keep academic labs, faculty, and students on the leading edge of technology.

Software available through the DreamSpark Premium program is provided at no charge to adopting departments through the Wiley and Microsoft publishing partnership.

Contact your Wiley rep for details.

For more information about the DreamSpark Premium program, go to Microsoft's DreamSpark website.

Note: Windows Server 2012 R2 can be downloaded from DreamSpark Premium for use by students in this course.

▪ Important Web Addresses and Phone Numbers

To locate the Wiley Higher Education Rep in your area, go to http://www.wiley.com/college and click on the "*Contact Us*" link at the top of the page, or call the MOAC Toll Free Number: 1 + (888) 764-7001 (U.S. & Canada only).

To learn more about becoming a Microsoft Certified Solutions Associate and exam availability, visit Microsoft's Training & Certification website.

Student Support Program

Book Companion Website (www.wiley.com/college/microsoft)

The students' book companion site for the MOAC series includes any resources, exercise files, and web links that will be used in conjunction with this course.

Wiley E-Text: Powered by VitalSource

Wiley E-Texts: Powered by VitalSource, are innovative, electronic versions of printed textbooks. Students can buy Wiley E-Texts for around 50% off the U.S. price of the printed text and get the added value of permanence and portability. Wiley E-Texts provide students with numerous additional benefits that are not available with other e-text solutions.

Wiley E-Texts are NOT subscriptions; students download the Wiley E-Text to their computer desktops. Students own the content they buy to keep for as long as they want. Once a Wiley E-Text is downloaded to the computer desktop, students have instant access to all of the content without being online. Students can also print the sections they prefer to read in hard copy. Students also have access to fully integrated resources within their Wiley E-Text. From highlighting their e-text to taking and sharing notes, students can easily personalize their Wiley E-Text as they are reading or following along in class.

Microsoft Windows Server Software

Windows Server 2012 R2 software is available through a DreamSpark student membership. DreamSpark is a Microsoft program that provides students with free access to Microsoft software for learning, teaching, and research purposes. Students can download full versions of Windows Server 2012 R2 and other types of software at no cost by visiting Microsoft's DreamSpark website.

■ Microsoft Certification

Microsoft Certification has many benefits and enables you to keep your skills relevant, applicable, and competitive. In addition, Microsoft Certification is an industry standard that is recognized worldwide—which helps open doors to potential job opportunities. After you earn your Microsoft Certification, you have access to a number of benefits, which can be found on the Microsoft Certified Professional member site.

Microsoft Learning has reinvented the Microsoft Certification Program by building cloud-related skills validation into the industry's most recognized certification program. Microsoft Certified Solutions Expert (MCSE) and Microsoft Certified Solutions Developer (MCSD) are Microsoft's flagship certifications for professionals who want to lead their IT organization's journey to the cloud. These certifications recognize IT professionals with broad and deep skill sets across Microsoft solutions. The Microsoft Certified Solutions Associate (MCSA) is the certification for aspiring IT professionals and is also the prerequisite certification necessary to earn an MCSE. These certifications integrate cloud-related and on-premise skills validation in order to support organizations and recognize individuals who have the skills required to be productive using Microsoft technologies.

On-premise or in the cloud, Microsoft training and certification empowers technology professionals to expand their skills and gain knowledge directly from the source. Securing these essential skills will allow you to grow your career and make yourself indispensable as the industry shifts to the cloud. Cloud computing ultimately enables IT to focus on more mission-critical activities, raising the bar of required expertise for IT professionals and developers. These reinvented certifications test on a deeper set of skills that map to real-world business context. Rather than testing only on a feature of a technology, Microsoft Certifications now validate more advanced skills and a deeper understanding of the platform.

Microsoft Certified Solutions Expert (MCSE)

The Microsoft Certified Solutions Expert (MCSE) certification is the globally recognized standard for IT professionals. MCSE certification proves your ability to build innovative solutions across multiple technologies, both on-premises and in the cloud. To begin your journey to MCSE Server Infrastructure certification, the prerequisite is the Microsoft Certified Solutions Associate (MCSA) certification for Windows Server 2012.

The MCSE Server Infrastructure certification validates that you have the skills needed to run a highly efficient and modern data center, with expertise in identity management, systems management, virtualization, storage, and networking. Earning an MCSE: Server Infrastructure certification will qualify you for such jobs as computer support specialist and information security analyst.

Exam 70-413, Designing and Implementing a Server Infrastructure, is part one of a series of two exams that validate the skills and knowledge necessary to design and implement an advanced Windows Server 2012 Infrastructure in an enterprise environment. If you're designing, implementing, configuring, or managing a Windows Server infrastructure or desktops and devices in your organization, consider making the MCSE for Windows Server 2012 your certification goal.

You can learn more about the MCSE certification at the Microsoft Training & Certification website. This MCSE certification requires you to show continued ability to perform in your chosen solution area by completing a recertification exam every three years.

Preparing to Take an Exam

Unless you are a very experienced user, you will need to use test preparation materials to prepare to complete the test correctly and within the time allowed. The Microsoft Official Academic Course series is designed to prepare you with a strong knowledge of all exam topics, and with some additional review and practice on your own, you should feel confident in your ability to pass the appropriate exam.

After you decide which exam to take, review the list of objectives for the exam. You can easily identify tasks that are included in the objective list by locating the exam objective overview at the start of each lesson and the Certification Ready sidebars in the margin of the lessons in this book.

To register for the 70-413 exam, visit Microsoft Training & Certifications Registration webpage for directions on how to register. Keep in mind these important items about the testing procedure:

- **What to expect.** Microsoft Certification testing labs typically have multiple workstations, which may or may not be occupied by other candidates. Test center administrators strive to provide a quiet and comfortable environment for all test takers.

- **Plan to arrive early.** It is recommended that you arrive at the test center at least 30 minutes before the test is scheduled to begin.

- **Bring your identification.** To take your exam, you must bring the identification (ID) that was specified when you registered for the exam. If you are unclear about which forms of ID are required, contact the exam sponsor identified in your registration information. Although requirements vary, you typically must show two valid forms of ID, one with a photo, both with your signature.

- **Leave personal items at home.** The only item allowed into the testing area is your identification, so leave any backpacks, laptops, briefcases, and other personal items at home. If you have items that cannot be left behind (such as purses), the testing center might have small lockers available for use.

- **Nondisclosure agreement.** At the testing center, Microsoft requires that you accept the terms of a nondisclosure agreement (NDA) and complete a brief demographic survey before taking your certification exam.

Patrick Regan has been a PC technician, network administrator/engineer, design architect, and security analyst for the past 24 years since graduating with a bachelor's degree in physics from the University of Akron. He has taught many computer and network classes at Sacramento local colleges (Heald Colleges and MTI Colleges) and participated in and led projects for Heald Colleges, Intel Corporation, Miles Consulting Corporation, and Pacific Coast Companies. For his teaching accomplishments, he received the Teacher of the Year award from Heald Colleges, and he has received several recognition awards from Intel. He is currently a senior network engineer and consultant supporting a large enterprise network at Pacific Coast Companies. As a senior system administrator, he supports approximately 140 servers and 1,500 users spread over 5 subsidiaries and 75 sites. Some of the systems that he has designed, implemented, and managed Microsoft Exchange, SharePoint, and SQL Server and System Center. He holds many certificates including the Microsoft MCSE and has a long history as an author of computer and networking books.

Garrett Stevens is a Systems Software Specialist for Black Hills State University (BHSU). He currently designs, tests, implements, and manages solutions for virtualization, messaging, storage, backup, server operations, and client support. The environment he supports includes over 160 servers, serving over 4,800 students, faculty, and staff. He has earned the following certifications: Microsoft Certified Trainer (MCT), Microsoft Certified Solutions Expert (MCSE): Server Infrastructure; Microsoft Certified Solutions Associate (MCSA): Server 2012, MCSA: Server 2008, Microsoft Certified IT Professional (MCITP): Enterprise Administrator on Windows Server 2008, MCITP: Enterprise Messaging Administrator on Exchange 2010, and HP Accredited Platform Specialist. In his free time, Garrett enjoys spending time with his wife and children, hiking in the Black Hills, disk golf, writing, and trap shooting.

Acknowledgements

We thank the MOAC faculty and instructors who have assisted us in building the Microsoft Official Academic Course courseware. These elite educators have acted as our sounding board on key pedagogical and design decisions leading to the development of the MOAC courseware for future Information Technology workers. They have provided invaluable advice in the service of quality instructional materials, and we truly appreciate their dedication to technology education.

Brian Bridson, Baker College of Flint

David Chaulk, Baker College Online

Ron Handlon, Remington College – Tampa Campus

Katherine James, Seneca College of Applied Arts & Technology

Wen Liu, ITT Educational Services

Zeshan Sattar, Pearson in Practice

Jared Spencer, Westwood College Online

David Vallerga, MTI College

Bonny Willy, Ivy Tech State College

We also thank Microsoft Learning's Tim Sneath, Keith Loeber, Michael McMann, Natasha Chornesky, Wendy Johnson, Brian Swan, Briana Roberts, Jim Clark, Anne Hamilton, Shelby Grieve, Erika Cravens, Paul Schmitt, Jim Cochran, Julia Stasio, and Heidi Johnson for their encouragement and support in making the Microsoft Official Academic Course programs the finest academic materials for mastering the newest Microsoft technologies for both students and instructors.

Brief Contents

Contents

Designing and Planning an Automated Server Installation Strategy

70-413 EXAM OBJECTIVE

Objective 1.1 – Design and plan an automated server installation strategy. This objective can include but is not limited to: Design considerations including images and bare metal/virtual deployment; design a server implementation using Windows Assessment and Deployment Kit (ADK); plan for deploying servers to Microsoft Azure infrastructure as a service (IaaS); plan for deploying servers to public and private cloud by using AppController and Windows PowerShell; plan for multicast deployment; plan for Windows Deployment Services (WDS).

LESSON HEADING	EXAM OBJECTIVE
Designing a Server Imaging Strategy • Selecting Image Characteristics • Selecting Image Types	Design considerations including images
Planning for Bare Metal/Virtual Deployments	Design considerations including images and bare metal/virtual deployment
Selecting an Appropriate Server Deployment Strategy	
Planning for Windows Deployment Services (WDS)	Plan for Windows Deployment Services (WDS)
Planning for Multicast Deployment	Plan for multicast deployment
Designing a Server Implementation Using Windows Assessment and Deployment Kit • Using Windows PE • Creating and Configuring a Reference Computer and Image • Creating and Using Answer Files with Windows SIM • Using Sysprep to Prepare the Reference Computer • Capturing a Reference Image by Using DISM • Performing an Unattended Installation by Using WDS	Design a server implementation using Windows Assessment and Deployment Kit (ADK)
Designing a Virtual Server Deployment	
Planning for Deploying Servers to the Cloud • Planning for Deploying Servers to Microsoft Azure Infrastructure as a service (IaaS) • Planning for Deploying Servers to Public and Private Clouds	Plan for deploying servers to Microsoft Azure infrastructure as a service (IaaS) Plan for deploying servers to public and private clouds by using App Controller and Windows PowerShell

KEY TERMS

answer file

bare metal server

boot image

cloud

Deployment Image Servicing and Management (DISM)

Discover image

file-based image

High Touch with Retail Media

High Touch with Standard Image

hybrid image

image

infrastructure as a service (IaaS)

install image

Lite Touch Installation (LTI)

Lite-Touch, High-Volume Deployment

Microsoft Azure

Microsoft Deployment Toolkit (MDT)

multicast

platform as a service (PaaS)

Preboot eXecution Environment (PXE)

private cloud

public cloud

reference computer

sector-based image

software as a service (SaaS)

sysprep.exe

System Image Manager (SIM)

thick image

thin image

unicast

virtual hard disk (VHD)

Windows Assessment and Deployment Kit (ADK)

Windows Deployment Services (WDS)

Windows Image Format (WIM)

Windows Preinstallation Environment (Windows PE)

Zero-Touch Installation (ZTI)

Zero-Touch, High-Volume Deployment

■ Designing a Server Imaging Strategy

↓ THE BOTTOM LINE

Images are a key component used to deploy Windows to server and client computers. Without images, you have to install Windows and all applications, update Windows and the applications, and configure Windows and the applications each time you want to deploy a server. Installing, updating, and configuring the computer can take several hours. When you have many servers to install within a relatively short period of time, you have to hire several people to perform these tasks or develop a faster way to deploy these servers. Images can reduce the time required to deploy a computer.

CERTIFICATION READY
Design considerations including images
Objective 1.1

An *image* is a single file or other storage device that contains the complete contents and structures of a disk or other data storage device used with computers and other computing devices. The image has the necessary information to be installed as a copy of Windows onto another machine. Often the images can contain additional software packages, drivers, and features, which also are deployed as a single complete package.

In the simplest method, an image is created from a reference or master computer. On the *reference computer*, you install Windows, install any necessary drivers, configure Windows, install additional software, and configure the additional software. You also should update and patch Windows and any applications that run on the computer. When you are done, the reference computer becomes a pristine computer that you can hand to a user, ready to use. Instead of giving the computer to a user, capture the content of the system of it by copying the drive's content to an image file. You can store and access this image from a central location so that you can copy it to other computers.

When you create the reference computer, you want to take a little bit of time and care to ensure that it is properly installed and configured, that Windows and the applications are running properly, and that the desktop environment is clean and ready for any user to use. You also need to ensure that the computer follows any policies established within your organization and that it fits into the security model established by the organization. By taking a little bit of extra time configuring the reference computer and creating the image, you will save lots of time and effort in the future as you deploy that image to a hundred or more computers.

Sometimes a system becomes corrupted or badly misconfigured causing the system to be unreliable or unresponsive. You can use images to refresh computers. So rather waste hours working on one computer that a technician might or might not be able to fix, you can use a new image to overwrite the computer drive, essentially making the computer new again. Of course, doing so would not fix a hardware failure unless that failure is caused by a corrupted driver. The hard device is the physical component, but the driver is the software component that controls the devices is faulty.

Selecting Image Characteristics

As explained earlier, a disk image is a single file that contains a disk's complete contents and structure. However, a disk image is just one of several different types of images. Before you choose a specific image type, you need to understand the various types of images.

When selecting the image type, you need to understand the following:
- Thin, thick, and hybrid images
- Sector-based and file-based formats
- Image type (boot, install, capture, or discover)
- Image format (VHD or WIM)

SELECTING THICK IMAGES, THIN IMAGES, AND HYBRID IMAGES

During the planning phase of a deployment project or as a standard procedure when deploying servers, you need to determine whether to create a thick image, thin image, or hybrid image. How you deploy applications varies, depending on the type of image you select.

Thick images are monolithic images that contain the operating system, all core applications, language packs, and other files. In this case, monolithic indicates massive or huge. Thick images have the following advantages over Thin images:
- Because they include all applications, they are simple to deploy.
- After a thick image is deployed, applications and language packs are available immediately to the end user.

Thick images also have the following disadvantages:
- Each image file is large.
- Creating and testing an image requires a lot of work.
- Updating a thick image (such as adding an application, adding a patch or update, or upgrading a new version of an application) requires rebuilding, retesting, and redistributing the image.
- Either all computers receive all applications whether they are needed or not, or many different thick images must be developed and maintained.

Thin images, as you can surmise, are the opposite of thick images. They contain the operating system and software updates. Typically, they contain no or few core applications but no language packs. When a new computer is deployed, the thin image is deployed first. Then after the thin image is successfully deployed, the system and software installation is customized, usually over the network. Thin images have the following advantages over thick images:
- Thin images cost less to build, maintain, and test.
- Storage costs are lower because the image size is smaller.
- Thin images are more flexible than thick images.

Thin images have the following disadvantages:

- The initial deployment of thin images, followed by applications and language packs, is more complex process then deploying thick images.
- Thin images usually require scripting and/or a software distribution infrastructure to deploy the additional software packages and language packs.
- Fully deploying a system takes longer because it is done in multiple parts back to back.
- Core applications and language packs are not available when end users first starts their computers.
- More traffic is generated over the network

Hybrid images mix thin and thick image strategies, which include applications that everyone uses or needs (such as the operation system, VPN software, antivirus software, and Microsoft Office). Therefore, as a hybrid image is deployed, users can quickly have the necessary applications to perform their jobs. Hybrid images still require longer install time than a thick image, but not as long as a thin image. Using hybrid images takes advantage of the single instancing in a Windows image by combining multiple hybrid images into a single WIM file.

SELECTING SECTOR-BASED IMAGES OR FILE-BASED IMAGES

Some system image programs use sector-based images, whereas others use file-based images. A *sector-based image* copies each sector to a file. One well-known example of a sector-based image is ISO images, which are images of a CD or DVD disk. Other well-known examples of sector-based images are Norton/Symantec Ghost and Acronis True Image. One problem with using sector-based images is that you have to take additional steps to rename a computer and to regenerate the security identifier (SID), which uniquely identifies a computer running Windows on a network. Sector-based images might not work on other computers that run on different hardware.

A *file-based disk image* captures images based on files on the disk. Because a file-based image is hardware independent, it can be deployed to different computers. It uses single-instance storage, which keeps a single copy of a file that might be referenced multiple times in a file system tree. When a file-based image is applied, it is non-destructive, which means that data files will still exist after the image is applied. Examples of file-based images include virtual hard disk (.vhd) and Windows Imaging Format (.wim).

SELECTING IMAGE FORMATS

The *Virtual hard disk (VHD)* format, traditionally used with virtual machines, represents a virtual hard disk drive. It can be found with Microsoft Virtual PC and Hyper-V. Starting with Windows 7, a computer can mount and start from an operating system stored within the .vhd file. Windows 8 Enterprise introduced Windows To Go, which allows Windows to start and run from a storage device such as a USB flash drive or an external hard disk drive. VHD images are limited to maximum size of 2 terabytes (2 TB) and are compatible with all versions of Hyper-V, as well as Microsoft Type 2 hypervisor products, such as Virtual Server and Virtual PC.

Windows 8 and Windows Server 2012 introduced an updated version of the virtual hard disk file called VHDx, whose specification is being made publicly available through the Microsoft Open Source Promise initiative. The VHDx format supports up to 64 TB. It can support 4 KB logical sector size, to provide compatibility with new 4 KB native drives. VHDx files can also use larger block sizes, up to 256 MB, to allow you to fine-tune the performance of a virtual storage subsystem based on the specific application and data types. To protect against data corruption during power failures, it logs updates to the VHDx metadata structures. Finally, VHDx files can add custom metadata to the file. Unfortunately, VHDx are not backward compatible and can be read only by Windows 8/8.1 Windows Server 2012, and Window Server 2012 R2.

Windows Image Format (WIM) is a file-based image format developed by Microsoft that allows a file structure (folders and files) to be stored inside a single WIM database. WIM files have the following features:

- They incorporate compression.
- A single WIM file allows multiple images.
- WIM files uses single instancing of files when multiple WIM files are appended.
- Because WIM image format is a file-based image, it can be used on different hardware platforms and various size disks.
- WIM file format supports offline servicing, which allows you to open a WIM file in Windows and directly add or remove folders, files, drivers, and operating system components.

A WIM file structure contains up to six components:

- *WIM header* defines the content of the WIM file, including file attributes (such as version, size, and compression type). It also acts as an index to locate the other components.
- *File resources* are packages that contain the captured data.
- *Metadata resource* contains information about captured files, including directory structure and file attributes. Each image in a WIM file has one metadata resource.
- *Lookup table* defines the memory location of resource files.
- *XML data* contains additional data about the image.
- *Integrity table* contains security hash (one-way encryption) information to verify integrity when the image is being applied.

A single WIM file can address many hardware configurations. It does not require that the destination hardware match the source hardware. This helps you greatly reduce the number of images, and gives you the advantage of having only one image to address the many hardware configurations.

One WIM file can store multiple images. This is useful because you can store images, with or without core applications, in a single image file. Another benefit is that you can mark one image as bootable, which means you can start a machine from a disk image that a WIM file contains.

By using WIM files for imaging, you can perform maintenance so that when the image is deployed to a new system, it will also include the updates (operating system updates, application updates, and driver updates) and changes without creating a new image from scratch and without deploying and recapturing the image.

If you will be imaging computers with Microsoft tools, you will most likely work with WIM files. You need to know how to update or modify a WIM file by using *Deployment Image Servicing and Management (DISM)*. As you recall from previous exams, DISM is a command-line tool that you can use to service and deploy WIM, VHD, and VHDX files. You also can use DISM to prepare Windows PE images.

 **MORE INFORMATION**

For more information on how to use DISM, refer to the 70-411 course material.

Selecting Image Types

To deploy Windows, you must create or use two types of images: a boot image (boot.wim) and an install image (install.wim). The Windows installation disk already includes basic copies of both images.

Like the name implies, the ***boot image*** starts the computer and can be used to start the operating system installation. Boot images are built with Windows PE, which is a lightweight version of Windows used to deploy client computers and servers and troubleshooting offline operating systems. Windows PE 4.0 is built with the Windows 8 code base and is included with Windows Assessment and Deployment Kit (ADK).

Most of the time, an installation can be done by performing a ***Preboot eXecution Environment (PXE)*** boot, whereas the computer loads the operating system directly from a boot image over the network. If you have a computer that does not support a PXE boot, you can start the computer from disk by using a ***discover image***. You can burn a discover image to a CD-ROM or other startup medium and then start the computer. You can use a discover image to connect directly to a Windows Deployment Services (WDS) server or to Microsoft System Center Configuration Manager and then start the operating system installation process. You can also deploy an image by using the Microsoft Deployment Toolkit (MDT).

You can configure discover images to use the following:

- ***Static discovery:*** An image that connects to a specific deployment server.
- ***Dynamic discovery:*** An image file that emulates the PXE boot process to find a deployment server.

An ***install image*** contains the operating systems you will deploy to client computers. Although the Windows installation disk has a default Install.wim file, you would typically create your own installation images by building a reference computer, modifying the reference computer, and then capturing the system to an install image.

To capture a reference computer, you restart the reference computer and boot the computer using mobile device (such as an optical disk or USB device) or a ***capture image***. The mobile device or capture images contain the files necessary to load an operating system, and the tools to capture an image (such as the DISM tools or the Windows Deployment Server Image Capture Wizard).

By using WIM files for imaging, you can perform maintenance on the image so that when it is deployed to a new system, it will also include the updates (operating system updates, application updates, and driver updates) and changes without creating a new image from scratch and without deploying and recapturing the image.

DETERMINING THE NUMBER OF IMAGES

When you plan the images, you need to determine the number of images based on operating system, hardware platform, drivers, and operating features. As mentioned earlier, sector-based and file-based images each have their own advantages and disadvantages. Sector-based images can be deployed faster than file-based images and work well with identical computers. So if you use sector-based images, you need at least one image for each computer type. If you have one set of applications on one some computers and another set of applications on others, you need to two images for each computer type you are installing to. If you want to make changes to the sector-based image, you will need to deploy the sector-based image, make the necessary changes, and recapture the image.

File-based images are hardware independent, can contain multiple images in a single file, can offer offline-servicing, and provide nondestructive deployment. So by using file-based images, you can use one image for several different computers, with different applications. As a result, you will use less space when storing the file-based images.

You can include device drivers in captured images, or you can install them after the image is deployed. Of course, critical drivers, such as storage and network drivers, have to be included within the image.

■ Planning for Bare Metal/Virtual Deployments

THE BOTTOM LINE

When you deploy servers, you can deploy Windows to a physical or to a virtual machine. A virtual deployment is deployment to a virtual machine, which is usually running on Hyper-V or VMware. A *bare metal server* is where the virtualization hypervisor is directly installed and executed on the hardware without any underlying operating system. The hypervisor then directly interfaces with the underlying hardware without going through an operating system.

CERTIFICATION READY
Designing considerations including images and bare metal/virtual deployment
Objective 1.1

When you first learned about computers and Windows, you mostly learned by running Windows on a desktop or mobile computer running on a physical system. Also, if you have a home computer, it consists of Windows running on a physical system (a desktop or mobile computer).

When you run Windows servers on a physical system in a production environment, Windows is the primary operating system on the server and the hardware is dedicated to Windows and the applications that are running on Windows.

When you use virtualization for a server environment, you use a few very powerful host systems onto which you install guest systems, known as *virtual machines (VMs)*. VMs behave like physical machines in almost every conceivable way. They must be patched, restarted, backed up, upgraded, decommissioned, replaced, fixed, and maintained. They are virtual versions of physical machines with CPUs, memory, disk, network, an operating system, and applications. Today, almost any operating system can be installed into a virtual machine and run on a host system.

The primary reason for virtualization is efficiency. Server hardware has become so powerful that much of it sat in data centers, with utilization numbers hovering in the 5 to 10 percent range. As a result, the server is grossly underutilized.

Virtualization increases utilization of computing hardware with server consolidation to minimize hardware footprints and to save money by "stacking" multiple, complementary services on these powerful systems. As server hardware became more powerful, with hardware-assisted virtualization from Intel and AMD, having consolidation ratios in the range of 20, 30, or more systems to one host system is common. With virtualization, you have lower computing costs associated with power, cooling, hardware expenditures, maintenance, rented data center rack space, and personnel. Also, virtualization vendors and third parties have created applications that allow physical and virtual systems to be managed in a single application.

Since virtualization was introduced, virtualization has matured into an efficient and dependable system and architecture. Today, the newest server technology is based on public cloud services, which provide a way to access information from anywhere at any time. The cloud can be defined in many ways. Microsoft defines a cloud as a web-based service hosted outside your organization. This means the information technology infrastructure (hardware, servers, software, and so on) is located somewhere other than your office and is managed by a third party (such as a hosted identity). With a cloud, an organization can use various network services, including virtual servers.

To allow a system to run more efficiently, you can deploy bare metal systems because you are cutting out the middleman. To perform a bare metal deployment, you must have a PXE capable system. The network also must be able to support large transfers.

To deploy bare metal servers, you will need the following:
- The server computer must be capable of network starting via PXE.
- The server computer must be configured to start without user interaction.
- If you are using Windows Deployment Services, you need to create two unattended installation files: one for the WDS screens and one for the setup process itself.

With WDS, to specify which boot image for a device to start from, you must first *prestage* the computer, in which you define the computer in Active Directory as a managed computer and define the globally unique identifier (GUID) derived from the MAC address. You would then use the following command:

```
WDSUTIL /Set-Device /Device:,name. /BootImage-
Path:,Relative Path.
```

Alternatively, you can set a default image globally for all clients on the Boot tab of the WDS server Properties dialog box.

You can use WDS to link physical computers to computer account objects in Active Directory Domain Services (AD DS). This is called prestaging the client. Prestaged clients are also called known computers. By prestaging the client, you can configure properties to control the client's installation. For example, you can configure the network startup program and the unattend file that the client should receive, as well as the server from which the client should download the network startup program.

■ Selecting an Appropriate Server Deployment Strategy

THE BOTTOM LINE

When you select a deployment method for Windows, you determine the best way to deploy Windows with minimal effort, resources, and time while minimizing problems during and after Windows deployment. Of course, although you need to look after your organization and users, you also need to follow all policies and guidelines established by the organization.

When selecting an appropriate server deployment strategy, you can choose from four models:

- High Touch with Retail Media
- High Touch with Standard Image
- Lite-Touch, High-Volume Deployment
- Zero-Touch, High-Volume Deployment

The *High Touch with Retail Media* strategy is the basic local installation strategy used by small organizations with fewer than 100 unmanaged client computers, a simple network infrastructure, and no staff to perform complicated or large deployments. The administrator will go from computer to computer to perform the installation, using a Window installation disk (usually the retail media). So the High Touch with Retail Media strategy is a hands-on, manual deployment in which you insert the Windows installation disk in the drive, install Windows, apply any patches, install any applications, and manually configure the computer. If you are using retail media, you also have to activate the computers online or by using a phone. If you need to install only a few computers, the strategy makes sense.

In many cases, a small company can purchase a new computer with Windows already installed. In these cases, you need to unbox the computer, connect it to the network, apply patches, install any necessary applications, and configure the computer. Other options would be bring in a consultant or service company that can provide IT support when needed.

Of these four strategies, High Touch with Retail Media requires the most work and time. You can reduce the burden by using scripts and/or answer files. You create the answer file (unattend.xml), place it on a USB storage device, and start the computer with the Windows installation disk. During the startup process, Windows looks for the answer file on the USB devices. If the answer file is found, the Windows setup program uses it to automate or partially automate the installation.

Unfortunately, creating the script and/or answer file requires some technical experience, which might not be available to small companies. Although you can create the answer file by downloading and installing the Windows Automated Installation Kit (AIK), and running the System Image Manager (SIM), a number of non-Microsoft websites provide unattend. xml files. However, if you download one of these answer files, you need to review it, using a text editor such as Notepad, to provide the proper product key and to use your own company information.

The *High Touch with Standard Image* strategy is usually aimed at organizations with 100 to 200 unmanaged client computers, in which the organization has at least one experienced IT professional or hires consultants. Rather than manually install Windows via the Windows installation disk, you use an operating system image that includes Windows, applications, and any necessary customization and configuring already performed. After creating and capturing the master images, the amount of effort to deploy a computer is much less than a High Touch with Retail Media deployment but still can require some hands-on to deploy Windows, as well as perform customization and configuration after Windows is deployed. Therefore, to use the High Touch with Standard Image strategy, you need a Windows installation disk, the Windows AIK, a USB storage device, and a reference computer (to make the image).

Using a standard image creates a standard environment across all deployed client computers, offers faster deployment, and includes many updates, configurations, and customizations already completed. However, this strategy works best when you only have one image to deploy that does not have to be changed often. Unfortunately, this strategy does not allow for upgrading an existing Windows installation, nor does it preserve the user's applications, settings, and files, because those will be overwritten when the image is deployed.

The *Lite-Touch, High-Volume Deployment* is aimed at medium-sized organization with 200 to 500 client computers and at least one site with more than 25 users. This strategy uses network infrastructure and servers to deploy Windows. The organization also uses various tools including answer files, scripts the Windows AIK, and the *Microsoft Deployment Toolkit (MDT)* to deploy Windows.

The MDT is a free download from Microsoft that provides a wide assortment of tools and recommended processes to perform *Lite-Touch Installation (LTI)* and *Zero-Touch Installation (ZTI)* deployment methods. The MDT is used in LTI deployments, whereas ZDI deployments are performed by using System Center Configuration Manager. The MDT provides a single console with a complete toolset and document to deploy Windows XP, Windows Vista, Windows 7, Windows 8/8.1, Windows Server 2008 R2, Windows Server 2012, Windows Server 2012 R2, Office 2012, and Office 365. It provides a central interface both for the creation of reference computer images and for the deployment of those images to the target workstations. Because the MDT 2013 relies on several Windows deployment tools, you would download the Windows 8.1 Assessment and Deployment Kit, Windows Automated Installation Kit, Application Compatibility Toolkit, and MSXML 6.0.

The Lite-Touch, High-Volume Deployment strategy is highly automated but requires a little interaction at the beginning of installation. However, if an organization configures a database and deploys Windows via the Windows Deployment Services role, you can reach nearly zero-touch deployment. Of course, using the Lite-Touch, High-Volume Deployment strategy requires more planning, and you need to do some work up front to install and configure the necessary components than the previous strategies.

The *Zero-Touch, High-Volume Deployment* strategy is for large organizations with more than 500 managed client computers and at least one location with more than 25 users. The Zero-Touch High-Volume Deployment strategy is similar to Lite-Touch, High-Volume Deployment, except that it uses System Center Configuration Manager, MDT, and Windows AIK to provide a fully automated deployment that requires no user interaction. Although System Center Configuration Manager has to be licensed and requires a little bit more effort to install and configure, the up-front cost and effort is offset by automated deployment of a large number of computers and by lower support costs because configurations are consistent across all client computers. This strategy also provides streamlined maintenance because System Center Configuration Manager handles applications, device drivers, and updates.

When you need to deploy multiple computers, you want the deployment to go smoothly. Therefore, for larger deployments, you should follow these basic steps:

1. *Plan:* Choose a strategy based on your organization's business requirements and needs.
2. *Test:* Test the deployment before you perform it (to ensure that the images and processes function properly) and before you touch the user computers. By testing, you can reduce the number of support and maintenance calls.
3. *Store images:* Select a file server on which to store the images. During the deployment process, these images will be applied to your server computers.
4. *Distribute:* Apply images across the network to the target server computers, or apply images from removable media such as a USB flash drive or a DVD.

■ Planning for Windows Deployment Services (WDS)

THE BOTTOM LINE

Windows Deployment Services (WDS) is a Windows server role used to deploy windows over the network with little or no user intervention. If the client can perform a PXE boot, you perform an installation over a network with no local operating system or local startup device on it. The WDS server will store and help administrators manage the boot and operating system image files used in the network installations.

CERTIFICATION READY
Plan for Windows Deployment Services (WDS)
Objective 1.1

When designing and planning for Windows Deployment Services, you need to determine the following:

- The number of Windows Deployment Services instances required
- Full Windows Deployment Services or the Transport Server Role
- Server resource requirements
- The file share fault-tolerance and consistency mechanism

To determine how many WDS servers you need, you first must look at current network infrastructure. If the WAN links have enough available bandwidth and low latency, you most likely need only one WDS server. However, you might need additional WDS servers for isolated networks, or sites that are connected with low bandwidth links or have high latency. For the best performance, you should place a WDS server at all large sites or locations.

For larger sites, you might need more than one server running WDS. This will be determined by the following:

- Number of computers
- Number of deployments that must be done at the same time or within a short period of time
- Time required to deploy a server
- Size and number of images

Because an operating system deployment can consume a large amount of bandwidth, if you have multiple sites, consider placing WDS servers at each site. If you do not do so, Windows deployments can consume large amounts of bandwidth between sites.

When planning WDS server resource requirements, the two most common constraints will be the amount of disk space to store images and the network bandwidth. If you plan to deploy many computers at the same time, you should consider coordinating the deployment and using multicast. Although WDS can be used with other services, deploying Windows Deployment services to its own server is recommended.

To increase fault tolerance, you can use fault-tolerant file shares, redundant network adapters, and clustering. You can also use Distributed File System (DFS) replication to copy the images from one WDS server to another to ensure that all servers have the same images.

As part of any organization's IT department, administrators must remember to provide the necessary tools for users to perform their jobs efficiently. When performing a deployment, administrators need to look at how the deployment affects other users and the network. To help reduce network load, consider doing the following:

- Perform the deployments after hours
- Stagger the deployment
- Use multicasting
- Use an isolated network

■ Planning for Multicast Deployment

THE BOTTOM LINE

When a host communicates directly to another host (single point to single point), the communication is *unicast*. If you need to use unicast to deploy Windows to 10 different computers at the same time, you wind up deploying Windows 10 times, generating 10 times the traffic. If you use multicasting communications, you send just one set of packets to the 10 computers at the same time. By default, Windows Deployment Services uses unicast when deploying Windows. However, if you need to deploy to multiple computers at the same time, you can use multicasting.

CERTIFICATION READY
Plan for multicast deployment
Objective 1.1

Multicast is when packets are sent from one host to multiple hosts (one point to a set of other points). Multicasting delivers the same packet simultaneously to a group of clients, which results in less bandwidth usage. For example, if you must send a live video to 100 computers, rather than send 100 sets of packets (unicast), you send one set of packets. When multicast packets reach a router, the packets are forwarded only to the networks that have receivers for the packets. In addition to sending live video or audio transmissions, multicast can be used in some instances when deploying multiple computers at the same time—you need to send only one set of packets to multiple computers.

To perform multicasting with WDS, your organization first must use routers that support multicasting. The routers also must have Internet Group Membership Protocol (IGMP) snooping enabled. This causes your network hardware to forward multicast packets only to those devices that request data. If IGMP snooping is turned off, multicast packets are treated as broadcast packets and will be sent to every device in the subnet. Only Windows Vista with SP1 clients and later supports multicasting.

Second, you need to create a multicast scope on the DHCP servers. In DHCP, multicast scopes—commonly known as a Multicast Address Dynamic Client Allocation Protocol (MADCAP) scopes—enable applications to reserve a multicast IP address for data and content delivery. For IPv4, Class D networks (224.0.0.0 to 239.255.255.255) are reserved for multicasting.

Creating and managing a multicast scope is similar to creating and managing a typical scope; however, multicast scopes cannot use reservations and you cannot set additional options such as DNS and routing. Also, because multicast is shared by groups of computers, the default duration of a multicast scope is 30 days.

To create a multicast transmission, follow these basic steps:

1. Establish the multicast address ranges.
2. Specify the multicast transfer settings.
3. Create the multicast transmission.

To specify and configure the multicast address ranges, open the Windows Deployment Services console, right-click the server, and click Properties. In the Properties dialog box, click the Multicast tab and configure one of the transfer settings:

- Keep all multicast clients in a session at the same speed.
- Separate clients into three sessions: slow, medium, or fast.
- Separate clients into two sessions: slow and fast.
- Automatically disconnect clients slower than this speed (in KBps).

■ Designing a Server Implementation Using Windows Assessment and Deployment Kit (Adk)

THE BOTTOM LINE

Windows Assessment and Deployment Kit (ADK) is a collection of tools and documentation designed to help IT professionals deploy Windows operating systems. Windows ADK is ideal for use in highly customized environments because you can use its tools to configure many deployment options. Depending on your business needs, you can choose to use all or part of the resources available in Windows ADK.

CERTIFICATION READY
Design a server implementation using Windows Assessment and Deployment Kit (ADK)
Objective 1.1

By default, Windows ADK is installed to C:\Program Files (x86)\Windows Kits. This directory contains all the tools and documentation included in the Windows ADK. The ADK includes the following tools:

- *Application Compatibility Toolkit (ACT)* helps identify which applications are compatible with the new versions of the Windows operating system and which require further testing.
- *Deployment Tools* enable you to customize, manage, and deploy Windows images. You can use these tools to automate Windows deployments, removing the need for user interaction during Windows setup. These tools include Deployment Image Servicing and Management (DISM), Windows System Image Manager (SIM), OSCDIMG, BCDBoot, DISMAPI, and WIMGAPI.
- *Windows Preinstallation Environment (Windows PE)* is a minimal operating system designed to prepare a computer for installation and servicing of Windows. You can use Windows ADK to create a customized Windows PE.
- *User State Migration Tool (USMT)* scriptable command-line tool is used to migrate user data from a previous Windows installation to a new Windows installation.
- *Volume Activation Management Tool (VAMT)* enables administrators to automate and centrally manage the activation of Windows. The VAMT can manage volume activation via retail keys (or single-activation keys), multiple-activation keys (MAKs), or Windows Key Management Service (KMS) keys.
- *Windows Performance Toolkit (WPT)* includes tools used to record system events (Event Tracing for Windows) and to analyze performance data in a graphical user interface. It also includes the Windows Performance Recorder, Windows Performance Analyzer, and Xperf.
- *Windows Assessment Toolkit* includes tools to discover and run assessments on a single computer, so that you can determine how to improve performance.

INSTALL THE WINDOWS ASSESSMENT AND DEPLOYMENT KIT

GET READY. To install the Windows Assessment and Deployment Kit (Windows ADK), perform the following steps:

1. On Server01, open the \\rwdc01\software\Windows Kits\8.1\ADK folder and double-click adksetup. When you are prompted to confirm that you want to run the file, click Run.

2. On the *Specify Location* page, click Next.

3. On the *Join the Customer Experience Improvement Program (CEIP)* page, click Next.

4. On the *License Agreement* page, click Accept.

5. On the *Select the features you want to install* page (as shown in Figure 1-1), select or clear the desired features. Click Install.

Figure 1-1

Selecting ADK features

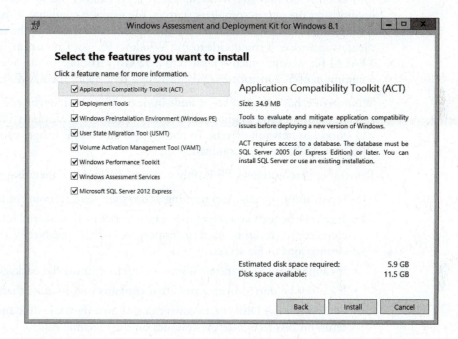

6. When the installation is complete, click Close.

Using Windows PE

Windows PE is the core deployment foundation for Windows 8.1 and Windows Server 2012 R2. Windows PE is a compact, special-purpose Windows operating system that prepares and initiates a computer for Windows operating system setup, maintenance, or imaging tasks, and recovers Windows operating systems such as Windows 8.1.

Windows PE is a lightweight bootable version of the Windows operating system. Typically when you start Windows PE, you are starting to a command prompt; however, some GUI-based tools run in Windows PE. Windows PE is used for the following:

- *Install Windows:* Prepares the system for Windows installation, such as by creating partitions and formatting drives.

- ***Troubleshoot Windows:*** Starts a computer and runs diagnostic tools such as the Startup Repair feature.
- ***Recovery:*** Builds customized startup disks to automate recovery and rebuilding of the Windows operating system.

You can start Windows PE 5.0 from almost any startup device, including CDs, DVDs, and USB devices. Windows PE supports both 32-bit and 64-bit hardware and supports installing both 32-bit and 64-bit versions of Windows. Unlike DOS, Windows PE supports the NTFS file system. It also supports network connections in which you can configure IP settings and connect to a network share. Because it is a disk image, Windows PE supports offline sessions, which allow servicing of the image. Finally, Windows PE supports some Windows-based applications and includes add-in modules for additional Windows-based components.

When you start Windows PE, the startup process creates a RAM disk (part of the RAM that is used as a disk) to store the Windows PE files. This allows you to remove the Windows PE start-up disk after the system completes startup. You can also configure Windows PE to perform a flat startup, which reads the files from the startup device and requires the startup disk to remain in the startup device. If you decide to run Windows PE as a flat startup, it needs to be installed on a FAT32 file system, which is limited to a 32 GB partition. To run Windows PE, you will need a minimum of 512 megabytes (MB) of RAM. By default, the RAM disk is assigned the letter X.

Windows PE has a limited set of built-in device drivers. Therefore, if you need to support specific hardware, you might need to create or modify a Windows PE image so that you can add storage or network drivers. To modify a Windows PE image, you can use DISM or the Windows ADK Drvload command.

Remember that Windows PE is only a minimal Windows operating system. Therefore,

- It will automatically stop running and restart after 72 hours of continuous use.
- It cannot be used as a server, nor can it create or host shared folders or terminal service connections. It can be used to connect to TCP/IP and NetBIOS over TCP/IP (NetBT) connections to file servers.
- It cannot be used to install Windows Installer (.msi) file packages.
- It cannot be started from a path that contains non-English characters.
- You cannot use Diskpart to convert a disk to a dynamic disk and have the Windows setup process recognize the volumes on the dynamic disk.
- The 64-bit version of Windows PE does not include Windows 32-bit on Windows 64-bit (WOW64). You must use 32-bit Windows PE to run 32-bit Windows Setup; you need to use 64-bit Windows PE to run 64-bit Windows Setup.
- If you are using a Unified Extensible Firmware Interface (UEFI-based) motherboard, you must install a 64-bit version of the Windows operating system. Therefore, you cannot install Windows using a 32-bit version of Windows PE.

You can use the following Windows ADK command-line tools to help deploy Windows via Windows PE:

- ***BCDboot*** initializes the Boot Configuration Data (BCD) store and copies the necessary startup environment files to the system partition so that it can start Windows.
- ***Bootsect*** updates the master startup code so that it can support the Windows Boot Manager (Bootmgr.exe) and Windows NT Loader (NTLDR).
- ***Copype*** creates and populates a directory structure for Windows PE files.
- ***Drvload*** adds third-party drivers to Windows PE.
- ***Expand*** expands one or more .cab files.
- ***Lpksetup*** installs language packs and configures international settings.

- ***Makewinpemedia*** creates startable Windows PE media.
- ***Oscdimg*** creates an .iso image file of a Windows PE image.
- ***Powercfg*** controls power settings such as hibernate and standby.
- ***Tzutil*** manages available time zones.
- ***Wpeinit*** The component that initializes Windows PE every time that it starts and installs Plug and Play devices, processes unattend.xml settings, and loads network resources when Windows PE is loaded.
- ***Wpeutil*** enables you to run commands during a Windows PE session, including shutting down or restarting Windows PE, enabling or disabling a firewall, or initializing a network.

You can add components to Windows PE. For example, you want to add language packs, third-party drivers, third-party components, and Windows PE updates.

 CONFIGURE A CUSTOM WINDOWS PE ENVIRONMENT

GET READY. To configure a custom Windows PE environment, perform the following steps:

1. Open the Start screen, right-click Deployment and Imaging Tools Environment, and then click Run as administrator.

2. In the *Administrator: Deployment and Imaging Tools Environment* window, type the following command, and then press Enter:

   ```
   Copype amd64 C:\WinPE_X64
   ```

   When the process completes, the Administrator: Deployment and Imaging Tools Environment window should display a *Success* message.

3. To mount a boot.wim file to the C:\winpe_x64\mount folder, in the *Administrator: Deployment and Imaging Tools Environment* window, type the following command, and then press Enter:

   ```
   DISM /mount-image
   /imagefile:C:\winpe_x64\media\sources\boot.wim
   /index:1 /mountdir:C:\winpe_x64\mount
   ```

   When the process completes, the Administrator: Deployment and Imaging Tools Environment window should display *The operation completed successfully*.

4. To add drivers to the Windows PE image (assuming that drivers are in the C:\Drivers folder), type the following command, and then press Enter:

   ```
   DISM /image:C:\winpe_x64\mount /add-Driver /driver:C:\Drivers /
   recurse /forceunsigned
   ```

   When the process completes, the Administrator: Deployment and Imaging Tools Environment window should show that drivers have been installed, and you should see a message that *The operation completed successfully*.

5. To add support for Windows PowerShell 3.0 to the Windows PE image, execute each of the following commands:

   ```
   CD "C:\Program Files (x86)\Windows Kits\8.1\Assessment and de-
   ployment kit\Windows preInstallation Environment\amd64\WinPE_OCs"
   DISM /image:C:\winpe_x64\mount /Add-Package /PackagePath:.\
   WinPE-NetFX4.cab
   DISM /image:C:\winpe_x64\mount /Add-Package /PackagePath:.\
   WinPE-Scripting.cab
   DISM /image:C:\winpe_x64\mount /Add-Package /PackagePath:.\
   WinPE-WMI.cab
   DISM /image:C:\winpe_x64\mount /Add-Package /PackagePath:.\
   WinPE-PowerShell3.cab
   CD C:\winpe_x64
   ```

6. To save the changes and unmount the image, type the following command:

   `DISM /unmount-image /mountdir:C:\winpe_x64\mount /commit`

   When the process completes, the Administrator: Deployment and Imaging Tools Environment window should display *The operation completed successfully.*

7. To create an ISO image that can be used to start media, run the following command:

   `Makewinpemedia /iso C:\winpe_x64 C:\winpe_x64\media\sources\`
   `winpe_x64.iso`

8. Close File Explorer and the Administrator: Deployment and Imaging Tools Environment window.

Creating and Configuring a Reference Computer and Image

As mentioned earlier, the reference computer is a pristine computer that is ready to be deployed. Windows ADK has several tools that can help you create a reference image of the reference computer. You can install from the image stored on a Windows DVD, USB flash drive, or network drive.

The following general steps explain how to use a USB device and a Windows installation disk to create a reference computer and retrieve an image:

1. Install and customize Windows PE. You need to copy a Windows PE image, add the necessary drivers, and include packages necessary for Windows PE to function on the reference computer. If you are using a USB device, you can use the `MakeWinPEMedia / UFD` command to create the startable USB device.

2. Create and modify answer files, which will be used to install Windows based on your organization's environment. To create and edit the answer file, use Windows SIM. Then copy the answer file to the root directory of the USB device with the name autounattend.xml. Create a profile that includes the CopyProfile setting, so that you can customize the default user profile, and copy the answer file profile to the root directory of the USB device as CopyProfile.xml.

3. Plug the USB device and start the computer with the Windows installation disk. The setup process will use the Autounattend.xml file to complete the installation. You will then customize the administrator profile.

4. To capture the image, use the Sysprep.exe command to generalize the system. To use the CopyProfile.xml file, use this command:

   `C:\Windows\System32\Sysprep\Sysprep.exe /generalize /oobe /shutdown`
   `/unattend:D:\CopyProfile.xml`

   Then start up the computer with the Windows PE USB device and use the DISM tool to copy the Windows partition to a network location or external hard drive.

5. Deploy the image to a test computer by starting the test system with the Windows PE USB device, using Diskpart to configure the hard drive, and using the Applyimage command to apply the previously captured image.

6. Verify and test that the computer image and profile settings are correct.

Starting with Windows Vista, Windows setup uses a process called image-based setup (IBS) to provide a single unified process for installing all versions of Windows. This process uses the install.wim file. The setup.exe used in the installation process supports the following command-line options:

- */installfrom:<path>* enables you to specify a custom .wim file to use for installation.
- */m:<folder_name>* causes Windows Setup to copy files from an alternative location. This option does not support a UNC path. The folder has a prescribed structure as described in the Windows ADK.
- */noreboot* instructs Windows Setup not to restart the computer after the first phase of the setup process completes.
- */tempdrive:<drive_letter>* instructs Windows Setup to create the temporary installation files on the specified partition.
- */unattend:<answer_file>* instructs Windows Setup to use the specified answer file to complete the installation.

During installation, Windows Setup goes through several different configuration passes, as follows. Unattended installation settings can be applied in one or more configuration settings.

1. *windowsPE:* Because Windows PE is used to start a computer to perform Windows installations and troubleshooting, this pass configures the Windows PE and basic Windows setup, including partitioning and formatting a disk, specifying networking parameters, specifying the Windows image to use for the deployment, and specifying any critical drivers needed to access the disk systems or network interfaces.

2. *offlineServicing:* This pass updates a Windows image via DISM.exe, including software fixes, language packs, and other security updates.

3. *generalize:* This pass removes system-specific information such as computer name and security ID.

4. *specialize:* This pass creates and applies system-specific information such as network settings, international settings, and domain information (including joining a computer to the domain). During this pass, unique SIDs are created.

5. *auditSystem:* This pass applies settings to the system if the computer is started in audit mode. Audit mode allows you to install and test additional device drivers, applications, and updates to an image. You can specify audit mode with the sysprep command.

6. *auditUser:* This pass applies settings after the user logs on if the computer is started in audit mode as specified with the sysprep command.

7. *oobeSystem:* Settings are applied to Windows before Windows Welcome starts. This pass configures Windows Shell options, creates user accounts, and specifies language and locale settings.

Creating and Using Answer Files with Windows SIM

To streamline the installation process, you can automate the installation of Windows by using an *answer file*, which is used to provide responses to the prompts that would typically appear during installation. For example, you can use the answer file to partition and format a disk, install additional device drivers, specify what Windows features to install, and specify the install language.

Because an answer file is just a text file based on XML, you can create one with a text editor or XML editor. However, Microsoft recommends that you use the *System Image Manager (SIM)*, which is part of the Windows ADK. SIM is a graphical interface tool used to create and manage unattended Windows setup answer files and to check answer files.

You can perform the following with the answer file:

- *Partition the hard disk:* You can create and format one partition or multiple partitions.
- *Install additional device drivers:* By installing additional drivers not included with Windows, you can ensure that the computers are ready to use immediately after installing the operating system. You can install drivers by scripting the installation of an executable file that installs the device driver onto the Windows installation disk.
- *Install applications:* You can have applications added automatically during installation by executing a file from a local disk or the network.
- *Apply updates:* You can install critical updates and security updates by running an executable file much like you would automatically install an application.
- *Configure settings:* You can customize hundreds of settings during deployment, including defining the computer, adding the computer to the domain, and defining the Internet Explorer home page.
- *Enable or disable features:* You can easily and automatically add or remove Windows features.
- *Minimize user interaction:* You can limit or reduce the amount of user interaction. In fact, you could use the answer file to avoid all user interaction during Windows installation. By reducing user interaction, you decrease the time to install Windows while minimizing user error.

To add a configuration setting to the answer file, browse through the available settings in the Windows Image pane, right-click the setting you want to add, and then select the configuration pass specifying when you want the setup program to configure the setting. The setting then appears in the Answer File pane, and the properties specific to that setting appear in the adjacent Properties pane. After the setting is added, you can modify the property values. If you need clarification on a setting, press F1 while a property or setting is highlighted to open the Unattended Windows Setup Reference Guide.

 CREATE AN ANSWER FILE

GET READY. To create an answer file, log on to the computer where you installed the Windows ADK and then perform the following steps:

1. Open File Explorer from the taskbar.
2. Create a folder named C:\DistFold.
3. Create a folder named C:\Images.
4. Copy the \sources\install.wim from the Windows installation disk to the C:\Images folder.
5. Copy the C:\Program Files (x86)\Windows Kits\8.1\Assessment and Deployment Kit\Deployment Tools\Samples\Unattend\Autounattend_x64_BIOS_sample.xml folder to the C:\Images folder.
6. Open the Start screen and click Windows System Image Manager.
7. When the *Windows System Image Manager* console opens, click Tools, and then click Create Distribution Share.
8. When the *Create Distribution Share* dialog box opens, in the Folder name text box, type C:\DistFold and click Open.

9. Click File, and then click Select Windows Image.

10. When the *Select a Windows Image* dialog box opens, in the file name text box, type C:\Images\install.wim and click Open.

11. The first time you load the image, it may require a couple of minutes to create a catalog file. Click Yes when prompted.at the prompt.

12. Click File and then click Open Answer File. Navigated to and click C:\Images\ Autounattend_x64_BIOS_sample.xml and then click Open. If you are asked to associate the answer file with the Windows Server 2012 R2 Windows image, click Yes. The answer file elements appear in the *Answer File* pane, as shown in Figure 1-2. To create a new answer file, open the File menu and select New Answer File.

Figure 1-2

Opening an answer file with
Windows System Image
Manager

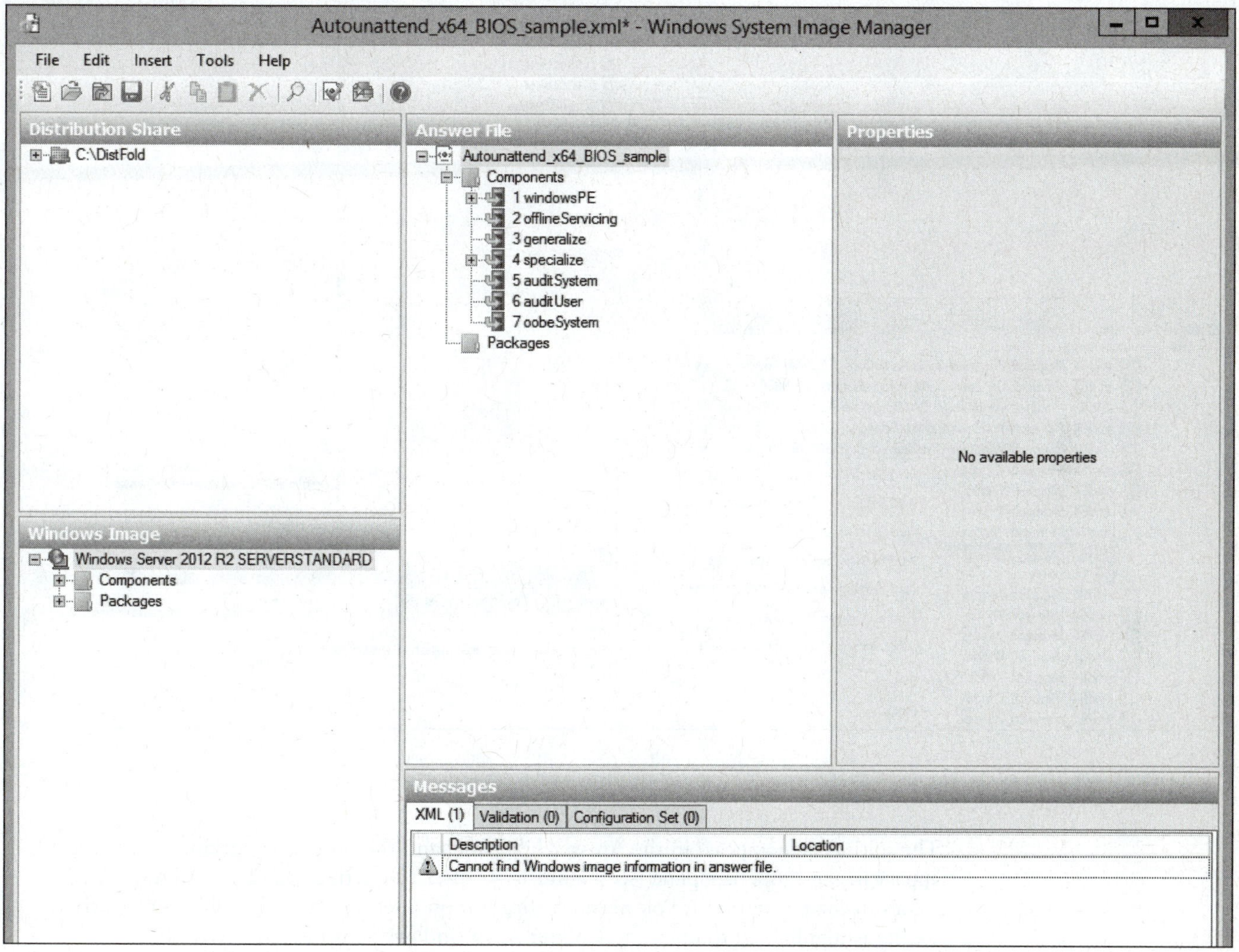

You can see in the Answer File pane the seven configuration passes, starting with WindowsPE and ending with oobeSystem. To add settings to the configuration pass (see Figure 1-3), go to the Windows Image pane, right-click the component that you want to add, and then click the configuration pass that you want to add the setting to.

Figure 1-3

Adding settings to a configuration pass

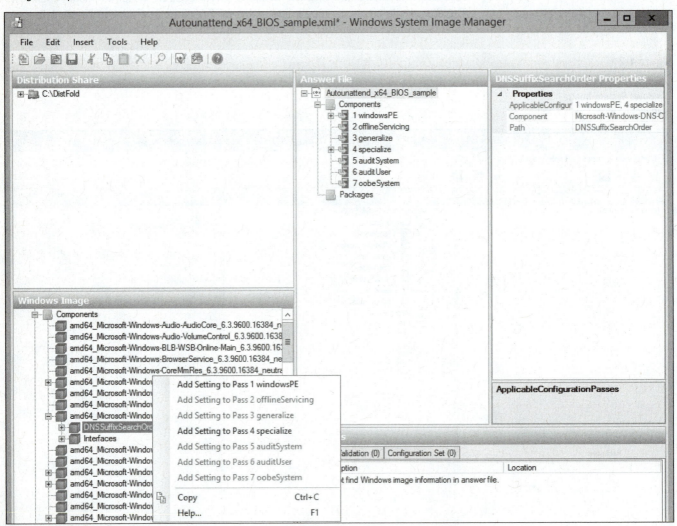

The setting then appears in the Answer File pane, and the properties specific to that setting appear in the Properties pane (see Figure 1-4). After the setting is added, you modify the values in the properties. If you need clarification on a setting, press F1 while a property or setting is highlighted to open the Unattended Windows Setup Reference Guide.

Figure 1-4

The Answer File pane and
adjacent properties

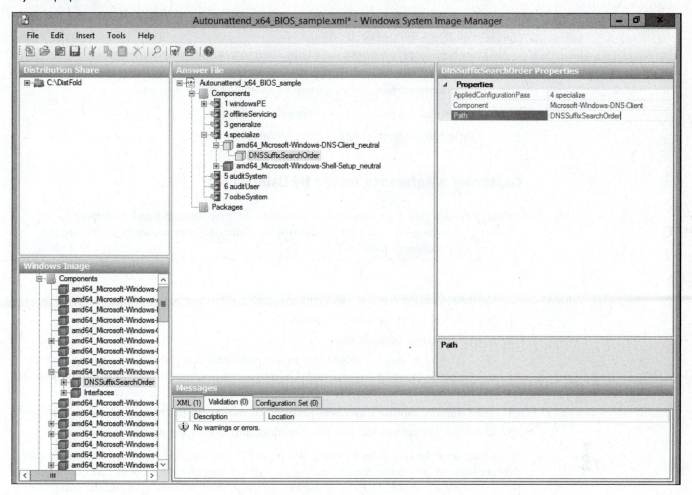

Using Sysprep to Prepare the Reference Computer

Before capturing a computer drive, you need to prepare the reference computer with
the Microsoft System Preparation Utility. *Sysprep.exe* prepares a Windows computer for
cloning by removing specific computer information, such as the computer name and SID.

For Windows 8.1, Sysprep.exe is located in the C:\Windows\System32\Sysprep folder. When
you restart the computer with the capture image, a wizard then guides you through the
process of capturing an image of the computer and uploading it to the WDS server.

The Sysprep.exe command supports the following options:

- **/generalize** instructs Sysprep to remove system-specific data, such as event logs, the
  computer name, and unique SIDs from the Windows operating system installation.
- **/oobe** instructs Windows to present the Windows Welcome wizard when the computer
  starts next time. The Windows Welcome wizard allows you to name the computer as
  well as generate a SID and any other required unique information.

- **/shutdown** instructs the computer to shut down and not restart.
- **/audit** instructs the Windows operating system installation to run in audit mode the next time the computer starts.
- **/reboot** instructs the computer to restart. Use this option if you want to verify that the OOBE phase runs correctly.
- **/quiet** runs Sysprep without displaying on-screen confirmation messages. If you automate Sysprep, use this option with an answer file.
- **/unattend:answerfile** applies settings in an answer file to Sysprep.

The basic command to prepare a computer for imaging is

```
sysprep /generalize /oobe /shutdown
```

Capturing a Reference Image by Using DISM

After you configure the reference computer use the Sysprep command to prepare a computer for imaging, and then shut down the computer, you are ready to capture the image of a partition manually.

To use DISM to capture the image manually, follow these steps:

1. Start the computer by using Windows PE.
2. Map a drive to a network share.
3. Use Diskpart to assign a drive letter to any partitions that you need to capture that do not have any driver letters assigned. Unless you customized the system partition, you do not have to create an image of it because it will automatically be re-created.
4. Use DISM to capture the system partition (if the system partition has been customized).
5. Use DISM to capture the primary partitions and any logical partitions.

When you start the computer by using Windows PE and, for some reason, accidentally start the computer to Windows, the OOBE command will start. If this happens, the computer will no longer be generalized. Therefore, you should finish the OOBE wizard, let the computer finish starting, and then run the Sysprep command again.

If you want to capture the system partition (or any volume that does not have a drive letter assigned to it), you need to assign a drive letter to the volume. After you start to Windows PE, start at the X: drive. You then execute the following commands:

```
Diskpart
Select disk 0
List partition
Select partition=1
Assign letter=s
Exit
```

The list partition command displays the partitions defined on the hard disk. Typically, the system partition will be partition 1. The assign letter command actually assigns the drive letter. The exit command closes the Diskpart command environment.

To capture the images using the DISM command and save the .wim files to the C drive, use the following commands:

```
DISM /Capture-Image /ImageFile:c:\windows-partition.wim
/CaptureDir:C:\ /Name:"Windows partition"
DISM /Capture-Image /ImageFile:s:\system-partition.wim
/CaptureDir:C:\ /Name:"System partition"
```

Note that you also could have saved the image directly to a network shared folder.

When you use the /Capture-Image option, you can use the following options:

- **/ConfigFile** specifies the location of a configuration file that lists exclusions for image capture and compress commands.
- **/Compress** specifies the type of compression (maximum, fast, or none) used for the initial capture operation.
- **/Bootable** marks a volume image as being bootable. This option can be used only with Windows PE images, and only one volume image can be marked as startable in a .wim file.
- **/CheckIntegrity** detects and tracks .wim file corruption when used with capture, unmount, export, and commit operations.
- **/Verify** checks for errors and file duplication.
- **/NoRpFix** disables the reparse point tag fix. A reparse point file contains a link to another file on the file system.

After you capture the image, you need a place to store it. Therefore, you need to share a folder so that it can be accessed over the network. After you start the reference computer with Windows PE, execute the following command:

```
Net Use G: \\Server01\Images
```

At the prompt, enter a username and password. Then use the following two commands to copy the image files to the network share:

```
copy C:\windows-partition.wim G:\Images\
copy c:\system-partition.wim G:\Images\
```

Performing an Unattended Installation by Using WDS

If you load the standard Windows image and startup files and then connect to WDS, you are still doing a manual installation in which you have to go through the Installation Wizard. If you have hundreds of installations, you probably want to perform an unattended installation where you start the computer and it automatically completes the installation.

To perform an unattended installation by using WDS, you need to upload two unattend files:

- **WDS client unattend file:** This file automates the WDS client procedure that begins when the client computer loads the boot image file. It is loaded from the server's Properties dialog box, on the Client tab.
- **Operating system unattend file:** This file installs a standard operating system containing responses to all the prompts that appear after the client computer loads the install image file. It is specified within the image's Properties dialog box.

Designing a Virtual Server Deployment

THE BOTTOM LINE

For a virtual server deployment, you can create a VHD by using a captured image from a reference computer. You can use that VHD to deploy to other machines. When using Hyper-V or VMWare, you can create a template from the VHD, and then copy or clone a virtual machine to new servers.

Although creating a VM from another VM is a simple process, you still need to design and plan your virtual server deployment. The first step in implementing a virtual server is to evaluate your current environment and determine what needs to be virtualized. Besides looking at what resources are required, you need to look at the reason or goals for the virtualization, such as server consolidation, application isolation, simplified server deployment, or higher server availability. You should also determine if the system will be part of a production environment, a test environment, or a development environment. Determining its usage will help you decide what resources the system will need and what the expected workload will be.

When you look at workload for virtualization, you must consider the physical host utilization and related hardware requirements such as processor, memory, network, and storage. Many servers are easy to virtualize. A web server typically produces low resource utilization; a file server typically requires low processor and memory requirements, but might require large amounts of disk space. Although multiple virtual machines can consume a large portion of the CPU processing cycles, recent physical hosts have enough available processing power to ensure that plenty of resources are available if needed.

Since virtualization technology has matured, you can pretty much virtualize any system, including servers running Microsoft SQL and Microsoft Exchange. However, not all machines are ideal to virtualize. If you have a machine that has high I/O applications or requires huge amounts of memory that would use all of the memory on a host machine (such as some databases implementations), are not good candidates to virtualize. Also, graphics-intensive applications, or applications requiring hardware cards or dongles, might not be available in a virtualized environment.

To support an automated system that can deploy standardized virtual machines, you can use System Center's Virtual Machine Manager 2012 R2 (VMM). With VMM, you can create and use a guest operating system profile, which contains a collection of operating system settings that the virtual machine deployment process imports into a virtual machine template. These settings include the following:

- Identity information
- Local administrator password
- Product key
- Time zone
- Operating system version
- Server roles and features
- Domain/workgroup membership
- Answer file references

You can also create application profiles to accommodate specialized applications such as Microsoft SQL Server, Microsoft Application Virtualization Server (Server App-V), or web applications. You can also use scripts to customize the server's settings and configuration.

■ Planning for Deploying Servers to the Cloud

↓ THE BOTTOM LINE

As briefly discussed earlier, cloud services provide a way to access information from anywhere at any time. Microsoft defines **cloud** as a web-based service hosted outside your organization. The IT infrastructure (hardware, servers, software, and so on) is located somewhere other than your office and is managed by a third party. If you use mobile banking, access web-based email, or store your photos online in one of the many services provided, you are interacting with "the cloud."

A **public cloud**, which is owned and operated by third-party service providers, shares the same infrastructure pool, which may limit configuration and security options. A public cloud is typically less expensive because the costs are spread across all users, thus allowing each individual client to operate on a low-cost, "pay-as-you-go" model. The public cloud infrastructure provides clients with seamless, on-demand scalability.

Using public cloud services such as OneDrive and Office 365 enable you to take advantage of hosted solutions. This means users can access their information from anywhere at any time across multiple devices. By using cloud-based services, your users can collaborate via calendars, email, and document sharing. From an administrative perspective, it means you gain access to services and programs without the additional overhead of maintenance and software upgrades.

A **private cloud** is an extension of an organization's data center, optimized to provide storage capacity and processor power for various functions. The resources are not shared with other clients, which allows for better security.

Software as a service (SaaS) is a software distribution model in which applications are hosted by a vendor or service provider. SaaS is made available to customers over a network, such as the Internet, typically as a web-based service. Because software is hosted remotely, the organization does not need to invest in additional hardware or worry about installing, setting up, or maintaining the hardware.

Infrastructure as a service (IaaS) is a computer infrastructure, such as virtualization, being delivered as a service. IaaS enables administrators to run applications in the cloud while maintaining full control over the virtual machines themselves. An organization can use IaaS to host websites, services, or applications that run as self-standing environments, or websites, services, or applications that run as extensions of an organization's data center. IaaS is usually billed monthly with a flat fee or based on usage.

Planning for Deploying Servers to Microsoft Azure Infrastructure as a service (IaaS)

Microsoft Azure (formerly known as Windows Azure) is a cloud-computing platform used for building, deploying, and managing applications and services throughout a global network of Microsoft-managed data centers.

CERTIFICATION READY
Plan for deploying servers to Microsoft Azure infrastructure as a service (IaaS)
Objective 1.1

Microsoft Azure includes the following features:

- Websites with support for ASP.NET, PHP, Node.js, or Python that can be deployed using FTP, Git, Mercurial, or Team Foundation Server
- Virtual machines that run both Windows Server and Linux virtual machines

- Cloud services including Microsoft's *platform as a service (PaaS)* environment that are used to create scalable applications and services
- Data management using SQL Database (formerly known as SQL Azure Database) that can integrate with Active Directory, Microsoft System Center, and Hadoop
- Media services that use PaaS to provide encoding, content protection, streaming, and/or analytics

When you use Microsoft Azure, you are leasing cloud resources provided by Microsoft. The Microsoft Azure resources can be self-contained in the cloud (such as when you want to have websites with databases), or you can extend your organization's data center to the cloud by using IaaS. By using IaaS, you can run applications in the cloud while maintaining full control over the virtual machines themselves.

If you decide to use Microsoft Azure to provide services for your organization, you need to treat the implementation of Microsoft Azure as a project. Therefore, you will need to include the following general steps in the planning process:

1. Determine business requirements
2. Define applications that will be migrated to Microsoft Azure.
3. Define performance and scalability needs.
4. Migrate the applications to Microsoft Azure.
5. Migrate data to Microsoft Azure.
6. Test thoroughly.
7. Optimize as needed.
8. Implement monitoring and maintenance procedures.

Planning for Deploying Servers to Public and Private Clouds

Because Microsoft Azure is a cloud service, planning to deploy servers to a public or private cloud is not much different then deploying to the organization data center. Before you choose to deploy servers to the cloud, you need treat the deployment as a project. Of course, before you jump to the cloud, make sure that you understand what you will get from the cloud. You do not want to jump to the cloud because it is the new IT thing. Instead, be sure you understand the benefits and the costs.

CERTIFICATION READY
Plan for deploying servers to public and private clouds by using App Controller and Windows PowerShell
Objective 1.1

When you plan to deploy servers to public or private clouds, you need to do the following:

1. Analyze business requirements, including defining applications that will be migrated to the servers. Also, be sure to define performance and scalability needed.
2. Define the servers needed to run the applications and services defined. You can also define what platform the servers will run on, such as a Hyper-V host running servers running Windows Server 2012 R2.
3. Migrate applications to the servers and perform detailed testing on the applications and services.
4. Migrate data to the servers and perform detailed testing of the application and data functionality. Perform optimization as needed.
5. Implement monitoring and maintenance procedures

As a virtual environment, you can create multiple virtual machines by deploying the Windows Server 2012 R2 operating system on the Hyper-V host or cloud service that it runs under. You can also upload a Windows Server 2012 R2 image template VHD file or a Windows Server 2012 R2 preconfigured image VHD file. You can then use the cloud tools to manage the hosted virtual machines.

Two tools that allow you to manage your servers located in the cloud is the System Center 2012 R2 App Controller and the related Windows PowerShell cmdlets. The System Center 2012 R2 App Controller allows you to manage applications across the private cloud and the Windows Azure platform from a single console. App Controller also allows you to manage the application components as a service rather than as a server directly from within your browser.

Also, when you load App Controller, you also load the App Controller command shell, which allows you to run App Controllers commands that can be used in scripts.

SKILL SUMMARY

IN THIS LESSON YOU LEARNED:

- An image is a single file or other storage device that contains the complete contents and structures of a disk or other data storage device used with computers and other computing devices. The image has the necessary information to install a copy of Windows onto another machine.

- On the reference computer, you install Windows, install any necessary drivers, configure Windows, install additional software, and configure the additional software.

- Microsoft developed Windows Image Format (WIM) file as a file-based image format that allows a file structure (folders and files) to be stored inside a single WIM database.

- When you plan the images, you need to determine the number of images based on operating system, hardware platform, drivers, and operating features. As mentioned earlier, sector-based images and file-based images each have their own advantages and disadvantages. Sector-based images can be deployed more quickly than file-based images and work well with identical computers.

- A bare metal server is one in which the virtualization hypervisor is directly installed and executed on the hardware without any underlying operating system. The hypervisor then directly interfaces with the underlying hardware without going through an operating system.

- Virtualization increases utilization of computing hardware with server consolidation to minimize hardware footprints and to save money by "stacking" multiple, complementary services on these powerful systems.

- To perform a Lite-Touch, High-Volume Deployment strategy, you need to use a volume-licensed (VL) media provided by Microsoft. You also need the following tools, all which are free from Microsoft: Windows Deployment Services (WDS), Microsoft Assessment and Planning Toolkit, and Microsoft Deployment Toolkit 2012.

- To perform a Zero-Touch, High-Volume Deployment, you need to install and configure System Center Configuration Manager. Next, you install Windows 8 Windows Automated Installation Kit and the Microsoft Deployment toolkit.

- Windows Deployment Services (WDS) is a Windows server role used to deploy Windows over the network with little or no user intervention. If the client can perform a PXE start, you can perform an installation over a network with no operating system or local startup device on it.

- Multicast is when packets are sent from one host to multiple hosts (one point to a set of other points). Multicasting delivers the same packet simultaneously to a group of clients, which results in less bandwidth usage.

- When you select a deployment method for Windows, you determine the best way to deploy Windows with minimal effort, resources, and time while minimizing problems during and after the deployment of Windows. Of course, although you need to look after your organization and users, you also need to follow all policies and guidelines established by the organization.

- The Windows Assessment and Deployment Kit (ADK) is a collection of tools and documentation designed to help IT professionals deploy Windows operating systems. Windows ADK is ideal for using with highly customized environments, because you can use its tools to configure many deployment options.

- For a virtual server deployment, you can create a VHD by using a captured image from a reference computer. You can use that VHD to deploy to other machines. When using Hyper-V or VMWare, you can create a template from the VHD, and then copy or clone a virtual machine to new servers.

- Cloud services provide a way to access information from anywhere at any time. Microsoft defines a cloud as a web-based service that is hosted outside your organization.

- Infrastructure as a service (IaaS) is a computer infrastructure, such as virtualization, being delivered as a service. IaaS enables administrators to run applications in the cloud while maintaining full control over the virtual machines themselves.

- Microsoft Azure (formerly known as Windows Azure) is a cloud-computing platform used for building, deploying and managing applications and services through a global network of Microsoft-managed data centers.

■ Knowledge Assessment

Multiple Choice

1. Your organization's 250 computers use several different motherboards and processors. To deploy Windows 8 to all 250 computers, which type of image would you use?
   a. disk-based image
   b. file-based image
   c. sector-based image
   d. folder-based image

2. Which of the following are advantages of using WIM files to deploy Windows 8? (Choose all that apply.)
   a. Supports offline servicing
   b. Uses file-based servicing
   c. Offers conditional images
   d. Uses compression

3. What is the advantage of VHDx over VHD files?
   a. Enables multiple images in a single VHDx file
   b. Supports up to 256 TB
   c. Enables master-child updating
   d. Uses larger block sizes up to 256 MB

4. You have a server named Server01 running Windows Server 2012 that is part of your Active Directory domain. You want to deploy Windows 8 to 500 client computers. Which image types will you use to deploy Windows? (Choose two.)
   - a. boot image
   - b. capture image
   - c. discover image
   - d. install image

5. You have a remote site with many computers that are not PXE-capable. However, you need to use WDS to deploy Windows to these computers. What type of image will you have to create to overcome this problem?
   - a. boot image
   - b. capture image
   - c. discover image
   - d. install image

6. What program is used to create and validate an answer file, which is used in the deployment of Windows?
   - a. Windows SIM
   - b. WDS
   - c. VDI
   - d. Sysprep.exe

7. Where is Windows SIM located?
   - a. WDS
   - b. VDI
   - c. Configuration Manager
   - d. Windows ADK

8. Which of the following is used to start a computer over the network?
   - a. multicast transmitter
   - b. System Preparation utility
   - c. PXE
   - d. answer file

9. Which of the following are necessary for deploying WDS for stand-alone mode? (Choose all that apply.)
   - a. AD DS
   - b. FAT32 or NTFS
   - c. DHCP
   - d. DNS

10. The answer file is made as a(n) _____ file.
    - a. XLS
    - b. SIM
    - c. XML
    - d. RTF

11. Which type of cloud is an extension of your data center but is not shared with other clients?
    - a. public cloud
    - b. private cloud
    - c. extended cloud
    - d. resource cloud

Best Answer

Choose the letter that corresponds to the best answer. More than one answer choice might achieve the goal. Select the BEST answer.

1. You are preparing 300 computers for classroom instruction. Which of the following is the quickest way to redeploy all 300 computers?
   a. Use WDS to deploy each computer one at a time.
   b. Use WDS to deploy all the computers at the same time while using unicast transmissions.
   c. Use WDS to deploy all the computers while using multicasting.
   d. Use TFTP to copy the image to each computer manually.

2. You are administering a computer that does not support PXE start. Which action should be taken to start the computer and install an image using WDS?
   a. Use a boot image.
   b. Use an install image.
   c. Use a discover image.
   d. Start with a DOS floppy disk.

3. Which of the following tools is part of the Windows 8.1 AIK? (Choose all that apply.)
   a. Deployment Workbench
   b. Sysprep
   c. Windows System Image Manager (SIM)
   d. ImageX

4. Over the next three months, you want to deploy hundreds of computers running Windows 8.1. Which strategy do you recommend?
   a. High-Touch with Retail Media
   b. High-Touch with Standard Image
   c. Lite-Touch, High-Volume Deployment
   d. Zero-Touch, High-Volume Deployment

5. You are the primary IT professional for a small company that supports 50 client computers. You want to deploy Windows 8 to 20 of the older computers. Which deployment strategy should you use?
   a. High-Touch with Retail Media
   b. High-Touch with Standard Image
   c. Lite-Touch, High-Volume Deployment
   d. Zero-Touch, High-Volume Deployment

Matching and Identification

1. Identify the following as High-Touch with Retail Media; High-Touch with Standard Image; Lite-Touch, High-Volume Deployment; or Zero-Touch, High-Volume Deployment.
   Best for more than 500 unmanaged client computers
   Uses WDS
   Best for less than 100 unmanaged client computers
   Best for 200-500 client computers
   Uses Configuration Manager
   Best for 100-200 unmanaged client computers
   Does not use images

Build a List

1. Order the following steps to create a startable ISO image:

    _____ Create the C:\WinPE_x64\ISO\Sources folder.

    _____ Rename the discover.wim file in the C:\WinPE_x64\ISO\Sources folder to boot.wim.

    _____ Copy the contents of the C:\Program Files (x86)\Windows Kits\8.0\ Assessment and Deployment Kit\Windows Preinstallation Environment\ amd64\Media folder to C:\WinPE_x64\ISO.

    _____ Create the C:\WinPE_x64\ISO folder.

    _____ Copy the etfsboot.com file from the C:\Program Files (x86)\Windows Kits\8.0\Assessment and Deployment Kit\Deployment and Imaging Tools\ amd64\Oscdimg folder to the C:\WinPE_x64 folder.

    _____ Create the bootable ISO by running the following command:

    ```
    oscdimg -b"c:\WinPE_X64\etfsboot.com" -n
    C:\WinPE_X64\ISO
    C:\WinPE_X64\WinPE_X64.iso
    ```

    _____ Install the Windows ADK.

    _____ Copy the discover image to the C:\WinPE_x64\ISO\Sources folder.

2. Order the following steps to create a new reference computer and retrieve an image from the reference computer:

    _____ Use DISM to capture the reference computer.

    _____ Create and modify the answer file. Copy the answer file to the USB startup device.

    _____ Prepare the computer by running Sysprep.

    _____ Install and customize Windows PE.

    _____ Plug the USB device and start the computer with the Windows installation disk.

■ Business Case Scenarios

Scenario 1-1: Determining the Images to Use

You are an administrator responsible for deploying 340 clients running Windows 8.1. These clients contain a mix of mobile computers and desktop computers, 32-bit computers and 64-bit computers. They will be distributed throughout a campus of three buildings and five subnets. Each subnet starts from a single DHCP server located on the server subnet. You have a newly installed WDS server (located on the server subnet) used to deploy Windows. You also have several older computers that do not support PXE. How many images do you need to deploy Windows to these clients and why do you need each of these images?

Scenario 1-2: Creating Images

You are an administrator who must deploy Windows to 300 clients by using Windows Server 2012 R2 with Windows Deployment Services. Therefore, you decide to create a master image. What would you need and how would you prepare the master image? After the image is created, what steps would you use to prepare the WDS server to use the image?

Scenario 1-3: Deploying Windows to Multiple Sites

As an administrator for a large corporation, you are currently using Windows Deployment Services (WDS) to deploy to computers through five primary sites. Each site has between 200 and 300 users. With this in mind, answer the following:

1. How can you configure WDS to efficiently use the network without saturating the WAN links doing regular business hours?

2. How would you replicate the images between sites?

3. What step or steps do you need to perform on the WSUS servers to use the replicated images?

Implementing a Server Deployment Infrastructure

70-413 EXAM OBJECTIVE

Objective 1.2 – Implement a server deployment infrastructure. This objective can include but is not limited to: Configure multisite topology and transport servers; implement a multiserver topology, including stand-alone and Active Directory–integrated Windows Deployment Services (WDS) servers; deploy servers to Microsoft Azure IaaS; deploy servers to public and private cloud by using App Controller and Windows PowerShell

LESSON HEADING	EXAM OBJECTIVE
Implementing a Server Deployment Infrastructure with WDS • Deploying WDS • Configuring Multicast Deployment in WDS • Configuring Multisite Topology and Transport Servers	Implement a multiserver topology including stand-alone and Active Directory-integrated Windows Deployment Services (WDS) servers Configure multisite topology and transport servers
Implementing a Server Deployment Infrastructure with Configuration Manager • Installing System Center 2012 R2 Configuration Manager • Configuring PXE Boot and Multicast Support • Configuring Task Sequences, Collections, and Advertisements • Configuring Multisite Topology and Distribution Points with System Center Configuration Manager	Configure multisite topology and transport servers
Implementing a Server Deployment Infrastructure with Microsoft Deployment Toolkit (MDT)	
Deploying Servers to Microsoft Azure IaaS	Deploy servers to Microsoft Azure IaaS
Deploying Servers to Public and Private Cloud by Using App Controller and Windows PowerShell	Deploy servers to public and private cloud by using App Controller and Windows PowerShell

KEY TERMS

advertisement

autocast

collection

Microsoft Deployment Toolkit (MDT) 2012

System Center 2012 R2 Configuration Manager

task sequence

■ Implementing a Server Deployment Infrastructure with WDS

THE BOTTOM LINE

As you learned in Lesson 1, Windows Deployment Services (WDS) is a Windows server role used to deploy Windows over the network with little or no user intervention. If the client can perform a PXE boot, you perform an installation over a network with no local operating system or local startup device on it. The WDS server stores and helps administrators manage the boot and operating system image files used in the network installations.

CERTIFICATION READY

Implement a multiserver topology, including stand-alone and Active Directory–integrated Windows Deployment Services (WDS) servers.

Objective 1.2

WDS supports deploying .vhd images and .wim files. If WDS deploys a .vhd file, it copies that file to the local hard drive, and then configures the local Boot Configuration Data (BCD) so that the file is used to start the computer.

Deploying WDS

With the 70-411 course/exam, you should already be familiar with Windows Deployment Services. Even though deployment of WDS is not new, some of the advanced configuration presented in this lesson is.

To use WDS with Active Directory, you need the following:

- The WDS server as a member of an Active Directory Domain Services (AD DS) domain, or as a domain controller for an AD DS domain
- An active DHCP server on the network
- An active DNS server on your network
- An NTFS file system partition on the server to store images

Starting with Windows Server 2012, you can deploy WDS in stand-alone mode, which means no dependency on Active Directory. To use WDS in stand-alone mode, you need the following:

- An active DHCP server on the network
- An active DNS server on your network
- An NTFS file system partition on the server to store images

In either case, you must be a member of the Local Administrators group to install WDS. WDS is a Windows server role that can be installed using the Server Manager console. WDS includes the following two role services:

- ***Deployment Server*** provides full functionality of WDS, including providing an image repository (such as boot images, install images, and other files necessary for remote installation over a network), a PXE server for remote computers to start, and a Trivial

File Transfer Protocol (TFTP) server to transfer files over the network. Deployment Server also includes tools to create and customize images.

- **Transport Server:** Although required by Deployment Server, the Transport role is a subset of WDS functionality but can also be used for custom solutions. Transport Server can also use multicasting.

Most likely, you will need Deployment Server.

 INSTALL WDS

GET READY. To install WDS on a computer running Windows Server 2012 R2, perform the following steps:

1. In Windows Server 2012 R2, click the Server Manager button on the taskbar.
2. At the top of the *Server Manager* console, select Manage and then click Add Roles and Features.
3. After the *Add Roles and Feature Wizard* opens, on the *Before you begin* page, click Next.
4. On the *Select installation type* page, select Role-based or feature-based installation and then click Next.
5. Click Select a server from the server pool, click the name of the server to install WDS to, and then click Next.
6. On the *Select server roles* page, scroll down and select Windows Deployment Services. In the *Add Roles and Features Wizard* dialog box, select Add Features.
7. Back on the *Select server roles* page, click Next.
8. On the *Select features* page, click Next.
9. On the *WDS* page, click Next.
10. On the *Select role services* page, ensure that the *Deployment Server* and *Transport Server* options are selected, and then click Next.
11. On the *Confirm installation selections* page, click the Install button.
12. When the installation is done, click Close.

After WDS is installed, you have to run the Windows Deployment Services Configuration wizard to perform the initial configuration.

 CONFIGURE WDS

GET READY. To configure WDS on a computer running Windows Server 2012 R2, perform the following steps:

1. In *Server Manager*, open the Tools menu and then click Windows Deployment Services.
2. In the *Windows Deployment Services* console, expand Servers, then right-click the WDS server and select Configure Server.
3. On the *Before You Begin* page, click Next.
4. On the *Install Options* page, click Integrated with Active Directory for an Active Directory–integrated WDS. (For a stand-alone installation, select Standalone server.) Click Next.
5. On the *Remote Installation Folder Location* page, specify the location of the remote installation folder. The default is *C:\RemoteInstall*. Using the system drive (C drive) is not recommended. Click Next.

   If you use the C drive, you should receive a warning that you have the selected the Windows system volume and that you should use a separate volume. To continue, click Yes. Of course, in a production environment, for performance and system reliability, you should create a separate volume to store the WDS images.

6. If your WDS server is also a DHCP server, an additional page appears that allows you to configure the server so that no port conflicts occur:

   • By default, when a DHCP client is looking for a DHCP server, it performs a broadcast, using UDP port 67. If your WDS server is also the DHCP server, you must tell WDS not to listen on port 67 so that DHCP can function properly. Select the Do not listen on DHCP and DHCPv6 ports option.

   • If the local DHCP server is a Microsoft DHCP server, you should select the Configure DHCP options for Proxy DHCP option so that the DHCP server is automatically configured to forward the PXE requests to the WDS server. If the local DHCP server is not a Microsoft DHCP server, you have to configure the DHCP server manually to forward the request to the WDS server.

   Click Next.

8. On the *PXE Server Initial Settings* page, select the appropriate options:

   • ***Do not respond to any client computers:*** If you select this option, WDS cannot perform installations. You typically would use this option to keep WDS disabled until you are ready to use it.

   • ***Respond only to known client computers:*** A known computer has an account prestaged or created in Active Directory before you perform the installation. By prestaging a computer, WDS responds to only computers you specify and not to unstaged or rogue systems.

   • ***Respond to all client computers (known and unknown):*** This least secure option allows WDS to respond to any client system that makes an installation request.

   Click Next.

9. When the task of configuring WDS is completed, the Add images to the server now option is already selected. If you do not want to load images, clear that option. Click the Finish button.

To further configure WDS, right-click the server in the Windows Deployment Services console, and then click Properties. The WDS server properties include the following tabs:

- *General* displays server name, mode, and location of the remote installation folder where images are stored.

- *PXE Response* enables you to specify which types of computers (known or unknown) can download and install images from the server. You also can specify the PXE boot delay in seconds (0 by default).

- *AD DS* allows you to determine the automatic naming format for WDS clients in AD DS that are not prestaged. It also allows you specify where the computer account will be created in Active Directory.

- *Boot* specifies the default network boot image for each architecture type (x86, x64, and ia64) and the PXE Boot Policy settings for known and unknown clients. It also allows you specify whether a user must press F12 to continue the PXE boot.

- *Client* allows you to enable and configure an unattended installation of the WDS clients. If you do not want to add a computer to the domain, select the *Do not join the client to a domain after an installation* option.

- *DHCP* allows you to enable or disable whether a server listens on the DHCP ports (port 67) and to configure DHCP option 60 automatically on a DHCP server.

- *Multicast* allows you to use one set of packets to install operating systems on multiple computers simultaneously. As a result, you minimize network traffic. The Multicast tab allows you to configure multicast transfer settings, as shown in Figure 2-1.

Figure 2-1

Configuring WDS multicast settings

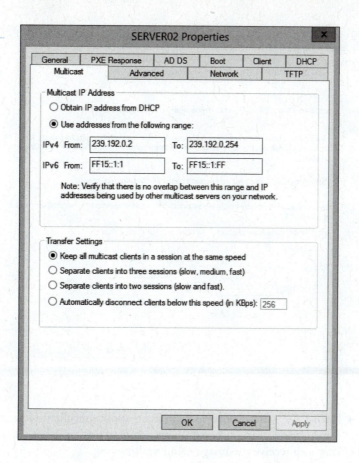

- *Advanced* allows you to authorize your WDS server in DHCP. It also allows you to specify a domain controller and global catalog or to enable WDS to discover them on its own.
- *Network* allows you to specify the UDP port ranges WDS uses. Typically, you would keep the default obtain dynamic ports from Winsock. Note that the *Network profile* option is grayed out in Windows Server 2012, which would allow you to specify the bandwidth of your network. Instead, the bandwidth is determined automatically.
- *TFTP* allows you to configure the maximum block size used for FTP transfers. The TFTP option is new to Windows Server 2012.

Configuring Multicast Deployment in WDS

To perform multicasting with WDS, your organization must use routers that support multicasting. The routers also must have Internet Group Membership Protocol (IGMP) snooping enabled. This causes your network hardware to forward multicast packets only to those devices that request data. If IGMP snooping is turned off, multicast packets are treated as broadcast packets and are sent to every device on the subnet. Only Windows Vista with SP1 clients and later support multicasting.

To create a multicast transmission, right-click the Multicast Transmission node, and then click Create Multicast Transmission. When you run the Multicast Transmission Wizard, select the image that you want to deploy, and then specify the multicast type (see Figure 2-2):

Figure 2-2

Specifying a multicast type when creating a multicast transmission

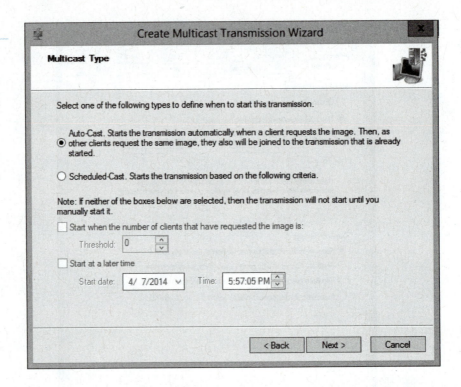

- *Auto-Cast* indicates that as soon as an applicable client requests the image, a multicast transmission of the selected image begins. Then, as other clients request the same image, they also receive the image using multicasting.
- *Scheduled-Cast* sets the start criteria for the transmission based on the number of clients requesting an image and/or a specific day and time. With Scheduled-Cast, only clients that join before the transmission is started receive the image using multicasting. Clients that join later receive the image using unicasting. If you do not select start criteria for the transmission, you must manually start it (by right-clicking the transmission and selecting Start).

Configuring Multisite Topology and Transport Servers

A multisite topology is typically found in large organizations where multiple sites are connected with slower WAN links. Multisite topologies place WDS servers with a centralized image store at each site so that Windows installations are performed locally. As a result, deployments are faster and do not consume valuable WAN link capacity.

CERTIFICATION READY
Configure multisite topology and transport servers.
Objective 1.2

To prevent replication conflicts, avoid modifying or servicing the same images from multiple servers at the same time. Creating a single master Windows Deployment Services server to act as a central point for all images and the images you modify is best practice.

When you configure DFS replication, you create and configure a replication group for the RemoteInstall folder, but exclude the \Mgmt, \Tmp, and \Stores folders. You then configure the BCD refresh policy, which makes the server regenerate the corresponding BCD by running the following command:

```
WDSUTIL /set-server /BcdRefreshPolicy /Enabled:yes
/RefreshPeriod:<time in minutes>
```

If you do not configure the BCD refresh policy or if the refresh period is too long, the network startups fail with a "The boot selection failed because a required device is inaccessible" error message.

Although WDS servers are not aware of other WDS servers, you can manage all WDS servers from one site. Right-click the Servers node, and then click Add Server to add a server to the WDS console. Then use prestage and assign clients to the local WDS server. You also need to configure DHCP option 66 to point to the local WDS server so that the local client performs a PXE boot from the local WDS server.

■ Implementing a Server Deployment Infrastructure with Configuration Manager

 THE BOTTOM LINE

Before you take the 70-413 exam, you should have taken or at least covered the material from the 70-410, 70-411, and 70-412 exams. The 70-411 exam covers installing and configuring WDS so that you can deploy Windows. However, none of these exams cover the System Center 2012 R2 Configuration Manager.

The *System Center 2012 R2 Configuration Manager* allows you to manage your PCs and servers, keep software up to date, deploy software, configure settings, and apply security policies. Configuration Manager can include a single site and server, a single site with one or more secondary servers, or a multisite hierarchy that contains a client administration site, one or more primary sites, and optionally one or more secondary sites.

The site roles used in Configuration Manager include

- The central administration site, at the top of the Configuration Manager hierarchy, enables centralized administration and reporting for the entire hierarchy. You can have only one central administration site for each hierarchy. When you install the central administration site, you define the site name and site code, which cannot be changed.
- Primary sites assigned to the central administration site are used to directly manage the clients.
- Secondary sites are optional site systems installed on small remote sites that use slow WAN links. They contain a management point and distribution point so that they can transfer client data and perform deployments.

When you install a site server, the following roles are installed by default:

- *Site server* provides core functionality for a site, which enables you to install or define additional roles.
- *Component server* runs the Configuration Manager services. It is installed automatically with all site systems except the distribution point.
- *SMS provider* provides an interface between the Configuration Manager console and the site database on the central administration site and primary sites.
- *Site system* hosts one or more of the site system roles or Configuration Manager site.
- *Site database server* hosts the SQL Server database used by Configuration Manager.
- *Management point* provides policy and content location information to Configuration Manager clients and receives hardware and software data from clients.
- *Distribution point* has the source files to perform a Windows software or update deployment. To minimize bandwidth, you can configure bandwidth throttling and perform deployment scheduling during nonpeak hours. To support Windows deployment, the distribution point supports PXE boot and multicasting.

You can add the following site roles:

- *Endpoint protection point* provides the ability to manage malware protection.
- *Fallback status point* helps monitor client installations and identify unmanaged clients.
- *Reporting services point* integrates with Microsoft SQL Server Reporting Services to create and run reports for Configuration Manager.
- *Software update point* interfaces with and manages Windows Server Update Services (WSUS) to synchronize the software update from Microsoft Update or an upstream WSUS server.
- *State migration point* migrates and stores user data when deploying the operating system.

Installing System Center 2012 R2 Configuration Manager

To install System Center 2012 R2 Configuration Manager, you first need to install the following on the server, in this order:

> System Center 2012 R2 Configuration Manager is an easy program to install. Because it is not included as part of Windows, you have to download System Center from Microsoft. You then need to install the Windows prerequisites. While the configuration manager is easy to install, how you configure it and where you deploy it requires planning and designing.

- Windows Server 2008 or higher (x64) operating system
- A supported version of SQL Server 2008 SP2 with CU6 or SQL Server 2008 R2 with SP1
- .NET Framework 3.5 and 4.0
- Internet Information Services (IIS) Manager with Web Distributed Authoring and Versioning (WebDAV), ASP.Net 3.5, ASP.NET 4.5, and IIS 6 Management Compatibility with IIS 6 Metabase Compatibility and IIS 6 WMI Compatibility
- Remote Differential Compression and Background Intelligent Transfer Service (BITS) features

 INSTALL SYSTEM CENTER 2012 CONFIGURATION MANAGER

GET READY. To install System Center 2012 Configuration Manager on a computer running Windows Server 2012 R2, perform the following steps:

1. To extend the Active Directory Schema with Schema Administrator's rights, execute the <CM2012R2RCMedia>\SMSSETUP\BIN\I386\extadsch.exe file.
2. From the Configuration Manager CM 2012 R2 install media, double-click Splash.hta.
3. When the *System Center 2012 R2 Configuration Manager* splash page opens, click Install.
4. On the *Before You Begin* page, click Next.
5. On the *Available Setup Options* page, click Install a Configuration Manager Central administration site, and then click Next.
6. On the *Product key* page, enter the key or select Install the evaluation edition of this product. Click Next.
7. On the *Microsoft Software License Terms* page, click I accept these license terms, and then click Next.
8. On the *Prerequisite license* page, click I accept these License Terms for Microsoft SQL Server 2012 Express, Microsoft SQL Server 2012 Native Client, and Microsoft Silverlight. Click Next.
9. On the *Prerequisite Downloads* page, in the top *Path* text box, type C:\Downloads, and then click Next. The C:\Downloads folder must exist.

10. On the *Server Language Selections* page, select your language and then click Next.

11. On the *Client Language Selection* page, select your language and then click Next.

12. On the *Site and Installation Settings* page, type the following:

    Site code: 001

    Site name: Corporate

    Click Next.

13. On the *Central Administration Site Installation* page, *Install as the first site in a new hierarchy* is already selected. Click Next.

14. On the *Database Information* page, click Next.

15. On the *SMS Provider Settings* page, click Next.

16. On the *Customer Experience Improvement Program* page, select I don't want to join the program at this time. Click Next.

17. On the *Settings Summary* page, click Next.

18. If any prerequisite is missing, the SCCM informs you before it starts the installation. Fix all prerequisites. When done, click Begin install.

19. When the installation is complete, click Close.

The System Center 2012 R2 Configuration Manager console is divided into the following workspaces:

- *Assets and Compliance* includes collections for managing users and devices (see Figure 2-3). You can also manage user state migration, asset intelligence, and software metering.

Figure 2-3

Using the System Center 2012 R2 Configuration Manager console

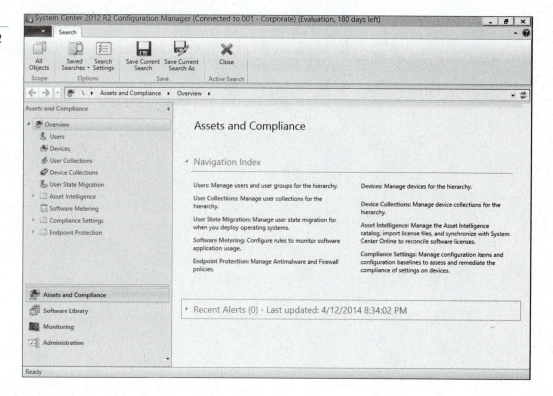

- *Software Library* includes options to manage applications, software updates, and operating system deployments.
- *Monitoring* allows the monitoring of the Configuration Manager infrastructure, including sites, components, distribution, replication and client health.
- *Administration* is used to manage the Configuration Manager infrastructure, security, and settings. It allows you to manage distribution points, site boundaries, resource discovery, and migration of data from System Center Configuration Manager 2007.

To provide the bulk of the Configuration Manager functionality for clients, you run the install the Configuration Manager client software, which installs an agent on the client. By default, the Configuration Manager uses the Local System account to perform most client operations. Whereas the Local System account has extensive privilege on the system, it does not have access to network resources. The Network Access account is used by clients from workgroups or non-trusted domains that require access to resources in the domain and during the Windows PE phase of operating system capture and deployment task sequences. The Network Access account that you choose to use should have the minimum appropriate permissions for the software distribution or operating system deployment content it needs to access. Because you can only have one Network Access account per site, the account must have function for all packages and task sequences that need to use it.

 CONFIGURE THE NETWORK ACCESS ACCOUNT

GET READY. To configure the Network Access Account, perform the following steps:

1. In the *Configuration Manager* console, in the navigation pane (bottom left pane), click Administration.
2. In the *Administration* workspace, expand Site Configuration, and then click the Sites node.
3. In the results pane, right-click a site, click Configure Site Components, and then click Software Distribution.
4. In the *Software Distribution Component Properties* dialog box, click the Network Access Account tab, as shown in Figure 2-4.

Figure 2-4

Specifying the Network Access
Account

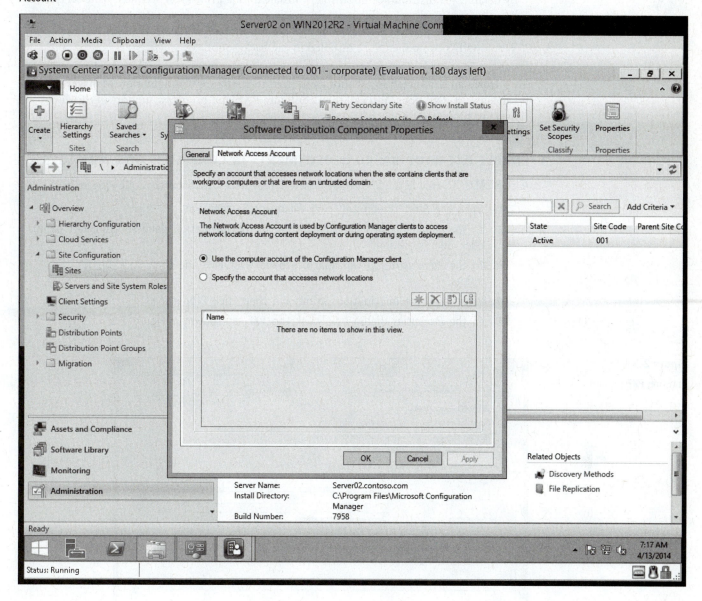

5. Click Specify the account that accesses network locations. click Set, and then click New Account.

6. In the *Windows User Account* dialog box, type a username in the *Domain\User* format. Type in the appropriate password in the *Password* and *Confirm password* text boxes, and click OK.

7. Click OK to close the *Software Distribution Component Properties* dialog box.

Configuring PXE Boot and Multicast Support

By default, the distribution point role is installed on a primary or secondary site server. You also can install a distribution point on a separate server. If you do not install Windows Deployment Services on a site system but configure PXE or multicast support, Windows DS components are installed in the background.

To perform an automated installation, you need to configure Configuration Manager so that it can support PXE boot. You can then configure PXE and multicast support in the distribution point properties.

 ENABLE PXE BOOT–BASED DEPLOYMENTS IN CONFIGURATION MANAGER

GET READY. To enable the PXE boot–based deployments, perform the following steps:

1. Open the Start screen and click Microsoft System Center 2012.
2. In the *Configuration Manager* console, in the navigation pane (bottom left pane), click Administration.
3. In the *Administration* workspace, expand Overview, and then click Distribution Points.
4. Right-click the distribution point, and then click Properties.
5. In the *Properties* dialog box, click the PXE, as shown in Figure 2-5.

Figure 2-5

Enabling PXE support

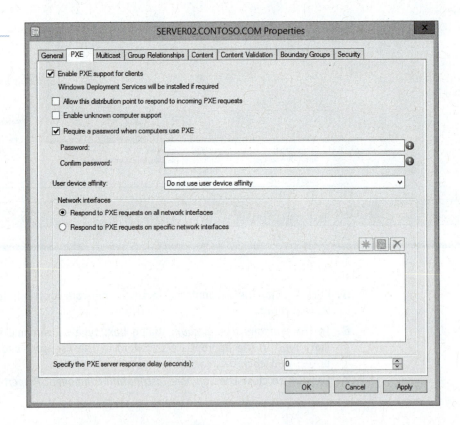

6. Click to select Enable PXE support for clients. In the *Review Required Ports for PXE boot* dialog box, notice that you can open the following ports for the Windows firewall:
   • For PXE requests: UDP ports 67, 68, 69, and 4011

- For operating system installation: UDP port 69

Click Yes.

7. By default, when the Configuration Manager PXE service point is installed, it will not respond to PXE requests. When you are ready to use PXE boot in your environment, you must select Allow this distribution point to respond to incoming PXE requests.

8. If you need to support unknown computers, click Enable unknown computer support.

9. If want to specify a password to start the PXE boot process, select Require a password when computers use PXE and then specify the password in the *Password* and *Confirm password* text boxes.

10. User device affinity establishes a relationship between users and computers in Configuration Manager. Select one of the following options:

- Allow user device affinity with auto-approval

- Allow user device affinity pending administrator approval

- Do not allow user device affinity

11. By default, *Respond to PXE request occurs on all network interfaces* is selected. If you want to listen on only certain network interfaces, select the Respond to PXE requests on specific network interfaces and then select the interfaces that you want to use.

12. If you want to delay the PXE server response, specify the number of seconds in the *Specify the PXE server response delay* (seconds) section.

13. Click OK to close the *Properties* dialog box.

When you enable multicast support, you can use the default settings, or you can customize multicast support. Of course, when you use multicast for operating system deployment, you must configure the multicast ranges and make sure that all routers and firewalls allow the necessary UDP ports.

The Multicast tab (see Figure 2-6) provides the following options:

Figure 2-6

Enabling Multicasting

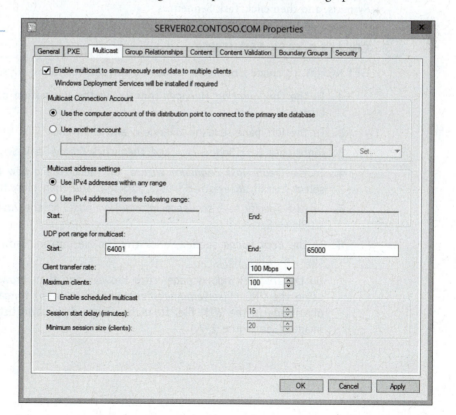

- *Multicast Connection Account* specifies the account to use when you configure Configuration Manager database connections for multicast.
- *Multicast address settings* specifies the IP addresses used in multicast deployments. You can select to use obtain addresses from a DHCP server, or you can specify a range of addresses.
- *UDP port range for multicast* specifies the range of UDP ports used to send data to the destination computers.
- *Client transfer rate* enables you to select the maximum transfer rate for Windows deployment.
- *Maximum clients* specifies the maximum number of multicast sessions that can be active at one time.
- *Enable scheduled multicast* allows you to schedule when multicast will occur.

By default, the Configuration Manager distribution point uses autocast mode for multicast. With *autocast*, the deployment starts on the first device. When you deploy a second device while the first deployment is running, the second device picks up the current stream. When the first deployment is finished, the second device goes back to pick up those bits missed. The only thing you have to do for autocast functionality is enable multicast.

Configuring Task Sequences, Collections, and Advertisements

Before you can deploy an operating system, you need to configure a task sequence, a collection, and an advertisement. The task sequence specifies what is being done, the collection specifies who or what the task is applied to, and the advertisement brings it all together by specifying when the task will be executed. •

Task sequences are used to automate the task steps on a client computer. To create a task sequence in the Configuration Manager Software Library workspace, expand Operating Systems, and then click Task Sequences.

 CREATE A TASK SEQUENCE

GET READY. To create a new task sequence, perform the following steps:

1. In the *Configuration Manager* console, in the navigation pane, click Software Library.
2. In the left pane, expand Overview, and then click Task Sequences.
3. Right-click Task Sequences, and then click Create Task Sequence.
4. In the *Create Task Sequence Wizard*, on the *Create a new task sequence* page, select Install an existing image package, and then click Next.
5. On the *Specify task sequence information* page, in the *Task sequence* text box, type Windows Server.
6. In the *Boot image* section, click the Browse button. Browse to a Boot image and click OK. Click Next.
7. On the *Install Windows* page, click Browse, and then browse to an image package using the UNC *(\\servername\sharename\install.wim)* format. If you have more than one image in the WIM file, from the *Image* drop-down list select the appropriate image. (See Figure 2-7.)

Figure 2-7

Installing the Windows operating system using a task sequence

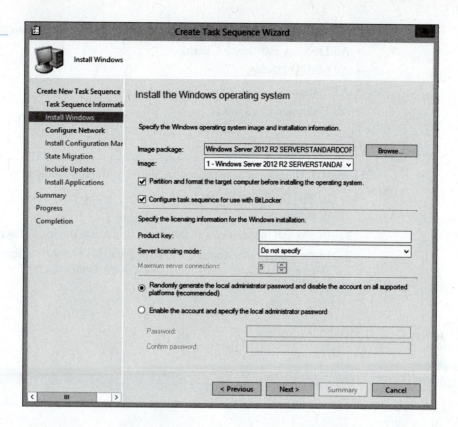

8. In the *Product key* text box, specify the product key. Click Next.

9. On the *Configure the network* page, click Join a domain.

10. Use the Browse buttons to specify the domain and domain organizational unit (OU).

11. In the *Account* section, click Set.

12. In the *Windows User Account* dialog box, in the *User name* section, type the name of the account that can add a computer account to the domain in the *domain\ user* format.

13. In the *Password* and *Confirm password* text boxes, type the password of the account and click Verify.

14. When the dialog box expands, click Test connection. When the connection has been verified, click OK.

15. Back on the *Configure Network* page, click Next.

16. To jump to the *Summary* page, click the Summary button.

17. On the *Summary* page, click Next.

18. On the Completion page, click Close.

When you deploy an operating system or application, you need to create a collection and advertisement. A ***collection*** is a group of objects (devices, computers, users, or groups) used to organize the objects that provides a target for advertisements and reports. To manage collections, open the Assets and Compliance workspace, expand Overview. and then click either User Collections or Device Collections.

When Configuration Manager is installed, the following collections are created:

- All Desktop and Server Clients
- All Mobile Devices
- All Systems
- All Unknown Computers

 CREATE A NEW COLLECTION

GET READY. To create a new collection, perform the following steps:

1. In the *Configuration Manager* console, in the navigation pane, click Assets and Compliance.
2. In the left pane, expand Overview, and click Device Collections.
3. In the *Assets and Compliance* workspace (as shown in figure 2-8), right-click Device Collections, and then click Create Device Collection.

Figure 2-8

Creating a new device collection

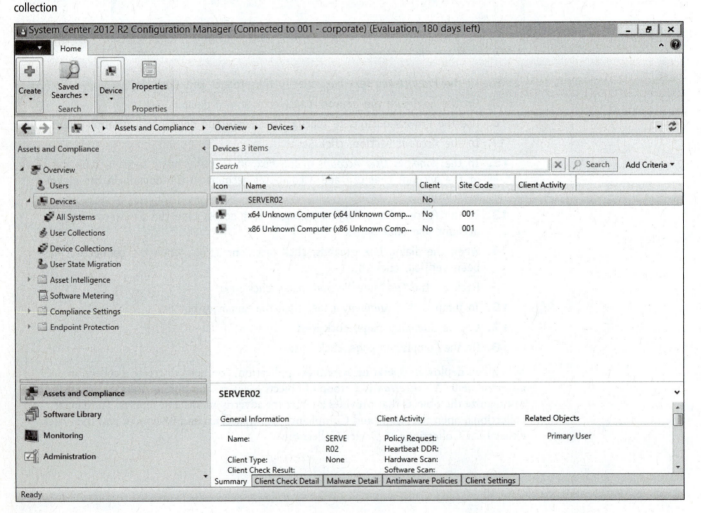

4. In the *Create Device Collection* Wizard, on the *General* page, type a name for the collection in the *Name* text box, such as Server Deployment.

5. To limit the collection to another collection, click the Browse button. In the *Select Collection* window, click the collection that you want to limit to (such as *All Systems*), and then click OK. Click Next.

6. To add a single computer to the collection, on the *Membership Rules* page, click Add Rule and then Direct Rule.

7. When the *Welcome to the Create Direct Membership Rule* Wizard opens, click Next.

8. On the *Search for Resources* page, the *Resource Class* is set to *System Resource*, and the *Attribute* name is set to *Name*. Because the percent sign (%) is the wildcard parameter in Configuration Manager, type % in the Value text box, and then click Next.

9. Because you used % by itself, it shows all computers. Click the computer that you want to add to the collection, and then click Next.

10. On the *Summary* page, click Next.

11. After the computer is added, click Close.

12. Back on the *Membership Rules* page, click Next.

13. On the *Summary* page, click Next.

14. After the collection is created, click Close.

To modify the collection after it is created, you just right-click it and then click Properties. You can add new members or delete old members on the Membership Rules tab.

An ***advertisement*** tells when a package is available to users and system center client computers. It specifies how the package is to be deployed, when it will be deployed, what package will run, and who can run the package.

 CREATE AN ADVERTISEMENT

GET READY. To create a new advertisement for an operating system deployment, perform the following steps:

1. In the *Configuration Manger* console, in the navigation pane, click Software Library.

2. In the *Software Library* workspace, expand Operating Systems, and then click Task Sequences.

3. Right-click the task sequence that you want to deploy, and click Deploy.

4. When the *Deploy Software* Wizard opens (as shown in Figure 2-9), click Browse next to the *Collection* text box. In the *Select Collection* dialog box, click Server Deployment. Click OK.

Figure 2-9

Selecting the collection using the Deploy Software Wizard

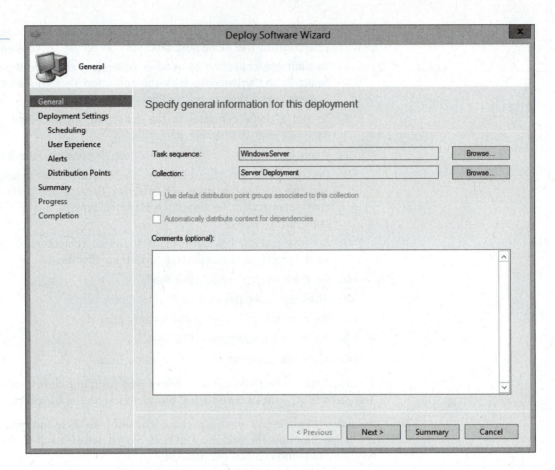

5. Back on the *General* page, click Next.

6. On the *Deployment Settings* page, select Configuration manager clients, media, and PXE. Click Next.

7. On the *Specify the schedule for the deployment* page, specify when the deployment will be available by selecting Schedule when the deployment will become available and Schedule when this deployment will expire, and then selecting the appropriate dates and times. Click Next.

8. On the *User experience* page, specify what users will see during the deployment. When done, click Next.

9. On the *Alerts* page, click Next.

10. On the *Distribution Points* page, *Download content locally when needed by running task sequence* is already selected for the deployment options. Click Next.

11. On the *Summary* page, click Next.

12. When the deployment has been configured, click Close.

You can then restart the computer and perform a PXE boot, or use a SCCM Boot CD to start the actual deployment.

Configuring Multisite Topology and Distribution Points with System Center Configuration Manager

> With Configuration Manager, you can use other servers at remote sites as distribution points for new packages and images. So when you deploy Windows, the client can retrieve the images from the local server.

After these packages and images are created, you select the distribution points from which the packages and images will be copied and available to target computers. After you configure a distribution point for a package, you need time for files to be copied to the distribution points before you can start using the files from the distribution point.

 CONFIGURE A DISTRIBUTION POINT

GET READY. To configure a distribution point, perform the following steps:

1. In the *Configuration Manager* console, in the navigation pane, click Software Library.
2. In the *Software Library* workspace, expand Overview, expand Operating Systems, and then click Task Sequences.
3. In the *preview* pane, click WindowsServer.
4. On the ribbon, on the *Home* tab, in the *Deployment* group, click Distribute Content.
5. When the *Distribute Content* Wizard opens, click Next.
6. On the *Content* page, review the content to distribute, and then click Next.
7. On the *Content Destination* page, click Add, and then click Distribution Point. Select the distribution point that you want to add and click OK. Click Next.
8. On the *Summary* page, click Next.
9. When the wizard is complete, click Close.

The advantage of using Configuration Manager is that with the operating system deployment, you can deploy additional packages including Windows User State Migration Toolkit (USMT) packages, device driver packages, and application packages. Therefore, you can deploy a standard operating system image, and then customize the deployed system with additional packages using the single operating system image. The package categories include the following:

- *Configuration Manager Client Software:* This package installs the Configuration Manager client on the system so that it can be fully managed (deploy applications, deploy updates, and perform inventory). By default, a Configuration Manager client package is created in the \\Server\Site\Client folder and is distributed to the default distribution point during installation.

- *USMT Package:* This package migrates the user state, including the Desktop folder, Documents folder, and Favorites, from one computer to another. Migrating the user state during operating system deployment migrates the data to a secure location, deploys the operating system, and then applies the user state to the new system. Configuration Manager SP1 creates the User State Migration Tool for Windows 8 package automatically. However, it is not distributed automatically to the default distribution point.

- *Driver Packages:* You can use device driver packages to group similar device drivers together and publish the drivers to a distribution point. The drivers can then be deployed to any Configuration Manager client.

- *Application Packages:* You can use a task sequence to install additional software applications.

When you install applications, you can use different task steps: Install Package and Install Application. The Install Package is used to install older style software packages that was used before System Center 2012. The Install Application task step is a new format with Configuration Manager 2012. Most software is deployed as an application, although the software package method also is available.

■ Implementing a Server Deployment Infrastructure with Microsoft Deployment Toolkit (MDT)

THE BOTTOM LINE

Although WDS can deploy an operating system image and even supports adding some drivers, you are limited on what you can do with WDS. However, when you combine WDS with Microsoft Deployment Toolkit (or combine Configuration Manager with MDT), you get a much more robust deployment solution.

The *Microsoft Deployment Toolkit (MDT) 2012* provides end-to-end guidance for the planning of, building, and deploying Windows 8.1 and Windows Server 2012 R2. It allows you to deploy Windows by using a Lite-Touch Installation (LTI) or Zero-Touch Installation (ZTI). MDT allows you to create a deployment share, which contains additional scripts and task sequences to customize the Windows installation process.

You first need to download the Microsoft Deployment Toolkit 2013 from Microsoft. The initial installation is simple enough; double-click MicrosoftDeploymentToolkit2013_x64.msi to run a simple installation wizard.

The Deployment Workbench centralizes multiple programs used in deployment. Therefore, in the Components node, the next step is to download and install those programs. Figure 2-10 shows that the Windows Automated Installation Kit (x64) is already download, but it still needs to be installed. So in this case, just click the Install button to perform the installation.

Figure 2-10

Installing the Windows
Automated Installation Kit

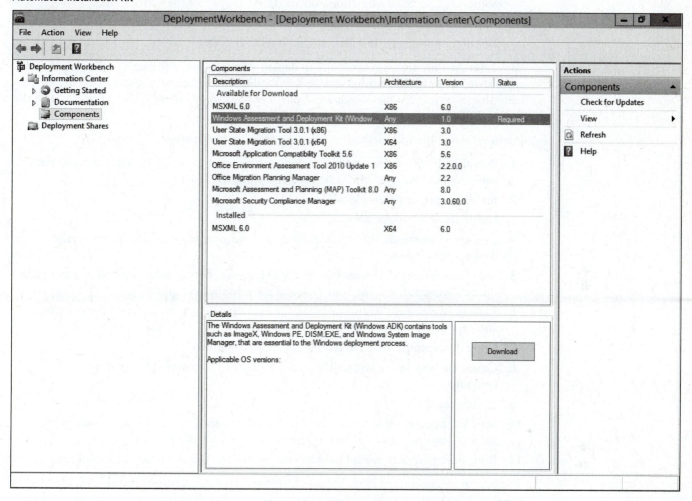

If needed, other components can be downloaded and installed. Therefore, you need to start Deployment Workbench, select the following components, then and click Download:

- Windows Automated Installation Kit (x86)
- User State Migration Tool 3.0.1 (x86)
- User State Migration Tool 3.0.1 (x64)
- Microsoft Application Compatibility Toolkit 5.6
- Office Environment Assessment Tool 2010 Update 1
- Office Migration Planning Manager
- Microsoft Assessment and Planning (MAP) Toolkit 8.0
- Microsoft Security Compliance Manager 3.0.60.0

You should also click Check for Updates so that the Deployment Workbench refreshes the components list, ensuring you have the latest version.

To perform a Lite-Touch, High-Volume Deployment strategy, you need to use a volume-licensed (VL) media provided by Microsoft. You will need to install the Windows Deployment Services (WDS) role. You also need the following tools, all which are free from Microsoft:

- Microsoft Assessment and Planning Toolkit
- Microsoft Deployment Toolkit 2013
- Windows User State Migration Toolkit (USMT) (part of the WAIK)
- Application Compatibility Toolkit (ACT)
- Windows Automated Installation Kit (WAIK)

You also need a network infrastructure to deploy Windows and a file server with shared folders to share store the distribution shares. You need a startup disk to connect to the deployment shares, or you can use Windows Deployment Services to allow PXE boot to perform the Windows deployment.

Preparing to use the LTI method involves the following basic steps:

1. Plan the MDT imaging strategy, including how you will build the MDT management computer and how you will store images and related files.
2. Install the prerequisites and MDT 2013.
3. Create the deployment share.
4. Create and customize the task sequences. Task sequences are used to automate the deployment process.
5. Start the reference computer with the MDT media. This transfers the task sequence files, the task sequence, and the boot image to the reference computer.
6. Run the deployment wizard to install the operating system on the reference computer and capture an image of the reference computer.
7. Copy the captured image to the management computer.
8. Create the boot image and task sequence to deploy the captured image to target computers.
9. Update the deployment share.
10. Start the target computer with the MDT media. This transfers the task sequence files, the task sequence, and the boot image to the reference computer.
11. Run the deployment wizard to install the operating system on the target computer.

To perform a Zero-Touch, High Volume Deployment strategy, you still need a VL media provided by Microsoft. You also will use many of the same tools that you would use in the Lite-Touch, High Volume Deployment strategy, including the following:

- MAP Toolkit 8.0
- MDT 2013
- Windows User State Migration Toolkit (USMT)
- Application Compatibility Toolkit (ACT)
- WAIK

Rather than use WDS, you use System Center Configuration Manager 2012 R2 to perform the hands-off deployment.

To perform a Zero-Touch, High-Volume Deployment, you need to install and configure System Center Configuration Manager. Next, you install Windows 8, WAIK, and MDT 2013, just as you would for an LTI deployment. Next, you need to run the Configure ConfigMgr Integration Wizard, which adds MDT functionality to Configuration Manager.

RUN THE CONFIGMGR INTEGRATION WIZARD

GET READY. To run the Configure ConfigMgr Integration Wizard, perform the following steps:

1. From the Start Menu, click All Programs. In the Microsoft Deployment Toolkit section, click Configure ConfigMgr Integration.
2. When the *Configure ConfigMgr Integration* Wizard opens, click Next.
3. If necessary, modify any options, and then click Next.
4. On the *Confirmation* page, click Finish.

Before performing an operating system deployment, you must perform a few preparation steps. With Configuration Manager, you can use other servers at remote sites as distribution points for new packages and images. Therefore, when you deploy Windows, the client can retrieve the images from the local server. The distribution point is automatically created on the server running Configuration Manager. Before you can use the distribution point, you need to configure the distribution point for use. In general, you need to perform the following planning and preparation steps:

1. Prepare the distribution point for PXE boot and multicast support.
2. Configure a Configuration Manager Network Access account.
3. Prepare boot images.
4. Import operating system installer packages.
5. Import device drivers.
6. Create additional packages such as USMT packages, driver packages, or application pages that are not included in the image.

■ Deploying Servers to Microsoft Azure IaaS

THE BOTTOM LINE

Microsoft Azure (formerly known as Windows Azure) is a cloud computing platform used for building, deploying, and managing applications and services through a global network of Microsoft-managed datacenters. Although Microsoft Azure has its own web-based tools, you can also use System Center 2012 R2 Virtual Machine Manager (VMM) and App Controller.

CERTIFICATION READY
Deploy servers to Microsoft Azure IaaS.
Objective 1.2

Microsoft provides several tools to deploy and manage servers running Windows Server 2012 R2 on public and private clouds:

- System Center 2012 R2 Virtual Machine Manager (VMM)
- Windows Azure virtual machine (VM) tools
- System Center 2012 R2 App Controller

System Center 2012 R2 Virtual Machine Manager (VMM) provides a single administrative tool for deploying virtual servers and managing a virtualization infrastructure, including hosts, virtual machines, storage, networks, and libraries. You can also use VMM to update virtual servers.

The Windows Azure web portal includes multiple tools for creating and managing virtual machines that are hosted on the Windows Azure cloud platform. With these tools, you can create VMs, attach disks, upload a Windows Server VHD file, load balance virtual machines, and manage availability of virtual machines.

The System Center 2012 R2 App Controller application allows administrators to deploy and manage services across the Microsoft private cloud services and the Microsoft public cloud services, such as Windows Azure. App Controller has a web-based interface that enables administrators to manage services rather than servers.

■ Deploying Servers to Public and Private Cloud by Using App Controller and Windows PowerShell

↓ THE BOTTOM LINE

System Center 2012 R2 App Controller allows you to manage applications across the private cloud and the Windows Azure platform from a single console. App Controller also allows you to manage the application components as a service rather than a server directly from within your browser.

CERTIFICATION READY
Deploy servers to public and private cloud by using App Controller and Windows PowerShell.
Objective 1.2

App Controller provides the self-service component by configuring, deploying, and managing services and virtual machines on private and public clouds, using a library of standard templates. You can also create, manage, and move services without needing to know what servers they are on, or without needing to use server-level tools. Job tracking and history views of jobs and actions taken are also available. Figure 2-11 shows the App Controller console.

Figure 2-11

The App Controller console

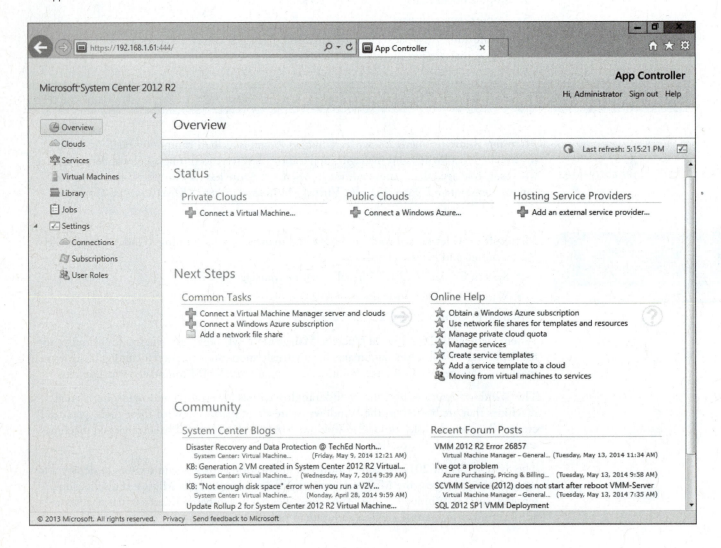

➡ INSTALL SYSTEM CENTER 2012 R2 APP CONTROLLER

GET READY. To install System Center 2012 R2 App Controller, perform the following steps:

1. From the System Center 2012 R2 App Controller installation folder or disk, double-click setup.exe.

2. When the *App Controller* splash page opens, click Install.

3. On the *Enter your product registration information* page, type your product key, and then click Next.

4. On the *Review the software license terms* page, select I have read, understand, and agree with the terms of the license agreement option. Click Next.

5. On the *Install missing software* page appears, click Install.

6. On the *Select the installation path* page, click Next.

7. On the *Configure the services* page, select Domain account. Then in the *Domain* and *User name* text box, type contoso\administrator. In the Password text box, type Pa$$w0rd. Click Next.

8. On the *Configure the website* page, click Generate-self-signed certificate. Click Next.

9. On the *Configure the SQL Server database* page, the *Server name* is already config-ured for localhost. For the *Instance name*, select MSSQLSERVER, and then click Next.

10. On the *Help improve App Controller for System Center 2012 R2* page, click No, I am not willing to participate. Click Next.

11. On the *Confirm the settings* page, click Install.

12. When the setup is completed successfully, click Finish.

The App Controller server runs the web-based Silverlight application to manage, build, configure, and deploy services to the cloud. The SQL database contains the necessary infor-mation for the connections to your Azure subscriptions and your VMM services. When you install App Controller, you can use the App Controller Windows PowerShell module to enable administrators to automate App Controller administration.

Because you still need to maintain security, App Controller allows administrators to delegate authority to application owners. You can use predefined templates to ensure compliance with company IT standards and policies. You also can create customized, role-based views of private and public cloud services, as well as a view of consumed and available resources. Application owners can customize all service components, including VMs, network resources, and load balancing.

You can use App Controller to move applications and components within public and private cloud environments, among Windows Azure subscriptions. You can also copy service tem-plates and resources from one VMM server to another.

To deploy a service to Windows Azure, you first create a Windows Azure configuration and pack-age files. You then upload these files to a Windows Azure storage account. When you select the configuration files, the diagram view loads and you then use hyperlinks to configure settings. When configured, you then click the Deploy button in the diagram view; the service becomes available.

After you connect to the cloud, you can use the Virtual Machine node's Deploy button to display a new deployment diagram view, which you can use to create a virtual machine. When it is all configured, you then click the Deploy button to deploy the virtual machine.

You can access the App Controller cmdlets on your App Controller server in one of two ways:

- Open the App Controller command shell (click Start, All Programs, Microsoft System Center 2012 R2, Windows PowerShell Module for App Controller).

- Open Windows PowerShell session and import the App Controller module by using the `Import-Module -Name` App Controller command.

SKILL SUMMARY

IN THIS LESSON YOU LEARNED:

- Windows Deployment Services (WDS) is a Windows server role used to deploy windows over the network with little or no user intervention.

- Multisite topologies install WDS servers with a centralized image store at each site so that Windows installations are performed locally. As a result, the deployments are faster and the deployments do not consume valuable WAN link capacity.

- The System Center 2012 R2 Configuration Manager allows you to manage your PCs and servers, keep software up to date, deploy software, configure settings, and apply security policies. The System Center 2012 R2 Configuration Manager can include a single site and server, a single site with one or more secondary servers, or a multisite hierarchy that contains a client administration site, one or more primary sites, and optionally one or more secondary sites.

- With Configuration Manager, you can use other servers at remote sites as distribution points for new packages and images. Therefore, when you deploy Windows, the client can retrieve the images from the local server.

- The Microsoft Deployment Toolkit (MDT) 2013 provides end-to-end guidance for the planning of, building, and deploying the Windows 8.1 and Windows Server 2012 R2 operating systems.

- Infrastructure-as-a-service (IaaS) is a computer infrastructure, such as virtualization, being delivered as a service. IaaS enables administrators to run applications in the cloud while maintaining full control over the virtual machines themselves.

- The System Center 2012 R2 App Controller allows you to manage applications across the private cloud and the Windows Azure platform from a single console. App Controller also allows you to manage the application components as a service rather than as a server directly from within your browser.

■ Knowledge Assessment

Multiple Choice

1. Which of the following are prerequisites to install System Center 2012 Configuration Manager? (Choose all that apply.)
   a. .NET Framework 3.5
   b. IIS with WebDAV
   c. Remote Differential Compression
   d. Background Intelligent Transfer Service

2. Which technology enables one set of packets to be sent to 10 different computers at the same time?
   a. multicasting
   b. prestaging clients
   c. PXE boot
   d. unattend boot

3. What are the primary tools used with Zero-Touch, High-Volume Deployment?
   a. Windows Deployment Services (WDS)
   b. System Center 2012 R2 Configuration Manager
   c. Windows Server Update Services (WSUS)
   d. Windows Automated Installation Kit (WAIK)

4. How do you integrate Microsoft Deployment Toolkit with System Center Configuration Manager?
   a. Install Microsoft Deployment Toolkit from within System Center Configuration Manager.
   b. Run the ConfigMgr Integration Wizard.
   c. Run the `MDT.exe /ConfigMgr` command.
   d. Install the Microsoft Deployment Kit, and then install System Center Configuration Manager.

5. For most WDS deployments, which WDS role services do you need? (Choose all that apply.)
   a. Deployment Server
   b. Image Creator
   c. Capture Utility
   d. Transport Server

6. In IPv4, what address ranges are used for multicasting?
   a. 1.0.0.0 to 126.255.255.255
   b. 128.0.0.0 to 191.255.255.255.0
   c. 192.255.255.255 to 224.0.0.0
   d. 224.0.0.0 to 239.255.255.255

7. Before you deploy operating systems to clients, what two things do you will need to create? (Choose two answers.)
   a. deployment rule
   b. advertisement
   c. collection
   d. image collection

8. Which of the following is needed for a Lite-Touch, High-Volume Deployment?
   a. Windows Automated Installation Kit (WAIK)
   b. System Center 2012 R2 Configuration Manager
   c. Microsoft Deployment Toolkit
   d. Windows Deployment Server

9. When you configure DFS replication for the RemoteInstall folder, between the corporate office and site servers, how can you configure the BCD refresh policy?
   a. `BCDRefresh /set-server /BcdRefreshPolicy /Enabled:yes / RefreshPeriod:<time in minutes>`
   b. `BCDUtil /set-server /BcdRefreshPolicy /Enabled:yes / RefreshPeriod:<time in minutes>`
   c. `BCDEdit /set-server /BcdRefreshPolicy /Enabled:yes / RefreshPeriod:<time in minutes>`
   d. `WDSUTIL /set-server /BcdRefreshPolicy /Enabled:yes / RefreshPeriod:<time in minutes>`

10. What option is used to ensure that the client starts from a local WDS server when deploying Windows?
    a. Modify the registry to point to local WDS Server.
    b. Configure DHCP option 66 to point to local WDS Server.
    c. Prestage the computer in the OU where the server exists.
    d. Configure the IP helper to point to the local WDS Server.

11. Which application allows you to manage services and virtual machines that are based in the cloud?
    a. System Center 2012 R2 Configuration Manager
    b. System Center 2012 R2 Virtual Machine Manager
    c. System Center 2012 R2 App Controller
    d. System Center 2012 R2 Operations Manager

Best Answer

Choose the letter that corresponds to the best answer. More than one answer choice could achieve the goal. Select the BEST answer.

1. Why would you use multicasting for WDS?
   a. It minimizes network traffic.
   b. It supports IPv6 and DHCPv6.
   c. It decreases deployment time.
   d. It requires less space on the client system.

2. You are an administrator for a large corporation. You installed System Center 2012 Configuration Manager on a server running Windows Server 2012 R2 called Server1. Although Server1 is located at the corporate office, you have a second server running Windows Server 2012 R2 called Server2, which is located at the manufacturing site. You want to perform a bare metal installation of Windows 8.1 on manufacturing machines over the network. Which of the following should you do? (Choose all that apply.)
   a. Configure Server2 as a distribution point.
   b. Enable PXE support for clients using the Configuration Manager console.
   c. Install the WSUS role.
   d. Install the Windows internal database feature on Server2.

3. You are ready to deploy Windows 8.1 to multiple clients. The clients are connected to the network using a 100 Mbps link or a 1 Gpbs link. You want to use multicasting. However, you do not want to have the clients connected at 1 Gbps to wait for the clients connected at 100 Mbps. What can you do?
   a. Select keep all multicast clients in a session at the same speed
   b. Select separate clients into three sessions (slow, medium, fast).
   c. Select separate clients into two sessions (slow and fast)
   d. Automatically disconnect clients below this speed (in KBps)

4. You are an administrator for the Contoso Corporation. The corporate office is located in New York. You have sites at Sacramento, Los Angeles, Miami, and Austin. You create several images in New York for WDS, which you want to share with WDS services at the other sites. What can you do?
   a. Use DFS replication.
   b. Use DFS Namespace.
   c. Connect a file server with multiple NICs, through which the images will be shared.
   d. Enable multicasting.

5. Where would you find the Office Migration Planning Manager?
   a. It is part of Windows Automated Installation Kit.
   b. It is part of the Windows Deployment Services.
   c. It is part of System Center suite.
   d. It has to be download and installed from Microsoft.

Matching and Identification

1. Match the tool with the tasks it can perform:
   _____ **a)** collection
   _____ **b)** Endpoint protection point
   _____ **c)** central administration site
   _____ **d)** advertisement
   _____ **e)** distribution point

   1. A computer that has the source files to perform a Windows software, update deployment, or operating system deployment
   2. Tells when a package is available to users and System Center client computers and specifies how the package is to be deployed such as when the package will be deployed and what package will run
   3. Used to manage malware protection
   4. A group of objects (devices, computers, users, or groups) used to organize the objects that provides a target for advertisements and reports.
   5. Top of the Configuration Manager hierarchy and enables centralized administration and reporting for the entire hierarchy.

Build a List

1. What steps do you need to do to use multicasting with WDS? In order of first to last, specify the steps used to enable and configuring multicasting. Not all answers will be used.
   _____ Create the multicast transmission.
   _____ Specify the multicast transfer settings.
   _____ Create a Multicast GPO to configure the clients IP addresses.
   _____ Establish the multicast address range.
   _____ Assign a multicast address to the WDS server.

2. You are an administrator for a large corporation with multiple sites. When planning for a large Windows 8.1 deployment, what do you need to determine? Specify the correct order of the steps required to deploy WDS. Not all steps will be used.
   _____ Determine the number of Windows Deployment Services instances required.
   _____ Specify the default block size.
   _____ Determine whether you will use site caching.
   _____ Determine the file share-tolerance and consistence mechanism.
   _____ Select between full Windows Deployment Services or Transport Services.
   _____ Determine the server resource requirements.

■ Business Case Scenarios

Scenario 2-1: Deploying Multiple Computers

As a system administrator, you need to deploy approximately 350 computers running Windows 8.1 over the next three months. All but five computers are used by office workers, and they require Windows 8.1, Microsoft Office 2013, and several company applications. However, you also have five lab computers that run Windows 8.1 and a specialized lab program. With this in mind, answer the following:

1. What is the best way to deploy the standard office computers?
2. What is the best method to deploy the lab computers?

Scenario 2-2: Deploying Windows to Multiple Sites

You are an administrator of a large corporation with 18 sites. You have 5,500 users throughout the United States. You are currently running Windows 7 and 8 with three types of desktop computers and three types of laptops. You need to deploy Windows 8.1 to about half of the computers with a small team of administrators over the next few months. How should you proceed to update these computers with the least amount of administrative effort when you perform the actual deployments?

Planning and Implementing Server Upgrade and Migration

70-413 EXAM OBJECTIVE

Objective 1.3 – Plan and implement server upgrade and migration. This objective can include but is not limited to: Plan for role migration; migrate server roles; migrate servers across domains and forests; design a server consolidation strategy; plan for capacity and resource optimization.

LESSON HEADING	EXAM OBJECTIVE
Planning a Windows Server 2012 R2 Upgrade	
Planning for and Implementing Role Migration • Developing a Deployment Plan • Using Proper License Keys and Activating Windows • Using the Microsoft Assessment and Planning (MAP) Toolkit • Using the Windows Server Migration Tools	Plan for role migration Migrate server roles
Migrating Servers Across Domains and Forests	Migrate servers across domains and forests
Designing a Server Consolidation Strategy	Design a server consolidation strategy
Planning for Capacity and Resource Optimization	Plan for capacity and resource optimization

KEY TERMS

Active Directory-Based Activation (ADBA)

Active Directory Migration Tool (ADMT)

in-place upgrade

interforest migration

intraforest migration

Key Management Service (KMS)

Microsoft Assessment and Planning (MAP) Toolkit

migration

Multiple Activation Key (MAK)

original equipment manufacturer (OEM) keys

Windows Server Migration Tools (WSMT)

■ Planning a Windows Server 2012 R2 Upgrade

↓ THE BOTTOM LINE

For organizations that move to Windows Server 2012 R2, you need to determine whether to upgrade older servers to Windows Server 2012 R2 or to install a new server running Windows Server 2012 R2 and migrate the application and data from the older server to the new server. Of course, as with any upgrade and migration, you want to ensure that you lose no data or functionality, while minimizing downtime.

When deciding whether to upgrade or migrate to Windows Server 2012 R2, you should determine the following:

- What are the organization's business needs?
- What is the current operating system, version, and edition?
- What is the current system's load?
- How do you want to expand or scale the capability of the old server?
- What operating system, version, and edition do you want to move to?
- What is the solution's cost and return on investment (ROI)?

Whatever solution you come up with, it must be the best solution for your organization and its users. As you look at these questions, you can easily to see that you first determine where you are and where you want to go. Then you need to determine whether the costs of the upgrade or migration is worth what you are proposing.

As you should recall from the 70-410 course/exam, Windows Server 2012 and Windows Server 2012 R2 come in four editions:

- *Windows Server 2012 R2 Datacenter:* This edition is designed for large and powerful servers with up to 64 processors and fault-tolerance features such as hot add processor support. It supports 64 sockets, up to 640 processor cores, and up to 4 (terabytes) TB of random-access memory (RAM). It also includes unlimited virtual machine licenses for virtual machines that are run on the same hardware for a server with up to two processors. An additional license is needed for each additional two processors.

- *Windows Server 2012 R2 Standard:* This edition includes the full set of Windows Server 2012 features, varying from the Datacenter edition only by the number of virtual machine instances permitted by the license. It supports up to 64 sockets and up to 4 TB of RAM. It also includes two virtual machine licenses for a server with up to two processors. An additional license is needed for each additional two processors.

- *Windows Server 2012 R2 Essentials:* This edition includes nearly all the features in the Standard and Datacenter editions, except for Server Core, Hyper-V, and Active Directory Federation Services. This edition is limited to one physical or virtual server instance and a maximum of 25 users.

- *Windows Server 2012 R2 Foundation:* This reduced version of the operating system is designed for small businesses that require only basic server features, such as file and print services and application support. It does not include Active Directory Domain Services (AD DS). This edition includes no virtualization rights, is limited to 15 users, and cannot be joined to a domain. It supports one processor core and up to 32 gigabytes (GB) of RAM. Lastly, Windows Server 2012 R2 Foundation is offered through original equipment manufacturer (OEM) program.

Windows Server 2012 and Windows Server 2012 R2 is available only in 64-bit architecture.

Larger organizations tend to use Standard and Datacenter editions over Essentials and Foundation. Unlike Windows Server 2008 R2 or earlier, Windows Standard and Datacenter includes the same features and capabilities. The primary difference is in the amount of memory and number of processors Windows recognizes, and the number of licenses included with virtualization.

The Windows Server 2012 R2 Standard operating system includes two virtual machine licenses, whereas the Windows Server 2012 R2 Datacenter operating system includes unlimited virtual machine licenses on systems of up to two physical processors. If the physical server has more than two processors, an additional license will be needed for each additional two processors. If your organization uses a large virtual environment, consider purchasing Windows Server 2012 R2 Datacenter. If you deploy non-virtual physical servers, select the Windows Server 2012 R2 Standard operating system.

As you also should recall from the 70-410 course/exam, Windows Server 2012 R2 requires the following:

- Processor architecture: x64
- Processor speed: 1.4 gigahertz (GHz)
- Memory (RAM): 512 megabytes (MB)
- Hard disk drive space: 32 GB

Of course, these are absolute minimum, and you should always consider significantly more for acceptable performance. You also might need to increase the computer resources even more based on

- The applications and the services that the server is running
- The number of users connected on the server
- Whether the solution is running in a physical or virtual environment.

If the load is too much for a single server, consider distributing the load among multiple servers. You also might need additional hardware for fault tolerance and high availability.

When you decide to move to Windows Server 2012 R2, you might encounter the following scenarios:

- If the older server cannot handle the new load running Windows Server 2012 R2, or if all the necessary drivers are not available for Windows Server 2012 R2, you have to migrate the applications, services, and/or data to a new server running Windows Server 2012 R2.
- If the older server can run Windows Server 2012 R2, either you have to use the existing hardware and upgrade the system to Windows Server 2012 R2, or you need to migrate the applications, services, and/or data to a new server.
- If the current operating system does not have an upgrade path to Windows Server 2012 R2 and the specific edition that you desire, you have to migrate the applications, services, and/or data to a new server.
- If you are upgrading from a x86 edition of Windows to Windows Server 2012 R2, you have to migrate the applications, services, and/or data to a new server.

An *in-place upgrade* is the process of upgrading a Windows Server operating system on a server that is running an earlier edition of Windows Server. When you perform an upgrade, you run the upgrade installation, which replaces the files from the earlier version of Windows to Windows Server 2012 R2. When you perform an upgrade, you preserve the files, settings, and applications that are installed on the server.

Because Windows Server 2012 R2 requires a 64-bit processor architecture, you can upgrade only the x64 edition of Windows Server operating systems. You can upgrade from Windows Server 2008, Windows Server 2008 R2, and Windows Server 2012. If you are upgrading from Windows Server 2008, you must have Service Pack 2 (SP2) installed. If you are upgrading from Windows Server 2008 R2, you must have Service Pack 1 (SP1) installed. Table 3-1 and Table 3-2 show the upgrade paths available for Windows Server 2012 and Windows Server 2012 R2.

Table 3-1

Upgrade paths to Windows Server 2012

From	To
Windows Server 2008 Standard or Windows Server 2008 Enterprise	Windows Server 2012 Standard or Windows Server 2012 Datacenter
Windows Server 2008 Datacenter	Windows Server 2012 Datacenter
Windows Web Server 2008	Windows Server 2012 Standard
Windows Server 2008 R2 Standard or Windows Server 2008 R2 Enterprise	Windows Server 2012 Standard or Windows Server 2012 Datacenter
Windows Server 2008 R2 Datacenter	Windows Server 2012 Datacenter
Windows Web Server 2008 R2	Windows Server 2012 Standard

Table 3-2

Upgrade paths to Windows Server 2012 R2

From	To
Windows Server 2008 R2 Datacenter	Windows Server 2012 R2 Datacenter
Windows Server 2008 R2 Enterprise	Windows Server 2012 R2 Standard or Windows Server 2012 R2 Datacenter
Windows Server 2008 R2 Standard	Windows Server 2012 R2 Standard or Windows Server 2012 R2 Datacenter
Windows Web Server 2008 R2	Windows Server 2012 R2 Standard
Windows Server 2012 Datacenter	Windows Server 2012 R2 Datacenter
Windows Server 2012 Datacenter	Windows Server 2012 R2 Datacenter

To perform an upgrade, you can insert the Windows Server 2012 R2 installation disk or execute the setup.exe from a shared folder or disk that contains the Windows Server 2012 R2 installation files. Of course, before you perform an in-place upgrade, you need to verify that all applications and devices will function on Windows Server 2012 R2 and understand any issues or risks that might occur. Probably more important, you should ensure that you have a current backup of the operating system, applications, and data. Lastly, you most likely want to perform the upgrade during off hours to minimize impact.

■ Planning for and Implementing Role Migration

↓ **THE BOTTOM LINE**

One reason to consider a server migration is when the hardware on the older server does not support Windows Server 2012 R2, or the hardware is near its end of life or is unreliable. Another reason to perform a migration is reduce the risk associated with an in-place upgrade such as server unavailability or data not being accessible if an issue occurs. Migration also gives you time to debug any problems that you might experience; to consolidate several servers, services, and applications into one server; or to split the services or applications across multiple servers. Therefore, you can perform a migration, and then when the new server is fully functional, you can divert the users to the new server or switch the servers name and/or IP addresses.

CERTIFICATION READY
Plan for role migration.
Objective 1.3

When you perform a *migration*, you transfer files and settings by using the Windows Server Migration Tools available with Windows Server 2012 R2. The ***Windows Server Migration Tools (WSMT)*** can transfer files and settings from computers that are running the following:

- Windows Server 2003
- Windows Server 2003 R2
- Windows Server 2008
- Windows Server 2008 R2
- Windows Server 2012

Software product migration is performed in a separate environment. For any software solution with an earlier edition of Windows Server, you must refer to the product documentation on how to migrate that solution to Windows Server 2012 R2. In some scenarios, currently used software products are not supported for installation on Windows Server 2012 R2, and newer editions of those software products are required. In this case, migration enables you to perform systematic installation of the operating system and the software products in a separate environment. This means that the migration does not affect the availability of current services provided by the software.

Typically before determining where you need to go, you need to first figure out where you are. Therefore, the first step would be to perform an assessment of your environment, which helps determine the state of the environment, including what software the current environment can handle. You should look to see what the minimum processor, minimum amount of memory, and the available disk space are. You should also look at the current operating systems used by the organization, the current service packs, and current software each system has.

Developing a Deployment Plan

While small and large organizations should take time to create a server upgrade and migration plan, planning is critical when upgrading or deploying a new operating system. You have to analyze the current IT infrastructure, choose an operating system edition, create a strategy for upgrade or migration, and create a strategy for backup, restoring, monitoring, and maintaining the operating system. You also need to look at operating system licensing and activation, as well as determine which roles can be migrated, which roles can be co-hosted, and which roles can be consolidated into a virtual environment.

When you want to upgrade or migrate to Windows Server 2012 R2, a development plan helps ensure that the upgrade and migration process runs smoothly and without interruption of services. The plan should provide detailed documentation and a checklist on the preparation, installation, and post-installation activities.

Your deployment plan should include the following general steps:

1. Analyze the current IT infrastructure.
2. Select the appropriate edition of Windows Server 2012 R2, determine whether to perform a full GUI installation or a Server Core deployment, and determine a physical or virtual environment.
3. Plan the in-place upgrade procedure and/or migration procedure.
4. Plan to install new servers.
5. Plan for backup, restoration, monitoring, and maintenance.

When you analyze the current IT infrastructure, you should assemble detailed information about your current IT resources. You should also look for any shortfalls or problems with your current environment, and how you can be better aligned with your organization's business requirements and needs.

Selecting in-place upgrade or migration means that you must prepare, test, and perform post-installation steps. In either case, you want to minimize downtime. You also need to determine when the best time to perform the upgrade or migration—for example, at night during off hours or during a weekend maintenance window. If you plan to deploy new servers, you need to develop a checklist of activities required for a successful deployment. You should also determine checkpoints that can be measure progress and determine a go/no-go decision before going onto the next step.

Even after the upgrade and deployment is complete, you are not quite done. You must convert the server from deployment to operations. To ensure that the server is reliable, and to prepare for disaster, you need to plan for backup, restoration, monitoring, and maintenance.

Lastly, consider that the deployment document is not a static document. As you perform each step within the deployment plan, you might learn things as each step occurs. Therefore, you might need to modify the plan as you progress step by step.

Using Proper License Keys and Activating Windows

During the installation of the server, you need to install the proper license key for Windows and any applications. You also need to activate Windows. Unlike earlier editions of the Windows Server operating system, you no longer have an activation grace period. If you do not activate Windows Server 2012 or Windows Server 2012 R2 immediately, you cannot perform an operating system customization.

You can activate Windows in two ways: manually or automatically. With manual activation, you must enter the product key and activate over the Internet to the special clearinghouse website, or over the phone by using a retail product key or a *multiple activation key (MAK)*. When you use a MAK, you can activate multiple computers, up to a set activation limit.

You can also use *Original Equipment Manufacturer (OEM)* keys with servers. Manufacturers provide OEM keys, which are typically tied to specific computers. OEM keys are usually distributed with systems running Windows 7, Windows 8, or Windows 8.1 but can be found on systems running Windows Server operating systems.

If you have a large number of clients and servers, consider setting up a Volume Activation Services server. When you install the Volume Activation Services server role, you can choose Key Management Service or Active Directory-Based Activation. After adding the Volume Activation Services role, you can use the Volume Activation Tools GUI to configure activation. When you use Volume Activation Services, each activated computer must contact the KMS server periodically to renew its activation status. To report on activated licenses, you can use the Volume Activation Management Tool (VAMT), which is part of the Windows Assessment and Deployment Kit (ADK).

Key Management Service (KMS) is a service that activates volume license versions of Windows Vista and later as well as Office 2010 and later. To activate operating systems, you need at least 25 client operating systems or 5 server operating systems. When you use Volume Activation Services, each activated computer must contact the KMS server periodically to renew its activation status. Activation lasts for 180 days and attempts to renew with the KMS host every 7 days by default. The KMS host is found by referencing an SRV record in DNS.

Active Directory-Based Activation (ADBA) is a new feature for Windows 8 and Windows Server 2012, which enables enterprises to activate computers when a computer is joined to the domain, as long as the computer has a Generic Volume License Key (GVLK) installed. No single physical computer is required to act as the activation object, because it is distributed throughout the domain. To activate an ADBA forest online, you need to specify a KMS host key, and optionally specify an Active Directory-based Activation Object display name.

Using the Microsoft Assessment and Planning (MAP) Toolkit

The ***Microsoft Assessment and Planning (MAP) Toolkit*** is a free, comprehensive agentless tool that can inventory, assess, and report on an organization's environment. You can install it on any system running Windows Vista through Windows 8.1 or Windows Server 2008 through Windows Server 2012 R2.

The MAP Toolkit analyzes the inventory of an organization's server infrastructure, performs an assessment, and then creates reports used for upgrade and migration plans. MAP is available for Windows 8, Windows 8.1, Windows Server 2012, and Windows Server 2012 R2, as well as for other products, such as SQL Server 2012. It can also determine the movement to cloud-based software, including Office 365 and Microsoft Azure.

You can use MAP to perform the following tasks:

- Perform an inventory of your organization's IT infrastructure and provide a detailed report about which machines can running Windows 8, Windows 8.1, Windows Server 2012, and Windows Server 2012 R2. MAP also will recommend specific upgrades that you can do to ensure that a computer can run Windows Server 2012 or Windows Server 2012 R2.

- Capture the performance metrics of the current IT infrastructure, which can be used to plan consolidation, server virtualization, or scaling of servers. Based on the metrics, you can estimate server usage before and after virtualization, determine which severs are the best candidates to be virtualized, and determine the hosts on which those virtual machines should be placed.

 INSTALL MAP

GET READY. To install MAP on a computer running Windows Server 2012 R2, perform the following steps:

1. In Windows Server 2012 R2, double-click MapSetup.exe. If you are asked to run this file, click Run.

2. When the *Microsoft Assessment and Planning Toolkit* Wizard opens, on the *Welcome* page, click Next.

3. On the License Agreement page, select I accept the terms in the License Agreement and click Next.

4. On the *Installation Folder* page, click Next.

5. On the *Customer Experience Improvement Program* page, select Do not join the program at this time. Click Next.

6. On the *Begin the installation* page, click Install.

7. When the installation is complete, click Finish.

8. Open the Start menu and click All Programs. Then under the *Microsoft Assessment and Planning Toolkit* section, click Microsoft Assessment and Planning Toolkit.

9. When the Microsoft Assessment and Planning Toolkit initially opens, the *Microsoft Assessment and Planning Toolkit* dialog box opens. In the *Create an inventory database* section, in the *Name* text box, type MAP. Click OK. Figure 3-1 shows the Microsoft Assessment and Planning Toolkit.

Figure 3-1

The Microsoft Assessment and Planning Toolkit

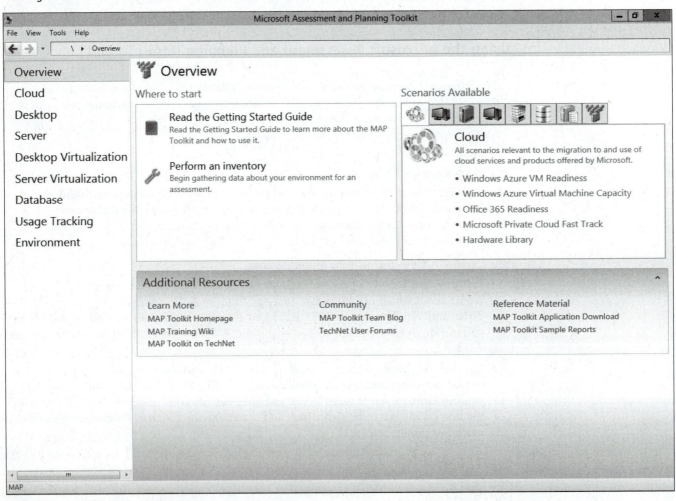

When you use MAP, you should consider the following six phases:

1. Choose goals

2. Gather data collection requirements

3. Prepare environment

4. Install MAP

5. Collect data

6. Review reports

MAP can be used in a number of inventory, assessment, capacity planning, and software usage tracking scenarios. Therefore, before you start using the tool, you should figure out what information you must gather. To help you perform data collection and organize the data, MAP uses wizards.

In the gather data collection requirements phase, you determine what is needed for MAP to communicate with the machine. This includes determining a username and password that can connect to and inventory the machines. You also might need to determine whether you need to configure any firewall and antivirus software settings so that MAP can connect to the computer and perform the inventory.

In phase 3, you configure MAP's communication protocols, including Windows Management Instrumentation (WMI), Active Directory Domain Services (AD DS), SQL Server commands, and VMware Web services, and secure shell with remote shell commands. During this phase, you also configure the firewalls and antivirus software packages.

MAP contains several helpful wizards to assist in the inventory process:

- Inventory and Assessment Wizard
- Performance Metrics Wizard
- Hardware Library Wizard
- Server Virtualization and Consolidation Wizard
- Prepare New Reports and Proposals Wizard

In phase 4, you install MAP. You can use either a Microsoft SQL Server 2012 Express database, or you can use a dedicated SQL server that is running SQL Server 2008, SQL Server 2008 R2, or SQL Server 2012. If you use a full database server, you must create a non-default instance named MAPS before running the MAP installer. Note that you cannot load MAP on a domain controller.

During phase 5, you collect data by selecting the inventory scenario, selecting the discovery method, and providing the credentials that will connect to and inventory the target machine. You can also use the Performance Metrics Wizard to collect specific performance-related information, such as the processor, memory, network and disk usage for Windows and Linux-based servers. As MAP runs, it shows the number of computers found, the number of machines inventoried, and the number of machines that still need to be inventoried.

In the last phase, you review the reports. If you click Desktop, Server, Desktop Virtualization, you can view information specific to a scenario such as Windows 8 Readiness or Windows 7 Readiness.

Before you deploy MAP, you should ensure the following:

- That the firewall allows WMI traffic from the inventory subnet
- That Remote Administration and File and Printer Sharing are allowed through firewalls
- If you are using network access policy, that local accounts are set to Classic mode

 PERFORM AN INVENTORY BY USING MAP

GET READY. To perform an inventory using MAP on a computer running Windows Server 2012 R2, perform the following steps:

1. Click the Start button to open the Start menu, and then click All Programs. Then under the *Microsoft Assessment and Planning Toolkit* section, click Microsoft Assessment and Planning Toolkit.

2. From *Overview*, click Perform an inventory.

3. When the *Inventory and Assessment* Wizard opens, on the *Inventory Scenarios* page (see Figure 3-2), select the desired inventory. Click Next.

Figure 3-2

Specifying an Inventory Scenario

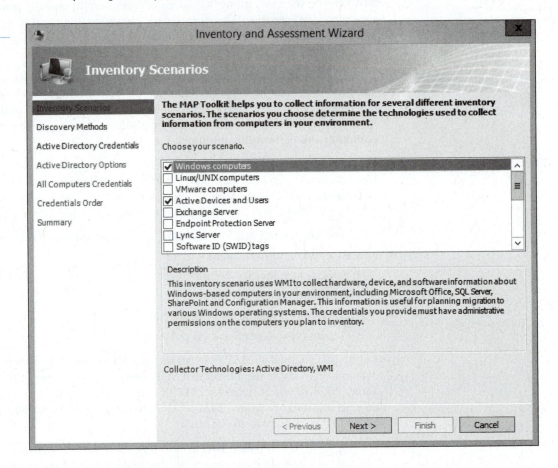

4. On the *Discovery methods* page, select which methods you want to use to discover computers such as use *Active Directory Domain Services (AD DS)* or *Use Windows networking protocols*. Click Next.

5. On the *Active Directory Credentials* page, in the *Domain* text box, type the name of the domain. In the *Domain account* text box, type a user account, using the *domain\user* format.

6. In the *Password* text box, type the password for the domain account. Click Next.

7. On the *Active Directory Options* page, click Next.

8. On the *All Computers Credentials* page, click Create.

9. On the *Account Entry* page, in the *Account name* text box, type a username, using the *domain\user* format.

10. In the Password and Confirm password text box, type the password for the account.

11. In the *Technology* section, *WMI* and *Active Directory* are already selected. Click Save.

12. Back on the *All Computers Credentials* page, click Next.

13. On the *Credentials Orders* page, click Next.

14. On the *Summary* page, click Finish. After some time, the *Overview* page shows the number of machines found and inventoried.

Using the Windows Server Migration Tools

Many roles included with Windows Server 2012 R2 involve a lot of configuring. A particular role might require policies, security, or other settings that you must configure before it can be used. Therefore, when you want to migrate such roles, you want to find a way that can migrate them and all their configuration settings to another server quickly and easily without having to install and configure the role from the beginning. If you search for *Migrating Roles and Features in Windows Server*, you should find a list of available migration guides, including how to use the Windows Server Migration Tools (WSMT) and how to migrate individual roles from one server to another.

CERTIFICATION READY
Migrate server roles.
Objective 1.3

You can migrate the following roles by using the WSMT from earlier versions of Windows to Windows Server 2012 R2 or another Windows Server 2012 R2 server:

- Active Directory Federation Services (AD FS) Role Services
- Hyper-V
- Network Policy Server
- Print and Document Services
- Remote Access
- Windows Server Update Services (WSUS)
- DHCP services

WSMT installation and preparation can be divided into the following stages:

1. Identify the source and destination servers.
2. Install WSMT on destination servers that run Windows Server 2012 R2 or Windows Server 2012.
3. Install all critical updates to the source server.
4. Prepare a migration store file location that source and destination servers can both access
5. Register WSMT on source servers.
6. Perform the actual migration.

The Windows Server Migration Tools role is installed like any other role, by using Server Manager. You can also load the WSMT by using the following Windows PowerShell command:

```
Add-PSSnapin
Microsoft.Windows.ServerManager.Migration
```

When you perform the actual migration, you export the configuration to the migration store by using the Windows PowerShell cmdlet `Export-SmigServerSettings`, and import the configuration from the migration store by using the cmdlet `Import-SmigServerSettings`.

 USE WINDOWS SERVER MIGRATION TOOLS

GET READY. To migrate the DHCP server from one server to another, perform the following steps:

1. On the source server, using Server Manager, open the Tools menu and click Services.
2. Right-click DHCP Server service and then click Stop.
3. On the source server, using Server Manager, open the Tools menu, and then click Windows Server Migration Tools > Windows Server Migration Tools.

4. In the *Windows Server Migration Tools* window, execute the following command:
   Export-SmigServerSetting -featureID DHCP -User All -Group
   -IPConfig -path \\rwdc01\software -Verbose

5. When prompted for a password, type Pa$$w0rd and press Enter.

6. On the target server, using Server Manager, open the Tools menu and click Services.

7. Right-click DHCP Server and click Stop.

8. On the target server, using Server Manager, open the Tools menu, and then click
   Windows Server Migration Tools > Windows Server Migration Tools.

9. From the *Windows Server Migration Tools* window, execute the following command:
   Import-SmigServerSetting -featureID DHCP -User All -Group
   -IPConfig -SourcePhysicalAddress "00-15-5D-01-32-24"
   -TargetPhysicalAddress "00-15-5D-01-32-1F" -path \\rwdc01\
   software -Verbose

10. Back on the *Services* console, right-click DHCP Server service, and then click Start.

If you think about it, not all servers have to be migrated with the WSMT. For example, instead of migrating an Active Directory Domain Controller, you can install a system with Windows Server 2012, install the Active Directory Domain Services role, and promote the server to a domain controller. When the server is promoted to a domain controller, all Active Directory information is replicated to the server. You can then demote the old domain controller and remote it from the domain.

■ Migrating Servers Across Domains and Forests

THE BOTTOM LINE

While it is uncommon, server migration can occur across domains and forest, as long as the roles do not depend on Active Directory Domain Services. For example, if a company purchases another company, you will need to migrate the resources from the purchases company into the organization's forest. Migrating objects between forests is known as an *interforest migration*, while migrating objects between domains within the same forest is known as *intraforest migration*.

To perform these migrations, you must have a trust between the two domains. After the trust is enabled, you can use tools such as *Active Directory Migration Tool (ADMT)* to migrate resources between domains. Interforest trusts are called Forest Trusts and can be a one-way trust or a two-way transitive trust. Lesson 14 discusses trusts in more detail.

ADMT version 3.2 simplifies the process of restructuring Active Directory resources such as user, groups, and computers between domains. ADMT also performs security translation Active Directory domains in different forests. After you migrate a computer between domains and forests, you must restart the computer.

■ Designing a Server Consolidation Strategy

THE BOTTOM LINE

When possible, you want to consolidate server roles by co-hosting multiple roles on a single server. By co-hosting, you can reduce the cost of servers. However, you should consolidate the servers only as long as you can maintain adequate performance, have sufficient disk space, and maintain security. You also want to maintain redundancy and security through separation of services.

When you consolidate server, you should follow these general steps:

1. Determine the scope of the project.
2. Create a list of workloads.
3. Select backup and fault-tolerance approaches.
4. Summarize and analyze workload requirements.

You first need to determine the project's scope. For example, although you can virtualize an entire datacenter, consolidation can be risky and require a hefty price tag as you purchase additional physical host servers. Instead, you might want to break the virtualization of the data center into several smaller projects.

Next, you need to create a list of workloads so that you can determine the current resources used by the servers and the required resources to run the servers. Of course, you might discover that some servers are underpowered. In such cases, you can decide to add resources when you consolidate those servers. To list the resources needed, you also can determine the administrators for the application or workload, and who needs to access the application or workload.

To determine the resource requirements, you can use the Microsoft Assessment and Planning (MAP) Toolkit, System Center Configuration Manager, or System Center Virtual Machine Manager (VMM), or you can collect the information manually. The MAP is free, but the System Center products incur licensing costs.

As you create the list of workloads, you should look at which applications and services are compatible with other applications and services, and which workload is not ideal for a virtualized environment. As mentioned earlier, if the server requires high I/O resources or specialized hardware, the server should not be virtualized.

When you create list of resource requirements, you should look at how the current workload or applications are being backed up and determine how the workload or application will be backed up in the future. You must ensure that the new backup method does not affect the workload or application.

Lastly, you should look at the current methods for fault tolerance and the planned fault tolerance method used in the future. Some options would include network load balancing, application-specific clustering, and host clustering.

During the last phase, you should group together the workloads that give you the performance, security, reliability, and regulatory requirements. You then can summarize the requirements and figure out the best way to migrate the servers and workloads.

■ Planning for Capacity and Resource Optimization

THE BOTTOM LINE

Mixed in with the other topics that this lesson has already covered has been talk about looking at resources used by the various servers, as well as their workload. You have to plan for capacity and resource optimization. Although you can use consolidation to combine servers for better use capacity and resources, you might discover that you need to increase the capacity or resources of a server or even split one over multiple servers. Therefore, although you can look at capacity and resources when you are ready to upgrade or migrate servers, you should also review current capacity and resources so that you can determine whether a server is overworked, determine trends, and know when to scale a server or break a server over multiple servers.

As mentioned earlier, to determine current loads, you can use MAP, System Center Configuration Manager, or System Center VMM, or you can collect the information manually. Windows Server 2012 R2 also includes the ability to perform data deduplication and trim storage.

The MAP Toolkit provides several reports useful for capacity planning and resource optimization. MAP primarily uses Windows Management Instrumentation (WMI) and accesses the registry remotely. WMI is a set of extensions to the Windows Driver Model that you can use to provide information and notification about a system. You can also write WMI scripts or applications to automate administrative tasks on remote computers.

To figure out what your organization's network contains, you can use one of these discovery methods:

- Use AD DS to examine computer objects.
- Import information from a file or enter it manually.
- Scan by IP address to discover computers.
- Discover computers through System Center Configuration Manager.
- Use the Windows network protocols that use the WIN32 LAN Manager Application Programming Interface (API) to search for computers available through the Computer Browser service.
- For Linux machines, use Secure Shell (SSH) as well as various APIs for other vendors.

When you collect information, the following is recommended:

- You should collect a minimum of two days' worth of performance data. However, seven days or more is recommended.
- Performance collection should be run during peak times (such as during end-of-month or quarterly activities), so that you can determine maximum usage.
- Do not leave long gaps between performance collections.

 COLLECT PERFORMANCE METRICS BY USING MAP

GET READY. To use MAP to collect performance metrics, perform the following steps:

1. Click the Start button to open the Start menu, and click All Programs. Then in the *Microsoft Assessment and Planning Toolkit* section, click Microsoft Assessment and Planning Toolkit.

2. Click Environment, and then click Collect performance data.

3. In the *Performance Metrics* Wizard, on the *Collection Configuration* page, *Windows-based machines* is already selected. If you want, you can also select Linux-based machines.

4. In the *End Time* section, specify the date and time that you want to end the performance collection. Click Next.

5. On the *Choose Computers* page, choose the computers from a list that you want to collect performance metrics from, and then click Next.

6. On the *Computer List* page (see Figure 3-3), select the computers from which you want to collect information, and then click Next.

Figure 3-3

Selecting Computers for
Performance Metrics

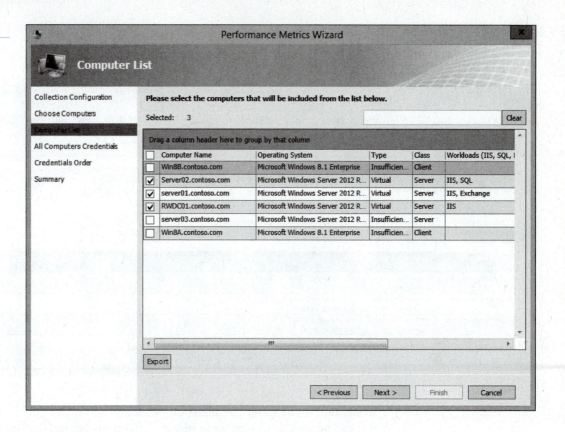

7. On the *All Computers Credentials* page, click Create.

8. In the *Account Entry* dialog box, in the *Account name* text box, type an account that has administrative permissions to the server, using the *domain\username* format.

9. In the *Password* and *Confirm password* text boxes, type the password.

10. Under the *Technology* section, *WMI* is already selected. Click Save.

11. Back on the *All Computers Credentials* page, click Next.

12. On the *Credentials Order* page, click Next.

13. On the *Summary* page, click Finish.

When the information is collected, under the Environment workspace, you can click Performance Metric. Then on the Performance Metric Summary page, you can click the performance metrics report to save the Excel spreadsheet. Figure 3-4 shows a example of the Excel spreadsheet.

Figure 3-4

Viewing a Performance Metrics report

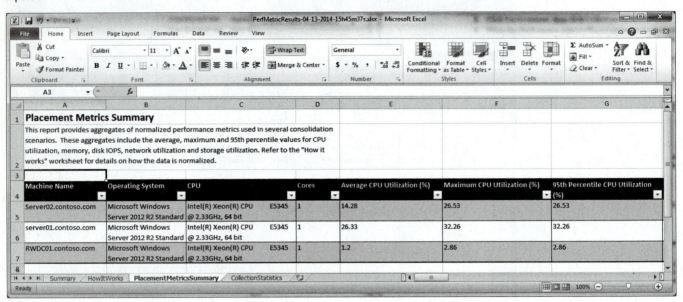

In addition to the server consolidation, Windows Server 2012 R2 includes two new features that can be used to reclaim some resources. Trim storage reclaims unused storage space, particularly when used in a storage area network (SAN) environment. Suppose that you have designated 100 GB for a virtual drive, but only 10 GB is being used, Of course, you can use dynamic expanding virtual hard disk, which uses only the necessary disk space but automatically expands up to the maximum size designated.

Data deduplication finds and removes duplicate data without compromising its integrity. By segmenting files into small variable-sized chunks ranging from 32 to 128 KB, identifying duplicate chunks, and maintaining a single copy of each chunk, you can use less disk space. Redundant copies of the chunk are replaced by a reference to the single copy. The chunks are then compressed and organized into special container files in the System Volume Information folder. As a result, you consume less disk space.

SKILL SUMMARY

IN THIS LESSON YOU LEARNED:

- For organizations that move to Windows Server 2012 R2, you need either to determine to upgrade older servers to Windows Server 2012 R2 or to install a new server running Windows Server 2012 R2 and migrate the application and data from the older server to the new server.

- As with any upgrade and migration, you want to ensure that you lose no data or functionality, while minimizing downtime.

- If the load is too much for a single server, consider distributing the load among multiple servers. Additional hardware might be needed for fault tolerance and high availability.

- An in-place upgrade is the process of upgrading a Windows Server operating system on the server running an earlier edition of Windows Server.

- One reason to consider a server migration is because the hardware on the older server does not support Windows Server 2012 R2, or the hardware is near its end of life or is unreliable. Another reason to perform a migration is to reduce the risk associated with an in-place upgrade, such as server unavailability or data being inaccessible if an issue occurs.

- When you perform a migration, you transfer files and settings by using the Windows Server Migration Tools (WSMT) available with Windows Server 2012 R2.

- The WSMT can transfer files and settings from computers running an earlier version of the Windows Server operating system.

- During the installation of the server, you need to install the proper license key for Windows and any applications. You also need to activate Windows.

- The Microsoft Assessment and Planning (MAP) Toolkit is a free, comprehensive agentless tool that can inventory, assess, and report on an organization's environment.

- To perform migrations between domains and forests, you must have a trust between the two domains. After the trust is enabled, you can use tools such as Active Directory Migration Tool (ADMT) to migrate resources between domains.

- When possible, you want to consolidate server roles by co-hosting multiple roles into a single server. By co-hosting, you can reduce the cost of servers, but you should consolidate the server only as long as you can maintain adequate performance, have sufficient disk space, and maintain security.

■ Knowledge Assessment

Multiple Choice

1. What is the minimum processor needed for Windows Server 2012 R2?
   a. x32 or x64 processor running at 1.4 GHz
   b. x64 processor running at 1.4 GHz
   c. x64 dual-core processor running at 1.4 GHz
   d. x64 processor running at 1.8 GHz

2. Which of the following are reasons to perform a migration instead of an in-place upgrade to Windows Server 2012 R2? (Choose all that apply)
   a. If the hardware is not sufficient to run Windows Server 2012 R2.
   b. You do not have all the correct drivers of Windows Server 2012 R2.
   c. You do not have an upgrade path to Windows Server 2012 R2.
   d. You want to run in a virtualized environment.

3. How do you perform an in-place upgrade?
   a. Start from a Windows Server 2012 R2 installation disk and choose Upgrade.
   b. Insert the Windows Server 2012 R2 installation disk into the computer while Windows is running and choose Upgrade.
   c. Perform a startup over the network and choose Upgrade.
   d. Open the Windows Update site and select Upgrade.

4. What tool can you use to migrate Print and Document Services and Remote Access running on Windows Server 2008 R2 to another server running Windows Server 2012 R2?
   a. Application Compatibility Toolkit
   b. Roles Migration Tools
   c. Server Manager
   d. Windows Server Migration Tools

5. Which type of key is tied to a single computer and cannot be moved to another computer?
   a. KMS
   b. OEM
   c. MAK
   d. Retail

6. What tool allows you to collect performance information and give recommendations on servers to consolidate?
   a. ACT
   b. MAK
   c. MAP
   d. AIK

7. Which of the following wizards are included in MAP? (Choose all that apply.)
   a. Software Compatibility Wizard
   b. Server Virtualization and Consolidate Wizard
   c. Hardware Library Wizard
   d. Inventory and Assessment Wizard

8. What Windows PowerShell cmdlet is used with the Windows Server Migration Tools to export a role?
   a. `ExportServerRole`
   b. `Export-Role`
   c. `Export-SmigServerSettings`
   d. `Export-RoleService`

9. What tool would you use to migrate a computer account to another domain?
   a. Active Directory Administrative Center
   b. Active Directory Domains and Trusts
   c. Active Directory Migration Tool
   d. Active Directory Users and Computers

10. What two tools can you use to determine Performance Metrics over a lengthy period of time?
    a. Performance Monitor
    b. Task Manager
    c. Microsoft Assessment and Planning Toolkit
    d. Automated Installation Kit

Best Answer

Choose the letter that corresponds to the best answer. More than one answer choice might achieve the goal. Select the BEST answer.

1. You have a server that is currently acting as a print server with the following requirements:
   - x64 Processor running at 1.8 GHz
   - 256 MB of RAM
   - 120 GB drive
   - 10/100 MHz network card

   What is preventing you from running Windows Server 2012 R2?
   a. The processor does not support Windows Server 2012 R2.
   b. The memory does not support Windows Server 2012 R2.
   c. The hard drive does not support Windows Server 2012 R2.
   d. The network card does not support Windows Server 2012 R2.

2. You have an extremely busy file server running Windows Server 2008 and holding 1.5 TB of data. You want to migrate the file server to a new server running Windows Server 2012 R2 with the following hardware:
   - x64 Processor running at 1.4 GHz
   - 512 MB of RAM
   - 2 TB drive
   - 1 Gbps network card

   What recommendations would you give?
   a. Increase the processor and memory.
   b. Increase the disk space.
   c. Increase the network card speed.
   d. Do not install Windows Server 2012 R2. Instead, install Windows Server 2012.

3. You have more than 250 servers and 1,000 client computers. Which type of keys would you prefer to use?
   a. KMS
   b. OEM
   c. MAK
   d. Retail

4. You want to collect performance metrics on three servers so that you can determine which servers to upgrade and which to consolidate. Which of the following would you recommend when collecting metrics? (Choose two answers.)
   a. Collect data on Monday
   b. Collect data on Wednesday
   c. Collect data for a week
   d. Collect data during the end-of-month or end-of-quarter period
   e. Collect data on the 15th of two consecutive months

5. What is the first step when developing a deployment plan of Windows Server 2012 R2?
   a. Perform an in-place upgrade or a migration
   b. Determine the best edition of Windows to use
   c. How to backup and maintain the systems
   d. Determine what you currently have

Build a List

1. In order of first to last, specify the steps used to deploy Windows Server 2012 R2.

   _____ Select appropriate edition of Windows Server 2012 R2 and, if it is full, GUI or Server Core installation

   _____ Plan for backup, restoration, monitoring, and maintenance

   _____ Analyze current IT infrastructure

   _____ Plan to install new servers

   _____ Plan the in-place upgrade procedures and/or migration procedures

2. In order of first to last, specify the six phases when using Microsoft Assessment and Planning (MAP) Toolkit.

   _____ Install MAP

   _____ Prepare environment

   _____ Review reports

   _____ Choose goals

   _____ Gather data collection requirements

   _____ Collect data

3. In order of first to last, specify the steps used when migrating roles from one server to another using the Windows Server Migration Tools (WSMT).

   _____ Prepare a migration store location

   _____ Identify the source and destination servers

   _____ Perform the actual migration

   _____ Install the source and destination servers

   _____ Register WSMT on the source server

   _____ Install all critical updates to the source server

4. In order of first to last, specify the steps used to consolidate servers.

   _____ Create a list of workloads

   _____ Determine the scope of the project

   _____ Summary and analyze workload requirements

   _____ Select backup and fault-tolerance approaches

■ Business Case Scenarios

Scenario 3-1: Select the Windows Server 2012 R2 Edition

You have nine virtual file servers on a single Hyper-V physical host that contains two eight-core processors. Currently, each server is running Windows Server 2012 Standard edition on one host. You are thinking of migrating these servers to Windows Server 2012 R2. You run MAP over a three-day period for these servers and discover the following:

	Avg Proc	95% CPU utilization
Server 1	25	5%
Server 2	25	3%
Server 3	35	6%
Server 4	15	5%
Server 5	15	3%
Server 6	10	6%
Server 7	25	5%
Server 8	20	3%
Server 9	30	6%

What type of license would you purchase? Why would you purchase this license if you upgrade these servers to Windows Server 2012 R2?

Scenario 3-2: Consolidate Servers

Like with Scenario 3-1, you have nine virtual file servers (assigned a single processor) on a single Hyper-V physical host that contains two eight-core processors. Currently, each server is running Windows Server 2012 Standard edition on one host. You are thinking of migrating these servers to Windows Server 2012 R2. You run MAP over a three-day period for these servers and you discover the following:

	Avg Proc	95% CPU utilization
Server 1	25	5%
Server 2	25	3%
Server 3	35	6%
Server 4	15	5%
Server 5	15	3%
Server 6	10	6%
Server 7	25	5%
Server 8	20	3%
Server 9	30	6%

Explain how you would consolidate the servers.

LESSON 4

Planning and Deploying Virtual Machine Manager Services

70-413 EXAM OBJECTIVE

Objective 1.4 – Plan and deploy Virtual Machine Manager services. This objective may include but is not limited to: Design Virtual Machine Manager service templates; plan and deploy profiles including operating system profiles, hardware and capability profiles, application profiles, and SQL profiles; plan and manage services including scaling out, updating, and servicing services; configure Virtual Machine Manager libraries; plan and deploy services to non-trusted domains and workgroups

LESSON HEADING	EXAM OBJECTIVE
Designing Virtual Machine Manager Service Templates • Installing Virtual Machine Manager	Design Virtual Machine Manager service templates
Designing Virtual Machine Manager Service Templates • Planning and Deploying Profiles	Plan and deploy profiles, operating system profiles, hardware and capability profiles, application profiles, and SQL profiles
• Planning and Managing Services	Plan and manage services including scaling out, updating, and servicing services
• Configuring Virtual Machine Manager Libraries	Configure Virtual Machine Manager libraries
• Managing Logical Networks	
• Planning and Deploying Services to Non-Trusted Domains and Workgroups	Plan and deploy services to non-trusted domains and workgroups

KEY TERMS

hardware profiles

host profile

logical networks

operating system profiles

physical computer profiles

Service Template Designer

service templates

services

tier

Virtual Machine Manager (VMM)

VMM library

■ Designing Virtual Machine Manager Service Templates

THE BOTTOM LINE

The Microsoft System Center line of products form a line of management and report tools designed for management of large number of computers. System Center 2012 R2 *Virtual Machine Manager (VMM)* enables centralized management of virtualized workloads. VMM allows you to manage the virtualized data center infrastructure, increase physical server utilization (including providing simple and fast consolidation of the virtual infrastructure), perform physical-to-virtual (P2V) migration, and perform intelligent workplace placement based on performance data and user-defined business policies.

To simplify the management of Hyper-V physical hosts, VMM allows you manage multiple Hyper-V physical host within the same console. You also can use VMM to manage VMWare and Citrix.

To simplify the process of deploying servers, VMM includes the following features:

- You can use virtual machine templates for common server configurations included with products such as VMM.
- Using VMM and Microsoft System Center 2012 R2 Service Manager, you can create virtual machine (VM) self-service portals that enable end users to provision approved servers and applications automatically, without assistance from the system administration team. For example, if you have a lab or development team that often needs new virtual machines, the lab personnel or devilment team can use the self-service portals to generate the servers.
- You can use P2V machine conversion to convert a physical server quickly into a virtual machine, which is then managed by the VMM environment.
- VMM uses bare-metal Hyper-V provisioning to automatically provision new Hyper-V hosts and bring them into the VMM environment to be managed.

Installing Virtual Machine Manager

Virtual Machine Manager has a similar installation as other System Center products. It requires a SQL server, such as Microsoft SQL Server (SQL Server 2008 R2 with SP1 or later).

To manage up to 150 hosts, you need the following:

- Processor: x64 processor running at 2 GHz
- RAM: 4 GB
- Hard disk space, without a local VMM database: 2 GB
- Hard disk space, with a local full version of Microsoft SQL Server: 80 GB

Having a dual-processor dual-core running at 2.8 GHz is recommended. Also recommended is that you have 40 GB free disk space without a local VMM database, and 150 GB with a local, full version of Microsoft SQL Server.

On a server running Windows Server 2012 R2, you must install the following:

- Windows Remote Management (WinRM)
- Microsoft .NET Framework 4.5
- Windows Assessment and Deployment Kit (Windows ADK)
- Windows Server Internet Information Services (IIS)

INSTALL SYSTEM CENTER 2012 R2 VIRTUAL MACHINE MANAGER

GET READY. To install the System Center 2012 R2 Virtual Machine Manager, perform the following steps:

1. Open the SC2012R2VMM disk and double-click setup.exe.

2. When the *Microsoft System Center 2012 R2 Virtual Machine Manager* splash screen opens, click Install.

3. When the *Microsoft System Center 2012 R2 Virtual Machine Manager Setup* Wizard opens, on the *Select features to add* page, select VMM management server and VMM console. Click Next.

4. On the *Product registration information* page, click Next.

5. On the *Please read this license agreement* page, select the I have read, understood, and agree with the terms of the license agreement option. Click Next.

6. On the *Customer Experience Improvement Program (CEIP)* page, select No, I am not willing to participate. Click Next.

7. On the *Microsoft Update* page, click On (recommended). Click Next.

8. On the Installation location page, click Next.

9. On the *Database configuration* page, specify the SQL server, such as Server02. *New database* is already selected and the default database is *VirtualManagerDB*. Click Next.

10. On the *Configure service account and distributed key management* page, *Domain account* is already selected. On the *username and domain* text box, type contoso\administrator. In the *Password* text box, type Pa$$w0rd. Click Next.

11. On the *Port configuration* page, click Next.

12. On the *Library configuration* page, *Create a new library share* is already selected. The default share name is *MSSCVMMLibrary*. Click Next.

13. On the *Summary* page, click Next.

14. When the installation is complete, click Close.

15. In the *Connect to Server* dialog box, click Connect. The Virtual Machine Manager opens, as shown in Figure 4-1.

Figure 4-1

Opening the Virtual Machine
Manager console

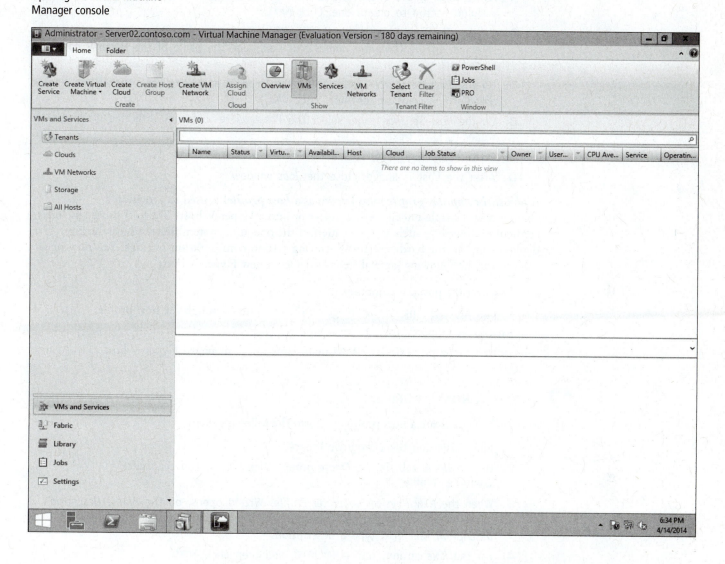

You can use VMM to manage Hyper-V, Citrix XenServer, and VMWare ESX hosts and clusters. To manage the hosts and clusters, you must add them to VMM.

 ADD A HYPER-V HOST TO VIRTUAL MACHINE MANAGER

GET READY. To add a Hyper-V Host to Virtual Machine Manager, perform the following
steps:

1. Open the *VMM* console and the *Fabric* workspace. Expand the Servers node, and
   then click All Hosts.

2. Right-click All Hosts, and then click Add Hyper-V Hosts and Clusters.

3. When the *Add Resource* Wizard opens, on the *Resource Location* page, *Windows
   Server computers in a trusted Active Directory domain* is already selected. Click
   Next.

4. On the *Credentials* page, *Use an existing Run As account* is already selected. Click
   the Browse button.

5. When the *Select a Run As Account* dialog box opens, double-click the desired Run As account. If the one that you want is not available, use the Create Run as Account button to create one. Click Next.

6. On the *Discovery Scope* page, *Specify Windows Server computers by names* is already selected. In the *Computer names* text box, type the name of the Hyper-V host. Click Next.

7. On the *Target resources* page, select the Hyper-V host, and then click Next. When asked if you want to continue, click OK.

8. On the *Host Settings* page, select the Reassociate this host with this VMM environment. Click Next.

9. On the *Summary* page, click Finish.

10. After the host is added, close the *Jobs* window.

A ***physical computer profile*** (also known as a ***host profile***) is used to provision a computer into a scale-out file server cluster or into a Hyper-V host. The host profile includes configuration settings such as the location of the operating system image to use during deployment and the hardware and operating system configuration settings. You now need to perform the following general steps to deploy a new Hyper-V host:

1. Discover the physical computer.
2. Deploy an operating system image on the computer through the host profile.
3. Enable the Hyper-V role on the computer.
4. Bring the computer under VMM management as a managed Hyper-V host.

 CREATE A HOST PROFILE

GET READY. To create a host profile, perform the following steps:

1. Open VMM and the *Library* workspace.
2. On the *Home* tab, in the *Create* group, click Create, and then click Physical Computer Profile.
3. When the *New Physical Computer Profiles* Wizard opens, on the *Profile Description* page, in the *Name* text box, type a name of the profile. Optionally, in the *Description* text box, type a description.
4. For the *Role* option, select VM Host, and then click Next.
5. On the *OS Image* page, click Browse. Browse to a generalized virtual hard disk file that you added to the library share, and then click OK. Click Next.
6. On the *Hardware Configuration* page, configure the hardware option similarly to the hardware settings found in a Hyper-V virtual machine. Click Next.
7. On the *OS Configuration* page, specify the following:
   - The domain to join
   - The Run As account used to join the domain.
   - The Admin password used for the local administrator account.
   - The Identity Information, including the Full name and Organization name boxes.
   - The Product Key
   - Time Zone
   - Answer File
   - [GUIRunOnce] Commands
8. On the *Summary* page, confirm the settings, and then click Finish.

■ Designing Virtual Machine Manager Service Templates

THE BOTTOM LINE

Servers are meant to provide services. With Virtual Machine Manager service, **services** are collections of virtual machines deployed together to provide a service or application. With Virtual Machine Manager service, however, you can create tiers or a tier-based infrastructure to provide the service. A **tier** has the configuration necessary for its portion of the service. The VMM **service templates** is a single object that contains multiple child templates, including VM templates, networking configuration, load balancing, applications, and storage.

CERTIFICATION READY
Design Virtual Machine
Manager service
templates
Objective 1.4

Before you can create a VMM service template, you need to already have created templates, virtual machines, and logical network configuration. VMM service templates are created and managed with the Service Template Designer.

CREATING VM TEMPLATES

You use virtual machine templates to create new virtual machines and configure tiers in a service template. You can create a virtual machine template based on an existing template or based on an existing virtual hard disk (VHD) that is stored in a library. You can also create a virtual machine template based on an existing VM that is stopped and already deployed on a host.

→ **CREATE A VM TEMPLATE**

GET READY. To create a VM Template using VMM, perform the following steps:

1. Open the VMM console and the Library workspace.
2. On the *Home* tab, in the *Create* group, click Create VM Template.
3. In the *Create VM Template Wizard* (see Figure 4-2), on the *Select Source* page, click Use an existing VM template or a virtual hard disk stored in the library, and then click Browse.

Figure 4-2

Opening the Create VM
Template Wizard

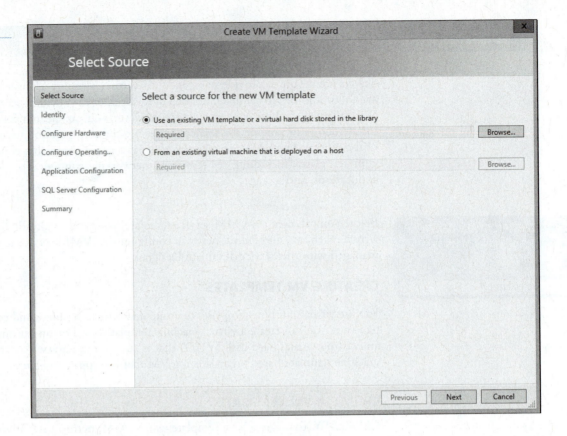

4. In *the Select VM Template Source* dialog box, click the appropriate virtual hard disk or virtual machine template, such as Blank Disk – Small.vhdx, click OK, and then click Next.

5. On the *Identity* page, specify the following, and then click Next:
   - In the *VM Template* name text box, type a name for the VM template.
   - In the *Description* text box, type an optional description.
   - For the *Generation* option, select Generation 1 or Generation 2.

6. On the *Configure Hardware* page (see Figure 4-3), configure the hardware settings. If you have an existing hardware profile that you want to use, in the *Hardware profile* list, click the desired hardware profile. After you configure the hardware settings, click Next.

Figure 4-3

Configuring hardware

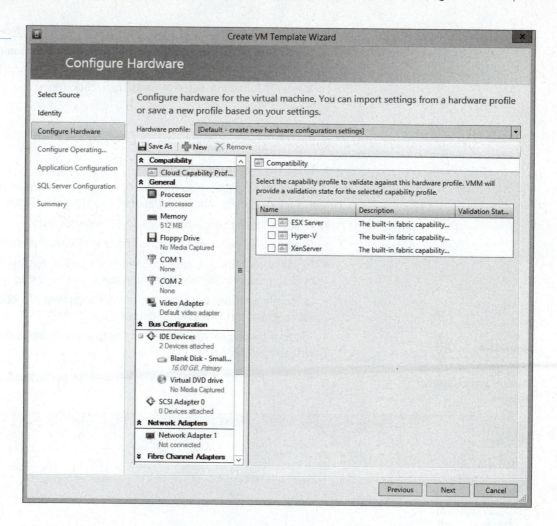

7. On the *Configure Operating System* page, from the *Guest OS profile* list select either a guest operating system profile or the type of operating system for which you want to create customized settings, such as Windows, Linux, or none. Click Next.

8. On the Application configuration page, select Windows Server 2012 R2 Standard, click Next.

9. On the *SQL Server configuration* page, click Next.

10. On the *Summary* page, click Create.

11. Close the *Jobs* window that opens. The template appears in the *Templates* node.

CREATING SERVICE TEMPLATES

To create a service template, you use the ***Service Template Designer***, which is launched from VMM. When you launch the designer, you can choose from predefined template such as single-tier, two-tier, and three-tier templates, or you can choose a blank template. You can then connect the host to a logical network.

 CREATE A SERVICE TEMPLATE

GET READY. To create a service template using VMM, perform the following steps:

1. Open the VMM console and the *Library* workspace.

2. On the *Home* tab, in the *Create* group, click Create Service.

3. In the *Create Service* dialog box, click Create a service template and then click OK.

4. In the *New Service Template* dialog box opens, in the *Name* text box, type a name for the template.

5. Click one of following Patterns, and then click OK:

   - Blank
   - Single Machine (V1.0)
   - Two Tier Application (V1.0)
   - Three Tier Application (v1.0)

6. If you selected *Single Machine (V1.0)*, you can do one of the following in the *Virtual Machine Service Template Designer* (as shown in Figure 4-4):

   - To add a VM network, click the Add VM Network button.
   - To add a load balancer, click the Add Load Balancer button.
   - To add a machine tier, click the Add Machine Tier button. You can also add a tier by dragging a virtual machine template onto the canvas.
   - To modify a virtual machine (including its application, operating system, processor, memory, and network cards), double-click it.
   - To add a second server, right-click the first server and select Copy. Then paste the virtual machine.

Figure 4-4

Using the Virtual Machine Manager Service Template Designer

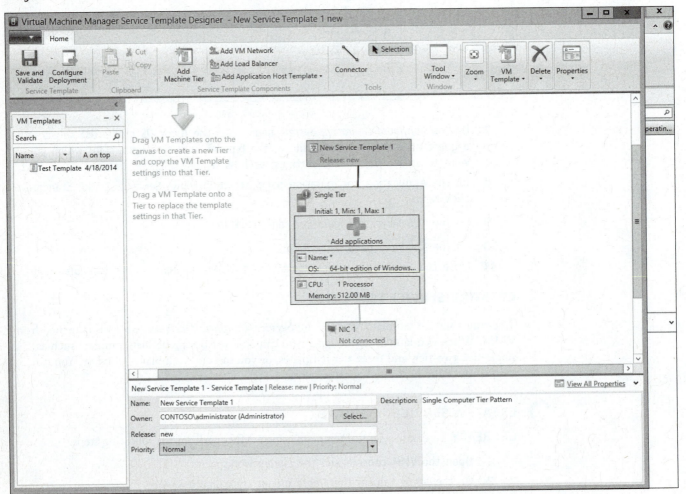

7. When done, on the *Home* tab, in the *Service Template* group, click Save and Validate to save the service template.

When you need to deploy a service, just click the Create Service button, select Use an existing service template, and then chose the desired service template. To scale a service out, the template needs to allow scaling. You can allow this by selecting the This Computer Tier Can Be Scaled Out check box and increasing the Maximum Instance Count accordingly.

Planning and Deploying Profiles

To modularize and simplify the deployment of virtual machines, you can create profiles, which are used with a template. Because certain VM settings are common between virtual machines, you can use the profiles to define those settings, which can be used repeatedly at any time. For example, the hardware profile specifies hardware settings that you want the VM to use when it is created and deployed. Operating system profiles are used to apply various settings that pertain to the operating system.

Virtual Machine Manager has the following profiles:
- Operating system profiles
- Hardware profiles
- Capability profiles
- Application profiles
- SQL profiles

PLANNING AND DEPLOYING OPERATING SYSTEM PROFILES

Operating system profiles are used to create standardized virtual machines by applying various settings to VMs and templates at the time of creation. After the VM is created, it can be changed without affecting other VMs or the template.

You can define operating system profiles in two ways:
- Manually with the New Guest OS Profile
- Automatically with a wizard within the New Template Wizard

 CREATE A GUEST OPERATING SYSTEM PROFILE

GET READY. To create a guest operating system profile using VMM, perform the following steps:

1. Open VMM and the Library workspace.
2. On the *Home* tab, in the *Create* group, click Create, and then click Guest OS Profile.
3. In the *New Guest OS Profile* dialog box, on the *General* tab, in the *Name* text box, enter a name for the guest operating system profile. You can also add an optional description in the *Description* text box.
4. Click the Guest OS Profile tab (see Figure 4-5), and then configure the desired settings:
   - **Operating system** allows you to specify the operating system.
   - **Identity Information** allows you to configure computer name. You can use an asterisk that can randomly generate a computer.
   - **Admin Password** allows you to specify a local administrator password.
   - **Product Key** allows you to specify the product key.

- **Time Zone** allows you to specify the time zone.
- **Roles** allows you to specify the Windows roles.
- **Features** allows you to specify the Windows features.
- **Domain/Workgroup** allows you to specify the workgroup or domain that the virtual machine should join.
- **Answer File** allows you to use an answer script for creating the VM.
- **[GUIRunOnce]** commands allow you to specify which commands to execute.

Figure 4-5

Configure a new guest OS profile

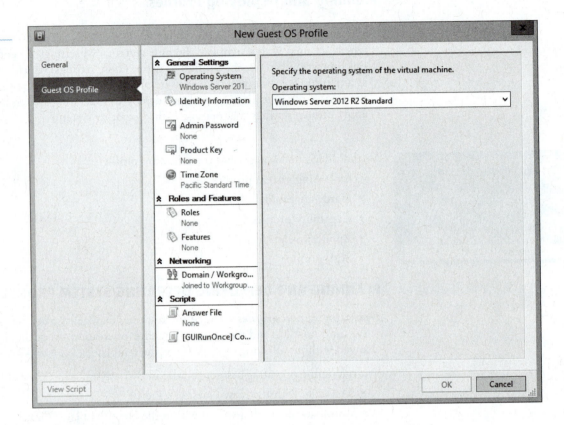

5. Click OK to close the *New Guest OS Profile* dialog box.

When you define a computer name, you can use an asterisk (*) or a hash tag (#) as wildcard characters. For example, if you type **server###**, the profile is used to create Server001, Server002, and so on.

PLANNING AND DEPLOYING HARDWARE AND CAPABILITY PROFILES

Hardware profiles specify the hardware settings that you want the virtual machine to use when it is created and deployed. Capability profiles are used to define the sets of capabilities allowed for the specified item. For example, VMM 2012 R2 ships with three capability profiles: Hyper-V, Xen Server, and ESX Server.

The hardware configuration defined in a hardware profile should be configured to match the systems workload. Some of the common settings in the hardware profile that you can configure are:

- Number of vCPUs
- RAM
- Floppy drive

- Video adapter (standard adapter or RemoteFX 3D adapter)
- DVD drive
- Network configuration such as a dynamic IP address or an address from one of the IP address pools that you created
- Availability options
- BIOS configuration
- CPU priority
- Memory weight

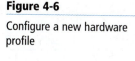 **CREATE A HARDWARE PROFILE**

GET READY. To create a hardware profile using VMM, perform the following steps:

1. Open VMM and the Library workspace.
2. On the *Home* tab, in the *Create* group, click Create, and then click Hardware Profile.
3. In the *New Hardware Profile* dialog box, on the *General* tab, in the *Name* box, enter a descriptive name for the hardware profile. Optionally, you can also type a description in the *Description* text box.
4. For the *Generation* option, select either Generation 1 or Generation 2.
5. On the *Hardware Profile* tab (see Figure 4-6), configure the desired hardware settings. You can also define the capability profile to use.

Figure 4-6

Configure a new hardware profile

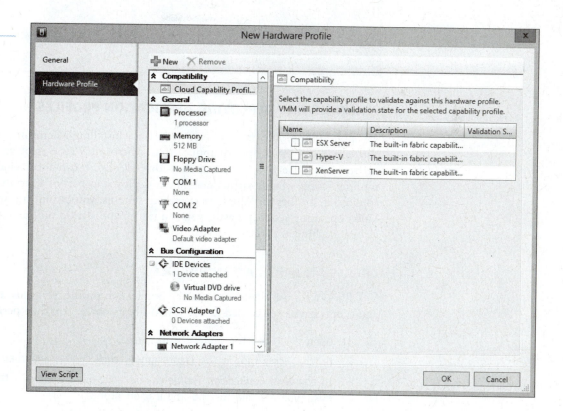

6. Click OK to close the *New Hardware Profile* dialog box.

Capability profiles are frequently used to ensure that the VM or service uses the minimum number of amount of resource, such as the minimum number of network adapters required. You can also use capability profiles to define whether a VM is created on a high availability cluster.

When you define Hyper-V, XenServer, or ESX server, you specify the ranges or limits of available settings for the respective platform. For example, the XenServer profile allows only a maximum of 32 GB of memory, whereas the Hyper-V profile can use up to 1,024 GB (see Figure 4-7).

Figure 4-7

Editing the Hyper-V capability profile

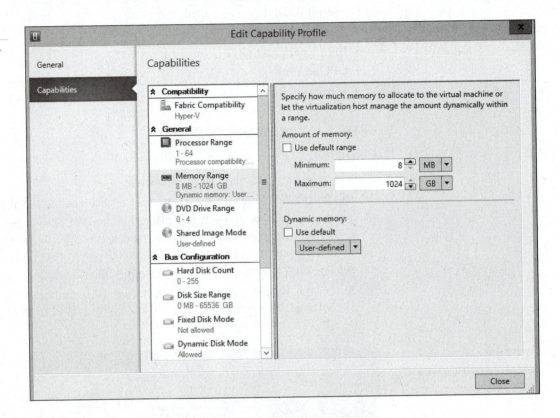

PLANNING AND DEPLOYING APPLICATION PROFILES

An application profile provides instructions for installing Microsoft Server Application Virtualization (Server App-V) applications, Microsoft Web Deploy applications, and Microsoft SQL Server data-tier applications (DACs). It can also include instructions for running scripts when a virtual machine is deployed as part of a service. While you can define application profiles for Windows operating systems, you cannot use application profiles for Linux operating systems. Lastly, you can use an application profile only when you deploy a virtual machine as part of a service.

 ### CREATE AN APPLICATION PROFILE

GET READY. To use VMM to create an application profile, you must ensure that all packages and scripts have been copied to the VMM library share. You then perform the following steps:

1. Open VMM and the Library workspace.
2. On the *Home* tab, in the *Create* group, click Create, and then click Application Profile.
3. In the *New Application Profile* dialog box, on the *General* tab, in the *Name* text box, type a name for the application profile.
4. On the *General* tab, in the *Compatibility* list, choose an appropriate option:
   - For deployment of any Microsoft Server Application and Virtualization (Server App-V) applications, SQL Server DAC packages, SQL Server scripts, or Web Application Hosts, or any combination, keep the default selection, General.

- For deployment of SQL Server DAC packages or SQL Server scripts to an existing instance of SQL Server in your environment, click SQL Server Application Host, which enables you to add only SQL Server DAC packages and SQL Server scripts to the application profile.

- For web applications that run Internet Information Services (IIS), click Web Application Host to add only Web Deploy packages and associated scripts to the application profile.

5. On the *Application Configuration* tab, click OS Compatibility (see Figure 4-8), and then select the guest operating systems on which the application is supported.

Figure 4-8

Using the Application Configuration tab to add applications and scripts

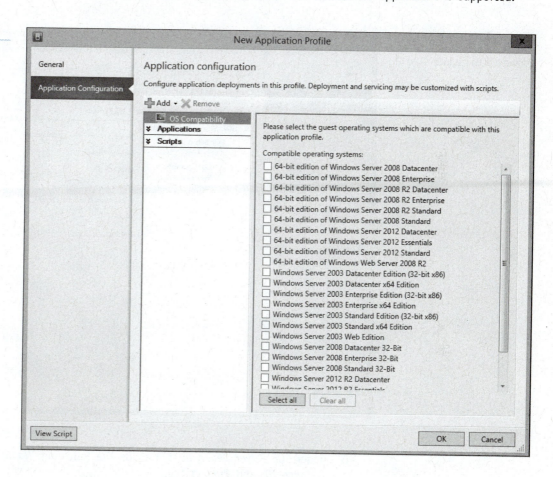

6. Click Add, and then click the type of application or script that you want to add to the application profile. Then use the Browse button to select the application or script. Repeat as needed to add more than one of each type of application.

7. Click OK to close the *New Application Profile* dialog box. The application profile appears in the *Profiles* pane.

PLANNING AND DEPLOYING SQL PROFILES

The SQL profile provides instructions for installing an instance of Microsoft SQL Server on a virtual machine. To use a SQL profile, you must use a virtual hard disk (VHD) that contains a prepared instance of SQL Server (SQL Server 2008 R2 or SQL Server 2012). Before using the VHD, it must be generalized by using the Sysprep tool.

CREATE A SQL PROFILE

GET READY. To create an SQL profile using VMM, perform the following steps:

1. Open VMM and the Library workspace.

2. On the *Home* tab, in the *Create* group, click Create, and then click SQL Server Profile.

3. In the *New SQL Server Profile* dialog box, on the *General* tab, in the *Name* text box, enter a name for the SQL Server profile.

4. On the *SQL Server Configuration* tab, next to *Add*, click SQL Server Deployment (see Figure 4-9).

Figure 4-9

Adding a SQL instance

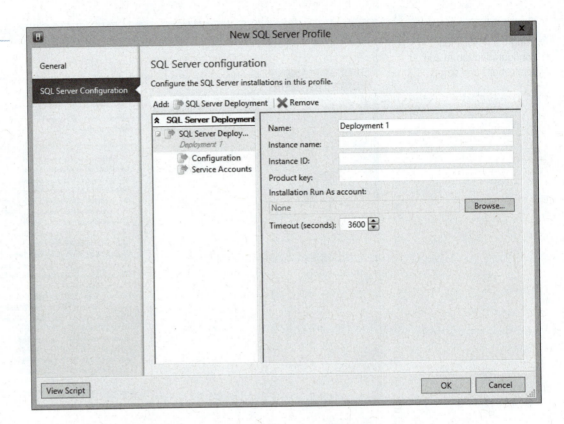

5. Under *SQL Server Deployment*, provide the following: *Name*, *Instance name*, *Instance ID*, and *Product key*.

6. To select the optional installation Run As account, click Browse. If one is not selected, the VMM Service account is used.

7. In the *Browse Run As Accounts* dialog box, select Use an existing Run As account or Use a configurable service settings. You can also click the Create Run As Account button to create a new Run As Account. Click OK to close the dialog box.

8. Click Configuration. In the results pane, enter the media source (the path to the SQL Server installation media folder where Setup.exe is located) and the SQL Server administrators.

9. Click Service Accounts. In the results pane, enter the *Run As accounts to use for SQL Server service Run As Account, SQL Server Agent service Run As Account*, and *Reporting Services Run As Account*.

10. Click OK to close the *New SQL Server Profile*. The SQL Server profile appears in the *Profiles* pane.

Planning and Managing Services

After a service is deployed, you can update the existing VMs or deploy new updated VMs. Updating existing virtual machines for smaller changes is best because doing so is a less time-consuming process than deploying a new VM. However, if you have larger changes, such as installing a service pack to a guest operating system, consider deploying new VMs.

System Center 2012 R2 Virtual Machine Manager keeps track of which service template was used to deploy a service. Therefore, you can make updates to the service template, and then use that updated service template to make changes to the deployed service.

To update a deployed service in VMM, you can make a copy of the service template on which the deployed service is based. You can then modify the copy of the service template.

 CREATE AN UPDATED SERVICE TEMPLATE

GET READY. To create an updated service template using VMM, perform the following steps:

1. Open VMM and the *Library* workspace. Expand the Templates node, and then click Service Templates.

2. In the *Templates* pane that lists the available service templates, select the service template that you want to copy.

3. On the *Service Template* tab, in the *Create* group, click Copy.

4. In the *Templates* pane, right-click the new service template and choose Properties.

5. In the *Properties* dialog box, on the *General* page, enter a new release value (such as 2.0).

6. Click OK to save and close the service template.

Before you can update a service using an updated template, you must first publish the updated service template. You can then replace the current template with an updated template.

 APPLY UPDATES TO A DEPLOYED SERVICE BY USING AN UPDATED SERVICE TEMPLATE

GET READY. To use an updated service template to apply updates to a deployed service, perform the following steps:

1. Open VMM and the *Library* workspace. Expand the Templates node, and then click Service Templates.

2. In the *Templates* pane, select the service template that you want to publish.

3. On the *Service Template* tab, in the *Actions* group, click Publish. If you no longer want to make the service template available, click Revoke.

4. Open the VMs and Service workspace and find the service that you want to update with the updated ser vice template. The *Update Status* column for the service should display *New Release Available*.

5. In the *VMs and Service* workspace, select the service that you want to update with the updated service template.

6. On the *Service* tab, in the *Update* group, click Set Template.

7. In the *Change Service Template* wizard, on the *Updated Service Template* page, select Replace the current template with an updated template for this service.

8. Click Browse, select the updated service template, click OK, and then click Next.

9. On the *Settings* page, configure any application settings that are listed, and then click Next.

10. On the *Update Method* page, select whether you want to make the updates in place to the existing virtual machines or whether you want to deploy new virtual machines with the updated settings. Then click Next.

11. On the *Updates Review* page, review your selections, and then click Next.

12. On the *Summary* page, review the settings, and then click Finish.

13. When you are ready to apply the updates to the deployed service (for example, during a regularly scheduled maintenance window), in the *VMs and Service* workspace, select the service that you want to update.

14. On the *Service* tab, in the *Upgrade* group, click Apply Template.

15. When the *Apply Service Template* dialog box opens, review the updates that will be made, and then click OK.

16. When the updates are complete, close the *Jobs* window.

You can use the scale-out functionality of VMM to deploy additional virtual machines to a tier of the service. For example, you can have several web servers in a tier. If your business grows, you can add web servers to handle the additional load.

When you create a tier in a service template, you can specify whether the tier can be scaled out. You can also specify the minimum and maximum number of VMs for the tier. If you scale the tier beyond the maximum number, you will receive a warning. Although VMM will not prevent you from scaling out the tier, it will show a status of Needs Attention in the VMs and Services workspace.

Configuring Virtual Machine Manager Libraries

The *VMM library* is a catalog of resources that provide access to file-based resources such as virtual hard disks (VHDs), virtual floppy disks, ISO images, scripts, driver files, and application packages.

To add images (such as a VHD or VHDX file) to VMM, choose Create Host Profile from the Library workspace. Then in the New Host Profile Wizard, you can import the VHD or VHDX image. When you install VMM, the MSSCVMMLibrary is already created from the C:\ProgramData\Virtual Machine Manager Library Files folder.

⊙ ADD A FILE-BASE RESOURCE TO THE LIBRARY

GET READY. To use VMM to add a file-based resource to the library, perform the following steps:

1. Open VMM and the *Library* workspace. Then expand the Library Servers node and a library server.

2. Right-click a library share, and then click Explore. The shared folder opens.

3. Using *File Explorer*, copy files to the shared folder.

4. Close the shared folder.

Alternatively, you can use the Import Physical Resource and Export Physical Resource options to import and export file-based resources between library shares.

Managing Logical Networks

> In VMM, you can create *logical networks* that can easily connect virtual machines to a network used for a particular function in your environment, such as the back-end, front-end, or backup network. It would define IP subnets and. if needed, virtual local area networks (VLANs).

The Fabric workspace in VMM enables you to create and configure logical networks. Besides defining subnets, you can also associate VLANs to the subnets. A VLAN is a logical network that isolate traffic to devices connected to it.

 CREATE A LOGICAL NETWORK

GET READY. To use VMM to create a logical network, perform the following steps:

1. Open the VMM console, and then open the Fabric workspace.
2. On the **Home** tab, in the **Show** group, click Fabric Resources.
3. In the **Fabric** pane, expand Networking, and then click Logical Networks.
4. In the **Create** group, click Create Logical Network. The **Create Logical Network Wizard** opens (see Figure 4-10).

Figure 4-10

Opening the Create Logical Network Wizard

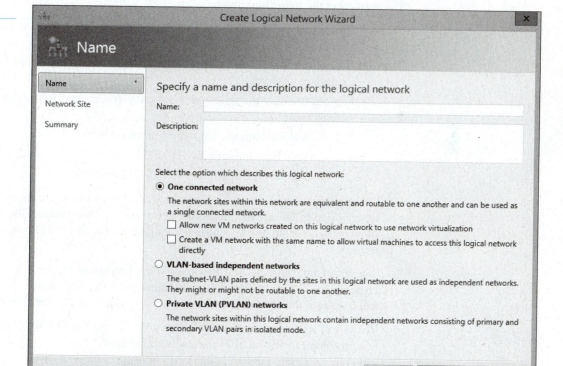

5. On the *Name* page, in the *Name* text box, type a descriptive name. For the *Description*, you can type an optional description of the logical network.
6. Select the option that describes the logical network. Options include *One connected network*, *VLAN-based independent networks*, or *Private VLAN (PVLAN) network*. Click Next.
7. On the *Network Site* page, click Add, and then select All Hosts.

8. Click Insert row, click Enter IP subnet, type a subnet such as 192.168.1.0/24, and then click Next.

9. On the *Summary* page, click Finish.

10. When the network is created, close the *Jobs* window.

Planning and Deploying Services to Non-Trusted Domains and Workgroups

Starting with System Center 2012 SP1, you can deploy services to virtual machines in a non-trusted domain or workgroup. This is useful when you want to deploy VMs to a perimeter network (also known as a demilitarized zone or DMZ), so that it can be accessed from the Internet.

In some situations, you can deploy an application or service, but for security concerns you do not want the application or service run within your company domain. Therefore, with System Center 2012 R2 VMM, you can deploy VMs based on service templates to hosts in a network perimeter or hosts in workgroups. You can also deploy to untrusted Active Directory domains or domains with one-way or two-way trust with the domain in which the VMM server is located.

To add Hyper-V hosts to a VMM management server in a domain in another tree, VMM must meet the following prerequisites:

- The VMM service must use an account that has permission to register its service principal name (SPN) in Active Directory Domain Services (AD DS).
- You must add the DNS suffix of the domain's tree in the TCP/IP settings of the VMM management server.
- You can use only the following Group Policy settings for Windows Remote Management:
  - Allow automatic configuration of listeners
  - Turn on Compatibility HTTP Listener
  - Turn on Compatibility HTTPS Listener

Other settings might cause the Virtual Machine Manager agent on the Hyper-V host that you are trying to install to fail. The Allow automatic configuration of listeners setting also must allow messages from any IP addresses. Unfortunately, this could potentially risk your overall security.

When you are using the Add Resource Wizard to install Hyper-V hosts, you must use the Hyper-V host's fully qualified domain name (FQDN). Of course, the Hyper-V host name will have to resolved to an IP address. Do not select the AD verification check box.

VMM will attempt to write an SPN into AD DS for the FQDN of the Hyper-V host. If it fails, you have to set the SPN manually, as follows:

```
setspn –A HOST/<FQDN> <NETBIOS Name>.
```

To add a Hyper-V host to an untrusted Active Directory domain that is managed by VMM, none of the Group Policy settings for Windows Remote Management should be enabled for setting access for a VMM management server in the trusted domain. Using a specific Run As account for the untrusted domain's Hyper-V hosts is recommended. The account should have local administrative rights on the Hyper-V hosts. Lastly, when you use the VMM Add Resource Wizard in an untrusted Active Directory, select the Windows Server computer radio button.

If you place the Hyper-V hosts in a perimeter network, you have to ensure that both firewalls are configured properly. You need to access VMM and the Hyper-V servers so that you can manage them from within the internal network, and you need to make sure that anyone who accesses the VMs, applications, or services from the Internet cannot access the internal network. You then need to install the Microsoft System Center Virtual Machine Manager Agent on the Hyper-V hosts in the perimeter network and then add the Hyper-V host as a resource to VMM.

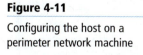 **ADD A HYPER-V HOST ON THE PERIMETER NETWORK TO VMM**

GET READY. To add a Hyper-V host on the perimeter network to VMM, perform the following steps:

1. On the Hyper-V host running within the perimeter network, double-click the VMM setup.exe.

2. When the *Virtual Machine Manager* splash screen opens, under *Optional Installations*, click Local Agent.

3. When the *Microsoft System Center Virtual Machine Manager Agent* Wizard opens, on the Welcome page, click Next.

4. On the *Microsoft Software Notice Terms* page, select I agree with the terms of this notice. Click Next.

5. On the *Destination Folder* page, click Next.

6. On the *Security File Folder* page, select This host is on a perimeter network, as shown in Figure 4-11.

Figure 4-11

Configuring the host on a perimeter network machine

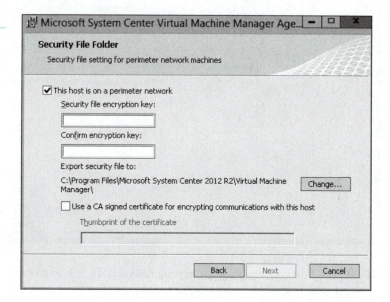

7. On the *Security File Folder* page, in the *Security file encryption key* and *Confirm encryption key* text boxes, type any value that you chose, similar to a password value. This encryption key is stored locally as SecurityFile.txt in a folder of your choosing. Click Next.

8. On the *Host network name* page, select Use IP address. Then type the IP address. Click xNext.

9. On the *Configuration settings* page, click Next.

10. On the *Ready to install Microsoft System Center Virtual Machine Manager Agent* page, click Install.

11. When the installation is complete, click Finish.

12. On the server running VMM, open Virtual Machine Manager.

13. Click the Fabric workspace.

14. Click Add Resources, and then select Hyper-V Hosts and Clusters.

15. In the *Add Resource* Wizard, on the *Resource Location* page, select Windows Server computers in a perimeter network. Click Next.

16. On the *Target resources* page, in the *Computer name* text box, type the name of the Hyper-V host.

17. In the *Encryption key* text box, type the encryption key you specified in step 7.

18. Use the Browse button to specify the location of SecurityFile.txt from step 7. Click Add. The target resource is displayed, as shown in Figure 4-12. Click Next.

Figure 4-12

Adding the target resources

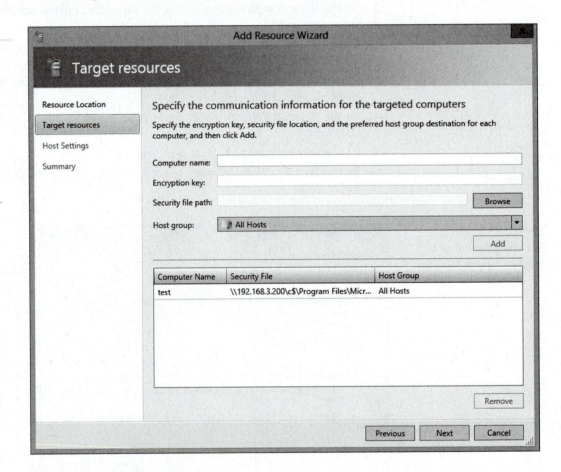

19. On the *Host settings* page, select the Reassociate this host with this VMM environment and click Next.

20. On the *Summary* page, click Finish.

21. When the computer is added, close the *Jobs* window.

SKILL SUMMARY

IN THIS LESSON YOU LEARNED:

- System Center 2012 R2 Virtual Machine Manager (VMM) enables centralized management of virtualized workloads. VMM allows you to manage the virtualized data center infrastructure; increase physical server utilization, including providing simple and fast consolidation of the virtual infrastructure; and perform physical-to-virtual (P2V) migration and intelligent workplace placement based on performance data and user-defined business policies.

- VMM has a similar installation as other System Center products. It requires a SQL server, such as Microsoft SQL Server (SQL Server 2008 R2 with SP1 or later).

- With Virtual Machine Manager Service, services are collections of virtual machines deployed together to provide a service or application. With Virtual Machine Manager Service, however, you can create tiers or a tier-based infrastructure to provide the service.

- The VMM service templates is a single object that contains multiple child templates, including VM templates, networking configuration, load balancing, applications, and storage.

- To create a service template, you use the Service Template Designer, which is launched from VMM.

- Operating system profiles are used to create standardized virtual machines by applying various settings to virtual machines and templates at the time of creation. After the VM is created, the VM can be changed without affecting other VMs and the template.

- Hardware profiles specify the hardware settings that you want the virtual machine to use when the virtual machine is created and deployed.

- You use capability profiles to define the sets of capabilities allowed for the specified item.

- The VMM library is a catalog of resources that provide access to file-based resources such as virtual hard disks, virtual floppy disks, ISO images, scripts, driver files, and application packages.

- In VMM, you can create logical networks that can easily connect virtual machines to a network used for a particular function in your environment. It would define IP subnets and, if needed, virtual local area networks (VLANs).

- Starting with System Center 2012 SP1, you can deploy services to virtual machines in a non-trusted domain or workgroup. This is useful when you want to deploy VMs to a perimeter network, so that it can be accessed from the Internet.

■ Knowledge Assessment

Multiple Choice

1. What tool is used to manage virtual machines with a Hyper-V infrastructure and provide simple and fast consolidation of the virtual infrastructure?
   a. System Center Configuration Manager
   b. System Center Operations Manager
   c. System Center Virtual Machine Manager
   d. System Center Essentials

2. Which tool is used to perform a physical-to-virtual machine conversion?
   a. System Center Configuration Manager
   b. System Center Operations Manager
   c. System Center Virtual Machine Manager
   d. Hyper-V Converter

3. Which of the following is a requirement for VMM management server)? (Choose all that apply.)
   a. Full version of Microsoft SQL Server
   b. Microsoft .NET Framework 4.5
   c. File and Storage Services
   d. Internet Information Services (IIS)

4. Which of the following can VMM manage? (Choose all that apply.)
   a. Microsoft Hyper-V
   b. Oracle VM Server
   c. Citrix XenServer
   d. VMWare ESX

5. Which of the following is a collection of virtual machines that are grouped together to deploy a network application?
   a. tier
   b. system profile
   c. hardware profile
   d. services

6. Which two items are used when defining a logical network? (Choose two answers.)
   a. DNS server
   b. IP subnet
   c. VLANs
   d. Default gateway

7. Which of the following is the primary tool to manage service templates?
   a. Service Template Designer
   b. Service Template Creator
   c. Service Template Manager
   d. Library Manager

8. You are an administrator for Contoso. You want to deploy Windows Server 2012 R2 to multiple virtual machines using VMM. Which of the following is used to apply various settings quickly and efficiently?
   a. Use Windows deployment profiles
   b. Use compatibility profile
   c. Use operating system profiles
   d. Use system profiles

9. When you deploy virtual machines, you want to cut down the time that it takes to specify the number of processors and amount of RAM. Which of the following can be used to reduce the time to deploy Windows VMs?
   a. compatibility profile
   b. service template
   c. system profile
   d. hardware profile

10. You want VMM to manage a Microsoft Hyper-V host. Which of the following actions adds the host to the VMM console?
    a. import the host
    b. deploy the agent
    c. deploy the host
    d. associate the host

11. VMM is installed on an internal server and you want to place 2 Hyper-V hosts on the perimeter network. Which of the following is needed in order to install on the Hyper-V hosts?
    a. The VMM console
    b. The VMM local agent
    c. The VMM communicator
    d. The VMM proxy

Best Answer

Choose the letter that corresponds to the best answer. More than one answer choice can achieve the goal. Select the BEST answer.

1. Which single object contains multiple child templates, including virtual machine templates, networking configuration, load balancing, applications, and storage?
   a. compatibility profile
   b. service template
   c. system profile
   d. hardware profile

2. You need to deploy an account software infrastructure that consists of a cluster to run the SQL Server and several front-end servers and portals. Which of the following actions deploys this infrastructure efficiently whenever needed?
   a. Create a customized standard VM and use multiple answer files.
   b. Configure the system on several hardware server, and run the P2V converter.
   c. Reassociate each VM to create a set of master templates.
   d. Use a service template.

3. You have a large Hyper-V infrastructure. You have created disk image templates over the last year that are located on various Hyper-V hosts. Which of the following actions best manages the images from VMM so that you can use them with any VM deployment?
   a. Copy the images to the MSSCVMMLibrary.
   b. Add the shared folders to the VMM library.
   c. Redeploy the VMs to the master VMM console server.
   d. Attach the Hyper-V hosts to the fabric. Be sure to enable the multi-share option.

4. VMWare released a new version of ESX that supports a larger number of processors and larger amount of RAM for each host and VM. Which of the following should be created so that you can get the most out of the ESX servers?
   a. compatibility profile
   b. service template
   c. system profile
   d. hardware profile

5. You are using VMM to create a test network. Which of the following actions ensures that all servers created on the test network are isolated from the production network?
   a. Define compatibility profile that allows communications to specified servers only.
   b. Create a test tier.
   c. Define VLANs in your logical networks.
   d. Create a second VMM console that will manage the test network.

Matching and Identification

1. Match the term with its definition:

_____ **a)** tier
_____ **b)** logical network
_____ **c)** service
_____ **d)** service template
_____ **e)** VMM library
_____ **f)** Fabric workspace

1. Collections of virtual machines deployed together to provide a service or application
2. A catalog of resources that provides access to file-based resources such as virtual hard disks, virtual floppy disks, ISO images, scripts, driver files, and application packages
3. Contains configuration necessary for its portion of the service
4. Defines IP subnets and, if needed, virtual local area networks (VLANs)
5. Allows you to create and configure logical networks
6. A single object that contains multiple child templates, including virtual machine templates, networking configuration, load balancing, applications, and storage

2. Match the policy with its definition:

_____ **a)** Hardware profile
_____ **b)** Compatibility profile
_____ **c)** Virtual machine
_____ **d)** Service template
_____ **e)** Operating system profile

1. A single object that contains multiple child templates, including virtual machine templates, networking configuration, load balancing, applications, and storage
2. Enables you to create standardized virtual machines by applying various settings to virtual machines and templates at the time of creation
3. Enables you to specify the ranges or limits of available settings for the respective platform
4. Enables you to specify the hardware settings that you want the virtual machine to use when the virtual machine is created and deployed
5. Used to create new virtual machines and configure tiers in a service template

Build a List

1. In order of first to last, specify the steps used to add a Hyper-V host to VMM.

_____ Specify the host name
_____ Specify a Run As account
_____ Associate the host with the VMM
_____ Right-click All hosts and click Add Hyper-V Hosts and Clusters

■ Business Case Scenarios

Scenario 4-1: Managing Hyper-V and ESX Servers

You are an administrator for the Contoso Corporation. You have 15 Microsoft Hyper-V hosts and 8 VMware ESX servers. You want manage all your hosts and virtual management using one centralized environment. You also need to deploy five more Microsoft Hyper-V hosts, which need to follow the standardized environment. What would you recommend, and how would you proceed?

Scenario 4-2: Implementing a Database Environment

You are ready to deploy a SAP database environment, which will include a cluster SQL server, four front-end servers, and four back-end servers. You need to deploy this environment into a test environment, a development environment, and a production environment. What would you use to deploy this environment and to ensure that the environments are standardized?

Planning and Implementing File and Storage Services

70-413 EXAM OBJECTIVE

Objective 1.5 – Plan and implement file and storage services. This objective may include but is not limited to: Planning considerations, including iSCSI SANs, Fibre Channel SANs, Virtual Fibre Channel, storage spaces, storage pools (including tiered storage) and data deduplication; configure the Internet Storage Name Server (iSNS); configure services for Network File System (NFS); plan and implement SMB 3.0 based storage; plan for Windows Offloaded Data Transfer (ODX).

LESSON HEADING	EXAM OBJECTIVE
Planning and Implementing Storage Technology • Planning and Implementing iSCSI SAN • Configuring the iSCSI Initiator • Configuring the iSCSI Target Server • Configuring the iSCSI MPIO Features • Configuring the Internet Storage Name Server (iSNS) • Using iSCSI Best Practices • Planning and Implementing Fibre Channel SANs • Planning and Implementing Virtual Fibre Channel • Installing Device-Specific Modules (DSMs) • Planning and Implementing Storage Spaces and Storage Pools	Planning considerations, including iSCSI SANs, Fibre Channel SANs, Virtual Fibre Channel, storage spaces, storage pools (including tiered storage) and data deduplication Configure the Internet Storage Name Server (iSNS) Plan and implement Storage Spaces and storage pools (including tiered storage)
Planning and Implementing Data Deduplication	Plan and implement data deduplication
Configuring Services for Network File System (NFS) • Obtaining User and Group Information • Creating an NFS Share • Installing and Configuring the NFS Datastore	Configure services for Network File System (NFS)
Planning and Implementing SMB 3.0 Based Storage	Plan and implement SMB 3.0 based storage
Planning for Windows Offloaded Data Transfer (ODX)	Plan for Windows Offloaded Data Transfer (ODX)

KEY TERMS

cluster-shared volume (CSV)	iSCSI qualified name (IQN)	Server Message Block (SMB) 3.0
copy offload	iSCSI Target	shared storage
data deduplication	iSCSI Target Storage Provider	simple resiliency type
device-specific modules (DSMs)	logical unit number (LUN)	storage area networks (SANs)
Discovery Domain (DD)	multipath I/O (MPIO)	storage pool
Fibre Channel	multiple connected session (MCS)	Storage Spaces
group identifier (GID)		thin provisioning
Identity Management for UNIX	network-attached storage (NAS)	three-way mirror resiliency type
Internet Small Computer System Interface (iSCSI)	Network File System (NFS)	tiered storage
Internet Storage Name Server (iSNS)	NFS Datastore	two-way mirror resiliency type
	parity resiliency type	user identifier (UID)
iSCSI Initiator	Scale-Out File Server (SoFS)	Windows Offloaded Data Transfer (ODX)

■ Planning and implementing storage technology

 **THE BOTTOM LINE**

Many servers used in an organization require large amounts of disk space to provide services and resources. For example, file servers need to store data files, and mail servers and database servers need to store large databases. Therefore, these servers typically need many hard drives connected directly to the machine, or the servers connect to shared storage. *Shared storage* devices have many hard drives to provide huge amounts of disk space.

CERTIFICATION READY
Planning considerations, including iSCSI SANs, Fibre Channel SANs, Virtual Fibre Channel, storage spaces, storage pools (including tiered storage) and data deduplication
Objective 1.5

Two network storage solutions are used in networking:

- *Network-attached storage (NAS)* is a file-level data storage device that is connected to the server over a computer network to provide shared drives or folders, usually using Server Message Block (SMB) or Network File System (NFS).
- *Storage area network (SAN)* is a storage architecture that allows systems to attach to the storage in the SAN and presents the drives to the server just as the drivers were locally attached.

Accessing the shared files on a NAS is like accessing a shared folder on a server. To provide fault tolerance and better performance, most NAS devices use redundant array of independent disks (RAID). NAS devices can be managed with a web interface, and some enterprise NAS devices include a command-line interface accessible with Secure Shell (SSH).

If a server fails, the data is still stored in the SAN. You can then bring up another server, present the same storage to the server, and have all your data intact. Typically when you use clustering in a production environment and for a virtual environment such as Hyper-V, using a SAN is common and recommended. Of course, robust SANs usually have a higher level of RAID such as RAID 10, spare drives, redundant power supplies, redundant network connections, and built-in monitoring tools.

Most SANs use the SCSI command for communication between servers and disk drive devices. By using the SCSI commands, you can connect disks to a server using copper Ethernet cables or fiber optic cables. The two standards used in SANs are Fibre Channel and iSCSI.

Each technology uses a fabric, which is a network topology in which devices are connected to each other through one or more high-efficient data paths. In addition to allowing multiple servers to access the SAN, both technologies allow the SAN to be in a different rack in the server room, a separate room, or even a separate building. Of course, deciding on what is an acceptable performance always comes down to bandwidth and latency.

A *logical unit number (LUN)* is a logical reference to a portion of a storage subsystem. The LUN can be a disk, part of a disk, an entire disk array, or part of the disk array. So when configuring servers to attach to a SAN, you usually configure the SAN to assign a LUN to a specific server. In other words, the LUN allows the administrator to break the SAN storage into manageable pieces. If the LUN is not mapped to a specific server, the server cannot see or access the LUN.

Planning and Implementing iSCSI SAN

Internet Small Computer System Interface (iSCSI) is a protocol that enables clients to send SCSI commands over a TCP/IP network using TCP port 3260. Unlike Fibre Channel, you use standard Ethernet cabling and switches to connect servers to the SAN. Because you connect to the SAN over the network, you should use a minimum of two network adapters on the server, one for the SAN communications and one for standard network communications. Currently, the fastest network connection is capable of 10 gigabits per second or more.

Unlike standard local SCSI drives, iSCSI allows data transfers over intranets and can be used over long distances. iSCSI allows clients (called *iSCSI initiators*) to send SCSI commands to iSCSI storage devices (*iSCSI targets*).

Storage devices provided by iSCSI are often used as storage devices that contain sensitive or critical data. Therefore, you need to protect the iSCSI infrastructure. The best approach for security is to use a defense-in-depth security strategy consisting of the following:

- Implementing policies, procedures, and awareness that include security best practices, enforcement of a strong user password policy and strong administrator password policy for accessing iSCSI storage devices, and computers that have iSCSI management software installed.
- Implementing physical security that protects servers and iSCSI storage devices that can be accessed by authorized personnel only.
- Establishing perimeter security that includes firewalls to protect attacks from outside the organization and prevent attacks on the iSCSI devices.
- Using network protection including authentication such as target access lists, Challenge-Handshake Authentication Protocol (CHAP), virtual LANs (VLANs), and physical isolation. You might also consider using Internet Protocol security (IPsec).
- Keeping your servers updated with the latest security updates.
- Protecting the data stored on the iSCSI storage devices, including encryption (using BitLocker and Encrypted File System [EFS]) and Access Control Lists (ACLs).
- Performing backups regularly and storing the backups in a safe place.

Of these, iSCSI targets and initiators have the following security features built in:

- They limit which iSCSI initiators can connect to an iSCSI target.
- They use CHAP to provide authentication between an iSCSI initiator and an iSCSI target.
- For encryption of traffic between an iSCSI Initiator and an iSCSI Target, you can use IPsec.

iSCSI qualified names (IQNs) are unique identifiers used to address initiators and targets on an iSCSI network. An IQN uses the following format:

- Literal IQN
- Date (yyyy-mm) that the naming authority took ownership of the domain
- Reversed domain name of the authority
- Optional : (colon) prefixing a storage target name specified by the naming authority

An example of an IQN is as follows:

```
iqn.1991-05.com.contoso:storage01-target1-target
```

When you configure an iSCSI target, you define which iSCSI initiators can connect to an iSCSI LUN by the client's IQN. You can also specify which servers can connect to the iSCSI target based on MAC addresses, IP address, and DNS name. iSCSI initiators use IQNs to connect to iSCSI targets. If name resolution is possible, you can also use IP addresses to identify initiators and targets.

Configuring the iSCSI Initiator

To connect to an iSCSI target, you use an iSCSI initiator. As mentioned previously, the iSCSI Initiator is already included with Windows.

After the targets are configured and registered, you open the iSCSI initiator, as discussed in the following procedure.

 CONFIGURE THE iSCSI INITIATOR

GET READY. To configure the iSCSI initiator, perform the following steps:

1. In *Server Manager*, click Tools > iSCSI Initiator. The *iSCSI Initiator Properties* dialog box opens. If it is the first time launching, Microsoft iSCSI will not be running. Therefore, when you are prompted to start automatically each time the computer restarts, click Yes.

2. The *Targets* tab is shown in Figure 5-1. If you just created a iSCSI target, and it does not show up, click Refresh. If it still does not show up, in the *Target* text box, type the address of the iSCSI Target Server or SAN and click Quick Connect. When the *Quick Connect* dialog box opens, click Done.

Figure 5-1

Connecting to a target

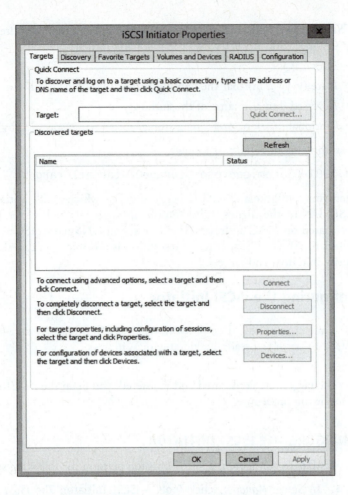

3. If the target is not connected, select it and click Connect. In the *Connect to Target* dialog box, if you need to specify the target portal IP address or a CHAP username, click Advanced to open the *Advanced Settings* dialog box. When you click OK to close the *Advanced Settings* dialog box and *Connect to Target* dialog box, the status should show *Connected*.

TAKE NOTE✱ If the target does not show up, verify that the initiator ID is specified correctly in the iSCSI target access server list.

4. On the *Volumes and Devices* tab, click Auto Configure. In the *Volume List*, the available iSCSI targets should appear.

5. If you need to configure CHAP or IPsec to connect to the iSCSI target, click the Configuration tab.

6. Click OK to close the *iSCSI Initiator Properties* dialog box.

After an iSCSI device is attached to a server running Windows Server 2012 or Windows Server 2012 R2, you might need to format the volume and assign a drive letter to the new volume. To accomplish this, you use Computer Management. After opening Computer Management, if the disk does not show up, right-click *Disk Management* and try to perform a disk rescan.

PREPARE AN iSCSI VOLUME

GET READY. To prepare an iSCSI volume, perform the following steps:

1. In *Server Manager*, click Tools > Computer Management. The *Computer Management* console opens.

2. Under *Storage*, click Disk Management. The *Disk Management* snap-in is displayed (see Figure 5-2).

Figure 5-2

Opening Disk Management

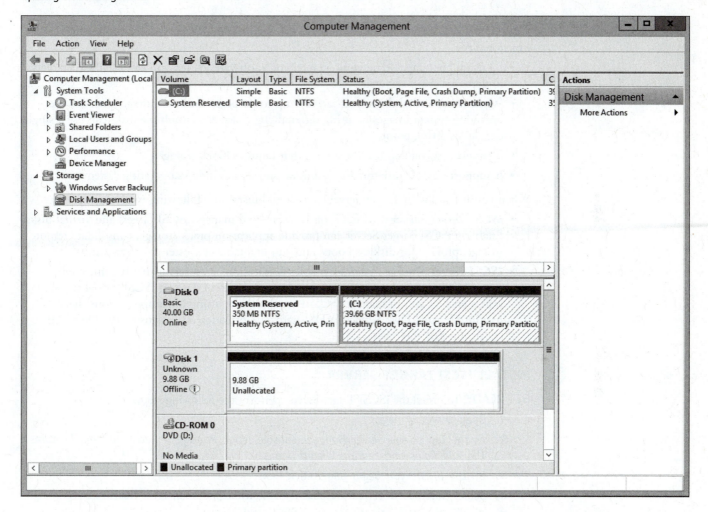

3. To bring Disk 1 online, right-click Disk 1 and choose Online. The status of Disk 1 changes to not initialized.

4. To initialize the disk, right-click Disk 1 and choose Initialize Disk.

5. In *the Initialize Disk* dialog box, click OK. The status of Disk 1 changes to *Basic, Online.*

6. Right-click the unallocated volume for Disk 1 and choose New Simple Volume.

7. When the *New Simple Volume* Wizard opens, click Next.

8. On the *Specify Volume Size* page, specify the size in megabytes of the volume and click Next.

9. On the *Assign Drive Letter or Path* page, select an unused drive letter and click Next.

10. On the *Format Partition* page, in the *Volume label* text box, type a name of the volume label and click Next.

11. When the wizard is done, click Finish.

Configuring the iSCSI Target Server

Starting with Windows Server 2012, you can install the iSCSI Target Server role so that other Windows servers can provide iSCSI storage to other clients (including other Windows servers). After you install the iSCSI Target Server role, you use Server Manager to create the volumes that will be presented to clients and specify what servers can access the iSCSI LUNs.

The iSCSI Target Server included in Windows Server 2012 R2 provides the following functionality:

- By using boot-capable network adapters or a software loader, you can use iSCSI targets to deploy diskless servers.
- When using virtual disks, you can save up to 90 percent of the storage space for the operating system images by using differencing disks, since multiple disks can use a single disk as a starting point.
- It supports server application storage that requires block storage.
- It supports iSCSI initiators for Windows and non-Windows operating systems.

When you install iSCSI Target Server, you should install the following two components:

- ***iSCSI Target Server*** provides tools to create and manage iSCSI targets and virtual disks. Enabling iSCSI Target Server can provide application block storage, consolidate remote storage, provide for diskless boots, and run in a failover cluster environment.
- ***iSCSI Target Storage Provider*** enables applications on a server that is connected to an iSCSI target to perform volume shadow copies of data on iSCSI virtual disks. It also enables you to manage iSCSI virtual disks by using older applications that require a Virtual Disk Service (VDS) hardware provider, such as using the DiskRAID command-line tool.

 INSTALL ISCSI TARGET SERVER

GET READY. To install the iSCSI Target Server, perform the following steps:

1. Open Server Manager.
2. At the top of the *Server Manager* console, click Manage > Add Roles and Features. The *Add Roles and Feature Wizard* opens.
3. On the *Before you begin* page, click Next.
4. Select Role-based or feature-based installation and then click Next.
5. On the *Select destination server* page, select the server that you are installing to and click Next.
6. On the *Select server roles* page, expand File and Storage Services, expand File and iSCSI Services, and click iSCSI Target Server and iSCSI Target Storage Provider (VDS and VSS hardware providers). Click Next.
7. On the *Select features* page, click Next.
8. On the *Confirm installation selections* page, click Install.
9. When the installation is complete, click Close.

Virtual disks or targets are created on an iSCSI disk storage subsystem that is not directly assigned to a server. Targets are created to manage the connections between an iSCSI device and the servers that need to access it. Rather than having its own console, iSCSI manages iSCSI virtual disks and iSCSI Targets through Server Manager.

⊙ CREATE AN iSCSI VIRTUAL DISK

GET READY. To create an iSCSI virtual disk, perform the following steps:

1. In *Server Manager*, click File and Storage Services, and then click iSCSI.
2. Click To create an iSCSI virtual disk, start the New iSCSI Virtual Disk Wizard (see Figure 5-3). Alternatively, in the *iSCSI Virtual Disks* section, you can click the Tasks menu and click New iSCSI Virtual Disk.

Figure 5-3

Managing iSCSI virtual disks

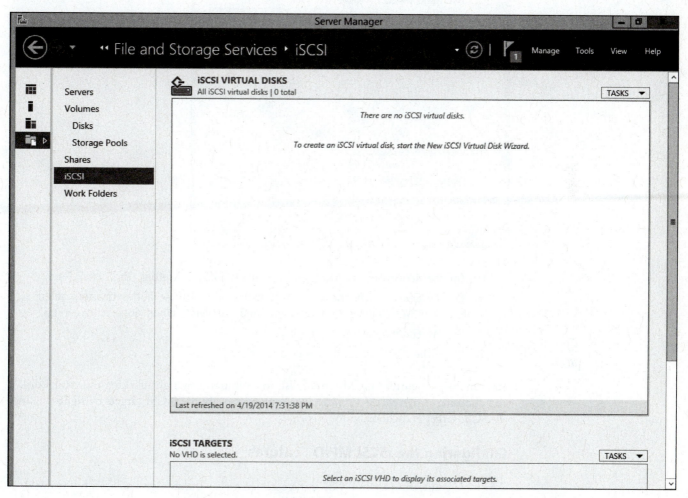

3. On the *Select virtual disk location* page, click a drive to store the iSCSI virtual disk, and then click Next.
4. On the *iSCSI Virtual Disk Name* page, in the *Name* text box, type the name of the iSCSI virtual disk. Click Next.
5. In the *iSCSI Virtual Disk Size* page, specify the size in gigabytes (GB) of the iSCSI virtual disk. Click Next.
6. On the *iSCSI Target* page, if targets been defined previously, you can click a target and then click Next. To create a new target, click New iSCSI target and then click Next.
7. If you chose the *New iSCSI target*, on the *Target Name and Access* page, type the name of the target. Click Next.
8. On the *Access Servers* page, click Add.

9. On the *Add initiator ID* page, for the type, select IQN, DNS Name, IP Address, or MAC address. Then in the *Value* text box, type the corresponding value for the initiator that matches the type (see Figure 5-4). Click OK.

Figure 5-4

Specifying the iSCSI initiators that can connect to the target

10. On the *Access Servers* page, add any other iSCSI initiators. Then click Next.

11. On the *Enable Authentication* page, if you want to use authentication, select Enable CHAP. Then type a username and password. When done, click Next.

12. On the *Confirmation* page, click Create.

13. When the iSCSI virtual disk is created, click Close.

You can assign a current iSCSI virtual disk to an initiator by right-clicking the virtual disk and choosing *Assign iSCSI Virtual Disk*. You can modify the iSCSI targets by right-clicking an iSCSI target and choosing *Properties*.

Configuring the iSCSI MPIO Features

A single connection to an iSCSI storage device makes the storage available, but it does not make the storage connections highly available. If the network connection or a switch fails, the server connecting to the iSCSI storage will lose access to its storage. Because many servers require high availability, you need to use high availability technologies such as multiple connected session (MCS) and multipath I/O (MPIO).

Multiple connected session (MCS) enables multiple TCP/IP connections from the initiator to the target for the same iSCSI session. If a failure occurs, all outstanding commands are reassigned to another connection automatically. Typically, MCS has better failover recovery and better performance than MPIO.

⊘ ENABLE A MULTIPLE CONNECTED SESSION

GET READY. To enable multiple connected sessions on Windows Server 2012 R2, perform the following steps:

1. In *Server Manager*, click Tools > iSCSI Initiator. The *iSCSI Initiator Properties* dialog box opens.

2. On the *Targets* tab, click Properties. The *Properties* dialog box opens.

3. On the *Sessions* tab, under the *Configure Multiple Connected Session (MCS)* section, click MCS. The *Multiple Connected Session (MCS)* dialog box opens (see Figure 5-5).

Figure 5-5

Configuring MCS

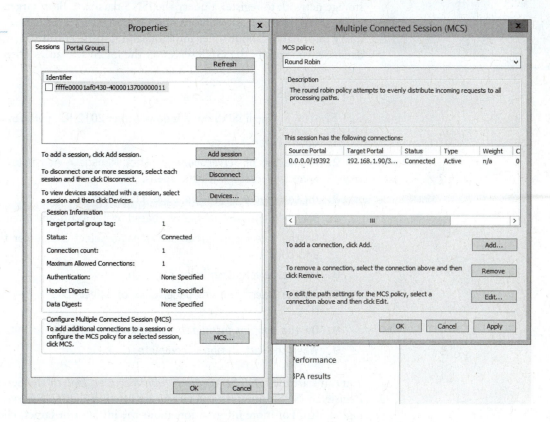

4. To add a second connection, click the Add button and then click Connect.

5. In the *Advanced* dialog box, in the *Initiator IP* text box, specify an IP address for a second local network card. In the *iSCSI target* text box, specify the second remote target portal.

6. Click OK to close the *Multiple Connected Session (MCS)* dialog box and then click OK to close the *Properties* dialog box.

7. Click OK to close *iSCSI Initiator Properties* dialog box.

Often organizations need to have redundancy to provide high availability. Because a SAN can provide central storage to be used by multiple servers, the entire SAN infrastructure needs to be highly available, including disks and connections. ***Multipath I/O (MPIO)*** is a multipath solution that supports iSCSI, Fibre Channel, and serial attached storage (SAS) SAN connectivity by establishing multiple sessions or connections to the storage array. Multipath solutions use redundancy path components such as adapters, cables, and switches to create logical paths between the server and the storage device. To use MPIO, you can install multipath I/O as a feature.

Configuring the Internet Storage Name Server (iSNS)

The **Internet Storage Name Server (iSNS)** protocol is used to discover, manage, and configure iSCSI devices automatically on a TCP/IP network. iSNS is used to emulate Fibre Channel fabric services to provide a consolidated configuration point for an entire storage network.

You can install iSNS as a feature. iSNS provides a registration function to enable entities in a storage network to register a query the iSNS database. Both targets and initiators can register in the iSNS database. After information is entered in the database, targets and initiators can query information about other initiators and targets. For information to be entered into the database, you specify the iSNS server on the iSCSI Initiator's Discovery tab.

 INSTALL iSNS

GET READY. To install iSNS on Windows Server 2012 R2, perform the following steps:

1. Open Server Manager.
2. At the top of *Server Manager*, click Manage > Add Roles and Features. The *Add Roles and Feature* Wizard opens.
3. On the *Before you begin* page, click Next.
4. Select Role-based or feature-based installation and then click Next.
5. On the *Select destination server* page, select the server that you are installing to and click Next.
6. On the *Select server roles* page, click Next.
7. On the *Select features* page, click to select iSNS Server service and then click Next.
8. On the *Confirm installation selections* page, click Install.
9. When the installation is complete, click Close.

You can start the iSNS Server from *Administrative Tools* or the Server Manager *Tools* menu. Registered iSCSI initiators and targets are listed in the iSNS Server Properties dialog box (see Figure 5-6). For more information about the initiator or target, click the iSCSI initiator or target and click *Details*.

Figure 5-6

Viewing registered iSCSI initiators and targets

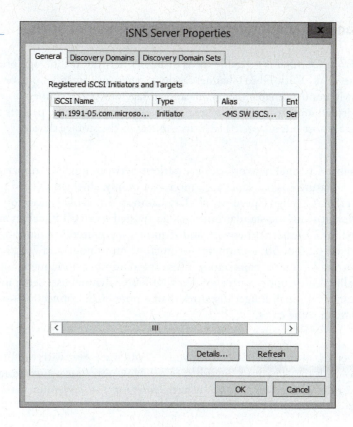

The **Discovery Domain (DD)** service allows the partitioning of storage nodes into management groupings (called *discovery domains*) for administrative and logon control purposes. The iSNS Server Properties start with the Default DD. You can create a new discovery domain by clicking *Creating* and typing the name of the discovery domain. Then click *Add* to add members.

Using iSCSI Best Practices

When designing and implementing iSCSI, you need to follow iSCSI best practices.

When designing your iSCSI storage solution, you should consider following best practices:

- You should deploy iSCSI on at least one 1 Gbps (gigabits per second) dedicated network.
- For production, you should design high availability, including redundant adapters, switches, and paths.
- Implement a security strategy for the iSCSI storage solution.
- For larger organizations, to ensure required performance levels, optimization, and security, be sure to engage various areas of specialization including Windows administrators, network administrators, storage administrators, and security administrators. Also consider engaging administrators for specific applications, such as Microsoft Exchange Server and Microsoft SQL Server.
- Be sure to review vendor-specific best practices for all network devices and adapters.
- Be sure to review best practices for specific applications such as Exchange Server and SQL Server.

Planning and Implementing Fibre Channel SANs

Fibre Channel is a gigabit-speed or higher network technology primarily used for a storage network. With Fibre Channel fabric, the network includes one or more Fibre Channel switches that enable the servers and storage devices to connect to each other through a virtual point-to-point connection. The switches route the packets in the fabric. Servers use a host bus adapter (HBA) to connect to the storage device.

A Fibre Channel network can use various network media. Copper alternatives include video or miniature coaxial cable and, more commonly, shielded twisted pair (STP) with DB-9 or HSSDC (High-Speed Serial Data Connection) cable connectors. These are distinctly different from the standard unshielded twisted pair (UTP) cables and RJ-45 connectors used for an Ethernet network and require a specialized installation. Fiber optic alternatives include 62.5 or 50 micrometer (or micron) multimode and 7 or 9 micrometer single mode, all using LC or SC connectors. These standard fiber optic media options are familiar to any qualified fiber optic contractor. Because Fibre Channel uses serial instead of parallel signaling, it can span much longer distances than a pure SCSI connection—up to 50 kilometers or more, in some cases.

TAKE NOTE ✳

When discussing Fibre Channel, you will often see *fibre* with the British spelling and *fiber* with the American English spelling. However, *fibre* is used to refer to the protocol that runs with Fibre Channel, whereas *fiber* (or *fiber optics*) refers to the media that Fibre Channel runs on.

Today, transmission speeds for Fibre Channel networks range from 1 Gbps to 10 Gbps for copper cables, and up to 16 Gbps for fiber optic. Maximum speeds depend on the type of cable the network uses, the lengths of the cable segments, and, in the case of fiber optic, the type of laser used to transmit the signals.

Fibre Channel networks can use any one of the following topologies:

- *Point-to-point (FC-P2P)* consists of two devices only, directly connected with a single cable.
- *Arbitrated loop (FC-AL)* consists of up to 127 devices, connected in a loop topology, similar to that of a token ring network. The loop can be physical, with each device connected to the next device, or virtual, with each device connected to a hub that implements the loop.
- *Switched fabric (FC-SW)* consists of up to 16,777,216 (224) devices, each of which is connected to a Fibre Channel switch. Unlike Ethernet switches, Fibre Channel switches provide redundant paths between the connected devices, forming a topology called a *mesh* or *fabric*. If a switch or a connection between switches fails, data can find an alternate path through the fabric to its destination.

Until recently, FC-AL was the most popular of the three topologies, because few SANs require more than 127 connections, and the arbitrated loop eliminates the need for expensive switches. The prices of Fibre Channel switches have dropped considerably over the last few years (perhaps due to competition from low-cost iSCSI components), and FC-SW has become the more popular Fibre Channel solution.

The Fibre Channel standards define five protocol layers:

- FC0 defines the physical elements of a Fibre Channel network, including cables, connectors, pinouts, and optical and electrical specifications.
- FC1 defines the data-link layer transmission protocol, including the 8b/10b encoding method used to generate Fibre Channel network signals.

- FC2 defines the basic transport mechanism of a Fibre Channel network, including the frame format and three service classes: a connection-oriented class, a connectionless class with acknowledgments, and a connectionless class without acknowledgments.
- FC3 defines a collection of common services often required by applications using Fibre Channel networks, including data striping, multicasting, and multiport hunt groups.
- FC4 defines the upper layer protocol mapping rules, which enable Fibre Channel networks to carry SCSI and other types of application layer traffic.

The most critical layer in the operation of a SAN is FC4, which enables the network to carry the SCSI traffic generated by the server and storage devices, replacing the lower layers native to the SCSI protocol. SANs typically use the Fibre Channel Protocol (FCP) to transmit SCSI traffic over the network. However, Fibre Channel networks can use a number of other protocols at the FC4 layer for storage area networking, as well as other applications.

Planning and Implementing Virtual Fibre Channel

Before Windows Server 2012, connecting a virtual client machine directly to Fibre Channel HBAs was difficult. Windows Server 2012 and Windows Server 2012 R2 support Virtual Fibre Channel for Hyper-V, which enables virtual client machines to connect directly to Fibre Channel \HBAs. Virtual Fibre Channel in Hyper-V guest also supports many related features, such as a virtual SAN (vSAN), live migration, quick migration, MPIO, Import and Export, Save and Restore, Pause and Resume, and host-initiated backups.

In Windows Server 2012 R2 and Windows Server 2012, you can have up to four virtual ports per virtual machine. Depending on your configuration, your hardware might restrict the number of virtual ports per HBA and the LUNs per port.

The virtual Fibre Channel feature has the following prerequisites:

- It requires a computer with one or more Fibre Channel HBAs or Fibre Channel over Ethernet (FCoE) converged network adapters.
- The HBAs and FCoE converged network adapters must use updated drivers that support virtual Fibre Channel. The HBA ports should be set up in a Fibre Channel topology that supports N_Port ID Virtualization (NPIV).
- It requires an NPIV-enabled storage area network (SAN).
- Virtual machines that are configured to use a virtual Fibre Channel adapter must use Windows Server 2012 R2, Windows Server 2012, Windows Server 2008 R2, or Windows Server 2008 as the guest operating system. No other guest operating systems are currently supported for use with virtual Fibre Channel.
- You must ensure that NPIV is enabled on your host bus adapter.
- Virtual Fibre Channel LUNs cannot be used as boot media. Fibre Channel tape devices are not supported.

➔ **ADD A VIRTUAL CHANNEL ADAPTER AND CONNECT TO A vSAN**

GET READY. To add and connect a virtual channel adapter to a vSAN, perform the following steps:

1. In *Server Manager*, click Tools, and then click Hyper-V Manager.
2. On the *Hyper-V Manager* screen, under *Virtual Machines*, click the name of the desired virtual machine.
3. In the *Action* pane, click Settings.

4. Under *Add Hardware*, notice a list of hardware options that you can add to your virtual machine. Click Fibre Channel Adapter and then click Add.

5. On the *Settings* page (see Figure 5-7), you must connect the virtual Fibre Channel adapter to a vSAN that you previously created. From the *Virtual SAN* drop-down list that shows *Not connected*, select the name of the required vSAN.

Figure 5-7

Connecting a Fibre Channel adapter to a virtual machine

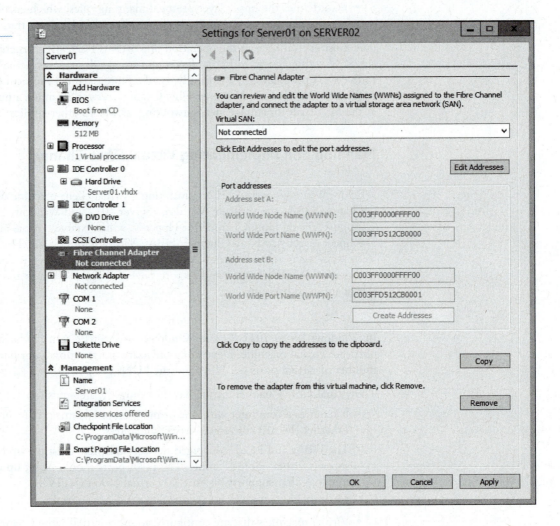

6. Configure your WWNNs (Set A and Set B) for your virtual Fibre Channel adapter. You can use the default automatically generated WWN or manually assign them. You need to configure both WWN sets to ensure a successful live migration of your virtual machines.

7. Click OK.

Installing Device-Specific Modules (DSMs)

Microsoft Multipath I/O provides a framework in which vendors can create *device-specific modules (DSMs)* that allow storage providers to develop multipath solutions for their devices or optimize connectivity with the storage arrays. For example, storage providers can provide high availability, load balancing, or clustering, or expand the standard MPIO capabilities by adding a DSM. MPIO is protocol-independent and can be used with Fibre Channel, Internet SCSI (iSCSI), and Serial-Attached SCSI (SAS) interfaces in Windows Server 2012 R2.

DSMs provided by third-party storage providers must be SPC-3 compliant. To enable the use of DSMs, you just install the Multipath I/O feature by using the Add Roles and Features Wizard in Server Manager. You then install the vendor's DSM setup program to install DSMs or use the INF file provided by the storage provider via the MPIO Administrative Tool. Figure 5-8 shows the MPIO Properties.

Figure 5-8

The MPIO Properties dialog box

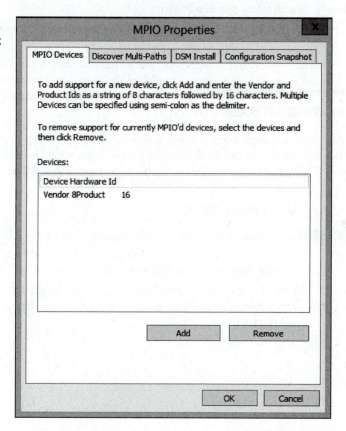

Planning and Implementing Storage Spaces and Storage Pools

Storage Spaces is a feature in Windows 8.1 and Windows Server 2012 R2 that allows you to combine multiple disks into a single logical volume that can be mirrored to protect against one or more drive failures.

The Storage Spaces feature in Windows Server 2012 R2 allows you to combine several physical drives, which the operating system will see as one large drive. The drives can be of any capacity and can consist of several different drive interfaces: Small Computer System Interface (SCSI), Universal Serial Bus (USB), and Serial Advanced Technology Attachment (SATA).

TAKE NOTE *

On Windows Server 2012 R2, you can use Storage Spaces with failover clusters, which are groups of computers connected via physical cables and by clustering software. When one fails, another member of the cluster takes over. To use Storage Spaces with this type of configuration, you are restricted to using Serial-Attached SCSI (SAS) devices. You can manage storage spaces from the Control Panel on Windows 8.1 clients and through the File and Storage Services role in Server Manager. You can also configure it via Windows PowerShell.

When the drives are combined, Windows places them into a ***storage pool***. These storage pools can then be segmented into multiple storage spaces, which are then formatted with a file system and can be used just like any other regular disk on your computer. New disks (internal or external) can be added to the storage pool as space requirements increase over time.

Although data can be stored on the drives, you cannot use Storage Spaces to host the Windows operating system files.

Storage Spaces offers two key benefits:

- By spreading data across multiple disks, you achieve data resiliency (fault tolerance), which can protect your data against hard disk failure.
- Volume sizes can be larger than the actual physical size of your drives in the storage pool (capacity). This is accomplished through a process called *thin provisioning*.

CREATING STORAGE POOLS

By creating a storage pool, you can combine multiple smaller drives that you might not otherwise be able to use by themselves into a larger, single logical volume. To create a storage pool on a Windows Server 2012 R2 client, you use Server Manager.

CREATE A STORAGE POOL

GET READY. To create a storage pool with Windows Server 2012 R2, perform the following steps:

1. In *Server Manager*, click File and Storage Services and then click Storage Pools.
2. On the *Storage Pools* page (see Figure 5-9), select the primordial space on the server where you want to create the pool. Then, from the Tasks menu, select New Storage Pool.

Figure 5-9

Managing storage pools with
Server Manager

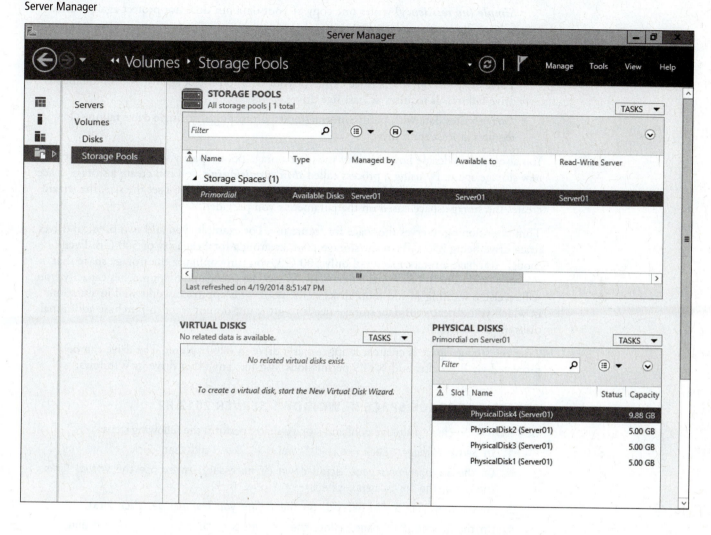

3. In the *New Storage Pool* Wizard, on the *Before you Begin* page, click Next.

4. On the *Storage Pool Name* page, in the *Name* text box, type a descriptive name for the storage pool. Select the server on which you want to create the pool, and then click Next.

5. On the *Select physical disks for the storage pool* page, select the check boxes for the disks you want to add to the pool and click Next.

6. On the *Confirm selections* page, click Create.

7. When the storage pool is created, click Close.

CREATING STORAGE SPACES

After selecting the drives to include in your storage pool, you are prompted to create the storage space. This involves entering a name, selecting a drive letter, identifying the type of resiliency you want to configure, and setting the maximum size you want to assign to the storage space.

When creating Storage Spaces, you can select from four resiliency types, but only three provide real fault-tolerance:

- **Simple (no resiliency)** writes one copy of your data but does not protect against drive failures. It requires at least one drive.
- **Two-way mirror** writes two copies of your data to protect against a single drive failure. It requires at least two drives.
- **Three-way mirror** writes three copies of your data to protect against two simultaneous drive failures. It requires at least five drives.
- **Parity** writes data with parity information to protect against single drive failures. It requires at least three drives.

You also need to decide how much of the total storage pool capacity you want to use for your new storage space. By using a process called **thin provisioning**, you can create a storage space that is larger than the available capacity of the storage pool. After you set the size, the wizard creates the storage space based on the parameters you provided.

Thin provisioning reserves the space for future use. For example, you add two physical drives (each drive being 250 GB) to the storage pool, creating a total capacity of 500 GB. Even though you have a total capacity of only 500 GB, you can configure the storage space that uses this pool to be 1 TB or greater capacity. When the storage pool approaches capacity, you will receive a warning to add more disks to the pool. This approach works well in situations in which you expect your data storage needs to grow but do not want to purchase additional disks immediately.

After the storage space is created, it appears as a drive in File Explorer. The drive can be protected via BitLocker and NTFS permissions, just like any other drive in Windows.

 CREATE A STORAGE SPACE IN WINDOWS SERVER 2012 R2

GET READY. To create a storage pool and storage space, perform the following steps:

1. In *Server Manager*, click File and Storage Services, and then click Storage Pools.
2. On the *Storage Pools* page, scroll down (if necessary) to expose the *Virtual Disks* tile. From the Tasks menu, select New Virtual Disk.
3. In the *New Virtual Disk* Wizard, on the *Before you begin* page, click **Next**.
4. On the *Storage Pool* page, select the storage pool that you just created and click Next.
5. On the *Virtual Disk Name* page, in the *Name* text box, type a descriptive name. In the *Description* text box, you can type an optional description of the virtual disk. Click Next.
6. On the *Storage Layout* page, select the appropriate layout (Simple, Mirror, and Parity), as shown in Figure 5-10. Click Next.

Figure 5-10

Specifying the storage layout

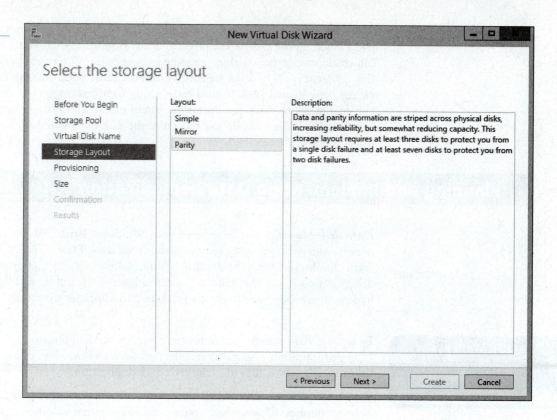

7. On the *Provisioning* page, for the *Provisioning type*, select either Thin or Fixed. Click Next.

8. On the *Size* page, select Specify size or Maximum size. If you select *Specify size*, type the number of gigabytes in the *Specify size* text box. Click Next.

9. On the *Confirmation* page, click Create.

10. When the virtual disk is created, click Close.

11. In the *New Volume* Wizard, on the *Before you Begin* page, click Next.

12. On the *Select the server and disk* page, click Next.

13. On the *Size* page, click Next.

14. On the *Drive Letter or Folder* page, click Next.

15. On the *File System Settings* page, click Next.

16. On the *Confirm selection* page, click Create.

17. When the volume is created, click Close.

If you use disks of different types, architecture, or speed, and you combine those disks into a single pool, you might not achieve the best throughput for the virtual disks provisioned in your pool. Therefore, when you create a pool, you should use the same type of physical disks.

Typically, faster disk space costs more than slower disk space. So although you would always want faster disk space, using all solid-state disks (SSDs) might not make economic sense. However, if you use the faster disk for often-used programs and access, you can achieve better performance while keeping costs down. Windows Server 2012 R2 offers *tiered storage*, in which you can combine the two types of disks into one virtual disk and volume. Keep in mind that you cannot remove storage tiers from a virtual disk after it is created. Storage tiers also require fixed provisioning.

With Windows Server 2012 and Windows Server 2012 R2, you can manually create the pools based on the type of the physical disks. Beginning with Windows Server 2012 R2, you can create storage tiers within the same storage pool. When the operating system recognizes that different types of disks are used within the same pool, you can create tiered virtual disks via the New Virtual Disk Wizard by selecting *Create storage tiers on this virtual disk*. When you enable storage tiers, the operating system moves files that are more frequently accessed to faster media. If the disks do not recognize the disk type, you can change the media type by using Windows PowerShell.

■ Planning and Implementing Data deduplication

THE BOTTOM LINE

Data deduplication was introduced with Windows Server 2012 to reduce disk space and preserve storage capacity by removing duplicate data. Data deduplication breaks data into small chunks, identifies the duplicates, and maintains a single copy of each chunk. Data deduplication is ideal for general shared folders such as public and home folders, offline folders, images, software deployment shares, and libraries that store VHD files.

CERTIFICATION READY
Plan and implement data deduplication
Objective 1.5

By default, data deduplication does not attempt to deduplicate a file until after three days. Data deduplication runs garbage collection once an hour. You can also define an exclusion list to specify which files to exclude from deduplication.

You can implement data deduplication on non-removable NTFS drives, but not on system or boot volumes. Cluster-share volumes (CSVs), system volumes, dynamic disks, and Resilient File System (ReFS) are not eligible for data deduplication. Lastly, files smaller than 32KB or encrypted are not processed.

⊙ INSTALL AND ENABLE DATA DEDUPLICATION

GET READY. To install and enable data deduplication, perform the following steps:

1. In *Server Manager*, from the Manage menu, select Add Roles and Features.
2. In the *Add Roles and Features* Wizard, on the *Before You Begin* page, click Next.
3. On the *Installation Type* page, *Role-based or features-based installation* is selected. Click Next.
4. On the *Select destination server* page, click Next.
5. On the *Select server roles* page, expand File and Storage Services, expand File and iSCSI Services, and select Data Deduplication. Then click Next.
6. On the *Select features* page, click Next.
7. On the *Confirmation* page, click Install.
8. When data deduplication is installed, click Close.
9. In *Server Manager*, click File and Storage Services, and then click Volumes.
10. Right-click a volume and choose Configure Data Deduplication.

11. In the *New Volume Deduplication Settings* dialog box (see Figure 5-11), for the *Data deduplication* option, select General purpose file server.

12. Click OK.

Figure 5-11

Configuring deduplication

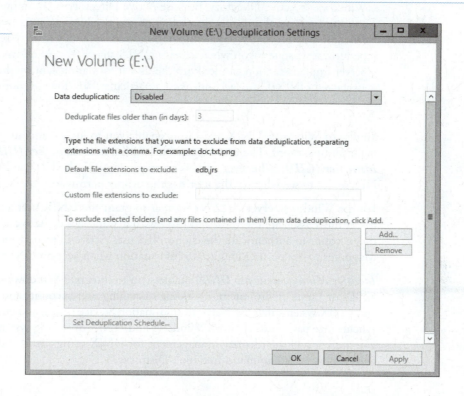

After data deduplication is installed, you can use the Ddpeval.exe command-line tool to estimate capacity savings on Windows. The Windows PowerShell Measure-DedupFileMetaData cmdlet determines the amount of disk that can be reclaimed by using deduplication.

■ Configuring Services for Network file System (NFS)

THE BOTTOM LINE

Network File System (NFS) is a distributed file system protocol used to access files over a network, similar to accessing a file via a shared folder in Windows (which uses Server Message Block [SMB] protocol). It is used primarily with UNIX and Linux file server clients and VMware. Therefore, to support these clients, Windows Server 2012 supports NFS.

CERTIFICATION READY
Configure services for Network File System (NFS).
Objective 1.5

NFS was originally developed by Sun Microsystems in the 1980s. It was later released to the public and, by 1995, the Internet Engineering Task Force (IETF) standardized it as RFC 1813, "NFS Version 3 Protocol Specification." Virtually all UNIX and Linux distributions available today include both NFS client and server support.

By installing the Server for NFS service and the Client for NFS feature, you can provide NFS Server and NFS Client capabilities. Unlike using a Universal Naming Convention (UNC), which uses a *servername**sharename* format, or mounting a UNC to a drive letter, NFS takes part of a remote file system and mounts or connects it to a local file system. The client can then access the server's files as though they were a local resource.

Obtaining User and Group Information

Natively, UNIX and Linux machines have their own user accounts, which are not part of Windows or Active Directory. Because Active Directory is common among corporations, you can use several technologies to link or add the UNIX/Linux machines to Active Directory. To prevent NFS clients running on UNIX or Linux systems from having to perform a separate logon when accessing NFS shares, the Windows Server 2012 NFS Server implementation can look up the user information sent by the client and the associated UNIX/Linux account with a particular Windows account.

Similar to Windows, UNIX and Linux enable you to log on and authenticate with an account name and password. The user is identified with a *user identifier (UID)* value and a *group identifier (GID)*. Whenever a file is accessed via NFS, the UID and GID are sent to the NFS server to see whether the user has the proper permissions to access.

For the Windows Server 2012 NFS server to grant the UNIX user access to the requested file, it must associate the UID and GID with a Windows or Active Directory account and use that account to authenticate the client. NFS uses Active Directory lookup and User Name Mappings to obtain user and group information when accessing NFS shared files.

Identity Management for UNIX enables you to integrate Windows users into an existing UNIX or Linux environment, including managing user accounts and passwords on Windows and UNIX systems that use Network Information Service (NIS), and enables you to automatically synchronize passwords between Windows and UNIX operating systems. To use this method, you must install the Identity Management for UNIX using the Deployment Image Servicing and management command-line tool, Dism.exe.

TAKE NOTE* Identity Management for UNIX is deprecated in Windows Server 2012 R2, which means that it will no longer be available in future Windows servers.

 INSTALL THE IDENTITY MANAGEMENT FOR UNIX BY USING DISM.EXE

GET READY. To install the Identity Management for UNIX using Dism.exe, perform the following steps on a Windows Server 2012 R2 domain controller:

1. Click Windows PowerShell to open the *Windows PowerShell* window.
2. To install the administration tools for Identity Management for UNIX, execute the following command:

   ```
   Dism.exe /online /enable-feature /featurename:adminui /all
   ```
   When you are prompted to restart the computer, type **N**.
3. To install the Server for NIS, execute the following command:

   ```
   Dism.exe /online /enable-feature /featurename:nis /all
   ```
   When you are prompted to restart the computer, type **N**.
4. To install Password Synchronization, execute the following command:

   ```
   Dism.exe /online /enable-feature /featurename:psync /all
   ```
5. When you are prompted to restart the computer, type **Y**.

When you install the Identify Management for UNIX role service, it extends the Active Directory schema by adding UNIX attributes. These attributes can be set with Active Directory Users and Computers (see Figure 5-12). When you use Active Directory lookup, NFS searches the Active Directory database for the UID and GID values in the NFS file access request and uses the accounts associated with those values to authenticate the client.

Figure 5-12

Setting UNIX attributes

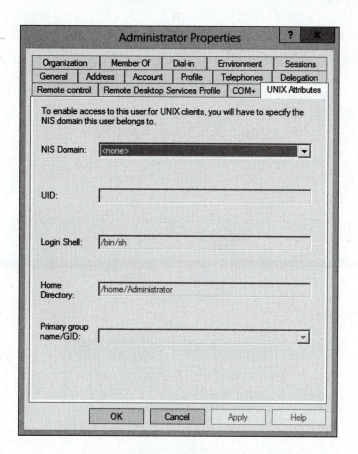

INSTALL THE SERVER AND CLIENT FOR NFS

GET READY. To install the Server for NFS and Client for NFS on Windows Server 2012 R2, perform the following steps:

1. In *Server Manager*, click Manage, and then click Add Roles and Features. The *Add Roles and Feature* Wizard opens.

2. On the *Before you begin* page, click Next.

3. Select Role-based or feature-based installation and then click Next.

4. On the *Select destination server* page, click Next.

5. On the *Select server roles* page, expand File and Storage Services, expand File and iSCSI Services, and then click to select Server for NFS. Click Next.

6. When you are prompted to add features required for Server for NFS, click Add Features.

7. On the *Select features* page, click to select Client for NFS and click Next.

8. Back on the *Select features* page, click Next.

9. On the *Confirm installation selections* page, click Install.

10. When the installation is complete, click Close.

 CONFIGURE ACCOUNT LOOKUPS

GET READY. To configure Account Lookup for NFS, perform the following steps:

1. In *Server Manager*, click Tools > Services for Network File System (NFS). The *Services for Network File System* console opens.

2. Right-click the Services for NFS node and choose Properties. The *Server for NFS Properties* dialog box opens (see Figure 5-13).

Figure 5-13

Configuring the identity mapping source

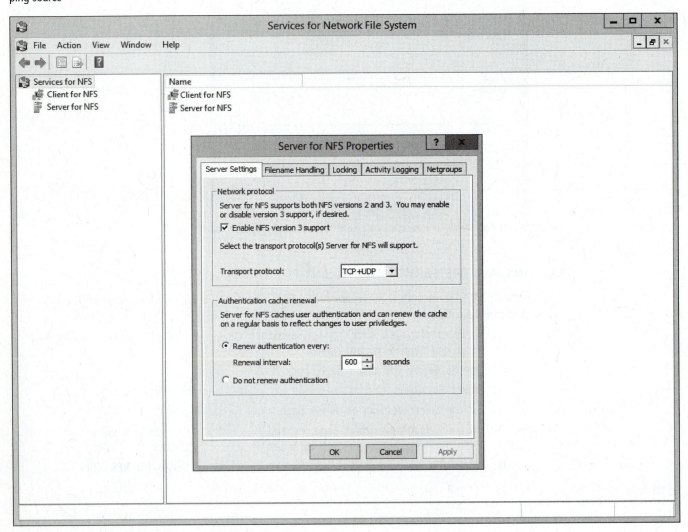

3. Select one of the following options to choose an identity mapping source:

- **Active Directory domain name**: Specify the name of the domain that Services for NFS should use to look up user UIDs and GIDs.

- **User Name Mapping**: Specify the name or IP address of the User Name Mapping server that Services for NFS should use to look up user UIDs and GIDs.

4. Click OK to close the *Server for NFS Properties* dialog box.

Creating an NFS Share

When you install the Services for NFS role service, an NFS Sharing tab is added to the properties of every volume and folder on the computer's drives.

To make a volume or folder available to NFS clients, you need to open the properties for the volume or folder and configure the appropriate values.

 CREATE AN NFS SHARE

GET READY. To create an NFS share, perform the following steps:

1. Browse to a volume or folder on a local NTFS drive, right-click it and choose *Properties*. The *Properties* dialog box opens.

2. On the *NFS Sharing* tab, click Manage NFS Sharing.

3. At the top of the *NFS Advanced Sharing* dialog box, select the Share this folder check box, as shown in Figure 5-14.

Figure 5-14

Sharing an NFS folder

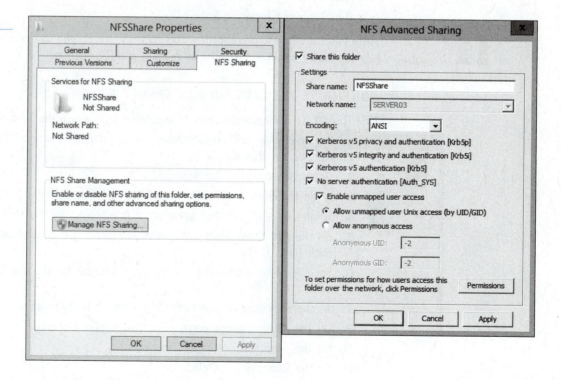

4. In the *Share Name* text box, type the name that you want NFS clients to use when accessing the folder, and then select one of the encoding schemes from the *Encoding* drop-down list.

5. If you want NFS clients to be able to access the share without authenticating, select Allow anonymous access, and then modify the *Anonymous UID* and *Anonymous GID* values, if necessary.

6. Click Permissions. The *NFS Share Permissions* dialog box appears.

7. By default, all NFS clients have read-only access to the share. If you want clients to have read-write, change the access type. You can also grant root access by clicking the Allow root access option.

8. You can click Add to select users or groups and create new permission assignments.

9. Click OK three times to close the *NFS Share Permissions*, *NFS Advanced Sharing*, and *Properties* dialog boxes.

Installing and Configuring the NFS Datastore

Starting with Windows Server 2012, you can now use Server for NFS with failover clustering, which means you can deploy NFS while providing fault tolerance. A shared folder within a cluster is known as a *NFS Datastore*.

To create an NFS shared folder on a cluster, you need to install the following on each cluster node:

- The File Services role
- The Server for NFS role service
- The Failover Clustering feature

After you install these prerequisites and create a cluster, you can configure the cluster to provide high availability for NFS and create an NFS share.

 CONFIGURE THE CLUSTER FILE SERVER ROLE

GET READY. To configure the cluster file server role, perform the following steps:

1. In *Server Manager*, click Tools > Failover Cluster Manager. The *Failover Cluster Manager* window opens.

2. Under *Actions*, click Configure Role.

3. When the *High Availability* Wizard starts, click Next.

4. When you are prompted to select a role, click File Server and then click Next.

5. On the *File Server Type* page, with *File Server for general use* already selected, click Next.

6. For the *Client Access Point* page, type a name for the cluster in the *Name* text box.

7. In the *Click here to type an address* text box, type an address for the cluster.

8. On the *Select Storage* page, click the available storage and click Next.

9. On the *Confirmation* page, click Next.

10. On the *Summary* page, click Finish.

To create an NFS share to use with the cluster, you need to choose an *NFS Share – Quick* or *NFS Share – Advanced*. The NFS Share – Quick is the quickest way to create an NFS file share. The Advanced profile allows you to set the folders' owners for access-denied assistance, configure default classification of data in the folder for management and access polices, and enable quotas. If you want to use NFS Share – Advanced, you need both the Server for NFS and File Server Resource Manager role servers installed.

CREATE A REDUNDANT NFS SHARE

GET READY. To create a redundant NFS share, perform the following steps:

1. In *Failover Cluster Manager*, click Roles in the left pane.
2. Right-click the cluster under *Roles* and choose Add File Share.
3. When the *New Share* Wizard opens, you are prompted to select a profile (see Figure 5-15). Click NFS Share – Quick and then click Next.

Figure 5-15

Selecting a profile for a file server failover cluster

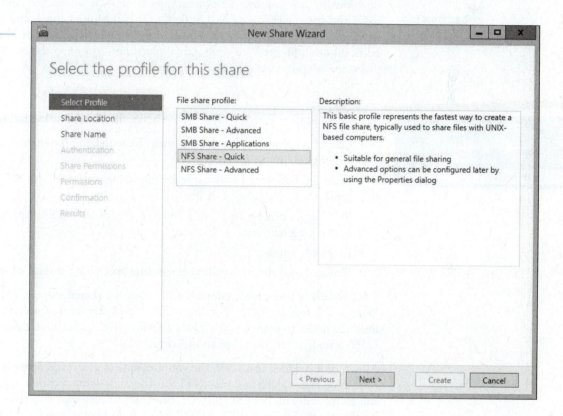

4. On the *Share Location* page, select the volume and click Next.
5. On the *Specify share name* page, type a share name in the *Share name* text box. In the *Local path to share* text box, specify the local path to share. If the folder does not exist, it will be created.
6. On the *Authentication* page, click the desired authentication method and click Next.
7. To specify the share permissions, click the Add button.
8. In the *Add Permissions* dialog box, *Host* is already selected. In the text box, type the name of the host that can access the NFS share. Then specify language encoding and Share permissions. If desired, you can click Allow root access. Click Add.

9. Repeat step 8 as necessary to add hosts or groups.

10. On the *Share Permissions* page, click Next.

11. On the *Permissions* page, you can customize the permissions by clicking the Customize permissions. When done, click the Next button.

12. On the *Confirmation* page, click Create.

13. When the share is created, click Close.

■ Planning and Implementing SMB 3.0 Based Storage

THE BOTTOM LINE

Server Message Block (SMB) 3.0 is the newest version of the SMB protocol, which was introduced with Windows 8 and Windows Server 2012. It brings significant changes to add functionality and improve performance, particularly in virtualized data center including SMB Transparent Failover, SMB Scale Out, SMB Multichannel, and SMB Encryption. In Windows Server 2012, SMB 3.0 file shares can be used as shared storage for Hyper-V hosts, allowing Hyper-V to store virtual machines, including the configuration, virtual disks, and snapshots, on the SMB file shares.

CERTIFICATION READY
Plan and implement
SMB 3.0-based storage
Objective 1.5

Storing application data for Hyper-V on SMB file shares has the following advantages:

- Ease of provisioning and management by managing file shares instead of storage fabric and logical unit numbers (LUNs)

- Increased flexibility by dynamically migrating virtual machines or databases in the data center

- Existing investment in existing converged network with no specialized storage networking hardware

- Reduced capital expenditures

- Reduced operating expenditures, because specialized storage expertise is not required

Traditionally, a single node controls a LUN on the shared storage. However, starting with Windows Server 2008 R2, Windows can use a *cluster-shared volume (CSV)*, which allows multiple nodes to share a single LUN concurrently. Rather than takes the control of the entire LUN, a node takes control of an individual file.

After a disk is added to a CSV, the volumes appear as Crystal Space Virtual File System (CSVFS). The CSVFS still uses NTFS as the underlying technology, and the volumes are still formatted with NTFS. However, because volumes appear as CSVFS, applications can quickly see that the volume is a CSV, so it knows how to handle the volume. So that they are available to all cluster nodes, the volumes use a single file namespace, with the same name and path on any node in a cluster.

CSVs were originally designed for virtual machines that run on a Hyper-V server in a failover cluster, whereas multiple cluster nodes have access to the LUN with multiple virtual machine files. But a virtual machine runs only on one node at a time, therefore avoiding two nodes accessing the same files at the same time. Starting with Windows Server 2012, CSVs can be used with other roles, including file sharing.

Another way to make a VM highly available is to store the VM files on a highly available SMB 3.0 file share, rather than use host or guest clustering. To accomplish this, you need the following:

- One or more computers must be running Windows Server 2012 or Windows Server 2012 R2, with the Hyper-V role installed.
- One or more computers must be running Windows Server 2012 or Windows Server 2012 R2, with the File and Storage Services role installed.
- The servers must be part of the same Active Directory domain.

After you have the servers in place, you create a scale-out file server cluster and deploy the new SMB file share for applications. When the file shares are ready, you can deploy new servers or migrate existing VMs to the SMB file share.

The Scale-Out File Server (introduced in Windows Server 2012) is intended for application data, such as Hyper-V VM files, and file shares that require reliability, manageability, and high performance. Different from a General Use File Server cluster, the **Scale-Out File Server (SoFS)** cluster is an active-active failover cluster where all files shares are online on all nodes simultaneously. Although the SoFS supports SMB, it does not support NFS, data deduplication, DFS Replication, or File Server Resource Manager.

To support multiple nodes to access the same volume at the same time, the SoFS uses a CSV. It also uses a CSV cache, which significantly improve performance in certain scenarios, such as virtual desktop infrastructure.

 DEPLOY A SCALE-OUT FILE SERVER

GET READY. To deploy a Scale-Out File Server, perform the following steps:

1. In *Server Manager*, click Tools > Failover Cluster Manager. The *Failover Cluster Manager* window opens.
2. Right-click Roles and choose Configure Roles. Alternatively, you can click the cluster and under *Actions*, click Configure Role.
3. In the *High Availability* Wizard, click Next.
4. On the *Select Role* page, click File Server and then click Next.
5. On the *File Server Type* page, click Scale-Out File Server for application data and click Next.
6. On the *Client Access Point* page, type the name that clients will use to access the file server. Click Next.
7. On the *Confirmation* page, click Next.
8. On the *Summary* page, click Finish.
9. Click Roles. Right-click the file server role and choose Add File Share.
10. When the *New Share Wizard* opens, click SMB Share – Quick, and then click Next.
11. On the *Share Location* page, click the file server name, and then click Select by volume. Click Next.
12. On the *Share Name* page, type the name of the share and click Next.
13. On the *Other Settings* page, verify that Enable continuous availability is selected, and then click Next.
14. On the *Permissions* page, configure the NTFS and Share permissions as needed by clicking Customize permissions. When done, click Next.
15. When the installation is complete, click Close.

■ Planning for Windows Offloaded Data Transfer (ODX)

THE BOTTOM LINE

Windows Offloaded Data Transfer (ODX), also known as ***copy offload***, enables direct data transfers within or between compatible storage devices without transferring the data through the host computer. As a result, storage arrays can directly transfer data within or between storage devices, bypassing the host computer. By offloading the file transfer to the storage array, ODX minimizes latencies, maximizes array throughput, and reduces resource usage such as CPU and network consumption on the host computer.

CERTIFICATION READY
Plan for Windows Offloaded Data Transfer (ODX)
Objective 1.5

By using ODX, you can rapidly import and export Hyper-V VMs stored on an ODX-capable storage array and accessed via iSCSI, Fibre Channel, or SMB file shares. You can also transfer large files such as databases or videos with increased speed and decreased CPU and network resource consumption on the host server.

To use ODX, your storage arrays must meet the following requirements:

- They must be certified compatible with Windows Offloaded Data Transfer (ODX) on Windows Server 2012 or Windows Server 2012 R2
- To support ODX between storage arrays, the copy manager for the storage arrays must support cross-storage array ODX
- Storage arrays must be from the same vendor
- They must be connected with iSCSI, Fibre Channel, Fibre Channel over Ethernet, or Serial Attached SCSI (SAS).
- Currently, the only configuration supported are one server with one storage array, one server with two storage arrays, two servers with one storage array, or two servers with two storage arrays.

Files can be transferred directly to or from this volume, or from one of the following containers:

- A Virtual Hard Disk (VHD) that uses the VHD or VHDX formats
- A file share that uses the SMB protocol

To use ODX, your environment must support the following:

- The computer initiating the data transfer must be running Windows 8, Windows 8.1, Windows Server 2012, or Windows Server 2012 R2.
- File system filter drivers such as antivirus and encryption programs need to allow ODX.
- Files must be on an unencrypted basic partition. Storage Spaces and dynamic volumes are not supported.
- Files must be on a volume formatted using NTFS. ReFS and FAT are not supported.
- The files must be 256 KB or larger.
- The application that performs the data transfer must be written to support ODX. Currently, Hyper-V manages operations that transfer large amounts of data such as creating fixed size virtual hard disk, merging snapshots, or converting virtual hard disks. File Explorer, copy commands in Windows PowerShell, and copy commands in Windows command prompt (including Robocopy) also support ODX.

ODX is not supported by the data deduplication and BitLocker Drive Encryption file system filter drivers. Lastly, files should not be highly fragmented, because highly fragmented files will reduce performance when transferring large files.

SKILL SUMMARY

IN THIS LESSON YOU LEARNED:

- Shared storage devices have many hard drives to provide huge amounts of disk space.

- Network-attached storage (NAS) is a file-level data storage device that is connected to the server over a computer network to provide shared drives or folders usually using Server Message Block (SMB) or Network File System (NFS).

- *Storage area networks (SANs)* is a storage architecture that allows systems to attach to the storage in the SAN and present the drives to the server just as it is locally attached.

- A Logical Unit Number (LUN) is a logical reference to a portion of a storage subsystem. The LUN can be a disk, part of a disk, an entire disk array, or part of the disk array.

- Internet Small Computer System Interface (iSCSI) is a protocol that enables clients to send SCSI commands over a TCP/IP network using TCP port 3260. Different from Fibre Channel, you use standard Ethernet cabling and switches to connect servers to the SAN.

- iSCSI allows clients, called iSCSI initiators, to send SCSI commands to iSCSI storage devices, which are known as iSCSI targets.

- A single connection to an iSCSI storage device makes the storage available, but it does not make the storage highly available. If the network connection or a switch fails, the server connecting to the iSCSI storage will lose access to its storage. Because many servers require high availability, you need to use high availability technologies such as multiple connected session (MCS) and multipath I/O (MPIO).

- The Internet Storage Name Server (iSNS) protocol is used to discover, manage, and configure iSCSI devices automatically on a TCP/IP network. iSNS is used to emulate Fibre Channel fabric services to provide a consolidated configuration point for an entire storage network.

- Fibre Channel is a gigabit-speed or higher network technology primarily used for a storage network. With Fibre Channel fabric, the network includes one or more Fibre Channel switches that enable the servers and storage devices to connect to each other through a virtual point-to-point connection.

- Microsoft Multipath I/O provides a framework in which vendors can create device-specific modules (DSMs) that allows storage providers to develop multipath solutions for their devices or optimize connectivity with the storage arrays.

- Storage Spaces is a feature in Windows 8.1 and Windows Server 2012 R2 that allows you to combine multiple disks into a single logical volume that can be mirrored to protect against one or more drive failures.

- Data deduplication, introduced with Windows Server 2012, reduces disk space by removing duplicate data to preserve storage capacity.

- Network File System (NFS) is a distributed file system protocol used to access files over a network, similar to accessing a file via a shared folder in Windows (which uses Server Message Block [SMB]). It is used with UNIX and Linux file server clients and VMware.

- Server Message Block (SMB) 3.0 is the newest version of the SMB protocol, which was introduced with Windows 8 and Windows Server 2012. It brings significant changes to add functionality and improve performance, particularly in virtualized data center.

- Windows Offloaded Data Transfer (ODX) enables direct data transfers within or between compatible storage devices without transferring the data through the host computer. As a result, storage arrays can directly transfer data within or between storage devices, bypassing the host computer.

■ Knowledge Assessment

Multiple Choice

1. Which of the following is *not* true about differences between network-attached storage (NAS) devices and storage area network (SAN) devices?
   a. NAS devices provide a file system implementation; SAN devices do not.
   b. NAS devices must have their own processor and memory hardware; SAN devices do not require these components.
   c. NAS devices must run their own operating system and typically provide a web interface for administrative access; SAN devices do not have to have either one.
   d. NAS devices require a specialized protocol, such as Fibre Channel or iSCSI; SAN devices use standard networking protocols.

2. Which of the following Fibre Channel layers contains the SCSI commands destined for storage devices on the SAN?
   a. FC1
   b. FC2
   c. FC3
   d. FC4

3. An iSCSI target receives commands from an initiator and passes them to a storage device. Which of the following is used to represent the storage device?
   a. logical unit number (LUN)
   b. iSNS database entry
   c. VDS hardware provider
   d. RS-232 port

4. Which protocol allows a server to connect to a SAN by sending SCSI commands over a TCP/IP network?
   a. Fibre Channel
   b. iSCSI
   c. SATA
   d. MPIO

5. Which port does iSCSI use?
   a. 1080
   b. 8080
   c. 3260
   d. 4800

6. Which client is called that connects to an iSCSI SAN?
    a. iSCSI Target
    b. iSCSI Source
    c. iSCSI Receiver
    d. iSCSI Initiator

7. Which of the following can be installed so that Windows Server 2012 R2 can be used to present iSCSI volumes to Windows servers?
    a. iSCSI Target
    b. iSCSI Source
    c. iSCSI Receiver
    d. iSCSI Initiator

8. Which of the following terms best describes a unique identifier used to identify iSCSI initiators and targets?
    a. iSNS
    b. IQN
    c. MPIO
    d. MPC

9. Which two technologies can help make iSCSI highly available? (Choose two answers.)
    a. MCS
    b. EFS
    c. LUNX
    d. MPIO

10. Which protocol is used for authentication for iSCSI?
    a. PAP
    b. CHAP
    c. MS-CHAPv2
    d. SPAP

11. Which of the following are requirements to create a VM highly available on an SMB 3.0 file share? (Choose all that apply.)
    a. Windows Server 2012 or Windows Server 2012 R2 with Hyper-V
    b. Windows Server 2012 or Windows Server 2012 R2 with File and Storage Services role
    c. Windows Server 2012 or Windows Server 2012 R2 with iSCSI Target loaded
    d. All servers must be part of the Active Directory domain
    e. The disks support ODX

12. Which of the following requirements are needed for Windows Offloaded Data Transfer (ODX) to work with Hyper-V? (Choose all that apply.)
    a. Files must be stored on NTFS or ReFS.
    b. Must load a ODX driver
    c. Disk array must support ODX
    d. Windows Server 2012 or Windows Server 2012 R2

Best Answer

Choose the letter that corresponds to the best answer. More than one answer choice can achieve the goal. Select the BEST answer.

1. You have around 30 servers, all running Windows Server 2012 and each using iSCSI storage. Your small team of administrators is complaining that locating the available iSCSI resources on the network is becoming difficult. What can you use to help administrators quickly locate iSCSI resources?
   a. DNS
   b. iSNS
   c. iSCSI Target Storage Provider
   d. Windows Standard-Based Storage Management feature

2. You are configuring an iSCSI Target Server role and multiple volumes that will be assigned to multiple servers via iSCSI initiators. Because these servers contain confidential information, you want to make sure that they are not accessed by other servers using an iSCSI initiator. What should you do?
   a. Specify the initiator ID that can connect when creating the iSCSI virtual disk.
   b. Specify the initiator ID that can connect when creating the iSCSI target.
   c. Enable IPSec.
   d. Configure the iSCSI ACL list when you configure the iSCSI initiator.

3. Which of the following is considered a best practice when deploying iSCSI? (Choose all that apply.)
   a. You should use redundant adapters, switches, and paths.
   b. Application servers should be in their own VLAN
   c. You should deploy at least 1 GB dedicated network
   d. For servers that require large loads, you should assign multiple LUNs.

4. Which of the following extends the Active Directory schema to store UNIX attributes?
   a. NFS Management console
   b. Server for NFS role
   c. Computer Management console
   d. Identity Management for UNIX

5. You are an administrator for an organization that has 70 sites in which users have their home and shared public folders. The 70 sites use DFS to replicate files to four subsidiary servers. Which of the following can be used to significantly reduce the file size while maintaining performance?
   a. EFS
   b. NTFS encryption
   c. data deduplication
   d. disk cleanup

Matching and Identification

1. Match the terms with their corresponding definitions:
   _____ **a)** switched fabric
   _____ **b)** VDS hardware provider
   _____ **c)** disk duplexing
   _____ **d)** JBOD
   _____ **e)** logical unit numbers
   _____ **f)** block I/O access
   _____ **g)** iSNS
   _____ **h)** Fibre Channel
   _____ **i)** iSCSI initiator
   _____ **j)** direct-attached storage

   1. Enables a database application to access specific records in a database file stored on a SAN drive array
   2. Identifies specific devices in a drive array
   3. Installed by default in Windows Server 2012 R2
   4. Provided with some SAN drive arrays
   5. Supports copper and fiber optic media
   6. Requires redundant drives and redundant host adapters
   7. Fibre Channel topology
   8. Hard drive installed inside a computer
   9. Maintains a database of targets and initiators
   10. Disk array that does not use RAID

Build a List

1. Identify the correct order of steps to be used when creating an iSCSI virtual disk by placing the number of the step in the appropriate space. Not all steps will be used.
   _____ Specify the access servers.
   _____ Specify the IP address of the iSCSI volumes.
   _____ Specify the size of the virtual disk.
   _____ Specify the location of the iSCSI virtual disk.
   _____ Specify the IPsec password.
   _____ Specify the name of the iSCSI virtual disk.
   _____ Specify the type of volume.

2. Identify the basic steps to configuring a server to use the iSCSI initiator to connect to an iSCSI volume by placing the number of the step in the appropriate space. Not all steps will be used.
   _____ Use Computer Management to partition the disk.
   _____ Use Computer Management to initialize the disk.
   _____ Use Computer Management to format the disk.
   _____ On the Connection tab, click the target and click Connect.
   _____ On the Targets tab, click the target and click Connect.
   _____ Click the Volumes and Devices tab and click Auto Configure.
   _____ Click the Attachment tab and click Auto Configure.
   _____ Click the Connection tab and click Auto Configure.

3. Identify the order of the IQN components that make up an IQN string.
   _____ `microsoft`
   _____ `1992-03`
   _____ `iqn`
   _____ `:storage01-targetnew-target`
   _____ `com`

■ Business Case Scenarios

Scenario 5-1: Using iSCSI Devices

You are an administrator for the Contoso Corporation. You have a large server running Windows Server 2012 R2 that has about 8 TB of disk space that you can allocate to be used by other servers. What can you do so that two other servers running Windows Server 2012 R2 can use the disk space just as if the disk space was local? Also, what would be required to deliver this solution?

Scenario 5-2: Supporting UNIX Machines

You are an administrator for a large organization. Your organization has a group of web developers that work on UNIX machines. You need to develop a solution so that the web developers can save their files on the Windows system and back them up with all your other data. Because the web servers are critical to the company, you must ensure that the data is available and backed up regularly.

Designing and Maintaining a Dynamic Host Configuration Protocol (DHCP) Solution

70-413 EXAM OBJECTIVE

Objective 2.1 – Design and maintain a Dynamic Host Configuration Protocol (DHCP) solution. This objective may include but is not limited to the following: Design considerations including a highly available DHCP solution including split scope, DHCP failover, DHCP failover clustering, DHCP interoperability, and DHCPv6; implement DHCP filtering; implement and configure a DHCP management pack; maintain a DHCP database.

LESSON HEADING	EXAM OBJECTIVE
Planning DHCP Design and Maintenance	
Designing and Maintaining DHCP High Availability • Configuring DHCP Failover • Configuring DHCP Split-Scope • Understanding DHCP Failover Clusters	Design a highly available DHCP solution including split scope, DHCP failover, and DHCP failover clustering.
Integrating DHCP Interoperability with Microsoft services • Configuring DHCP Interoperability with Domain Name Systems (DNS) • Configuring DHCP Interoperability with Active Directory Domain Services (AD DS) • Configuring DHCP Interoperability with Routing and Remote Access (RRAS) • Configuring DHCP Interoperability with Network Access Protection (NAP) • Configuring DHCP Interoperability with IP Address Management (IPAM) • Understanding DHCP Interoperability with Windows Internet Name Service (WINS)	Design for DHCP interoperability
Implementing DHCPv6 • Configuring DHCPv6	Design for DHCPv6
Implementing DHCP Access Restrictions and Policies • Configuring DHCP Policies • Configuring DHCP Link-Layer Filters	Implement DHCP filtering

LESSON HEADING	EXAM OBJECTIVE
Implementing Microsoft System Center 2012 Management Pack for Windows Server 2012 DHCP • Configuring the Microsoft System Center 2012 Management Pack for Windows Server 2012 DHCP	Implement and configure a DHCP management pack
Maintaining a DHCP Database • Performing a DHCP Database Backup • Restoring a DHCP Database • Compacting the DHCP Database • Reconciling the DHCP Database • Performing a DHCP Migration	Maintain a DHCP database

KEY TERMS

Client ID Tracking	load balancing	policy-based assignments
delayed response	load sharing	stateful address autoconfiguration
DHCP failover	Managed Address Configuration flag	stateful DHCPv6
DHCP failover cluster	Maximum Client Lead Time (MCLT)	stateless address autoconfiguration (SLAAC)
DHCP split-scope	message authentication	state switchover interval
failover relationship	Network Access Protection (NAP)	User Name Tracking
Host Name Tracking	Other Stateful Configuration flag	
hot standby		
interoperability		
IP Address Tracking		

■ Planning DHCP Design and Maintenance

THE BOTTOM LINE

Designing a Dynamic Host Configuration Protocol (DHCP) solution and aligning the design with best practices will ensure that future growth can be met with reliability, resilience and high availability. A well-thought-out design ensures that all clients can maintain network access in a secure DHCP environment.

Designing a DHCP environment from the ground up must include several considerations.

The first step in designing a server is assessing the system requirements. Can the server be virtualized, or are requirements for physical resources available only on a dedicated server? By starting with the basics in system requirements as a baseline, begin to plan out your environment. Also consider the need for additional resources, because more resources will be required. DHCP servers often use few resources, can experience little growth after deployment, and can work extremely efficiently in a virtualized environment. Virtualizing a DHCP solution decreases the cost of ownership and increases server availability. Physical servers can be expensive and are more vulnerable to failure than a virtualization solution designed for high availability.

Next, analyze and estimate the amount of clients in your environment. Also consider future growth and network trends. Many DHCP solutions designed more than five years ago no longer meet today's requirements. Nearly all environments need to consider the usage of mobile devices, including cell phones, tablets, laptops, desktops, wireless access points, Voice over Internet Protocol (VoIP) phones, guests, video surveillance, and even lighting. Some environments might allow for gaming devices to connect to an isolated network, online streaming devices, and paperless book devices. How many of these devices and future devices will require an IP address for network connectivity and management configuration? Plan for subnet segregation, option configurations, access restrictions, and policies to meet the requirements of your environment. How many addresses per subnet, and how many subnets will be required? What needs to get where, what should access different areas of the network, and what will be denied?

Some system administrators believe two types of servers exist: those that have failed and those that are about to fail. Plan for server failure, no matter the situation or size of the environment. Clients require uptime and access to resources to perform their job duties and utilize resources. What would be the consequences if you assign DHCP addresses to video surveillance cameras but a server goes down and cannot lease addresses to a camera at a critical location during an unfortunate situation? Plan for a highly available DHCP solution to take a proactive measure against server failure.

In addition to high availability, keeping up-to-date documentation and backups of DHCP server settings and databases is extremely important. How soon can you get the server back online, or how long will it take to load a new server and attach the database without error?

Many environments, from small businesses to large enterprises, can have multiple physical locations, some several hundred miles away from each other. Some environments might also have a disaster recovery site to keep services running if a disaster strikes the primary location. Consider the WAN links between locations, firewall requirements, and scope lease expectations if a server does fail.

Server and network security is important to all network clients, even those that might be unhealthy. Plan for the security of the clients and DHCP servers in the environment.

With IPv4 addresses being extinguished, will DHCPv6 be a required configuration? Will a DHCP server need to be configured to handle DHCPv6 requests?

If you have an environment with several DHCP servers, how will they all be managed from a central location? Plan for server management from a single management portal or application. Plan for solutions that allow for monitoring and alerting to prevent reactionary resolutions.

Plan for server migrations and upgrade paths. As new features and advancements are released with the release of a new operating system, how will you get from the old operating system to the new one in the most efficient amount of time and with as little downtime as possible?

■ Designing and Maintaining DHCP High Availability

THE BOTTOM LINE

DHCP servers, like all other services, need to be highly available. As DHCP services have evolved throughout the past 20 years, DHCP has grown from being a solution of independent server(s) not communicating with one another to, now, a failover infrastructure that is now highly resilient.

CERTIFICATION READY
Design a highly available DHCP solution including split scope, DHCP failover, and DHCP failover clustering
Objective 2.1

As enterprises grow, so does the need for redundant solutions throughout the enterprise. Three available solutions allow DHCP to be more redundant and highly available.

DHCP failover clusters, not to be confused with the new DHCP failover, allow for a redundant and resilient solution. Unfortunately, several risks and considerations are involved. A failover cluster requires additional hardware to perform and maintain a cluster quorum, such as a database that is shared between two servers. Due to the fact that one database is shared between two servers, if the database becomes corrupted, there is not a fallback database or server for network devices to retrieve addresses from. Similar to database corruption, if the shared database is stored on a disk improperly configured for hardware redundancy, the loss of that shared disk means the loss of the database.

DHCP split-scope configuration allows for hardware, software, and server failure. Two servers are configured independently, with separate databases and scopes. With the split-scope configuration, the DHCP Split-Scope Configuration Wizard connects to the second, independent server and configures an identical scope with identical options, reservations, filters, and settings, but allocates a configured percentage of addresses between the servers. Commonly configured in an 80/20 ratio, the DHCP servers allocate IP addresses from a primary server first, and then from the secondary server if the primary server becomes unreachable. This capability is enabled by configuring the delay configuration within the scope properties. A split-scope configuration can also provide a method of load balancing between two servers.

DHCP servers configured for failover clusters and split-scope do not actively communicate with one another. If one server goes down, the other server will not know and will be unable to service clients requesting leases. This will cause problems and will not allow for true high availability. Suppose that you have a split-scope configuration configured between two servers, one that handles 80 percent of the leases and the other that handles 20 percent. If the primary (80 percent) server fails but the administrator and secondary server do not know about the failure, and if it is down long enough, the secondary server will run out of addresses because the primary server was configured to handle the 80 percent.

DHCP failover is new to Windows Server 2012 and has been designed to further enhance DHCP high availability. Instead of two independent servers sharing the same database (DHCP failover cluster), or two independent servers sharing an allocated amount of addresses (split-scope), DHCP failover creates a failover relationship that allows replication of scopes and settings between two servers. With both DHCP servers actively communicating with one another, the partner server can take over for all leases during unplanned or planned downtime.

Configuring DHCP Failover

DHCP failover provides high availability and replication between two independent DHCP servers by using failover relationships. DHCP failover is a huge advancement compared to its predecessors in terms of high availability and meeting continued service requirements.

DHCP failover consists of two DHCP servers sharing DHCP scopes using failover relationships. *Failover relationships* share all scope information between two DHCP servers. A single scope cannot have a failover relationship with more than two servers. Multiple scopes can share the same failover relationship.

A DHCP server can have multiple failover relationships (up to 31) between more than two partner servers. For environments with only two DHCP servers, all scopes can be designed with one failover relationship between the two. But in environments that have multiple DHCP servers, a server can have a failover relationship for one scope with one server, and a failover relationship for another scope with another server.

Unlike previous high-availability solutions for DHCP, the two configured failover servers now know what each other is doing as they communicate through the failover relationship. This prevents duplicate addresses from being issued and also eliminates the headache of setting up additional hardware and software configurations to cluster two servers together.

Using the Configure Failover Wizard, you can configure DHCP failover in two ways:

- ***Load sharing*** allows the two DHCP servers to lease addresses and immediate replicate the client information. If a server fails, the scope information and leases remain and all addresses are still available from the non-failed server. When creating a load-sharing configuration, you must provide a relationship name, Maximum Client Lead Time (MCLT), and a load-balancing percentage for both the local server and the partner server. If a state switchover interval or message authentication is planned, those also can be configured during the Configure Failover Wizard setup.

- ***Hot standby*** allows two DHCP servers to be online, but only one leases addresses. Scope replication still actively takes place. If the primary server fails, the hot standby server takes over the address allocation until the primary server comes back online. When creating a hot standby configuration, you must provide a relationship name, MCLT, role of partner server (active or standby), and the percentage of addresses reserved for the standby server (by default, 5 percent). The state switchover interval or message authentication can also be configured during wizard setup.

A DHCP failover relationship can be in one of three different states:

- **Normal:** When both servers in the failover relationship are replicating as designed and no problems are occurring, they are in the Normal state.

- **Communication Interrupted:** When communication is lost between the local and partner servers, they go into a Communication Interrupted state (server restart, temporary power off/power on, network loss, or server failure). After the local server is in Communication Interrupted state for the length specified in the ***Maximum Client Lead Time*** (MCLT), the partner server takes ownership of all scope leases. The MCLT is the amount of time the DHCP server waits for communication to be reinitialized between it and the partner server before taking ownership of the relationship scopes. By default, the MCLT is one hour.

- **Partner Down:** You configure this state manually when a server failure is known and being addressed, or when the state switchover interval is configured and its time has been met.

The ***state switchover interval*** is the amount of time the DHCP server waits for its partner server when it is in a Communication Interrupted state before moving the relationship automatically to a Partner Down state.

Message authentication is a way to secure the replication communication between the local server and the partner server by using a shared secret.

Figure 6-1 shows the configurable options.

Figure 6-1

Configuring DHCP failover

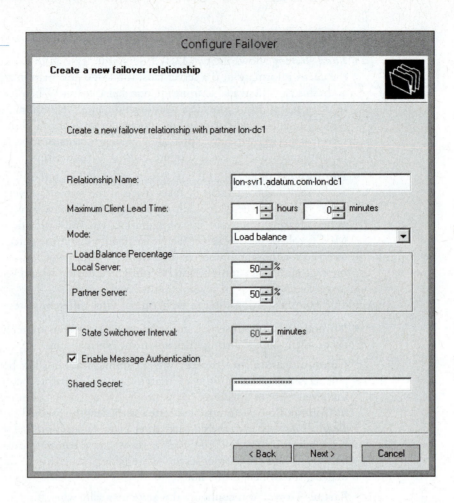

DHCP failover communication occurs over TCP port 647. In environments with multiple locations across a wide area network (WAN) link, the port must be opened in any firewalls to maintain failover communication. On the server itself, the port is opened in the firewall, both inbound and outbound, during the DHCP server role installation.

DHCP FAILOVER AND WINDOWS POWERSHELL

Table 6-1 lists the Windows PowerShell commands that you can use to create, remove, and manage DHCP failover.

Table 6-1

Windows PowerShell Cmdlets to Use with DHCP Failover

CMDLET	DESCRIPTION
Add-DhcpServerv4Failover	Creates a new failover relationship between DHCP servers. You can use the following switches: Name ScopeId PartnerServer ComputerName MaxClientLeadTime AutoStateTransition StateSwitchInterval SharedSecret LoadBalancePercent ReservePercent ServerRole
Add-DhcpServerv4FailoverScope	Creates a new failover relationship between DHCP server scopes. When running this command, you must specify the ScopeId. You also can use the Name and ComputerName switches,
Get-DhcpServerv4Failover	Lists existing failover relationships.
Remove-DhcpServerv4Failover	Removes the specified DHCP failover relationship.
Remove-DhcpServerv4FailoverScope	Removes the specified DHCP failover scope.
Set-DhcpServerv4Failover	Enables you to change failover settings. You can use the following switches: Name ComputerName AutoStateTransition MaxClientLeadTime SharedSecret StateSwitchInterval PartnerDown LoadBalancePercent ReservePercent Mode
Invoke-DhcpServerv4FailoverReplication	Replicates failover relationships. You can also run this command on a scope level by using the ScopeId switch.

 CONFIGURE A DHCP FAILOVER SCOPE TO BALANCE LOAD

GET READY. To configure a DHCP failover scope, perform the following steps in a test environment with two servers configured for DHCP:

1. Open the *DHCP Management* console and expand the DHCP server.
2. Right-click IPv4 and choose Configure Failover. In the *Configure Failover* Wizard, notice that the default option is *Select all*. Click Next.
3. Click the Add Server button. Select the partner server and click OK.
4. Back in the *Configure Failover* Wizard's *Specify the partner server to use for failover* page, click Next.

5. On the *Create a new failover* relationship page, in the *Relationship Name* text field, enter Load Balance – All Scopes. Review but do not modify the settings for *Maximum Client Lead Time, Mode, Load Balance Percentage, State Switchover Interval,* and *Enable Message Authentication.* In the *Shared Secret* text box, type in a secure password and then click Next.

6. On the summary screen, verify that all that failover relationship information is correct. Click Finish. The *Configure Failover Progress of failover configuration* window displays.

7. Verify that all actions have been successful. Click Close.

After the failover relationship is created, you can view the existing failover configuration in the IPv4 Properties dialog box on the Failover tab (see Figure 6-2).

Figure 6-2

Viewing DHCP failover properties

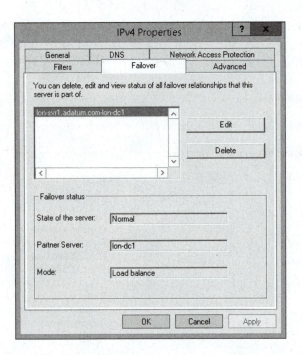

> **+ MORE INFORMATION**
> Practice creating DHCP failover relationships in DHCP Manager and Windows PowerShell. Before implementation, ensure that failover works as designed.

Configuring DHCP Split-Scope

Another form of fault tolerance is the DHCP split-scope configuration. Configuring split-scopes has been simplified in Windows Server 2008 through the use of a wizard. By using the DHCP Split-Scope Configuration Wizard, you can load balance or provide a backup server in case the primary DHCP server fails.

CERTIFICATION READY
Design a highly available DHCP solution including split scope, DHCP failover, and DHCP failover clustering
Objective 2.1

A DHCP split-scope contains two independent servers with a ratio of address leases to meet fault-tolerance requirements. During configuration, the wizard automatically connects to the partner server and makes the required changes. After the wizard completes, the servers operate independently of one another but serve the same scope, with different ranges and exclusions.

Shared scopes can be split based on percentage. Considered best practice, configuring the percentage of split to be 80/20 allows the primary server to maintain DHCP leases for 80 percent of the IP addresses within the address range. If the primary server fails, any new clients that have not already received their active lease from the primary server will acquire an IP address from the secondary server.

You can configure *delayed responses* for both DHCP servers. When the delayed response is configured to a higher millisecond value on the secondary server versus the primary server, when the client sends the DHCP discovery request, the secondary server waits that amount of time before issuing a DHCP offer to the client.

You can also send *load balancing* DHCP requests by configuring the DHCP offer delay time to be identical on both servers. If identical DHCP offer times are used, when both servers receive the request, they each send a response. Whichever offer is accepted by the client first assigns the IP in that server.

When a split-scope configuration is created, the scope is initially created on one server and configured with all the options and settings required for the scope. On the partner server, you can run the DHCP Split-Scope Configuration Wizard to integrate the scope with the two servers.

CREATE A DHCP SPLIT-SCOPE

GET READY. To create a split-scope, perform the following steps:

1. In the *DHCP Management* console, expand the DHCP server.
2. Expand IPv4 and select the scope you want to split with a partner server, hover over Advanced, and select Split-Scope.
3. In the *Dhcp Split-Scope Configuration Wizard*, on the *DHCP Split-Scope* page, click Next.
4. On the *Additional DHCP Server* page, for the *Additional DHCP Server*, click the Add Server button.
5. In the *Add Server* dialog box, choose the partner DHCP server and click OK.
6. Back on the *Additional DHCP Server* page. Click Next.
7. On the *Percentage of Split* page (see Figure 6-3), review but do not modify the slider as well as the *Percentage of IPv4 Addresses Serviced, Start IPv4 Address,* and *End IPv4 Address* configuration settings. Click Next.

Figure 6-3

Configuring split-scope
percentage range

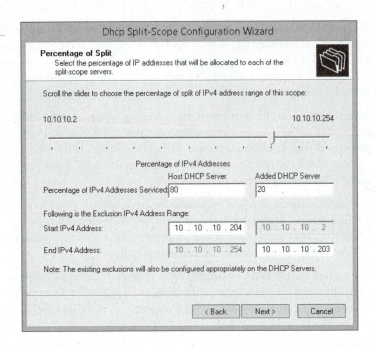

7. On the *Delay in DHCP Offer* page, for the *Added DHCP Server* option, specify the *Delay in DHCP Offer (milliseconds)* as 10. Click Next.

8. On the *Summary of Split-Scope Configuration* page, verify that all configuration settings are accurate. Click Finish.

9. On each server, verify that all configurations have been added to the scope and the configuration has completed successfully. Click Close.

After the split-scope is configured, review the scope's address pool. Take note of the address range for distribution as well as the IP addresses that have been excluded from being distributed on the server. Notice that the range of addresses were configured based on the percentage of IPs available to the range when the split-scope configuration was created. If you look at the other server, you should notice the same type of configuration; however, the IP addresses excluded from distribution are being distributed to the partner server.

Understanding DHCP Failover Clusters

Failover clusters are being slowly pushed out of the recommended DHCP fault-tolerant solutions because of the complexity of configuration, cost, and management requirements. Having two virtual servers, each with their own simple database, which are serving scopes in a DHCP environment is now cheaper.

CERTIFICATION READY
Design a highly available
DHCP solution including
split scope, DHCP
failover, and DHCP
failover clustering
Objective 2.1

If two servers can be configured, not share the same disk, be in different sites, and still be highly available to their clients—that is the route a DHCP design will likely take.

If failover clusters are still in the design plan and will be configured, the failover clustered scopes can be configured to take part in the DHCP failover solution for additional redundancy. This also increases the total cost of ownership.

■ Integrating DHCP Interoperability with Microsoft Services

↓
THE BOTTOM LINE

Interoperability with Microsoft services provides numerous benefits between DHCP and the services that can communicate with the DHCP service. By integrating these services with DHCP, you can have more control and monitoring over the network and the clients it serves.

CERTIFICATION READY
Design for DHCP
interoperability
Objective 2.1

Integration with other Microsoft services enables you to provide increased security to domain computers and also workgroup computers. Services that can interoperate with DHCP include DNS, Active Directory Domain Services (AD DS), Routing and Remote Access Service (RRAS), Network Access Protection (NAP), IP Address Management (IPAM), Windows Deployment Services (WDS) and Windows Internet Name Service (WINS).

- Integrating DNS with DHCP can provide secure DNS updates and host record registration.
- Integrating AD DS with DHCP allows only authorized DHCP servers to lease addresses.
- Integrating RRAS with DHCP allows the RRAS server to segregate the DHCP server from the remote access clients.
- Integrating NAP with DHCP allows for health checks to be performed against the client.
- Integrating IPAM with DHCP allows for additional server management, monitoring, and tracking.

During the design process, consider using existing or planned environments resources and services and how they can better improve or enhance DHCP usage.

Configuring DHCP Interoperability with Domain Name Systems (DNS)

Name resolution is critical in any network. DHCP interoperability with DNS allows the DHCP server to register and remove DNS records on behalf of clients, perform secure DNS registrations, and allow non-Windows clients DNS registration options. These settings for interoperability with DNS can be configured at the server level, scope level, and policy level.

As you can see in Figure 6-4, you can configure DHCP to update authoritative DNS servers automatically with the host (A) and pointer (PTR) records on behalf of the DHCP clients.

Figure 6-4

Configuring DHCP server
DNS settings

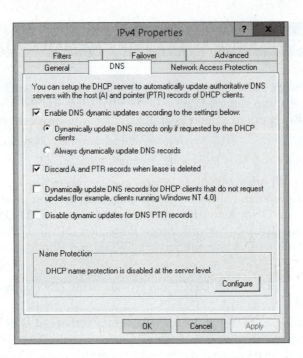

You can force a DHCP server to update records dynamically. Whether or not the DHCP client requests, the server can allow for updating on the clients' behalf only when the client requests it. DHCP clients that cannot perform DNS requests, including hardware devices and clients running Windows NT 4.0, can have their records dynamically updated in DNS by the DHCP server. The server can also discard the assigned DNS records on behalf of the client when the lease has ended.

Now in Windows Server 2012 R2, you can disable dynamic updates for DNS PTR records at the server and scope level. If you do not configure reverse lookup zones, you can disable dynamic updates for DNS PTR records to prevent unwanted errors that can occur if PTR records are attempting to be registered. However, in some scenarios disabling PTR record registration can be beneficial at some scopes, but not in others.

DHCP name protection can prevent a client with the same name as another client from registering in DNS. Configuring name protection forces the DHCP server to honor all requests for Windows DHCP clients, dynamically performs DNS registrations for all non-Windows DHCP clients, and discards the A and PTR records after the lease is deleted. If a clients has a unique name but a changing Media Access Control (MAC) address (some virtual machine configurations might do this), or if the previous reservation is for a different MAC address but has the same name, the current client cannot gain a lease.

When a DHCP policy is configured with fully qualified domain name (FQDN) conditions, you can modify the policy the DNS configuration settings for the clients falling within the DHCP policy.

Take Note

You can configure DHCP policies to be extremely granular. However, documenting all DHCP policy settings, what they do, what they apply to, and how it affects the client and end user is important. When troubleshooting a problem, you must take DHCP policies into consideration.

→ DISABLE DYNAMIC UPDATES FOR DNS PTR RECORDS

GET READY. To disable dynamic updates for DNS PTR records on all scopes, perform the following steps:

1. In *DHCP Manager*, expand the DHCP server so that the root of *IPv4* is visible.
2. Right-click IPv4 and choose Properties.
3. In the *IPv4 Properties* dialog box, on the *DNS* tab, review and understand the available options. Then select Disable dynamic updates for DNS PTR records And click OK.
4. Close the *DHCP Manager* console.

Many options found at the server level can be found at the individual scope level. Making changes at the server level can affect all server scopes. Changes made at the server level can be overridden at each scope. If you are not careful and apply a change at the wrong level with numerous scopes involved, it might cause results not immediately noticed and even could cause unplanned outages.

Configuring DHCP Interoperability with Active Directory Domain Services (AD DS)

In Active Directory Domain Services (AD DS) environments, domain joined Windows DHCP servers must be authorized to service DHCP client requests. By forcing DHCP servers to be authorized, clients are protected from rogue domain joined Windows DHCP servers that might maliciously affect network clients. This authorization does not prevent rouge access points, non-domain joined devices, or other devices from issuing addresses. Those types of devices must be restricted through the use of port security.

Unidentified machines entering the network, clients becoming unhealthy with viruses and malware, and even clients turning into rogue DHCP servers will always be risks. If a domain client becomes a rogue DHCP server because of malicious software that has been installed, it can then service clients and spread viruses and worms throughout the network. A rogue DHCP server can point clients to a poisoned DNS cache server and cause havoc throughout the enterprise. Clients cannot authenticate and will be vulnerable to external and internal risks, and network traffic might come to a standstill. This is where DHCP AD DS authorization comes in.

As a security measure in AD DS environments, domain joined Windows DHCP servers must be authorized against Active Directory to ensure that a rogue DHCP server cannot lease addresses to domain clients.

When a DHCP server in a domain environment is brought online in an AD DS environment, it is checked to see whether it is authorized. If it is not authorized, it is identified as an unauthorized DHCP server and will not lease IP addresses to DHCP clients.

To authorize a DHCP server, the DHCP server role must be installed on a domain member server or on a domain controller.

Additional considerations for AD DS interoperability include the following:

- The user authorizing the server to AD DS must be a member of the Enterprise Admins group.
- If DHCP is installed on a domain controller, the DHCP server is authorized at the time of role installation.
- The FQDN of the DHCP server cannot exceed 64 characters. If this is the case, you can authorize the server by using its IP address instead of the FQDN.

AUTHORIZE A DHCP SERVER IN AN AD DS ENVIRONMENT

GET READY. To restrict a user account to run a single Windows Store app, perform the following steps:

1. Log on to *DHCP Manager* as a member of the Enterprise Admins group.
2. Right-click the *DHCP Manager* at the top level and choose Manage authorized servers.
3. In the *Manage Authorized Servers* dialog box (see Figure 6-5), click Authorize.

Figure 6-5

Authorizing a DHCP server

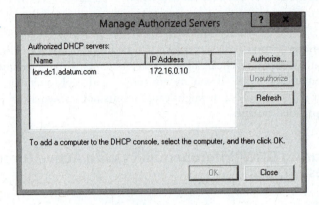

4. In the *Authorize DHCP Server* dialog box, type the FQDN or IP address of the DHCP server to be authorized and then click OK.
5. In the *Confirm Authorization* dialog box, verify that the DHCP server name and IP address are correct. Click OK.
6. In the *Manage Authorized Servers* dialog box, verify that the newly authorized DHCP server is listed as an authorized DHCP server. Click Close.
7. Close the remaining windows and snap-ins.

Configuring DHCP Interoperability with Routing and Remote Access Service (RRAS)

> By performing the DHCP offers and leases on behalf of DHCP, Routing and Remote Access Service (RRAS) supplies remote access clients IP addressing and DHCP options to the requesting client.

When a client connects to a network through RRAS, the RRAS server provides it with a DHCP lease and with access to network resources. Essentially, the RRAS server acts as a DHCP server for remotely connecting clients.

When a RRAS server configured to use DHCP to assign remote TCP/IP addresses server starts, it requests ten IP addresses from the DHCP server. The RRAS server uses these addresses to provide leases to remotely connecting clients. When the remote session is terminated, the IP address is released back to the RRAS server for the next client connection. This ensures that the DHCP server itself does not need to keep track of client leases that RRAS knows to not be in use. The only information it retrieves from the DHCP server is the following:

- IP address of the DHCP server
- Client leased IP addresses
- Lease assignment time

- Lease expiration time
- Duration of lease

Other configured DHCP options are not retrieved from the DHCP server. Any DNS settings are provided by the RRAS server itself.

Configuring DHCP Interoperability with Network Access Protection (NAP)

Network Access Protection (NAP) helps protect networks from computers that can be vulnerable to viruses because they are not up to date with antivirus software, antivirus definitions, and critical security patches. With NAP, DHCP can be configured to place unhealthy or noncompliant clients onto a restricted network. Placement onto a restricted network limits the client's network access to remediation servers until the quarantined client becomes compliant.

Although NAP, with the Remote Access server role, has been deprecated in Windows Server 2012 R2, you can still install and configure it to interoperate with DHCP. Solutions that replace NAP keep remote machines up to date and secure include DirectAccess and Web Application Proxy. For internal machines, Microsoft System Center Configuration Manager is recommended to keep clients up to date and secure.

At the time of client connection, the Windows Security Health Validator (WSHV) can check the following configuration settings and take action as required (see Figure 6-6):

- A firewall is enable for all network connections.
- An antivirus application is on.
- Antivirus is up to date.
- An antispyware application is on.
- Antispyware is up to date.
- Automatic updating is enabled.

Figure 6-6

Configuring the Windows Security Health Validator

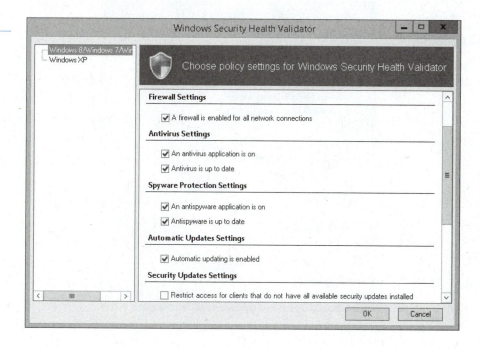

After checking these settings, you can restrict access for clients that do not have all available security updates installed. If any of the settings configured are not met, they are placed in the restricted network, through DHCP.

When NAP is integrated with DHCP and an unhealthy client machine tries to connect to the network, DHCP assigns it to the scope of addresses with limited network resources. In the quarantined network, the client can then access configured internal WSUS servers or externally accessible Microsoft Update servers or internal servers that can provide remediation services to the client. As soon as the client becomes healthy, it is reassigned to a new address, placing it in a scope with the intended network access.

 ENABLE NETWORK ACCESS PROTECTION IN DHCP

GET READY. To enable Network Access Protection (NAP) in DHCP, perform the following steps:

1. In *DHCP Manager*, expand the DHCP server so that the root of *IPv4* is visible.

2. Right-click IPv4 and choose Properties.

3. In the *IPv4 Properties* dialog box, on the *Network Access Protection* tab, review the available options. In the *Network Access Protection Settings* section, click Enable on all scopes.

4. In the *DHCP notification* dialog box, you will be informed that "This will overwrite Network Access Protection settings of all the scopes." Click Yes.

5. You are returned to the *IPv4 Properties* dialog box, click OK.

6. Back in the *DHCP Manager*, expand IPv4, right-click a scope (if none are created, create a test one) and choose Properties.

7. In the *Scope Properties* dialog box, on the *Network Access Protection* tab, review the available options, particularly the options enabled from the server level (see Figure 6-7. You can configure them granularly at the scope level. Click Cancel.

8. Close any open windows and snap-ins.

Figure 6-7

Viewing Network Access Protection DHCP properties

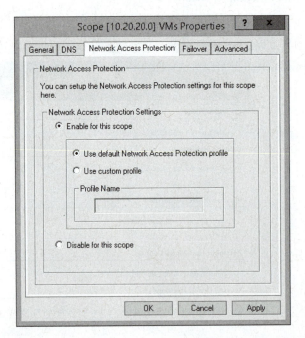

NAP must be configured for these DHCP settings to take effect. Performing these actions on the DHCP server does not secure your network without the integration of a NAP server.

> **Take Note** *
>
> NAP health checks and interoperability with DHCP do not affect clients with static IP addresses assigned. This means that if an unhealthy computer attempts to connect to the network, it might be able to bypass NAP DHCP enforcement because the DHCP server cannot assign it a temporary IP for access into the quarantine network.

Configuring DHCP Interoperability with IP Address Management (IPAM)

> IP Address Management (IPAM) is a tool new to Windows Server 2012 that integrates with DNS, AD DS, and DHCP. Through this integration, administrators can take a deeper look into what is happening on the network in the way of IP addressing and monitoring.

When IPAM is configured, the following Group Policies are created that force DHCP servers to connect to IPAM for monitoring and maintenance:

- **IP Address Tracking**: Based on lease assignment, IPAM can query against the DHCP database and its own to find out which MAC address, host, and user had the IP address reservation.
- **Client ID Tracking**: This is useful when attempting to track down a client by MAC address to see when it was last on the network and what IP address it had.
- **User Name Tracking:** Use this setting when only a user name is known but tracking needs to be performed to find out the host name, MAC address, and IP address of the client that was in use by that user.
- **Host Name Tracking**: Use this setting when the host name of the client is known. You can see who logged into the client and when, what the MAC address is, and what IP address it had.
- **Monitoring and Management of DHCP:** Use this for environments with multiple DHCP servers that can be managed from one console.
- **IP Address Utilization:** Use this to actively monitor and manage IP address utilization.

> **TAKE NOTE** *
>
> With its integration with DHCP, IPAM is a great tool to use when tracking down users and devices when an incident occurs.

Understanding DHCP Interoperability with Windows Internet Name Service (WINS)

> Although Windows Internet Name Service (WINS) is not widely used in enterprise environments, those that still maintain applications and clients requiring the service can integrate it with DHCP. WINS is deprecated but still available to enable as a server feature in Windows Server 2012 R2.

> **TAKE NOTE** *
>
> Some tools are installed when the WINS server feature is installed. Because DHCP and WINS both use a Jet database, the tools are interchangeable with one another.

WINS resolves NetBIOS names for pre-Windows Vista clients and applications that can require NetBIOS settings for operation and name resolution.

When DHCP configured to integrate with WINS, options are set to direct DHCP clients to the WINS server and configure WINS node types. If WINS is configured, you must configure the WINS and DHCP lease times to match or to be as close to one another as possible to prevent inconsistencies between one another.

■ Implementing DHCPv6

With DHCPv6, you can issue clients DHCPv6 addresses and network settings, or just network settings based on two states: stateful and stateless.

As explained earlier in this lesson, IPv4 addressing is now a thing of the past. Moving forward, design processes must include the usage of IPv6. Over the past several years, enterprises, Internet service providers (ISPs) and small businesses have moved toward using IPv6. In fact, if you own a PC running Windows Vista or later, you are already using IPv6, whether or you configured it. One key benefit of DHCPv6 is that compatible clients have their own IP addresses already configured. As you design your network infrastructure, you must consider both DHCP and statically assigned addresses. Many websites are already IPv6 ready and con-figured to use IPv6 before IPv4 if a client communicates with the site using IPv6.

Configuring DHCPv6

DHCPv6 can be autoconfigured for two states: stateless and stateful. Based on router advertisements, the client is directed to use its existing link-local addressing or to retrieve a combination of addressing and configurations from the DHCPv6 server.

CONFIGURING FOR STATELESS AND STATEFUL AUTOCONFIGURATION

Stateless address autoconfiguration (SLAAC) does not use a DHCPv6 server to obtain an IPv6 address. However, the client can use the DHCPv6 server to obtain additional network configuration settings—for instance, DNS server addresses.

With *stateful address autoconfiguration*, clients connect to the DHCPv6 server to obtain an IP address and additional network configuration settings. These network settings are based on flags issued by the closest router in the form of router advertisements:

- **Managed Address Configuration flag (M flag):** When configured to 1, this flag directs the network device to obtain and use a stateful address.
- **Other Stateful Configuration flag (O flag):** When configured to 1, this flag directs the network device to obtain other configuration settings.

The flags can be combined as follows:

- **M and O flags are both configured with 0:** This combination is typically used in net-works that do not take advantage of DHCPv6 for addressing. Clients use statically assigned IPv6 addresses.
- **M and O flags are both configured with 1:** The client uses DHCPv6 to acquire an IPv6 address and to apply configuration settings. This configuration is also known as *stateful DHCPv6.*
- **M flag is configured with 0 and O flag is configured with 1:** The client does not use DHCPv6 to acquire an address, but instead uses DHCPv6 to acquire other configuration settings. The client uses the advertised non–link-local address prefix issued by the router and DHCPv6 assigned settings.
- **M flag is configured with 1 and O flag is configured with 0:** The client uses DHCPv6 to acquire an address but does not use DHCPv6 to acquire other configuration settings. Any clients in this situation must have their settings configured manually. This configu-ration is typically not used because a client needs to have DNS, gateway, and Network Time Protocol (NTP) servers configured before it can fully utilize network resources.

Autoconfigured addresses can be in one or more of the following states:

- **Tentative**: This state is for the amount of time required for the IPv6 address to be declared unique.
- **Preferred**: The address has been determined to be unique and will remain so until it is deprecated.
- **Deprecated**: During the deprecated state, the address is still valid but will not be used for future communications. All existing sessions will remain until the address becomes invalid.
- **Valid**: The time range from which an address goes from being declared preferred to being declared invalid.
- **Invalid**: The valid lifetime has expired and the address can no longer send communications.

CONFIGURING ADVANCED DHCPV6 SETTINGS

Like with DHCPv4, you can configure DHCPv6 to register DNS records on behalf of the client or to always dynamically update the DNS records. You can configure DHCPv6 to register and discard host (AAAA) and pointer (PTR) records.

Lease durations for Non Temporary Addresses (IANA) autoconfigured address states can also be configured to determine the length of time a device can use an IPv6 address.

- **Preferred Lifetime**: Configured within the Properties of the DHCPv6 scope, this is the time range at which an IPv6 address goes from being tentative to being deprecated.
- **Valid Lifetime**: Configured within the Properties of the DHCPv6 scope, this is the time range at which an IPv6 address goes from being preferred to being invalid.

CONFIGURING DHCPV6 WITH WINDOWS POWERSHELL

Table 6-2 lists the Windows PowerShell commands that you can use to configure DHCPv6.

Table 6-2

Windows PowerShell Cmdlets to Configure DHCPv6

CMDLET	DESCRIPTION
Add-DhcpServerv6Class	Creates an IPv6 vendor or user class
Add-DhcpServerv6ExclusionRange	Creates an exclusion range to an IPv6 scope
Add-DhcpServerv6Lease	Creates a new IPv6 lease
Add-DhcpServerv6OptionDefinition	Creates option definitions
Add-DhcpServerv6Reservation	Creates an IPv6 address reservation to a defined scope
Add-DhcpServerv6Scope	Creates an IPv6 scope
Get-DhcpServerv6Binding	Gets IPv6 interfaces bound to a DHCP server
Get-DhcpServerv6Class	Gets an IPv6 vendor and user class
Get-DhcpServerv6DnsSetting	Applies IPv6 DNS settings to scope, reservations, or server
Get-DhcpServerv6ExclusionRange	Lists IPv6 address exclusion ranges

(continued)

Table 6-2

(continued)

CMDLET	DESCRIPTION
Get-DhcpServerv6FreeIPAddressLists	Lists free and unassigned IPv6 addresses from the defined scope
Get-DhcpServerv6Lease	Lists IPv6 leases
Get-DhcpServerv6OptionDefinition	Lists IPv6 option definitions
Get-DhcpServerv6OptionValue	Lists IPv6 option values
Get-DhcpServerv6Reservation	Lists IPv6 reservations
Get-DhcpServerv6Scope	Provides IPv6 scope information
Get-DhcpServerv6ScopeStatistics	Provides IPv6 statistics for the defined scope
Get-DhcpServerv6StatelessStatistics	Lists IPv6 subnet prefixes containing stateless clients
Get-DhcpServerv6StatelessStore	Provides IPv6 stateless store properties for the defined subnet
Get-DhcpServerv6Statistics	Provides IPv6 server statistics
Remove-DhcpServerv6Class	Removes the defined vendor or user class
Remove-DhcpServerv6ExclusionRange	Removes the configured IPv6 exclusion range
Remove-DhcpServerv6Lease	Removes the configured IPv6 lease
Remove-DhcpServerv6OptionDefinition	Removes the configured IPv6 option definition
Remove-DhcpServerv6OptionValue	Removes the IPv6 option value configured at the scope, reservation, or server level
Remove-DhcpServerv6Reservation	Removes the configured IPv6 reservation
Remove-DhcpServerv6Scope	Removes the configured IPv6 scope
Set-DhcpServerv6Binding	Defines the server IPv6 interface binding state
Set-DhcpServerv6Class	Modifies the configured IPv6 vendor or user class
Set-DhcpServerv6DnsSetting	Modifies the configured DNS settings applied to scope, reservation, or server
Set-DhcpServerv6OptionDefinition	Modifies the configured IPv6 option definitions
Set-DhcpServerv6OptionValue	Modifies the configured IPv6 option value at scope, reservation, or server level
Set-DhcpServerv6Reservation	Modifies the configured IPv6 reservation properties
Set-DhcpServerv6Scope	Modifies the configured IPv6 scope properties
Set-DhcpServerv6StatelessStore	Modifies the configured IPv6 stateless store properties

Implementing DHCP Access Restrictions and Policies

↓
THE BOTTOM LINE

You can configure additional management restrictions and policies to prevent, allow, and direct IP allocation based on specific criteria. By configuring policies and filtering, you can have more granular control over devices, virtual machines, and clients configured with an FQDN.

CERTIFICATION READY
Implement DHCP filtering
Objective 2.1

The ability to further configure, group, and isolate devices based on an enterprise's need has tremendously grown. With the amount of devices, vendors, and new innovations coming out, DHCP is no longer just about issuing IP addresses. Appling policies allow you to configure device more granularly.

Link-layer (MAC) filtering used to be the only option to perform any filtering within DHCP. MAC filtering allowed you to supply a list of machines allowed and/or a list of machines denied from acquiring DHCP addresses.

With DHCP policies, you can now filter based on several criteria. When the client connects and requests an address, it is run against DHCP policies. From there, if it matches a policy or policies affecting it, DHCP assigns a defined set of options, scope assignment, or denial.

Configuring DHCP Policies

DHCP policies or policy-based assignments (PBAs) are created to configure DHCP client IP addresses and options based on criteria and met client conditions. This allows targeted administration and configuration to client devices.

Policy-based assignments can be used in multiple scenarios. When several PBAs are in placed, assignments are processed in order starting with the first policy, policy 1; the closer to 1 the policy is, that policy takes precedence over assigned options in other policies. Also, as a client begins processing policies, it applies only those policies that it meet the defined criteria and conditions.

Some examples of managing PBAs include following:

- **Multiple device types:** Because many enterprises include devices that need to be segregated, you can configure PBAs to assign options, lease durations, and assign scopes to these devices. For instance, if a company has several hundred VoIP phones deployed that do not require access to other networks, those phones can be assigned to a policy that will allow them to access networks or vLANs defined by the administrator.

- **Multiple roles:** You can configure PBAs to maintain the dynamics that occur on networks, including addresses needed for multiple mobile devices, laptops, desktops, and servers. Trying to keep them all within the same role can be detrimental to the availability of addresses within a scope. Being able to configure a policy for mobile devices that issue an IP for only an hour, provide laptops with an eight-hour lease, and provide desktops with a seven-day lease will keep addresses free and available for additional clients that might need to connect.

- **Virtualization:** In enterprise environments, virtual desktops are often refreshed frequently and dynamically to meet demand. During these refreshes, they also can be assigned different MAC address suffixes. If leases are kept for too long and MAC addresses are truly being randomly generated at each refresh, you must shorten the lease of the virtual machines to ensure that multiple leases for the same machine are not registered in DHCP. If MACs are not being refreshed and being maintained, consider assigning static IP addresses to them and excluding those IPs from the DHCP lease pool.

You can configure the following PBA criteria:

- **Vendor class:** You can configure vendor-managed DHCP option assignments with a prepending or trailing wildcard.
- **User class:** You can configure non-standard DHCP option assignments with a prepending or trailing wildcard.
- **MAC address:** You can configure the MAC address of a client with a prepending or trailing wildcard.
- **Client identifier:** You can configure the MAC address or network interface card GUID with a prepending trailing wildcard.
- **Fully qualified domain name (FQDN):** You can configure this to register foreign clients by using a guest DNS suffix.
- **Relay agent information:** You can configure this based on DHCP Option 82 configurations sent from the DHCP relay agent.

CONFIGURING DHCP POLICIES WITH WINDOWS POWERSHELL

For the exam, you need to know how to configure and practice configuring DHCP policies (policy-based assignments) by using Windows PowerShell. Table 6-3 lists the Windows PowerShell commands that you can use to configure DHCP policies.

Table 6-3

Windows PowerShell Cmdlets
to Configure DHCP Policies

CMDLET	DESCRIPTION
Add-DhcpServerv4Policy	Creates a new policy in the defined scope or server level
Add-DhcpServerv4PolicyIPRange	Adds an IP range to a policy at the scope level
Get-DhcpServerv4Policy	Lists configured policies at the scope or server level
Get-DhcpServerv4PolicyIPRange	Lists configured IP ranges on the defined scope
Set-DhcpServerv4Policy	Modifies the configured policy at the scope or server level
Remove-DhcpServerv4Policy	Removes the configured policy from the defined scope or server level
Remove-DhcpServerv4PolicyIPRange	Removes the configured IP range from the defined scope

 CONFIGURE A DHCP POLICY FOR HYPER-V VIRTUAL MACHINE LEASE DURATION

GET READY. To configure a DHCP policy for Hyper-V virtual machine lease expiration, perform the following steps:

1. In *DHCP Manager*, expand the DHCP server, and then expand IPv4.
2. Right-click Policies and choose New Policy.
3. In the *DHCP Policy Configuration Wizard*, on the *Policy based IP Address and Option Assignment* page, in the *Policy Name* text box, type a unique, easily recognizable name. In the *Description* text box, type a descriptive comment about the policy. Then click Next.
4. On the *Configure Conditions for the policy* page, click the Add button.
5. In the *Add/Edit Condition* dialog box (see Figure 6-8), from the *Criteria* drop-down list, select MAC Address. From the *Operator* drop-down list, select Equals. In the *Within the Value* text box, type 00155D, and then select the Append wildcard (*) check box. Click Add and then click OK to return to the *DHCP Policy Configuration Wizard*.

Figure 6-8

Configuring DHCP policy with
MAC address criteria

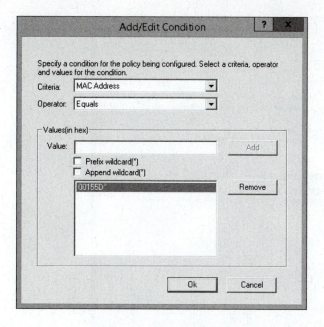

6. Back on the *Configure Conditions for the policy* page, click Next.

7. On the *Configure settings for the policy* page, review the configurable client options that match the conditions specified in the previous step. Click Next and then click Finish to return to the DHCP Manager.

8. In the *Policies* folder, verify that the policy you recently created exists. Right-click the newly created policy and choose Properties.

9. In the *Policy Properties* dialog box, select Set lease duration for the policy. The *Lease duration for DHCP* clients' options become available.

10. Verify that the *Limited to* option is selected. Change the *Days* field to 0, change the *Hours* field to 2, and then click OK. Now when a client obtains a DHCP address that starts with 00155D, it obtains a lease that expires after two hours.

11. Close the DHCP Manager and any open snap-ins.

You can also perform these steps at a scope level for additional management options. For instance, if you prefer that only MAC addresses meeting the criteria be placed within a specified IP range within the scope, you can do so.

Configuring DHCP Link-Layer Filters

You can configure link-layer filtering (also known as MAC filtering) to allow and/or deny DHCP services to configured MAC addresses.

You can configure link-layer filters at the server level and at the scope level. Configuring link-layer filters at the scope level must be done by using DHCP policies (policy-based assignments).

Server-level link-layer filtering must first be enabled from the IPv4 properties before the filters can be applied. You can enable an allow list and/or a deny list to allow only devices or to restrict devices from leasing an address from the server (see Figure 6-9).

Figure 6-9

Configuring MAC filters

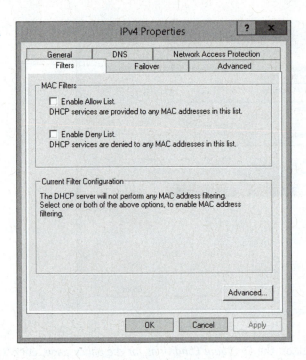

Both the allow and deny filters filter by MAC address. The MAC address applied to the filter can include trailing wildcards and can be in any of the following formats:

- 01-AB-23-*-*-*
- 01-AB-23-CD-45-*
- 01-AB-23-CD-*-*
- 01AB23CD45EF
- 01AB*

When you enable the allow list, DHCP services are allowed only to those IP addresses listed in the allow filter. Before you restrict addressing to allow only specified MAC addresses, you must analyze the DHCP environment. If the Enable Allow List check box is selected and the settings are applied, any devices that attempt to renew their IP address or receive a new lease with the server are denied access if their MAC or MAC pattern are not configured in the allow filter.

When you enable the deny list, DHCP services are not allowed to those IP addresses listed in the deny filter. Deny filters take priority over allow filters.

 ENABLE AND CONFIGURE LINK-LAYER FILTERING DENY RULES

GET READY. To enable and configure link-layer filtering deny rules, perform the following steps:

1. In *DHCP Manager*, expand the DHCP server, then right-click IPv4 and choose Properties.

2. In the *IPv4 Properties* dialog box, on the *Filters* tab, in *MAC Filters*, select Enable Deny List. Review the *Current Filter Configuration*. Click OK to close the *IPv4 Properties* dialog box and return to the *DHCP Manager*.

3. Expand Filters, then right-click the Deny folder and choose New Filter.

4. In the *New Filter* dialog box, in the *MAC address* text box, enter the MAC address of the device that will be denied. In the *Description* text box, enter a detailed description of what is being blocked and why. Click Add. The MAC address is now listed within the *Deny* folder and pane.

5. With the *New Filter* dialog box still open, click Close.

6. Verify that the MAC address recently configured does exist within the *Deny* folder, as shown in Figure 6-10. Close the *DHCP Manager* and any open snap-ins.

Figure 6-10

Verifying denied devices

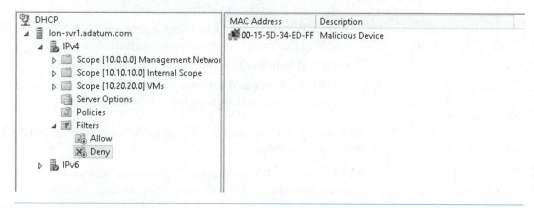

■ Implementing Microsoft System Center 2012 Management Pack for Windows Server 2012 DHCP

THE BOTTOM LINE

You can integrate administrative reporting, management, and configuration for DHCP with Microsoft System Center 2012 to achieve proactive notifications and support for DHCP servers.

CERTIFICATION READY
Implement and configure
a DHCP management pack
Objective 2.1

Configuring the Microsoft System Center 2012 Management Pack for Windows Server 2012 DHCP

The Microsoft System Center 2012 Management Pack for Windows Server 2012 DHCP is used for monitoring the DHCP server role on servers running Windows Server 2012 and Windows Server 2012 R2.

You can configure the System Center Management Pack for Windows Server 2012 DHCP to monitor and provide notifications for the following items:

- **DHCP Server Health:** At the server level, this monitors the health, availability, security, and configuration of all DHCP components. Server Health is also an aggregate of other monitors.

- **DHCP Service Health:** At the service level across the network, this monitors the health, availability, security, and configuration of all DHCP components. Service Health aggregates other health monitors and monitors servers across the enterprise.

- **DHCP Core Component Health:** This monitors DHCP services, networking bindings, and AD DS authorization.

- **DHCP Database Health:** This monitors the health of the DHCP databases. It also ensures that all scopes and super scopes are available to the database. Finally, it monitors disk availability to the drive the database is located as well as database integrity.

- **DHCP Security Health:** This monitors for security-related issues. It verifies that the DHCP server is performing secure updates with DNS and monitors for rouge DHCP servers that have been detected on the network.

- **DHCP Performance Health:** This monitors server queue health and verifies that DHCP servers are responding to queries efficiently.
- **DHCP Configuration Changes:** This monitors and detects configuration changes to the DHCP server and alerts on changes.
- **DHCP Performance Counter Collection:** This collects performance information to be able to chart and report on recent performance.
- **DHCP Policies:** This monitors DHCP policy health.
- **DHCP Cluster and Failover Server Relationships:** This monitors communication with partner servers and clustered nodes for health.

All System Center Management Pack for Windows Server 2012 DHCP workflows use Windows PowerShell.

When a Run As account is required, you must provide the user account with the minimum required permissions. The following least privilege permissions are required:

- Read permissions to the Registry
- Full access to the HKLM\CurrentControlSet\Services\DhcpServer\Performance key and all subkeys
- Event Log read permission
- Member of DHCP Users or DHCP Administrators
- Server Operators group
- Full access to create temporary files in the service account temp directory

For DHCP failover cluster environments, you must also download and install the Cluster Management Pack for Microsoft System Center 2012.

■ Maintaining a DHCP Database

 THE BOTTOM LINE

Maintaining a DHCP database must be a routine and well-practiced method to ensure database health, safety, and security. You need to know where the database and backup are located, how you can recover from a failure, and how to be proactive through maintenance.

CERTIFICATION READY
Maintain a DHCP database
Objective 2.1

Throughout the design process and in addition to the resilience and high availability of the DHCP server's databases, routine maintenance is a critical process that cannot be neglected.

Figure 6-11 shows the following default locations for the DHCP server database path and the backup path. Before modifying these settings, verify that a backup is performed because data loss can occur.

- **Database path:** By default, the database path is located in the following directory: %SYSTEMROOT%\system32\dhcp\
- **Backup path:** By default the backup database path is located in the following directory: %SYSTEMROOT%\system32\dhcp\backup

Figure 6-11

Viewing DHCP default
database paths

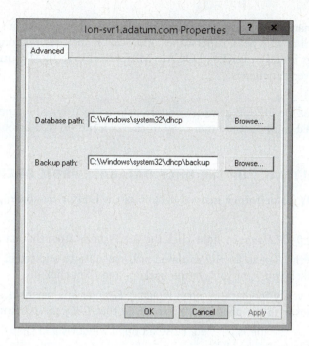

Database maintenance keeps your DHCP solution running smoothly and provide proactive measures in preparing for server failure or inconsistencies. As with any other server or service, you must know how to run and maintain an active backup and to store it in a location separate from the DHCP server.

Along with understanding how to create a backup, you must also test the backup by routinely restoring the production database into a lab environment. Maintaining, testing, and consistently practicing good backup and restore processes provides your enterprise a well-planned and resilient environment.

Another routine maintenance task is monitoring database growth compared to actual usage. If the database begins to approach or grows over 30 MB, you are recommended to compact the database to free up whitespace and maintain the database's integrity.

Finally, sometimes you need to resolve inconsistencies within your database by reconciling it.

Performing a DHCP Database Backup

Knowing how to perform a manual backup and restore of a database in the event of a disaster is critical. Separating the backup path from the default DHCP database location can be beneficial. If you have ever had a failed disk that contained both the DHCP database and the backup database, the design for DHCP resiliency was not properly planned.

The Dhcp.mdb file automatically backs up synchronously every 60 minutes by default. To change the interval of automatic backups, using Registry Editor, you can modify the following registry key REG_DWORD:

HKEY_LOCAL_MACHINE\SYSTEM\CurrentControlSet\Services\DHCPServer\Parameters\BackupInterval

You also can manually or synchronously back up the Dhcp.mdb file up from the DHCP console or by using Windows PowerShell. To back up the DHCP database manually, you must be a member of the DHCP Administrators group on the DHCP server.

Both the manual and automated backup processes described earlier backs up the entire database, as well as all scopes, superscopes, multicast scopes, reservations, leases, options, and keys and settings found in HKEY_LOCAL_MACHINE\SYSTEM\CurrentControlSet\Services\DHCPServer\Parameters.

Take Note A backup of the DHCP database does not store DNS dynamic update credentials. These settings need to be restored manually in case of a full DHCP database restore.

MANUALLY BACK UP THE DHCP DATABASE FROM DHCP MANAGER

GET READY. To perform a manual backup of the DHCP database, perform the following steps:

1. In *DHCP Manager*, right-click the DHCP server from the list and choose Backup.
2. In the *Browse for Folder* dialog box, navigate to and select the destination path to which you want to save the backup, and then click OK.
3. To verify the backup, open *Windows Explorer* and navigate to the destination path chosen in the previous step to verify that *DHCP.cfg* exists in the correct location.
4. After the file is verified, close all open windows and snap-ins.

Although backups occur automatically (every 60 minutes by default), you should take a manual backup and store it in a safe location before any changes to a DHCP production environment.

MANUALLY BACK UP THE DHCP DATABASE BY USING WINDOWS POWERSHELL

GET READY. To perform a manual backup of the DHCP database by using Windows PowerShell, perform the following steps:

1. Identify the destination file path where the backup will be stored. This will be used as the *<Destination>* in Step 2.
2. At the Windows PowerShell prompt, type **Backup-DHCPServer – Path *<Destination>*** and then press Enter.

   Depending on the size of the database, the backup may take a few minutes to complete. Once the backup has completed, you will be returned to the Windows PowerShell prompt.
3. To verify the backup, open *Windows Explorer* and navigate to the destination path chosen in Step2. Verify that *DHCP.cfg* exists.
4. After the file is verified and is in the correct location, close all open windows and snap-ins.

Although backups occur automatically, every 60 minutes by default, you should take a manual backup of your database and store it in a safe location before making any changes to a DHCP production environment.

Restoring a DHCP Database

Restoring the DHCP database restores those settings backed up during the backup process, including all scopes, superscopes, multicast scopes, reservations, leases, all options, and all keys and settings found in the aforementioned registry path. You can perform a restore within the DHCP console or by using Windows PowerShell.

Again, after a restore is completed, you need to reenter the DNS dynamic update credentials. During the restore process, if the DHCP server being restored is serving clients, they cannot receive an address until the DHCP service is started when the restore process is complete.

 RESTORE THE DHCP DATABASE BY USING DHCP MANAGER

GET READY. To perform a manual restore of the DHCP database, perform the following steps:

1. In *DHCP Manager*, right-click the DHCP server from the list and choose Restore.
2. In the *Browse for Folder* dialog box, navigate to and select the source path to which you want to save the backup, and then click OK.

   Depending on the size of the database, this may take some time. The DHCP Server service will stop, the database will be restored and the DHCP Server service will start. Upon completion you will receive a notification that "The database was restored successfully."
3. To verify the restore, confirm changes made between the last backup and the restore no longer exist.
4. Close all open windows and snap-ins.

 RESTORE THE DHCP DATABASE BY USING WINDOWS POWERSHELL

GET READY. To perform a manual backup of the DHCP database by using Windows PowerShell, perform the following steps:

1. Identify the destination file path where the backup is stored. This will be used as the *<Source>* in Step 2.
2. At the Windows PowerShell prompt, type Restore-DHCPServer – Path *<Source>* and then press Enter. The following message appears:

   ```
   Confirm
   The DHCP server database will be restored from the file
   <Source>. Do you want to want to perform this action?
   [Y] Yes [N] No [S] Suspend [?] Help (default is "Y"):

   WARNING: Please restart the DHCP server for the restored data-
   base to take effect.
   ```
3. Press Enter.
4. Restart the DHCP Server service by entering the following command: **Restart-Service "DHCP Server"**.

Compacting the DHCP Database

You need to compact the DHCP database if it becomes too large. During the compaction process, the database is copied to a temporary database and compacted, the original DHCP database is deleted, and the temporary database is migrated to be the live database. The temporary database is then removed.

Compacting the DHCP database requires the use of Jetpack.exe, which is installed when the WINS server feature is installed on the DHCP server.

COMPACT THE DHCP DATABASE

GET READY. To compact the DHCP database using a Windows command prompt, perform the following steps:

1. If not already installed, install the WINS server feature on the DHCP server from Server Manager, but do not configure it.

2. At a command prompt, type **cd %SYSTEMROOT%\System32\dhcp** and then press Enter.

3. Type **net stop dhcpserver** and then press Enter.

4. To begin the compaction process, type **jetpack dhcp.mdb temp.mdb** and then press Enter.

5. When compaction has completed, type **net start dhcpserver** and then press Enter (see Figure 6-12).

6. Close the command prompt window.

Figure 6-12

Running Jetpack.exe

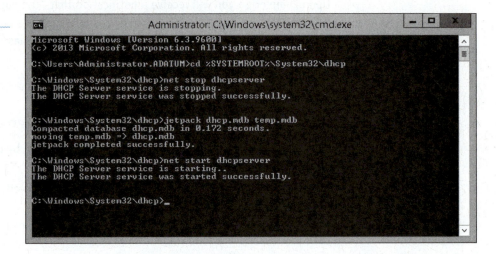

Reconciling the DHCP Database

Reconciling the DHCP database checks for inconsistencies between lease records in the registry and the DHCP database. If inconsistencies are found, the lease is reassigned to the client or a new lease is created until the client performs a DHCP discovery again.

 RECONCILE THE DHCP DATABASE VIA DHCP MANAGER

GET READY. To reconcile the DHCP database, perform the following steps:

1. In *DHCP Manager*, expand the DHCP server.

2. Right-click IPv4 and choose Reconcile All Scopes.

3. In the *Reconcile All Scopes* dialog box, click Verify to begin the scope repair procedure.

It might complete the procedure immediately or it might take a few minutes, depending on the size of the database and amount of items needed to be reconciled. Any inconsistencies found are displayed.

4. When the *DHCP* window displays with the message *The database is consistent*, click OK.

5. After the file is verified and is in the correct location, close all open windows and snap-ins.

 RECONCILE THE DHCP DATABASE VIA WINDOWS POWERSHELL

GET READY. To perform a manual backup of the DHCP database by using Windows PowerShell, perform the following steps:

1. At the *Windows PowerShell* prompt, type **Get-DhcpServerv4Scope | Repair-DhcpServerv4IPRecord** and then press Enter.

2. When prompted to check for consistencies for each scope, press Enter to confirm.

3. When the reconciliation is complete, close Windows PowerShell.

Performing a DHCP Server Migration

> Migrations are recommended when moving from a previous version of Windows Server to a new version.

To perform a migration from Windows Server 2008 to Windows Server 2012 and later, use the following commands within Windows PowerShell with their required switches:

- From the source server: `Export-DhcpServer`
- From the destination server: `Import-DhcpServer`

To perform a migration from Windows Server 2003 to Windows Server 2012 and above, use the following commands with their switches:

- From the source server: `netsh dhcp server export`
- From the destination server: `netsh dhcp server import`

The preceding commands simplify the migration, compared to using the Windows Server Migration Tool commands and their switches:

- From the source server: `Export-SmigServerSetting`
- From the destination server: `Import-SmigServerSetting`

 PERFORM A DHCP SERVER MIGRATION WITH WINDOWS POWERSHELL

GET READY. With the migration prerequisites ready, and with Windows Server Migration Tools installed on both the source server and destination server, perform the following steps:

1. Log on to the Source DHCP server and run Windows PowerShell under a domain administrator user account.

2. Type Export-DHCPServer –ComputerName <SourceFQDN> **-Leases –File C:\export.xml -verbose** and then press Enter. In this code, *<SourceFQDN>* represents the fully qualified domain name of the source DHCP server.

3. Copy the recently exported xml file, export.xml, to the clipboard. Log on to the destination DHCP server and paste the file to the C drive. Verify that export.xml now exists on the drive on the destination server.

4. While still logged on to the destination server, run Windows PowerShell under a domain administrator user account.

5. Type **Import-DHCPServer –ComputerName** *<DestinationFQDN>* **-Leases –File C:\export.xml -verbose** and then press Enter. *<DestinationFQDN>* represents the fully qualified domain name of the destination DHCP server.

6. When prompted to confirm the import, press Y then press Enter.

SKILL SUMMARY

IN THIS LESSON YOU LEARNED:

- High availability and DHCP have now integrated into a resilient, partner-server aware, and failover solution called DHCP failover.

- DHCP policies, or policy-based assignments (PBAs), can help you configure and assign DHCP settings based on met conditions and operations.

- Interoperability with IP Address Management (IPAM) allows you to manage several DHCP servers, scopes, and settings from a centralized location.

- You can block devices by configuring DHCP link-layer (MAC) deny filters at the server level. You also can configure allow rules to allow only devices by MAC or MAC*.

- Microsoft System Center Operations Manager can import the Management Pack for DHCP 2012. This allows DHCP to be proactively monitored and provides alerting.

- You can back up, restore, repair, and migrate the DHCP database by using Windows PowerShell.

- DHCP integrates with DNS in several ways through PTR record registration, DHCP policy assignments, DHCP options, and secure records updates.

- Migrating from Windows Server 2003 DHCP to Window Server 2012 R2 requires using the NETSH DHCP SERVER EXPORT and NETSH DHCP SERVER IMPORT commands. Migrating from Windows Server 2008 to Windows Server 2012 R2 requires using the EXPORT–DHCPSERVER and IMPORT–DHCPSERVER commands.

- To protect against rogue DHCP servers in a domain environment, Windows DHCP servers must be authorized in Active Directory Domain Services (AD DS) to lease addresses to clients.

- DHCP can integrate with NAP to direct clients to a remediation network, providing them access to remediation servers and network resources. This allows the client to get from an unhealthy state to a healthy state and back on the secure network.

■ Knowledge Assessment

Multiple Choice

1. Which high-availability option provides the best uptime if a server were to fail for a long period of time?
   a. Failover Cluster
   b. Failover
   c. Split-Scope
   d. Split-Failover

2. Which of the following domain groups must a user be in to authorize a DHCP server in Active Directory?
   a. DNS Admins
   b. DHCP Admins
   c. Domain Admins
   d. Enterprise Admins

3. Which two Windows PowerShell commands are used with Windows Server Migration Tools to export and import a DHCP Database?
   a. `Import-SmigServerSetting`
   b. `Export-DHCPServerv4Scope`
   c. `Import-DHCPServerv4Scope`
   d. `Export-SmigServerSetting`

4. Which interoperability service can allow PTR records to not be updated automatically?
   a. RRAS
   b. IPAM
   c. DNS
   d. NAP

5. Which tool is used to compact a DHCP database that has grown to more than 30MB in size?
   a. Windows PowerShell
   b. DHCP Manager
   c. `Repair-DhcpServer -Compact`
   d. Jetpack.exe

6. Which service prevents clients without up-to-date antivirus or security patches from connecting to the network?
   a. System Center Endpoint Protection
   b. Windows Server Update Services
   c. Network Access Protection
   d. Software Restriction Policies

7. Which feature allows an administrator to lease an IP range to devices that match a domain name?
   a. DNS
   b. DHCP Policy
   c. WINS
   d. RRAS

8. Which service can monitor the overall health of all DHCP servers?
   a. DHCP Manager
   b. System Center Configuration Manager
   c. System Center Operations Manager
   d. System Center Endpoint Protection

9. By default, where is the DHCP database located?
   a. C:\Windows\dhcp
   b. C:\Windows\System\dhcp
   c. C:\Windows\System32\dhcp
   d. C:\Windows\SysWOW64\dhcp

10. Which Windows PowerShell command backs up the DHCP database?
    a. `Backup-DHCPDatabase`
    b. `Backup-DHCPDatabaseScopes`
    c. `Backup-DHCPDatabaseScopesRegistry`
    d. `Backup-DHCPServer`

Best Answer

Choose the letter that corresponds to the best answer. More than one answer choice can achieve the goal. Select the BEST answer.

1. When performing a DHCP server migration from Windows Server 2012 to Windows Server 2012 R2, which command is used on the source server?
   a. NETSH
   b. Export-SmigServerSetting
   c. Export-DHCPServer
   d. Copy-Item

2. Where do you disable PTR record registration for a single IP range?
   a. DHCP Server Properties
   b. IPv4 Properties
   c. Scope Properties
   d. DHCP Policies

3. Which high-availability option allows full communication and replication between two DHCP servers?
   a. DHCP failover cluster
   b. Windows Cluster Services
   c. DHCP failover
   d. DHCP split-scope

4. Which interoperability service provides secure access to the network by using health monitors?
   a. IPAM
   b. NAP
   c. RRAS
   d. AD DS

5. Which setting blocks a range of MAC addresses from being issued DHCP server addresses?
   a. MAC filters
   b. DHCP policies
   c. Reservations
   d. Server options

Matching and Identification

1. Match the Windows PowerShell command to the correct task:
   _____ a) Backup-DHCPDatabase
   _____ b) Get-DhcpServerv4Scope
   _____ c) Import-SmigServerSetting
   _____ d) Invoke-DhcpServerv4FailoverReplication
   _____ e) Add-DhcpServerv4Policy
   1. Imports a DHCP server by using Windows Server Migration Tools
   2. Performs a backup of the DHCP database
   3. Lists all DHCP IPv4 scopes
   4. Forces failover replication across relationship members
   5. Adds a new policy to the server level or scope level

2. Write the command for the specified function or scenario:

_____ Reconcile the DHCP database

_____ Compact the DHCP database

_____ Import a DHCP database into Windows Server 2012 R2 from Windows Server 2003

_____ Create an IPv4 failover relationship

Build a List

1. Specify the correct order of the steps to migrate DHCP from Windows Server 2008 to two Windows Server 2012 R2 servers.

_____ Run `Import-DhcpServer` from the destination server.

_____ Create a DHCP failover.

_____ Copy the export results to the destination server.

_____ Run `Export-DhcpServer` from the source server.

_____ Install the DHCP server role on the destination server

2. Specify the correct order of the steps that must be completed to add a new user to your Office 365 portal.

_____ Right-click DHCP from the top of the tree view.

_____ Choose Manage Authorized Servers.

_____ Click the Authorize button.

_____ Log on as a member of the Enterprise Admins group.

_____ Enter the name of the server to authorize.

_____ Confirm the authorization and close the wizard.

_____ Open DHCP Manager.

■ Business Case Scenarios

Scenario 6-1: Troubleshooting DNS issues on non-Windows devices

Your network includes 225 wireless access points that are not and cannot be domain joined. They get their IP addresses assigned through DHCP. A DHCP policy has been created to place them all within the same scope and to provide them with several DHCP option configurations. After deployment of the devices, the wireless controller cannot resolve the access point host names through the primary DNS server. The wireless solution as a whole continues to fail until it can resolve the host names of all access points. The DNS settings are set correctly on the controller and the DHCP options. You can also ping the host name of the wireless controller from all access points. What should be configured?

Scenario 6-2: Running JetPack.exe

A DHCP database has grown to more than 50 MB in size, and various, random issues have been happening. Attempting to run `jetpack dhcp.mdb temp.mdb` from C:\Windows\System32\dhcp does not work. You realize that jetpack.exe can be found only within the sub-directories of C:\Windows\WinSxS\. You copy jetpack.exe from within that subdirectory and place it into the C:\Windows\System32\dhcp folder and attempt to run `jetpack dhcp.mdb temp.mdb` again, only to find a different error arises. How can you successfully run the jetpack executable with the least amount of headache?

Designing a Name Resolution Strategy

LESSON **7**

70-413 EXAM OBJECTIVE

Objective 2.2 – Design a name resolution strategy. This objective may include but is not limited to: Design considerations, including Active Directory–integrated zones, DNSSEC, DNS Socket Pool, cache locking, disjoint namespaces, DNS interoperability, migration to application partitions, IPv6, Single-Label DNS Name Resolution, zone hierarchy, and zone delegation.

LESSON HEADING	EXAM OBJECTIVE
Creating a Name Resolution Strategy • Reviewing DNS Names and Zones • Reviewing DNS Resource Records	
Designing a Zone Hierarchy and Zone Delegation • Designing a Zone Hierarchy • Designing Disjoint Namespaces • Designing a Physical DNS Infrastructure • Designing a Zone Delegation • Designing DNS Interoperability • Supporting IPv6 with DNS • Designing Migration to DNS Application Partitions	 Design a zone hierarchy Design disjoint namespaces Design a zone delegation Design DNS interoperability Design IPv6 Design migration to application partitions
Designing Secure Name Resolution • Designing Active Directory-Integrated Zones • Designing Secure Dynamic Updates • Designing DNSSEC • Designing a DNS Socket Pool • Designing DNS Cache Locking	 Design Active Directory–integrated zones Design DNSSEC Design a DNS Socket Pool Design cache locking
Designing a Single-Label DNS Name Resolution • Understanding WINS • Designing a GlobalNames Zone	Design a Single-Label DNS Name Resolution

KEY TERMS

automated key rollover

Berkeley Internet Name Domain (BIND)

disjoint namespace

DNS cache locking

DNS Security (DNSSEC)

DNS Socket Pool

DNSSEC resource records

domainDNS zones application partition

Domain Name System (DNS)

domain

dynamic updates

forestDNS zones application partition

forwarder

fully qualified domain names (FQDNs)

GlobalNames zone (GNZ)

iterative query

key signing key (KSK)

Name Resolution Policy Table (NRPT)

Name Server (NS) record

recursive query

referral

resource record (RR)

second-level domains

signing the zone

Start of Authority (SOA) record

top-level domains

trust anchor

Windows Internet Name Service (WINS)

zone

zone signing key (ZSK)

zone-signing parameters

zone transfer

■ Creating a Name Resolution Strategy

THE BOTTOM LINE

As all enterprise administrators know, network devices typically have names, because names are easier to remember and work with than addresses. The length and hexadecimal notation of IPv6 addresses makes this more evident. When designing an enterprise network, you must develop policies for creating effective names and also plan for the implementation of name resolution mechanisms such as Domain Name System (DNS).

Domain Name System (DNS), a naming service used by TCP/IP networks, is an essential service used for the Internet. Every time a user accesses a web page, he must type a URL. Before the client computer can communicate with the web server, it needs to use DNS to retrieve the IP address of the web server, similarly to someone using a phone book to find a phone number. When an enterprise client needs to communicate with a corporate server, it also uses DNS to find the IP address of the corporate service. DNS servers are often referred to as name servers.

The Transmission Control Protocol/Internet Protocol (TCP/IP) is the most popular networking protocol suite used in the world and is the same protocol used with the Internet. Of course, the Internet is a worldwide network that links billions of computers. For a client computer or host to communicate on a TCP/IP network, a client must have an IP address.

Traditional IP addresses based on IPv4 were based on a 4-byte address written in a four-octet format. Each octet ranges from 0 to 255. Examples of IP addresses are 24.64.251.189 and 192.168.1.53. Most users would have difficulty remembering hundreds of telephone numbers and hundreds of IP addresses. Name resolution enables administrators to assign logical names to a server or network resource by IP address and translate a logical name to an IP address.

With early TCP/IP networks, name resolution was done with hosts files, which were stored locally on each computer. Hosts files were simple text files with a host name and IP addresses on each line. (In Windows, the hosts file is located in the C:\Windows\System32\Drivers\etc folder.) The disadvantage of using hosts files is that every time you need to add a new entry, you need to add or modify the hosts file on every computer in your organization—not exactly a practical way to provide up-to-date name resolution.

DNS was developed as a system and as a protocol to provide up-to-date name resolution. The benefits of DNS include the following:

- *Ease of use and simplicity:* DNS allows users to access computers and network resources with easy-to-remember names.
- *Scalability:* DNS allows the workload of name resolution to be distributed across multiple servers and databases.
- *Consistency:* DNS allows the IP addresses to be changed while keeping the host names consistent, making network resources easier to locate.

A resolver service uses the DNS protocol to query for information about DNS servers via UDP and TCP port 53.

Reviewing DNS Names and Zones

DNS uses *fully qualified domain names (FQDNs)* to map host names to IP addresses. An FQDN describes the exact relationship between a host and its DNS domain. For example, computer1.sales.microsoft.com represents an FQDN; the computer1 host is located in the sales domain, which is located in the Microsoft second-level domain, which is located in the .com top-level domain.

DNS is a hierarchical distributed naming system used to locate computers and services on a TCP/IP network. DNS clients send queries to a DNS server, and the Domain Name Service receives and resolves queries such as translating a host or domain name to an IP address. Because it is so closely tied to the Internet and TCP/IP network, DNS is an essential service that enables the Internet and networks to function. DNS is required by many network services, including Active Directory.

DNS is known as a distributed naming system because the information stored with it is not found on a single DNS server. Instead, the information is distributed among multiple DNS servers, all of which are linked into a hierarchical structure.

UNDERSTANDING DNS NAMES AND ZONES

The DNS is a hierarchical system consisting of a tree of domain names. At the top of the tree is the root zone (see Figure 7-1). The tree can then be divided into *zones*, each served by a name (DNS) server. Each zone can contain one domain or many domains. The administrative responsibility over any zone can be delegated or divided by creating a subdomain, which can be assigned to a different name server and administrative entity.

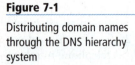

Figure 7-1

Distributing domain names through the DNS hierarchy system

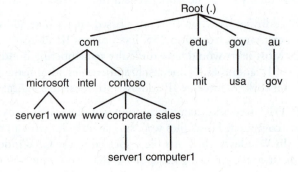

Each node or leaf in the tree is a *resource record (RR)*, which holds information associated with the domain name. The most common resource record is the host address (A or AAA), which lists a host name and the associated IP address.

A domain name consists of one or more labels. Each label can be up to 63 characters. The full domain name cannot exceed a total length of 253 characters.

The right-most label designates the top-level domain. For example, *microsoft.com* consists of two labels. The top-level domain is com. The hierarchy of domains descends from right to left. Each label to the left specifies a subdomain of the domain or label on the right. Therefore, in our example, *microsoft* is a subdomain of the *com* domain.

Traditionally, top-level domains consist of generic top-level domains and, internationally, country codes (such as *us* for United States, *uk* for United Kingdom, *de* for Germany, and *jp* for Japan). Traditional generic *top-level domains* include the following:

.*com* Commercial

.*org* Organization (originally intended for nonprofit organizations)

.*edu* Educational

.*gov* U.S. governmental entities

.*mil* *U.S. military*

.*net* Network (originally intended for the portal to a set of smaller websites)

Over the years, many other generic domains have been added such as aero, biz, coop, info, int, jobs, name, and pro. More recently, organizations can purchase their own top-level domains.

Second-level domains are registered to individuals or organizations:

microsoft.com	Microsoft Corporation domain
mit.edu	Massachusetts Institute of Technology
gov.au	Australian government

Second-level DNS domains can have many subdomains, and any domain can have hosts.

A host is a specific computer or other network device in a domain. For example, *computer1. sales.contoso.com* is the host called *computer1* in the sales subdomain of the *contoso.com* domain. A host has at least one IP address associated with it. For example, *www.microsoft.com* represents a particular address.

If you have *server1.corporate.contoso.com, com* is the top domain, *contoso* is a subdomain of com, and corporate is a subdomain of *contoso*. In the *corporate* domain, you can have one or more addresses assigned to *server1*, such as 192.168.1.53. As a result, when you type *server1.corporate. contoso.com* into your browser, the client sends a query to a DNS server asking what the IP address is for *server1.corporate.contoso.com*. The DNS server responds back with the 192.168.1.53 address. The client then communicates with the server with the address of 192.168.1.53.

UNDERSTANDING THE ADDRESS RESOLUTION MECHANISM

Every time a user accesses a network resource by a domain or host name, and the name has to be resolved to an IP address, the name and IP address are added to a cache so that you do not have to constantly contact the DNS server to resolve the IP address. If the name is not in the cache, the client contacts the first DNS server specified in the system's IP configuration. If the DNS server is available but cannot determine the address, the client does not ask another DNS server. However, because the DNS is distributed hierarchical system, the local DNS server might need to contact other DNS servers to resolve the IP address.

Figure 7-2

Using recursive query, which
performs DNS forwarding
when needed

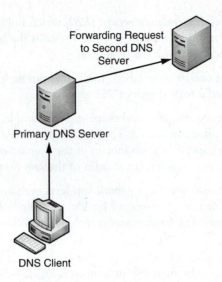

Forwarding Request
to Second DNS
Server

Primary DNS Server

DNS Client

The DNS client is known as the DNS resolver. Because a client computer or server depends on a DNS server to resolve IP addresses and identify certain network services, client computers and servers alike can be DNS clients.

When a DNS client queries a DNS server, it performs a ***recursive query***, in which the host asks the DNS server to respond with the requested data or respond that the domain does not exist. If the DNS server is does not know the answer and is a forwarder is configured, the DNS server will forward the request to the specified DNS server as shown in Figure 7-2. If a forwarder is not configured, it will perform a recursive query with another DNS server to determine the answer. The other DNS server will either know the answer or determine the answer.

When the DNS server receives the response, it first checks its own cache. It then checks to see whether it is the authority for the requested domain. If it knows the answer, it responds with the answer.

If the client DNS server does not know the answer and is not configured to forward requests to another DNS server, the client DNS server uses the DNS hierarchy to determine the correct answer. Rather than perform a recursive query, the client DNS server performs an ***iterative query***, which gives the best current answer back if it does not know the exact answer. For example, when a user types *www.contoso.com* in his or her browser and the client DNS server does not know the answer, the client DNS server contacts one of the root DNS servers to determine the addresses of a *com* name server. The client DNS server then contacts the *com* name server to get the name server for *contoso.com*. The DNS server contacts the *contoso.com* name server to get the IP address of *www.contoso.com*. The client DNS server responds to the client with the resolved IP address. It also adds the address to its cache for future queries. Figure 7-3 shows an iterative query.

Figure 7-3

Performing an iterative query

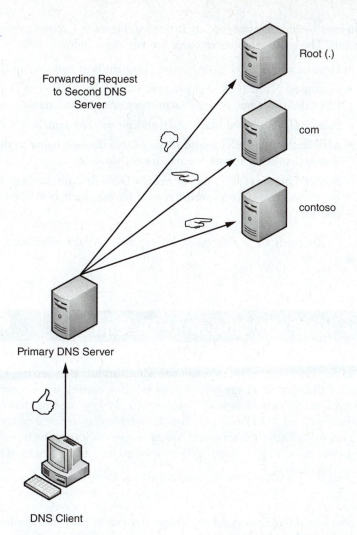

In some instances, the client DNS server does not know and cannot determine the answer, so it responds to the client that the answer cannot be found or the query is a nonexistent domain.

Most DNS clients are configured with two or more DNS servers. The second DNS server is contacted for DNS queries only when the first server is not available. If the first server cannot answer the query, the second DNS server is not used.

Reviewing DNS Resource Records

When you create a user account, certain attributes define the user account, such as first name, last name, and logon name. When you define a printer in Active Directory, you define a name of the printer and a location. A printer does not have a first name or a last name. Just as you have different types of objects in Active Directory, you also have different types of resource records in DNS, with different fields.

When you create a new zone, two types of records are automatically created:

- *Start of Authority (SOA) record* specifies authoritative information about a DNS zone, including the primary name server, the email of the domain administrator, the domain serial number, and the expiration and reload timers of the zone.
- *Name Server (NS) record* specifies an authoritative name server for the host.

You have to add resource records as needed. Figure 9-1 shows a zone with common resource records. The most common resource records are as follows:

- Host (A and AAAA) record maps a domain/host name to an IP address.
- Canonical Name (CNAME) record, sometimes referred to as an alias, maps an alias DNS domain name to another primary or canonical name.
- Pointer (PTR) record maps an IP address to a domain/host name.
- Mail Exchanger (MX) record maps a DNS domain name to the name of a computer that exchanges or forwards email for the domain.
- Service Location (SRV) record maps a DNS domain name to a specified list of host computers that offer a specific type of service, such as Active Directory domain controllers.

The PTR records are in the reverse lookup zone. All the other record types are in the forward lookup zone.

■ Designing a Zone Hierarchy and Zone Delegation

THE BOTTOM LINE

One primary function of an enterprise administrator is to establish policies that can be applied throughout a large organization without consulting the policymakers. For example, you will need to establish policies concerning how to naming items such as domains, computers, and AD DS objects. You do not want to receive a phone call from every branch office each time someone creates a new subdomain or installs a new server, asking you what name to give it, nor do you want to have to call them to find out what name they have chosen.

A domain naming strategy for an enterprise is a set of rules that administrators at any level can apply both when they have to create a new name and when they are attempting to locate a particular resource. For example, when a user from a branch office calls the help desk to report a problem accessing a server, the support staff should know immediately what server the user is talking about and be able to find it in the AD DS hierarchy. A good top-to-bottom naming policy would also include server names that identify the location of the computer and perhaps its function.

Designing a Zone Hierarchy

Working from the top down, you first need to consider naming the domains your organization will use. The term *domain* refers to an organizational division, but with two distinct uses in enterprise networking. Internally, a domain refers to an AD DS domain, but externally it refers to an Internet domain.

CERTIFICATION READY
Design a zone hierarchy
Objective 2.1

Internally, AD DS domains can enable you to emulate geographical or departmental divisions in the AD DS hierarchy. Users look in particular domains to find the network resources they need, such as servers and printers. On the Internet, domains enable users to locate your organization's web servers and other public resources.

Of course, a boundary must exist between these two types of domains. You want internal users to be able to access resources on the Internet, but you absolutely do not want Internet users to be able to access your internal resources.

With these necessities in mind, you can use three possible strategies when creating your internal and external domains:

- **Use the same domain internally and externally.** Using the same second-level domain, such as *contoso.com,* is possible for both internal and external resources. The domain name you choose must be registered in a top-level domain, such as *.com* or *.org,* so that it is accessible from the Internet and should be owned by the organization that is trying to use it. Using a single domain name provides a unified experience and corporate identity for all users. However, administrators must maintain separate DNS zones with the same name for internal and external records, which can be confusing. This solution also leads to problems when internal users must access the organization's external servers, because the internal DNS zone resolves the domain name to internal, not external, resources. You must duplicate the external zone on the internal DNS servers for this reason. From an administrative and security perspective, this is the least desirable of the naming options. However, if you are working with an existing DNS namespace, this might be the most expedient option.

- **Create separate domains in the same hierarchy.** When you register a second-level domain, such as *contoso.com,* for use on the public Internet, you also gain the right to create additional subdomain levels beneath that domain. Therefore, you can conceivably use *contoso.com* for your external resources and create a third-level domain, such as *internal.contoso.com,* for your internal resources. The biggest problem with this solution is that the FQDNs of your internal resources can be unmanageably long.

- **Create separate internal and external domains.** Creating entirely separate domains for your internal and external resources, such as *contoso.local* and *contoso.com,* respectively, is generally considered to be the optimum solution for administrative and security reasons. The internal domain can be, but does not have to be, registered. In this case, *.local* is not a valid top-level domain, so Internet users cannot possibly resolve the names associated with your internal resources, which provides additional security. Because the domain names are different, internal users do not have any problems accessing external resources. For organizations in which a particular domain name is intimately associated with a corporate branding effort, using another domain name, even internally, might raise non-technical objections. However, you can use aliases and other techniques to keep the internal domain name almost completely hidden, even from internal users.

TAKE NOTE *

An internal domain name can use either a valid or an invalid top-level domain name. If you choose to create an internal domain by using a valid top-level domain name, such as .com or .org, you are not required to register the domain for use on the Internet. However, registering the name is still a good idea, because if someone else on the Internet registers the name, your internal users' attempts to resolve that name will direct them to the Internet domain instead of the internal one.

Whichever naming strategy you choose to use, keeping the internal DNS records separated from the external ones is imperative. In most cases, enterprise networks maintain separate DNS servers for this purpose. In addition, Enterprise networks usually have multiple DNS servers, for domain delegation and fault-tolerance purposes.

The external server responsible for the *contoso.com* domain is the authoritative source for information about that domain on the Internet. This DNS server should contain only the records for Internet-accessible resources, such as web and mail servers.

The internal server responsible for the *contoso.local* domain contains records for internal resources only. This includes the AD DS domain controller records and possibly records for all the computers on the network, which is why they must be secured. When internal users attempt to access resources on the Internet, the internal DNS server is configured to forward those Internet name resolution requests to the external DNS server.

This arrangement is basically the same if you choose to use a single domain name or separate domain in the same hierarchy. Only the zone names are different. You still must make the external records available to the Internet while protecting the internal records from Internet access.

CREATING AN INTERNAL DOMAIN NAMING HIERARCHY

The external DNS namespace is usually quite simple, often consisting of only a single domain name with a few resource records. If your organization consists of several companies, you might have multiple second-level domain names registered and different content associated with each one. In that case, you might have multiple zones on your external DNS server, or perhaps even separate DNS servers for each domain name.

The internal naming hierarchy, however, can often be more complex in a large enterprise. In most cases, the domain namespace for an enterprise is based—at least in part—on the design of its AD DS hierarchy. The same circumstances that can lead to the creation of multiple AD DS domains should lead administrators to create separate DNS domains as well.

Most enterprise administrators design their domain hierarchies along geographic or departmental lines, or sometimes a combination of both. For example, the *contoso.local* internal domain mentioned earlier might have child domains named for the cities in which branch offices are located. In this example, the child DNS domains correspond to the AD DS domain tree, and the same servers that perform AD DS name resolution also enable users to access Internet resources.

ADDING AD DS DOMAINS TO AN EXISTING DNS HIERARCHY

The previous example assumes an enterprise built around Active Directory Domain Services. But what about an enterprise with an existing DNS namespace to which you are adding AD DS? The existing DNS infrastructure might consist of non-Windows DNS servers that provide users with name resolution services for Internet resources and UNIX servers on the network.

To introduce AD DS domain onto a network with an existing DNS namespace, you again have three options:

- **Use the existing domains for AD DS.** You can use the existing internal domain names for AD DS, either by using the existing non-Windows DNS servers or by replacing them with Windows Server 2012 R2.
- **Create new domains for AD DS.** You can create a new second-level domain, such as contoso.local, to function as the root domain for your AD DS tree.
- **Create child domains for AD DS.** You can leave the existing namespace intact and add a third-level child domain, such as *ad.contoso.local,* to function as the root domain for your AD DS tree.

Administrators generally base this decision on the enterprise's physical DNS infrastructure, as discussed later in this chapter.

Designing Disjoint Namespaces

A *disjoint namespace* occurs when one or more domain member computers have a primary DNS suffix that does not match the DNS name of the Active Directory domain of which the computers are members. For example, a computer that uses the DNS suffix of *corporate.contoso.com* is disjointed from an Active Directory domain *na.corporate.contoso. com.* However, a disjoint namespace can also occur in a multi-domain Active Directory forest with a single DNS namespace or zone or after one organization merges with another organization.

Domain member computers and domain controllers automatically function in a disjoint namespace. When a client registers its IPv4 host (A) resource record and IP version 6 (IPv6) host (AAAA) resource record in a disjoint DNS name, the domain controller automatically registers the global and site-specific (SRV) records into the DNS domain. The SRV records are also placed in the _msdcs zone.

Designing a Physical DNS Infrastructure

The DNS naming strategy you devise for your enterprise network does not necessarily have to correspond to your DNS server infrastructure. As you probably know, to host a domain on a DNS server, you create a zone. A single DNS server can host multiple zones. In each zone, you create resource records that contain information about the computers on the network. A DNS server hosting a zone becomes an authoritative source for information about the resources in that zone.

Each resource record on a Microsoft DNS server consumes 100 bytes of memory. At that rate, 10,000 records requires 1 million bytes, or 1 megabyte (MB). A single DNS server can therefore support a network of almost any conceivable size, theoretically. Thus, factors other than record capacity, such as the following, must compel administrators to install multiple DNS servers on their networks:

- **Security:** To prevent users on the Internet from accessing records for internal DNS resources, they must be stored on a separate server from the external resource records, not just a separate zone. This is true even if you are using the same domain name for your internal and external resources.

- **Fault tolerance:** DNS is a critical service that must be available at all times. For external services, a DNS failure can mean that Internet users cannot access your web sites and incoming email bounces back to the sender. For internal users, without DNS, all AD DS authentication and authorization stops. Therefore, the recommended practice is to have at least two copies of every zone on at least two different servers.

- **Performance:** Although one single DNS server could probably handle all name resolution requests for your entire enterprise, this is usually not a practical solution, especially if you have offices at remote locations connected by wide area network (WAN) links. Nearly every network operation that a user performs begins with a DNS name resolution request, and delays as these requests pass over relatively slow WAN links can cause performance to degrade noticeably. Therefore, whenever possible, you should provide users with access to a local DNS server.

As a result of these factors, a typical enterprise network will have a minimum of two DNS servers on the perimeter network with the servers accessible to the Internet, and two on the internal network. Larger branch offices might also have their own DNS servers, possibly coupled with a read-only domain controller (RODC).

In many cases, enterprise administrators install one external DNS server of their own on the perimeter network and contract with an ISP to maintain a replica. Because the two servers are located at different sites and often use different backbones to connect to the Internet, this arrangement can provide a greater degree of fault tolerance than two servers located in the same data center.

TAKE NOTE

DNS servers installed in branch offices or other locations for performance reasons do not have to be an authoritative source for a zone. They can function as caching-only DNS servers, which simply provide name resolution services to clients on the network.

Designing a Zone Delegation

DNS servers traditionally store their resource records in text files. This is the method that Microsoft DNS Server uses when you create a primary or secondary zone. To create multiple copies of a zone, you first create a primary zone, and then one or more secondary zones. Then you configure zone transfers to occur regularly. A *zone transfer* simply copies the records from the primary zone to a secondary zone.

CERTIFICATION READY
Design a zone delegation
Objective 2.2

A Windows Server 2012 R2 DNS server can host both primary and secondary zones on the same server, so you do not have to install additional servers just to create secondary zones. You can configure each of your DNS servers to host a primary zone, and then create secondary zones on each server for one or more of the primaries on other servers. Each primary can have multiple secondaries located on servers throughout the network. This provides not only fault tolerance, but also prevents all the traffic for a single zone from flooding a single subnet.

On networks using AD DS, however, administrators more commonly create Active Directory–integrated (ADI) zones, which store their resource records in the Active Directory database. The advantages of this option are as follows:

- **Fault tolerance:** The DNS data is stored on domain controllers throughout the network.
- **Security:** By using Windows permissions, you can control access to the DNS zones.
- **Compatibility:** You can perform zone transfers of ADI zones to standard secondary zones, if desired.
- **Replication:** AD DS replicates the DNS data along with the rest of its information. Unlike zone transfers, AD DS replication is multi-master (you can modify the data on any server) and compressed (for better traffic utilization on slow WAN links).

TAKE NOTE*

By default, Windows Server 2012 R2 replicates the database for a primary zone stored in Active Directory to all the other domain controllers running the DNS Server role in the AD DS domain where the primary is located. You can also modify the scope of zone database replication to keep copies on all domain controllers throughout the enterprise or on all domain controllers in the Active Directory domain, whether or not they are running the DNS server. You can also create a custom replication scope that copies the zone database to the domain controllers you specify.

Although Active Directory–integrated zones provide definite advantages, you do not want to use them everywhere. For example, for the external DNS servers on your perimeter network, you do not want to expose your AD DS information to the Internet, so you should create standard file-based primary or secondary zones on these servers.

USING FORWARDERS

As mentioned earlier, the DNS relies heavily on communication between servers, especially in the form of referrals. A *referral* is the process by which one DNS server sends a name resolution request to another DNS server.

In most cases, configuring one DNS server to send a recursive query to another DNS server is improper. For example, if DNS servers started sending recursive queries instead of iterative queries to the root name servers, the additional burden on the root name servers would be immense and would probably cause the entire Internet to grind to a halt.

The only time a DNS server sends recursive queries to another server is in the case of a special type of server called a *forwarder*, which is specifically intended to interact with other servers in this way. For example, in the DNS server arrangement described earlier, with external servers on the perimeter network and internal servers on the other side of the firewall, the external DNS servers typically function as forwarders for the internal servers.

When the clients on the internal network attempt to access Internet resources, they send a recursive name resolution query to their local DNS server, on the internal network. This DNS server is not directly accessible from the Internet, so you configure it to forward the name resolution query to the external DNS server on the perimeter network. This is a recursive query, because you want the external DNS server to handle all the individual queries to the authoritative root name, top-level, and second-level servers. Only when the external DNS server can actually resolve the name requested by the client does it return a response to the internal DNS server, which responds in turn to the client resolver.

The difference in a forwarder arrangement is in the nature of the query, so you do not have to modify the configuration of the server that will act as the forwarder. However, you do have to configure the other server to use a specific computer as a forwarder. To configure a Microsoft DNS server to use a forwarder, you open the server's Properties dialog box in the DNS Manager console and click the Forwarders tab (see Figure 7-4). On this tab, you specify the IP addresses of the DNS servers you want to use as forwarders, if the server cannot resolve a requested name on its own.

Figure 7-4

The Forwarders tab of a DNS server's Properties dialog box

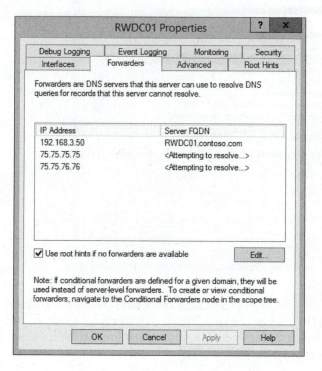

You might want to use forwarders in other situations as well. For example, if a branch office has a slow link to the Internet, you might want to configure its local DNS server to use the DNS server at the home office as a forwarder. This would enable the home office server to use its faster Internet connection to perform the interim resolution steps, only returning the final resolved name to the branch office server over the slow link.

Designing DNS Interoperability

To ensure that Microsoft DNS can operate with other DNS servers outside your organization, Microsoft DNS complies with the relevant DNS-related RFCs, thus making interoperability possible with other servers.

In an enterprise with an existing DNS infrastructure to which you want to add AD DS, you will likely have non-Microsoft DNS servers currently in service. The most common DNS server is the *Berkeley Internet Name Domain (BIND)*, also known as named (pronounced *name-dee*), which is supplied with many UNIX and Linux distributions.

If you need to support BIND, you have to select the Enable BIND Secondaries check box on the Advanced tab of the DNS server Properties dialog box (see Figure 7-5). This enables the Windows-based DNS server to interact with a server running the BIND name server.

Figure 7-5

Enabling the Enable BIND Secondaries option

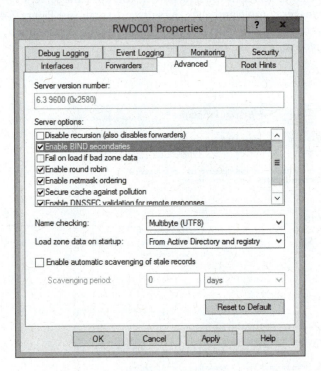

The only special requirement for a DNS server to function with AD DS is support for the Service (SRV) resource record, which enables clients to use a DNS query to locate domain controllers on the network. The current version of BIND, version 9.x, supports the SRV record, as do most other DNS server implementations.

TAKE NOTE*

Primary zones, secondary zones, and zone transfers are all part of the DNS standards, which all DNS server implementations support. BIND servers cannot store zone information in the AD DS database, however; for this feature, you must use the Microsoft DNS server.

If you choose to create new domains or child domains for AD DS, whichever DNS server versions you elect to use, you can create forwarders to ensure that queries for AD DS resources are referred to the correct servers.

Supporting IPv6 with DNS

Windows Server 2012 R2 supports IPv6 DNS hosts with no configuration needed. As mentioned earlier in the lesson, address records are known as AAAA in IPv6 rather than A records for IPv6 DNS hosts, as shown in Figure 7-6.

Figure 7-6

The Contoso.com zone with IPv4 and IPv6 resource records

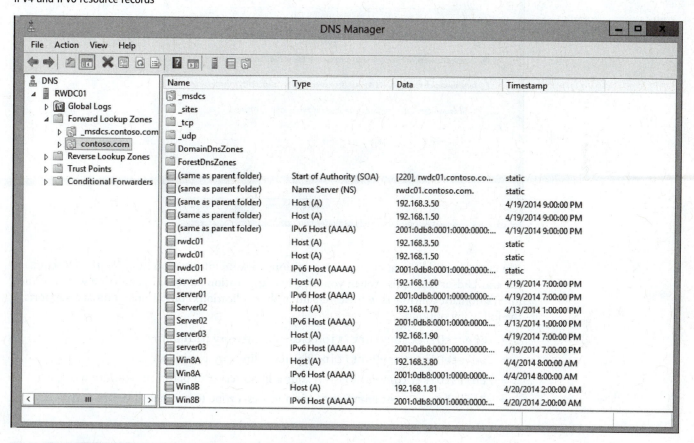

CERTIFICATION READY
Design IPv6
Objective 2.2

When designing your DNS environment, you need to ensure that the DNS server has IPv6 enabled and the clients can access the DNS server with IPv6. Also be sure to configure the clients manually or through DHCP the IPv6 address of the DNS server.

Designing Migration to DNS Application Partitions

When you install DNS, it creates two application partitions: the ***domainDNS zones application partition*** and the ***forestDNS zones application partition***. Domain controllers that have DNS installed automatically receive a copy of the domainDNS zones application partition for the domain they are part of. All domain controllers within the forest that have the DNS server installed also receive a forestDNS zones application partition for the forest that they are part of.

CERTIFICATION READY
Design migration to
application partitions
Objective 2.2

When you create a DNS zone, you specify the Active Directory Zone Replication scope (see Figure 7-7). By default, the zone replication scope is *To all DNS servers running on domain controllers in this domain.*

Figure 7-7

Specifying the Active Directory zone replication scope

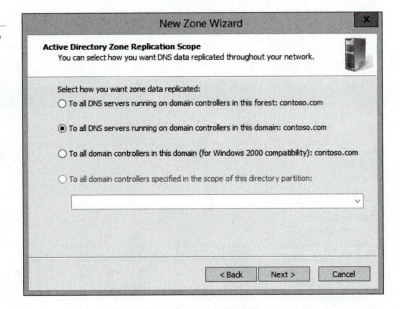

You can create additional application partitions to store information by using the Dnscmd.exe and Utdsutilexe tools. When you create an application partition, you define which of the forest's domain controllers will participate in the replication. For example, `dnscmd` supports the following options:

- `/CreateDirectoryPartition` creates a directory partition.
- `/DeleteDirectoryPartition` deletes a directory partition.
- `/EnlistDirectoryPartition` adds a DNS server to partition replication scope.
- `/ZoneChangeDirectoryPartition` moves a zone to another directory partition.

■ Designing Secure Name Resolution

THE BOTTOM LINE

Windows Server 2012 R2 includes a number of features for DNS security. Securing the DNS server and DNS records prevents false records from being added and prevents clients from receiving incorrect DNS query responses, which can lead them to visit phishing sites or worse. To prevent DNS from being used to attack systems, you can implement DNS Security (DNSSEC), Cache Locking, and other security measures.

After you deploy and configure DNS servers successfully, you need to secure them and their caches from spoofing, man-in-the-middle, and cache-poisoning attacks. In today's world, securing all areas of functionality is a sad necessity. DNS is a common area for attack by interception and tampering. A client that uses DNS to connect is always vulnerable to redirection to an attacker's servers unless the zone has been secured using DNSSEC.

Designing Active Directory–Integrated Zones

Today, DNS can instead be stored in and replicated with Active Directory as an Active Directory–integrated (ADI) zone. By using ADI zones, DNS follows a multi-master model, in which each server enables all DNS servers to have authoritative read-write copies of the DNS zone. When a change is made on one DNS server, it is replicated to the other DNS servers.

CERTIFICATION READY
Design Active Directory–integrated zones
Objective 2.2

Microsoft recommends using Active Directory to store DNS for good reasons:

- **Fault tolerance:** Because each server is an authoritative read-write copy of DNS, you have the DNS information stored on multiple servers. You also can update the DNS records from any DNS server.
- **Security:** Zone transfers are securely replicated as part of Active Directory. Like with Active Directory objects, you can manage who can access which records by using discretionary access control lists (DACLs). You also can configure secure dynamic updates, which allow records to be updated only by the client that first registered the record.
- **Efficient replication:** Zone transfers are replicated more efficiently when using Active Directory, especially if the information must be replicated over slow WAN links.

Three different replication scopes are available for ADI zones:

- To all domain controllers in the domain (the only replication scope available in Windows 2000)
- To all domain controllers that are DNS servers in the local domain (default), which is known as the DomainDNSZones application partition
- To all domain controllers that are also DNS servers in the entire forest, which is known as the ForestDNSZones application

In the following exercise, you create an ADI zone.

 CREATE AN ACTIVE DIRECTORY–INTEGRATED STANDARD FORWARD LOOKUP PRIMARY ZONE

GET READY. To create a standard forward lookup primary zone, perform the following steps:

1. In *Server Manager*, click Tools > DNS to open the *DNS Manager* console.
2. If necessary, expand the *DNS Manager* console to a full-screen view.
3. Expand the server so that you can see the *Forward Lookup Zones* and *Reverse Lookup Zones* folders.
4. Right-click Forward Lookup Zones and then click New Zone.
5. On the *Welcome to the New Zone Wizard* page, click Next.
6. On the *Zone Type* page, select Primary zone.
7. Make sure the *Store the zone in Active Directory* option is selected and click Next.
8. On the *Active Directory Zone Replication Scope* page, make sure that *To all DNS servers running on domain controllers in this domain* is selected and click Next.
9. On the *Zone Name* page, in the *Zone name* text box, enter the name of the domain, such as contoso.com, and then click Next.
10. On the *Zone File* page, ensure that *Create a new file with this file name* is selected, and then click Next.

11. On the *Dynamic Update* page, ensure that *Do not allow dynamic updates* is selected, and then click Next.

12. On the *Completing the New Zone Wizard* page, click Finish.

Designing Secure Dynamic Updates

DNS supports *dynamic updates*, in which client resource records are created and updated automatically at the host's primary DNS server. For ADI zones, these records are automatically replicated to the other DNS servers. However, because standard dynamic updates are insecure, Microsoft added secure dynamic updates.

For years, Windows DNS has supported dynamic updates, in which a DNS client host registers and dynamically updates the resource records with a DNS server. If a host's IP address changes, the resource record (particularly the A record) for the host is automatically updated, while the host uses the DHCP server to dynamically update its Pointer (PTR) resource record. Therefore, when a user or service needs to contact a client PC, it can look up the host IP address. With larger organizations, this becomes an essential feature, especially for clients that frequently move or change locations and use DHCP to automatically obtain an IP address. For dynamic DNS updates to succeed, the zone must be configured to accept dynamic updates.

Unfortunately, standard dynamic updates are not secure because anyone can update a standard resource record. However, if you enable secure dynamic updates, only updates from the same computer can update a registration for a resource record.

Designing DNSSEC

DNS Security (DNSSEC) is a suite of protocols defined by the Internet Engineering Task Force (IETF) for use on IP networks. DNSSEC provides DNS clients, or resolvers, with proof of identity of DNS records and verified denial of existence. DNSSEC does *not* provide availability or confidentiality information.

CERTIFICATION READY
Design DNSSEC
Objective 2.2

The process for securing a zone with DNSSEC is called *signing the zone*. Any queries on a signed zone will return a digital signature along with the usual DNS resource record that is used to verify the server via the public key of the server or zone from the *trust anchor*. To make this usable, the DNSSEC uses trust anchors represented by public keys that define the top of a chain of trust. The trust anchor verifies that a digital signature and associated data is valid.

When a zone is signed, a number of new *DNSSEC resource records* become available:

- The DNSKEY records are used to sign the records.
- The RRSIG record, along with the A record, is returned to the client in response to a successful query.
- The NSEC record is returned to deny positively that the requested A record exists in the zone.

These records are in addition to the standard A, NS, and SRV records in an unsigned zone.

DNSSEC uses a series of keys to secure the server and the zones: *key signing key (KSK)* and *zone signing key (ZSK)*. The KSK authentication key signs all the DNSKEY records at the root of the zone and is part of the chain of trust. The ZSK is used to sign zone data. *Automated key rollover* is the process by which a DNSSEC key management strategy for key management is made easier with automated key regeneration.

You can enable DNSSEC on an ADI zone or on a primary zone. As with all security measures and particularly advanced implementations, planning is important. Which zones do you want to secure? Who has access to the zone? Who has access to the server and the administration of the server security? The answers to these and many other questions always depend on your organization's security requirements. By the time you are ready to implement DNSSEC on your DNS server, the security documentation should have already been created and approved.

DNSSEC is installed as part of the DNS Server role. To enable DNSSEC, Windows Server 2012 R2 provides a DNSSEC Zone Signing Wizard, which is run from the DNS console. This wizard configures the **_zone-signing parameters_** all the settings required for ensuring that the zone is signed correctly and securely. Follow the steps to configure DNSSEC for the ADatum.com ADI zone.

 CONFIGURE DNSSEC ON AN ACTIVE DIRECTORY–INTEGRATED ZONE

GET READY. Log on with administrative privileges to the computer where you installed the DNS Server role and the ADatum.com ADI zone. To configure DNSSEC on an Active Directory–integrated zone, perform the following steps:

1. In _Server Manager_, click Tools > DNS.
2. In the _DNS Manager_ console, expand _DNS Server_ by clicking the arrow to the left of the server name.
3. Expand the _Forward Lookup Zones_ by clicking the arrow to the left of them.
4. Right-click the ADatum.com zone and click DNSSEC > Sign The Zone.
5. The _Zone Signing Wizard_ opens. Click Next.

TAKE NOTE* Examine all the options in the Zone Signing Wizard. Test items often require you to know where to set a particular choice.

6. The _Signing options_ page (see Figure 7-8) provides three options to define the parameters used to sign the zone. Select Customize zone signing parameters, and then click Next.

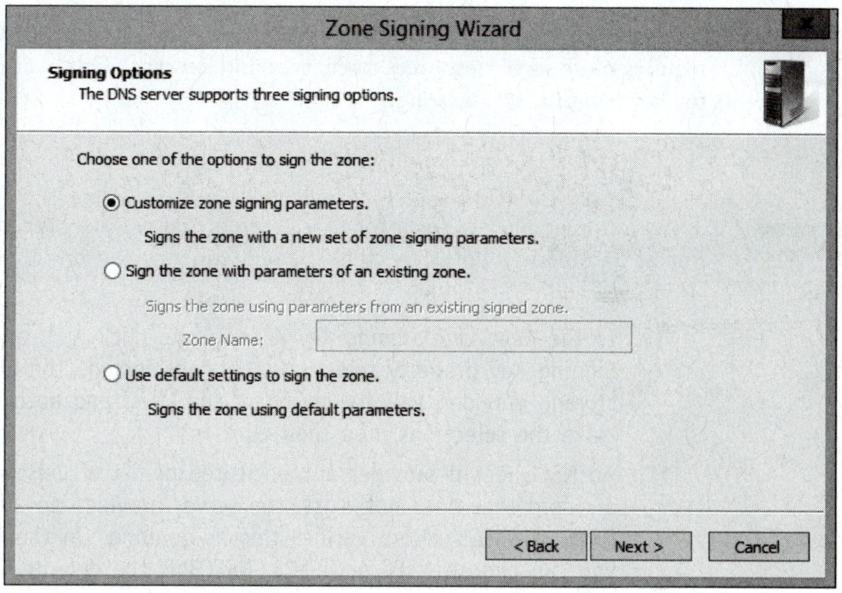

Figure 7-8

Selecting the signing options

Zone Signing Wizard

Signing Options
The DNS server supports three signing options.

Choose one of the options to sign the zone:

◉ Customize zone signing parameters.

    Signs the zone with a new set of zone signing parameters.

○ Sign the zone with parameters of an existing zone.

    Signs the zone using parameters from an existing signed zone.

    Zone Name:

○ Use default settings to sign the zone.

    Signs the zone using default parameters.

< Back   Next >   Cancel

7. On the *Key Master* page, select the DNS server that will manage the keys for the zone. The default is the current server. Click Next.

8. On the *Key Signing Key (KSK)* page, click Next.

9. On the *New Key Signing Key (KSK)* page, click Add.

10. In the *New Key Signing Key (KSK)* dialog box, configure settings to generate keys, and specify the algorithm, key length, replication, and auto rollover (see Figure 7-9). Click OK after you make the selections. Click Next, and then click Next again.

Figure 7-9

Creating a new Key Signing Key (KSK)

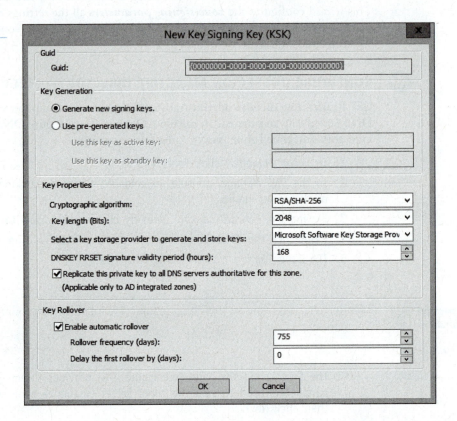

The greater the key length (in bits), the more secure the DNSSEC keys are. A long key requires more server resources to encrypt and decrypt. This overhead can be noticeable if the key length is set too long.

TAKE NOTE*

To set automatic key rollover for DNS servers that are not part of a domain, select the Enable automatic rollover check box. The frequency and initial delay is also set here.

TAKE NOTE*

11. In the *New Zone Signing Key (ZSK)* page, click Add, and then make the Zone Signing Key property selections. Settings include the algorithm, key length, key storage provider, validity period of the keys, and auto rollover. Click OK after you make the selections, and then click Next.

12. An NSEC record provides authenticated denial of existence. If a DNS client requests a record that does not exist, the server provides an authoritative denial and the NSEC or NSEC3 record verifies this as genuine. On the *Next Secure (NSEC)* page, you can choose NSEC or NSEC3. NSEC3 is the default. Click Next.

13. If the DNS server is also a domain controller, when trust anchor distribution is enabled, every other DNS server that is also a domain controller in the forest will receive the trust anchors for the zone. This speeds up key retrieval. Automated key rollover should be set if trust anchors are required on non-domain-joined computers. On the *Trust Anchor's (TAs)* page, click Next.

14. On the *Signing and Polling Parameters* page, you can configure delegation key record algorithm (DS record) and the polling intervals for the delegated zones. Accept the defaults by clicking Next > Next.

15. The wizard signs the zone. Click Finish. You can now see the new DNSSEC records in the DNS Manager.

When you apply DNSSec to a zone, the zone will include a padlock at the root to show that the zone is signed (see Figure 7-10). Also notice the additional records visible in the zone: DNSKEY (Public Key for the zone), RRSIG, and NSEC3. Indeed, each original entry now has four records: the A, RRSIG for the A, NSEC3, and the RRSIG for the NSEC3 record.

Figure 7-10

Displaying the signed zone

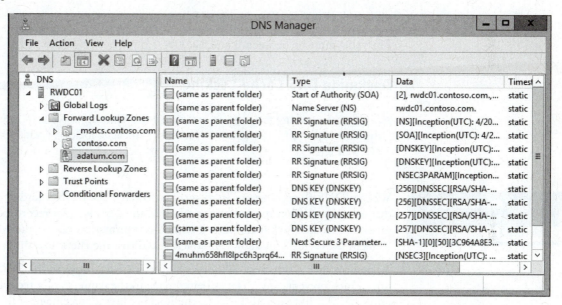

When the zone is signed, two more options become available on the zone DNSSEC context menu: Properties and Unsign the Zone. The Properties dialog box contains the settings you made in the wizard. Unsign the Zone removes all the records and disables DNSSEC for this zone.

The **Name Resolution Policy Table (NRPT)** contains a list of rules for DNS client access and response to the DNS server. NRPT is usually set through Group Policy when a zone is signed using DNSSEC.

TAKE NOTE* When signed, a zone cannot be removed from the Active Directory unless it is unsigned first.

Designing a DNS Socket Pool

The *DNS Socket Pool* is a tool used to allow source port randomization for DNS queries, which reduces the chances of an attacker guessing which IP address and port (socket) the DNS traffic uses. The DNS socket pool protects against DNS-spoofing attacks. To be able to tamper with DNS traffic, an attacker needs to know the correct socket and the randomly generated transaction ID.

DNS socket pooling is enabled by default in Windows Server 2012 R2. The default size of the DNS socket pool is 2500, and the available settings range from 0 to 10,000. The larger the number of ports available to the pool, the more secure the communication.

Windows Server 2012 R2 also allows for an exclusion list to be created. The preferred method to set the socket pool size is through the use of the `dnscmd` command-line tool:

1. Launch an elevated command prompt.
2. Type the following command:

```
dnscmd /Config /SocketPoolSize <value>
```

The value must be between 0 and 10,000.

Designing DNS Cache Locking

DNS cache locking prevents an attacker from replacing records in the resolver cache while the Time to Live (TTL) is still in force. When cache locking is enabled, records cannot be overwritten.

When a DNS client or server (resolver) has received the DNS record of a requested resource, that entry is stored in the resolver cache until the TTL for that record expires. (The TTL is set on the record itself at the zone level.) This information can be altered by an attacker while it sits in the cache. This allows an attacker to divert the client to a different (unsafe) resource.

To prevent such a situation, Windows Server 2012 R2 provides the DNS Cache Locking feature, which prevents any changes being made to the contents of a record in the resolver cache until the TTL has expired. DNS Cache Locking uses a percentage of the TTL to set the lock. For example, if the cache locking value is set to 75, the record would not be available to be overwritten until at least 75 percent of the TTL expires. The optimum setting, 100, prevents any record from being overwritten during the time its TTL is valid.

The preferred method to set the DNS cache locking value is through the use of the `dnscmd` command-line tool:

1. Launch an elevated command prompt.
2. Type the following command:

```
dnscmd /Config /CacheLockingPercent <percent>
```

3. Restart the DNS Service to apply the new settings. From the command prompt, enter `net stop DNS`, wait for the service to stop, and then enter `net start DNS`.

USING WINDOWS POWERSHELL

To change the cache locking value via Windows PowerShell, run the following cmdlet from a Windows PowerShell window: `Set-DnsServerCache -LockingPercent 100`

■ Designing a Single-Label DNS Name Resolution

↓
THE BOTTOM LINE

Windows Server 2012 R2 DNS provides support for single-label names without the need for NETBIOS or WINS. This allows a large multi-DNS environment to support a single name, such as *addressbook*, rather than an FQDN, such as *addressbook.contoso.com*.

CERTIFICATION READY
Design a Single-Label
DNS Name Resolution
Objective 2.2

By default, when you use the single name to try to access a computer, Windows takes the single name and appends the DNS suffixes specified in the IP configuration. By default, it appends the parent suffix of the primary DNS suffix. Therefore, if you are part of the *contoso.com* domain, it automatically appends contoso.com to *addressbook*, resulting in *addressbook.contoso.com*. You can append additional DNS suffixes on the Advanced TCP/IP Settings dialog box's DNS tab, as shown in Figure 7-11. This can also be configured using DHCP.

Figure 7-11

Specifying the DNS suffixes

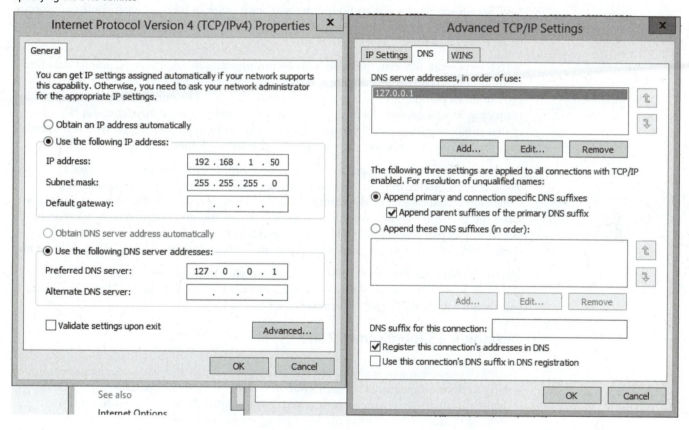

Understanding WINS

Before the introduction of Active Directory in Windows 2000, Windows used simple 15-character NetBIOS names to identify computers on the network. The NetBIOS namespace is flat, not hierarchical like that of DNS, and is designed only for use on private networks, not the Internet. To use these names with TCP/IP—a combination called NetBIOS over TCP/IP (NetBT)—a name resolution service is needed, but DNS is not suitable for these types of names.

Windows can use various NetBIOS name resolution mechanisms, but the one most suited for the enterprise is **Windows Internet Name Service (WINS)**. WINS is a client/server application that registers NetBIOS names and IP addresses as computers connect to the network and fulfills requests for the addresses associated with those names.

If you have computers on your network running earlier versions of Windows than Windows 2000, they rely NetBIOS names for identification, and you are probably running a WINS server to provide them with NetBIOS name resolution services. WINS is more advanced than the original DNS service in that it registers computer names automatically and stores its information in a database rather than a text file.

If all the Windows computers on your network are running Windows 2000 or later with AD DS, the network is not using NetBIOS names, and you do not have to run WINS servers for NetBIOS name resolution as a result. You can also disable the NetBIOS over TCP/IP (NetBT) protocol on your computers by using the controls in the NetBIOS Setting box, which is located on the WINS tab in the Internet Protocol Version 4 (TCP/IPv4) Properties/Advanced TCP/IP Settings dialog box.

You can run multiple WINS servers to provide fault tolerance and service thousands of clients. WINS servers can also communicate with each other to replicate their database information. This enables you to maintain a composite picture of your entire NetBIOS namespace on all your WINS servers.

WINS servers can replicate their databases by pushing data to other servers, pulling data from them, or both. When you configure a WINS server as a push partner, the server sends messages to all its pull partners whenever the database changes. The pull partners then respond by requesting an update, and the push partner transmits any new database records. A WINS server that you configure as a pull partner issues requests to its push partners for database records with version numbers higher than the last record it received during the previous replication.

The basic difference between push and pull partnerships is that push partners trigger replication events when a specific number of database changes have occurred, but pull partners initiate replication according to a predetermined schedule. Therefore, push partnerships are preferable when the WINS servers are connected by a fast link and you do not care if replication occurs at any time. Pull partnerships are preferable for servers connected by slower links, such as WAN connections, because you can schedule replication to occur during off hours, when traffic is low.

Unless you have pre-Windows 2000 computers on your network that use NetBIOS names and NetBT, WINS most likey is not needed. WINS also does not support IPv6. Therefore, you should start making plans to remove or replace WINS.

Designing a GlobalNames Zone

In an environment that includes several DNS suffixes, such as *contoso.com*, *adatum.com*, and *fabrikam.net*, you must create a **GlobalNames zone (GNZ)** manually within DNS to allow a single-label name to be resolved. For example, the company address book is accessed throughout the enterprise by entering *addressbook* into an Internet Explorer address bar. Without the use of a GlobalNames zone, in this scenario, the name would not be resolved. In an environment with a single DNS suffix such as *contoso.com*, the suffix would be appended automatically and the name would be resolved.

The only other way to achieve this would be to use a WINS server. However, WINS is a deprecated technology; the GlobalNames zone is now the preferred method for achieving single-label name resolution.

Windows Server 2012 R2 provides built-in support for a GlobalNames zone. However, it must be configured manually and enabled in several steps, as shown in the following steps.

CONFIGURE A GLOBALNAMES ZONE

GET READY. Log on with administrative privileges to the computer where you installed the DNS Server role. Ensure that the ADatum.com ADI zone is present. Then, to configure a GlobalNames zone, perform the following steps:

1. From the start screen, type CMD, right-click the CMD icon, and then click Run As administrator at the bottom of the screen.

2. In the command window, type dnscmd <servername> /Config /EnableGlobalnames-support 1 and wait for the *Command completed successfully* message.

3. Close the command window, and repeat steps 1 and 2 on every DNS server in the forest.

4. In *Server Manager*, click Tools > DNS.

5. In the *DNS Manager* console, expand the DNS server by clicking the arrow to the left of the server name.

6. Right-click the DNS server. Click New Zone to start the New Zone Wizard. Click Next four times. This creates a new primary forward lookup zone replicated to all DNS servers in the domain.

7. Enter the name GlobalNames (this is not case-sensitive), and then click Next.

8. Select Do not allow dynamic updates. Because all entries in this zone will be created manually, allowing dynamic updates is not required and would be a security loophole (as you read earlier in this lesson). Click Next > Finish.

To access the addressbook, create a CNAME record in the GlobalNames zone that points to any records that already exist in the other zones on the Forest DNS servers. In this instance, a single CNAME record of addressbook in the zone pointing to *addressbook.adatum.com* would allow any client to resolve this FQDN by entering the *addressbook* label.

SKILL SUMMARY

IN THIS LESSON YOU LEARNED:

- The Domain Name System (DNS) naming service is used by TCP/IP networks and is an essential service used by the Internet. Every time a user accesses a computer or web page by name, the DNS server provides naming resolution that translates the name to an IP address.

- DNS uses fully qualified domain names (FQDNs) to map a host name to an IP address. An FQDN describes the exact relationship between a host and its DNS domain.

- DNS is a hierarchical distributed naming system used to locate computers and services on a TCP/IP network. DNS clients send queries to a DNS server, and the Domain Name Service receives and resolves queries such as translating a host or domain name to an IP address.

- The DNS is a hierarchical system consisting of a tree of domain names. At the top of the tree is the root zone. You can delegate or divide the administrative responsibility over any zone by creating a subdomain, which can be assigned to a different name server and administrative entity.

- Each node or leaf in the tree is a resource record (RR), which holds information associated with the domain name. The most common resource record is the host address (A or AAA), which lists a host name and the associated IP address.

- Working from the top down, the first issue to consider is that of naming the domains your organization will use. The term *domain* refers to an organizational division but has two distinct uses in enterprise networking. Internally, a domain refers to an AD DS domain, but externally it refers to an Internet domain.

- A disjoint namespace occurs when one or more domain member computers have a primary DNS suffix that does not match the DNS name of the Active Directory domain of which the computers are members.

- To ensure that Microsoft DNS can operate with other DNS servers outside your organization, it complies with the relevant DNS-related RFCs, thus making interoperability possible with other servers.

- When you install DNS, it creates two application partitions: the domainDNS zones application partition and the forestDNS zones application partition.

- Windows Server 2012 R2 includes a number of new features to DNS security. Securing the DNS server and DNS records prevents false records from being added and prevents clients from receiving incorrect DNS query responses, which can lead them to visit phishing sites or worse. To prevent DNS being used to attack systems, DNS Security (DNSSEC), Cache Locking, and other security measures are implemented.

■ Knowledge Assessment

Multiple Choice

1. Which of the following is *not* one of the elements of the Domain Name System (DNS)?
   a. resolvers
   b. relay agents
   c. name servers
   d. name space

2. What is the maximum length for a fully qualified domain name (FQDN), including the trailing period?
   a. 50 characters
   b. 63 characters
   c. 255 characters
   d. 255 characters for each individual domain name

3. Which of the following would be the correct FQDN for a resource record in a reverse lookup zone, if the computer's IP address is 10.75.143.88?
   a. 88.143.75.10.in-addr.arpa
   b. 10.75.143.88. in-addr.arpa
   c. in-addr.arpa.88.143.75.10
   d. arpa.in-addr. 10.75.143.88

4. Which of the following are types of zone transfers supported by the DNS server in Windows Server 2012 R2? (Choose all that apply.)
   a. network zone transfers
   b. full zone transfers
   c. incremental zone transfers
   d. partial zone transfers

5. In the FQDN *www.sales.contoso.com*, which of the following is the second-level domain?
   a. www
   b. sales
   c. contoso
   d. com

6. You have DNS and Active Directory domain called *contoso.com*. You then decide to create a DNS subdomain called *support.contoso.com*, to be used to support external customers. Which type of namespace does this scenario describe?
   a. split namespace
   b. disjoint namespace
   c. multi-namespace
   d. Forwarding namespace

7. What is the most common external DNS server used with non-Microsoft DNS Servers?
   a. SRV
   b. Citrix
   c. UCS
   d. BIND

8. By default, when you create a DNS zone, which partition is it assigned to?
   a. domainDNS
   b. forestDNS
   c. treeDNS
   d. CacheDns

9. Which type of keys are used in DNSSEC? (Choose all that apply.)
   a. KSK
   b. PLK
   c. ZSK
   d. VFK

10. Which of the following statements about the GlobalNames zones in Windows Server 2012 R2 DNS Server role are true?
    a. GlobalNames zone is domain-specific.
    b. GlobalNames zones require dynamic updates disabled.
    c. GlobalNames zones are useful in multi-DNS domain systems.
    d. GlobalNames zones are enabled by default.

Best Answer

Choose the letter that corresponds to the best answer. More than one answer choice can achieve the goal. Select the BEST answer.

1. Which security group provides the privileges required for managing DNS within a single domain?
   a. Enterprise Admins
   b. DNS Admins
   c. Power Users
   d. Domain Admins

2. Which key length, in bits, should you choose for a zone signing key (ZSK) that is secure but does not provide too much processing overhead?
   a. 4096
   b. 1024
   c. 2624
   d. 3712

3. Which DNS Cache locking setting should you choose?
   a. 30 percent
   b. 0 percent
   c. 100 percent
   d. 50 percent

4. To provide single-name resolution, which of the following should you enable?

a. WINS

b. NETBIOS

c. GlobalNames support

d. netmask ordering

5. To provide location-specific name resolution for DNS clients, which of the following should you enable?

a. DNS round-robin

b. Hardware load-balancing cluster

c. Netmask ordering

d. Microsoft Network Load Balancing cluster

Matching and Identification

1. Identify which of the following are DNSSEC resource records.

_____ **a)** SRV

_____ **b)** AAAA

_____ **c)** NSEC

_____ **d)** MX

_____ **e)** RR

_____ **f)** NS

_____ **g)** RRSIG

_____ **h)** TXT

_____ **i)** TSIG

_____ **j)** DNSKEY

2. For each of the following message exchanges that can occur during a DNS name resolution procedure, specify whether the sending computer generates an iterative query or a recursive query:

_____ Resolver to designated DNS server

_____ Designated DNS server to top-level domain server

_____ Designated DNS server to forwarder

_____ Designated DNS server to second-level domain server

_____ Forwarder to root name server

Build a List

1. Identify the correct order in which a GlobalNames zone and GlobalNames zone record are created. Not all steps will be used.

_____ Sign the zone.

_____ Enable GlobalNames support.

_____ Enable dynamic updating.

_____ Manually create a host record in the GlobalNames zone.

_____ Create a GlobalNames forward lookup zone.

_____ Create a GlobalNames reverse lookup zone.

_____ Disable dynamic updating on the GlobalNames zone.

Business Case Scenarios

Scenario 7-1: Deploying DNS Servers

Harold is a freelance networking consultant who has designed a network for a small company with a single location. The owner of the company wants to use an Active Directory domain, so Harold installs a Windows Server 2012 R2 domain controller with the Active Directory Domain Services and DNS Server roles. Harold also uses DHCP to configure all the network workstations to use the DNS services provided by the domain controller.

Soon after the installation, however, the owner of the company reports extremely slow Internet performance. After examining the traffic passing over the Internet connection, you determine that it is being flooded with DNS traffic. What can you do to reduce the amount of DNS traffic passing over the internet connection?

Scenario 7-2: Managing Access to App1

You are responsible for DNS within the enterprise and need to provide access to a company-wide application named *App1*. This web-based application exists in the *contoso.com* domain with a FQDN of *App1.contoso.com*. Every user throughout the forest must be able to access the application by typing *App1* into an Internet browser address bar. The forest contains the following DNS zones:

- Contoso.com
- Fabrikam.net
- ADatum.com

The DNS servers have been installed by default and have each had their single zone added. What must you do to allow this application to work in this way?

LESSON | # Designing and Managing an IP Address Management Solution

70-413 EXAM OBJECTIVE

Objective 2.3 – Design and manage an IP address management solution. This objective may include but is not limited to: Design considerations including IP address management technologies including IPAM, Group Policy–based, manual provisioning, and distributed, centralized, hybrid placement, and database storage; configure role-based access control; configure IPAM auditing; migrate IPs; manage and monitor multiple DHCP and DNS servers; configure data collection for IPAM; integrate IPAM with Virtual Machine Manager (VMM)

LESSON HEADING	EXAM OBJECTIVE
Designing and Managing an Address Management System	
• Planning IP Address Management Technologies	Design considerations including IP address management technologies including IPAM, Group Policy–based, manual provisioning, and distributed, centralized, hybrid placement, and database storage
• Configuring Data Collection for IPAM	Configure data collection for IPAM
• Configuring Role-Based Access Control (RBAC)	Configure role-based access control
• Configuring IPAM Auditing	Configure IPAM auditing
• Managing and Migrating IP Addresses	Migrate IPs
• Managing and Monitoring Multiple DHCP and DNS Servers	Manage and monitor multiple DHCP and DNS servers
Integrating IPAM with Virtual Machine Manager (VMM)	Integrate IPAM with Virtual Machine Manager (VMM)

KEY TERMS

IP Address Management (IPAM)   IP address range   IPAM provisioning

IP address block   IPAM client   IPAM server

IP addresses

■ Designing and Managing an Address Management System

↓ THE BOTTOM LINE

IP Address Management (IPAM) is a feature within Windows Server 2012 and Window Server 2012 R2, but it is not a new network function. Planning, management, tracking, and auditing of IP addresses have been problems for every network administrator for many years. The only method of managing such facilities prior to Windows Server 2012 was by using the Dynamic Host Configuration Protocol (DHCP) and Domain Naming Service (DNS) management consoles, third-party databases or applications, spreadsheets, or in some cases even scraps of paper with details of every network node recorded. The advent of IPAM in Windows Server 2012 removes the need for all these alternative methods.

IPAM provides a single point of administration for all DNS and IP management features within an Active Directory forest. Before implementing IPAM, you need to understand a number of key terms, requirements, and functional limitations:

- **IP address block:** IP address blocks are the highest level conceptual entity in an IP address space. They are marked with a starting and ending IP address. For public IP addresses, the address block is assigned by the Internet registry (for smaller ranges, this is delegated by your Internet service provider). Network administrators use address blocks to split an entity into address ranges, which is the basis of DHCP scopes. You can use IPAM to add, import, edit, and delete IP address blocks. IPAM automatically tracks the address ranges belonging to an address block.

- **IP address range:** IP address ranges are the next hierarchical level of an IP address space, beneath the address block. Typically, an address range is a subnet marked by a starting and ending address, using a subnet mask. An IP address range usually maps to a DHCP scope. IP address ranges can be added or imported by IPAM.

- **IP addresses:** IP addresses are the individual addresses contained in an IP address range. IPAM allows complete end-to-end management of IPv4 and IPv6 addresses. IPAM automatically maps IP addresses to the correct range by using the start and end address of a range. You can add IP addresses manually or have IPAM import them from external sources.

Planning IP Address Management Technologies

By using Server Manager, you can easily install the IPAM role. IPAM requires several steps to successfully configure the server, discovery, and address space management. The planning stage is fairly simple, but the servers, services, and administrators must all be configured carefully to ensure the feature adds full value.

IPAM has two main components:

- **IPAM server** collects data from the managed DNS and DHCP servers within the discovery scope. If Windows Internal Database (WID) is used IPAM server manages the Windows Internal Database (WID). In Windows Server 2012 R2, IPAM can also use a Microsoft SQL Server. The server also provides the Role-Based Access Control (RBAC) for the IPAM installation. All the IPAM security groups and roles are managed from the IPAM server.

- **IPAM client** provides the interface with which the IPAM administrator manages and configures the server. The client interfaces with the server and invokes the Windows PowerShell commands to carry out DHCP and DNS tasks as well as any remote management functions. The IPAM client is automatically installed on the IPAM server when the IPAM feature is installed. You also can install the IPAM client on an alternative Windows Server 2012 without the IPAM server feature. Finally, you can manage IPAM using the IPAM client from a Windows 8 client with the Remote Server Administration Tools (RSAT) installed.

UNDERSTANDING IPAM REQUIREMENTS

To successfully deploy IPAM, you need to meet the following general requirements:

- An IPAM server *must* be a domain member but *cannot* be a domain controller.
- The IPAM server should be a single-purpose server. Installing DHCP, DNS, or any other roles on the IPAM server is not recommended.
- The IPAM server can manage only the IPv6 address space if IPv6 is enabled on that server.
- Always log on to the IPAM server with a domain account, *not* with a local account.
- Ensure that the IPAM administrator is a member of the correct local IPAM security group on the IPAM server.
- To use IPAM to track and audit IP addresses, ensure that auditing is enabled for Audit Account Logon Events on all domain controllers and NPS servers.

TAKE NOTE *

When installing an IPAM server, the computer must be a domain member, not a domain controller.

For an IPAM server to be deployed to Windows Server 2012 or Windows Server 2012 R2, it must meet the following hardware requirements:

- A dual-core processor of at least 2.0 GHz
- 4 gigabytes (GB) or more of RAM
- 80 GB of free hard disk space

To be able to manage the DHCP and DNS roles of a Windows Server 2008 using IPAM on Windows Server 2012 R2, you need to install the following requirements on the Windows Server 2008 or Windows Server 2008 R2 systems:

- Service Pack 2 on Windows Server 2008
- .NET Framework 4.0 full installation
- Windows Management Framework (WMF) 3.0, which provides Windows PowerShell 3.0
- Windows Remote Management (WinRM) must be enabled

The IPAM feature has a number of published specifications:

- Understanding that an IPAM server never communicates with another IPAM server is important. For example, IPAM servers maintain their own IP address spaces and do not share that information within their databases. To effectively manage multiple IPAM servers within a forest, you must configure the discovery scope of each server manually.
- IPAM manages only Microsoft DHCP and DNS services; Windows Server 2012 R2 IPAM will manage third-party solutions.
- IPAM supports only domain-joined DNS, DHCP, and NPS servers.
- IPAM running on Windows Server 2012 R2 supports WID and Microsoft SQL Server. It does not run on MYSQL or any other third-party solution.
- A single IPAM server supports a maximum of 150 DHCP servers and 500 DNS servers.
- A single IPAM server supports up to 6,000 DHCP scopes and 150 DNS zones.
- IPAM stores up to three years of forensic IP data (IP address leases, MAC address details, and logon and logoff details) for up to 100,000 users.

Unfortunately, non-Microsoft devices such as routers and switches are not managed or monitored by IPAM.

UNDERSTANDING GROUP POLICY-BASED AND MANUAL PROVISIONING

IPAM provisioning is the process of allowing the IPAM server to configure and manage the necessary features and functions of the servers, services, and domain objects required for IPAM. You can provision the IPAM server in two ways:

- Automatic Group Policy–based provisioning
- Manual provisioning

⚠ WARNING Remember that when chosen, the automatic Group Policy provisioning method cannot be undone without a complete IPAM reinstall.

The default is Group Policy–based. When this is selected and provisioned, the only method for reversing that decision is to uninstall IPAM and then reinstall. The Group Policy–based provisioning method creates the following Group Policy Objects (GPOs), which allow the required access settings on all the IPAM managed servers:

- IPAM1_DHCP for DHCP servers
- IPAM1_DNS for DNS servers
- IPAM1_DC_NPS for domain controllers and NPS servers

Also, the IPAM security groups are created, the IPAM database is created and role-based access is configured, and access to the IPAM tasks and folders is configured.

USING WINDOWS POWERSHELL

The following example shows how you can use the `Invoke-IpamGpoProvisioning` cmdlet to create IPAM-provisioning GPOs:

```
Invoke-IpamGpoProvisioning-Domain contoso.com -GpoPrefixName IPAM1 -
IpamServerFqdn ipam1.contoso.com -DelegatedGpoUser user1
```

In this example, three GPOs are created (IPAM1_DHCP, IPAM1_DNS, and IPAM1_DC_NPS) and linked to the *contoso.com* domain. These GPOs enable access for the server *ipam1.contoso.com*, using the domain administrator account user1. In this example, the hostname of the IPAM server is used as a GPO prefix; however, this is not required.

The manual provisioning method is not preferred because it is more complex and less consistent than the Group Policy–based method. You typically would use manual provision only when the number of managed servers is small. When you choose manual provisioning, you must configure settings on each managed server. Settings must also be removed manually if the server becomes unmanaged.

If you chose to provision IPAM manually, you need to do the following:

- Configure Windows Firewall on a managed DHCP server:
  - To allow the management of DHCP servers, the DHCP Server (RPC-In) and DHCP Server (RPCSS-In) inbound firewall rules must be enabled on the DHCP servers.
  - To allow access to the DHCP audit share, the File and Printer Sharing (NB-Session-In) and File and Printer Sharing (SMB-In) inbound firewall rules must be enabled on the DHCP server.
  - To allow read access to DNS, the DNS Service RPC and DNS Service RPC Endpoint Mapper inbound firewalls must be enabled.
  - To allow access to the event logs and to monitor the DHCP and DNS services, the Remote Event Log Management (RPC) and Remote Event Log Management (RPC-EPMAP) inbound firewall rule—Remote Service Management—must be enabled on the DHCP, DNS, domain controllers and NPS servers.

- Add the IPAM server to the domain IPAM User Group (IPAMUG).
- The IPAM server must also be a member of the local DHCP Users and Event Log Readers security groups.
- On the DHCP server, share the %windir%\system32\dhcp folder with the sharename of dhcpaudit. Ensure that the IPAMUG has Read access.
- To activate new security group memberships on the DHCP server, restart the DHCP Server service.

UNDERSTANDING DISTRIBUTED, CENTRALIZED, AND HYBRID PLACEMENT

Windows Server IPAM can manage only one Active Directory Forest. IPAM can be deployed in one of three topologies:

- **Centralized placement:** A single IPAM server is used for the whole forest.
- **Distributed placement:** An IPAM server is deployed to every site in the forest.
- **Hybrid placement:** A central IPAM server and dedicated site-based IPAM servers are deployed at some sites.

Because different IPAM servers have no automatic built-in communication or database sharing, if you deploy multiple IPAM servers, you can customize the scope of discovery for each server or filter the list of managed servers. However, you can use Windows PowerShell export and import functions for IPAM to periodically update IP address range and address information between multiple IPAM servers.

You can also customize the role of different deployed IPAM servers. For example, you can use one IPAM server to manage your organization's IP addressing and another IPAM server to monitor the DNS zone health or to configure the DHCP scopes.

SETTING UP DATABASE STORAGE

When you provision IPAM, you have to select which database to use. Whereas Windows Server 2012 supported only WID, Windows Server 2012 R2 allows you to choose WID or Microsoft SQL Server. If you choose WID, the IPAM database is located on the system root drive (the operating system drive). Because of that, you must ensure that enough disk space is available on the system root drive to accommodate this data. Although SQL Server uses more resources, it allows additional scalability, disaster recovery, and reporting scenarios.

IPAM uses several data collection tasks to gather data from managed servers:

- DHCP scopes
- DHCP scope utilization
- DNS zones
- DNS zone events
- DHCP lease logs
- IPAM configuration events
- DHCP configuration events
- network authentication events

These tasks run in the background and regularly update the IPAM database.

To store five years of data, you must ensure that you have the following disk space available:

- To hold IP address blocks, IP address ranges, IP address records, custom fields, DHCP configuration data, DHCP scopes, and other static managed server information, you should have 1.0 GB of free space.

- To keep track of usage for IP address blocks, IP address ranges and DHCP scopes so that utilization trends can be displayed graphically, you will need 1.0 GB of data for every 10,000 IP address ranges for each month. Therefore, if you have to keep this data for five years and have 2,000 IP address ranges—1 GB/month $\times$ 5 years $\times$ 12 months/year—you will need to allocate 60 GB of disk space.

Configuring Data Collection for IPAM

IPAM requires several steps to successfully configure the server, discovery, and address space management. The planning stage is fairly simple, but the servers, services, and administrators must all be configured carefully to ensure the feature adds full value.

CERTIFICATION READY
Configure data collection for IPAM
Objective 2.3

After the IPAM server is installed, configuring it successfully requires a number of steps. These are all shown on the main IPAM client screen (see Figure 8-1).

Figure 8-1

Displaying IPAM server tasks

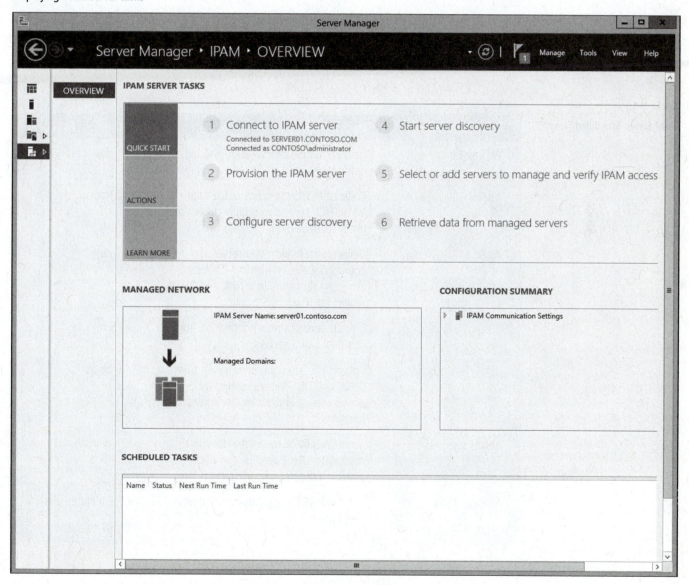

The following IPAM tasks are required to configure the IPAM server installation.

1. **Connect to IPAM Server:** This step is automatically carried out when the client is running on an IPAM server. If the client is running from a remote server (not an IPAM server), the administrator needs to connect to the chosen IPAM server.

2. **Provision the IPAM Server:** IPAM provisioning is the process of allowing the IPAM server to configure and manage the necessary features and functions of the servers, services, and domain objects required for IPAM.

3. **Configure Server Discovery:** Server Discovery is the process of defining which domains in the forest that contain servers will be managed by this IPAM server.

4. **Start Server Discovery:** *IPAM discovery* is the process of retrieving a list of all domain controllers, DNS servers, and DHCP servers from the active directory.

5. **Select or add servers to manage and verify IPAM access:** When the IPAM discovery is complete, the IPAM administrator can select which servers, roles, and services will be managed from the list in server inventory.

6. **Retrieve Data from Managed Servers:** This final task launches various data collection tasks on the IPAM server to collect data from all the servers managed by this IPAM server.

When the IPAM server tasks are complete, the IPAM server creates a schedule of tasks to repeat at various intervals. Table 8-1 lists these tasks.

Table 8-1

IPAM Server Scheduled Tasks

Task Name	Description	Default Frequency
AddressExpiry	Tracks IP address expiry state and logs notifications	1 day
AddressUtilization	Collects IP address space usage data from DHCP servers to display current and historical utilization	2 hours
Audit	Collects DHCP and IPAM server operational events; also collects events from domain controllers, NPS, and DHCP servers for IP address tracking	1 day
ServerAvailability	Collects service status information from DHCP and DNS servers	15 minutes
ServerConfiguration	Collects configuration information from DHCP and DNS servers for display in IP address space and server management functions	6 hours
Server Discovery	Automatically discovers the domain controllers, DHCP servers, and DNS servers in the domains you select	1 day
Service Monitoring	Collects DNS zone status events from DNS servers	30 minutes

Now that the IPAM server tasks are completed, the full server inventory appears (after a refresh) in the Server Manager IPAM console. The server inventory contains a list of managed servers and a panel containing the full relevant details for the selected server (see Figure 8-2).

Figure 8-2

Displaying the IPAM server inventory

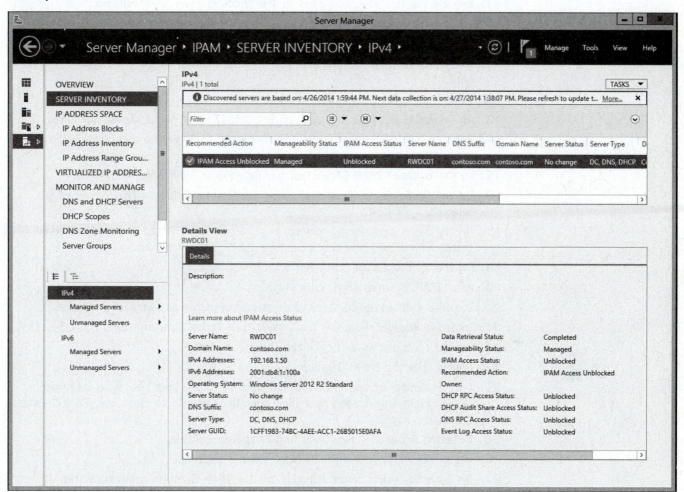

 INSTALL AND CONFIGURE IPAM

GET READY. To install and configure IPAM on a server running Windows Server 2012 R2, perform the following steps:

1. On Server01, in the *Server Manager* console, open the Manage menu and then click Add Roles and Features.

2. In the *Add Roles and Features* Wizard, click Next.

3. On the *Select installation type* page, click Next.

4. On the *Select destination server* page, click Server01.contoso.com, and then click Next.

5. On the *Select server roles* page, click Next.

6. On the *Select features* page, select IP Address Management (IPAM) Server. When prompted to add additional features, click Add Features.

7. Back on the *Select features* page, click Next.

8. On the *Confirm installation selections* page, click Install.

9. When the installation is complete, click Close.

10. On the server, open *Windows PowerShell* by clicking the Windows PowerShell icon on the taskbar.

11. Execute the following command in the Windows PowerShell window:

   Invoke-IpamGpoProvisioning -Domain contoso.com

   -GpoPrefixName IPAM1 -IpamServerFqdn server01.contoso.com

   When prompted to confirm that you want to perform this action, type Y and press Enter.

12. Close the *Windows PowerShell* window.

13. On Server01, in *Server Manager*, click IPAM. If IPAM is not shown, press F5.

14. Because the IPAM server is already connected to Server01, click step 2, Provision the IPAM server.

15. In the *Provision IPAM* Wizard, on the *Before you begin* page, click Next.

16. On the *Configure database* page, *Windows Internal Database (WID)* is already selected. Click Next.

17. On the *Select provisioning method* page, *Group Policy Based* is already selected. In the *GPO name prefix* text box, type IPAM1 and click Next.

18. On the *Summary* page, click Apply.

19. After IPAM is provisioned, click Close.

20. Log into RWDC01 as contoso\administrator with the password of Pa$$w0rd.

21. In *Server Manager*, from the Tools menu click Active Directory Users and Computers.

22. Expand contoso.com and click the Users container.

23. Double-click the IPAMUG group.

24. On the *Member of* tab, click the Add button. In the text box, type Enterprise admin; Event Log Readers and then click OK. Click OK to close the *IPAMUG Properties* dialog box.

25. Close the *Active Directory Users and Computers* console.

26. Reboot RWDC01. Wait until RWDC01 finishes booting.

27. On Server01, using *Server Manager*, on the *IPAM Overview* page, click step 3: Configure server discovery.

28. In the *Configure Server Discovery* dialog box, the root domain (contoso.com) is already selected. Click Add.

29. Click OK to close the *Configure Server Discovery* dialog box.

30. On the *IPAM Overview* page, click step 4: Start server discovery. Wait until Server Discovery is done; this might take 5-10 minutes. Under *Scheduled Tasks* at the bottom of the screen, the Server Discovery status should display *Ready*.

31. On the *IPAM Overview* screen, click step 5: Select or add servers to manage and verify IPAM access.

32. On the *IPv4* page, rwdc01 is blocked. Right-click RWDC01, and then click Edit Server.

33. On the *Add or Edit Server* page, change the *Manageability* status *Unspecified* to Managed. Also, make sure that *DC, DNS server*, and *DHCP server* are selected. Click OK.

34. Right-click the RWDC01 server and select Refresh Server Access Status. If a status dialog box appears, click OK. When the list is refreshed, click F5 to refresh the screen.

35. Click Overview again in the left pane.

36. Click step 6: Retrieve data from managed servers. Again, this might take a few minutes.

Configuring Role-Based Access Control (RBAC)

Network administration is a vast topic with many varied and differing roles required to carry it out successfully. Within IP address management are several sets of tasks that might require separate staff to carry them out. For this reason, IPAM relies on role-based access control (RBAC) to provide the necessary delegated administrative features.

CERTIFICATION READY
Configure role-based
access control
Objective 2.3

When the IPAM feature is installed, the provisioning process (if you selected automatic Group Policy–based provisioning) creates the RBAC roles to enable simple delegated administration of the whole IPAM infrastructure.

Use the previously mentioned IPAM local security groups to control the roles. These groups allow delegation of tasks to individuals whom you do not want to have full administrative access to your IPAM server and data. Simply place the necessary users or groups in the correct Local group on the IPAM server:

- **IPAM Users:** Users who are members of this group can view Server Discovery, IP address space, and server management information. Group members can also view IPAM and DHCP server operational events, but they cannot view IP address tracking information.

- **IPAM MSM Administrators:** Members of this group have IPAM Users privileges and can perform common IPAM multi-server management (MSM) tasks and server management tasks.

- **IPAM ASM Administrators:** Members of this group have IPAM Users privileges and can perform common IPAM address space management (ASM) tasks and IP address space tasks.

- **IPAM IP Audit Administrators:** Members of this group have IPAM Users privileges, can perform common IPAM management tasks, and can view IP address tracking information.

- **IPAM Administrators:** Members of this group have the privileges to view all IPAM data and perform all IPAM tasks.

You can view the built-in roles and the allowed operations through Server Manager, as shown in Figure 8-3. You can create additional roles from the Tasks menu by selecting Add User Role.

Figure 8-3

Viewing the IPAM Roles

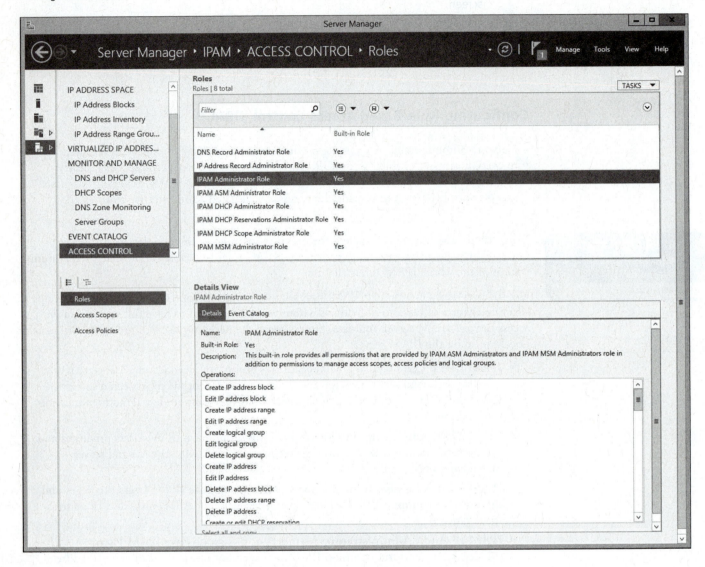

Configuring IPAM Auditing

You can use IPAM to audit address utilization, policy compliance, and other information based on the type of servers IPAM is managing. To configure the IPAM auditing, use the Event Catalog (see Figure 8-4).

Figure 8-4

Viewing the IPAM
Configuration Events

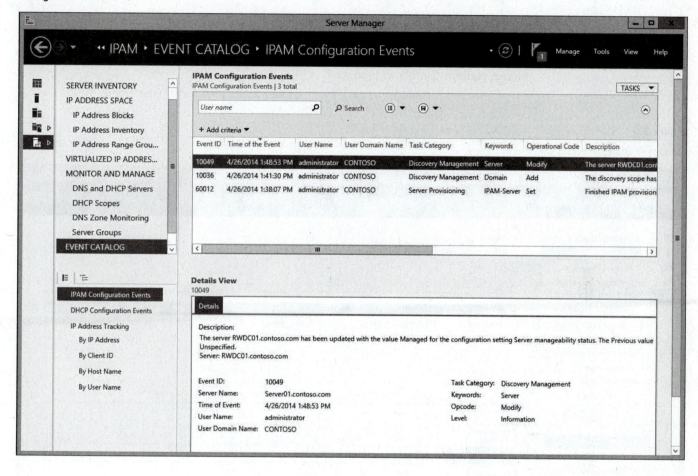

IPAM collects user information from the DHCP server, domain controllers, and network policy servers. The information includes the user's assigned IP address, host name, and client identifier (MAC address for IPv4 or DUID for IPv6).

By default, the IPAM configuration events are shown. However, you can configure IPAM to show other events as well as create reports using the data stored within the database. Also, IPAM provides a query tool and search box, and criteria can be added to a query filter. After the data is retrieved, it can be exported to a comma-separated value (CSV) file.

Managing and Migrating IP Addresses

CERTIFICATION READY
Migrate IPs
Objective 2.3

Most IP address space management is now carried out by using a mixture of spreadsheets, third-party applications, and printed materials. After installing the IPAM feature and configuring the provisioning and discovery, you can choose to migrate all the IP address space data into the IPAM database.

The starting point for the configuration of IP address blocks and IP address ranges is the main IPAM screen, which is reached through Server Manager. The first stage is to allocate IP address blocks for the server to track and manage.

 CREATE AN IP ADDRESS BLOCK

GET READY. Log on to the IPAM server with administrative privileges. To create IP address blocks, perform the following steps:

1. In *Server Manager*, click IPAM > IP Address Blocks, Tasks (see Figure 8-5).

Figure 8-5

Creating IP address blocks

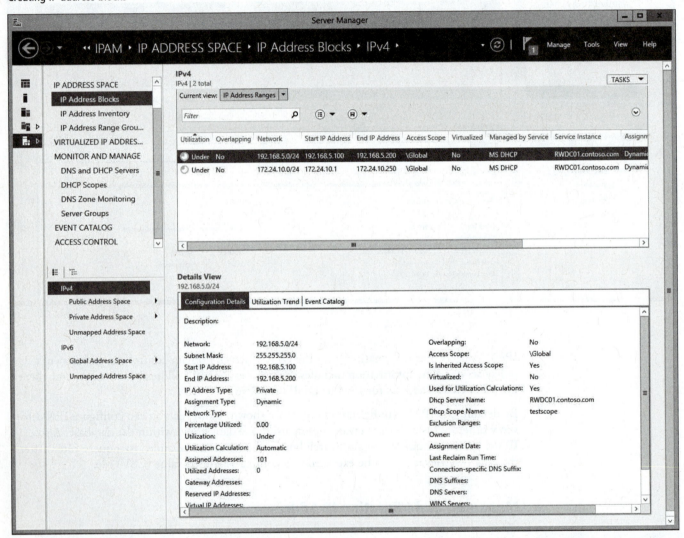

2. From the Tasks menu, click Add IP Address Block.

3. In the *Add or Edit IPv4 Address Block* dialog box (see Figure 8-6), complete the fields with the required IP block data, and then click OK.

Figure 8-6

Adding an IP address block

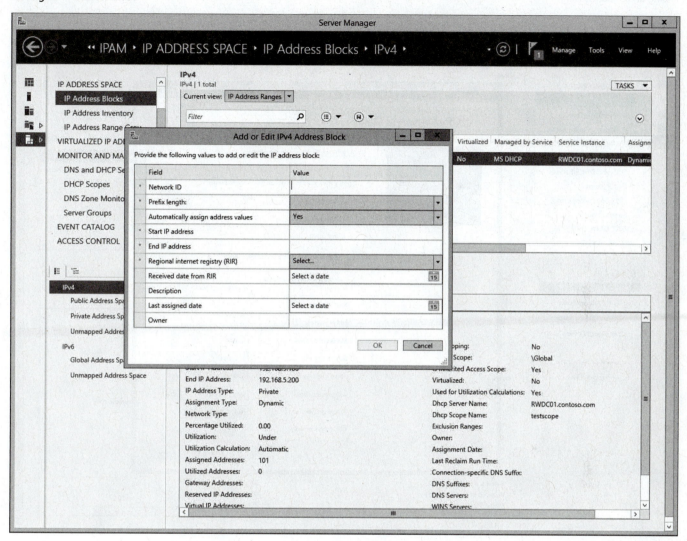

The newly added IP address block is now listed in the top panel and the configuration details in the bottom panel of the IPAM IP address blocks section of the console.

After you create the IP address block, the next stage is to split the IP address block into IP address ranges. This procedure is also done through the IPAM console in Server Manager.

 CREATE AN IP ADDRESS RANGE

GET READY. Log on to the IPAM server with administrative privileges. To create an IP address range, perform the following steps:

1. In *Server Manager*, click IPAM > IP Address Range Groups, Tasks.
2. From the Tasks menu, click Add IP Address Range.
3. In the *Add or Edit IPv4 Address Range* dialog box, complete the fields with the required Basic IP Range configuration data (see Figure 8-7).

Figure 8-7

Adding an IP address range

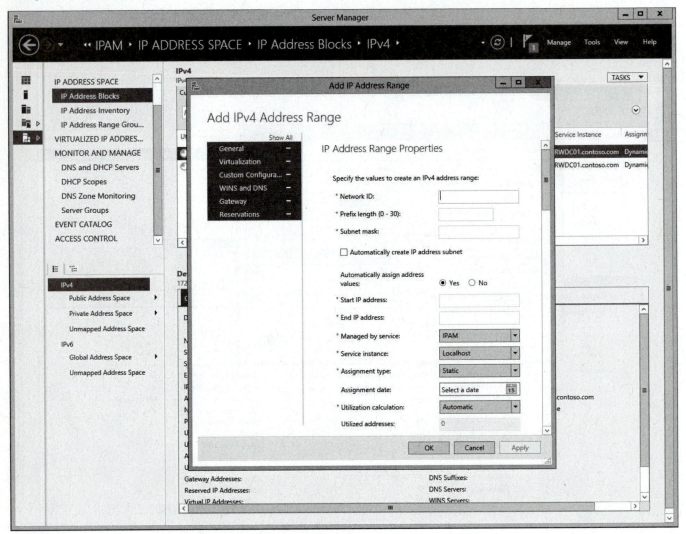

4. In this version of the dialog box are additional custom configuration options that enable you to associate the IP address range with a number of selectable criteria (AD Site, Building, and so on). Selecting several user-entered values is possible. Click Add and select the chosen options, entering the required user data, and then click OK.

5. Click OK to finish the creation of the IP address range.

Now that the IP configuration is complete, the IPAM server can maintain accurate records of utilization and allocations. If the IPAM server manages several IP address ranges, the custom configuration proves most useful to reducing clutter in the console.

From the IP Address Range Groups console page, you can carry out a number of actions on each range, such as modify a DHCP scope or add a DHCP reservation. These options significantly reduce the workload of an IPAM administrator. Remotely logging on to a DHCP server and querying the data directly is not required.

The IPAM client console options for importing IP address data from a comma-separated values (CSV) file include the following:

- Import IP Address Block
- Import IP Address Ranges
- Import IP Addresses
- Import and Update IP Address Ranges

When you open the Add or Edit Ipv4 Address Range dialog box, use the Managed By Service drop-down list to select how the address block or range is being managed. Choices include:

- IPAM (as shown)
- non-Microsoft DHCP solution
- Microsoft Virtual Machine Manager (VMM)
- another method

By selecting the correct option, you can import the IP address space within IPAM but still have the assigned address managed by the current method. When ready, the IP address can be moved under IPAM management as appropriate.

An export option exports all IP address data to a user-selected CSV file. Also consider that when the IPAM server is backed up, the Windows Internal Database must also be backed up to secure the IPAM data.

+ MORE INFORMATION

To ensure that you format the CSV file correctly, prepare an export to capture the header information required to import IP address data into the database.

Managing and Monitoring Multiple DHCP and DNS Servers

IPAM can monitor DHCP and DNS servers form any physical location in the organization, as well as simultaneously manage multiple DHCP servers or scopes that exist among multiple DHCP servers.

CERTIFICATION READY
Manage and monitor
multiple DHCP and DNS
servers
Objective 2.3

You can use IPAM to view and check the status and health of selected sets of Windows Server DNS and DHCP servers from a single console. It can also display recent configuration events. Based on your needs, you can also organize the managed servers into logical server groups.

For DHCP servers, you track various server settings, server potions, the number of scopes, and the number of active leases configured on the server. From the IPAM console, you can perform the following actions:

- Edit DHCP server properties
- Edit DHCP server options
- Create DHCP scopes
- Configure predefined options and values
- Configure the user class across multiple servers simultaneously
- Create and edit new and existing user classes across multiple servers simultaneously
- Configure the vendor class across multiple servers simultaneously
- Start the management console for a selected DHCP server
- Retrieve server data from multiple servers

For DNS, you can track all configured zones, the zone type details, and the health of the zones. The DNS Zone Monitoring view displays all the forward-lookup and reverse-lookup zones on all DNS servers that IPAM is currently managing. For the forward-lookup zones, IPAM also displays all servers that are hosting the zone.

Integrating IPAM with Virtual Machine Manager (VMM)

You can integrate IPAM and Virtual Machine Manager (VMM) so that IP address settings associated with the logical networks and the virtual machine networks are stored in the IPAM server. You can then use the IPAM server to monitor the usage of VM networks that have been configured or changed in VMM. However, you still must configure the VM networks with VMM.

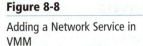

CERTIFICATION READY
Integrate IPAM with Virtual Machine Manager (VMM)
Objective 2.3

When you configure IPAM, you should use a service account that is a member of IPAM ASM Administrators or Remote Management Users. Make sure that the IPAM server and the VMM are kept in time synchrony.

ADD AN IPAM SERVER IN VMM

GET READY. To add an IPAM server to System Center 2012 R2 Virtual Machine Manager, perform the following steps:

1. Open the VMM console and then open the Fabric workspace.
2. On the *Home* tab, in the *Show* group, click Fabric Resources.
3. In the *Fabric* pane, expand *Networking*, and then click Network Service. Network services include gateways, virtual switch extensions, network managers (which include IPAM servers), and top-of-rack (TOR) switches.
4. On the *Home* tab, in the *Add* group, click Add Resources, and then click Network Service.
5. In the *Add Network Service* Wizard (see Figure 8-8), on the *Name* page, in the *Name* and *Description* text boxes, type a name and optional description, and then click Next.

Figure 8-8

Adding a Network Service in VMM

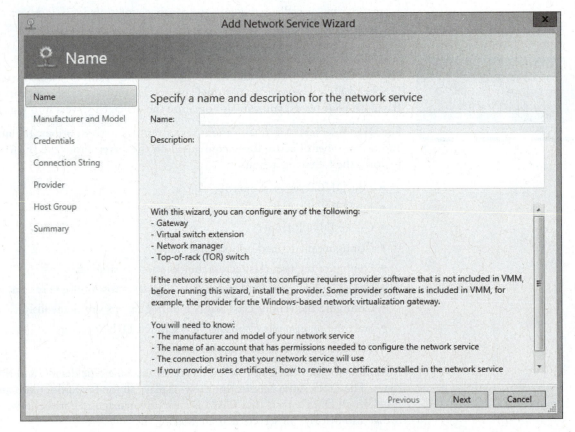

6. On the *Manufacturer and Model* page, in the *Manufacturer* list, click Microsoft. In the *Model* list, click Microsoft Windows Server IP Address Management. Then click Next.

7. On the *Credentials* page, click Browse. In the *Select a Run As Account* dialog box, specify the service account. If the account is not created, click Create Run As Account to create a new Run As account. Click Next.

8. On the *Connection String* page, in the *Connection string* text box, type the fully qualified domain name (FQDN) of the IPAM server, and then click Next.

9. On the *Provider* page, in the *Configuration provider* list, select Microsoft IP Address Management Provider, and then click Test to run basic validation tests with the provider. If tests indicate that the provider works as expected with the IPAM server, click Next.

10. On the *Host Group* page, select one or more host groups for which you want integration between the IPAM server and the VMM server. Click Next.

11. On the *Summary* page, review and confirm the settings, and then click Finish.

12. Confirm that the IPAM server is listed under *Network Services*. Whenever you want to send or receive the latest settings to and from the IPAM server, you can right-click the listing for the IPAM server and then click Refresh.

SKILL SUMMARY

IN THIS LESSON YOU LEARNED:

- IP Address Management (IPAM), a feature within Windows Server 2012 and Window Server 2012 R2, is used to plan, manage, track, and audit IP addresses.

- IPAM provisioning allows the IPAM server to configure and manage the necessary features and functions of the servers, services, and domain objects required for IPAM.

- Windows Server IPAM can manage only one Active Directory forest. You can deploy IPAM into one of three topologies: Centralized, Distributed, and Hybrid.

- Within IP address management are several sets of tasks that might require separate staff to carry them out. For this reason, IPAM relies on RBAC to provide the necessary delegate administrative features.

- After installing the IPAM feature and configuring the provisioning and discovery, you can choose to migrate all the IP address space data into the IPAM database.

- IPAM can monitor DHCP and DNS servers from any physical location in the organization, as well as simultaneously manage multiple DHCP servers or scopes that exist among multiple DHCP servers.

- You can integrate IPAM and Virtual Machine Manager (VMM) so that IP address settings associated with the logical networks and the virtual machine networks are stored in the IPAM server. You can then use the IPAM server to monitor the usage of VM networks that have been configured or changed in VMM.

■ Knowledge Assessment

Multiple Choice

1. Which of the following GPOs is not created when you provision IPAM by using the automatic Group Policy method?
   a. IPAM1_DHCP
   b. IPAM1_DNS
   c. IPAM1_NPS
   d. IPAM1_DC_NPS

2. How many DNS servers can be managed from a single IPAM server?
   a. 25
   b. 500
   c. 250
   d. 50

3. How much RAM is required to install an IPAM server?
   a. 1 GB
   b. 2 GB
   c. 4 GB
   d. 8 GB

4. How many DHCP scopes can a single IPAM server support?
   a. 150
   b. 500
   c. 2,000
   d. 6,000

5. You are an administrator for a large organization. Which IPAM topology would you use if you deploy an IPAM to every site?
   a. Centralized
   b. Distributed
   c. Hybrid
   d. Isolated

6. You have IPAM loaded on a server running Windows Server 2012. Because the IPAM database has grown larger then you expected, you decided to migrate the database to a centralized SQL server. What should you do?
   a. Upgrade the server to Windows Server 2012 R2
   b. Export the database to a backup file, and import the database in the dedicated SQL server
   c. Run the Migrate utility to move the database to the SQL server
   d. Rerun the IPAM provisioning program

7. Which IPAM security group allows access to IP address tracking information but not full administration of an IPAM server? (Choose two answers)
   a. IPAM Audit administrators
   b. IPAM ASM Administrators
   c. IPAM Users
   d. IPAM Administrators

8. What tool is used to monitor the usage of VM networks that have been configured with Virtual Machine Manager (VMM)?
   a. Ensure that IPAM is in the same subnet as VMM
   b. Add the VMM server to IPAM
   c. Add the IPAM server to VMM
   d. Add the IPAM server to the Monitor VMM group

9. IPAM servers should be installed on which Windows Server 2012 R2?
   a. domain controller
   b. non-domain joined
   c. DNS server
   d. domain-joined dedicated server

10. How long does IPAM store forensic IP data?
    a. 6 months
    b. 1 year
    c. 3 years
    d. 5 years

Best Answer

Choose the letter that corresponds to the best answer. More than one answer choice can achieve the goal. Select the BEST answer.

1. Which of the following IPAM provisioning methods should you use?
   a. Manual
   b. Group Policy
   c. Automatic Group Policy
   d. Active Directory

2. How do you share information between different IPAM servers?
   a. Use Windows PowerShell to export and import functions
   b. Create a federation link between the IPAM servers
   c. Use the same shared database
   d. Configure IPAM as the Distributed topology

3. You have 2,000 IP addresses running at one time and need to keep IP information for 1 year. How much disk space will you need?
   a. 1 GB
   b. 2.5 GB
   c. 10 GB
   d. 25 GB

4. You install a new domain controller and DNS server. However, when you open the IPAM console, you see that it is blocked. What should you do?
   a. You need to add the server to the IPAM server group
   b. You need to ensure that the new server is in the domain controller organizational unit
   c. You need to load the IPAM agent
   d. You need to change the manageability status to Managed

5. You have several switches that can assign IP addresses to devices. How should you proceed in monitoring the switches with IPAM?
   a. Create a service account that matches the account on the switch
   b. Export the data from the switch and import the data into IPAM by using Windows PowerShell
   c. Create a SQL Query that will query the switches
   d. Use a GPO to provision the switch

Matching and Identification

1. Identify which of the following are IPAM server tasks.

   _____ **a)** AuditTracking
   _____ **b)** IPAM discovery
   _____ **c)** DNSDataCollection
   _____ **d)** ServerConfiguration
   _____ **e)** GPOCollection
   _____ **f)** Audit
   _____ **g)** DHCpDataCollection
   _____ **h)** ForestCollection
   _____ **i)** ServerAvailability
   _____ **j)** EFS recovery
   _____ **k)** AddressExpiry

Build a List

1. Identify the correct order in which IPAM post configuration tasks are carried out. Not all steps will be used.

   _____ Select or add servers to manage.
   _____ Start Forest Discovery.
   _____ Provision the IPAM server.
   _____ Template.
   _____ Configure Server Discovery.
   _____ Start Server Discovery.
   _____ AD Discovery.
   _____ Connect to IPAM server.
   _____ Retrieve data from managed servers.

2. Identify in order the steps in which IP address management is carried out. Not all steps will be used.

   _____ Create IP addresses (static).
   _____ Create DHCP scopes.
   _____ Create IP address blocks.
   _____ Create DNS zones.
   _____ Collect all IP data from servers.
   _____ Create IP address ranges.

■ Business Case Scenarios

Scenario 8-1: Planning IPAM Deployment

You are an administrator for Contoso Corporation. Contoso has a forest root domain called contoso.com with subdomains in three trees: Eu.Contoso.com, US.contoso.com, and adatum.com. The CTO has asked you to recommend an IPAM deployment option but wants each domain administrator to have full control of the infrastructure in his or her own domain. What do you recommend?

Scenario 8-2: Planning Another IPAM Deployment

You are setting up an IPAM solution for your Active Directory forest. The forest contains a single domain, adatum.com, with 10 large sites and 10 small sites. The large sites have between 800 to 1,000 users; the small sites have 100-200 users. All domain controllers are now running Windows Server 2008, Windows Server 2008 R2, and Windows Server 2012. The forest and domain functional levels are at Windows Server 2008 R2. Your CTO has asked you to ensure that you can manage all DHCP and DNS servers from the IPAM server. You also need to keep the data for three years. Explain what you would do, including how you would deploy and configure IPAM.

9 LESSON

Designing a VPN Solution

70-413 EXAM OBJECTIVE

Objective 3.1 – Design a VPN solution. This objective may include but is not limited to: Design considerations including certificate deployment, firewall configuration, client/site to site, bandwidth, protocol implications, connectivity to Microsoft Azure IaaS, and VPN deployment configuration with Connection Manager Administration Kit (CMAK).

LESSON HEADING	EXAM OBJECTIVE
Planning and Designing a VPN Solution	
• Selecting a Tunneling Protocol	
• Deploying Security Certificates	Design considerations including certificate deployment
• Designing VPN Solution with Firewalls	Design considerations including firewall configuration
• Designing Client-to-Site VPN Solutions	Design considerations including client to site
• Designing Site-to-Site VPN Solutions	Design considerations including site to site
• Planning for Bandwidth and Protocol Implications	Design considerations including bandwidth and protocol implications
• Using Connection Manager Administration Kit (CMAK)	VPN deployment configuration with Connection Manager Administration Kit (CMAK)
• Planning for Microsoft Azure IaaS	Connectivity to Microsoft Azure IaaS

KEY TERMS

back-to-back firewalls

bastion host

certification authority (CA)

certificate chain

Challenge Handshake Authentication Protocol (CHAP)

Connection Manager (CM)

Connection Manager Administration Kit (CMAK)

demilitarized zone (or DMZ)

digital certificate

Extensible Authentication Protocol (EAP-MS-CHAPv2)

firewalls

Internet Key Exchange v2 (IKEv2)

Layer 2 Tunneling Protocol (L2TP) with IPsec

Microsoft CHAP version 2 (MS-CHAP v2)

multihomed firewall

Password Authentication Protocol (PAP)

perimeter network

Point to Point Tunneling Protocol (PPTP)

public key infrastructure (PKI)

Secure Socket Tunneling Protocol (SSTP)

split tunnel

virtual private networks (VPNs)

■ Planning and Designing a VPN Solution

↓ **THE BOTTOM LINE**

Virtual private networks (VPNs) link two computers or network devices through a wide-area network (WAN) such as the Internet. Because the Internet is considered insecure as a public network, the data sent between the two computers or devices is encapsulated and encrypted.

You can use VPNs in the following scenarios:

- A client connects to the Remote Access Service (RAS) server to access internal resources from off-site.
- Two remote sites connect by creating a VPN tunnel between a RAS server located at each site.
- Two different organizations create a VPN tunnel so that users from one organization can access the resources in the other organization.

VPN connections provide the following:

- **Encapsulation:** Private data is encapsulated or placed in a packet with a header containing routing information that allows the data to traverse the transit networks such as the Internet.
- **Authentication:** This proves the identity of the user or computer that tries to connection.
- **Data encryption:** Encryption ensures that confidentiality is maintained by the sender encrypting the data before it is sent, so that unauthorized people cannot read the private data. When the data is received, the intended recipient decrypts it. Of course, the encryption and decryption depend on the sender and receiver. Both must have a common or related encryption key; larger keys offer better security.
- **Data integrity:** This verifies that the data sent over the VPN connection has not been modified in transit. The verification process is usually done with a cryptographic checksum that is based on an encryption key known only to the sender and receiver. When the data is received, the same checksum calculation is performed and the result is compared to the one that was calculated before the data was sent. If the values match, the data has not been tampered with.

Authentication for VPN connections takes one of the following forms:

- **User-level authentication by using Point to Point Protocol (PPP):** User-level authentication usually means username and password. With a VPN connection, if the VPN server authenticates, the VPN client attempts the connection by using a PPP user-level authentication method and verifies that the VPN client has the appropriate authorization. If the method uses mutual authentication, the VPN client also authenticates the VPN server. By using mutual authentication, clients are ensured that they do not communicate with a rogue server masquerading as a VPN server.
- **Computer-level authentication that uses Internet Key Exchange (IKE)** to exchange either computer certificates or a pre-shared key: Microsoft recommends using computer-certificate authentication because it is a much stronger authentication method. Computer-level authentication is performed only for Layer 2 Tunneling Protocol/IP Security (L2TP/IPsec) connections.

When using VPNs, Windows 8.1 and Windows Server 2012 R2 support the following forms of authentication:

- ***Password Authentication Protocol (PAP):*** This method uses plain text (unencrypted passwords). PAP is the least secure authentication and is not recommended.

- *Challenge Handshake Authentication Protocol (CHAP):* This challenge-response authentication method uses the industry standard md5 hashing scheme to encrypt the response. CHAP was an industry standard for years and is still quite popular.
- *Microsoft CHAP version 2 (MS-CHAP v2):* This method provides two-way authentication (mutual authentication). MS-CHAP v2 provides stronger security than CHAP. Also, MS-CHAP v2 is the only authentication protocol provided by Windows Server 2012 that allows you to change an expired password during the connection process.
- *Extensible Authentication Protocol (EAP-MS-CHAPv2):* This universal authentication framework allows third-party vendors to develop custom authentication schemes, including retinal scans, voice recognition, fingerprint identifications, smart cards, Kerberos, and digital certificates. It also provides a mutual authentication method that supports password-based user or computer authentication.

TAKE NOTE If you want to use smart cards for remote connections, you need to use Extensible Authentication Protocol (EAP)

If you have multiple remote access servers, you can choose to use a RADIUS server, which provides authentication, authorization, and accounting for remote access clients.

Selecting a Tunneling Protocol

When selecting the appropriate VPN protocol to use, you must take into consideration operating systems, authentication requirements, and limitations.

The following types of tunneling protocols are used with a VPN/RAS server running on Windows Server 2012 R2:

- Point to Point Tunneling Protocol (PPTP)
- Layer 2 Tunneling Protocol (L2TP) with Internet Protocol Security (IPsec)
- Internet Key Exchange v2 (IKEv2)
- Secure Socket Tunneling Protocol (SSTP)

When selecting the appropriate VPN protocol to use, you must take into consideration the following:

- Operating systems you will be using and their ability to traverse firewalls, NAT devices, and web proxies
- Authentication requirements, for computers as well as users
- Implementations, such as site-to-site VPN or a remote access VPN

In most situations, using VPN Reconnect (also referred to as IKEv2) should provide you the best option for security and uninterrupted VPN connectivity. You can then use SSTP for your VPN solution as a fallback mechanism.

UNDERSTANDING PPTP

Point to Point Tunneling Protocol (PPTP) has widespread support with nearly all versions of Windows. It is a VPN protocol based on the legacy Point to Point (PPP) protocol used with modems. PPTP uses a Transmission Control Protocol (TCP) connection for tunnel management and a modified version of Generic Route Encapsulation (GRE) to encapsulate PPP frames for tunneled data. PPTP uses TCP port 1723 and IP protocol ID 47.

Payloads of the encapsulated PPP frames can be encrypted, compressed, or both. The PPP frame is encrypted with Microsoft Point-to-Point Encryption (MPPE) with RC4 (128-bit key) by using encryption keys that are generated from the MS-CHAPv2 or EAP-TLS authentication process. PPTP is easy to set up but has weak encryption technology.

PPTP provides confidentiality, meaning that it prevents the data from being viewed but does not provide data integrity (proof that the data was not modified in transit) or data origin authentication (proof that the data was sent by the authorized user). In other words, it does not protect the packet from being intercepted and modified.

> ➕ **MORE INFORMATION**
>
> You can encrypt data only with PPTP if you use MS-CHAPv2 and EAP-TLS as the authentication protocols. PPTP is supported natively by Windows client operating systems (Windows XP and later) and Windows server operating systems (Windows Server 2003 through Windows Server 2012 R2). It is used typically for remote access and site-to-site VPNs; works with IPv4; and uses Network Address Translation (NAT), which is supported via PPTP-enabled NAT routers. It uses PPP for user authentication and RC4 for data confidentiality.

UNDERSTANDING L2TP/IPSEC

Whereas PPTP supports authentication of only the user, *Layer 2 Tunneling Protocol (L2TP)* with IPsec requires that the computers mutually authenticate themselves to each other. The computer-to-computer authentication takes place before the user is authenticated.

L2TP is the industry standard when setting up secure tunnels. L2TP provides a support mechanism for pre-shared keys, digital certificates, or Kerberos for mutual authentication. Pre-shared keys are basically passwords and should be used only on test networks when you do not want to set up a Public Key Infrastructure (PKI). Digital certificates, which are stored in a format that cannot be modified, offer a more secure option. They are issued by certification authorities that you trust. Kerberos is the native authentication protocol for Windows Server 2003 and later and provides the easiest way to secure VPN connections in a domain-based environment.

By using IPsec, L2TP/IPsec VPN connections provide data confidentiality, data integrity, and data authentication. IPsec provides mutual authentication, anti-replay, and non-repudiation just like digital certificates. Kerberos can be used only when both computers involved in the L2TP tunnel are in the same forest. L2TP uses IPsec to encrypt the PPP packets. L2TP/IPsec provides data confidentiality and data integrity as well as proof that an authorized individual sent the message.

The L2TP message is encrypted with either Advanced Encryption Standard (AES) or Triple Data Encryption Standard (3DES) by using encryption keys that the IKE negotiation process generates. L2TP uses UDP Port 500, UDP Port 1701, UDP Port 4500, and IP Protocol ID 50.

> ➕ **MORE INFORMATION**
>
> L2TP/IPsec is supported by Windows client operating systems (Windows XP and later) and Windows server operating systems (Windows Server 2003 through Windows Server 2012 R2). It is used typically for remote access and site-to-site VPNs; works over IPv4 and IPv6; and supports NAT. It uses IPsec with 3DES (168-bit key) and uses UDP Ports (500, 1701, 5500). It uses IPsec for machine authentication followed by PPP for user authentication.

UNDERSTANDING SECURE SOCKET TUNNELING PROTOCOL (SSTP)

Secure Socket Tunneling Protocol (SSTP) improved on the PPTP and L2TP/IPsec VPN tunneling protocols. It works by sending PPP or L2TP traffic through a Secure Sockets Layer (SSL) 3.0 channel.

The SSTP protocol uses SSL and TCP port 443 to relay traffic. TCP port 443 will work in network environments in which other VPN protocols might be blocked when traversing firewalls, network address translation (NAT) devices, and web proxies. SSTP uses a 2,048-bit certificate for authentication and implements stronger encryption, which makes it the most secure VPN protocol.

+ MORE INFORMATION

SSTP is supported by Windows client operating systems (Windows Vista SP1 through Windows 8.1) and Windows server operating systems (Windows Server 2008 through Windows Server 2012 R2). It is designed for remote access VPN, works over IPv4 and IPv6 networks, and traverses NAT, firewalls and web proxies. SSTP uses a generic port that firewalls rarely block. It uses PPP for user authentication and RC4/AES for data confidentiality.

UNDERSTANDING IKEv2

Internet Key Exchange v2 (IKEv2) consists of three protocols: IPsec tunnel mode, Encapsulating Security Payload (ESP), and IKEv2 Mobility and Multihoming (MOBIKE). IPsec uses IKEv2 for key negotiations, ESP for securing the packet transmissions, and MOBIKE for switching tunnel endpoints. MOBIKE ensures that if a break occurs in connectivity, the user can continue without restarting the connection. Therefore, the VPN connection is more resilient when moving from one wireless hotspot to another or switching from wireless to a wired connection. IKEv2 is supported only on Windows 7, Windows Server 2008 R2 and newer operating systems.

VPN Reconnect (also known as IKEv2) is a feature introduced with Routing and Remote Access Services (RRAS) in Windows Server 2008 R2 and Windows 7. It is designed to provide users with consistent VPN connectivity and automatically reestablish a VPN when users temporarily lose their Internet connection.

VPN Reconnect was designed for those remote workers who are sitting in the coffee shop, waiting at the airport for their next plane to arrive, trying to submit that last expense report from their hotel room or working at any location where Internet connections are less than optimal.

It varies from other VPN protocols in that it will not drop the VPN tunnel associated with the session. Instead, VPN Reconnect keeps the connection alive for 30 minutes by default after it is dropped. This allows you to reconnect automatically without having to go through the process of reselecting your VPN connection and reauthenticating yourself.

+ MORE INFORMATION

You can find the IKEv2 setting (network outage) in the RRAS console by right-clicking the RRAS server and selecting Properties > IKEv2 tab.
VPN Reconnect is supported by Windows client operating systems (Windows 7, Windows 8, and Windows 8.1) and Windows server operating systems (Windows Server 2008 R2 through Windows Server 2012 R2). Designed for remote access VPN, it works well over IPv4 and IPv6 networks and traverses NAT. It also supports user or machine authentication via IKEv2 and uses 3DES and AES for data confidentiality.

TAKE NOTE* If you need to use a VPN connection behind a firewall that allows only https, you have to use SSTP.

Deploying Security Certificates

With some VPN technologies, such as IPsec authentication or IP-HTTPS server, you must deploy digital certificates. A ***digital certificate*** is an electronic document that contains a person's or organization's name, a serial number, expiration dates, a copy of the certificate holder's public key, and the digital signature of the certification authority (CA). The holder's public key is used for encrypting messages and creating digital signatures. The digital certificate can be used to prove the identity of a user or computer system.

CERTIFICATION READY
Design considerations including certificate deployment
Objective 3.1

The most common digital certificate is X.509 version 3. This standard specifies the format for the public key certificate, certificate revocation lists, attribute certificates, and a certificate path validation algorithm.

Digital certificates carry information about their functions and capabilities in various fields, including the following:

- **Version** identifies the version of the X.509 standard used to format the certificate.
- **Serial number** specifies a value assigned by the CA that uniquely identifies the certificate.
- **Signature algorithm** specifies the algorithm that the CA used to calculate the certificate's digital signature.
- **Issuer** specifies the name of the entity that issued the certificate.
- **Valid from** specifies the beginning of the period during which the certificate is valid.
- **Valid to** specifies the end of the period during which the certificate is valid.
- **Subject** specifies the name of the entity for which the certificate is issued.
- **Public key** specifies the type and length of the public key associated with the certificate.
- **Enhanced key usage** specifies the functions for which the certificate can be used.
- **Key usage** specifies additional functions for which the certificate can be used.
- **Thumbprint algorithm** specifies the algorithm used to generate a digest of the certificate data.
- **Thumbprint** contains a digest of the certificate data, used for digital signing.
- **Friendly name** specifies a common name for the entity listed in the Subject field.
- **Certificate policies** describes the policy that the CA followed to originally authenticate the subject.
- **CRL distribution points** specifies the location of the certificate revocation list (CRL), a document maintained and published by a CA that lists revoked certificates.

Figure 9-1 shows the certificate details and chain.

Figure 9-1

Viewing a digital certificate

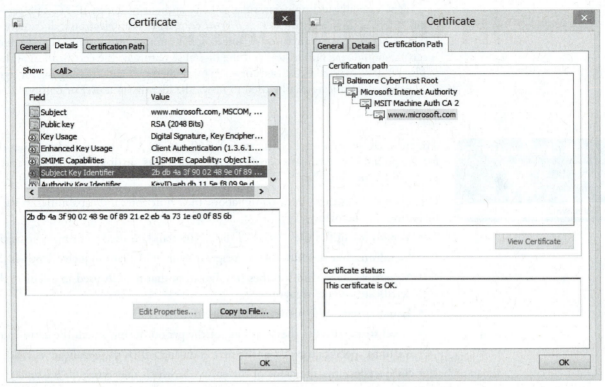

The **public key infrastructure (PKI)** system consists of hardware, software, policies, and procedures and creates, manages, distributes, uses, stores, and revokes digital certificates. PKI consists of certification authorities (CAs) and registration authorities that verify and authenticate the validity of each entity involved in an electronic transaction through the use of public key cryptography. Within the PKI, the **certification authority (CA)** binds a public key with respective user identities and issues digital certificates containing the public key. The CA assigns the digital certificate so that a recipient can verify that the certificate is real.

Within the PKI, the certification authority binds a public key with respective user identities and issues digital certificates containing the public key. For this system to work, the CA must be trusted. Typically within an organization, you can install a CA on a Windows server—specifically, a domain controller—thus making it trusted within your organization.

If you need to trust a CA outside of your organization, you have to use a trusted third-party CA such as Verisign or Entrust. It is the established commercial CA's responsibility to issue certificates that are trustworthy in most web browsers. Only so many root CA certificates are assigned to commercial third-party organizations. Therefore, when you acquire a digital certificate from a third-party organization, you might need to use a certificate chain to obtain the root CA certificate. You also might need to install an intermittent digital certificate that links the assigned digital certificate to a trusted root CA certificate. The **certificate chain**, also known as the *certification path*, is a list of certificates used to authenticate an entity. It begins with the certificate of the entity and ends with the root CA certificate.

By using digital certificates with remote access, you can enhance security by using longer keys and by using a unique key for each user and/or system. Certificate deployment involves several planning stages, including planning the computer name and adding a static IP. Other steps include configuration of the certification authority itself.

To use certificates for IPsec, you need the following:

- You should set up an enterprise CA such as Microsoft Certificate Authority.
- You should use Group Policy–based autoenrollment to ensure that all domain members receive the certificate automatically from an enterprise CA.
- The certificate needs to have client authentication Extended Key Usage (EKU).
- The trust chains for the client and server certificates should connect to the same root certificate.

A valid certificate for SSTP must meet the following requirements:

- The certificate is configured with the Server Authentication purpose or the All Purposes purpose in the Enhanced Key Usage (EKU) extensions.
- The certificate's subject name is the IP address of the external interface on the remote access server, or a regular expression containing a DNS name that resolves to that IP address. If the remote access server is located behind a NAT device, the IP address or DNS name must be that of the external interface of the NAT device.

Designing VPN Solution with Firewalls

Security devices such as firewalls are the main defense for a company's networks, whether they are LANs, WANs, intranets, or extranets. *Firewalls* are used to protect a network from malicious attack and unwanted intrusion. They are the most commonly used type of security device in an organization's perimeter. Firewalls are an essential component to keep the network infrastructure secure, particular when the network is connected to a public network such as the Internet. In addition to being places on the network perimeter, it can also be found on client computers and servers. To keep a network safe, protocols are blocked by default. Therefore, until the protocol is unblocked, the protocol cannot communicate through the firewall.

CERTIFICATION READY
Design considerations
including firewall
configuration
Objective 3.1

Many of today's firewalls have two types of firewall technologies built into them: SPI and NAT. However, you should be aware of several other types of firewall methodologies:

- Packet filtering inspects each packet that passes through the firewall and accepts or rejects it based on a set of rules. Packet filtering comes in two varieties: stateless packet inspection and stateful packet inspection (SPI). A stateless packet filter, also known as *pure packet filtering*, does not retain memory of packets that have passed through the firewall. As a result, a stateless packet filter can be vulnerable to IP spoofing attacks. However, a firewall running stateful packet inspection usually is not vulnerable to this because it keeps track of the state of network connections by examining the header in each packet. It should be able to distinguish between legitimate and illegitimate packets. This function operates at the network layer of the Open Systems Interconnection (OSI) model.
- NAT filtering, also known as *NAT endpoint filtering*, filters traffic according to ports (TCP or UDP). This can be done in three ways: by using basic endpoint connections, by matching incoming traffic to the corresponding outbound IP address connection, or by matching incoming traffic to the corresponding IP address and port.
- Application-level gateway (ALG) supports address and port translation and checks whether the type of application traffic is allowed. For example, your company might allow FTP traffic through the firewall, but it might decide to disable Telnet traffic. The ALG checks each type of packet coming in and discards those that are Telnet packets. This adds a layer of security; however, it is resource intensive.
- Circuit-level gateway works at the session layer of the OSI model, where a TCP or UDP connection is established. As soon as the connection is made, packets can flow between

the hosts without further checking. Circuit-level gateways hide information about the private network but do not filter individual packets.

You can use many possible firewall configurations. However, the three most commonly used firewall configurations are as follows:

- **Bastion host:** A single-point firewall that connects the internal network and the Internet. You typically find the Bastion host on small networks to protect against attacks on resources on the internal network.

- **Multihomed firewall:** A single firewall that contains multiple network connections. One adapter is connected to the internal private network; a second adapter is connected to the Internet. Other adapters can be used to create a perimeter network. The multihomed firewall uses different filters for traffic, depending on the network for which the traffic is destined.

- **Back-to-back firewalls:** Two firewalls used to create a perimeter network (see Figure 9-2). The perimeter network connects the private internal network and the external Internet. Larger networks often use this configuration. Back-to-back firewalls use different filters for traffic, depending on the network for which the traffic is destined.

Figure 9-2

Using two firewalls to create a perimeter network

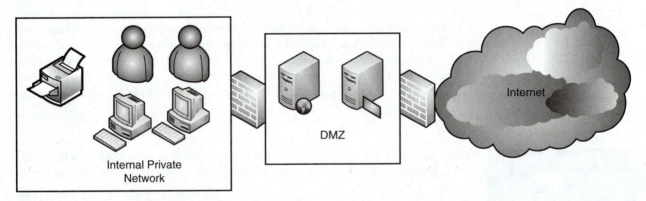

A **perimeter network** (also known as a **demilitarized zone** or *DMZ*) is a small network set up separately from a company's private local area network (LAN) and the Internet. It is called a perimeter network because it is usually on the edge of a LAN. A perimeter network allows users outside a company LAN to access specific services located on it. However, when the perimeter network is set up properly, those users are blocked from gaining access to the company LAN. Users on the LAN quite often connect to the perimeter network also but without having to worry about outside attackers gaining access to their private LAN. The perimeter network might house a switch with servers connected to it that offer web, email, and other services.

Services or network applications typically found on a perimeter network include the following:

- **Email:** Often you would place the front-end server on the perimeter network and the back-end server in the internal network. Email protocols include Post Office Protocol 3 (POP3), Internet Message Access Protocol 4 (IMAP4), Simple Mail Transfer Protocol (SMTP), Microsoft Outlook Web App (HTTPS), Outlook Anywhere (HTTPS), and Microsoft Exchange ActiveSync (HTTPS).

- **External Web servers:** You would place external-facing web servers so that they could be accessed by Internet users. Web server protocols include HTTP and HTTPS.

- **Directory services:** Placing a domain controller on the perimeter network is not advisable. However, if you need directory services, you can deploy a server running Lightweight Directory Access Protocol (LDAP).
- **Web conferencing:** This allows for online meetings (such as with Microsoft Lync Server) with internal users, customers, vendors, consultants, and partners, including sharing desktops, audio, and video. Web conference protocols include HTTPS, Session Initiation Protocol (SIP), Persistent Shared Object Model (PSOM), Real-time Transport Protocol (RTP), and Real-Time Control Protocol (RTCP).
- **Instant messaging:** This standard technology is used for instant messaging on computers and mobile devices. The most common protocol is SIP.

Today, firewalls are based on the protocol and IP version. Therefore, you might need to consider opening one or more of the following ports:

- For PPTP:
  - Used by PPTP control path: TCP Port 1723
  - Used by PPTP data path (GRE): IP Protocol Type 47

- For L2TP:
  - Used by IKEv1 IPsec control path: UDP Port 500
  - Used by IKEv1 IPsec control path: UDP Port 4500
  - Used by L2TP control/data path: UDP Port 1701
  - Used by ESP: IP Protocol Type 50
  - Used by Authentication Header (AH): IP Protocol Type 51

- For SSTP:
  - Used by SSTP control and data path: TCP Port 443

- For IKEv2:
  - Used by IKEv2 IPsec control path: UDP Port 500
  - Used by IKEv2 IPsec control path: UDP Port 4500
  - Used by L2TP control/data path: UDP Port 1701
  - Used by data path (ESP): IP Protocol Type 50

- For Teredo: UDP port 3544
- For 6to4: IP Protocol Type 41

➕ MORE INFORMATION

For more information, search for *Service overview and network port requirements for Windows* at *Microsoft.com* for discussions on the required network ports, protocols, and services used by Microsoft client and server operating systems, server-based programs, and the subcomponents in the Microsoft Windows Server system.

Host-based firewall solutions use software to provide a firewall solution on the client or server. Implementing host-based firewalls improves security by imposing another security layer. When using host-based firewalls, consider the following:

- To protect against unknown connections, block all inbound connections by default. Then create inbound rules to allow access to local applications when necessary.
- To increase security, prevent outbound connections by default. Use outbound rules to prevent communication with specific software. Then create outbound rules to allow necessary applications to communicate with other devices or sites. (Identifying all the

allowed applications requires significant administrative work,) Then create rules that allow them to communicate on the network.

- If you are using Windows Firewall with Advanced Security, consider using connection security rules to authenticate and encrypt network communications.

Designing Client-to-Site VPN Solutions

A remote access client allows a remote access VPN connection to a VPN server that connects the remote access client to a private network. In some situations, clients connect to partner or vendor private networks by using a VPN client. In other situations, you need your own users as well as consultants or partners to access your private network over the Internet.

If you have only one or two users who connect to a vendor or partner private network, using a client-to-site VPN solution is best. However, if you have multiple users who frequently connect from the organization's private network to a vendor or partner private network, you should consider using a site-to-site VPN solution.

A more common scenario is that users from your organization need to access the organization's private network when traveling, visiting customers, or working from home. In this case, you need an external IP address to connect to an internal remote access server, usually protected with NAT and firewalls.

Most users have difficulty creating a VPN connection in Windows 8.1. Therefore, you need to create the VPN connection on their laptops or use the Connection Manager Administration Kit (CMAK) to create an executable, which can then be deployed to the users' mobile computers.

To control who can access a VPN server, you can require users to have an Active Directory user account, in which they need to type in a username or password. If you chose L2TP with IPsec, you can require that a digital certificate be installed on the computer to restrict that only designated computers can connect through a VPN. Depending on your solution, you can use the Active Directory Users and Computers User console user's Dial-In tab to allow or deny access option (as shown in Figure 9-3), or use an NPS Network Policy to control access by a group or other attribute. Lastly, you could use a custom solution that uses EAP, which allows you to add an add-on component for authentication such as a biometric component or a smart card.

Figure 9-3

Controlling who can dial in through a VPN server

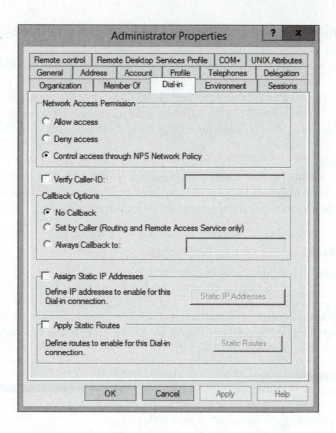

By default, when you use the default configuration to connect to a VPN, all web browsing and network traffic goes through the default gateway on the remote network unless you are communicating with local home computers. Having this option enabled helps protect the corporate network because all traffic also goes through firewalls and proxy servers, which prevent a network from being infected or compromised.

If you want to route Internet browsing through your home Internet connection rather than go through the corporate network, you can disable the *Use Default Gateway on Remote Network* option in the VPN Connection Advanced TCP/IP Settings. Disabling this option is called using a ***split tunnel***.

Designing Site-to-Site VPN Solutions

Many organizations use a VPN solution to connect sites or data centers to each other or to provide redundant connections between sites. Site-to-site VPN solutions also can be used to connect organizations, as one organization is acquired by another organization or the two organizations have a partnership.

CERTIFICATION READY
Design considerations
including site to site
Objective 3.1

Although organizations can use private connections between sites, they also can use a site-to-site VPN connection over a public network such as the Internet. Doing so can provide the following:

- A lower-cost solution when compared to private connections
- A redundant or backup connection for a private connection
- Multiple entry points, which can be determined manually by the client, a global load balancer, or an automatic probe based on proximity

Of course by using a VPN tunnel, you can encrypt the data that travels over the public network.

Planning for Bandwidth and Protocol Implications

Any time you use a VPN connection (client or site-to-site), you always have to look at the bandwidth needed to travel over the VPN connections and the protocols or applications that will use the VPN connections. If you have a connection that cannot handle the load, the applications will not run efficiently. If you have a fast connection but do not utilize the bandwidth, you might be paying more then you need to for the connection.

CERTIFICATION READY
Design considerations including bandwidth and protocol implications
Objective 3.1

Besides looking at the network applications, you also need to look at client needs. Do your clients need to get updates, or do you need to deploy applications over the VPN connection? Some factors that you should consider include the following:

- What number of users are connected all at once?
- What tasks is each user performing?
- From where are the users connecting?
- What level of security is required?

After you collect this information, you need to select a service provider that meets your needs for a Service Level Agreement (SLA), including uptime and recovery requirements for outages. You also should always consider cost.

A remote access server can be a dedicated hardware server or device or a software-based solution such as Windows Server 2012 R2 Routing and Remote Access Services (RRAS). If you choose to use a Windows Server 2012 R2 solution, you can use other roles, features, or applications running on Windows Server 2012 R2.

Besides ensuring that the remote server can handle the load, you also must look at how the clients will be connected. For example, if you are providing VPN access, clients must have the necessary hardware to connect to their Internet provider. This can require a wireless connection, Ethernet, or other connection type.

No matter which solution you select, you need to determine where to place the VPN server. Many firewall solutions can be configured as VPN servers, but some of these solutions can require complex firewall rules. You can place the VPN server in front of an organization firewall; although doing so is simple to implement, the VPN server is not protected. In many situations, you can use two firewalls to create a perimeter network, and then place the VPN server in the perimeter network.

When you use site-to-site VPN solutions to connect sites within an organization, you should consider defining an Active Directory site. You should also consider placing an Active Directory domain controller and/or DNS server at each site. If the site is considered unsecure, you should consider using a read-only domain controller. The site server can be used to increase performance when doing DNS and Active Directory queries, as well as deploy applications and store data locally.

Using Connection Manager Administration Kit (CMAK)

Connection Manager (CM) is a client network connection tool that helps administrators simplify the management of remote connections. CM uses profiles that consist of settings that allow connections from the local computer to a remote network.

CERTIFICATION READY
VPN deployment configurations using Connection Manager Administration Kit (CMAK)
Objective 3.1

You use the *Connection Manager Administration Kit (CMAK)* to create and customize the profiles for Connection Manager and to distribute them to users. The profile, when completed, contains all the settings necessary for users to connect, including the IP address of the VPN server.

Connection Manager supports different features in a profile, depending on which operating system is running on the client computer. You must create a connection profile on a computer that uses the same architecture (32-bit or 64-bit) as the clients on which you will install the profile. The CMAK Wizard will ask you to specify the operating system on which the Connection Manager profile will be run:

- Windows Vista or later
- Windows Server 2003, Windows XP, or Windows 2000

After you use the CMAK Wizard to create the executable file, you can then deploy the executable file using a Group Policy Object (GPO) or System Center 2012 R2 Configuration Manager.

 INSTALL CMAK ON WINDOWS SERVER 2012 R2

GET READY. To install CMAK on Windows Server 2012 R2, perform the following steps:

1. In *Server Manager*, click Manage > Add Roles and Features.
2. On the *Before you begin* page, click Next.
3. On the *Select installation type* page, click Role-based or feature-based installation.
4. On the *Select destination server* page, select a server from the server pool and then click Next.
5. On the *Select server roles* page, click Next.
6. On the *Select features* page, click RAS Connection Manager Administration Kit (CMAK).
7. Confirm Installation selections and then click Install.
8. Confirm installation completes and then click Close.
9. Select Tools > Connection Manager Administration Kit.

 SET UP A SIMPLE VPN-ONLY PROFILE BY USING CMAK

GET READY. To set up a simple VPN-only profile using CMAK, perform the following steps:

TAKE NOTE*

This activity is designed to expose the features and options available when creating a Connection Manager profile using CMAK from Windows Server 2012 R2. As you walk through each step, be sure to read the explanation behind it to gain more insight into how CMAK could be used in your specific network environment.

1. Start *Connection Manager* by clicking Server Manager > Tools > Connection Manager Administration Kit.
2. After reading the CMAK Wizard *Welcome* message, click Next.
3. On the *Select the Target Operating System* page, click Windows Vista or above and then click Next.
4. On the *Create or Modify a Connection Manager profile* page, click New Profile and then click Next.
5. On the *Specify the Server Name and the File Name* page, in the *Service name* and *File name* text boxes, type MyVPN and then click Next.
6. On the *Specify a Realm Name* page, click Do not add a realm name to the user name and then click Next.

7. On the *Merge Information from Other Profiles* page, when prompted to merge information with another profile, click Next. If you had an additional profile, you could merge phone book information, access numbers and VPN host address information.

8. On the *Add Support for VPN Connections* page, click Phone book from this profile. Then in the *Always use the same VPN server* text box, type RemoteServer.contoso. com and then click Next.

9. On the *Create or Modify a VPN Entry* page, click Edit to view the settings that can be configured for this VPN profile.

10. Click OK to close the *Edit VPN Entry* dialog box.

11. Back on the *Create or Modify a VPN entry* page, click Next.

12. On the *Add a Custom Phone Book* page, clear the Automatically download phone book updates option and then click Next.

13. On the *Configure Dial-up Networking Entries* page, click Next.

14. On the *Specify Routing Table Updates* page, ensure that the Do not change the routing tables option is selected and then click Next.

15. On the *Configure Proxy Settings for Internet Explorer* page, ensure that Do not configure proxy setting is selected and then click Next.

16. On the *Add Custom Actions* page, click Next to *not* add any custom actions.

17. On the *Display a Custom Logon Bitmap* page, click Next to display a default graphic or select one of your own.

18. On the *Display a Custom Phone Book Bitmap* page, click Next to display a default graphic for a custom phone book.

19. On the *Display Custom Icons* page, click Next to use a default icon for the Connection Manager user interface.

20. On the *Include a Custom Help File* page, click Next to use the default help file.

21. On the *Display Custom Support Information* page, add any text you want to appear in the logon dialog box and then click Next. (For example, type Contact Support at 800-123-1234.)

22. On the *Display a Custom License Agreement* page, when prompted to display a custom license agreement, click Next.

23. On the *Install Additional Files with the Connection Manager profile* page, specify any additional files that the Connection Manager profile will require and then click Next.

24. On the *Build the Connection Manager Profile and Its Installation Program* page, select the Advanced customization option and then click Next.

25. On the *Make Advanced Customizations* page, set the following values and then click Apply:

    Filename: MyVPN.cms

    Section name: Connection Manager

    Key name: Dialup

    Value: 0

26. Note the location where the profile will be saved to. By default, this will be
    `c:\Program Files\CMAK\Profiles\Windows Vista and above\MyVPN\ MyVPN.exe`

27. Click Finish.

Planning for Microsoft Azure IaaS

> You can create a virtualized AD DS forest to organize and manage the leased resources, or you can create a virtual network in the Microsoft Azure cloud and connect it to your private network with a site-to-site link via a VPN device. You can also create a Windows Server 2012 R2 virtual machine in the cloud and configure it as a replica domain controller for an existing domain.

CERTIFICATION READY
Connectivity to Microsoft
Azure IaaS
Objective 3.1

Configuring a point-to-site connection to Microsoft Azure provides a secure connection from your computer or VPN device. To create a point-to-site connection, you have to configure the following:

- Virtual network and a dynamic routing gateway
- Certificates
- VPN client configuration

 CREATE A VIRTUAL DYNAMIC ROUTING GATEWAY

GET READY. To create a virtual network and dynamic routing gateway, perform the following steps:

1. Log on to the Microsoft Azure Management Portal.
2. In the lower left-hand corner of the screen, click New.
3. In the navigation pane, click Network Services, and then click Virtual Network. Click Custom Create to begin the configuration wizard.
4. On the *Virtual Network Details* page, enter the following information, and then click the next arrow on the lower right.
   - *Name:* Name your virtual network
   - *Affinity Group:* The affinity group is directly related to the physical location where you want your resources (VMs) to reside. If the affinity group does not exist, click Create a new affinity group.
   - *Region:* If you create a new affinity group, you need to associate it with an Azure region.
   - *Affinity Group Name:* Name your affinity group.
5. On the *DNS Servers and VPN Connectivity* page, in the *DNS server name* and *IP address* text boxes, enter the DNS server name and IP address. If you want to use the Azure default name resolution service, leave this section blank.
6. Select the Configure Point-To-Site VPN check box. Click the next arrow on the lower right.
7. On the *Point-To-Site Connectivity* page, specify the IP address range by from which your VPN clients will receive an IP address when connected. Enter the following information, and then click the next arrow.
   - *Address Space:* Include the Starting IP and CIDR (Address Count).
   - *Add address space:* Add this only if required for your network design.
8. On the *Virtual Network Address Spaces* page, specify the address range that you want to use for your virtual network. These addresses are assigned to VMs and other role instances that you deploy to this virtual network. Enter the following information:
   - *Address Space:* Add the internal IP address range that you want to use for this virtual network, including Starting IP and Count.
   - *Add subnet:* Additional subnets are not required, but you might want to create a separate subnet for VMs that have static DIPS.

- *Add gateway subnet:* The gateway subnet is required for a point-to-site VPN.

9. Click the Create checkmark to begin creating your virtual network.

CREATE A DYNAMIC ROUTING GATEWAY

GET READY. To create a dynamic routing gateway, perform the following steps:

1. Log in to the Microsoft Azure Management Portal.

2. In the *Management Portal,* on the *Networks* page, click the virtual network that you just created, and then navigate to the *Dashboard* page.

3. Click Create Gateway. When a message appears asking *Do you want to create a gateway for virtual network 'yournetwork'?,* click Yes to begin creating the gateway. Creating the gateway can take around 15 minutes.

Certificates are used to authenticate VPN clients for point-to-site VPNs. To generate certificates, you would use the following basic steps:

1. Generate a self-signed root certificate. Only self-signed root certificates are supported at this time.

2. Upload the root certificate file to the Management Portal.

3. Generate a client certificate.

4. Export and install the client certificate.

You can also create a site-to-site VPN using the Management Portal. To perform a site-to-site VPN, you need an externally facing IPv4 IP address for your VPN device.

SKILL SUMMARY

IN THIS LESSON YOU LEARNED:

- Virtual private networks (VPNs) link two computers or network devices through a wide-area network (WAN) such as the Internet. Because the Internet is public and is considered insecure, the data sent between the two computers or devices is encapsulated and encrypted.

- VPN connections provide encapsulation, authentication, data encryption, and data integrity.

- Public key infrastructure (PKI) is a system consisting of hardware, software, policies, and procedures that create, manage, distribute, use, store, and revoke digital certificates.

- Within the PKI, the certification authority (CA) binds a public key with respective user identities and issues digital certificates containing the public key. The CA assigns the digital certificate so that a recipient can verify that the certificate is real.

- Firewalls are essential to keeping the network infrastructure secure, particular when the network is connected to a public network such as the Internet. Besides being placed on the network perimeter, firewalls can also be found on client computers and servers.

- A perimeter network (also known as a demilitarized zone or DMZ) is a small network set up separately from a company's private local area network (LAN) and the Internet.

- To keep a network safe, protocols are blocked by default. Until the protocol is unblocked, it cannot communicate through the firewall.

- You use the Connection Manager Administration Kit (CMAK) to create and customize the profiles for Connection Manager and to distribute them to users.

■ Knowledge Assessment

Multiple Choice

1. Which of the following is the strongest authentication protocol supported by Windows Server 2012 R2?
   a. Microsoft Encrypted Authentication version 2
   b. Challenge Handshake Authentication Protocol (CHAP)
   c. Password Authentication Protocol (PAP)
   d. Extensible Authentication Protocol (EAP)

2. Which of the following methods enables the server to support authentication with smart cards or other types of digital certificates?
   a. Extensible Authentication Protocol-Transport Level Security (EAP-TLS)
   b. Protected EAP (PEAP)&&&
   c. Microsoft CHAP version 2 (MS-CHAP v2)
   d. Encrypted Authentication

3. Which VPN technology allows for VPN Reconnect?
   a. PPTP
   b. L2TP with IPsec
   c. SSTP
   d. IKEv2

4. Which of the following contains a digest of the certificate data used for digital signing?
   a. certificate policies
   b. friendly name
   c. thumbprint algorithm
   d. thumbprint

5. You are an administrator for a large organization. You have a root CA, an intermediate CA, and a subordinate CA. Which of the following terms best describes a structure that shows a certificate was assigned by the subordinate CA, which is under the intermediate, which is under the root?
   a. certificate topology
   b. certificate chain
   c. certificate structure
   d. certificate line

6. You want to create a VPN solution that can be accessed by using SSL. Which VPN solution should you use?
   a. PPTP
   b. L2TP with IPsec
   c. SSTP
   d. IKEv2

7. Which of the following ports would you need to use for L2TP with IPsec? (Choose all that apply.)
   a. 80
   b. 443
   c. 500
   d. 1701
   e. 1723
   f. 4500

8. You want to place the VPN server within your perimeter network. How do you connect the Internet address to the perimeter address of the remote access server?
   a. Use NAT
   b. Use SSTP
   c. Use CMAK
   d. Use IKE

9. You have a cable connection at home that runs at 50 Mb/s. However, when you connect to your company network, you can download files from the Internet at only 1 Mb/s. How can you use your Internet connection to download the files?
   a. Re-create the VPN connection and define the speed of your network connection.
   b. Turn off packet acknowledgements.
   c. Re-create the VPN connection and use PPTP.
   d. Use split tunneling.

10. Which port is used by SSTP?
    a. 80
    b. 443
    c. 500
    d. 1701
    e. 4500

Best Answer

Choose the letter that corresponds to the best answer. More than one answer choice can achieve the goal. Select the BEST answer.

1. You have 500 users that use a VPN connection to your organization network. Which of the following is the best way to deploy the VPN connection to the 500 users?
   a. Use the Connection Manager Administration Kit (CMAK) to create an executable and deploy the executable with a Group Policy Object (GPO).
   b. Configure GPO settings that define the VPN settings.
   c. Create a script that will create the VPN connections and deploy the script with a GPO.
   d. Use Remote Desktop to connect to each computer and create the VPN connections.

2. Your clients have computers running Windows 7 and Windows 8. Many of these users visit customer locations, hotels, and remote sites. Unfortunately, these places often have firewalls that limit connectivity to the Internet. Which VPN solution would you recommend?
   a. PPTP
   b. L2TP with IPsec
   c. SSTP
   d. IKEv2

3. Which of the following is the best way to connect Microsoft Azure sites and services to your organization network?
   a. Create a virtualized AD DS forest.
   b. Create a CMAK executable file that connects to the Microsoft Azure site and deploy the executable to your clients.
   c. Create a virtual network in the Microsoft Azure cloud and connect to a private network using a site-to-site VPN link.
   d. Create a service account that has administrative access to your organization network on the Microsoft Azure management site.
   e. Install a Microsoft Azure tunnel that will connect to the Microsoft Azure cloud.

4. You have a mix of 32-bit and 64-bit computers running Windows 7. Windows 8, and Windows 8.1. How many executable files are necessary for creating with CMAK?
   a. 1
   b. 2
   c. 3
   d. 4

5. Which VPN technology would you use to provide a secure connection that uses computer certificates and supports Windows XP, Windows 7, Windows 8, and Windows 8.1?
   a. PPTP
   b. L2TP with IPsec
   c. SSTP
   d. IKEv2

Matching and Identification

1. Identify the appropriate VPN protocol (PPTP, L2TP, IKEv2, or SSTP).
   _____ **a)** Uses MPPE
   _____ **b)** Uses SSL
   _____ **d)** Has the weakest encryption technology
   _____ **e)** Used with IPsec to encrypt the payload
   _____ **f)** Features include VPN Reconnect

2. Identify the protocol port used.
   _____ AH
   _____ L2TP control/data path
   _____ PPTP
   _____ SSTP
   _____ IPsec control path
   _____ ESP

Build a List

1. Order the following steps from first to last as required to configure and enable VPN remote access:
   A. Choose Server Manager > Tools > Routing and Remote Access.
   B. On the *VPN Connection* page, select the external network card that is connected to the Internet.
   C. Right-click the server and select Configure and Enable Routing and Remote Access.
   D. On the *IP Address Assignment* page, select from a specified range of addresses.
   E. On the *Remote Access* page, select VPN.
   F. Fill in the Start IP address and End IP address.

■ Business Case Scenarios

Scenario 9-1: Designing a Remote Connection

You are an administrator for the Contoso Corporation. You want to develop a solution that will allow your users to work from home and to allow remote connections to stay connected when traveling on a train or car. The corporate office contains several subnets, which are used by the client users. You also have server and perimeter subnets used for the corporate web servers. What solution would you use that allows a secure connection of authorized computers? Also, how would you install and configure the remote access server?

Scenario 9-2: Managing VPN Connections

You are an administrator for the Contoso Corporation. Many of your users have laptops that they take when they meet with customers or work from home. The laptops are running Windows 7 and Windows 8. Some laptops are 32-bit machines; others are 64-bit. You have two remote access servers, each located at two different sites. If users cannot connect to one remote access server, they can connect to the other remote access server. Your remote servers support L2TP with IPsec. For IPsec, you assign digital certificates to users with the domain. Because consultants and vendors are not part of the domain, you use a passkey for IPsec instead of digital certificates. How can you simplify the configuring of a VPN connection on each mobile computer?

Designing a DirectAccess Solution

70-413 EXAM OBJECTIVE

Objective 3.2 – Design a DirectAcess Solution. This objective can include but is not limited to: Design considerations including deployment topology, migration from Forefront UAG, One-Time Password (OTP), and use of certificates issued by enterprise Certificate Authority (CA).

LESSON HEADING	EXAM OBJECTIVE
Designing a DirectAccess Solution	
• Understanding the DirectAccess Connection Process	
• Understanding DirectAccess Enhancements in Windows Server 2012 R2	
• Understanding DirectAccess Requirements	
• Designing a DirectAccess Deployment Topology	Design a deployment topology
• Migrating from Forefront UAG	Migrate from Forefront UAG
• Designing a DirectAccess Server Infrastructure and Deployment	Use certificates issued by enterprise Certificate Authority (CA)
• Using the Getting Started Wizard to Set Up a Remote Access Server	Use a One-Time Password (OTP)

KEY TERMS

Behind an Edge Device

DirectAccess

Edge

Forefront Unified Access Gateway (UAG)

Name Resolution Policy Table (NRPT)

network location server (NLS)

One-Time Password (OTP)

WMI filter

■ Designing a DirectAccess Solution

THE BOTTOM LINE

DirectAccess is a feature introduced with Windows 7 and Windows Server 2008 R2 that provides seamless intranet connectivity to DirectAccess client computers when they are connected to the Internet. Unlike traditional virtual private network (VPN) connections, DirectAccess connections are automatically established, and they provide always-on seamless connectivity.

DirectAccess overcomes VPN limitations by automatically establishing a bi-directional connection from client computers to the organization's network by using IPsec and IPv6. For organizations that have not deployed IPv6, you can use transition mechanisms such as 6to4 and Teredo IPv6 transition technologies for connectivity across the IPv4 Internet and the Intra-Site Automatic Tunnel Addressing Protocol (ISATAP) IPv6 transition technology, so that DirectAccess clients can access IPv6-capable resources across your IPv4-only intranet. As a result, remote client computers are automatically connected to the organization's network so that they can be easily managed and kept up to date with critical updates and configuration changes.

> **+ MORE INFORMATION**
>
> For more information about planning and designing a DirectAccess solution, search for and download the *Infrastructure Planning and Design IPD) guide for DirectAccess* from the Microsoft TechNet site.

Understanding the DirectAccess Connection Process

A DirectAccess connection to a target intranet resource is initiated when the DirectAccess client connects to the DirectAccess server through IPv6. IPsec is then negotiated between the client and server. Finally, the connection is established between the DirectAccess client and the target resource.

DirectAccess works by establishing two IPsec tunnels from the client to the DirectAccess server. The IPv6 packets, protected via IPsec, are encapsulated inside IPv4 packets to make the transition across the Internet.

This general process can be broken into the following specific steps:

1. The DirectAccess client computer running Windows 8, Windows 8.1, Windows 7 Enterprise, or Windows 7 Ultimate detects that it is connected to a network.

2. The DirectAccess client computer determines whether it is connected to the intranet. If the client is connected to the intranet, it does not use DirectAccess.

3. The DirectAccess client connects to the DirectAccess server by using IPv6 and IPsec.

4. If the client is not using IPv6, it will try to use 6to4 or Teredo tunneling to send IPv4-encapsulated IPv6 traffic.

5. If the client cannot reach the DirectAccess server by using 6to4 or Teredo tunneling, it tries to connect by using IP over Secure Hypertext Transfer Protocol (IP-HTTPS). IP-HTTPS uses a Secure Sockets Layer (SSL) connection to encapsulate IPv6 traffic.

6. As part of establishing the IPsec session for the tunnel to reach the intranet DNS server and domain controller, the DirectAccess client and server authenticate each other via computer certificates.

7. If Network Access Protection (NAP) is enabled and configured for health validation, Network Policy Server (NPS) determines whether the client is compliant with system health requirements. If it is compliant, the client receives a health certificate, which is submitted to the DirectAccess server for authentication.

8. When the user logs on, the DirectAccess client establishes a second IPsec tunnel to access the resources of the intranet. The DirectAccess client and server authenticate each other by using a combination of computer and user credentials.

9. The DirectAccess server forwards traffic between the DirectAccess client and the intranet resources to which the user has been granted access.

As shown in Figure 10-1, the first tunnel is an infrastructure tunnel used to communicate with the DNS server and domain controller to obtain Group Policy and to request

Figure 10-1

Direct Access Tunnels

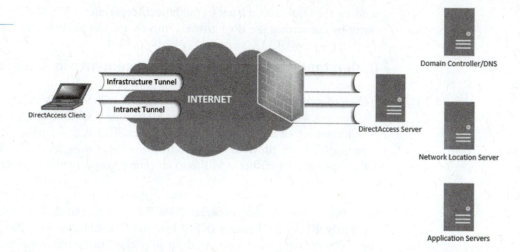

authentication. The second tunnel is used to authenticate the user and to provide access to resources inside the network.

The *Name Resolution Policy Table (NRPT)* is used to determine the behavior of the DNS clients when issuing queries and processing so that internal resources are not exposed to the public via the Internet and to separate traffic that is not DirectAccess Internet traffic from DirectAccess Internet traffic. By using the NRPT, the DirectAccess clients can use the intranet DNS servers for internal resources and Internet DNS for name resolution of other resources. You can manage the NRPT via Group Policies—specifically, Computer Configuration\Policies\Windows Settings\Name Resolution Policy.

DirectAccess clients use the *network location server (NLS)* to determine their locations. The NLS is an internal web server that can be installed directly on the remote access server or on another server in the network. If the client detects that it is on the corporate network, the DirectAccess client components are not enabled. If it cannot connect to the NLS, it assumes that it is not on the corporate network and enables DirectAccess. The secret to how this works is a URL written into the client's registry by way of Group Policy created during the deployment of the remote access server. The client uses the URL and DNS to attempt to locate the NLS.

To configure a network location server, install Internet Information Services (IIS) on a Windows server. Then for a website, bind a name such as nsl.contoso.com and associate a NLS DNS name to the IP address. Finally, to ensure that this server is highly available, use technology such as Network Load Balancing (NLB) and make sure that you have redundant hardware.

To ensure that DirectAccess clients can correctly detect when they are on the Internet, you can configure the IIS server to deny connections from Internet-based clients with the IP and Domain Restrictions Web server (IIS) role service. Alternatively, you can ensure that the Certificate Revocation List (CRL) distribution point location in the certificate being used for network location cannot be accessed from the Internet.

The DirectAccess clients use IPv6 to connect to resources on the intranet or to other DirectAccess clients. If you have servers providing resources running on the intranet that do not support IPv6, have disabled IPv6, or use applications that do not work natively with IPv6, you need to provide access to these devices for the DirectAccess clients. This is accomplished through Windows Server 2012 R2 by implementing a protocol translation and name resolution gateway that supports NAT64 and DNS64.

NAT64 receives packets from the DirectAccess client and converts them into IPv4 before sending it to the resource on the intranet. It converts IPv4 packets to IPv6 packets before sending the information back to the DirectAccess client. DNS64 handles the client's DNS query by converting the IPv4 answers into an associated IPv6 mapping on NAT64.

Understanding DirectAccess Enhancements in Windows Server 2012 R2

DirectAccess is designed for use by domain-based clients: Windows 7 (Enterprise and Ultimate), Windows 8 and Windows 8.1 (Enterprise), Windows Server 2008 R2, Windows Server 2012, and Windows Server 2012 R2). Routing and Remote Access Services (RRAS) provides traditional VPN access for legacy clients, non-domain clients, third-party VPN clients, and site-to-site connections between servers.

In earlier releases (Windows Server 2008 R2), you had to deploy DirectAccess and RRAS separately. RRAS implements IKEv2 Internet Protocol security (IPsec) and configures incoming and outgoing packet filters to drop all packets using transition technologies. Conversely, DirectAccess uses IPv6 transition technologies to establish client connections and IPsec denial of service (DoS) protection to drop all IPv4 traffic and IPv6 traffic not protected with IPsec. So in Windows Server 2008 R2, DirectAccess and RRAS on the same system would conflict with each other.

In Windows Server 2012 and Windows Server 2012 R2, Microsoft resolved these issues by modifying the IKEv2 policies to allow IPv6 transition technology traffic and modifying the DoS protection to allow VPN traffic. Windows Server 2012 R2 also removes the requirement to use public key infrastructure (PKI), which was a major obstacle to deploying DirectAccess in Windows Server 2008 R2 and Windows 7. Windows Server 2012 R2 does this by configuring the clients to send authentication requests to a Kerberos proxy service that runs on the DirectAccess server. The Kerberos proxy service sends the requests to a domain controller for authentication.

DirectAccess does not use a traditional VPN connection. Whereas a traditional VPN required users to manually initiate and disconnect a VPN connection when they wanted to connect to their corporate office, DirectAccess is designed to establish connectivity whenever an Internet connection is available. This occurs whether or not users are logged on. From an administrator perspective, this allows you to manage and monitor the remote computer to apply patches and check for compliance enforcement.

Additional remote access features in Windows Server 2012 and Windows Server 2012 R2 include the following:

- Force tunneling (sends all traffic through the DirectAccess connection)
- NAP compliance
- Support for locating the nearest remote access server from DirectAccess clients distributed across different geographical locations.
- Deployment of DirectAccess for only remote management

You can configure the DirectAccess server with two network adapters at the network edge or behind an edge device, or with a single network adapter running behind a firewall or Network Address Translation (NAT) device. By using a single adapter, you remove the requirement of needing dedicated public IPv4 addresses for DirectAccess deployments. Clients use IP-HTTPS to connect with the DirectAccess server.

Understanding DirectAccess Requirements

Compared to other forms of remote access, DirectAccess is more complex, which has more required components. Of course, with the complexity, you get much more functionality than you did with other remote access technologies.

In addition to installing DirectAccess on the VPN server, you need to make sure that you prepare the network, the server, and the clients. A little planning goes a long way when implementing DirectAccess.

UNDERSTANDING DIRECTACCESS SERVER REQUIREMENTS

The DirectAccess server requires the following:

- It must be part of an Active Directory domain.
- It must be running Windows Server 2008 R2, Windows Server 2012, or Windows Server 2012 R2.
- If it is connected to the intranet and published over Microsoft Forefront Threat Management Gateway (TMG) or Microsoft Forefront Unified Access Gateway (UAG) 2010, a single network adapter is required. If the DirectAccess server is connected as an edge server, it will need two network adapters: one for the Internet and one for the intranet.
- Implementation of DirectAccess in Windows Server 2012 R2 does not require two consecutive static, public IPv4 addresses as was required with Windows Server 2008 R2. However, to achieve two-factor authentication with a smart card or operational data provider deployment, a DirectAccess server still needs two public IP addresses.
- You can deploy Windows Server 2012 R2 DirectAccess behind NAT support, which avoids the need for additional public addresses. However, only IP over HTTPS (IP-HTTPS) is deployed, allowing a secure IP tunnel to be established via a secure HTTP connection.
- With Windows Server 2012 or Windows Server 2012 R2, you can use NLB (up to eight nodes) to achieve high availability and scalability for both DirectAccessand RRAS.

You also need the following in your network infrastructure:

- An Active Directory domain that runs a minimum of Windows Server 2008 R2 domain functional level.
- Group policy for central administration and deployment of DirectAccess client settings.
- One domain controller running Windows Server 2008 SP2, Windows Server 2008 R2, Windows Server 2012, or Windows Server 2012 R2.
- PKI to issue computer certificates for authentication and health certificates when NAP is deployed, and computer certificates for authentication. The SSL certificates installed on the DirectAccess server must have a CRL distribution point that can be reached from the Internet. Finally, the certificate subject file must contain the Fully Qualified Domain Name (FQDN) that can be resolved to a public IPv4 address assigned to the DirectAccess server by using DNS on the Internet.

- DNS running on at least Windows Server 2008 R2, Windows Server 2008 with the Q958194 hotfix, Windows Server 2008 SP2 or later, or a third-party DNS server that supports DNS message exchanges over ISATAP.

- IPsec policies. DirectAccess uses IPsec policies that are configured and administered with Windows Firewall with Advanced Security.

- Internet Control Message Protocol Version 6 (ICMPv6) Echo Request traffic. You must create separate inbound and outbound rules that allow ICMPv6 Echo Request messages. DirectAccess clients that use Teredo for IPv6 connectivity to the intranet use the ICMPv6 message when establishing communication.

- IPv6 and transition technologies such as ISATAP, Teredo, and 6to4 available for use on the DirectAccess server. For each DNS server running Windows Server 2008 or higher, you need to remove the ISATAP name from the global query block list.

- Optionally, NAP to provide compliance checking and enforce security policy for DirectAccess clients over the Internet. Unlike Windows Server 2008 R2, Windows Server 2012 and Windows Server 2012 R2 DirectAccess provides the capability to configure NAP health checks directly from the setup user interface.

UNDERSTANDING DIRECTACCESS CLIENT REQUIREMENTS

To use DirectAccess, clients must be Windows 7 Enterprise Edition, Windows 7 Ultimate Edition, Windows 8, Windows Server 2008 R2, or Windows Server 2012. You cannot deploy DirectAccess for Windows Vista or earlier or Windows Server 2008 or earlier. Finally, the client must be joined to an Active Directory domain.

Designing a DirectAccess Deployment Topology

DirectAccess supports multiple topologies based on where the DirectAccess server is placed, how it is connected to the network, and/or how it is connected to the Internet. During deployment of the DirectAccess server, you will be asked to choose which topology you are using, as shown in Figure 10-2.

Figure 10-2

Selecting a DirectAccess
topology

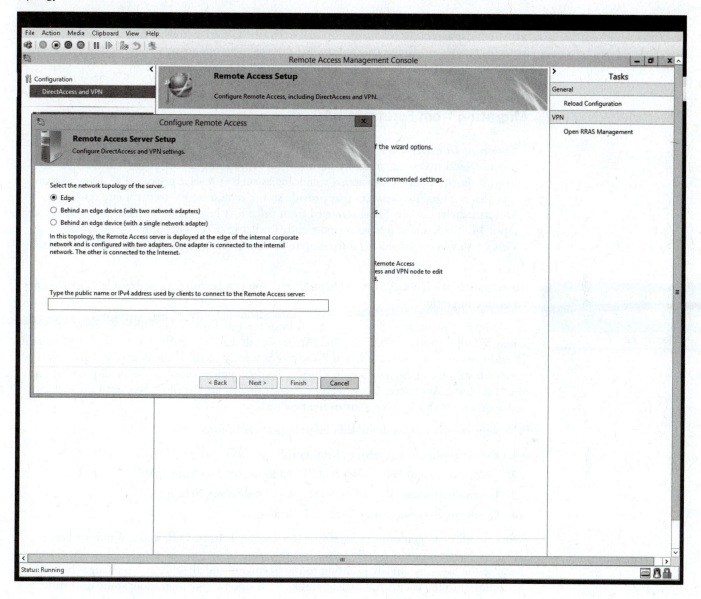

CERTIFICATION READY
Design a deployment
topology
Objective 3.2

DirectAccess has three topologies available:

- Edge
- Behind an Edge Device (with two network adapters)
- Behind an Edge Device (with a single network adapter)

When you select **_Edge_**, the DirectAccess server is the edge device with two network adapters: one connected directly to the Internet and one connected to the internal network. The Internet connection will be assigned one or more public IPv4 addresses.

When you select **_Behind an Edge Device (with two network adapters)_**, you are deploying the DirectAccess server behind a dedicated edge firewall or device, such as Forefront Threat Management Gateway 2010, Unified Access Gateway 2010, or a third-party hardware firewall device. One network adapter will be connected to the perimeter network while the other adapter is connected to the internal network. To use this option, the external network adapter is network access translated with an external IPv4 public address.

When you select **Behind an Edge Device (with a single network adapter)**, you have one network adapter connected to the internal network. The edge firewall passes traffic to the DirectAccess server. To use this option, the external network adapter is network access translated with an external IPv4 public address.

Migrating from Forefront UAG

Forefront Unified Access Gateway (UAG) is a Microsoft software solution that provides secure remote access to corporate networks for remote employees, consultants, and partners. It incorporates remote access technologies such as reverse proxy, VPN, DirectAccess, and Remote Desktop Services that provide secure remote access to corporate resources. Unfortunately, UAG is being removed from price lists July 1, 2014, free support ends April 14, 2015, and extended support ends April 14, 2020. Therefore, if you are using UAG, you will eventually need to migrate Forefront UAG DirectAccess to DirectAccess.

CERTIFICATION READY
Migration from Forefront
UAG
Objective 3.2

To migrate UAG DirectAccess to DirectAccess, you can perform a side-by-side migration or an offline migration.

A side-by side migration allows you to run both the Forefront UAG DirectAccess server with a new Windows Server 2012 R2 DirectAccess simultaneously. Both servers will have different IP addresses and host names. When Windows Server 2012 R2 DirectAccess is deployed, new users will start using the new server. During the deployment process, users still pointing to the Forefront UAG DirectAccess server can continue to use the old server until the client's configuration is changed to point to the new server.

The steps involved in a side-by-side migration are as follows:

1. Export configuration settings from Forefront UAG.
2. Record all Group Policy Objects (GPOs) in use for Forefront UAG.
3. Install the Remote Access role on the Windows Server 2012 server.
4. Configure the remote access server, including GPOs.

With an offline migration, the Forefront UAG server is turned off, and a Windows Server 2012 R2 Server is brought online that uses the same IP address, host name, and certificates. Because the users are already pointing to the hostname and IP address, no changes have to be deployed to the clients. Of course, unlike with side-by-side migration, some downtime is involved while you switch servers.

After you take the existing server offline, you use the following overall steps to complete the offline migration:

1. Shut down the UAG DirectAccess server.
2. Install the Remote Access role on Windows Server 2012 R2.
3. Configure IP addresses to match the old Forefront UAG server.
4. Install a certificate for IP-HTTPS connections.
5. Prepare GPOs for the remote access server.
6. Configure DirectAccess.

Designing a DirectAccess Server Infrastructure and Deployment

Compared to traditional remote access deployments, DirectAccess is more complex and requires planning before deploying. Therefore, you need to treat DirectAccess implementation as a project.

When deploying the Remote Access role on the server, you need to make several decisions. These decisions include the topology to use; whether to support Windows 7, Windows 8, and Windows 8.1 clients; and whether to implement a VPN for clients that do not support DirectAccess. You also need to identify your IP addressing requirements; review your firewall settings, certificate requirements, and DNS server information; and must address Network Location Service information issues. When designing a DirectAccess server infrastructure, you must consider the following:

- Microsoft's Remote Access role supports one-adapter and two-adapter topologies. When a single adapter is used, the server should be installed behind a device such as a firewall or router. If you set up a remote access server with two adapters, one adapter is connected to the internal network and the other to either a perimeter network or directly to the Internet. With two adapters, you need to ensure that they are detected appropriately during the setup process. To make this process easier, name one of them *internal* and the other *external* before starting the installation of the Remote Access role.

- If you are supporting Windows 7, Windows 8, and Windows 8.1 remote clients, you need to perform additional advanced configuration steps to enable them to connect via DirectAccess.

- If you are supporting remote clients that do not support DirectAccess or are unmanaged, you need to provide VPN access. The Getting Started Wizard configures VPN IP addresses to be distributed by a Dynamic Host Configuration Protocol (DHCP) server and the VPN clients to be authenticated via Active Directory.

- You need to review firewall settings if you are placing the RAS on an IPv4 subnet to ensure that traffic is allowed to pass through: 6to4 traffic requires IP port 41 for both inbound and outbound, and IP-HTTPS requires Transmission Control Protocol (TCP) destination port 443 and TCP source port 443 outbound. If RAS is deployed with a single adapter and you install the network location service functionality, you need to exempt TCP port 62000.

- During the setup of the Remote Access role, you need to specify an IP address or FQDN. This information, called the ConnectTo address, is matched with the self-signed certificate used in IP-HTTPS connections and must be available via the public DNS. It is also used by the remote clients to connect to the server.

- If you configured your remote access server to use SSTP VPN, the wizard integrates the certificate used by SSTP for IP-HTTPS. If SSTP VPN is not configured, the wizard checks to see whether one has been configured for IP-HTTPS. If it cannot find one, the wizard provisions a self-signed certificate and automatically enables Kerberos for authentication.

- DirectAccess clients use DNS to locate the network location server (NLS). If they can reach the NLS, the clients assume they are on the local network, will not use DirectAccess, and will rely on the DNS server configured on their local adapter for name resolution. If the client cannot locate the NLS, it assumes it is on the Internet and will use DirectAccess. This means it will consult its Name Resolution Policy Table (NRPT) to select a DNS server to use when resolving names. The NLS is basically a website. Using the Getting Started Wizard to set up RAS will result in the NLS being set up on the server itself and a self-signed certificate being generated.

Designing a DirectAccess deployment involves four high-level steps:

1. Define the scope of the DirectAccess Project.
2. Determine network requirements.
3. Design a DirectAccess server infrastructure.
4. Design web servers and certificate infrastructure.

DETERMINING THE SCOPE OF THE DIRECTACCESS PROJECT

As with any IT project, you must always determine the scope of the DirectAccess project. At this point you should start imaging what will be the final goal. While doing this, you need to answer the following questions:

- Who will use DirectAccess? Which parts of the organization will participate? Which geographical areas will be included?
- What kind of load do you expect? Determine the number of users, the access peak time, and the maximum number of concurrent connections.
- What internal resources and applications will users need to access?
- What type of access do users need for internal resources and applications? Do users need a specified access, or do different groups need different levels of access?
- What operating system is running on the domain controllers and DNS servers?
- What operating system do the internal resources use that the DirectAccess clients will access?
- Do you need to manage the remote computers that use DirectAccess?
- Do you need to monitor or audit the web traffic of specific users or machines?

The next major step is to determine the network requirements, including what is needed to make your network DirectAccess-ready.

DETERMINING NETWORK REQUIREMENTS

By determining the network requirements, you determine how DirectAccess clients will connect to intranet resources. A DirectAccess client can connect to the DirectAccess server using one of the following methods:

- Directly, over the IPv6 Internet
- By using 6to4
- By using Teredo
- By using IP-HTTPS

If users have IPv6 connectivity, the clients are ready to connect to the DirectAccess infrastructure. However, if users are still using IPv4, you need to implement one or more of the IPv6 transitional technologies. As a result, you need to configure the DirectAccess server to perform the following functions:

- Teredo server and relay
- 6to4 relay
- IP-HTTPS server
- ISATAP router
- Native IPv6 router
- IPsec tunnel endpoint and gateway

When you place the DirectAccess servers, they must be joined to an AD DS domain and must be running Windows Server 2008 R2, Windows Server 2012, or Windows Server 2012 R2. Although DirectAccess servers must be members of an AD DS domain, they cannot be domain controllers.

DESIGNING A DIRECTACCESS DEPLOYMENT

When planning your client deployment, you must decide whether you want to make DirectAccess available to mobile computers only or to any computer. The Getting Started Wizard, which you can run after installing the Remote Server role, will by default configure DirectAccess for mobile computers that are members of the Domain Computers security group only. This can be done by creating a Windows Management Instrumentation (WMI) filter for the DirectAccess Client Settings GPO.

A *WMI filter* is used to control the application of the GPO. The WMI filter is evaluated on the target computer during the processing of the Group Policy. The GPO will be applied only if the WMI filter evaluates as true. In this case, even though other computers are members of the Domain Computers security group, they will not receive the DirectAccess policy because they are not considered to be mobile computers.

Windows Server 2012 R2 has simplified DirectAccess deployment by providing an Express Setup for small and medium deployments. Express Setup includes the following characteristics:

- Although PKI deployment is option, you can use self-signed certificates without the need for CRLs, which uses HTTPS-based Kerberos proxy. The HTTPS-based Kerberos proxy accepts client authentication requests and sends them to domain controllers on behalf of the client.
- It uses single IPsec tunnel configuration.
- It uses single factor authentication only.

Unfortunately, Express Setup works only for client computers running Windows 8 and Windows 8.1.

DESIGNING AN ENTERPRISE CERTIFICATE DEPLOYMENT

The DirectAccess server requires the following certificates:

- The IP-HTTPS listener on the DirectAccess server requires a website certificate. Also, the DirectAccess client must be able to contact the server hosting the CRL for the certificate. If the CRL check fails, the IP-HTTPS connection fails. Using a third-party commercial certificate for the IP-HTTPS listener is recommended.
- The DirectAccess server requires a computer server to establish the IPsec connections with the DirectAccess clients.

You need a public CA certificate for clients to have the best compatibility with HTTPS-based Remote Access. You should also follow these guidelines:

- The certificate's Subject field should specify the IPv4 address or the FQDN of the remote access server.
- The common name of the certificate should match the name of the site or use a wildcard certificate.
- The Enhanced Key Usage (EKU) field should use the Server Authentication object identifier.
- The certificate must be imported into the personal store, which can be automatically deployed with Group Policy.

The SSL certificate for the DirectAccess server should have a CRL distribution point that can be reached from the Internet. You do not have to use an external certificate.

Each DirectAccess client must have a computer certificate to establish the IPsec connection to the DirectAccess server and IP-HTTPS connection. The computer certificates are usually assigned by using the Microsoft Certificate Authority via Group Policy–based computer certificate autoenrollment. On the *Remote Access Server Setup* page, you specify the root or intermediate CA that will issue the certificates, as shown in Figure 10-3.

Figure 10-3

Specifying the source of computer certificates

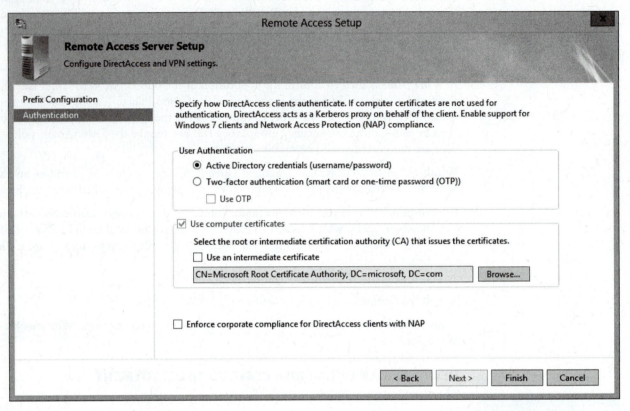

Because DirectAccess tends to be used for larger organizations, you will have many clients that will connect to the DirectAccess infrastructure. Because users will need digital certificates, you should implement a PKI that uses autoenrollment. Autoenrollment ensures that all domain members obtain a computer certificate from an enterprise CA.

DirectAccess clients use the NLS to determine their locations. You can configure the DirectAccess server as the NLS, or you can designate another web server. Because DirectAccess depends on connectivity, you should make the web server highly available. If the client computer can connect with HTTPS to the URL specified, the client computer assumes it is on the intranet and disables DirectAccess components. If the client cannot reach the NLS, it assumes it is on the Internet. The URL for the NLS is distributed via a GPO.

To implement certificates on the NLS, the certificate for the network location server's website must have the following properties:

- In the Subject field, either an IP address of the intranet interface of the NLS or the FQDN of the network location URL
- For the Enhanced Key Usage field, the Server Authentication object identifier (OID)

To configure a network location server, install IIS on a Windows server. Then for a website, bind a name such as *nsl.contoso.com* and associate a NLS DNS name to the IP address. Finally, to make sure that this server is highly available, use technology such as NLB and ensure that you have redundant hardware.

You need an internal CRL as part of your PKI so that clients can determine whether the NLS is using a valid certificate. You must publish the intranet CRL by using a domain name that is not included in the namespace, which is defined by DirectAccess as the internal network. The CRL can be hosted on multiple servers. It also can be hosted by various methods, including on an intranet web, file, or LDAP server, and it can be published to multiple locations.

To ensure that DirectAccess clients can correctly detect when they are on the Internet, you can configure IIS server to deny connections from Internet-based clients with the IP and Domain Restrictions Web server (IIS) role service. Alternatively, you can ensure that the CRL distribution point location in the certificate being used for network location cannot be accessed from the Internet. The certificate used with NLS should use the IP address or FQDN of the network location URL for the Subject field in the certificate, and the EKU field uses the Server Authentication object identifier.

USING ONE-TIME PASSWORD (OTP) WITH DIRECTACCESS

CERTIFICATION READY
Use a One-Time
Password (OTP)
Objective 3.2

A ***One-Time Password (OTP)*** is valid for only one logon session or transaction. By using an OTP, you avoid the vulnerability of static passwords to replay attacks in which a user guesses until he or she figures out the password. By using the *Authentication* page shown in Figure 10-3, you can enable two-factor authentication such as a smart card or OTP. If you want to use OTP, you must select the *Use OTP* option.

The general steps to configure DirectAccess with OTP authentication are as follows:

1. Implement a single server remote access deployment.
2. Configure the Remote Authentication Dial-In User Service (RADIUS) server.
3. Configure the remote access server for OTP.
4. Verify DirectAccess with OTP.

When you configure the RADIUS server, you need to do the following:

1. Configure the necessary license, software, and/or hardware distribution token to be used with DirectAccess.
2. Create a new user account called DAProbeUser and assign the password DAProbePass.
3. Because the RADIUS server must have user accounts that correspond to the users in Active Directory that will use DirectAccess with OTP, you must synchronize the server with Active Directory.
4. Configure the RADIUS authentication agent.

CHOOSING AN ACCESS METHOD

By default, DirectAccess requires IPsec authentication and encryption between the DirectAccess client and server. If you require additional security, you can also extend the authentication to selected application servers that are in a security group containing the servers (see Figure 10-4). You can also limit server access in the specified security groups and infrastructure servers, or you can specify that end-to-end traffic is authenticated but not encrypted.

Figure 10-4

Choosing an access method

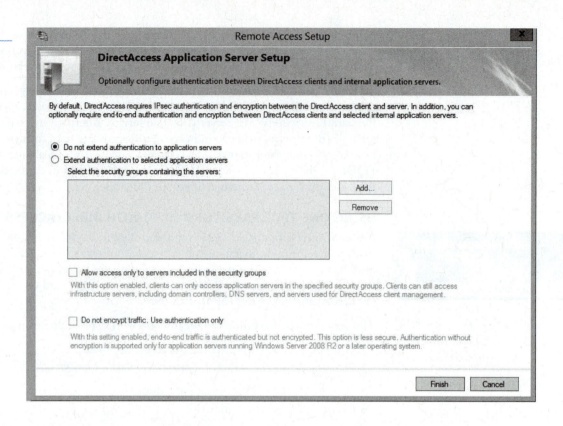

Using the Getting Started Wizard to Set Up a Remote Access Server

When setting up the remote access server, you can use the Getting Started Wizard to complete the post-installation setup.

The wizard backs up existing GPOs and then creates two GPOs that are used by the server and the clients:

- DAServerSettings is filtered to apply only to the DirectAccess server computer account.
- DAClientSettings is filtered to apply to mobile computers in the Domain Computers global security group. If you change this default behavior, you must create a new security group for your DirectAccess clients.

These policies are linked to the root of your Active Directory domain automatically if the install is run under the domain administrator's account.

The Getting Started Wizard also performs the following tasks:

- It configures the Kerberos proxy to eliminate the need to set up a PKI. You can also configure DirectAccess to use certificates issued by a PKI certification authority.
- It enables NAT64 and DNS64, which are used for protocol translation in IPv4-only network environments.
- It generates, self-signs, and verifies an IP-HTTPS certificate on the DirectAccess server.
- The wizard identifies the domain's infrastructure servers.
- It registers DNS entries used to check client connectivity.
- It creates client policies
- It applies GPOs to remote access servers.

INSTALL RRAS/DIRECTACCESS

GET READY. To install RRAS and DirectAccess, perform the following steps.

TAKE NOTE * This exercise requires a Windows Server 2012 R2 member server, a domain controller, and a DNS server present on the network.

1. Log on with domain administrative credentials to a Windows Server 2012 R2 member server.
2. In *Server Manager*, click Manage > Add Roles and Features.
3. On the *Before You Begin* page, click Next.
4. On the *Installation Type* page, select Role-based or featured-based installation and then click Next.
5. On the *Server Selection* page, in the *Server pool* section, select the member server and then click Next.
6. On the *Server Roles* page, select the Remote Access role and then click Add Features. Click Next.
7. Back on the *Server Roles* page, click Next.
8. On the *Remote Access* page, read the information regarding Remote Access and then click Next.
9. Click DirectAccess and VPN (RAS) and then click Next.
10. Read the Web Server role and then click Next.
11. Click Next.
12. After confirming your installation selections, click Install.

 DEPLOY RRAS/DIRECTACCESS WITH THE GETTING STARTED WIZARD

GET READY. To deploy RRAS and DirectAccess with the Getting Started Wizard, perform the following steps.

TAKE NOTE * You can also start this wizard from within the Remote Access Management Console by clicking the Run the Getting Started Wizard link.

1. After installation completes, click Open the Getting Started Wizard.
2. Select Deploy both DirectAccess and VPN (recommended).
3. For the *Network Topology*, click Edge and then type the public name (FQDN) or IPv4 address used by clients to connect to the Remote Access Server. Click Next.

   In this topology, the remote access server is deployed at the edge of the internal corporate network and is configured with two network adapters: one connected to the internal network, the other to the Internet.
4. Click Finish to apply the settings.
5. Select More details to monitor the tasks performed by the wizard.
6. When the process is completed, click Close.
7. Click Finish.
8. In the *Remote Access Management Console* (see Figure 10-5), click Operations Status to confirm that the server is working properly.

Figure 10-5

Operations Status showing
several problems

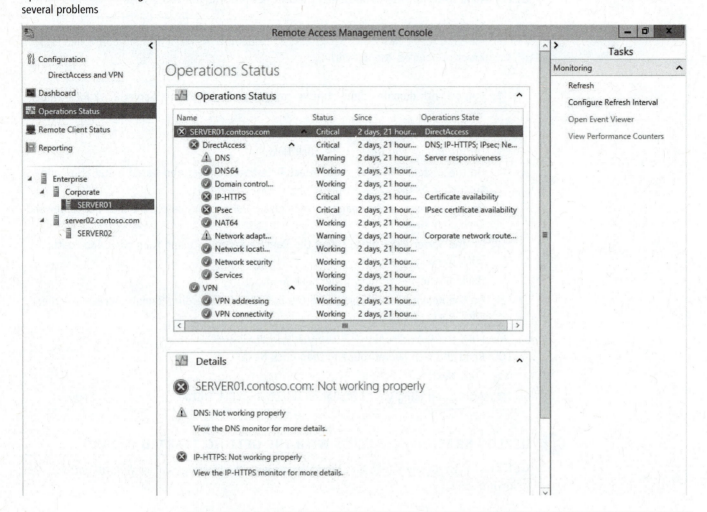

 VERIFY DIRECTACCESS DEPLOYMENT ON A MOBILE COMPUTER

GET READY. To verify that DirectAccess was deployed to a Windows 8 mobile computer,
perform the following steps while connected to the domain:

1. Connect the DirectAccess mobile client to your corporate network and obtain the
   DAClientSettings GPO.
2. Open Windows PowerShell with administrative privileges.
3. Type gpresult/r and press Enter.
4. In the *COMPUTER SETTINGS* section of the output, confirm that the DirectAccess Client
   Settings GPO has been applied.
5. Exit Windows PowerShell.
6. In the notification area, click the Network connection icon.
7. Click the Workplace Connection option. Notice that you are connected to the network
   locally.
8. Disconnect the computer and reconnect it to an external network. You should be able
   to access the DirectAccess server.

SKILL SUMMARY

IN THIS LESSON YOU LEARNED:

- DirectAccess is a feature introduced with Windows 7 and Windows Server 2008 R2 that provides seamless intranet connectivity to DirectAccess client computers when they are connected to the Internet.

- Unlike the traditional virtual private network (VPN) connections, DirectAccess connections are automatically established and provide always-on seamless connectivity.

- If you select the Edge topology when deploying DirectAccess, the DirectAccess server is the edge device that has two network adapters: one connected directly to the Internet and one connected to the internal network. The Internet connection will be assigned one or more public IPv4 addresses.

- Forefront Unified Access Gateway (UAG) is a Microsoft software solution that provides secure remote access to corporate networks for remote employees, consultants, and partners. It incorporates remote access technologies such as reverse proxy, virtual private network (VPN), DirectAccess, and Remote Desktop Services that provide secure remote access to corporate resources.

- To migrate UAG DirectAccess to DirectAccess, you can perform a side-by-side migration or an offline migration.

- Compared to traditional remote access deployments, DirectAccess is more complex and requires planning before deploying. Therefore, you need to treat the implementation of DirectAccess as a project. When deploying the Remote Access role on the server, you must make several decisions.

- To run DirectAccess, you must deploy an SSL certificate to the DirectAccess server, which has a certificate revocation list (CRL) distribution point that can be reached from the Internet.

■ Knowledge Assessment

Multiple Choice

1. What is the main advantage of using DirectAccess over VPN connections?
   a. Users do not have to connect manually to the remote network.
   b. DirectAccess uses IPv4 rather than IPv6.
   c. DirectAccess supports more operating systems than VPNs.
   d. DirectAccess connections are unidirectional.

2. Which of the following is not a prerequisite for a DirectAccess server?
   a. Membership in an AD DS domain
   b. Two network interface adapters
   c. Two consecutive, public IPv4 addresses
   d. A NAT connection to the Internet

3. Which of the following steps in the DirectAccess connection establishment process occurs first?
   a. The client and the DirectAccess server authenticate each other by using their computer certificates.
   b. The client attempts to connect to a designated network detection server on the intranet.
   c. The client establishes a connection to the domain controller and performs a standard AD DS user authentication.
   d. The client submits a health certificate to a Network Policy Server (NPS) on the host network.

4. Which technology is used to automatically connect to the company network whenever organization users have Internet access?
   a. BranchCache
   b. VPN Autoconnect
   c. DirectAccess
   d. Protected Extensible Authentication Protocol (PEAP)

5. Which protocol does DirectAccess rely on?
   a. Challenge Handshake Authentication Protocol (CHAP)
   b. BranchCache
   c. Protected Extensible Authentication Protocol (PEAP)
   d. IPv6

6. Which VPN protocol does DirectAccess use?
   a. Point to Point Tunneling Protocol (PPTP)
   b. IPsec
   c. MS-CHAPv2
   d. Secure Socket Tunneling Protocol (SSTP)

7. Which type of server is the network location server (NLS)?
   a. Domain Name System (DNS) server
   b. Dynamic Host Configuration Protocol (DHCP) server
   c. Web server
   d. Active Directory domain controller

8. If the client cannot reach the DirectAccess server by using 6to4 or Teredo tunneling, which protocol does the client tries to connect with?
   a. IP-HTTPS
   b. HTTP
   c. DHCP
   d. HTTPS

9. The Run the Remote Access Setup Wizard breaks the installation into four separate installations that give you a great deal of control over settings and configurations. Identify the correct description for the installation of infrastructure servers.
   a. Configure the network connections based on one or two network cards and specify which adapters are internal and which adapters are external. You can also specify the use of smart cards and specify the certification authority (CA) to use for DirectAccess to provide secure communications.
   b. Specify which clients within your organization can use DirectAccess. You specify the computer groups that you want to include and whether you want to include Windows 7 clients.
   c. Configure how the clients access the core infrastructure services such as Active Directory domain controllers and DNS servers. You also specify an internal web server that can provide location services for infrastructure components to your DirectAccess clients.
   d. Configure your end-to-end authentication and security for the DirectAccess components. The installation of infrastructure servers also provides secure connections to individual servers.

10. You want to use DirectAccess for your remote users. According to your security policy, all traffic destined for the Internet must be routed through the corporate network. What do you need to do?
    a. Enable split tunneling
    b. Enable force tunneling
    c. Disable Teredo
    d. Enable Teredo

Best Answer

Choose the letter that corresponds to the best answer. More than one answer choice can achieve the goal. Select the BEST answer.

1. Which of the following statements reflects the best reason for deploying DirectAccess connectivity for remote users?
   a. You can easily manage and keep the remote users' computers up to date.
   b. The remote users' computers connect automatically.
   c. Remote computers can connect via encrypted links over the Internet.
   d. Remote users can access corporate resources.

2. Which Remote Access Management interface gives you the most control?
   a. Remote Access Management console
   b. Getting Started Wizard
   c. Remote Access Setup Wizard
   d. Command-line Dnscmd.exe command

3. You are now using UAG DirectAccess. You cannot afford to have DirectAccess down. Therefore, how can you migrate to Windows Server 2012 R2 DirectAccess?
   a. Perform a side-by-side migration.
   b. Perform an offline migration.
   c. Perform a safe migration.
   d. Perform backup migration.

4. Which step should be used to enable one-time password (OTP) for DirectAccess?
   a. Remote clients
   b. Remote access server
   c. Infrastructure servers
   d. Application servers

5. You are going to connect the Windows Server 2012 R2 server directly to the Internet. Which topology should you configure?
   a. Edge
   b. Edge (with two network adapters)
   c. Behind an Edge Device (with two network adapters)
   d. Behind an Edge Device (with a single network adapter)

Matching and Identification

1. Match the term with the appropriate description
   _____   a) WMI filter
   _____   b) DAServerSettings
   _____   c) network location server (NLS)
   _____   d) DAClientSettings
   _____   e) WMI filter

   1. This GPO is filtered to apply only to the DirectAccess server computer account.
   2. This controls the application of the GPO by evaluating on the target computer during processing of the Group Policy.
   3. GPO is filtered to apply to mobile computers in the Domain Computers global security group.
   4. DirectAccess clients use this to determine their locations.
   5. This is used to control the application of the GPO.

Build a List

1. In order of first to last, specify the steps to migrate from Forefront UAG to Windows Server 2012 R2 DirectAccess offline migration. Not all steps will be used.

   _____ Record all Group Policy Objects (GPOs) in use for Forefront UAG.

   _____ Configure the remote access server, including GPOs.

   _____ Configure IP addresses to match the old Forefront UAG server.

   _____ Export configuration settings from Forefront UAG.

   _____ Install the Remote Access role on the Windows Server 2012 server.

   _____ Install a certificate for IP-HTTPS connections.

2. In order of first to last, specify the steps to deploy DirectAccess using the Getting Started Wizard.

   _____ Identify the infrastructure servers in the domain.

   _____ Enable NAT64 and DNS64 for protocol translation in IPv4-only network environments.

   _____ Register DNS entries used to check client connectivity.

   _____ Create client policies.

   _____ Apply GPOs to remote access servers.

   _____ Have an IP-HTTPS generated, self-signed, and verified on the DirectAccess server.

   _____ Configure the Kerberos proxy to eliminate the need to set up a public key infrastructure. Also configure DirectAccess to use certificates issued by a PKI certification authority.

3. Put the following steps in order to design a DirectAccess deployment.

   _____ Define the scope of the DirectAccess project.

   _____ Design web servers and certificate infrastructure.

   _____ Design DirectAccess server infrastructure.

   _____ Determine network requirements.

■ Business Case Scenarios

Scenario 10-1: Maintaining Clients

You are an administrator with the Contoso Corporation, which has about 1,400 users. Among those 1,400 users are 400 users who use VPN to connect to the organization's network when they are not in the office. However, you realize that you are having trouble keeping the clients updated and performing other maintenance tasks as needed because these clients are often not connected to the network. What should you do?

Scenario 10-2: Upgrading to Windows Server 2012 R2 DirectAccess

You have a Microsoft Unified Access Gateway (UAG) configured for your network. Because UAG is no longer available by Microsoft, you decide to migrate to Windows Server 2012 R2 DirectAccess. Therefore, you want to choose one weekend to migrate to a new server. How would you proceed?

Designing a Web Application Proxy Solution

70-413 EXAM OBJECTIVE

Objective 3.3 – Design a Web Application Proxy solution. This objective may include but is not limited to: design considerations including planning for applications, authentication and authorization, Workplace Join, devices, Multi-Factor Authentication, Multi-Factor Access Control, Single Sign-On (SSO), certificates, and planning access for internal and external clients.

LESSON HEADING	EXAM OBJECTIVE
Understanding Active Directory Federation Services • Installing AD FS • Configuring Claims Provider Trust Rules	
Designing a Web Application Proxy Solution • Planning for Applications, Authentication, and Authorization • Planning for Single Sign-On (SSO) • Using Multi-Factor Authentication with AD FS • Using Multi-Factor Access Control • Adding Devices with Workplace Join • Configuring CAs and Certificates	Design considerations including planning for applications, authentication and authorization Plan for Single Sign-On (SSO) Plan for Multi-Factor Authentication Plan for Multi-Factor Access Control Plan for Workplace Join Plan for devices Plan for certificates Planning access for internal and external clients

KEY TERMS

account organizations

Active Directory Federation
  Services (AD FS)

AD FS preauthentication

attribute store

bring-your-own-device (BYOD)

claim rules

claims

claims-based authentication

claims provider trust

claims provider

Device Registration Service (DRS)

federated trust relationship

federation server

federation server proxy

form-based authentication

Integrated Windows
  authentication

Multi-Factor Access Control

Multi-Factor Authentication
(MFA)

pass-through preauthentication

preauthentication

relying parties

relying party trust

resource organizations

Single Sign-On (SSO)

token

trusted identity provider

Web Application Proxy

Workplace Join

■ Understanding Active Directory Federation Services

THE BOTTOM LINE

The ***Active Directory Federation Services (AD FS)*** role allows administrators to configure ***Single Sign-On (SSO)*** for web-based applications across a single organization or multiple organizations without requiring users to remember multiple usernames and passwords, although it is not required. This enables you to configure Internet-facing business-to-business (B2B) applications between organizations. For example, a user from *contoso.com* can use contoso.com credentials to access a web-based application hosted by *adatum.com*.

Traditionally, if users from one organization or domain need to access a website provided by another organization or domain, you can do it one of two ways:

- Depending on the web application, you can create web or domain accounts for users and have them log on with a second account. Unfortunately, this does not provide an SSO solution.
- You can create a virtual private network (VPN) between the two organizations and establish a trust relationship between the two Active Directory domains. Although this provides an SSO solution, it is difficult to set up and maintain.

AD FS–enabled applications are claims-based, which allows a much more scalable authentication model for Internet-facing applications. Therefore, AD FS is an identity access solution that allows any browser-based clients to access a website with a single logon to one or more protected Internet-facing applications, even when the user accounts and applications are on different networks and exists within different organizations via a federated trust relationship.

An AD FS configuration consists of two types of organizations:

- ***Resource organizations*** own the resources or data that are accessible from the AD FS–enabled application, similar to a trusting domain in a traditional Windows trust relationship.
- ***Account organizations*** contain the user accounts that access the resources controlled by resource organizations.

Because federation can be used within a single organization, the single organization serves as the resource organization and the account organization.

Of course, to establish an identity federation partnership, both partners agree to create a ***federated trust relationship***. Each partner defines what resources are accessible to the other organization and how access to the resources is enabled. User identities and their associated credentials are stored, owned, and managed by the organization where the user is located.

Claims-based access control uses a trusted identity provider to provide authentication. The trusted identity provider issues a token to each user, which is then presented to the application or service as proof of identity. In other words, with claims-based authentication, users can authenticate to the Active Directory located within their organization and be granted a claim based on that authentication. The claim is then presented to an application that is running in a different organization.

The organization that accepts the claim and has the application the user is trying to access will require key information in the claim—for example, an email address or User Principal Name (UPN) to identify the user, and group membership to specify the access allowed within the application by the user.

To keep the claims secure, all communications occur over HTTPS. Of course, both organizations need to agree on the format for exchanging claims. To simplify this process, a set of specifications identified as web services have been identified, which can be used when implementing AD FS.

Web services are based on Extensible Markup Language (XML), Simple Object Access Protocol (SOAP), Web Services Description Language (WSDL), and Universal Discovery Description and Integration (UDDI). It also uses Security Assertion Markup Language (SAML), which is an XML-based standard for exchanging claims between an identity provider and a service or application provider. The communication between federation servers is based around an XML document that stores the X.509 certificate for token signing and stores the SAML 1.1 or 2.0 token.

AD FS uses the following components:

- *Federation server:* The server that issues, manages, and validates requests involving identity claims. A federation server is needed in each participating forest.
- *Web Application Proxy:* An optional component that is usually deployed on a perimeter network that can receive externally and forward the packets to the internal federation server.
- *Claims:* A statement made by a trusted entity about an object, such as a user, that includes key information identifying the object.
- *Claim rules:* Rules that determine what makes up a valid claim and how claims are processed by the federation servers.
- *Attribute store:* A database, such as Active Directory Domain Services (AD DS), that is used to look up claim values.
- *Claims provider:* The server that issues claims and authenticates users.
- *Relying parties:* The application or web service that accepts claims from the claims provider. The relying party server must have the Microsoft Windows Identity Foundation installed or use the AD FS 1.0 claims-aware agent.
- *Claims provider trust:* Configuration data that specifies which client can request claims from a claims provider and subsequently submits them to a relying party.
- *Relying party trust:* Configuration data used to provide claims about a user or client to a relying party.

In the simplest scenario, an organization can deploy a federation server to be used with its own web applications. If the web application is running on Windows and is part of the same domain as the users who are accessing the web application, you can bypass the federation server and grant access directly to the Active Directory users. However, in more complicated scenarios, an organization might require AD FS:

- The application is not running on Windows or does not support AD DS authentication.
- The Windows server is not part of the domain and requires SAML or web services for authentication or authorization.
- A larger organization consists of multiple domains or multiple forests and has multiple identities.
- Users from outside the organization need access to internal servers and are not part of the domain.

When a single organization uses AD FS, you need only one federation server (not including what might be needed for high availability). If the network with the federation server is completely isolated, you need a second server to act as a *federation proxy server*. For AD FS to provide SSO for a single organization, the following would happen:

1. The client computer accesses a web-based application on a web server by sending an HTTPS request.
2. When the web server receives the request and identifies that the client computer does not have a claim, the web server redirects the client computer to the federation server proxy, if a proxy is being used. If not, it will forward the request to the federation server.

3. If the AD FS is using a proxy, the client computer sends an HTTPS request to the federation server proxy. Depending on the configuration and setup, the federation server proxy might use the current Windows logon (Integrated Windows authentication) or prompt for a logon.

4. If the AD FS is using the proxy, the federation server proxy passes the request and the credentials to the federation server.

5. The federation server uses AD DS to authenticate the user.

6. If authentication is successful, the federation server collects AD DS information about the user and generates the user's claims.

7. The claim is put into a security token, which is passed back to the client computer.

8. The client presents the token to the web server and uses the claims to access to the application.

Installing AD FS

Installing the Active Directory Federation Services role and creating the federation server is a simple process with Server Manager. To configure the federation server, you need a Secure Sockets Layer (SSL) certificate.

With Windows Server 2012, the AD FS role includes the Federation Service, AD FS 1.1 Web Agents, and federation server proxy. With Windows Server 2012 R2, AD FS only includes the Federation Service. If necessary, rather than install the federation server proxy, you would install the Remote Access role, specifically the Web Application Proxy role service. The Web Application Proxy configuration is stored on the AD FS servers in your organization.

Before you can create the stand-alone federation server, you must have a managed service account, which is used to run the federation services. You also need an SSL digital certificate. You can import the digital certificate from a .pfx file, which includes the public and private key.

 INSTALL THE ACTIVE DIRECTORY FEDERATION SERVICES

GET READY. To install the Active Directory Federation Services, perform the following steps:

1. On *Server01*, click the Server Manager button on the task bar to open *Server Manager*.

2. At the top of *Server Manager*, click Manage and then click Add Roles and Features. The *Add Roles and Feature* Wizard opens.

3. On the *Before you begin* page, click Next.

4. On the *Server Select* page, select Role-based or feature-based installation and then click Next.

5. On the *Server Roles* page, select Active Directory Federation Services and click Next.

6. On the *Select features* page, click Next.

7. On the *Active Directory Federation Services (AD FS)* page, click Next.

8. On the *Confirm installation selections* page, click Install.

9. When the installation is complete, click Close.

→ **CREATE A STAND-ALONE FEDERATION SERVER**

GET READY. To create a stand-alone federation server, perform the following steps:

1. On *Server01*, in *Server Manager*, click Configure the federation service on this server.

2. In the *Active Directory Federation Services Configuration* Wizard, on the *Welcome* page, *Create the first federation server in a federation server farm* is already selected. Click Next.

3. On the *Connect to AD DS* page, click Next.

4. On the *Specify Service Properties* page, select the certificate for the federation server. If a certificate is not available, click the Import button to import one from a .pfx file.

5. In the *Federation Service Name* text box, type the name of the Federation Service, such as Contoso Corporation (see Figure 11-1). Click Next.

Figure 11-1

Specifying the Service Properties

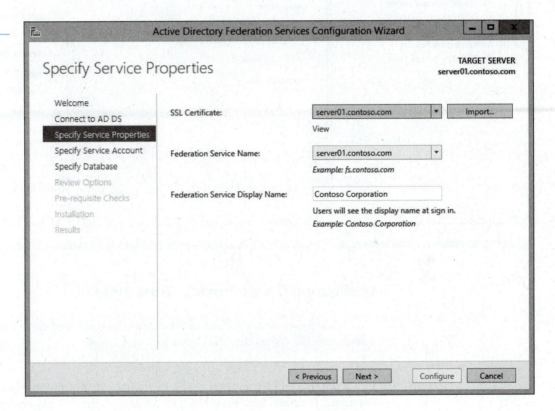

6. On the *Specify Service Account* page, select Use an existing domain user account or group Managed Service Account. Then click Select.

7. In the *Select User or Service Account* dialog box, in the *Enter the object name to select* text box, type the name of a service account (such as adfs) and click OK.

8. Back on the *Specify Service Account* page, in the *Account Password* text box, type in the password for the *adfs* service account. Click Next.

9. On the *Specify Configuration Database* page, *Create a database on this server using Windows Internal Database is already* selected. Click Next.

10. On the *Review Options* page, click Next.

11. On the *Pre-requisite Checks* page, click Configure.

After the federation server is created, you can manage the Federation Service by using the AD FS console (see Figure 11-2) or by using Windows PowerShell. In both methods, you can manage certificates within AD FS, create and manage claims provider trusts, relying party trusts, attribute stores, and authentication policies.

Figure 11-2

Accessing the AD FS console

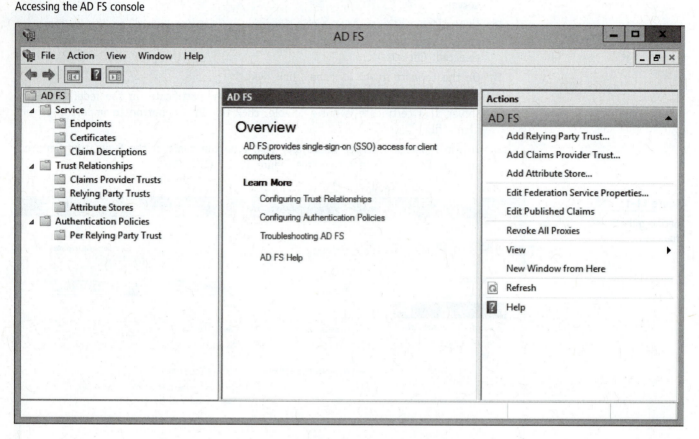

Configuring Claims Provider Trust Rules

A *claims provider trust* identifies the claims provider and describes how the relying party consumes the claims that the claims provider issues.

By default, the AD FS server is configured with a claims provider trust named Active Directory. It defines how the AD FS server accepts the AD DS credentials, including which user names, security identifiers (SIDs), and group SIDs to the relying party. If you are communicating with other organizations, you need to create additional claims provider trusts for each federated organization.

The claims provider trust has similar options for the relying party trusts:

- Import data about the claims provider through the federation metadata.
- Import data about the claims provider from a file.
- Manually configure the claims provider trust.

CONFIGURE THE ACTIVE DIRECTORY CLAIMS PROVIDER TRUST

GET READY. To configure the Active Directory claims provider trust, perform the following steps:

1. In the *AD FS* console, expand Claims Provider Trusts.
2. In the middle pane, right-click Active Directory, and then click Edit Claim Rules.
3. In the *Edit Claims Rules for Active Directory* dialog box, on the *Acceptance Transform Rules* tab, click Add Rule.
4. In the *Add Transform Claim Rule* Wizard, in the *Select Rule Template* page, under *Claim rule template*, select Send LDAP Attributes as Claims, and then click Next.
5. On the *Configure Rule* page, in the *Claim rule name* text box, type Outbound LDAP Attributes Rule.
6. From the *Attribute Store* drop-down list, select Active Directory.
7. In the *Mapping of LDAP attributes to outgoing claim types* section, select the following values for the *LDAP Attribute* and the *Outgoing Claim Type*:
   - E-Mail-Addresses: E-Mail Address
   - User-Principal-Name: UPN
   - Display-Name: Name
8. Click Finish, and then click OK.

Designing a Web Application Proxy Solution

↓
THE BOTTOM LINE

The **Web Application Proxy** is a new Remote Access role service available in Windows Server 2012 R2 that provides reverse proxy functionality for web applications inside an organization's network so that users can access the application externally no matter what device they are using. Also, the Web Application Proxy preauthenticates access to web applications by using AD FS and functions as an AD FS proxy.

A *reverse proxy* is a proxy server that retrieves resources from servers on behalf of a client. The resources are then relayed through the proxy server to the client. As far as the client is concerned, the resources originate from the server itself. You can use the Web Application Proxy to hide the existence of the resource server. It can selectively access the necessary applications on the servers inside the organization from the outside. Therefore, by using a reverse proxy, you protect applications from external threats and help protect internal resources by providing a defense-in-depth approach.

The Web Application Proxy is integrated into the Remote Access Management console, which allows you to manage your Web Application Proxy servers and other Remote Access technologies by using one console.

TAKE NOTE*

The Web Application Proxy configuration is stored on the AD FS servers in your organization; therefore, Web Application Proxy servers require connectivity to the AD FS servers.

To configure the Web Application Proxy server, perform the following general steps:

1. Configure the Web Application Proxy server.
2. Use the Web Application Proxy Configuration Wizard to connect the Web Application Proxy server to the AD FS server.
3. Publish the application.
4. Attempt to connect to the application by using the default AD FS authentication scheme.

 INSTALL THE WEB APPLICATION PROXY ROLE SERVICE

GET READY. To install the Web Application Proxy Role Service, perform the following steps:

1. On the edge server, open Server Manager.
2. From the Manage menu, select Add roles and features.
3. When the *Add Roles and Features Wizard* opens, on the *Before you begin* page, click Next.
4. Select Role-based or feature-based installation and then click Next.
5. Click Select a server from the server pool, click the name of the server to install the Remote Access role to, and then click Next.
6. On the *Select server roles* page, select Remote Access, and then click Next.
7. On the *Features*, page, click Next.
8. On the *Remote Access* page, click Next.
9. In the *Select role services* dialog box, select Web Application Proxy, click Add Features, and then click Next.
10. On the *Confirm installation selections* dialog box, click Install.
11. When the installation is complete, click Close.

CONFIGURE THE WEB APPLICATION PROXY

GET READY. To configure the Web Application proxy, perform the following steps:

1. In *Server Manager*, click the yellow triangle with the black exclamation point. Then click Configure the federation service on this server.
2. In the *AD FS Federation* Wizard, for the *SSL Certificate*, select the certificate for the server running AD FS. For the *Federation Service Display* name, type an identifier such as Contoso Corporation. Click Next.
3. On the *Specify Service Account* page, *Create a Group Managed Service Account* is already selected. For the *Account name*, specify an account that will be used for the Group Managed Service account, such as CONTOSO\ADFS. Click Next.
4. On the *Specify Configuration Database* page, click Next.
5. On the *Review Options* page, click Next.
6. On the *Pre-requisite Checks* page, click Configure.
7. Click Close.

You might receive a message saying that you must configure the Service Principal Name (SPN) for the service account. For example, if AD FS is running on server01.contoso.com and the Group Managed Service Account is contoso\adfs, you would execute the following command on a domain controller:

```
setspn -S http/server01.contoso.com adfs
```

PUBLISH AN APPLICATION

GET READY. To publish an application, perform the following steps:

1. In *Server Manager*, open the Remote Access Management console.
2. On the Web Application Proxy server, using the *Remote Access Management* console, click Web Application Proxy. Then in the *Tasks* pane (as shown in Figure 11-3), click Publish.

Figure 11-3

Using Remote Access Management console to publish a web application

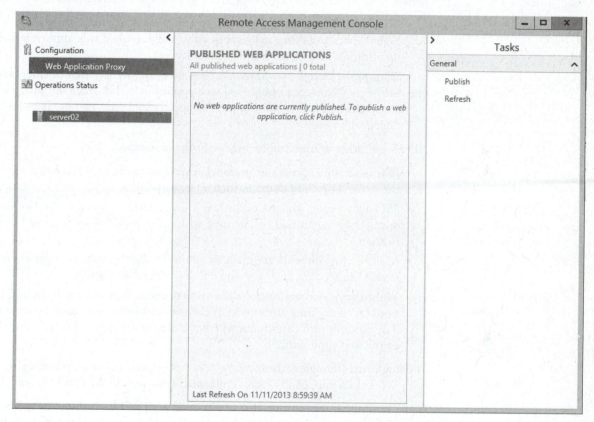

3. When the *Publish New Application* Wizard opens, click Next.
4. On the *Preauthentication* page, select Pass-through and then click Next.
5. On the *Publishing Settings* page, enter the following and click Next:
   - *Name:* This name is used only in the list of published applications in the Remote Access Management console.
   - *External URL:* Enter the external URL for this application.
   - *External certificate list:* Select a certificate whose subject covers the external URL.
   - *Backend server URL:* The URL of the back-end server is entered automatically when you enter the external URL. You should change it only if the back-end server URL is different.
6. On the *Confirmation* page, review the settings, and then click Publish.
7. On the *Results* page, make sure that application published successfully, and then click Close.

Planning for Applications, Authentication, and Authorization

Preauthentication is the process by which users and devices are authenticated before they access an application. Web Application Proxy supports two forms of preauthentication: AD FS preauthentication and pass-through preauthentication. After a user or device is authenticated, the authentication is used for authorization.

When you publish applications through Web Application Proxy, the process by which users and devices are authenticated before they gain access to applications is known as *preauthentication*. Web Application Proxy supports two forms of preauthentication:

- With *AD FS preauthentication*, users must authenticate to the AD FS server before Web Application Proxy redirects them to the published web application. AD FS preauthentication uses claims-based authentication.
- With *pass-through preauthentication*, users are not required to enter credentials before they connect to published web applications. The main advantage of pass-through authentication is that you can publish applications that are not claims-aware to external organization users.

AD FS preauthentication can be used with the following:

- Workplace Join allows you to associate devices to the workplace that are not members of the Active Directory domain, such as smart phones, tablets, or non-company laptops.
- SSO allows users who are preauthenticated by AD FS to enter their credentials only once. Those credentials will be used with other applications that use AD FS for authentication.
- Multi-Factor Authentication allows you to configure multiple types of credentials to strengthen security, such as using a password and a smartcard.
- Multi-Factor Access Control allows you to strengthen security in publishing web applications by configuring authorization claim rules so that they issue a permit or deny claim. The claim in turn determines whether a user or a group will be allowed or denied access to the web application.

Although pass-through authentication does not require any extra planning, it cannot be used with Workplace Join, Multi-Factor Authentication, and Multi-Factor Access Control.

Some forms of authentication that can be used with AD FS include the following:

- Claims-based authentication
- Integrated Windows authentication
- Microsoft Office Forms Based Authentication
- Windows Store app clients

The next section explains claims-based authentication.

PLANNING FOR INTEGRATED WINDOWS AUTHENTICATION

With *Integrated Windows authentication* (formerly called NTLM, and also known as Windows NT Challenge/Response authentication), the user name and password (credentials) are hashed before being sent across the network. If you require integrated Windows authentication, the Web Application Proxy server must preauthenticate the user.

You need the following to use Integrated Windows Authentication:

- The AD FS server must have a nonclaims-aware relying party trust for the application.
- The Web Application Proxy server must be part of an AD DS domain. It should be noted that the server does not have to be the AD DS domain where the resources reside.

- The Web Application Proxy server must be able to provide delegation for the users who need access to the application.
- The application must be running on a computer that is running Windows Server 2012 R2 or Windows Server 2012.

PLANNING FOR MICROSOFT OFFICE FORMS BASED AUTHENTICATION CLIENTS

With *form-based authentication*, you fill out and submit a web-based form or page to log on to a system or service. To publish an application for clients that use Microsoft Office Forms Based Authentication, you must add a relying party trust for the application to the AD FS server. Web Application Proxy supports access from Microsoft Office clients such as Microsoft Word that access documents and data on back-end servers. Depending on the application, you can use claims-based authentication or Integrated Windows authentication.

PLANNING FOR WINDOWS STORE APP CLIENTS

With the growth of mobile phones and related mobile store apps, a web application can be accessed from a Windows Store app. Therefore, to allow authentication, you need the following:

- The Windows Store app must support Open Authorization (OAuth) 2.0.
- The OAuth endpoint in AD FS must be proxy-enabled.
- You must use the Windows PowerShell cmdlet Set-WebApplicationProxyConfiguration to configure the Web Application Proxy server with the URL for the AD FS server.

Planning for Single Sign-On (SSO)

> *Claims-based authentication* uses a trusted identity provider to provide authentication. The *trusted identity provider* issues a token to the user, who then presents it to the application or service as proof of identity. Identity is based on a set of information. Each piece of information is referred to as a claim (such as who the user or computer claims to be) and is stored as a *token*, which is a digital key. The token is digital identification for the user or computer accessing a network resource. The token has a digital signature of the identity provider to verify the authenticity of the information stored within the token. As users or computers need access to resources, they present the tokens to access the resources.

CERTIFICATION READY
Plan for Single Sign On (SSO).
Objective 3.3

When claims-based applications are published and then accessed from a browser, the general authentication flow is as follows:

1. The client attempts to access a claims-based application using a web browser.
2. The web browser sends an HTTPS request to the Web Application Proxy server, which redirects the request to the AD FS server.
3. The AD FS server authenticates the user and the device and redirects the request back to Web Application Proxy with an edge token. Because the user has already been authenticated, AD FS server adds a Single Sign-On (SSO) cookie.
4. Web Application Proxy validates the token, adds its own cookie, and forwards the request to the back-end server.
5. The back-end server redirects the request to the AD FS server to get the application security token.
6. Adding the application token and SSO cookie, the request is redirected to the back-end server by the AD FS server, allowing the user access to the application without having to enter a user name or password.

To use claims-based authentication, you must meet the following prerequisites:

- The AD FS server must have a claims-aware relying party trust for the application.
- The Web Application Proxy server does not need to be part of an Active Directory domain.
- Applications must be configured to use AD FS for SSO.

By default, AD FS uses AD DS, which can be used by SSO. The simplest configuration would be all users are member of the same Active Directory forest, and all applications run on servers that are part of the Active Directory forest.

However, you can use AD FS in the following situations:

- The applications might be running on servers that do not have Windows Server installed, servers that do not support Active Directory authentication, servers that have Windows Server installed but are not domain-joined, and servers that are running a non-Microsoft web server service.
- The applications might require SAML or web services for authentication and authorization.
- Large organizations with multiple domains and forests.
- External users need access to applications running on internal servers.

If the organization has a single Active Directory forest, the organization needs to have only a single federation server. The AD FS server will operate as the claims provider and provide authorization for application access. Using AD FS does not necessarily mean that users will not be prompted for authentication. However, Windows Server 2012 R2 supports SSO. In either case, because users can continue to use the AD DS credentials, they do not have to remember another set of credentials.

Using Multi-Factor Authentication with AD FS

With Windows Server 2012 R2, AD FS access control is enhanced with *Multi-Factor Authentication (MFA)*, which uses two or more methods for authentication. It can include user, group, device, location, and authentication data. Unlike Windows Server 2012, Windows Server 2012 R2 includes new claim types such as client application, device operating system type, device operating system version, public key, thumbprint, inside corporate network, and password expiration time.

By now, you should already be familiar with the benefits of MFA. By using two or more methods for authentication allows for a more secure environment. By default, the primary authentication for AD FS is as follows:

- The extranet requires forms-based authentication. You can optionally enable users to choose between forms-based authentication or certificate-based authentication.
- Intranet resources require Integrated Windows authentication. You can optionally enable users to choose between Integrated Windows authentication, forms-based authentication, or certificate-based authentication.

To configure Multi-Factor Authentication in Windows Server 2012 R2, you must do the following:

- Select an additional authentication method.
- Set up MFA policy.

CONFIGURE ADDITIONAL AUTHENTICATION METHODS

GET READY. To configure AD FS additional authentication methods, perform the following steps:

1. On your federation server, in the *AD FS Management* Console, navigate to the Authentication Policies node.

2. Under the *Multi-factor Authentication* section, click the Edit link next to the *Global Settings* subsection.

3. In the *Edit Global Authentication Policy* dialog box, on the *Primary* tab, select Certificate Authentication as an additional authentication method (see Figure 11-4), and then click OK.

Figure 11-4

Selecting certificate authentication

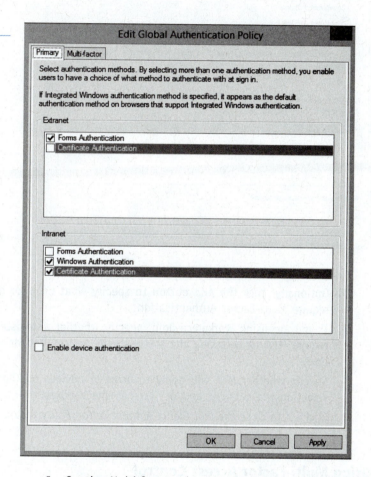

4. On the *Multi-factor* tab, near the bottom, select Certificate Authentication (see Figure 11-5).

Figure 11-5

Selecting Multi-Factor
Authentication

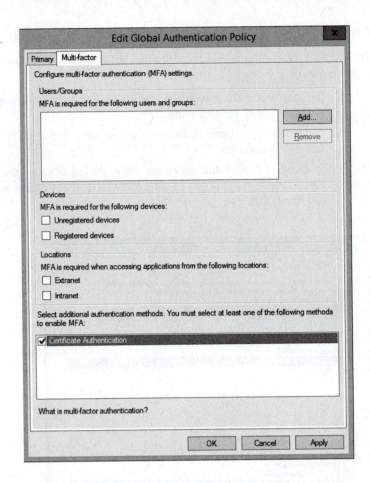

5. Optionally, click the Add button to specify what users or groups you want to require Multi-Factor Authentication.

6. If you are using Workplace Join, specify whether unregistered or registered devices require MFA by selecting the Unregistered devices and/or Registered devices check boxes.

7. Specify whether MFA will apply to users or devices on the extranet or intranet by selecting the Extranet and/or Intranet check boxes.

8. Click OK to close the *Edit Global Authentication Policy* dialog box.

Using Multi-Factor Access Control

CERTIFICATION READY
Plan for Multi-Factor
Access Control
Objective 3.3

For an extra layer of security, you can also use *Multi-Factor Access Control*, which AD FS implements with authorization claim rules that can be used to permit or deny claims for a group of users to access secured resources. Multi-Factor Access Control uses multiple factors including user, device, location, and authentication data.

Windows Server 2012 R2 AD FS Multi-Factor Access Control offers the following benefits:

- Flexible and expressive per-application authorization policies that can permit or deny access based on user, device, network location, and authentication state
- Issuance authorization rules for relying party applications
- Rich UI experience for common Multi-Factor Access Control scenarios

- Rich claims language and Windows PowerShell support for advanced Multi-Factor Access Control scenarios
- Custom (per relying party application) "Access Denied" messages

CONFIGURE MULTI-FACTOR ACCESS CONTROL POLICY

GET READY. To configure Multi-Factor Access Control policy based on user data, perform the following steps:

1. In the *AD FS Management* Console, expand Trust Relationships > Relying Party Trusts.

2. Select the relying party trust that represents your application, and then in the *Actions* pane, click Edit Claim Rules.

3. In the *Edit Claim Rules* dialog box, on the *Issuance Authorization Rules* tab, click Add Rule.

4. In the *Add Issuance Authorization Claim Rule* Wizard, on the *Select Rule Template* page, select the Permit or Deny Users Based on an Incoming Claim claim rule template and then click Next.

5. On the *Configure Rule* page (shown in Figure 11-6), in the *Claim rule name* text box, type a name for the claim rule.

Figure 11-6

Editing claim rules

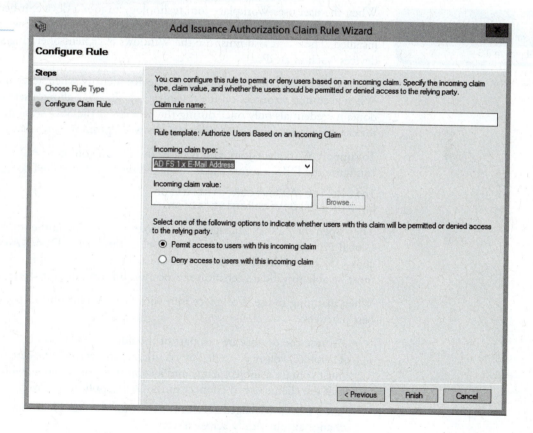

6. For the *Incoming claim type*, select a group SID, by clicking Browse. When the *Select User, Computer, or Group* dialog box opens, type the name of a user or group, and click OK.

8. Select Deny access to users with this incoming claim.

9. Click Finish.

10. The *Permit Access to All Users* rule was created by default when you created this relying party trust. Therefore, back in the *Edit Claim Rules* dialog box, select Permit Access to All Users and then click Remove Rule.

Adding Devices with Workplace Join

Over the last several years, smart phones and tablets have become powerful devices that offer the convenience of mobile technology. Therefore, users commonly use multiple computers and devices to access email and other business-related applications services. Also, many organizations are implementing ***bring-your-own-device (BYOD)*** policies, which help administrators manage users who use their personal devices to access organizational resources. ***Workplace Join*** allows users to associate their devices to the organization's network without joining the device to the Active Directory domain. You can then manage access based on a wide range of attributes.

CERTIFICATION READY
Plan for Workplace Join
Objective 3.3

CERTIFICATION READY
Plan for devices
Objective 3.3

When you use Workplace Join to join a device, ***Device Registration Service (DRS)*** registers a non-domain–joined device in Active Directory and installs a certificate on the device. By joining the device, Workplace Join provides a secure SSO mechanism while controlling which resources can be accessed by the device.

When the user uses Workplace Join technology to join a device, it becomes a *known* device. To use Workplace Join, you must have Windows Server 2012 R2 with the AD FS role service installed. The client also must use the Windows 8.1 client operating system or iOS-based devices (such as an iPad).

The certificate will be used to represent device identity when accessing organization resources. When accessing resources on the organization, the SSO allows users to be prompted for their domain credentials only once during the lifetime of the SSO session. However, an administrator can specify resources that enforce a password prompt or reauthentication.

To support Workplace Join, you need to install and configure AD FS and the new DRS. To configure the DRS, execute the following Windows PowerShell commands:

```
Initialize-ADDeviceRegistration
Enable-AdfsDeviceRegistration
```

Then open the AD FS Management console, navigate to Authentication Policies, click Edit Global Primary Authentication, click to select the Enable Device Authentication, and then click OK. Lastly, the client must trust the SSL certificate used for the federation server and must be able to validate certificate revocation information for the certificate.

When planning to use Workplace Join with Web Application Proxy, you should follow these best practices:

• Because the devices are not part of the domain, they do not automatically trust the CA. Therefore, you need to deploy certificates to devices. The certificate that AD FS uses must contain a subject name and a subject alternate name, which should be same name that the clients use to connect to the Web Application Proxy server.

• Use a Group Managed Service Account for the AD FS services so that passwords would change automatically across servers.

• Determine which applications will allow access to Workplace Joined–devices. When a device is Workplace Joined, the application can retrieve information about the device from Active Directory, which can then be used to generate device claims. Based on your security needs, you can determine whether the device is a Workplace Joined device or from a domain-joined device, which can be used if you want the web application cached on the device.

→ **JOIN A DEVICE**

GET READY. To join a device, perform the following steps:

1. Log on to the client device with a Microsoft account.
2. On the *Start* screen, open the Charms bar, click the Settings charm, and then click Change PC Settings.
3. On the *PC Settings* page, click Network > Workplace.
4. In the *Enter your UserID to get workplace access or turn on device management* dialog box, type the user name (such as **JSmith@contoso.com**) and then click Join.
5. When prompted for credentials, type the username and the associated password and then click OK. You should now see the message *This device has joined your workplace network.*

Configuring CAs and Certificates

Essentially, AD FS allows a web-based application to be published externally with the Web Application Proxy. Therefore, HTTPS traffic requires having digital certificates.

CERTIFICATION READY
Plan for certificates
Objective 3.3

Each Web Application Proxy server requires the following certificate in the certificate store:

- A certificate whose subject covers the federation service name. If you want to use Workplace Join, the certificate must also contain the following subject alternative names (SANs): *<federation service name>.<domain>* and enterpriseregistration.*<domain>*.
- A wildcard certificate, a subject alternative name (SAN) certificate, several SAN certificates, or several certificates whose subjects cover each web application.
- A copy of the certificate issued to external servers when using client certificate preauthentication.

Although the certificate could be a third-party CA or an enterprise CA, the certificate subject name should be an externally resolvable FQDN that can be reached from the Internet. Also, the certificate revocation list (CRL) distribution point should be reachable from a publicly resolvable FQDN.

Planning Access for Internal and External Clients

AD FS can be used for internal and external clients. By using the Web Application Proxy to provide a protection layer against malicious HTTP requests that originate from the Internet, the Web Application Proxy offers preauthentication, network isolation, selective publishing, and protection against distributed denial of service (DDoS) attacks.

CERTIFICATION READY
Planning access for internal and external clients
Objective 3.3

For internal users to access AD FS, you would configure the DNS entry to point to the internal server running AD FS. For external users, the DNS entry points to the firewall that connects to the Web Application Proxy. The firewall will forward the intended packets to the Web Application Proxy, which will forward to the federation servers.

The Web Application Proxy needs to be placed at one of the following:

- Behind a front-end firewall to separate it from the Internet
- Between two firewalls: a front-end firewall to separate it from the Internet and a back-end firewall to separate it from the corporate network

Having the Web Application Proxy behind a firewall adds network-level protection and reduces the attack surface of the Web Application Proxy server. If the Web Application Proxy server is located in front of a firewall that separates it from the corporate network, you must make sure that the firewall does not block HTTP and HTTPS traffic meant for the back-end servers. All firewalls must be configured to allow HTTPS so that the Web Application Proxy in the perimeter network to access the federation server in the corporate network. Also, device registration uses Workplace Join, and all federation server communications to and from client devices use HTTPS. Lastly, to use client certificate authentication, you must also configure the firewall to allow traffic on port 49443.

SKILL SUMMARY

IN THIS LESSON YOU LEARNED:

- The Active Directory Federation Services (AD FS) role allows administrators to configure Single Sign-On (SSO) for web-based applications across a single organization or multiple organizations without requiring users to remember multiple usernames and passwords. This enables you to configure Internet-facing business-to-business (B2B) applications between organizations.

- The Web Application Proxy is a new Remote Access services role available in Windows Server 2012 R2 that provides reverse proxy functionality for web applications inside an organization's network so that users can access the application externally no matter what device they are using. Also, the Web Application Proxy preauthenticates access to web applications by using AD FS and functions as an AD FS proxy.

- Preauthentication is the process by which users and devices are authenticated before they access an application. Web Application Proxy supports two forms of preauthentication: AD FS preauthentication and pass-through preauthentication. After a user or device is authenticated, the authentication is used for authorization.

- With Windows Server 2012 R2, AD FS access control is enhanced with Multi-Factor Authentication (MFA), which uses two or more methods for authentication. It can include user, group, device, location, and authentication data.

- For an extra layer of security, you can also use Multi-Factor Access Control, which AD FS implements with authorization claim rules that can be used to permit or deny claims for a group of users to access secured resources. Multi-Factor Access Control uses multiple factors including user, device, location, and authentication data.

- Workplace Join allows users to associate their devices to the organization's network without joining the device to the Active Directory domain. You can then manage access based on a wide range of attributes.

Knowledge Assessment

Multiple Choice

Select the correct answer for each of the following questions.

1. In Active Directory Federation Services, which of the following is the default claim provider?
   a. SQL server
   b. Active Directory
   c. LDAP
   d. Active Directory Lightweight Directory Services

2. Which role or feature is used to provide reverse proxy functionality in Windows Server 2012 R2?
   a. AD FS Proxy
   b. Internet Security and Acceleration (ISA)
   c. Internet Information Services (IIS)
   d. Web Application Proxy

3. Which service or feature does the Web Application Proxy depend on to store the configuration information?
   a. Active Directory Federation Services (AD FS)
   b. Internet Security and Acceleration (ISA)
   c. Internet Information Services (IIS)
   d. Windows Internal Database (WID)

4. Which of the following include Web Application Proxy? (Choose all that apply.)
   a. Windows Server 2008
   b. Windows Server 2008 R2
   c. Windows Server 2012
   d. Windows Server 2012 R2

5. For an intranet, which of the following is the default form of authentication used with AD FS?
   a. forms-based authentication
   b. Integrated Windows authentication
   c. certificate-based authentication
   d. pin authentication

6. For AD FS, which of the following are the available forms of authentication for extranet connections? (Choose all that apply.)
   a. forms-based authentication
   b. Integrated Windows authentication
   c. certificate-based authentication
   d. pin authentication

7. In AD FS, which type of control allows you to permit or deny claims based on membership of a group?
   a. Multi-Factor Authentication (MFA)
   b. Multi-Factor Access Control
   c. Criteria-based
   d. Database controls
   e. Active Directory–based

8. Which technology would you use to enable a mobile device that is not part of your domain to function with AD FS?
   a. Multi-Factor Access Control
   b. bring your own device (BYOD)
   c. Workplace Join
   d. workplace folders

9. Which type of preauthentication is done by entering credentials right before they connect to the published AD FS web application?
   a. AD FS preauthentication
   b. pass-through preauthentication
   c. Workplace Join preauthenitcation
   d. SSO preauthentication

10. Which of the following is the simplest configuration to use SSO for AD FS?
    a. application and users are part of same AD forest.
    b. Users are imported into a SQL database.
    c. When autosync occurs between SQL and Active Directory
    d. The Application Web Proxy has the Active Directory agent.

Best Answer

Choose the letter that corresponds to the best answer. More than one answer choice can achieve the goal. Select the BEST answer.

1. You want to enable SSO. Which type of authentication should you configure?
   a. AD FS preauthentication
   b. pass-through preauthentication
   c. Windows Store App client authentication
   d. proxy authentication

2. Which of the following can be used to with an IPad to provide an SSO on mechanisms when accessing company resources?
   a. Network Policy Server
   b. site-link bridge
   c. workplace folders
   d. Workplace Join

3. As an administrator for a large corporation, you are responsible for deploying a new web application for company users to manage their company profiles. You want the application to be available from the Internet, but security must be maintained. Which of the following do you recommend?
   a. Use a server running the Web Application Proxy role that is connected to the Internet through a firewall.
   b. Connect the Web Application Proxy server directly to the Internet.
   c. Place the federation server on a perimeter network that is connected to the Internet through a firewall.
   d. Connect the federation server directly to the Internet

4. You need to ensure that your company web applications are secure and not available to non-authorized users. Which of the following options should you use? (Choose all that apply.)
   a. Single Sign-On (SSO)
   b. Multi-Factor Authentication (MFA)
   c. multi-factor auditing
   d. Multi-Factor Access Control

5. In AD FS, how do you enable support for device support for workplace devices?
   a. Create a claim rule.
   b. Configure the Device Registration Service.
   c. Enable the Global Primary Authentication policy.
   d. Modify the Multi-Factor Authentication policy.

Matching and Identification

1. Match the term with its definition:
   _____ a) Pass-through preauthentication
   _____ b) Multi-Factor Authentication
   _____ c) Reverse proxy
   _____ d) Multi-Factor Access Control
   _____ e) Web Application Proxy
   _____ f) AD FS preauthentication
   1. A proxy server that retrieves resources from servers on behalf of a client.
   2. A new Remote Access role service available in Windows Server 2012 R2 that provides reverse proxy functionality for web applications inside an

organization's network so that users can access the application externally no matter what device they are using.

3. Used when users are not required to enter credentials before they connect to published web applications.

4. Allows you to configure multiple types of credentials to strengthen security, such as using a password and a smartcard.

5. Used when users must authenticate to the AD FS server before Web Application Proxy redirects them to the published web application.

6. Allows you to strengthen security in publishing web applications by configuring authorization claim rules so that they issue a permit or deny claim.

Build a List

1. In order of first to last, specify the steps to configure Web Application Proxy server.

_____ Publish an application.

_____ Use the Web Application Proxy Configuration Wizard to connect the Web Application Proxy server to the AD FS server.

_____ Configure the Web Application Proxy server.

_____ Connect to the application by using the default AD FS authentication scheme.

2. In order of first to last, specify the steps to install and configure Workplace Join. Not all steps will be used.

_____ Use the Configure AD FS Configuration wizard to configure AD FS.

_____ Run the `Enable-ADDeviceRegistration` Windows PowerShell command.

_____ Run the `Initialize-ADDeviceRegistration` Windows PowerShell command.

_____ Install AD FS and the new Device Registration Service.

_____ Edit the Global Primary Authentication policy.

_____ Install the digital certificate on the AD FS server.

_____ Edit the Multi-Factor Authentication policy tab.

■ Business Case Scenarios

Scenario 11-1: Sales App

Your development team just created a new Sales application for Windows and Apple mobile devices. It is designed for the sales team when they are traveling from customer to customer to access sales and manufacturing records. What do you need in order for your sales team to access the application securely?

Scenario 11-2: Multiple Mobile Applications

You need to deploy several mobile applications for your sales team, which will access the apps over the Internet while meeting with customers. Because they allow access to all sales and current bids, you need to tighten up the security for these mobile apps. You also want to simplify the logon that users must use. How should you proceed?

12 LESSON

Implementing a Scalable Remote Access Solution

70-413 EXAM OBJECTIVE

Objective 3.4 – Implementing a scalable Remote Access solution. This objective may include but is not limited to: Configure site-to-site VPN; configure packet filters; implement packet tracing; implement multisite Remote Access; configure Remote Access clustered with Network Load Balancing (NLB); implement an advanced DirectAccess solution; configure multiple RADIUS server groups and infrastructure; configure Web Application Proxy for clustering.

LESSON HEADING	EXAM OBJECTIVE
Configuring Site-to-Site VPN	Configure site-to-site VPN
Configuring Packet Filters • Exploring the WFAS Profiles • Understanding Inbound Rules, Outbound Rules, and Connection Security Rules • Addressing Conflicts with Firewall Rules • Exporting Firewall Configuration Rules	Configure packet filters
Implementing Packet Tracing	Implement packet tracing
Implementing Multisite Remote Access	Implement multisite Remote Access
Configuring Remote Access Clustered with Network Load Balancing (NLB)	Configure Remote Access clustered with Network Load Balancing (NLB)
Implementing an Advanced DirectAccess Solution	Implement an advanced DirectAccess solution
Configuring Multiple RADIUS Server Groups and Infrastructure • Installing and Configuring Network Policy Server • Configuring Multiple RADIUS Servers	Configure multiple RADIUS server groups and infrastructure
Configuring Web Application Proxy for Clustering	Configure Web Application Proxy for clustering

KEY TERMS

access client

Authentication, Authorization, and Accounting (AAA)

authorization

connection security rules

domain profile

inbound rules

Network Connectivity Assistant (NCA)

Network Load Balancing (NLB)

Network Location Server (NLS)

Network Policy Server (NPS)

outbound rules

packet filters

packet tracing

private profile

public profile

RADIUS clients

RADIUS proxy

Remote Authentication Dial-In User Service (RADIUS)

■ Configuring Site-to-Site VPN

THE BOTTOM LINE

In the previous two lessons, you have installed and configured servers to provide VPN connections for the clients using either the Routing and Remote Access console or the Remote Access Management console. For this lesson, you will learn how to configure a site-to-site VPN between two VPN servers or devices.

CERTIFICATION READY
Configure site-to-site VPN
Objective 3.4

A **site-to-site VPN connection** connects two private networks. Site-to-site VPN connections can be used to connect branch offices to an organization's primary site, or to connect one organization to the network of another organization. This VPN connection allows routed connections to the remote site or network while helping to maintain secure communications over the Internet. When networks are connected over the Internet, a VPN-enabled router forwards packets to another VPN-enabled router across a VPN connection.

To control who can connect to the VPN server, the calling VPN server or router must authenticate itself to the answer server or router. To ensure that the calling server or router is talking to the correct VPN server (mutual authentication), the remote server must authenticate itself to the calling device.

 CONFIGURE AND ENABLE ROUTING AND REMOTE ACCESS

GET READY. To configure and enable Routing and Remote Access, perform the following steps:

1. In *Server Manager*, open Routing and Remote Access Server.
2. Right-click the server and choose Configure and Enable Routing and Remote Access.
3. In the *Routing and Remote Access Server Setup* Wizard, on the *Welcome* page, click Next.
4. On the *Configuration* page, select Secure connection between two private networks (see Figure 12-1). Click Next.

Figure 12-1

Configuring the routing and Remote Access server

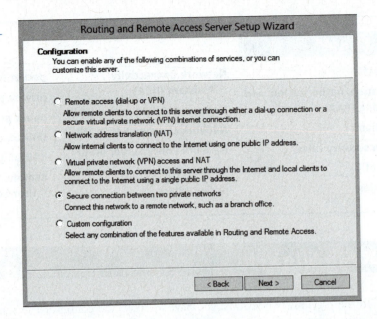

5. On the *Demand-Dial Connections* page, click Next.

6. On the *IP Address Assignment* page, select From a specified range of addresses. Click Next.

7. On the *Address Range Assignment* page, click New.

8. In the *New IPv4 Address Range* dialog box, type the following:

   Start IP address: 192.168.1.201

   End IP address: 192.168.1.205

   Then click OK.

9. Back on the *Address Range Assignment* page, click Next.

10. On the *Completing the Routing and Remote Access Server Setup Wizard* page, click Finish. The *Demand-Dial Interface Wizard* opens.

 CONFIGURE A DEMAND-DIAL INTERFACE

GET READY. To configure Demand-Dial Interface, perform the following steps:

1. With the *Demand-Dial Interface Wizard* already open, on the *Welcome* page, click Next.

2. On the *Demand-Dial Interface Wizard* page, click Next.

3. On the *Connection Type* page, *Connect using virtual private networking (VPN)* is already selected. Click Next.

4. On the *VPN Type* page, select the appropriate VPN type, and then click Next.

5. On the *Destination Address* page, enter the IP address or name of the VPN server or device (such as 192.168.5.1). Click Next.

6. On the *Protocols and Security* page, *Route IP packets on this interface* is already selected. Select Add a user account so that a remote router can dial in.

7. On the *Static Routes for Remote Networks* page, click Add.

8. In the *Static Route* dialog box (see Figure 12-2), in the *Destination* text box, type the destination network address. In the *Network Mask* text box, type the subnet mask for the network. In the *Metric* text box, type a metric or cost for the router. Click OK.

Figure 12-2

Configuring a static route

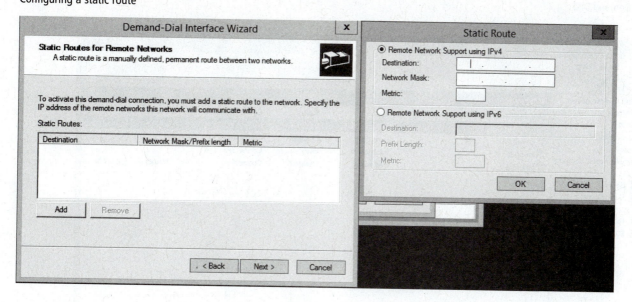

9. Back on the *Static Routes for Remote Networks* page, click Next.

10. On the *Dial-in Credentials* page, *Remote Router* is the default user name. In the *Password* and *Confirm password* text boxes, enter a password such as Pa$$w0rd.

11. On the *Dial-Out Credentials* page, in the *Username* and *Domain* text boxes, enter a username and domain. Then in the *Password* and *Confirm password* text boxes, enter a password such as Pa$$w0rd. Click Next.

12. On the *Completing the Demand-Dial Interface* Wizard page, click Finish.

The Demand Dial Interface appears in the Network Interfaces list, as shown in Figure 12-3. Also, the Remote Router account appears as a local user on the computer, which has been created allow access for the Network Access Permission.

Figure 12-3

Viewing the Demand Dial
Interface

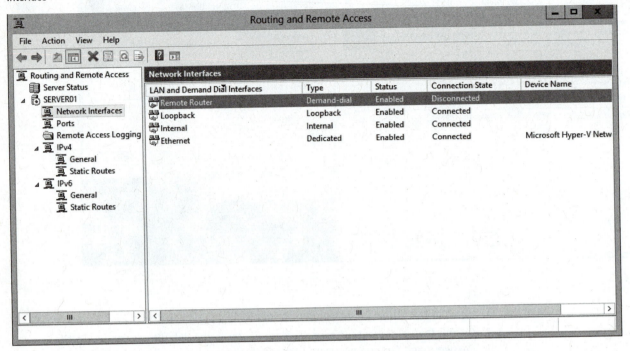

Routing and Remote Access				

Network Interfaces

LAN and Demand Dial Interfaces	Type	Status	Connection State	Device Name
Remote Router	Demand-dial	Enabled	Disconnected	
Loopback	Loopback	Enabled	Connected	
Internal	Internal	Enabled	Connected	
Ethernet	Dedicated	Enabled	Connected	Microsoft Hyper-V Netw

Tree (left pane):
- Routing and Remote Access
  - Server Status
  - SERVER01
    - Network Interfaces
    - Ports
    - Remote Access Logging
    - IPv4
      - General
      - Static Routes
    - IPv6
      - General
      - Static Routes

Configuring Packet Filters

THE BOTTOM LINE

To keep a network secure, you want to limit what traffic can enter and leave the network perimeters. Because the Remote Access/VPN servers are acting as routers, you can configure *packet filters* to allow desirable traffic while minimizing undesirable traffic. With Windows Server 2012 R2, packet filtering is done with Windows Firewall.

CERTIFICATION READY
Configure packet filters
Objective 3.4

Windows Firewall with Advanced Security (WFAS) is a tool that allows you to manage the Windows Firewall (a stateful host-based firewall) with IPsec. Windows Firewall is designed to protect against attacks that originate from within your network or those that might bypass network perimeter firewall(s). Windows firewall inspects both IPv4 and IPv6 packets that enter and leave your computer and then compares them against the criteria contained in the firewall's rules. If the packet matches a rule, the action configured in the rule is applied. If the packet does not match a rule, the firewall discards it and records an entry in its log files.

Exploring the WFAS Profiles

WFAS is network location–aware, so it can determine the type of network you are connecting to. After it identifies the type of network, it applies the appropriate profile to provide protection against attacks that can originate from inside and outside of your network.

You can use the following WFAS profiles to apply settings to your computer (see Figure 12-4):

Figure 12-4

WFAS profiles

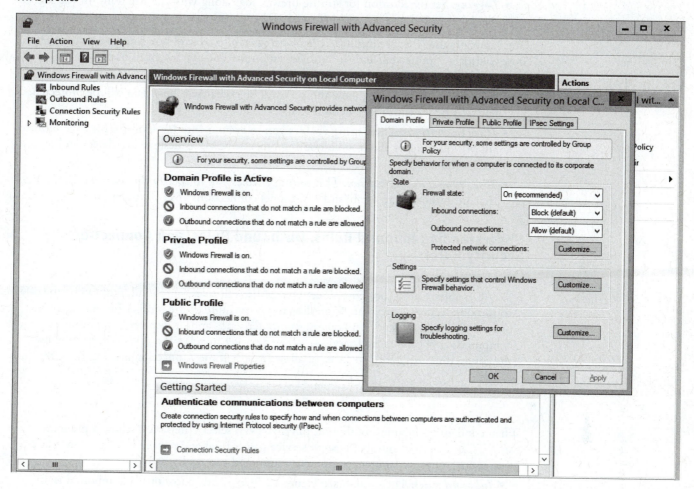

- Use a ***domain profile*** when your computer is connected to its corporate domain and can authenticate to the domain controller through one of its connections.
- Use a ***private profile*** when your computer is connected to a private network location (home or small office network) and is located behind a firewall and/or a device that performs Network Address Translation (NAT). If you are using this profile with a wireless network, you should implement encryption (WPAv2).
- Use a ***public profile*** when your computer is connected to a public network (for example, directly connected to the Internet). It is assigned to the computer when it is first connected to a new network; rules associated with this profile are the most restrictive.

You can click the Windows Firewall Properties link to see the range of settings available within each of the three profiles. These settings include the following:

- ***Firewall state:*** Set to On or Off.
- ***Inbound connections:*** Set to Block, Block all connections, or Allow.
- ***Outbound connections:*** Set to Allow or Block.
- ***Protected network connections:*** Select the connections/interfaces you want Windows Firewall to help protect.

- *Settings:* Choose to display notifications when a program is blocked from receiving inbound connections; allow unicast response to multicast or broadcast network traffic; and perform rule merging (allow rules created by local administrators to be merged with rules distributed via Group Policy).
- *Logging:* Set the location for storing firewall logs along with the size limit for the log file; log dropped packets; and log successful connections.

You can configure IPsec settings (the IPsec settings tab) to control how keys are exchanged, how your data is protected, and the authentication methods you want to use:

- *IPsec defaults:* These settings determine how your computer will establish a secure connection by identifying how the keys will be exchanged, how data will be protected, and which authentication method to use.
- *IPsec exemptions:* This setting enables you to exempt Internet Control Message Protocol (ICMP) to simplify the troubleshooting process. ICMP is designed to detect and report error conditions.
- *IPsec tunnel authorization:* This setting enables you to specify the users and computers that are authorized to establish IPsec tunnel connections with your computer.

Understanding Inbound Rules, Outbound Rules, and Connection Security Rules

WFAS enables you to configure three types of firewall rules—inbound, outbound, and connection security—that can be applied to one or more of the profiles (domain, private, or public). These rules govern how the computer sends and/or receives traffic from users, computers, applications, and services. When a packet matches the rule's criteria, it allows the connection, explicitly blocks it, or allows it only if the connection is using IPsec to secure it.

When configuring inbound/outbound rules, you can select criteria to include a program name, TCP/UDP port number, system service name, local and remote interfaces, interface types, users/groups, computers/computer groups, and protocols:

- *Inbound rules:* These rules (see Figure 12-5) explicitly allow or block inbound traffic that matches the criteria set in the rule. To set up an inbound rule, select the type (program, port, predefined, or custom), select the entity to which the rule applies (for example, specify program all or provide a path to a specific .exe, or specify a port name/number), determine the action (allow, block, or allow if it is secure), select the profile it applies to (domain, private, or public), and provide a name for the rule. When your system is set up, it is automatically configured to disallow unsolicited inbound traffic. If you decide to set up a service on your computer (a test website) and want others to connect to it, configure an inbound rule that allows traffic to the web service (typically running on TCP port 80).

Figure 12-5

Window Firewall with Advanced Security inbound rules

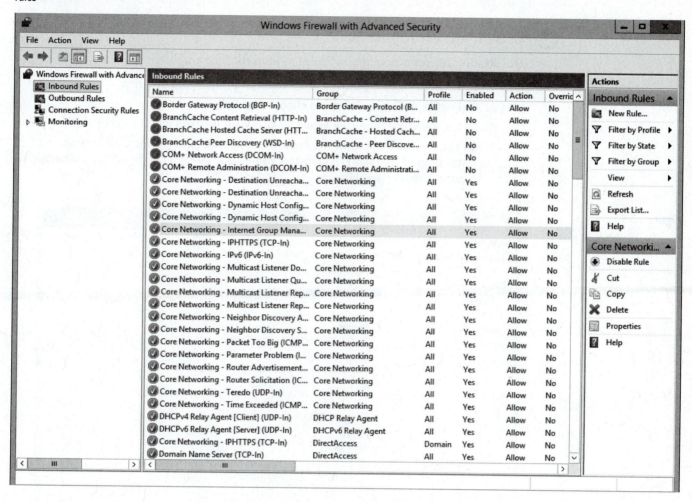

- *Outbound rules:* These rules explicitly allow or deny outbound traffic that originates from the computer when it matches the criteria set in the rule. The setup for an outbound rule is identical to the options discussed in the inbound rule. Because outbound traffic is allowed by default, you create an outbound rule to block traffic that you did not want.

Connection security rules: These rules secure the connection with both authentication (Kerberos, digital certificates, and preshared keys) and encryption protocols. Connection security rules are used to determine how the traffic between the computer and others is secured. The process for creating a connection security rule involves setting the type of connection security you want to create (isolation, authentication encryption, server-to-server, or tunnel), when you want authentication to occur on inbound/outbound connections (request but do not require it, require it for inbound but request for outbound, or require for both), select the authentication method to use, choose which profile to apply the rule to (domain, private, or public), and then provide a name for the rule.

TAKE NOTE*

Many roles and applications will automatically configure the needed Windows Firewall rules.

TAKE NOTE Connection security rules specify how and when authentication occurs, but they do not allow connections. You need to create an inbound or outbound rule to allow the connection.

➔ CREATE AN OUTBOUND RULE

GET READY. To create an outbound rule, perform the following steps.

1. In *Server Manager*, open Windows Firewall with Advanced Security.
2. Right-click Outbound Rules and choose New Rule.
3. On the *Rule Type* page (see Figure 12-6), select Program and then click Next.
4. On the *Program* page, click Browse and then navigate to the location of your installation of Internet Explorer. This can usually be found at c:\%ProgramFiles%\ Internet Explorer\iexplore.exe.

Figure 12-6

Creating an outbound rule

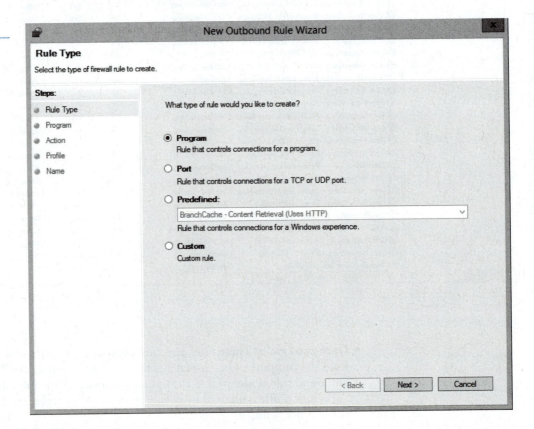

5. Select iexplore.exe and then click Open.
6. In the *New Outbound Rule* Wizard, click Next.
7. On the *Action* page, select Block the connection and then click Next.
8. On the *Profile* page, select Domain, Private, and Public; then, click Next.
9. On the *Name* page, for the name of the profile, type IE Restriction; for the description, type Restricts IE from connecting to the Internet.
10. Click Finish.
    Do not close the *Windows Firewall with Advanced Security* dialog box.
11. Use Internet Explorer to try to access the Internet. You should see the message *This page can't be displayed*.

12. Close the *Internet Explorer* window.

13. In the *Windows Firewall with Advanced Security* window, from the top menu, click Action and then choose Export Policy.

14. Navigate to a folder that you can access from your Windows Server 2012 R2 domain controller. In the *File name* field, type IE Restriction and then click Save.

    Note where you stored this policy, because you will use it in the next exercise.

15. When the message *Policy successfully exported* appears, click OK.

16. Return to the *Windows Firewall with Advanced Security* dialog box and click Outbound Rules.

17. Locate the Internet Explorer restriction rule you created earlier, right-click it, and then choose Delete. Click Yes to confirm you want to delete the rule.

18. Use Internet Explorer again to try to access the Internet. You should be successful this time.

19. Close *Internet Explorer* and *Windows Firewall with Advanced Security*.

To secure traffic, you can create connection security rules, which are used to evaluate network traffic, and then block or allow messages based on the criteria you established in the rule. If you configure settings that require security for a connection (in either direction), and the two computers cannot authenticate each other, the connection is blocked. Windows Firewall with Advanced Security uses IPsec to enforce these rules.

Windows Firewall rules that you can configure are as follows:

- An *isolation rule* isolates computers by restricting connections based on credentials.

- An *authentication exemption rule* designates connections that do not require authentication. You can designate computers by specific IP address, IP address range, subnet, or predefined group such as a gateway.

- A *server-to-server rule* protects connections between specific computers. When you create the rule, you specify the network endpoints between which communications are protected, and the requirements and the authentication that you want to use.

- A *tunnel rule* allows you to protect connections between gateway computers. Typically, you use such a rule when connecting across the Internet between two security gateways. You must specify the tunnel endpoints by IP address, and then specify the authentication method.

- Use a *custom rule* to authenticate connections between two endpoints when you cannot set up the authentication rules by using the other rules available in the new Connection Security Rule Wizard.

To specify how authentication is applied to inbound and outbound connections, you use the Connection Security Rule Wizard. If you request authentication, communications are enabled even if authentication fails. If you require authentication, the connection drops if authentication fails.

The following is a list of options for configuring authentication:

- ***Request Authentication for Inbound and Outbound Connections:*** Select this option to specify that all inbound and outbound traffic is authenticated, yet allow the connection even if authentication fails. If authentication succeeds, traffic is protected.

- ***Require Authentication for Inbound Connections*** and ***Request Authentication for Outbound Connections:*** Use the first option if you require that all inbound traffic be authenticated or be blocked. Outbound traffic can be authenticated but is allowed even if authentication fails. If authentication succeeds for outbound traffic, that traffic is authenticated.

- *Require Authentication for Inbound and Outbound Connections:* Use this option to require that all inbound and outbound traffic either be authenticated, or blocked.

When creating these rules, you have the following authentication methods available:

- Computer and User (Kerberos version 5 (V5) protocol)
- Computer (Kerberos V5 protocol)
- User (Kerberos V5 protocol)
- Computer certificate

Some considerations for designing connection security rules are as follows:

- To create an IPsec connection, compatible connection security rules must exist on both hosts.
- When a connection security rule is in place, other rules can be enforced based on the user or computer.
- Use Kerberos V5 authentication to allow both user and computer authentication.
- Because rules can conflict, avoid applying IPsec policies and connection security rules to the same computer.
- Any IPsec policies applied through connection security rules will override IPsec policies applied through Group Policy.
- To automate the deployment of firewall rules and to help prevent errors, use Group Policy to deploy rules to a large number of computers.
- Before using IPsec, define its purpose as part of your security plan or policy.
- Because IPsec policies can stop communications between computers, you must thoroughly test IPsec rules before implementing them. A best practice is to request IPsec authentication and then verify functionality before requiring IPsec authentication.

> **TAKE NOTE** *
>
> Using Kerberos V5 authentication for connection security rules that involve domain controllers can result in the domain becoming inoperable.

Addressing Conflicts with Firewall Rules

As soon as an incoming packet matches a rule, that rule is applied and processing stops. From time to time, as you create rules, you will discover that traffic is allowed when it should be blocked, or that traffic is blocked when it should be allowed. Although you might have one rule that specifies traffic being allowed or blocked, it could conflict with another rule.

When firewall rules conflict, they are applied in the following order:

1. *Authenticated bypass rules* allow a connection even if the existing firewall rules would block it. For example, you might block a specific type of traffic but then want to allow a certain group of users and computers to bypass the block. These types of rules require that the authenticated computers utilize IPsec to prove their identity.
2. *Block connection rules* block matching inbound traffic.
3. *Allow connection rules* allow matching inbound traffic.
4. *Default profile behavior* and blocks unsolicited inbound traffic allows all outbound traffic.

Exporting Firewall Configuration Rules

Configuring multiple firewall rules is a lot of work. If you have multiple VPN servers, you want to find a simpler way to establish firewall rules on all the VPN servers. To accomplish this, you can export the firewall configuration rules and import the firewall settings into a Group Policy object (GPO), which can be applied to all your VPN servers.

After you export the current firewall configuration from the Action menu in the Windows Firewall with Advanced Security window, you can then import it on another stand-alone system or copy it to a folder to use as a backup in case you make changes to the policy and need to return it to a known state. Policy files are exported as (*.wfw) files.

If you want to deploy the firewall configuration to multiple computers in your domain, create a Group Policy Object (GPO) and import the firewall settings into the policy.

IMPORT A WINDOW FIREWALL RULE INTO A GROUP POLICY OBJECT

GET READY. To import the firewall policy you created earlier into a GPO and restrict the use of Internet Explorer for your domain, log on with administrative privileges to your domain controller and then perform the following steps:

1. If Server Manager does not open automatically, click the Server Manager icon on the task bar.
2. Click Tools > Group Policy Management.
3. Expand the *contoso.com* domain folder, right-click Group Policy Objects choose New.
4. For the name, type IE Restriction and then click OK.
5. Double-click the *Group Policy Objects* folder and click IE Restriction.
6. Right-click and choose Edit.
7. Expand Computer Configuration > Policies > Windows Settings > Security Settings > Windows Firewall with Advanced Security.
8. Right-click the Windows Firewall with Advanced Security policy and choose Import Policy.
9. When you are prompted to confirm that you want to import a policy now, click Yes.
10. Browse to the folder where you saved the IE Restriction policy in the previous exercise. Click the IE Restriction policy and then click Open.
11. When you see *Policy successfully imported*, click OK.
12. Click the Outbound Rules folder. The IE Restriction policy is now listed in the GPO.
13. Close the *Group Policy Management Editor* window.
14. In the *Group Policy Management* console, right-click the contoso.com domain and choose Link an Existing GPO.
15. Click IE Restriction and then click OK.
16. Close the *Group Policy Management* console window. The GPO is now applied to your domain.

■ Implementing Packet Tracing

THE BOTTOM LINE

Sometimes when you encounter a problem, its cause and resolution might not be obvious. Sometimes you need to search through the packets being passed over the network or through a Remote Access server. To accomplish this, you perform *packet tracing* or packet capturing so that you can analyze the packets.

CERTIFICATION READY
Implement packet tracing
Objective 3.4

To enable packet tracing of a Remote Access server, click Start Tracing in the dashboard's Monitoring task pane of the Remote Access Management Console. From here, you can then configure how and where the logs will be stored.

START A PACKET TRACE

GET READY. To start a packet trace using the Remote Access Management console, perform the following steps:

1. From *Server Manager*, open Remote Access.
2. In the *Remote Access Management* Console, click the Remote Access server.
3. In the *Tasks* pane, click Start Tracing.
4. In the *Start Tracing* dialog box (see Figure 12-7), click Start Tracing.

Figure 12-7

Starting a trace

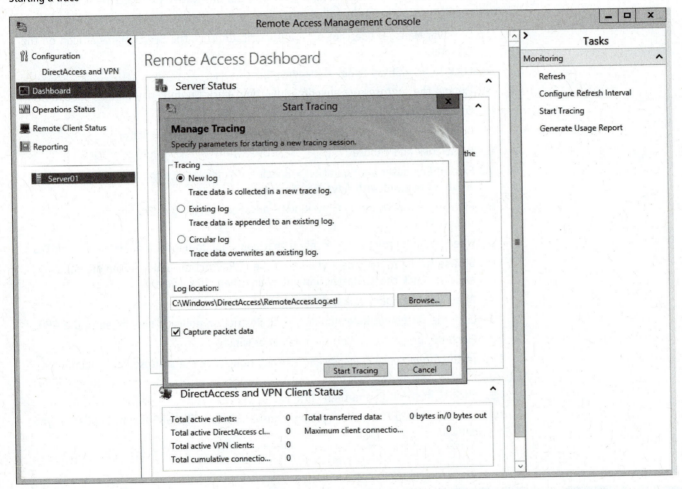

5. After the trace collects enough packets, in the *Tasks* pane, click Stop Tracing.
6. In the *Manage Tracing* dialog box, click Stop Tracing.

In some situations, you might want to use a protocol analyzer/network analyzer, which allows you to view the actual packets on the network and usually contains tools to analyze the packets. Three popular software protocol analyzers are WireShark, Microsoft Network Monitor, and Microsoft Message Analyzer.

A protocol analyzer grabs every packet on a network interface, puts a timestamp on each packet, and stores the packets in a storage area. You would use a filter to specify the packets to display. Then open each packet to look at the various TCP/IP layers to see what is happening. The packets can be saved to a file so that they can be analyzed later.

When you first capture packets on an interface, you should quickly notice hundreds of packets. Usually, most packets can be ignored because they have nothing to do with the problem you are trying to analyze. In these cases, you need to use a filter to show only the packets that you are concerned with.

Implementing MultiSite Remote Access

↓ THE BOTTOM LINE

Larger organizations have multiple DirectAccess entry points across geographic locations. Windows 8 and Windows 8.1 clients allow users to connect from the Internet to access resources within the organization's network efficiently regardless of where they are located by automatically connecting to the closest DirectAccess server. If one of the access points is not available, the clients failover to another entry point.

CERTIFICATION READY
Implement multisite
Remote Access
Objective 3.4

To configure multisite Remote Access, click the Enable Multisite link in the Tasks pane to start the Enable Multisite Deployment Wizard. When you run this wizard, you will enable multisite, and define the initial entry point. You then can add entry points.

For multisite Remote Access deployment, both the Network Location Server and the IP-HTTPS server must use trusted certificates and cannot use self-signed certificates. The Remote Access server role must be configured on the server to be added to the multisite configuration. However, Remote Access should not be configured on that new server.

 ENABLE MULTISITE REMOTE ACCESS

GET READY. To enable multisite Remote Access via the Remote Access Management console, perform the following steps:

1. From *Server Manager*, open Remote Access.

2. In the *Remote Access Management* Console, click DirectAccess and VPN in the left pane.

3. Under the *Tasks* pane, click Enable Multisite.

4. In the *Enable Multisite Deployment* Wizard, on the *Before You Begin* page, click Next.

5. On the *Multisite Deployment and Entry Point Name* page, the default multisite deployment name is *Enterprise*. In the *First entry point name* text box, type Corporate. Click Next.

6. On the *Entry Point Selection* page, leave *Assign entry points automatically, and allow clients to select manually* selected. Click Next.

7. On the *Global Load Balancing Settings* page, select Yes, use global load balancing. In the *Type the global load balancing FQDN to be used by all entry points* text box, type a name such as directaccess.contoso.com. In the *Type the global load balancing IP address for this entry point* text box, type the public IP address of the previous of the global load balancing fully qualified domain name (FQDN). Click Next.

8. On the *Client Support* page, leave *Limit access to client computers running Windows 8 or a later operating system* selected. Click Next.

9. On the *Summary* page, click Commit.

10. When the configuration is applied, click Close.

11. Click Close to close the *Enable Multisite Deployment* Wizard.

After multisite Remote Access is enabled, you then add entry points by running the Add an Entry Point Wizard via the Remote Access Management Console on the first server. In fact, you can use the server that you enabled Multi-Site using Remote Access Management Console to manage all your DirectAccess servers.

 ADD AN ENTRY POINT

GET READY. To add an entry point via the Remote Access Management console that has the Remote Access role installed, perform the following steps:

1. From *Server Manager*, open Remote Access.
2. In the *Remote Access Management* Console, click DirectAccess and VPN in the left pane.
3. Under the *Tasks* pane, click Add an Entry Point.
4. In the *Add an Entry Point* Wizard, on the *Entry Point Details* page, in the *Remote Access server* and *Entry point name* text boxes, type server02.contoso.com. Click Next.
5. On the *Global Load Balancing Settings* page, in the *Type the global load balancing IP address for this entry point* text box, type the external IP address. Click Next.
6. On the *Network Topology* page, select one following topologies and click Next:
   - Edge
   - Behind an edge device (with two network adapters)
   - Behind an edge device (with a single network adapter)
7. On the *Network Name or IP address* page, in the *Type in the public name or IP address used by clients to connect to the Remote Access server* text box, type a name or IP address for the Remote Access entry point.
8. On the *Network adapters* page, click the Browse button to select a digital certificate to be used with IP-HTTPS. Click Next.
9. On the *Prefix Configuration* page, click Next.
10. On the *Client Support* page, click Next.
11. On the *Server GPO Settings* page, click Next.
12. On the *Network Location Server* page, use the Browse button to select a digital certificate. Click Next.
13. On the *Summary* page, click Commit.
14. When the configuration is applied, click Close.
15. Click Close to close the *Add an Entry Point* Wizard.

In the left pane, you can see all DirectAccess servers/entry points, as shown in Figure 12-8. If you need to remove an entry point, simply select the DirectAccess server with the entry point and, under Tasks, click Remove Entry Point.

Figure 12-8

Managing entry points

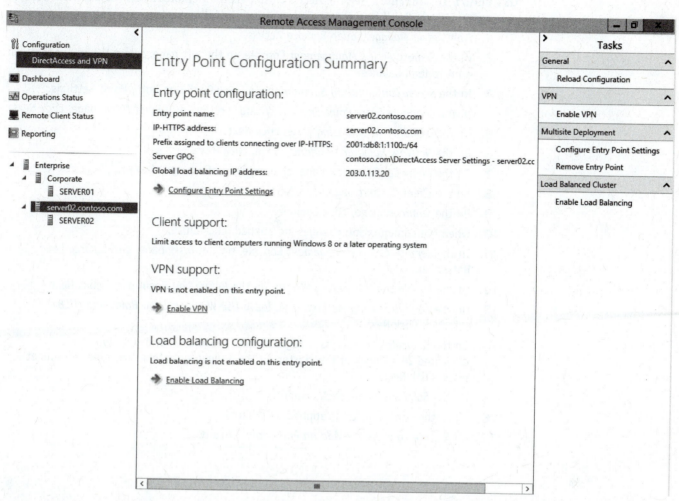

■ Configuring Remote Access Clustered with Network Load Balancing (NLB)

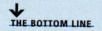 **THE BOTTOM LINE**

Because remote users depend on a Remote Access connection, most organizations want to make sure that the Remote Access server is always available. *Network Load Balancing (NLB)* can be used with Remote Access to provide greater availability as well as load sharing among multiple servers.

CERTIFICATION READY
Configure Remote Access clustered with network load balancing (NLB)
Objective 3.4

Before you can use NLB with Remote Access, you first must install NLB. You can then use the Enable Load Balancing Wizard to configure NLB. Like with configuring NLB for file serving, you specify the dedicated IP address. Because IPv6 addressing is used for VPN, the IPv6 prefix should be 59 bits.

CONFIGURE A REMOTE ACCESS CLUSTER

GET READY. To configure a Remote Access cluster via the Remote Access Management console on a server with the NLB feature installed, perform the following steps:

1. From *Server Manager*, open Remote Access.

2. In the *Remote Access Management* Console, in the left pane, select the server that you want to load balance.

3. In the *Server Configuration Summary* pane, click Configure Entry Point Settings.

4. In the *Configure Entry Point Settings* Wizard, on *the Entry Point Name* page, click Next.

5. On the *Global Load Balancing* page, click Next.

6. On the *Network Name or IP address* page, click Next.

7. On the *Prefix Configuration* page, change the prefix length (*/xx*) to */59*. Click Next.

8. On the *Client Support* page, click Next.

9. On the *Summary* page, click Commit.

10. When the configuration changes are applied, click Close.

11. In the *Remote Access Management* Console, on the *Tasks* pane, click Enable Load Balancing.

12. In the *Enable Load Balancing* Wizard, on the *Before You Begin* page, click Next.

13. On the *Load Balancing Method* page, leave *Use Windows Load Balancing (NLB)* selected. Click Next.

14. On the *Dedicated IP Addresses* page, in the *IPv4 address* text box, type the dedicated IP address for the cluster. In the *Subnet mask* text box, type the subnet mask. Click Next.

15. On the *Summary* page, click Commit.

16. When the configuration is applied, click Close.

17. Click Close to close the *Add an Entry Point* Wizard.

■ Implementing an Advanced DirectAccess Solution

 THE BOTTOM LINE For more control, you can run the Run the Remote Access Setup Wizard. You also can execute the Remote Access Setup Wizard during the initial installation or anytime afterward to fine-tune a deployment.

CERTIFICATION READY
Implement an advanced
DirectAccess solution
Objective 3.4

The Run the Remote Access Setup Wizard breaks the installation to the following steps, as shown in Figure 12-9:

Figure 12-9

Using the Access Setup Wizard

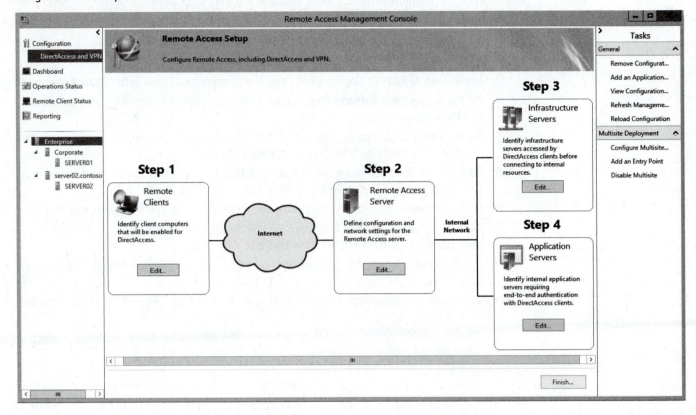

1. **Remote Clients:** You can specify which clients within your organization can use DirectAccess. You specify the computer groups that you want to include and whether you want to include Windows 7 clients.

2. **Remote Access Server:** You can configure the network connections based on one or two network cards and specify which adapters are internal and which are external. You can also specify the use of smart cards and the certificate authority (CA) to use for DirectAccess to provide secure communications.

3. **Infrastructure Servers:** You can configure how the clients access the core infrastructure services, such as Active Directory domain controllers and DNS servers. You also can specify an internal web server that can provide location services for infrastructure components to your DirectAccess clients.

4. **Application Servers:** You can configure your end-to-end authentication and security for the DirectAccess components. You also can provide secure connections with individual servers to which you want to establish secure connections.

In Window 7 and Windows Server 2008 R2, DirectAccess used the DirectAccess Connectivity Assistant (DCA), which is a free solution accelerator installed on the DirectAccess clients that adds an icon to the notification area of the desktop. The DCA provides tools to help users reconnect if a problem occurs and to help with diagnostics used by the help desk. It helps detect whether One-Time Passwords (OTPs) are required and helps your system determine whether it is connected to the intranet or the Internet.

In Windows 8, the DCA was replaced by the ***Network Connectivity Assistant (NCA).*** Although the DCA has to be downloaded from Microsoft, the NCA is included in the Windows 8 operating system, and installation and deployment are not required.

CONFIGURE REMOTE CLIENTS

GET READY. To configure remote clients, perform the following steps:

1. From *Server Manager*, click Tools > Remote Access Management.
2. In the *Remote Access Management* console, on the left pane, click DirectAccess and VPN, and the click the top node of your DirectAccess infrastructure.
3. Under *Step 1, Remote Clients*, click Edit. The *DirectAccess Client Setup Wizard* opens.
4. On the *Deployment Scenario* page, select Deploy full DirectAccess for client access and remote management.
5. On the *Select Groups* page, select Add. Type the name of the group of computers that you want to include as DirectAccess clients and click OK.
6. Back on the *Select Groups* page, if Forefront UAG is configured to use force tunneling for DirectAccess clients, select Use force tunneling. Click Next.
7. On the *Network Connectivity Assistant* page, double-click a blank resource space.
8. In the *Configure Corporate Resources for NCA* dialog box, specify HTTP or ping and then specify an URL or FQDN in the text box. Click Add.
9. In the *Helpdesk email address* text box, specify an address for the organization's help desk.
10. By default, the DirectAccess connection name is *Workplace Connection*. If you wish to change it, do so.
11. If you want DirectAccess clients to use local DNS servers for name resolution, select Allow DirectAccess clients to use local name resolution.
12. Click Finish.

By using the Remote Access Server Setup Wizard, you can configure the DirectAccess server to specify what method of authentication to use.

 CONFIGURE THE DIRECTACCESS REMOTE ACCESS SERVER

GET READY. To configure the DirectAccess Remote Access server, perform the following steps:

1. Continuing with the *Remote Access Setup Configuration* page, under *Step 2, Remote Access Server*, click Edit. The *Remote Access Server Setup Wizard* starts.
2. On the *Network Topology* page, select the appropriate topology and specify the public name or IPv4 address used by clients to connect to the Remote Access server. Click Next.
3. On the *Network Adapters* page, ensure that the appropriate network adapters are selected for the external and internal networks.
4. Specify the digital certificate that you want to use for HTTPS connections or select Use a self-signed certificate created automatically by DirectAccess. Click Next.
5. On the *Prefix Configuration* page, specify the internal network IPv6 and IPv6 prefix assigned to DirectAccess client computers. Click Next.
6. On the *Authentication* page, specify whether to use Active Directory credentials (username/password) or Two-factor authentication. If you choose *Two-factor authentication*, you can select Use OTP.
7. If desired, you can use computer certificates. If you select the Use computer certificates, you have to choose the root or intermediate certification authority (CA). If you decide to use intermediate certification authority (CA), you need to select the Use an intermediate certificate.

8. Optionally, to allow Windows 7 clients, enable Enable Windows 7 client computers to connect via DirectAccess.

9. If you want to use Network Access Protection (NAP), select Enforce corporate compliance for DirectAccess clients with NAP.

10. Click Finish.

After you configure the DirectAccess server, you need to configure the infrastructure servers to support DirectAccess. For example, you need to configure the DNS servers, as well as specify your management servers, such as WSUS servers.

DirectAccess clients use the *network location server (NLS)* to determine their locations. The network location server is an internal web server. If the client computer can connect with HTTPS to the specified URL, the client computer assumes it is on the intranet and disables DirectAccess components. If the client cannot reach the NLS, it assumes it is on the Internet. The URL for the NLS is distributed via a GPO.

To configure an NLS, you need to install Internet Information Services (IIS) on a Windows server. Then for a website, bind a name such as *nsl.contoso.com* and associate an NLS DNS name to the IP address. Finally, to ensure that this server is highly available, you should use technology such as NLB and make sure that you have redundant hardware.

To ensure that DirectAccess clients can correctly detect when they are on the Internet, you can configure IIS server to deny connections from Internet-based clients with the IP and Domain Restrictions Web Server (IIS) role service. Alternatively, you can ensure that the CRL distribution point location in the certificate being used for network location cannot be accessed from the Internet.

⊙ CONFIGURE THE DIRECTACCESS INFRASTRUCTURE SERVERS

GET READY. To configure the DirectAccess infrastructure servers, perform the following steps:

1. Continuing with the *Remote Access Setup Configuration* page, under *Step 3, Infrastructure Server*, click Edit. The *Infrastructure Server Setup* Wizard opens.

2. On the *Network Location Server* page, type the URL of the network location in the appropriate box. Click Next.

3. On the *DNS* page, verify the DNS suffixes and internal DNS servers. Then, click Next.

4. On the *DNS Suffix Search List* page, verify the domain suffixes and click Next.

5. On the *Management* page, in the *Management Servers* box, double-click the first line.

6. In the *Add a Management Server* dialog box, add the names of your management servers, such as your Windows Update server. Click OK.

7. Click Finish.

As mentioned earlier, you can add an extra level of authentication and encryption to those servers that you must protect at all costs. By using the DirectAccess Application Server Setup Wizard, you can configure those servers.

⊙ CONFIGURE APPLICATION SERVERS FOR DIRECTACCESS

GET READY. To configure the application servers for DirectAccess, perform the following steps:

1. Continuing with the *Remote Access Setup Configuration* page, under *Step 4, Application Servers*, click Edit. The *DirectAccess Application Server Setup* Wizard starts.

2. On the *DirectAccess Application Server Setup* page, to add a layer of authentication and encryption between the DirectAccess clients and selected internal application servers, select the Extend authentication to selected application servers option.

3. If you selected to extend authentication, click Add. Then type in the name of the server for which you want to extend authentication and click OK.

4. Back on the *DirectAccess Application Server Setup* page, click Finish.

5. At the bottom of the *Remote Access Management console*, click Finish to apply all the changes for steps 1 through 4.

■ Configuring Multiple RADIUS Server Groups and Infrastructure

THE BOTTOM LINE

Remote Authentication Dial-In User Service (RADIUS) is a networking and client/server protocol that provides centralized ***authentication, authorization, and accounting (AAA)*** management for computers that connect and use a network service. It can be used in wireless and Remote Access connection technologies, 802.1x switches, and Remote Desktop Services Gateway.

RADIUS is defined in the Internet Engineering Task Force (IETF) RFCs 2865 and 2866. Microsoft's RADIUS server is part of ***Network Policy Server (NPS)***. By installing and configuring RADIUS, you can create and enforce network-wise access policies for client health, connection request authentication, and connection request authorization.

As mentioned earlier, RADIUS is used for authentication, authorization, and accounting. ***Authorization*** is the process that determines what a user is permitted to do on a computer system or network. After a client or device is authenticated, the client or device must be authorized to access any type of network resource. The *authorization* controls what resources an authenticated user can and cannot access. Finally, *accounting* keeps track of what resources a user has accessed or attempted to access.

When you implement RADIUS, Windows Server 2012 R2 computers running Routing and Remote Access Service (RRAS) and/or wireless access points can forward access requests to a single RADIUS server. The RADIUS server then queries the domain controller for authentication and applies NPS Network Policies to the connection requests.

TAKE NOTE*

RADIUS clients (also referred to as access servers) are servers (such as servers running RRAS) and devices (such as wireless access points and 802.1X switch) that forward RADIUS requests to a RADIUS server. An ***access client*** is a computer or device that contacts or connects to a RADIUS client, which requires authentication and authorization to connect.

When NPS is used as a RADIUS server, AAA follows these steps:

1. When an access client accesses a VPN server or wireless access point, a connection request is created and sent to the NPS server.

2. The NPS server evaluates the Access-Request message.

3. If required, the NPS server sends an Access-Challenge message to the access server. The access server processes the challenge and sends an updated Access-Request to the NPS server.

4. The user credentials are checked and the dial-in properties of the user account are obtained by using a secure connection to a domain controller.

5. When the connection attempt is authorized with both the dial-in properties of the user account and network policies, the NPS server sends an Access-Accept message to the access server. If the connection attempt is either not authenticated or not authorized, the NPS server sends an Access-Reject message to the access server.

6. The access server completes the connection process with the access client and sends an Accounting-Request message to the NPS server, where the message is logged.

7. The NPS server sends an Accounting-Response to the access server.

RADIUS has been officially assigned UDP ports 1812 for RADIUS Authentication and 1813 for RADIUS Accounting by the Internet Assigned Numbers Authority (IANA). However, before IANA officially allocated ports 1812 and 1813, ports 1645 and 1646 were used for authentication and accounting. Although Microsoft RADIUS servers default to port 1812 and 1813, others can still use 1645 an 1646. Therefore, if the RADIUS server is separated by a firewall, you should open all four ports.

Installing and Configuring Network Policy Server

Installing NPS is a simple process done with Server Manager. After NPS is installed, you use the Network Policy Server console to configure NPS.

 INSTALL NETWORK POLICY SERVER

GET READY. To install NPS, perform the following steps:

1. Click the Server Manager button on the task bar to open *Server Manager*.
2. At the top of *Server Manager*, select Manage and then click Add Roles and Features. The *Add Roles and Feature* Wizard opens.
3. On the *Before you begin* page, click Next.
4. Select Role-based or feature-based installation, and then click Next.
5. Click Select a server from the server pool, click the name of the server to install Network Policy and Access Services to, and then click Next.
6. On the *Server Roles* page, select Network Policy and Access Services and click Next.
7. When you are prompted to add features required for Network Policy and Access Services, click Add Features.
8. Back on the *Select server roles* page, click Next.
9. On the *Select features* page, click Next.
10. On the *Network Policy and Access Services* page, click Next.
11. On the *Select role services* page, with the NPS selected, click Next.
12. On the *Confirm installation* page, click Install.
13. When the installation is complete, click Close.

Configuring Multiple RADIUS Servers

If you have multiple RADIUS servers, you can configure RADIUS clients to use a primary RADIUS server and alternate RADIUS servers. If the primary RADIUS server becomes unavailable, the request is sent to the alternate RADIUS server.

Another multiple RADIUS server infrastructure is to place a **RADIUS proxy** between the RADIUS server and the RADIUS clients (see Figure 12-10). A RADIUS proxy forwards authentication and accounting messages to other RADIUS servers. When NPS is a RADIUS proxy, the NPS becomes a central switching or routing point through which RADIUS access and account messages flow.

Figure 12-10

Using a RADIUS proxy server

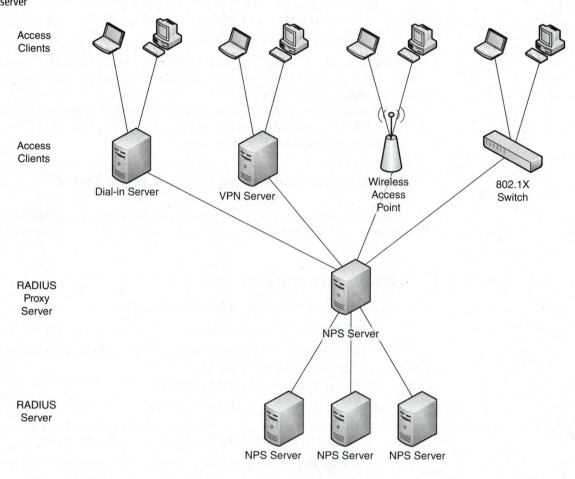

When you configure NPS as a RADIUS proxy, you create a new connection request policy that NPS uses to determine which connection requests to forward to other RADIUS servers. Also, the connection request policy is configured by specifying a remote RADIUS server group that contains one or more RADIUS servers, which tell NPS where to send the connection requests that match the connection request policy.

To configure load balancing, you must have more than one RADIUS server per remote RADIUS server group. Based on load and resources, you can configure the following:

- **Priority:** Priority specifies how important the RADIUS server to the NPS proxy server. The lower the number, the higher priority of the NPS proxy, with the highest priority being 1. When the NPS proxy sends connection request, it will first send to the RADIUS server with the highest priority. If the RADIUS server is not available, it will send to the RADIUS server with the next highest priority. You can also assign the same priority to multiple RADIUS servers to load balance the servers.

- **Weight:** Weight determines how many connections are sent to a RADIUS server when multiple RADIUS servers have the same priority level. While the Weight settings is assigned a value between 1 and 100, the number of connections are based on the weight as compared to other RADIUS weight settings. If two servers are assigned the same priority and weight, the connection requests are distributed evenly between the two servers.

• ***Advanced settings:*** If the remote RADIUS server is unavailable, you can start sending connection requests to other RADIUS servers. The Advanced settings determine when it considers the server is not available and sends the requests to the next RADIUS server.

 ADD A REMOTE RADIUS SERVER GROUP

GET READY. To add a remote RADIUS group, perform the following steps:

1. In *Server Manager*, click Tools > Network Policy Server. The *Network Policy Server console* opens.

2. In the console tree, double-click RADIUS Clients and Servers, right-click Remote RADIUS Server Groups and choose New. The *New Remote RADIUS Server Group* dialog box opens.

3. For *Group name*, type a name for the remote RADIUS server group.

4. Click Add. The *Add RADIUS Servers* dialog box opens.

5. Type the IP address of the RADIUS server that you want to add to the group or type the FQDN of the RADIUS server.

6. On the *Authentication/Accounting* tab, in the *Shared secret* and *Confirm shared secret* text boxes, type the shared secret that you used for the RADIUS server.

7. If you are not using Extensible Authentication Protocol (EAP) for authentication, click Request must contain the message authenticator attribute.

8. Verify that the authentication and accounting port numbers are correct for your deployment. The default port is 1813.

9. If you use a different shared secret for accounting, in Accounting, clear the Use the same shared secret for authentication and accounting check box. Then, in the *Shared secret* and *Confirm shared secret* text boxes, type the accounting shared secret.

10. If you do not want to forward network access server start and stop messages to the remote RADIUS server, clear the Forward network access server start and stop notifications to this server check box.

11. On the *Load Balancing* tab (see Figure 12-11), you can specify how often requests are sent to a specific server in a group by specifying the weight assigned to the server.

Figure 12-11

Configuring load balancing

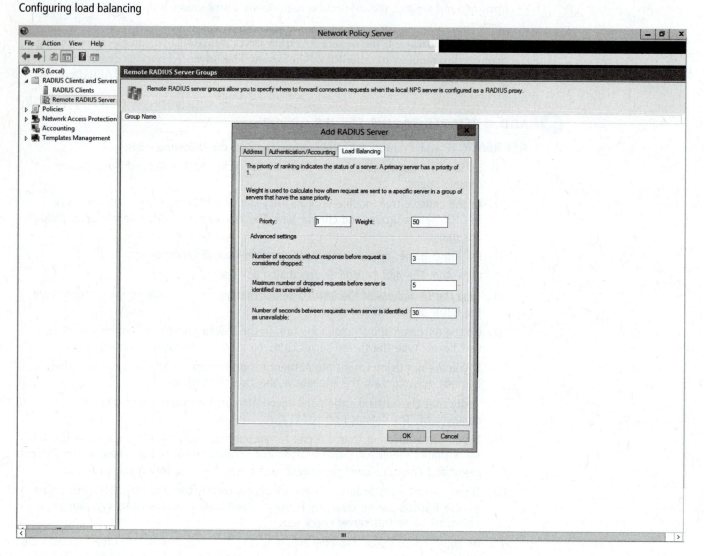

12. Click OK to close the *Add RADIUS Server* dialog box.

13. Click OK to close the *New Remote RADIUS Server* group.

If you want more control in the configuration, use NPS Advanced Configuration options in the Network Policy Server console. In addition to modifying the RADIUS clients, network policies, and accounting, you can configure the NAP Health Policy server and the RADIUS proxy (as shown in Figure 12-12).

Figure 12-12

Looking at NPS Advanced
Configuration

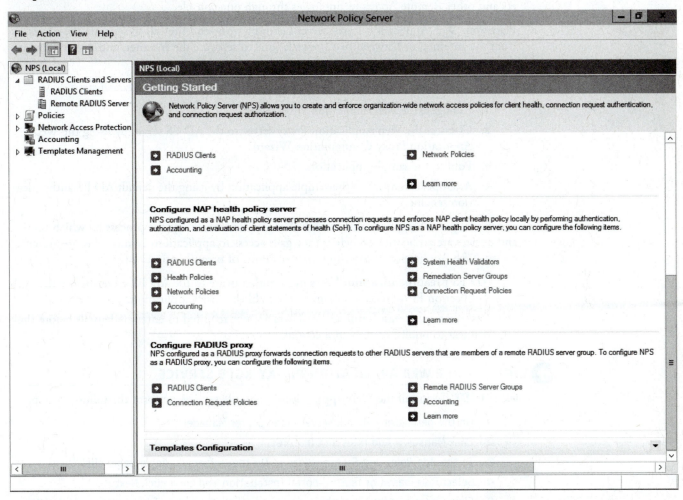

Configuring Web Application Proxy for Clustering

THE BOTTOM LINE

The Web Application Proxy provides reverse proxy functionality for web applications inside an organization's network so that users can access the application externally no matter what device they are using. Also, the Web Application Proxy preauthenticates access to web applications by using Active Directory Federation Services (AD FS) and functions as an AD FS proxy. You can install multiple Web Application proxy servers to form a cluster.

CERTIFICATION READY
Configure Web
Application Proxy for
clustering
Objective 3.4

A reverse proxy is a proxy server that retrieves resources from servers on behalf of a client. The resources are then relayed through the proxy server to the client. As far as the client is concerned, the resources originate from the server itself. You can use a Web Application Proxy to hide the existence of the resource server. It can selectively access the necessary applications on the servers inside the organization from the outside. Therefore, by using a reverse proxy, you protect applications from external threats and help protect internal resources by providing a defense-in-depth approach.

Starting with Windows Server 2012 R2, a reverse proxy is provided by a Remote Access role service, the Web Application Proxy. The Web Application Proxy is integrated into the Remote Access Management console, which allows you to manage your Web Application Proxy servers and other Remote Access technologies through one console.

Place your Web Application Proxy server behind a front-end firewall to separate the server from the Internet, or between two firewalls (one to separate the Internet, and one to separate the corporate network).

Configuring the Web Application Proxy server involves the following general steps:

1. Configure the Web Application Proxy server.
2. Connect the Web Application Proxy server to the AD FS server by using the Web Application Proxy Configuration Wizard.
3. Publish the sample application.
4. Attempt to connect to the sample application by using the default AD FS authentication scheme.

When you publish applications through Web Application Proxy, the process by which users and devices are authenticated before they gain access to applications is known as preauthentication. Web Application Proxy supports two forms of preauthentication:

- **AD FS preauthentication:** Users must authenticate to the AD FS server before the Web Application Proxy redirects them to the published web application.
- **Pass-through preauthentication:** Users are not required to enter credentials before they connect to published web applications.

 INSTALL THE WEB APPLICATION PROXY ROLE SERVICE

GET READY. To install the Web Application Proxy role service, perform the following steps:

1. On the perimeter network server, open Server Manager.
2. Click Manage > Add roles and features.
3. In the *Add Roles and Features Wizard*, On the *Before you begin* page, click Next.
4. Select Role-based or feature-based installation and then click Next.
5. Click Select a server from the server pool, click the name of the server to install the Remote Access role to, and then click Next.
6. On the *Select server roles* page, select Remote Access and then click Next.
7. On the Features page, click Next.
8. On the Remote Access page, click Next.
9. In the *Select role services* page, select Web Application Proxy, click Add Features, and then click Next.
10. In the *Confirm installation selections* dialog box, click Install.
11. When the installation is complete, click the Close button.

 CONFIGURE THE WEB APPLICATION PROXY

GET READY. To configure the Web Application Proxy, perform the following steps:

1. In *Server Manager*, click the yellow triangle with the black exclamation point. Then click Open the Web Application Proxy Wizard.
2. On the *Welcome* page, click Next.
3. On the *Federation Server* page, in the *Federation service name* text box, type the federation service name, such as adfs.contoso.com. Then in the *User name* and

Password text boxes, type the name of an administrator and password for the federation server. Click Next.

4. On the *AD FS Proxy Certificate* page, select the digital certificate used with AD FS and click Next.

5. On the *Confirmation* page, click Configure.

6. On the *Results* page, click Close.

Because the Web Application Proxy configuration is stored on the AD FS servers within the organization, you can easily create a cluster by installing additional Web Application Proxy servers. When you run the Web Application Proxy Configuration wizard on additional Web Application Proxy servers, the configuration is automatically transferred to the new server. Figure 12-13 shows the Web Application Proxy cluster.

Figure 12-13

A Web Application Proxy cluster

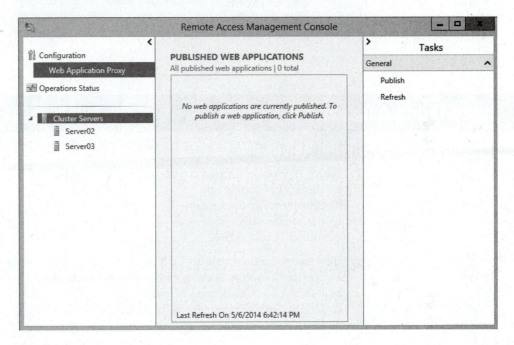

SKILL SUMMARY

IN THIS LESSON YOU LEARNED:

- A site-to-site VPN connection connects two private networks. When networks are connected over the Internet, a VPN-enabled router forwards packets to another VPN-enabled router across a VPN connection.

- To keep a network secure, you want to limit what traffic can enter and leave the network perimeters. Because the Remote Access/VPN servers are acting as routers, you can configure packet filters to allow desirable traffic while reducing undesirable traffic packets. With Windows Server 2012 R2, packet filtering is done with Windows Firewall.

- Sometimes you need to search through the packets being passed over the network or through a Remote Access server. To accomplish this, you perform packet tracing or packet capturing so that you can analyze the packets.

- Larger organizations have multiple DirectAccess entry points across geographic locations. If one of the access points is not available, the clients failover to another entry point.

- Because remote users depend on a Remote Access connection, most organizations want to make sure that the Remote Access server is always available. Network Load Balancing (NLB) can be used with Remote Access to provide greater availability as well as load sharing among multiple servers.
- For more control, you can run the Run the Remote Access Setup Wizard. You also can execute the Remote Access Setup Wizard during the initial installation or anytime afterward to fine-tune a deployment.
- If you have multiple RADIUS servers, you can configure RADIUS clients to use a primary RADIUS server and alternate RADIUS servers. If the primary RADIUS server becomes unavailable, the request is sent to the alternate RADIUS server.
- The Web Application Proxy provides reverse proxy functionality for web applications inside an organization's network so that users can access the application externally no matter what device they are using. You can install multiple Web Application Proxy servers to form a cluster.

■ Knowledge Assessment

Multiple Choice

1. Which type of connection connects two private networks?
   a. client VPN connection
   b. routable VPN connection
   c. site-to-site VPN connection
   d. sub-VPN connection

2. How can you ensure that no TCP port 63 can communicate with a server?
   a. Use the Windows Firewall with Advanced Security.
   b. Use Internet Connection Firewall.
   c. Disable Internet Connection Sharing.
   d. Use a packet sniffer.

3. Which software is used to manage IPsec connections with a local computer?
   a. Windows Security console
   b. IPSec console
   c. Certificate Authority console
   d. Windows Firewall with Advanced Security

4. Which WFAS profile is used when the user is at home connected to the Internet?
   a. public profile
   b. domain profile
   c. private profile
   d. firewall profile

5. Which type of rule would you use to prevent a client to connect to a server over TCP port 152?
   a. inbound rule
   b. outbound rule
   c. connection security rules
   d. server rule

6. Which program is the simplest to use to perform packet tracing of a Remote Access connection?
   a. Remote Access Management Console
   b. Windows Firewall with Advanced Security

   c. Microsoft Network Monitor

   d. Microsoft Message Analyzer

7. Which of the following is not a default configuration of Windows Firewall?

   a. The firewall is turned on.

   b. Incoming traffic is blocked unless it matches a rule.

   c. The firewall is turned off.

   d. Outgoing traffic is allowed unless it matches a rule.

8. What is the maximum number of cluster nodes that you can have with a Remote Access cluster?

   a. 2

   b. 4

   c. 8

   d. 32

9. If you are using the Remote Access Setup Wizard to configure DirectAccess, which step is used to specify the internal web server that provides location services?

   a. remote clients

   b. Remote Access server

   c. infrastructure servers

   d. application servers

10. How is the location of the DirectAccess network location server distributed to the clients?

   a. GPO

   b. NAP console

   c. DHCP broadcast

   d. DNS entry

Best Answer

Choose the letter that corresponds to the best answer. More than one answer choice can achieve the goal. Select the BEST answer.

1. Which type of Windows Firewall rule would you use to encrypt traffic going between a client and a server?

   a. inbound rules

   b. outbound rules

   c. connection security rules

   d. crypto rules

2. You have an NPS proxy server that needs to authenticate users by forwarding the request to a RADIUS server. To ensure that the system is highly available, you configured two RADIUS servers. However, you want one server to be the primary server, and the other server be the backup server. What do you need to configure so that the primary server gets the entire request?

   a. Configure the primary server with a priority of 1.

   b. Configure the primary server with a weight of 1.

   c. Configure the primary server with a priority of 100.

   d. Configure the primary server with a weight of 100.

3. You capture packets for three minutes to diagnose a problem with Dynamic Host Configuration Protocol (DHCP). However, when you review the packets, you realize that you have hundreds of packets to go through. What should you do?

   a. Filter the packets to show only the DHCP packets.

   b. Filter the packets that only show communications between the DHCP server and the client.

    c. Sort the packets by IP address.
    d. Sort the packets by timestamp.

4. You want to make DirectAccess highly available. What should you do?
    a. Create an NLB cluster for DirectAccess.
    b. Install multiple RADIUS servers.
    c. Configure a Web Application Proxy cluster.
    d. Implement multiple access points.

5. How do you make the Web Application Proxy highly available?
    a. Create an NLB cluster for the Web Application Proxy.
    b. Configure a Web Application Proxy cluster.
    c. Specify two AD FS servers in the Web Application Proxy console.
    d. Configure pass-through preauthentication.

Build a List

1. Specify the correct order of how Windows Firewall rules are applied.
    _____ Allow connection
    _____ Authenticated bypass rules
    _____ Default profile behavior
    _____ Block connection

2. Specify the correct order to configure a Remote Access cluster.
    _____ Open the Configure Entry Point Settings Wizard.
    _____ In the Remote Access console, enable load balancing.
    _____ Install the NLB feature.
    _____ Specify a dedicated IP address.
    _____ Change the prefix configuration to /59 prefix length.

3. Specify the correct order when running the Remote Access Setup Wizard.
    _____ Remote Access Server
    _____ Infrastructure Servers
    _____ Application Servers
    _____ Remote Clients

■ Business Case Scenarios

Scenario 12-1: Standardizing Firewall Settings

You are an administrator for a corporation that has 1,500 client computers running Windows 7 and Windows 8. You need to ensure that Windows Firewall is enabled for all users and that each machine has the same standardized firewall rules. How can you accomplish this?

Scenario 12-2: Multiple RADIUS Servers

You want to use RADIUS servers for central authentication of remote users. However, because authentication must always be available, you want to make the RADIUS servers highly available. How can you make these servers highly available?

Designing and Implementing a Network Protection Solution

70-413 EXAM OBJECTIVE

Objective 3.5 – Design and implement a network protection solution. This objective may include but is not limited to: Design considerations including Network Access Protection (NAP) enforcement methods for DHCP, IPSec, VPN, and 802.1x, capacity, placement of servers, firewall, Network Policy Server (NPS), and remediation network; configure NAP enforcement for IPsec and 802.1x; monitor for compliance.

LESSON HEADING	EXAM OBJECTIVE
Designing Network Access Protection (NAP)	
• Choosing a NAP Enforcement Method	Design Network Access Protection (NAP) enforcement methods for DHCP, IPSec, VPN, and 802.1x
• Designing for NAP Capacity	Design for capacity
• Designing placement of Servers, Firewall, Network Policy Server, and Remediation Network	Design for placement of servers, firewall, Network Policy Server (NPS), and remediation network
• Configuring NAP Enforcement for IPsec	Configure NAP enforcement for IPsec
• Configuring NAP enforcement for 802.1x	Configure NAP enforcement for 802.1x
• Configuring System Health Validators (SHVs)	
• Configuring Health Policies	
• Configuring Isolation and Remediation	
• Monitoring NAP Compliance	Monitor for compliance

KEY TERMS

802.1x enforcement

DHCP enforcement

health policy server

Health Registration Authority (HRA)

health requirements server

Internet Protocol Security (IPsec) enforcement

Network Access Protection (NAP)

NAP agent

NAP client-side components

NAP enforcement points

NAP health policy server

remediation servers

statement of health (SoH)

system health agents (SHAs)

system health validators (SHVs)

VPN enforcement

Designing Network Access Protection (NAP)

THE BOTTOM LINE

Microsoft *Network Access Protection (NAP)* is software for controlling network access for computers based on the host's health, which depends on the newest security patches and a current antivirus/antimalware software package. You can use NAP on any computer that runs Windows and supports NAP. As a computer connects to the network, its health status is evaluated based on health policies to determine whether it should be allowed to connect to the network. If a computer is not compliant with the system health requirements, it can be denied network access or given restricted network access. In some situations, automatic remediation can occur to bring the computer into compliance.

The following types of computers can connect to an organization's network:

- **Desktop computers:** These Windows computers typically do not move much and are part of the domain. Because they are part of the domain, they are easier to manage with Group Policy Objects, managed antivirus/antimalware systems, and administrative control.

- **Roaming laptops:** These Windows computers move often and might not be connected to the organization's network office. Because they are typically part of the domain, they can be managed but might not get the newest updates because they are not always connected to the network.

- **Unmanaged home computers:** These Windows computers usually do not connect directly to the network but instead connect through a virtual private network (VPN). Because they are usually personal computers, they are not part of the domain. Therefore, they usually do not get security updates and might not have an up-to-date antivirus/antimalware software package.

- **Visiting laptops:** These unmanaged Windows computers are often used by consultants or vendors who need to connect to your organization's network. Because they are unmanaged, they might not have the latest up-to-date security patches and an up-to-date antivirus/antimalware software package.

Each NAP enforcement method has its strengths and weaknesses. Although combining enforcement methods enables you to eliminate most of the weaknesses of your NAP deployment, using multiple NAP implementations makes the implementation complex to initiate and manage.

The overall architecture of NAP involves the following components:

- *NAP client-side components:* Windows Server 8, Windows 7, Windows Vista, Windows XP with SP3, Windows Server 2012 R2, Windows Server 2012, Windows Server 2008 R2, and Windows Server 2008. Microsoft also provides third-party vendors that can use the NAP API to write additional clients for additional operating systems such as Macintosh and Linux computers.

- *NAP enforcement points:* A server or device that enforces compliance. Depending on the enforcement method in use, a NAP enforcement point can take a number of different forms, such as an 802.1X-capable Wireless Access Point (WAP) for 802.1X enforcement, a Windows Server 2008 Dynamic Host Configuration Protocol (DHCP) server for the DHCP enforcement method, or a Health Registration Authority (HRA) that can obtain health certificates from client computers when the IPsec enforcement method is used.

- *NAP health policy server:* A server running the Network Policy Server (NPS) server role that receives information from NAP enforcement points. The health policy server stores NAP health requirement policies and provides health state validation for NAP clients.

- *System health agents (SHAs):* A component that maintains information and reporting on one or more elements of the health of a NAP client. Newer versions of Windows have a built-in Windows SHA that monitors the settings configured in the Windows Security Center. Third-party vendors can use the NAP API to write additional SHAs to plug into third-party products.

- *Statement of health (SoH):* Each SHA creates a SoH that transmits to the NAP agent. Each SHA generates a new SoH whenever the status is updated, such as when an update to the antivirus package is released but has not been installed on the client.

- *NAP agent:* A component that maintains information about the health of the NAP client computer and transmits information between the NAP enforcement clients and the SHAs. The NAP agent combines the SoH from each SHA into a single system statement of health (SSOH), which it then passes to the enforcement clients. The enforcement clients then use this SSOH to request network access by passing the SSOH information on to the NAP server components.

- *Health Registration Authority (HRA):* A computer that runs Windows Server 2012 R2 and Internet Information Services (IIS). It obtains health certificates from a certification authority (CA) for compliant computers.

- *Health requirements server:* A server that provides the current health state information to the NPS health policy server. Examples of health requirements include an antivirus software management server, or a Windows Server Update Services (WSUS) or System Center Configuration Manager (SCCM) server that sends updates to client computers.

- *Remediation servers:* An optional component that can be deployed to allow noncompliant client computers to achieve network compliance and gain network access. Examples include antivirus software or a WSUS server.

The following describes the NAP connection process:

1. When the NAP client connects to a network that requires NAP, each SHA on the NAP client validates its system health and generates a SoH.

2. The NAP client combines the SoHs from multiple SHAs into an SSoH and sends the information to a NAP health policy server that is defined with the NAP lenforcement point.

3. The NAP health policy server uses its installed SHVs and the health requirements policies to determine whether the NAP client meets health requirements.

4. The NAP health policy server combines the statement of health responses (SoHRs) from the multiple SHVs into a system statement of health response (SSoHR) and sends the SSoHR back to the NAP client through the NAP enforcement point.

5. If the client is compliant, the enforcement point allows the connection. If the client is noncompliant, the computer can be connected to a remediation network.

6. If the computer is noncompliant, the noncompliant computer can attempt to come into compliance.

7. If the status of the computer changes, the entire process starts over.

TAKE NOTE With Windows Server 2012 R2, NAP is deprecated. This means that NAP is available in Windows Server 2012 R2 and the material can be found on the 70-413 exam, but it will not be available in future versions of Windows servers.

Choosing a NAP Enforcement Method

NAP supports four enforcement methods: IPsec, 802.1X, VPN, and DHCP enforcement. When selecting a NAP enforcement method, you need to consider the benefits of each method. You must also understand how your users work and how their computers connect to your network.

CERTIFICATION READY
Design Network Access Protection (NAP) enforcement methods for DHCP, IPSec, VPN, and 802.1x
Objective 3.5

The **DHCP enforcement** method uses DHCP configuration information to ensure that NAP clients remain in compliance. If a computer is out of compliance, NAP provides a DHCP configuration that limits a person's access to the network until the computer is compliant. DHCP enforcement works only for IPv4 clients. If the client computer is noncompliant, a lease is given with the following settings:

- A default gateway of 0.0.0.0
- A subnet mask of 255.255.255.255
- Static routes to remediation servers

Three components are involved in a NAP deployment for DHCP:

- A DHCP NAP enforcement server
- A NAP DHCP enforcement client with NAP-capable clients
- A Network Policy Server (NPS)

NAP is configured on the DHCP management console. When configuring NAP on a server that does not run the DHCP service, you need to install the Network Policy Server (NPS) role on the DHCP server and then configure NPS to act as a Remote Authentication Dial-In User Service (RADIUS) proxy to forward connections to the local NPS server. Because DHCP enforcement works only when the client interacts with a DHCP server to request an initial lease or renew a lease, it is considered the weakest form of NAP enforcement because the client computer can bypass it by using static IP addresses.

The **Internet Protocol Security (IPsec) enforcement** method uses IPsec, which is secured by specially configured public key infrastructure (PKI) certificates known as health certificates. These certificates are issued to clients that meet defined compliance standards. If clients cannot provide the necessary health certificate, they cannot participate in IPsec-secured traffic. NAP with IPsec requires the following components:

- A health certificate server
- A Health Registration Authority (HRA)
- A Network Policy Server (NPS)
- A NAP IPsec enforcement client with NAP-capable clients

NAP with IPsec requires the HRA to have the NPS installed. The HRA NPS server is then configured as a RADIUS proxy to forward connections to the local NPS server. IPsec enforcement is considered the strongest form of NAP enforcement. DirectAccess uses IPsec enforcement and can set enforcement requirements for clients down to the individual IP address and/or port (TCP/UDP).

The **VPN enforcement** method restricts the level of network access that remote access clients can obtain, based on the health information that the client computers present when the VPN connection is made. VPN enforcement has two components:

- A VPN enforcement server
- NAP-capable clients running the NAP Remote Access and Extensible Authentication Protocol (EAP) enforcement clients

VPN enforcement ensures that roaming laptops or home computers do not introduce malware to your network. VPN enforcement means that health policies are enforced when a client connects to the VPN. When a computer is noncompliant, the VPN connection is still authenticated. However, IP filters restrict access to only remediation servers. This requires the Remote Access role, and the NPS must be configured as the primary RADIUS server. The VPN servers also must be configured as RADIUS clients.

The ***802.1x enforcement*** method uses 802.1x-aware network access points, such as network switches or wireless access points, to restrict network access of noncompliant resources. NAP for 802.1x uses the following components:

- 802.1X networking components such as wireless access points or switches
- NAP-capable clients with the NAP service and an EAP enforcement client

Although each NAP enforcement method has strengths and weaknesses, by combining enforcement methods, you can eliminate most of the weaknesses of your NAP deployment. However, deploying multiple NAP enforcement methods makes the deployment more complex and harder to manage.

Designing for NAP Capacity

When designing a system, you must always plan for capacity. For NPS deployment, you need to consider how to use each server and which roles each server will be responsible for. You also need to think about the location of the servers within your topology.

CERTIFICATION READY
Design for capacity
Objective 3.5

The following will affect the number of NAP client computers that can be supported by a NAP enforcement server:

- A shorter SoH validity period will result in more frequent access requests to the enforcement server.
- An enforcement server that provides other services or has limited processor speed will process fewer client requests.
- An enforcement server can support more clients if access requests are evenly distributed over time.
- For the IPsec enforcement method, a NAP client computer will attempt to renew its network access when it receives an update to Group Policy.
- A dedicated HRA server that meets the minimum hardware requirements can support 20 or more network request per second. In a typical environment, that equates to 50,000 or more clients with a certificate validity period of 24 hours.
- If the servers have cryptography requirements, the extra processing will affect performance.
- The ***health policy server*** provides authentication, including the health status of the client computer through the NPS RADIUS service. Although a typical server can handle a large number of requests without much impact to performance, NPS can be load balanced through a RADIUS server group.
- Although a stand-alone CA can perform slightly better than an enterprise CA for issuing health certificates, NAP CA servers are used when you use IPsec enforcement.

Designing Placement of Servers, Firewall, Network Policy Server, and Remediation Network

NAP is used to maintain the health of clients and remediate those that are considered unhealthy. The various enforcement methods are designed to protect the network and hosts connected to the network. While you are planning the capacity of each server, you also need to determine where to place each server. Of course, health requirement servers need to communicate with the health policy server, which dictates their placement within the NAP deployment.

On a typical network, remediation servers should not have to be used heavily because you should have update servers and antivirus/antimalware servers already keeping the organization computers compliant. Because the remediation servers are used to isolate noncompliant servers, you need to place them on a network separate from the main corporate network. Although most noncompliant computers will not contain malware, you need to assume that they can be infected and must be verified that they are not infected before being allowed to communicate on the production network.

Configuring NAP Enforcement for IPsec

NAP IPsec provides the strongest and most flexible method for maintaining client computer compliance with network health requirements. It provides secure communications with compliant clients based on IP address or port number.

To deploy NAP with IPsec and HRA, you must configure the following:

1. Configure connection request policy, network policy, and NAP health policy using NPS.
2. So that the NAP IPsec enforcement clients will work with the policies configured in the previous step, you need to enable the NAP IPsec enforcement client and the NAP service on NAP-capable client computers.
3. For the clients to know how to interact with the NAP IPsec enforcement clients, install HRA on the local computer or on a remote computer. If HRA is not installed on the local computer, you will need to install NPS on the server that is running HRA, and then configure the NPS as a RADIUS proxy server that will forward connection request to the local NPS server.
4. To issue health certificate for the NRA servers, install and configure Active Directory Certificate Services (AD CS), and then configure the appropriate Certificate Templates.
5. To configure the client computers for your deployment, you will configure Group Policy.
6. Configure the appropriate Windows Security Health Validator (WSHV) and install and configure other system health agents (SHAs) and system health validators (SHVs).

INSTALL NETWORK POLICY SERVER AND HEALTH REGISTRATION AUTHORITY

GET READY. To install Network Policy Server and Health Registration Authority, perform the following steps:

1. On *Server01*, using *Server Manager*, click Manage > Add Roles and Features. The *Add Roles and Feature Wizard* opens.

2. On the *Before you begin* page, click Next.

3. On the *Installation Type* page, select Role-based or feature-based installation, and then click Next.

4. On the *Server Selection* page, click Select a server from the server pool, click the name of the server to install Network Policy and Access Services to, and then click Next.

5. On the *Server Roles* page, select Network Policy and Access Services and click Next.

6. When you are prompted to add required features for Network Policy and Access Services, click Add Features.

7. On the *Select server roles* page, click Next.

8. On the *Select features* page, click Next.

9. On the *Network Policy and Access Services* page, click Next.

10. On the *Select server roles* page, expand *Network Policy and Access Services*. With the *Network Policy Server* selected, select Health Registration Authority.

11. In the *Add Roles and Features Wizard* dialog box, click Add Features.

12. Back on the *Select server roles* page, click Next.

13. On the *Select role services* page, click Next.

14. On the *Network Policy and Access Services* page, click Next.

15. If the CA is located on the current sever, select Use the local CA to issue health certificates for this HRA server. If the CA is on another server, select Use an existing remote CA and then specify the name of the server. Click Next.

16. On the *Authentication Requirements* page, select Yes, required requestors to be authenticated as members of a domain (recommended). Click Next.

17. On the *Confirm installation selection* page, click Install.

18. When the installation is complete, click Close.

 CONFIGURE THE NAP POLICY FOR IPsec

GET READY. To configure the NAP policy for IPsec, perform the following steps:

1. In *Server Manager*, click Tools > Network Policy Server. The *Network Policy Server* console opens (see Figure 13-1).

Figure 13-1

Starting the Network Policy
Server console

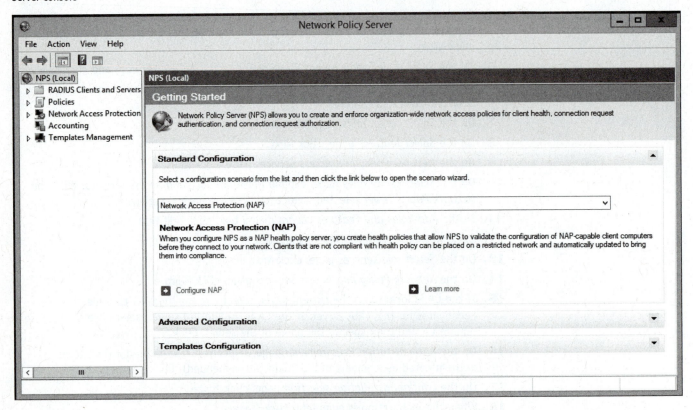

2. In the main pane, click Configure NAP to start the *Configure NAP* Wizard.

3. When the *Configure NAP* wizard starts, For the *Network connection method* option, select IPsec with Health Registration Authority (HRA).

4. In the *Policy name* text box, type a name for the policy. The default name is *NAP IPsec with HRA*. Click Next.

5. On the *Specify NAP Enforcement Servers Running HRA* page, for the RADIUS clients, click Add.

6. In the *New RADIUS Client* dialog box, type Server01. In the *Address (IP or DNS)* text box, type 192.168.1.60.

7. In the *Shared secret* and *Confirm shared secret* text boxes, type a password such as Pa$$w0rd. Click OK.

8. Back on the *Specify NAP Enforcement Servers Running HRA* page, click Next.

9. On the *Configure Machine Groups* page, click Add. In the *Select Group* dialog box, in the *Enter the object name to select* text box, type the name of the group that you created, such as IPsec Enabled. Click OK. If you do not specify a group, the policy is applied to all users.

10. Back on the *Configure Machine Groups* page, click Next.

11. On the *Define NAP Health Policy* page, leave the *Windows Security Health Validator* and *Enable auto-remediation of client computers* options selected (see Figure 13-2). Click Next.

Figure 13-2

Defining NAP health policies

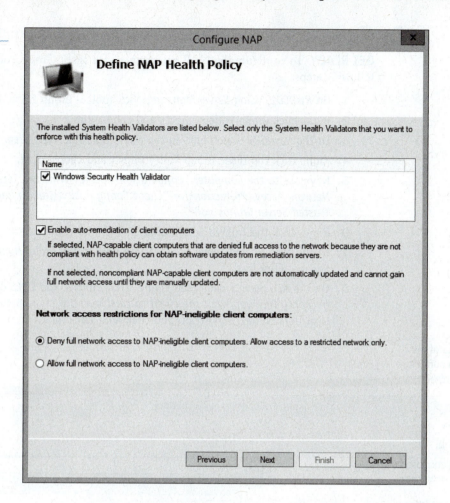

12. On the *Completing NAP Enforcement Policy and RADIUS Client Configuration* page, click Finish.

When the wizard is finished, the following configurations and policies are applied to your NPS server:

- A connection request policy named NAP IPsec with HRA is created that will configure the server to evaluate NAP IPsec requests.
- Two network policies are created: NAP IPsec with HRA Compliant and NAP IPsec with HRA Noncompliant.
- Two health policies are created: NAP IPsec for HRA Compliant and NAP IPsec with HRA Noncompliant.

Next, you need to configure the NAP clients by using the Computer Configuration\Policies\Windows Settings\Security Settings\Network Access Protection\NAP Client Configuration\Health Registration Settings\Trusted Server Groups and to Computer Configuration\Policies\Windows Settings\Security Settings\Network Access Protection\NAP Client Configuration\Enforcement Clients GPO settings. You must also ensure that computers have the following enabled:

- NAP agent service, which is the client-side service that allows the client to be NAP aware
- Security Center, which allows the NAP client service to provide information about the current state of the machine.

CONFIGURE NAP ENFORCEMENT FOR IPsec GROUP POLICY OBJECTS

GET READY. To configure the NAP enforcement for IPsec Group Policy Objects, perform the following steps:

1. On *RWDC01*, using *Server Manager*, click Tools > Group Policy Management.

2. Right-click Group Policy Objects and choose New.

3. In the *New GPO* dialog box, in the *Name* text box, type IPsec and click OK.

4. Right-click the IPsec Group Policy Object and choose Edit.

5. Navigate to the *Computer Configuration\Policies\Windows Settings\Security Settings\ Network Access Protection\NAP Client Configuration\Health Registration Settings\ Trusted Server Groups* node.

6. Right-click the Trusted Server Groups node and choose New.

7. In the *New Trusted Server Group* dialog box, in the *Group Name* text box, type IPsec Servers. Click Next.

8. On the *Add Servers* page (see Figure 13-3), in the *Add URLS of the health registration authority that you want the client to trust* text box, type https://server01.contoso. com/domainhra/hcsrvext.dll and click Add. Click Next.

Figure 13-3

Specifying the URLs of the health registration authority servers

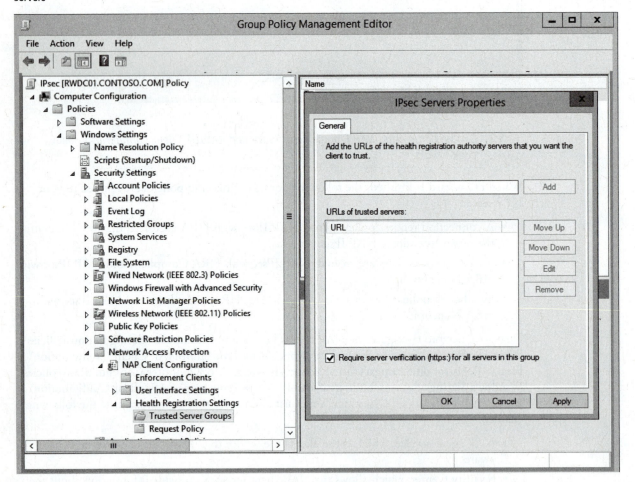

9. On the *Completing the new trusted server group wizard* page, click Finish.

10. In the details pane (see Figure 13-4), double-click IPsec Relying Party. In the *IPsec Relying Party Properties* dialog box, select Enable this enforcement client and then click OK.

Figure 13-4

Managing NAP Client
enforcement methods

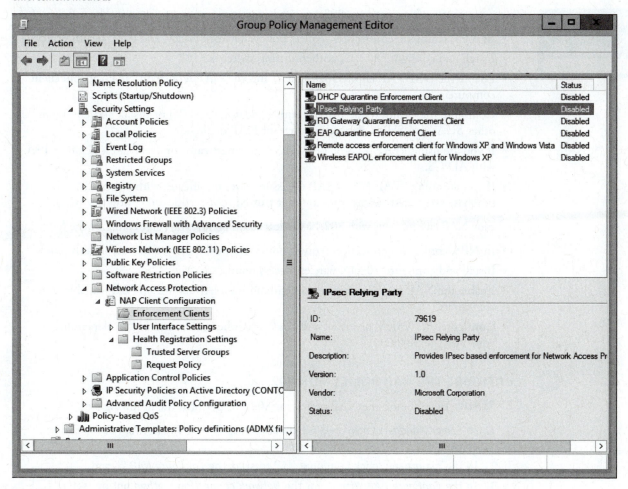

11. Navigate to *Computer Configuration/Policies/Windows Settings/Security Settings/ System Services*.

12. In the details pane, double-click Network Access Protection Agent.

13. In the *Network Access Protection Agent Properties* dialog box, select Define this policy setting, select Automatic, and then click OK.

14. Navigate to the *Computer Configuration\Policies\Administrative Templates\Windows Components\Security Center* node.

15. Close the *Group Policy Management Editor*.

16. Close the *Group Policy Management* console.

Configuring NAP Enforcement for 802.1x

NAP enforcement for 802.1x port-based network access control is deployed with a server running Network Policy Server (NPS) and an EAP host enforcement client component. With 802.1x port-based enforcement, the NPS server instructs an 802.1x authentication switch or 802.1x compliant wireless access point to place the noncompliant 802.1x clients on the remediation network.

CERTIFICATION READY
Configure NAP enforcement for 802.1x
Objective 3.5

To deploy NAP enforcement for 802.1x wired switches, you must configure the following:

- In NPS, configure connection request policy, network policy, and NAP health policy.
- Install and configure 802.1X authenticating switches.
- Enable the NAP EAP enforcement client and the NAP service on NAP-capable client computers.
- Configure the Windows Security Health Validator (WSHV) or install and configure other SHAs and SHVs, depending on your NAP deployment.
- If you are using PEAP-TLS or EAP-TLS with smart cards or certificates, deploy a PKI with AD CS.
- If you are using PEAP-MS-CHAP v2, issue server certificates with either AD CS or purchase server certificates from another trusted root certification authority (CA).

To deploy NAP enforcement with 802.1x wireless access points, you must configure the following:

- In NPS, configure connection request policy, network policy, and NAP health policy.
- Install and configure 802.1X wireless access points.
- Enable the NAP EAP enforcement client and the NAP service on NAP-capable client computers.
- Configure the WSHV or install and configure other SHAs and SHVs, depending on your NAP deployment.

 CONFIGURE THE NAP POLICY FOR 802.1X

GET READY. To configure the NAP policy for 802.1X, perform the following steps:

1. In *Server Manager*, click Tools > Network Policy Server. The *Network Policy Server* console opens.
2. In the main pane, click Configure NAP to start the *Configure NAP* Wizard.
3. In the *Configure NAP Wizard*, for the *Network connection method* option, select IEEE 802.1X (Wired) or IEEE 802.1X (Wireless).
4. In the *Policy name* text box, type a name for the policy. The default name is *NAP 802.1X (Wired)* or *IEEE 802.1X (Wireless)*. Click Next.
5. On the *Specify 802.1X Authentication Switches or Access Points* page, for the RADIUS clients, click Add.
6. In the *New RADIUS Client* dialog box, type a name for a switch or access point such as HP Procurve. In the *Address (IP or DNS)* text box, type the address of the switch such as 192.168.1.21.
7. In the *Shared secret* and *Confirm shared secret* text boxes, type a password such as Pa$$w0rd. Click OK.
8. Back on the *Specify 802.1X Authentication Switches or Access Points* page, click Next.
9. On the *Configure Machine Groups* page, click Add. In the *Select Group* dialog box, in the *Enter the object name to select* text box, type the name of the group that you

created, such as IPsec Enabled. Click OK. If you do not specify a group, the policy will be applied to all users.

10. Back on the *Configure Machine Groups* page, click Next.

11. On the *Configure an Authentication Method* page, select a certificate. Click the Choose button. In the *Windows Security* dialog box, choose the appropriate certificate and click OK.

12. In the *EAP types* section, leave *Secure Password (PEAP-MS-CHAP v2)* selected, as shown in Figure 13-5. Click Next.

Figure 13-5

Configure an authentication method

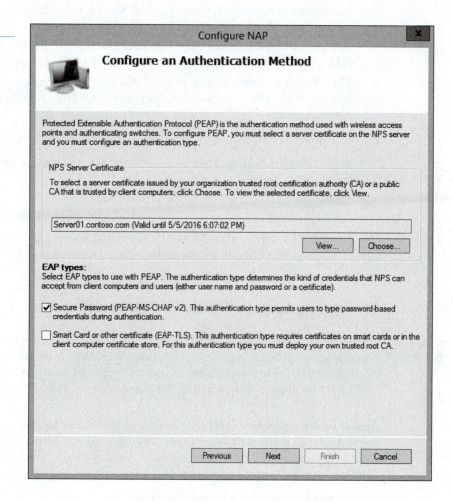

13. In the *Configure Traffic Controls* page, you can configure the RADIUS attributes for full access network and restricted access network. Click Next.

14. On the *Define NAP Health Policy* page, leave the *Windows Security health Validator* and *Enable auto-remediation of client computers* options selected. Click Next.

15. On the *Completing NAP Enforcement Policy and RADIUS Client Configuration* page, click Finish.

When the wizard is finished, the following configurations and policies are applied to your NPS server:

- A connection request policy named NAP 802.1X (Wired/Wireless) is created, which will configure the server to evaluate NAP IPsec requests.
- Two network policy rules are created: NAP 802.1X (Wired/Wireless) Compliant and NAP 802.1X (Wired/Wireless) Non NAP-Capable Noncompliant.
- Three health policies are created: NAP 802.1X (Wire/Wireless) Compliant, NAP 802.1X (Wire/Wireless) Noncompliant, and NAP 802.1X (Wire/Wireless) Non NAP-Capable.

On the organization's managed devices, you need to set at least four settings:

- Ensure that the NAP and Wired AutoConfig services are configured as Automatic and are started.
- Enable the EAP Quarantine Enforcement Client.
- For the network connections, enable 802.1X and select PEAP.
- For the Microsoft Protected EAP (PEAP) settings, select *Validate server cert* and your certificate authority, and set the authentication method to *other certificate*.

Configuring System Health Validators (SHVs)

The system health agents (SHAs) and system health validators (SHVs) provide health-state status and validation. Windows 8 includes a Windows Security Health Validator SHA that monitors the Windows Security Center settings. Windows Server 2012 R2 includes a corresponding Windows Security Health Validator SHV.

System health validators (SHVs) define the requirements for client computers that connect to your network. You configure them through the Network Policy Server console. Double-clicking a SHV opens the Windows Security Health Validator box (see Figure 13-6). Configuring a SHV involves two sets of configurations:

- Windows 8, Windows 7, and Windows Vista
- Windows XP

Figure 13-6

Configuring a Windows SHV

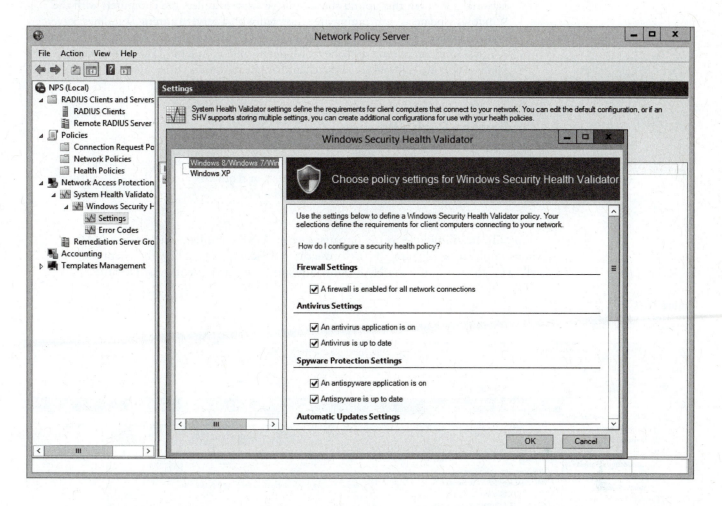

The settings for each include the following options:

- **Firewall Settings:** These specify whether a firewall (Windows Firewall or firewall software that is compatible with Windows Security Center) is enabled for all network connections. If the client computer does not run firewall software or runs a firewall that is not compliant with Windows Security Center, the client computer is restricted to a remediation network until firewall software is installed and running. If you enable NAP autoremediation and WSHA on the client computer reports that no firewall is enabled, then WSHV directs WSHA on the client computer to turn on Windows Firewall.

- **Antivirus Settings:** These specify whether a compatible antivirus application runs on the client computer. If the anti-virus application is not up to date, the client computer is restricted to a remediation network until the computer becomes compliant.

- **Spyware Protection Settings:** These specify whether an antispyware application (such as Windows Defender or other spyware protection software that is compatible with the Windows Security Center) runs on the client computer. If the antispyware application is not up to date, the client computer is restricted to a remediation network until the computer becomes compliant.

- **Automatic Updates Settings:** When Automatic Updates are enabled but Microsoft Update Services is not enabled on the client computer, the client computer is restricted to a remediation network until Microsoft Update Services is enabled.

- **Security Updates Settings:** If you select *Restrict access for clients that do not have all available security updates installed*, the client computer is restricted to a remediation network. However, this option should not be selected unless the computers with the Windows Update agent running are registered with a server running Windows Server Update Service (WSUS) or similar. You can specify the minimum severity of the updates (Critical Only, Important and above, Moderate and above, and Low and above) and the number of hours allowed since the client has checked for security updates (maximum of 72 hours).

Configuring Health Policies

Health policies consist of one or more system health validators and other settings that enable you to define client computer configuration requirements for the NAP-capable computers that attempt to connect to your network.

Typically, health policies come in pairs: one for NAP-compliant and one for NAP-noncompliant (see Figure 13-7). To use the NAP-compliant policy, the client must pass all SHV checks; to use the NAP-noncompliant policy, the client must fail at least one SHV check.

Figure 13-7

Viewing health policies

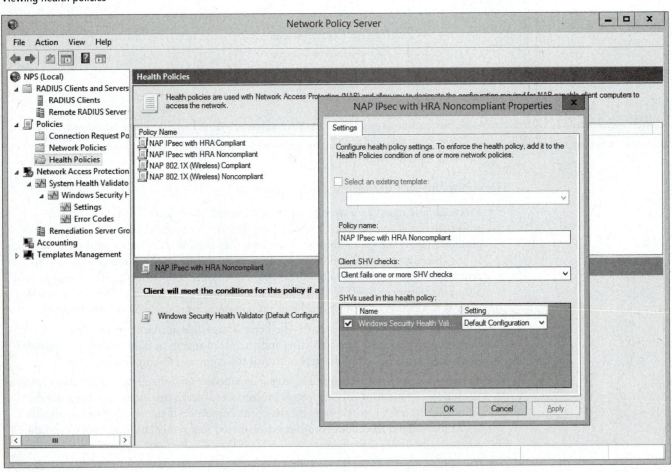

Figure 13-8 shows the Network Policy properties. In the Overview tab, you can see if the policy is enabled, if access is granted or denied with the policy, and you can see the type of network access server. The Conditions tab specifies the health policy that it is connected to.

Figure 13-8

Displaying the conditions of a health policy

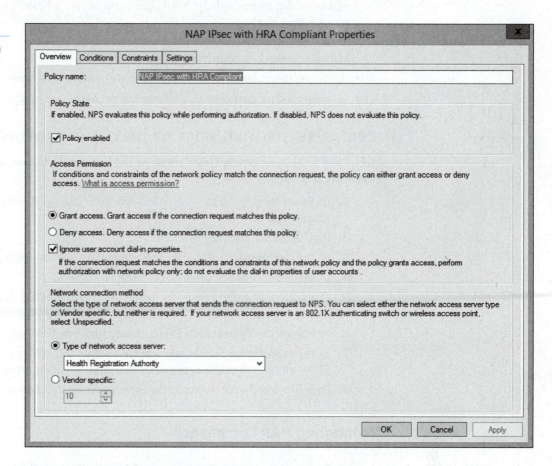

Configuring Isolation and Remediation

As discussed earlier, if a computer is noncompliant, it should be isolated from the production network. When you configure NAP, you can configure either a monitor-only policy or an isolation policy.

Although a monitor-only policy cannot prevent PCs from gaining access to your network, the compliance state of each remote PC that attempts a connection will be logged. Typically, you use a monitor-only policy when you first implement NAP so that you can test the implementation to verify which computers are blocked and which are granted access to the production network by viewing the security logs in the Event Viewer on the NAP server. After you tweak the policies and NAP is working properly, you then switch the policy to isolation mode.

To provide assistance to users of noncompliant computers when requiring NAP health enforcement, you can configure a remediation server group and troubleshooting URL that is available to users if they fail the compliance check. Each organization has its own remediation server depending on the requirements of the SHVs. Remediation servers typically consists of the following:

- DHCP servers to provide IP configuration
- Naming servers, including DNS servers and WINS servers

- Active Directory domain controllers (read-only domain controllers are recommended to minimize security risks)
- Internet proxy servers so that noncompliant NAP clients can access the Internet
- HRAs so that noncompliant NAP clients can obtain a health certificate for the IPsec enforcement method
- Web server that contains the troubleshooting URL server, so users can access information on compliance
- Antivirus/antimalware servers to retrieve antivirus/antimalware updates
- Software update servers so that clients can get Windows updates

 CONFIGURE ISOLATION MODE OR THE LIST OF REMEDIATION SERVERS

GET READY. To configure isolation mode or the list of remediation servers, perform the following steps:

1. In *Server Manager*, click Tools > Network Policy Server. The *Network Policy Server* console opens.
2. Under *Policies*, click Network Policies.
3. In the right pane, double-click the appropriate network policy.
4. In the network policy window, click the Settings tab.
5. To modify NAP enforcement, including whether the policy has full network access or limited access, click NAP Enforcement.
6. To change the Remediation Servers Group and Troubleshooting URL, click Configure.
7. In the *Remediation Servers and Troubleshooting URL* dialog box, under *Remediation Server* group, select the appropriate remediation server group.
8. Click OK to close the *Remediation Servers and Troubleshooting* URL dialog box.

Monitoring NAP Compliance

After NAP is deployed, you should monitor how many NAP clients are not compliant and how many clients have undergone remediation, the most frequently requested software updates, and any errors that have occurred. You can use the `netsh nap client show group`, `netsh nap client show config`, and `netsh nap client show state` commands to view the policies being applied to a computer. However, using `netsh` is not practical for monitoring the entire organization. For a detailed look for the entire organization, you should use System Center 2012 R2 End Point Protection.

CERTIFICATION READY
Monitor for compliance
Objective 3.5

You can sort the policy reports by category. NAP has 13 built-in reports, including the following:

- List of NAP-eligible computers
- List of Network Access Protection policies
- List of noncompliant computers in remediation from last polling interval
- List of remediation failures for specified time period
- List of software updates installed through remediation

The Client Status node and the System Center 2012 Endpoint Protection Status node contain information about events related to client compliance. Compliance-related settings are set in the Assets and Compliance workspace within Configuration Manager. Lastly, the Compliance Settings node enables both Configuration Items and Configuration Baselines to be created.

SKILL SUMMARY

IN THIS LESSON YOU LEARNED:

- Microsoft Network Access Protection (NAP) is software for controlling network access for computers based on the host's health, which depends on the newest security patches and a current antivirus/antimalware software package.

- As a computer connects to the network, its health status is evaluated based on health policies to determine whether it should be allowed to connect to the network.

- If a computer is not compliant with the system health requirements, it can be denied network access or given restricted network access. In some situations, automatic remediation can occur to bring the computer into compliance.

- NAP supports four enforcement methods: IPsec, 802.1X, VPN, and DHCP enforcement. When selecting a NAP enforcement method, you need to consider the benefits of each method.

- NAP IPsec provides the strongest and most flexible method for maintaining client computer compliance with network health requirements.

- NAP enforcement for 802.1x port-based network access control is deployed with a server running Network Policy Server (NPS) and an EAP host enforcement client component. With 802.1x port-based enforcement, the NPS server instructs an 802.1x authentication switch or 802.1x compliant wireless access point to place the noncompliant 802.1x clients on the remediation network.

- After NAP is deployed, you should monitor how many NAP clients are not compliant and how many clients have undergone remediation, the most frequently requested software updates, and any errors that have occurred.

- For a detailed look at policies for the entire organization, you should use System Center 2012 R2 End Point Protection.

Knowledge Assessment

Multiple Choice

1. Which of the following can be used to ensure that computers have had their up-to-date antivirus software packages and recent Windows Updates applied?
   a. Network Connectivity Assistance
   b. RADIUS
   c. Windows Firewall with Advanced Security
   d. Network Access Protection

2. Where do you configure NAP when using DHCP enforcement?
   a. NAP server
   b. DHCP server
   c. RADIUS server
   d. domain controller

3. When a computer is noncompliant because it does not have the current Windows Updates, where is it redirected?
   a. NAP health policy server
   b. health requirement servers
   c. infrastructure servers
   d. remediation servers

4. How can a user bypass NAP DHCP enforcement?
   a. Use a static IP address.
   b. Use a dynamic IP address.
   c. Use a reserved IP address.
   d. Use IPsec.

5. Which NAP enforcement method is the strongest?
   a. DHCP
   b. IPsec
   c. VPN
   d. 802.1x

6. Which type of NAP enforcement is used to enforce authentication when connecting to a wireless access point?
   a. DHCP
   b. IPsec
   c. VPN
   d. 802.1x

7. Which server role is used create health policies, which are used with NAP?
   a. DHCP server
   b. domain controller
   c. Network Policy Server
   d. remote access server
   e. RADIUS server

8. What is the easiest way to configure NAP client settings?
   a. Modify the DHCP options for a zone.
   b. Copy an NRA file to the C:\Windows\System32 folder.
   c. Modify the registry.
   d. Use Group Policy Objects.

9. Which of the following is required for NAP IPsec enforcement? (Choose all that apply.)
   a. Health Registration Authority (HRA)
   b. Network Policy Server (NPS)
   c. NAP-capable client
   d. remote access server
   e. health certificate server

10. How many requests can be handled by a dedicated HRA server?
    a. 10/second
    b. 20/second
    c. 40/second
    d. 50/second

Best Answer

Choose the letter that corresponds to the best answer. More than one answer choices can achieve the goal. Select the BEST answer.

1. You are an administrator for an organization with approximately 1,200 client computers. You have two clients that, when at the office, always get a default gateway of 0.0.0.0 and a subnet mask of 255.255.255.255 from the DHCP server. What is the problem?
   a. The host is connected to the wrong subnet.
   b. The DHCP scope is not configured properly.
   c. The users have reserved addresses within the DHCP scope.
   d. The computers are using the NAP enforcement method and are considered noncompliant.

2. Which of the following helps protect against malware being brought in through a client VPN tunnel? (Choose two answers.)
   a. Using NAP 802.1x enforcement
   b. Requiring strong passwords
   c. Requiring that digital certificates be used with IPsec
   d. Not allowing split-tunneling

3. Where should the remediation servers be located?
   a. Their own isolated network
   b. The perimeter network
   c. The central corporate network
   d. The primary server subnet

4. You need to choose a NAP enforcement method. You want to ensure that all client computers have an up-to-date antimalware package and the latest Windows updates. Which enforcement method should you choose?
   a. DHCP
   b. IPsec
   c. VPN
   d. 802.1x
   e. Multiple enforcement methods

5. Which component is used to provide information about the status of Windows updates and the status of antivirus software?
   a. NAP validator
   b. Status service
   c. NAP Agent service
   d. Security Center

Matching and Identification

1. Which of the following are considered remediation server?
   _____ a) DHCP servers
   _____ b) DNS servers
   _____ c) file server
   _____ d) Active Directory domain controller
   _____ e) antivirus deployment server
   _____ f) print server
   _____ g) SQL server
   _____ h) mail server
   _____ i) Windows Update server
   _____ j) System Center Configuration Manager server

2. Which of the following are settings for the System Health Validator (SHV)?
   _____ a) firewall settings
   _____ b) DHCP scope settings
   _____ c) automatic update settings
   _____ d) spyware protection settings
   _____ e) antivirus settings
   _____ f) IPsec settings
   _____ g) host file settings
   _____ h) security update settings

Build a List

1. In order of first to last, specify the general steps used to configure NAP enforcement for IPsec.

_____ Install and configure the Active Directory Certificate Services (AD CS).
_____ Install MRA on the local computer or on a remote computer.
_____ Enable the NAP IPsec enforcement client and the NAP service on the NAP-capable client computer.
_____ Configure the Windows security health validators.
_____ Use a Group Policy Object to configure NAP-related settings.
_____ In NPS, configure the connection request policy, network policy, and NAP health policy.

Business Case Scenarios

Scenario 13-1: Configuring IPsec

You are an administrator at a corporation with military contracts. You need to ensure that you networks are safe from malware and that all communications is encrypted. What should you do?

Scenario 13-2: Implementing NAP

You are an administrator for a corporation that has approximately 2,000 client computers. You also have an additional 50 consultants and vendors that connect to your network each week directly through the VPN. How can you ensure that all computers connected to the network have an updated antivirus software package, an updated antispyware package, and the newest security patches?

Designing a Forest and Domain Infrastructure

70-413 EXAM OBJECTIVE

Objective 4.1 – Design a forest and domain infrastructure. This objective may include but is not limited to: Design considerations including multi-forest architecture, trusts, functional levels, domain upgrade, domain migration, forest restructure, Microsoft Azure Active Directory, and DirSync.

LESSON HEADING	EXAM OBJECTIVE
Designing a Forest and Domain Infrastructure	
• Using Microsoft Operations Framework	
• Gathering Information	
• Designing a Multi-Forest Architecture	Design multi-forest architecture
• Designing a Domain Structure	
• Designing Trust Relationships	Design trusts
• Designing Functional Levels	Design functional levels
Migrating to Windows Server 2012 R2	
• Designing a Domain Migration	Design domain migration
• Designing Domain Upgrades	Design domain upgrade
Designing Forest Restructure	Design forest restructure
Designing Microsoft Azure Active Directory	Design Microsoft Azure Active Directory
Using DirSync	Design DirSync

KEY TERMS

Active Directory Migration Tool (ADMT)

administrative autonomy

administrative isolation

domain functional levels

domain restructure migration

domain trees

domain upgrade migration

domains

external trusts

forest functional levels

forest root domain

forest trusts

forests

Microsoft Azure Active Directory (Microsoft Azure AD)

Microsoft Azure Active Directory Sync (DirSync) tool

Microsoft Operations Framework (MOF)

non-transitive trust relationship

one-way trust

organizational units (OUs)

organizational forest model

realm trusts

resource forest model

restricted access forest model

shortcut trusts

transitive trust relationship

trusted domain

trusting domain

trusts

two-way trust

upgrade-then-restructure migration

Designing a Forest and Domain Infrastructure

 THE BOTTOM LINE

Active Directory domains, trees, and forests are logical representations of your network organization, allowing you to organize them in the best way to manage them. To identify domains, trees, and forests, Active Directory is closely tied to the Domain Name System (DNS).

You can look at Active Directory from two sides: logical and physical. The logical components (which administrators create, organize, and manage) include the following:

- *Organizational units (OUs):* These domain containers allow you to organize and group resources for easier administration, including delegating administrative rights.
- *Domains:* These make up an administrative boundary for users and computers that are stored in a common directory database. A single domain can span multiple physical locations or sites and can contain millions of objects.
- *Domain trees:* These domain collections are grouped in hierarchical structures and share a common root domain. A domain tree could have a single domain or many domains. A domain (known as the parent domain) can have a child domain. Likewise, a child domain can have its own child domain. Because the child domain is combined with the parent domain name to form its own unique DNS name, the domains with a tree have a contiguous namespace.
- *Forests:* These form collections of domains trees that share a common schema. A forest can contain one or more domain trees or domains, all of which share a common logical structure, global catalog, directory schema, and directory configuration, as well as automatic two-way transitive trust relationships. A forest can consist of a single domain tree or even a single domain. The first domain in the forest is called the forest root domain. If you have multiple domain trees, each domain tree would consist of a unique namespace.

A Windows domain is a logical unit of computers and network resources that define a administrative boundary. A domain uses a single Active Directory database to share its common security and user account information for all computers within the domain, allowing centralized administration of all users, groups, and resources on the network.

TAKE NOTE *

While a domain can be thought of as a security boundary when considering the management aspects of Active Directory, it does not provide autonomy and security isolation between domains within the forest. Autonomy is the ability of the administrators of an organization to independently manage. For example, because all domains in a forest trust each other users from one domain could access resources from another domain. In addition, the enterprise administrator account of the forest root domain has administration privileges for all forest domains. Because some organizations contain thousands of users and thousands of computers, breaking an organization into more than one domain might make sense. However, with Windows Server 2012 and Windows Server 2012 R2, the number of users and computers isn't a factor since each domain controller can handle 2.15 billion objects during its lifetime. Instead, Microsoft suggests reasons to deploy multiple domains include the following:

- To minimize replication traffic
- You have large number of users in remote sites with limited bandwidth between sites
- You need a different password or account lockout policies at the domain level. Note: with the introduction of fine-grained password and account policies, you can assign different policies to users and groups.
- You need to meet some administrative requirements

An Active Directory forest contains one or more transitive, trust-linked trees, with each tree linked in a transitive trust hierarchy so that users and computers from one domain can access resources in another domain. Active Directory is very closely tied to DNS and, in fact, requires it.

A tree is made of one or more domains (although most people think of a tree as two or more domains) with contiguous name space. For example, you can have one domain assigned to an organization's developers and another domain assigned to its salespeople:

Developers.contoso.com

Sales.contoso.com

The Developers and Sales domains would both be child domains of the *contoso.com* domain. A forest is made of one or more trees (although most people think of a forest as two or more trees). Unlike a tree, a forest uses disjointed namespaces between the trees. For example, in a forest, you can have *contoso.com* as the root for one tree. Suppose that Contoso then purchases another company called Adatum, and *adatum.com* then becomes the root of another tree. Both trees could be combined into a forest using external trusts, yet each tree's identity could be kept separate.

To allow users in one domain to access resources in another domain, Active Directory uses trust relationships. Domains with a tree and forest are automatically created as two-way transitive trusts. A transitive trust is based on the following concept:

If domain A trusts domain B, and domain B trusts domain C, then domain A trusts domain C.

However, if you have a partnership with another company and need users from one domain within one organization to access resources in another domain, you can configure an explicit nontransitive trust to be either one way or two way.

Creating Active Directory Domain Services (AD DS) objects, such as forests and domains, is easy. Windows Server 2012 R2 provides wizards to walk you through the process in a few simple steps. However, understanding why you should create a forest or domain is not so simple.

Every AD DS infrastructure starts with a single forest containing a single domain. This simple structure can service a great many organizations—even very large ones—perfectly well. Many administrators feel compelled to create additional domains or additional forests, simply because they can. A competent enterprise administrator is someone who, when designing an Active Directory hierarchy, adds domains and forests only when the organization's requirements call for them.

Designing an AD DS hierarchy is a high-level process that is concerned with business and management issues as much as it is with technical ones. An enterprise administrator must know what Active Directory can do as well as what the organization needs it to do. The design process is a matter of finding a common ground between those AD DS capabilities and the organization's requirements.

The first part of the design process consists of gathering information about the infrastructure of the organization and of the existing technical resources. Then you create a design for a forest structure and, within each forest, a domain structure. Finally, you consider any modifications that might be necessary to satisfy your organization's requirements.

Using Microsoft Operations Framework

Depending on the size and nature of the organization, designing an Active Directory hierarchy can be an extremely large and complex project. To organize and define projects of this type, Microsoft created a collection of documents called the *Microsoft Operations Framework (MOF)*.

Now in version 4.0, the MOF defines the entire lifecycle of an IT service, such as Active Directory, by splitting it into three distinct phases:

- **Plan:** An agreement between IT and management on a set of business requirements provided by the service, a mechanism to monitor the service's reliability, and a budget to support the service
- **Deliver:** The actual planning, testing, and deployment of the service
- **Operate:** Procedures for the operation, support, and eventual retirement of the service

TAKE NOTE
The Microsoft Operations Framework 4.0 package is available free of charge from the Microsoft Download Center.

The three phases of the project are all supervised by a Manage layer.

The MOF does not contain instructions for specific project types; instead, it is an organization and planning tool that consists of a series of white papers called service management functions (SMFs). SMFs define processes for specific elements of each phase and management reviews that are to occur at specific milestones.

Gathering Information

Before you can actually begin to design the forest and domain structure for your enterprise network, you must gather information about the organization that AD DS will service and about the infrastructure on which you will build.

The information-gathering process generally falls into two categories: business and technical. In both cases, a well-run organization should have certain types of information readily available; also, you might have to discover other types yourself or wheedle them out of colleagues who might or might not be cooperative.

DETERMINING THE ROLE OF AD DS

Arguably the most important question you have to answer is what role the AD DS database will play in your organization. More specifically, what kind of information will be stored in the AD DS database?

In your server administer training, you learned about the default network operating system (NOS) functions of Active Directory. AD DS is a directory service. In its basic form, it is essentially the digital equivalent of a telephone book. The AD DS database contains information about users, computers, printers, and services, which enables users to access those resources and administrators to control access to them.

Some enterprises limit their use of AD DS to these basic NOS functions. However, as a directory service, AD DS is almost infinitely expandable, capable of storing a great deal more information about its existing objects and of supporting additional object types.

> **TAKE NOTE***
>
> Despite its apparent complexity in large enterprise installations, AD DS is still just a database that consists of two basic elements: objects and attributes.
>
> Network or company resources are represented in AD DS by objects. Objects can represent physical resources (such as users and computers) or virtual ones (such as domains and groups). Each object, whatever it represents, is just a collection of attributes. A user object has as its attributes various types of information about the user, such as names and addresses. A group object has as its attributes a list of its members.
>
> The Active Directory schema dictates the structure of an AD DS database—that is, the types of objects it can contain and the attributes allowed for each object type. You can modify the schema to create new object types or new attributes for existing objects. This is what gives AD DS almost unlimited scalability.

After consulting with management, you and your organization might decide to use AD DS as a full-fledged enterprise directory. An enterprise directory is a repository for more extensive information about an organization's resources, which users consult daily.

The default AD DS schema defines a variety of informational attributes for user objects, including common name, office, telephone number, and email address. Figure 14-1 shows John Smith Properties from Active Directory Users and Computers. Also, the ADSI Edit shows all the attributes assigned to the John Smith account.

Figure 14-1

The General tab from the user
in the Active Directory Users
and Computers and the ADSI
attributes for John Smith

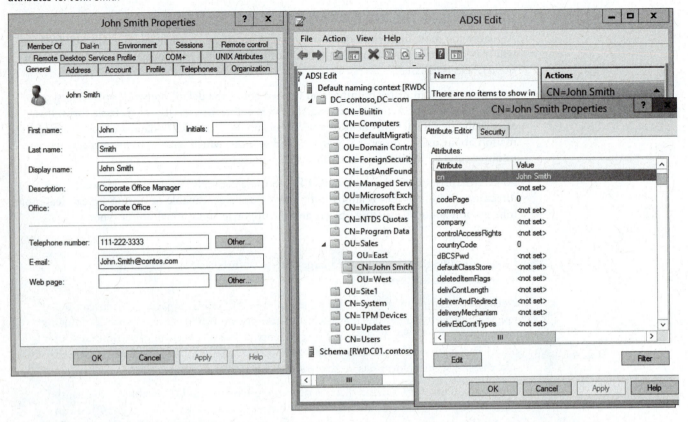

These attributes do not serve any network operating system function; they are a means for storing enterprise directory information. When administrators keep these fields updated, users can search for staff telephone numbers by using AD DS as a "white pages" directory, replacing whatever other telephone directory list or application the organization would otherwise use.

The potential for AD DS as an enterprise directory goes far beyond simple white pages information, however. By altering the directory schema, you can use AD DS to store all kinds of information about its resources. For example, user objects can include employee records and payroll information. Computer and printer objects can include maintenance records and technical support contacts. Another potential use for AD DS is as an external directory that stores customer data, including contact information and order histories.

Using AD DS as an enterprise or external directory can present you with factors that complicate the AD DS design process. Security is the most obvious factor because, by default, all domain users have read access to the entire AD DS database. If that database contains confidential user information or customer information that must be protected by law, you must include security considerations in the AD DS design.

Although these security considerations at first might seem a matter of modifying permission assignments to specific object attributes—a process that occurs much later in the AD DS deployment—many administrators find best to store in a dedicated database built for such data. Also, because of certain legal statutes, such as the U.S. Health Insurance Portability and

Accountability Act (HIPAA), creating a separate storehouse for external data, such as customer or client information, might be necessary. These factors require consideration at the very beginning of the AD DS design process, when you are deciding how many forests to create.

DIAGRAMMING THE CURRENT INFRASTRUCTURE

Enterprise AD DS deployments usually are not created out of nothing. An existing AD DS infrastructure might be in place, but even if not, you always must consider some existing business and technical infrastructure in your design.

Before you can begin designing your forests and domain, you must collect the following information:

- **Organizational infrastructure:** The political divisions of your organization, including companies, divisions, and departments
- **Geographical infrastructure:** The locations of the organization's various elements, both large scale and small scale, including continents, countries, states, and counties or cities
- **Network infrastructure:** The network facilities at each of the organization's locations, including all the links between them and their speeds

All three elements can take the form of a diagram. In most large organizations, these should already exist. If not, management should most likely be responsible for creating the first two, and IT the last.

In addition to these three elements, you should also consider other IT-related infrastructures that might already exist within the organization, such as the following:

- **IT administration:** The current IT administration paradigm will likely be the model for future AD DS designs. For example, if each of the organization's offices maintains its own autonomous IT staff, you might have to establish barriers between the offices as they are reflected in the new AD DS hierarchy.
- **IP addressing:** What IP versions do your network devices support, and what progress has been made in the transition to IPv6? How is the enterprise network subnetted, and what addresses are they using?
- **Name resolution:** What DNS names is the organization now using for its domains and hosts, and what is the policy for creating those names? What DNS server software is the network using, and how are the zones and zone replication configured?
- **Active Directory:** How many forests and domains does the current AD DS hierarchy have? What trusts exist between the forests? What are the current forest and domain functional levels? How many domain controllers and global catalog servers do you have?

TAKE NOTE*

The current Active Directory infrastructure is one of the most important factors to consider in the design of a new or expanded AD DS hierarchy. You must balance the cost of building on an existing infrastructure that might be less than ideal with that of constructing an entirely new hierarchy from the ground up.

DETERMINING BUSINESS REQUIREMENTS

With a business decision, implementing or extending an Active Directory infrastructure must yield some palpable benefits to the organization—benefits beyond the satisfaction and convenience of the IT staff. Any type of service deployment in a large organization is liable to be expensive in terms of time, manpower, and lost productivity, and those expenses must be justified. As a result, usually a project must meet a list of business requirements before the management approves it. These requirements obviously can vary widely but might include elements such as the following:

- **Functional requirements:** Stipulations of services that the project will be able to provide, capabilities that the project will enhance, or problems that the project will solve.
- **Legal stipulations:** Compliance with specific codes governing areas such as information storage and data confidentiality. International organizations might face different legal requirements for different countries.
- **Service-level agreements:** Stipulations that the service, when complete, will meet specified levels of performance and availability.
- **Security requirements:** Specifications for system, data, network, and application security.
- **Project constraints:** Agreements that the project will be completed according to a specified schedule and budget.

Designing a Multi-Forest Architecture

The first question in Active Directory design is whether to use one forest or multiple forests. The main reason this question comes first is because splitting one forest into two or joining two forests into one is difficult. Therefore, considering the possible reasons for creating multiple forests at the beginning of the design process is best.

CERTIFICATION READY
Design multi-forest architecture
Objective 4.1

Active Directory forests are designed to keep separated things such as directory information and administrative permissions. Within a single forest, the default behavior is to share mation unless you expressly prohibit that sharing.

If your organization consists mostly of individuals, departments, and divisions that are accustomed to working together cooperatively and reliably, they can very likely coexist within a single forest. If, on the other hand, certain elements of your organization's business model are more used to operating independently and have different business requirements, multiple forests might be the better choice.

To create the simplest possible example, consider an organization that consists of two separate companies. Perhaps they were independent companies that are now merged. The companies have different names, separate facilities, separate computer networks, separate IT staffs, and separate management infrastructures, except for the executives at the very top of the corporate tree.

In a scenario like this, creating two separate forests makes sense. If you used one forest, the AD DS administrators would probably spend more time building barriers between the companies than they would creating connections between them with two forests. Forests are naturally separated. The only changes needed in this situation are a few connections between the two forests at the top of the hierarchy.

The converse example is also true. If you have two companies that share many of the same resources, such as one IT staff and one computer network, erecting the necessary barriers in a single forest would be easier than creating many connections between two separate forests.

SHARED FOREST ELEMENTS

To fully understand the circumstances under which creating multiple forests is preferable, you need to understand the differences between them. A single forest shares each of the following elements:

- **Global catalog:** A forest has a single global catalog, which enables computers and users to locate objects in any domain in the forest.
- **Configuration directory partition:** All domain controllers in a forest share a single partition in which AD DS stores configuration data for Active Directory–enabled applications.

- **Trust relationships:** All domains in a forest are connected by two-way transitive trust relationships, enabling users and computers in one domain to access resources in other domains.
- **Schema:** The domains in a forest all share a single schema. If one business element requires schema modifications, those modifications affect all other elements in the forest.
- **Trustworthy administrators:** Any individual with the permissions needed to administer an AD DS domain controller can make changes that affect the entire forest. Therefore, a certain level of trustworthiness is necessary for all forest administrators.

If your business requirements call for any of these elements to be separated for part of your network, additional forests might be in order.

WHY CREATE MULTIPLE FORESTS?

As a general rule of Active Directory design, you should stick to one forest unless you have an explicit reason to create more. The following sections describe some of the most common reasons.

PERIMETER NETWORKS

Many organizations create separate networks—called *perimeter networks*—for their Internet servers, such as those hosting web sites and email services. Because these servers can be accessed from the Internet, they are isolated from the internal network by a firewall and usually are not part of the internal AD DS hierarchy.

However, administrators sometimes find that the services provided by AD DS are too useful to forego on these servers, so they create a separate forest for the perimeter network, isolated from the internal network.

INCOMPATIBLE SCHEMA

Active Directory–enabled applications often modify the schema, adding their own objects and attributes. If you must deploy two such applications for different pools of users, and the schema modifications those applications make are not compatible with each other, the only solution is to deploy the applications in separate forests.

TRUST RELATIONSHIPS

As mentioned earlier, all domains in a forest have two-way transitive trusts to the other domains. Breaking these trusts is not possible. If, for any reason, you must restrict the inter-domain access and collaboration that these trusts provide, the only way to do so is to create separate forests.

INFORMATION PROTECTION

In some cases, legal or contractual requirements force administrators to keep information generated by a particular business unit completely separate from other business units. The only way to do this is by creating separate forests.

ADMINISTRATIVE ISOLATION

In Active Directory, distinguishing between two conditions of administrative separation is important:

- *Administrative autonomy* is when an individual is granted complete administrative control over some part of a forest: an organizational unit (OU), a domain, or the entire forest. However, that individual does not have exclusive control over that element; enterprise administrators also have control and can rescind the individual autonomy.
- By contrast, *administrative isolation* is when an individual has complete and exclusive control over some part of a forest. No one can rescind the individual's control, and no one else can exercise control unless the individual grants them permission.

Granting someone administrative autonomy within a forest is possible, but the only way to provide administrative isolation is to create a separate forest.

 TAKE NOTE *

> You almost never have sufficient technical reason to create multiple forests. A single forest can have multiple domains, with each domain containing hundreds of thousands of objects, so more than likely no enterprise network exists that is too big for a single forest.

CHOOSING A FOREST MODEL

After you decide to create multiple forests, you can use several models to separate the enterprise resources, as described in the following sections.

ORGANIZATIONAL FOREST MODEL

In the *organizational forest model*, the divisions between the forests are based on organizational or political divisions within the enterprise. Administrators frequently use this model when an enterprise consists of distinctly separate business units because of acquisitions, mergers, or geographical separation. For example, Figure 14-2 shows an enterprise network with three forests representing isolated divisions on three continents. Trusts between the forests in this model are optional, but by creating them, you and users can still gain access to resources throughout the enterprise.

Figure 14-2

The organizational forest model

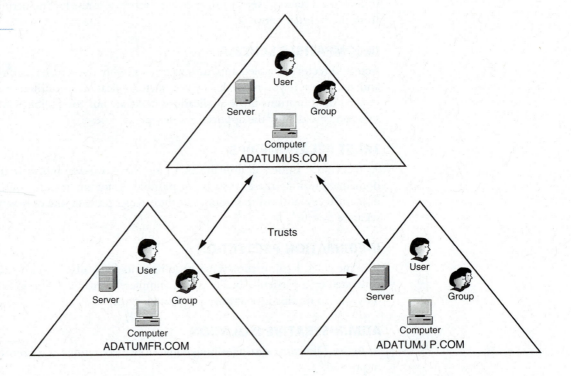

TAKE NOTE *

An enterprise that consists of a single forest is still considered to be using the organizational forest model.

RESOURCE FOREST MODEL

In the *resource forest model* (see Figure 14-3), you create one or more forests containing users and group objects, and one or more separate forests containing the resources that the users and groups will access, such as servers and applications. By separating the users from the resources, you can give each administrative isolation.

Figure 14-3

The resource forest model

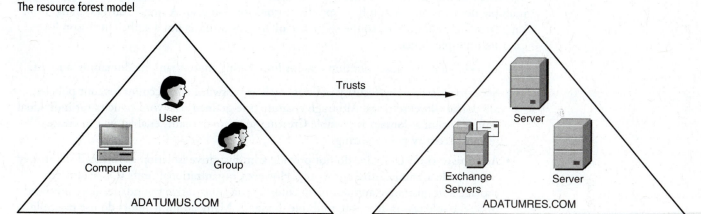

For this model to function, you must create trust relationships between the forests. The most common arrangement is to create one-way trusts running from the forests containing the users to the forests containing the resources. The trusts can be one-way because the users must access the resources, but the resources do not have to access the users.

RESTRICTED ACCESS FOREST MODEL

The *restricted access forest model* is intended for an enterprise with a business unit that must remain completely isolated from the rest of the network. The forest arrangement is like the organizational forest model, except that no trust relationships exist between the forests, as shown in Figure 14-4. This means that for users to access resources in both forests, they must have a separate user account in each one and separate workstations joined to each forest.

Figure 14-4

The restricted access forest model

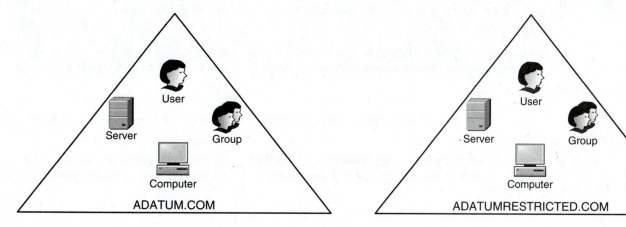

Designing a Domain Structure

After you determine how many forests to create in your enterprise, you next need to move down one level in the AD DS hierarchy and have each forest populated with one or more domains. The question here is the same one you asked with forests: Should you create multiple domains in each forest, or is one sufficient?

The default configuration is to have one domain per forest and, as before, you should create multiple domains only if you have specific reasons for doing so. A single AD DS domain can support millions of objects, so the sheer size of your network is not a sufficient reason for creating multiple domains.

The following are the most common reasons for creating more than one domain in a forest:

- **Security:** Certain key security policies, such as password and account lockout policies, are domain-level settings. Although creating fine-grained password policies for individual groups within a domain is possible Creating separate domains enables you to create separate security policy settings.

- **Administration:** Domains do not provide administrative isolation as forests do, but they can provide administrative autonomy. However, organizational units (OUs) also can provide administrative autonomy, so enforcing administrative boundaries does not need to be the sole reason to create multiple domains. Many administrators do use multiple domains for this purpose, though.

- **Namespaces:** Sometimes the different business units in a single enterprise must maintain different namespaces—for branding purposes or because mergers and acquisitions have brought businesses together. Different domains in a single forest can maintain different namespaces without affecting their interdomain access.

- **Replication:** All domain controllers in a domain replicate the domain directory partition and the contents of the SYSVOL folder among themselves, which can generate a lot of network traffic. By comparison, replication traffic between domains is relatively light. When parts of a network are connected by relatively slow wide area network (WAN) links, or when relatively little bandwidth is available between sites, creating separate domains can be preferable.

TAKE NOTE *

Planning for AD DS replication traffic is not just a matter of comparing the speeds of the WAN links connecting the organization's sites. You must also consider the bandwidth available on those links. Two sites might have a high-speed link connecting them, but if that link is already saturated with traffic, adding more by creating an AD DS domain that encompasses both sites can cause performance degradation in other areas. Conversely, a relatively slow link that is underused might be able to support the addition of domain replication traffic.

Network traffic conditions tend to change over time, so a major AD DS deployment project should always include a reassessment of the traffic levels on all enterprise WAN links.

You should also consider some of the disadvantages of creating multiple domains, including the following:

- **Group Policy:** The application of Group Policy is limited by domain boundaries. Therefore, you must create separate Group Policy Objects (GPOs) for each domain.

- **Moving objects:** Moving objects between OUs is much easier to do than between domains. If your organization tends to reorganize frequently, this might be a factor worthy of consideration.

- **Domain controllers:** Each domain that you create should have at least two domain controllers for fault-tolerance purposes. An enterprise network with multiple domains most likely will require more servers than a single domain.

- **Administration policies:** Even when domains are autonomous, enterprise administration policies will always need to be disseminated, implemented, and enforced.

- **Access control:** For users who require access to resources in other domains, you must assign permissions across domain boundaries and rely on interdomain trusts for reliable access.

- **Global catalog:** With multiple domains, administrators must be conscious of which domain controllers they designate as global catalog servers, so that users throughout the enterprise have adequate access to the catalog.

CREATING A FOREST ROOT DOMAIN

When you create a new forest and assign it a name, that name becomes the name of the first domain in the forest, called the ***forest root domain***. The forest root domain performs critical forest-level functions, such as the following, that make it vital to the operation of the other domains in the forest:

- **Forest-level administration groups:** The forest root domain contains the Enterprise Admins and Schema Admins groups, membership in which should be limited to only the most trustworthy administrators.

- **Forest-level operations masters:** The forest root domain contains the domain controllers that function as the domain naming master and the schema master. These roles are vital to the creation of new domains and the modification of the schema for the forest.

- **Interdomain authentication and authorization:** Users throughout the enterprise must have access to the forest root domain when they log on to other domains and when they access resources in other domains.

TAKE NOTE*   After you create a forest, the first domain in it is permanently designated the forest root domain. You cannot reassign this role to another domain. If the forest root domain should be irretrievably lost, you have no other choice than to rebuild the forest from scratch.

If you cannot use a single domain forest, you need to determine if you want to use a dedicated forest root domain or a regional domain as a forest root domain. A dedicated root domain is a forest root domain that performs only those critical forest-level functions; it contains no users or resources other than those needed to manage the forest. When you create your domain hierarchy, you build it off of the dedicated root domain, as shown in Figure 14-5.

Figure 14-5

A forest with a dedicated root domain

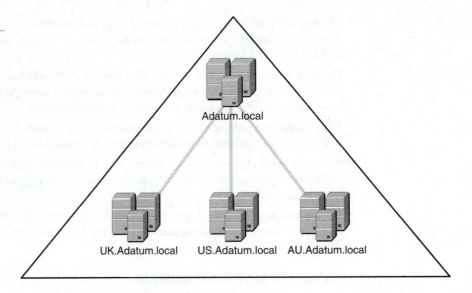

Creating a dedicated root domain provides a number of benefits, including the following:

- You have an operational separation of forest service administrators from domain service administrators.
- You have protection from operational changes in other domains.
- The root domain acts a neutral country or region so that it appears that other countries or regions are subordinates of others.

If you select a regional domain to function as a forest root domain, the domain is the parent domain of all of the other regional domains and will be the first domain that you deploy. It contains user accounts (including Enterprise Admins and Schema Admins groups) and is managed in the same way that the other regional domains are managed.

CREATING A DOMAIN HIERARCHY

After you decide to create multiple domains within an AD DS forest, the question remains of what divisions to use as the model for the domain hierarchy. The most common models that enterprise administrators use to create multiple domains are as follows:

- **Geographical divisions:** Divisions across geographical lines, such as countries, cities, or even buildings on a campus, are typically the result of the need to limit AD DS replication traffic on WAN links between sites.
- **Business unit divisions:** Divisions based on company or departmental lines are usually the result of the desire for administrative autonomy in specific areas of the enterprise, or the need to maintain separate namespaces. In some cases, business unit divisions are combined with geographical divisions.
- **Account and resource divisions:** Creating separate domains for user accounts and shared resources was a common practice in Windows NT 4.0, and some administrators still adhere to it. However, in AD DS, the ability to delegate administrative autonomy to individual OUs and the virtually unlimited scalability of a domain eliminates the need for this practice.

When creating domains within a forest, you can create one domain tree in which all domains share the same namespace, or different trees. The geographical domain model typically uses a single tree, with each domain forming a branch off of a second-layer domain name. For domains created along business unit divisions, however, administrators more commonly create multiple trees with separate namespaces, as shown in Figure 14-6.

Figure 14-6

A forest with multiple domain trees

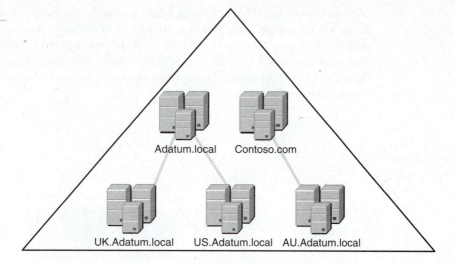

Functionally, the question of whether to use one domain tree or multiple trees has little bearing on the operation of a forest. The trust relationships that AD DS automatically creates between domains in the same forest enable users in any domain to log on to any other domain and access its resources, whether or not they are in the same tree. However, in a large forest with multiple trees and multiple domain levels in each tree, the default trust relationships can conceivably result in performance delays.

By default, every parent domain in a tree has a trust relationship with its child domains. Also, the root domain of every tree has a trust relationship with the root domains of the other trees. Therefore, in a large complex forest, the network of trust relationships can look like the diagram on Figure 14-7.

Figure 14-7

Trust relationships in a forest with multiple domain trees

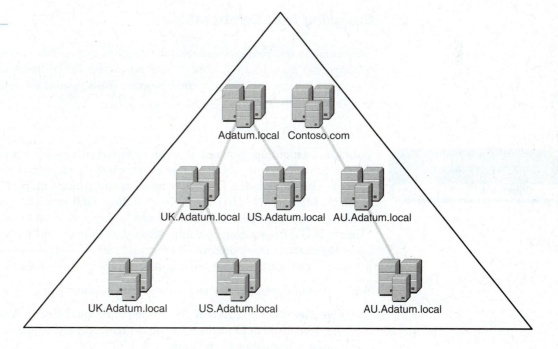

The potential problem with this arrangement occurs when a user from a domain at the bottom of a tree attempts to log on to a domain at the bottom of another tree. In Figure 14-7, if a user in the *Glas.UK.Adatum.local* domain tries to access a server in the Glasgow domain of the company's other division (Synd.*AU.Contoso.com*), access is possible, but the logon request must be referred all the way up one tree to its root, over to the root of the other tree, and then down through the levels to the desired domain. This can be a lengthy process (Glas.UK.Adatum.local > UK.Adatum. local > Adatum.local > Contoso.com > AU.Contoso.local > Sydn.AU.Contoso.local). To improve the situation, you can create shortcut trusts between domains at the lower levels of the trees, as shown in Figure 14-8.

Figure 14-8

Shortcut trusts in a forest with multiple domain trees

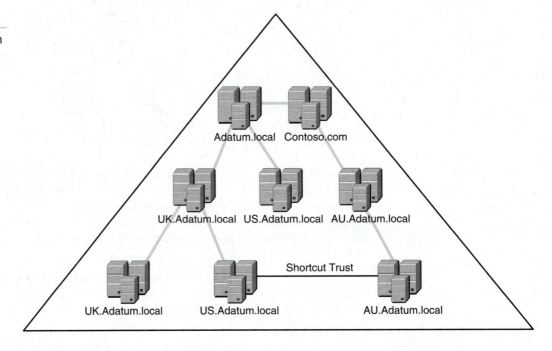

Designing Trust Relationships

When building an enterprise network that spans multiple domains and Active Directory forests, you must plan for access to resources across the entire organization and look for ways to optimize the authentication process. Trusts provide the foundation on which authorization to resources can be built.

CERTIFICATION READY
Design trusts
Objective 4.1

Trusts are relationships between domains or forests that enable a user to be authenticated by domain controllers from another domain. Through trusts, users can access and share resources across security boundaries. Domain controllers authenticate users via either Kerberos v5 or NT LAN Manager (NTLM). Kerberos v5 is the default protocol, but NTLM is still available when Kerberos is not possible. Clients using Kerberos v5 must obtain their Ticket Granting Tickets (TGTs) from a domain controller in their domain and present it to the domain controller in the trusting domain. If the client uses NTLM, the server that contains the resource must contact the domain controller in the user's domain to validate their credentials.

You need to understand a few terms about trust relationships:

- ***One-way trust:*** A trust that goes in one direction. Domain A is trusted by Domain B; therefore, users in Domain A can access resources in Domain B, but Domain B users cannot access resources in Domain A.

- ***Two-way trust:*** A trust that goes in both directions. Domain A is trusted by Domain B, and Domain B is trusted by Domain A. Users in each domain can access resources in each other's domains.

- *Trusted domain:* The domain that contains the user accounts that want to gain access to the other domain.
- *Trusting domain:* The domain that contains the resources that can be accessed by user accounts in the trusted domain.
- *Transitive trust relationship:* Trust extended between all trusted and trusting domains. All domains trust all other domains.
- *Non-transitive trust relationship:* Trust not extended across domains. Domain A trusts Domain B, and Domain B trusts Domain C. Domain A does not trust Domain C.

The following section covers the types of trust relationships that you can configure.

EXTERNAL TRUSTS

You can create *external trusts* (see Figure 14-9) between a domain in a forest and a Windows NT 4.0 (or later) domain or a domain in another forest that is not joined by a forest trust. For example, if Contoso acquires Adatum, and you want Contoso employees located in the *East.contoso.com* domain to be able to access resources in the *West.adatum.com* domain, you can create an external trust relationship between those two domains. If it is configured as a one-way trust, employees located in the *West.adatum.com* domain would not have access to resources in the *East.contoso.com* domain.

- **Direction:** One-way or two-way. In a one-way trust, the trusted domain is the domain whose accounts can be given access to resources in the trusting domain. If you want the trust to extend both ways, you have to create two one-way external trusts.
- **Transitivity:** Non-transitive. This trust does not extend to other domains.

Figure 14-9

Accessing resources using an external trust (one-way)

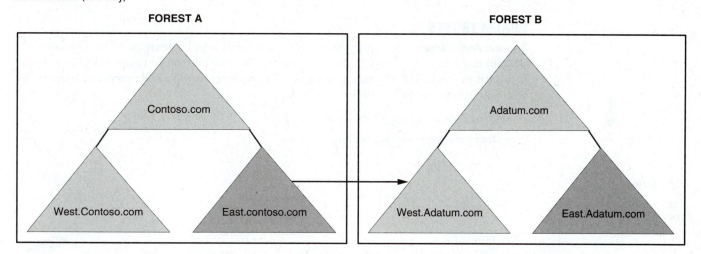

FOREST TRUSTS

You can create *forest trusts* (see Figure 14-10) between two forest root domains if the forest functional level is Windows Server 2003 or later. For example, if Contoso acquires Adatum and both are running Windows Server 2003 or later forests, you can create a forest trust to allow access for users in both forests. The access depends on whether it is a one-way or two-way trust.

- **Direction:** One-way or two-way
  - In a one-way forest trust, members of the trusted forest can use resources that are located in the trusting forest. Example: Forest A (trusted) and Forest B (trusting). Members of Forest A can access resources located in Forest B, but Forest B members cannot access resources in Forest A.

• If a two-way trust is set up between Forest A and Forest B, members from Forest A can access Forest B, and vice versa.

• **Transitivity:** Transitive

• This trust extends to other domains.

Figure 14-10

Accessing resources using a forest trust (two-way)

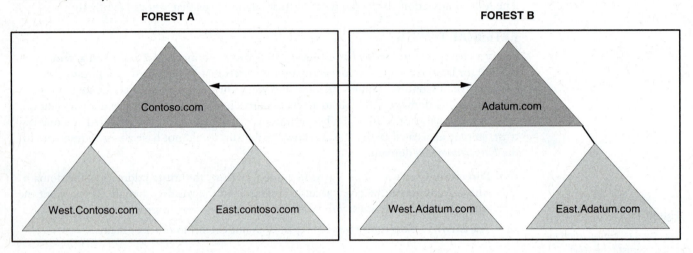

REALM TRUSTS

You use *realm trusts* (see Figure 14-11) to form relationships between an Active Directory domain and a non–Windows Kerberos realm. For example, if Contoso acquired another company that runs a UNIX network, you can create a realm trust to provide users at Company B with access to Contoso resources.

• **Direction:** One-way or two-way

• **Transitivity:** Transitive or non-transitive

Figure 14-11

Configuring a realm trust with UNIX (one-way)

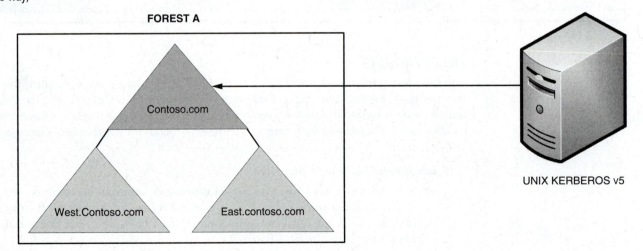

SHORTCUT TRUSTS

You can use ***shortcut trusts*** (see Figure 14-12) to optimize the authentication process. Even if domains within a forest trust each other, authentication must take a trust path from the child domain to the parent domain. You can create a shortcut trust between two domains within the forest to optimize this process. This works well when users must cross multiple domains to access resources or if a parent domain is located across a slower wide area network (WAN) link.

Figure 14-12

Optimizing authentication using a shortcut trust (two-way)

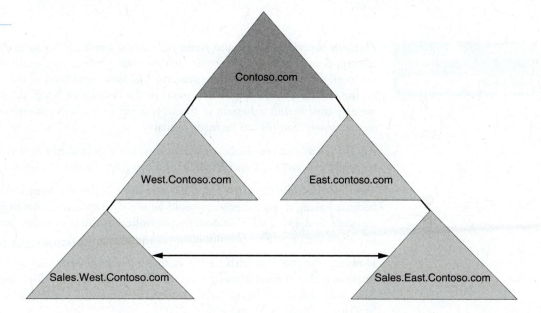

For example, if employees in the *Sales.East.Contoso.com* domain and employees in the *Sales.West.Contoso.com* domain are heavy users of resources in each other's domain, a two-way shortcut trust between the two optimizes the authentication process.

Without a shortcut trust in place, the following occurs. When a user in the *Sales.West.Contoso.com* domain wants to access a resource in the *Sales.East.Contoso.com* domain, he must request a session ticket from the *Sales.West.Contoso.com* domain controller. This domain controller must make the request with a domain controller in the *West.Contoso.com* domain, which then makes a request of a domain controller in the *Contoso.com* domain, and so on. This process continues until the request reaches a domain controller in the *Sales.East.Contoso.com* domain. This domain controller, located in the same domain as the resource computer, issues the session ticket and passes it back to the user in the *Sales.West.Contoso.com* domain.

- **Direction:** One-way or two-way
- **Transitivity:** Transitive

TAKE NOTE ⁎

You can set up trusts by using the Active Directory Domains and Trusts snap-in. To create and manage trusts, you must be a member of the Domain Admins or the Enterprise Admins group. You also can set up trusts from a command line by using the NetDom utility.

Designing Functional Levels

To provide backward compatibility with older systems, Windows domains and forests can run at various levels of functionality. However, to get the most out of the domain controllers and use all available features, you need to upgrade the domain controllers to Windows Server 2012 R2 and raise the domain and forest functional level to Windows Server 2012 R2. Moving to the newer domain and forest functional levels might prevent older systems from operating in the upgraded environment, however.

CERTIFICATION READY
Design functional levels
Objective 4.1

Domain functional levels and *forest functional levels* allow you to enable Active Directory features domain-wide or forest-wide within your network environment while maintaining compatibility for older operating systems. The functional level of the domain or forest depends on the version of the domain controllers in the domain or forest. After all domain controllers are upgraded within a domain or forest, you can upgrade the domain or forest functional level so that newer features can be made available.

AD DS, in all but the smallest installations, requires multiple servers to function as domain controllers. A large enterprise installation can have dozens of domain controllers.

The domain controllers in a particular domain can run different versions of Windows Server, because having it any other way would be utterly impractical. An organization can hardly be expected to upgrade all their domain controllers at the same time, leaving the entire network idle until the upgrades are complete.

However, the problem with having domain controllers running different Windows Server versions is that the older domain controllers do not support the new AD DS features Microsoft introduces in the later versions of Windows. This is where the concept of functional levels comes in.

By raising the functional level of a domain or a forest, you enable certain new AD DS features. To raise a functional level, all domain controllers involved must be running a certain Windows Server version or later.

For example, to raise a forest to the Windows Server 2012 R2 forest functional level, all domain controllers in the forest must be running at least Windows Server 2012 R2. Thus, the functional level available for a particular forest or domain is equivalent to the oldest Windows Server version running on one of its domain controllers.

Table 14.1 lists the Active Directory features provided by each forest functional level.

Table 14-1

Forest Functional Level
Features

FOREST FUNCTIONAL LEVEL	FEATURES
Windows 2000	All default Active Directory features Supported domain controllers: Windows 2000, Windows Server 2003, Windows Server 2008, and Windows Server 2008 R2
Windows Server 2003	All default Active Directory features plus the following: • Forest trusts • Domain renaming • Linked value replication • Read-only domain controllers running Windows Server 2008 • Improved Knowledge Consistency Checker (KCC) algorithms and scalability • Ability to create a dynamic auxiliary class instance called *dynamicObject* in a domain directory partition • Ability to convert an *inetOrgPerson* object instance into a *User* object instance • Ability to create application basic groups and Lightweight Directory Access Protocol (LDAP) query groups to support role-based authorization • Deactivation and redefinition of schema attributes and classes Supported domain controllers: Windows Server 2003, Windows Server 2008, Windows Server 2008 R2, Windows Server 2012, and Windows Server 2012 R2
Windows Server 2008	All Windows Server 2003 features Supported domain controllers: Windows Server 2008, Windows Server 2008 R2, Windows Server 2012, and Windows Server 2012 R2
Windows Server 2008 R2	All Windows Server 2008 features plus the following: • Active Directory Recycle Bin Supported domain controllers: Windows Server 2008 R2, Windows Server 2012, and Windows Server 2012 R2
Windows Server 2012	All Windows Server 2008 R2 features, but no additional features Supported domain controllers: Windows Server 2012 and Windows Server 2012 R2
Windows Server 2012 R2	All Windows Server 2012 features, but no additional features Supported domain controller: Windows Server 2012 R2

Table 14-2 lists the Active Directory features provided by each domain functional level.

Table 14-2

Domain Functional Level
Features

DOMAIN FUNCTIONAL LEVEL	FEATURES
Windows 2000 Native	All default Active Directory features plus the following: • Universal groups • Group nesting • Group conversion • Security identifier (SID) history Supported domain controllers: Windows Server 2000, Windows Server 2003, Windows Server 2008, and Windows Server 2008 R2

(continued)

Table 14-2

(continued)

DOMAIN FUNCTIONAL LEVEL	FEATURES
Windows Server 2003	All Windows 2000 native features plus the following: • Domain renaming • Updated logon timestamp • The *userPassword* attribute on the *inetOrgPerson* object and *User* objects • Redirectable Users and Computers containers • Storage of Authorization Manager policies • Constrained delegation, allowing Kerberos authentication for applications • Selective authentication for users accessing resources in a trusting forest Supported domain controllers: Windows Server 2003, Windows Server 2008, Windows Server 2008 R2, Windows Server 2012, and Windows Server 2012 R2
Windows Server 2008	All Windows Server 2003 features plus the following: • Support for SYSVOL in Distributed File System Replication • Advanced Encryption Services (AES) for Kerberos • Information about the last interactive logon • Fine-grained password policies Supported domain controllers: Windows Server 2008, Windows Server 2008 R2, Windows Server 2012, and Windows Server 2012 R2
Windows Server 2008 R2	All Windows Server 2008 features plus the following: • Authentication assurance Supported domain controllers: Windows Server 2008 R2, Windows Server 2012, and Windows Server 2012 R2
Windows Server 2012	All Windows Server 2008 R2 features plus the following: • Key Distribution Center (KDC) support for claims, compound authentication, and Kerberos armoring KDC administrative template policy, which has two settings (Always provide claims and Fail unarmored authentication requests) that require Windows Server 2012 domain functional level Supported domain controllers: Windows Server 2012 and Windows Server 2012 R2
Windows Server 2012 R2	All Windows Server 2012 features plus the following: • Domain controller (DC)-side protection for protected users, in which users can no longer use authenticate with NTLM authentication, use DES or RC4 cipher suites in Kerberos pre-authentication, be delegated with unconstrained or constrained delegation, renew user tickets (TGTs) beyond the initial four-hour lifetime • Authentication policies • Authentication Policy silos Supported domain controller: Windows Server 2012 R2

Before you can raise the domain functional level, you need to ensure that all domain controllers within that domain are running the required version of the Windows operating system. For example, to raise the domain functional level to Windows Server 2012 R2, you must upgrade or retire any domain controllers with Windows Server 2012 or earlier.

With older versions of Windows, raising the domain functional level is a one-way process that cannot be reversed, short of performing an authoritative restore of Active Directory. However, with Windows Server 2008 R2, Windows Server 2012, and Windows Server 2012 R2, you can roll back the domain functional level back if the forest has not been upgraded.

RAISE THE DOMAIN FUNCTIONAL LEVEL

GET READY. To raise the domain functional level, perform the following steps:

1. Log on to a domain controller such as *RWDCO1* as contoso\administrator with a password such as Pa$$w0rd.

2. In *Server Manager*, open Active Directory Domains and Trusts.

3. Right-click a domain and choose Raise Domain Functional Level.

4. In the *Raise Domain Functional Level* dialog box, select the desired domain functional level (see Figure 14-13) and click Raise.

Figure 14-13

Selecting the desired domain functional level

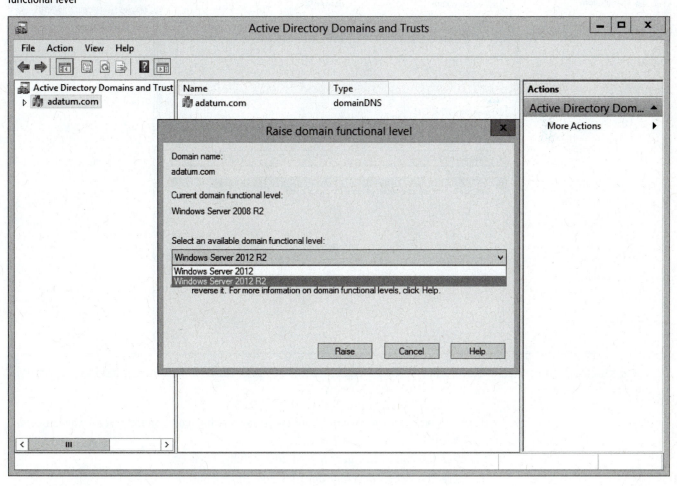

5. When you receive a warning message saying that the process cannot be reversed, click OK.

6. After the functional level is raised successfully, click OK.

7. Close the *Active Directory Domains and Trusts* console.

 RAISE THE FOREST FUNCTIONAL LEVEL

GET READY. To raise the forest functional level, perform the following steps:

1. Log on to a domain controller such as *RWDC01* as contoso\administrator with a password such as Pa$$w0rd.

2. In *Server Manager*, open Active Directory Domains and Trusts.

3. Right-click Active Directory Domains and Trusts and choose Raise Forest Functional Level.

4. In the *Raise Domain Functional Level* dialog box, select the desired forest functional level (see Figure 14-14) and click Raise.

Figure 14-14

Selecting the desired forest functional level

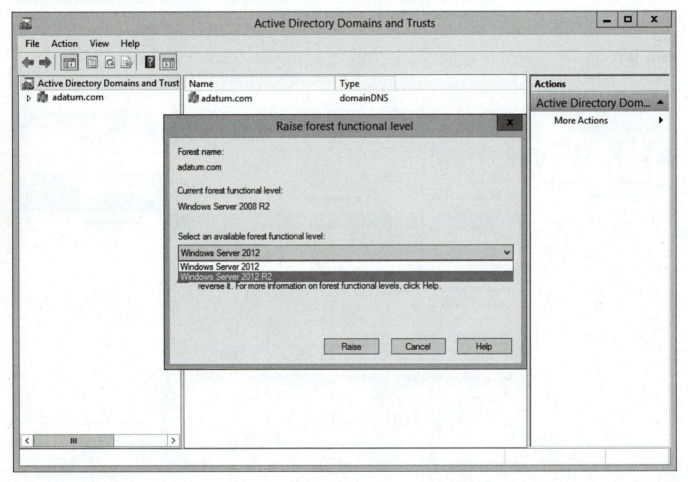

5. When you receive a warning message saying that you cannot reverse the process, click OK.

6. After the forest has been raised successfully, click OK.

7. Close the *Active Directory Domains and Trusts* console.

■ Migrating to Windows Server 2012 R2

For many enterprise administrators, deploying Windows Server 2012 R2 is a matter of integrating the new operating system into a network that already has servers running earlier Windows versions. As with the other aspects of AD DS administration, migration to Windows Server 2012 R2 requires careful planning to ensure a successful completion without any interruption of services.

Adding computers running Windows Server 2012 R2 to an existing Windows Server 2008 R2 or Windows 2012 Server network as member servers does not require any special planning or preparation. However, upgrading existing servers to Windows Server 2012 R2 comes with certain limitations.

In-place upgrades to Windows Server 2012 R2 are supported in Windows Server 2008 R2 with SP1 and in Windows Server 2012 as long as the platform, architecture, edition, and language are the same.

Generally speaking, you cannot upgrade across platforms or architectures, but you can upgrade across editions if the Windows Server 2012 R2 edition is the same or higher than its precedent. For example, you can upgrade Windows Server 2008 R2 Standard to Windows Server 2012 R2 Standard or Datacenter, but you cannot upgrade a Datacenter edition to Standard. You can upgrade Windows Server 2008 R2 Enterprise with SP1 to Windows Server 2012 R2 Standard because Windows Server 2012 R2 has no Enterprise edition. You also cannot upgrade a full installation to Server Core or the other way around.

Designing a Domain Migration

Upgrading member servers is a relatively simple matter, but migrating domain controllers is considerably more complicated. You cannot add a domain controller running Windows Server 2012 or Windows Server 2012 R2 to a Windows Server 2008 R2 Active Directory domain without upgrading the functional level of AD DS. While you will have to upgrade the schema to accommodate the newer version of the domain controllers, older domain controllers will still function the same.

A directory service migration is the process that takes you from a *source* directory—that is, your current Active Directory infrastructure—to a *target* directory, which is a Windows Server 2012 R2 AD DS infrastructure. Three migration paths are possible from the source to the target:

- **Domain upgrade:** In a ***domain upgrade migration***, you either upgrade one of the existing domain controllers in your source domain to Windows Server 2012 R2 or install a new domain controller running Windows Server 2012 R2 into the domain. In this case here, you extend the schema, upgrade a domain controller to Windows Server 2012 or Windows Server 2012 R2 or install a new domain controller running Windows Server 2012 or Windows Server 2012 R2. You can then upgrade other domain controllers, install additional domain controllers, and decommission/demote domain controllers you do not wish to use any more. Lastly, you update the forest and domain functional levels. Users should not see any downtime for AD DS.

- **Domain restructure:** In a ***domain restructure migration***, you create an entirely new Windows Server 2012 R2 domain on a newly installed domain controller, and then copy or move objects from your original source domain to the new target. With this model, the source domain remains operational throughout the migration process, and you can redesign the domain as you migrate the objects. You also can migrate objects selectively, eliminating those that are no longer needed and moving others to different domains or forests.

- **Upgrade-then-restructure:** An *upgrade-then-restructure migration* is a two-phase process in which you first upgrade your existing forest and domains to Windows Server 2012 R2 and then restructure the AD DS database by migrating objects into other domains within the same forest.

Like with nearly every activity in your job description, migrating to AD DS involves a great deal of planning and decision-making before the hands-on part of the project even begins. One of the first steps in the planning process is to decide which of the preceding migration paths you want to use. Some criteria you should use to make that decision are as follows:

- **Design:** If you are satisfied with the design of your Active Directory infrastructure—the forests, domains, and OUs that make up your directory—you might want to consider the domain upgrade migration path. A domain upgrade leaves everything where it is and is by far the simplest and most expedient of the migration paths. Otherwise, if you believe that your existing domain infrastructure is not satisfactory—perhaps because it is outdated or because you inherited a poorly designed directory—a domain restructure migration to Windows Server 2012 R2 provides an opportunity to redesign your domains.

- **Time:** The domain upgrade migration path is much faster and requires less planning and interaction than a domain restructure migration. Domain restructure migrations are often long-term projects that occur gradually in phases, whereas a domain upgrade must be completed all at the same time. The time required for the upgrade depends on the size and number of objects in the Active Directory database.

- **Budget:** A domain upgrade is usually less expensive than a domain restructure migration because, in many cases, it can use the same domain controller hardware. However, if your existing domain controllers cannot run Windows Server 2012 R2 and you have to replace them anyway, you might want to consider incorporating a domain restructure into your migration.

- **Productivity:** One advantage of a domain restructure migration is that it requires no downtime and therefore no loss of productivity from network users. The source directory remains continuously operative throughout the process while administrators construct and test the target domains. Then, the transition from source to target can be seamless. By contrast, the source domains are offline during a domain upgrade process—for how long depends on the database size.

- **Manpower:** The domain upgrade migration process is largely automated, so in most cases the manpower demands for the project are minimal. This can change, however, if the upgrade requires the installation of new servers. A domain restructure migration requires considerably more effort, both for planning and for the actual deployment of the new domains, which is largely a manual process.

Designing Domain Upgrades

Upgrading Windows Server 2008 R2 or Windows Server 2012 domain to Windows Server 2012 R2 domain is basically a matter of introducing a Windows Server 2012 R2 domain controller onto the network. However, you must perform a few steps first.

CERTIFICATION READY
Design domain upgrade
Objective 4.1

To prepare the forest and the domain for the upgrade, you must modify the schema of your existing Active Directory installation. Then you can upgrade one of the domain controllers to Windows Server 2012 R2 or install a new Windows Server 2012 R2 domain controller.

PREPARING THE FOREST

To prepare the forest for the upgrade, you must modify the schema of the existing Active Directory database using the Adprep.exe utility included with Windows Server 2012 R2. Only one domain controller—the schema operations master—can write changes to the schema. Therefore, when you update the schema, you can perform the update from any domain controller; however, the schema operations master must be available, so you must perform this procedure on that domain controller.

 PREPARE A FOREST

GET READY. Log on to the down-level domain controller that serves as the schema operations master for the forest, using an account with Enterprise Admins and Schema Admins privileges. Then perform the following steps:

> **TAKE NOTE** ★
>
> The schema modifications that you must perform before upgrading a domain to Windows Server 2012 or Windows Server 2012 R2 are irreversible. Be sure to back up the Active Directory database before you begin this procedure.

1. Disconnect the schema operations master computer from the network by disabling the local area connection or disconnecting the network cable. This prevents the system from replicating the changes you make to the schema to other domain controllers until you are sure the changes are completed successfully.

2. Insert the Windows Server 2012 R2 installation DVD into the computer's drive.

3. Open a *Command Prompt* window and switch to the DVD's *support\adprep* folder.

4. Type adprep /forestprep and press Enter. A warning message appears, prompting you to confirm that all domain controllers in the forest are running Windows 2003 or later.

5. To continue, type C and press Enter. The program displays a series of results as it imports and modifies individual Active Directory elements.

6. In the *Event Viewer* console, check the system log for any errors that might have occurred during the schema upgrade. If any errors have occurred that you cannot correct with the usual troubleshooting procedures, you should restore the schema operations master computer from your backup without reconnecting it to the network.

7. If the command completes successfully and no errors have occurred, reconnect the computer to the network to allow the schema changes to replicate to the other domain controllers.

Before you proceed to prepare the domain for the upgrade, as described in the next section, you must wait for the forest schema changes you have made to replicate to the other domain controllers throughout the forest, particularly to the infrastructure operations master for the domain you intend to upgrade. If the forest consists of multiple sites, you might have to wait for some time.

PREPARING THE DOMAIN

The process of preparing individual domains for an upgrade is similar to that of preparing a forest. You can prepare the domain from any domain controller, however, the infrastructure operations master must be available, not the schema operation master.

PREPARE A DOMAIN

GET READY. Log on to the down-level domain controller that serves as the infrastructure operations master for the domain, using an account with Enterprise Admins and Domain Admins privileges. Then perform the following steps:

1. Insert the Windows Server 2012 R2 installation DVD into the computer's drive.
2. Open a *Command Prompt* window and switch to the *support\adprep* folder on the DVD.
3. Type adprep /domainprep /gpprep and press Enter. The program updates the domain and the permissions on the Group Policy Objects in the directory.
4. In the *Event Viewer* console, check the system log for any errors that might have occurred during the schema upgrade.
5. If the command completes successfully and no errors have occurred, the preparation for the domain upgrade is complete.

As with the forest preparation, you must wait for the changes you have made to replicate throughout the enterprise before you proceed to upgrade the operating system on the domain controllers.

UPGRADING A DOMAIN

After you complete the preparation procedures for your forest and domain, you can proceed to upgrade one of the domain controllers to Windows Server 2012 R2 or install a new computer running Windows Server 2012 R2 and promote it to a domain controller. As long as down-level domain controllers remain, you cannot raise the forest or domain functional levels to Windows Server 2012 R2.

Designing Forest Restructure

THE BOTTOM LINE

Forest restructure can mean one of two things: you can move one domain within the forest, or you need to move items from one domain to another or even from one forest to another. In either case, you need to plan how you will migrate items from one place to another with no or very little down time.

If you plan to move a domain within a forest, use the rendom tool. If you need to migrate objects from one domain to another within the same forest (intraforest migration) or migrate objects between domains in two separate forests (interforest), use a tool that is not included with Windows. At the time of this writing, Microsoft's **Active Directory Migration Tool (ADMT)** 3.2 supports only up to Windows Server 2008 R2 and does not officially supported Windows Server 2012 or Windows Server 2012 R2. For now, the recommended workaround is to add a Windows Server 2008 R2 domain controller and then install the ADMT on the Windows Server 2008 R2 domain controller. Eventually, Microsoft will introduce new software that will allow you to perform the migration to Windows Server 2012 or Windows Server 2012 R2 with software running on Windows Server 2012 or Windows Server 2012 R2.

When you use the ADMT, you should use the following best practices:

- Perform regular backups of domain controllers in both the source and target domains throughout the course of the migrations.
- Perform a test migration by creating a test user, adding the test user to the appropriate global groups, and then verifying resource access before and after migration.

- Test your migration scenarios in a test environment before migrating objects in the production environment.
- Have a recovery plan and ensure that your it works during the test phase of your migration.
- Decrypt files that have been encrypted by means of Encrypting File System (EFS). If the files are still encrypted, users cannot decrypt the files after they are migrated.
- Ensure that the system time is synchronized in each domain from which objects are migrated.

When you perform user and group account migration, you should follow these best practices:

- Perform regular backups of domain controllers in both the source and target domains throughout the course of the migrations.
- To make the migration process more manageable, migrate users in batches, such as in batches of 100 or so users.
- Use the *Migrate and merge conflicting objects* option on the *Conflict Management* page of the *User Account Migration* Wizard and the *Group Account Migration* Wizard to remigrate users and groups as often as necessary throughout the migration.
- To maintain access to resources, ensure that group membership adheres to the following guidelines:
  - Use global groups to group users.
  - Use local groups to protect resources.
  - Place global groups into local groups to grant members of the global groups access to a resource.
- Adhere to the guidelines in the following list when you translate user profiles:
  - When migrating roaming profiles, select the *Translate roaming profiles* option on the *User Options* page of the *User Account Migration* Wizard, which will translate the local user profiles immediately after you migrate those users.
  - When migrating local profiles, translate local profiles as a separate step from the user account migration process by selecting the *User profiles* option on the *Translate Objects* page of the *Security Translation* Wizard.
  - Unmanaged user profiles will lose their existing profiles when user accounts are migrated.

When you perform computer migration, you should use the following best practices:

- Perform regular backups of domain controllers in both the source and target domains throughout the course of the migrations.
- If you are migrating computers that contain file shares to perform security translation, also backing up those computers throughout the migration is recommended.
- Verify that workstations and member servers have restarted immediately after you join them to the target domain.
- Communicate to end users that their computers must be connected to the network at the time that their computer is scheduled to be migrated. Of course, you perform these migrations during off hours.

➕ MORE INFORMATION

For more information, including checklists on Active Directory Domain Restructure and Intraforest Active Directory Domain Restructure, search for the "ADMT Guide: Migrating and Restructuring Active Directory Domains" from http://technet.microsoft.com.

■ Designing Microsoft Azure Active Directory

Microsoft Azure Active Directory is a cloud-based infrastructure-as-a-service (IaaS) that you can use for identity management and access control. It allows you to manage your applications and identity services without having to manage a computer.

Microsoft Azure AD is a cloud-based infrastructure as a service (IaaS) that you can use for identity management and access control. Microsoft Azure AD has been the identity provider for Office 365 since before Microsoft Azure AD was made available to the public.

Microsoft Azure AD provides the following features:

- Active Directory authentication services in public or private clouds
- Cloud-based storage for directory service data
- Federation services
- A service for extending an on-premises Active Directory environment to cloud services

Microsoft Azure AD provides high availability and scalability. It can integrate with on-premises AD DS, including directory synchronization and Single Sign-On (SSO). You also can limit the data that synchronizes to Windows Azure Active Directory. Lastly, Microsoft Azure AD provides an application programming interface to perform management tasks and to query the directory data.

To authenticate through Microsoft Azure AD, you can use one of the following web-based authentication protocols:

- OAuth 2.0 is an open standard for authorization that provides granular access control to destination services as specified in RFC 6749. Access can be provided temporarily.
- Security Assertion Markup Language 2.0 (SAML 2.0) is an open standard XML protocol made up of security tokens and claims. The security token used with SAML contains claims, which are typically Active Directory attributes that the workflow application uses to make decisions for authorization and access.
- Web Services Federation (WS-Federation) is a security mechanism that allows identity federation so that users in one realm (or directory) can access resources in another realm.

To integrate with an on-premises Active Directory environment, you can use one of the following:

- *Microsoft Azure Active Directory Sync (DirSync) tool* runs on an on-premises domain-joined computer to provide directory synchronization to Microsoft Azure AD. Used primarily to synchronize user objects and user attributes, DirSync is a requirement for SSO.
- Active Directory Federation Services (AD FS) is deployed onsite and provides SSO for applications and services that reside onsite or in Microsoft Azure. AD FS enables all authentications to take place in the on-premises Active Directory and offers Multi-Factor Authentication (MFA).
- On-premises AD DS is the authentication provider and the source of directory data. AD DS is a requirement for DirSync, AD FS, and SSO.

If you have configured synchronization between Active Directory and Microsoft Azure, you can manage your user accounts with the standard Active Directory tools such as Active Directory Users and Computers. If you are not using directory synchronization, you can manage your accounts in Microsoft Azure using the Microsoft Azure AD management portal or the Microsoft Azure Directory Module for Windows PowerShell.

■ Using DirSync

> **THE BOTTOM LINE**
>
> The Microsoft Azure AD DirSync tool provides synchronization between Active Directory and Microsoft Azure. It is the same tool that is also used with Office 365.

CERTIFICATION READY
Design DirSync
Objective 4.1

Because DirSync sends confidential information outside the domain, you must carefully plan how to synchronize information between Active Directory and Microsoft Azure. Without out proper planning, the synchronization could reduce performance and create administrative overhead.

You can filter the Active Directory user objects that use DirSync from the on-premises Active Directory domain to Microsoft Azure AD in three ways:

- Filtering by organizational unit (OU)
- Filtering by domain
- Filtering by user object attributes

You can install the DirSync tool on a domain computer but not on a domain controller. To maintain security, you should install the DirSync tool on a highly secure server that is accessible only by domain administrators or other trusted administrators.

Before you perform the initial synchronization, you should synchronize in a pre-production environment. For large organizations, you should perform the initial synchronization after hours. Microsoft Azure AD synchronizes every three hours by default.

When you configure the directory synchronization, a service account named MSOL_AD_SYNC is created. If you are synchronizing more than 50,000 objects, a full installation of Microsoft SQL Server is required.

SKILL SUMMARY

> **IN THIS LESSON YOU LEARNED:**
>
> - Active Directory domains, trees, and forests are logical representations of your network organization, allowing you to organize them in the best way to manage them. To identify domains, trees, and forests, Active Directory is closely tied to the Domain Name System (DNS).
>
> - Before you can actually begin to design the forest and domain structure for your enterprise network, you must gather information about the organization that AD DS will service and about the infrastructure on which you will build.
>
> - As a general rule of Active Directory design, you should stick to one forest unless you have an explicit reason to create more. Some of the common reasons would be for a separate network such as a perimeter network, incompatible schema, trust relationships, information protection, or administrative isolation.
>
> - The default configuration for a domain structure is to have one domain per forest and, as before, you should create multiple domains only if you have specific reasons for doing so. A single AD DS domain can support millions of objects, so the sheer size of your network is not a sufficient reason for creating multiple domains.
>
> - When you create a new forest and assign it a name, that name becomes the name of the first domain in the forest, called the forest root domain. The forest root domain performs critical forest-level functions that make it vital to the operation of the other domains in the forest.

- When building an enterprise network that spans multiple domains and Active Directory forests, you must plan for access to resources across the entire organization and look for ways to optimize the authentication process. Trusts provide the foundation on which authorization to resources can be built.

- To provide backward compatibility with older systems, Windows domains and forests can run at various levels of functionality. However, to get the most out of the domain controllers and use all the available features, you need to upgrade the domain controllers to Windows Server 2012 R2 and raise the domain and forest functional level to Windows Server 2012 R2. Moving to the newer domain and forest functional levels might prevent older systems from operating in the upgraded environment, however.

- For many enterprise administrators, deploying Windows Server 2012 R2 is a matter of integrating the new operating system into a network that already has servers running earlier Windows versions. As with the other aspects of AD DS administration, migration to Windows Server 2012 R2 requires careful planning to ensure a successful completion without any interruption of services.

- The Microsoft Azure AD DirSync tool provides synchronization between Active Directory and Microsoft Azure. It is the same tool that is also used with Office 365.

- The Microsoft Azure AD DirSync tool provides synchronization between Active Directory and Microsoft Azure.

■ Knowledge Assessment

Multiple Choice

1. Active Directory consists of a database. Which two components make up the AD DS database?
   a. objects
   b. users
   c. attributes
   d. computers

2. Before you can design forests and domains, which three items do you have to collect? (Choose all that apply.)
   a. geographical infrastructure
   b. political infrastructure
   c. organizational infrastructure
   d. network infrastructure

3. Which of the following are shared within a multi-domain forest? (Choose all that apply.)
   a. schema
   b. trust relationships
   c. global catalog
   d. domain administrators

4. Which of the following are reasons to create multiple forests? (Choose all that apply.)
   a. administration isolation
   b. information protection
   c. geographical divisions
   d. incompatible schema
   e. account and resource divisions

5. Which type of trusts do the domains have within a forest?
   a. transitive trust relationship
   b. non-transitive trust relationship
   c. external trusts
   d. realm trusts

6. Which type of trust do you use to optimize the authentication by shortening the path between two domains?
   a. forest trust
   b. shortcut trust
   c. realm trust
   d. external trust

7. Which domain functional level is the lowest you can have that supports domain controllers running Windows Server 2012 R2?
   a. Windows 2003
   b. Windows Server 2008
   c. Windows Server 2008 R2
   d. Windows Server 2012

8. Which of the following features were added to the Windows Server 2012 R2 functional level? (Choose two answers.)
   a. KDC support for claims, compound authentication, and Kerberos armoring KDC administrative template policy
   b. authentication assurance
   c. authentication policies
   d. DC-side protection for Protected Users

9. You need to upgrade a domain to Windows Server 2012 R2. Which of the following allows you to create a new Windows Server 2012 R2 domain and forest on a newly installed domain controller, and then copy the objects into the new domain?
   a. domain upgrade migration
   b. domain restructure migration
   c. upgrade-then-restructure
   d. dynamic restructure migration

10. You are an administrator for the Contoso Corporation. You have a main office in the North America and two branch office offices in Asia and Europe. You need to ensure that the contact information for offices cannot be seen by the other offices and that the local administrators need to manage the users in their respective offices. Which of the following do you recommend?
    a. one forest with one domain
    b. three forests with three domains
    c. one forest with three domains
    d. two forests with three domains each

Best Answer

Choose the letter that corresponds to the best answer. More than one answer choice can achieve the goal. Select the BEST answer.

1. You just deployed some servers using Microsoft Azure. You now need to ensure that the same users and groups are available to the new servers. What should you do?
   a. Enable OAuth.
   b. Configure SSO.
   c. Use DirSync to keep the accounts in sync.
   d. Manually crate the user accounts using the Microsoft Azure AD portal.

2. You are told that you have to keep all contracts and warranties for 10 years. Which type of business requirement does this fulfill?
   a. functional
   b. security
   c. service level agreement
   d. legal stipulation

3. You are partnering with a company on a new product. What type of trust relationship would you configure where the partner company's employees can access documents from your network?
   a. shortcut trust
   b. transitive trust
   c. forest trust
   d. external trust

4. You have a new server on Microsoft Azure with a new sales application. You want to ensure that only the sales users (located within the Sales group and OU) are authenticated to Microsoft Azure via DirSync. What can you do?
   a. Use Active Directory Federation Services (AD FS)
   b. filter by organizational unit
   c. filter by domain
   d. filter by user object attributes

5. You have a multiple domain forest. Your company wants to purchase a new company, and management would like to keep their identities separate. What should you do?
   a. Create two administrators groups.
   b. Create a new DNS server.
   c. Create the new company's own forest and create a trust between the two.
   d. Create the new company's own domain.

Matching and Identification

1. Match the following terms with the related description or usage.

   _____ a) One-way trust
   _____ b) Two-way trust
   _____ c) Trusted domain
   _____ d) Trusting domain
   _____ e) Transitive trust relationship
   _____ f) Non-transitive relationship
   _____ g) External trust
   _____ h) Short-cut trust
   _____ i) Realm-cut trust

   1. A trust that allows users to access files from the other domain
   2. A trust that does not extend across domains
   3. A trust that allows users to access files on a domain.
   4. Used to connect to a UNIX system
   5. The domain that contains the resources
   6. Used to connect to a partner's domain
   7. A trust that optimizes that shortens the authentication process
   8. The domain that has the users
   9. The trusts that allow you to access domains from another trusts

2. Identify the functional level at which a feature was introduced:
   a) Domain renaming
   b) Active Directory Recycle Bin
   c) DFS replication for SYSVOL
   d) Authentication Policy silos
   e) KDC support for claims
   f) Fine-grained password policy

Build a List

1. You have a domain running at the Windows Server 2008 R2 domain functional level with no Windows Server 2012 or Windows Server 2012 R2 domain controllers. In order of first to last, specify the steps to use to upgrade the domain to Windows Server 2012 R2.

   _____ Upgrade each domain controller to Windows Server 2012 R2
   _____ Run `Adprep /domainprep`
   _____ Run `ADPrep /forestprep`
   _____ Upgrade the domain functional level to Windows Server 2012 R2
   _____ Upgrade the forest functional level to Windows Server 2012 R2

Business Case Scenarios

Scenario 14-1: Upgraded to Windows Server 2012 R2

You have a domain running with five domain controllers (four running Window Server 2008 R2 and one running Windows Server 2012). The domain is now running the Windows Server 2008 forest functional level and the Windows Server 2008 R2 domain functional level. What do you need to do to make the domain and forest Windows Server 2012 R2 functional level?

Scenario 14-2: Organizing Forests/Domains

You are a new administrator with the Contoso Corporation. You discover that you have one forest with five domains. Currently, you have 5,000 users spread out between 10 cities throughout the United States. How would you determine the best way to organize your forest/domains?

15 LESSON

Implementing a Forest and Domain Infrastructure

70-413 EXAM OBJECTIVE

Objective 4.2 – Implement a forest and domain infrastructure. This objective may include but is not limited to: Configure domain rename; configure Kerberos realm trusts; implement a domain upgrade; implement a domain migration; implement a forest restructure; deploy and manage a test forest including synchronization with production forests.

LESSON HEADING	EXAM OBJECTIVE
Configuring Domain Rename	Configure domain rename
Configuring Forest and Domain Trusts	
Configuring Kerberos Realm Trusts	Configure Kerberos realm trusts
Implementing a Domain Upgrade	Implement a domain upgrade
Implementing a Domain Migration	Implement a domain migration
Implementing a Forest Restructure	Implement a forest restructure
Deploying and Managing a Test Forest	Deploy and manage a test forest including synchronization with production forests

KEY TERMS

forest-wide authentication

selective authentication

■ Configuring Domain Rename

THE BOTTOM LINE

The renaming of a domain is one of the more serious changes that you can make with Active Directory. Because users, computers, and applications use Active Directory for authentication and authorization, when you rename a domain, you are changing the entire networking environment. Therefore, you must plan the renaming of a domain and then implement the change during the off hours. You should also ensure that you have good backups, and you should test the procedure on a test environment before performing the changes on a production environment.

CERTIFICATION READY
Configure domain
rename
Objective 4.2

Renaming a domain involves two main phases:

- Preparation
- Renaming

The preparation phase involves the following general steps:

1. Ensure that the forest functional level is Windows Server Windows Server 2003 or higher. If you have Windows Server 2012 or Windows Server 2012 R2 domain controllers, the domain and forest functional level are already set to Windows Server 2003 or higher.

2. To restructure the domains with the forest, create trust relationships between domains so that the new forest structure has two-way, transitive trust paths between every pair of domains in the target forest.

3. Prepare Domain Name System (DNS) zones by making a list of DNS zones for the domain operations and then create new DNS zones as necessary.

4. Relocate folder redirection and roaming user profiles to a stand-alone Distributed File System Namespace (DFS-N) so that when you change the domain name, the folder redirection and roaming user profiles will continue to function.

5. By default, the DNS suffix changes as part of the domain rename. To avoid the traffic generated by the computer rename, use a Group Policy Object (GPO) to apply a new primary DNS suffix. It is recommended that the GPO setting should include old and new primary DNS suffix.

6. Prepare certification authorities (CAs) so that Lightweight Directory Access Protocol (LDAP) URLs for its CRL Distribution Point (CDP) or Authority Information Access (AIA) include the new domain name by renewing the existing CA hierarchy and all issued End Entity certificates. You also must reissue cross-certificates with the appropriate End Entity certificates.

7. If you have Microsoft Exchange Server, run the Exchange Domain Rename Fix-up Tool to update Exchange attributes.

The renaming phase involves the following general steps:

1. Back up all domain controllers, including the system state.

2. Configure an administrative computer that is a member of the domain but not a domain controller. It will need the Remote Server Administrative Tools for Windows Server 2012 R2.

3. Freeze the forest configuration by discontinuing the following activities:

   - Creating new domains in or removing existing domains from your forest
   - Creating new application directory partitions in or removing existing application directory partitions from your forest
   - Adding domain controllers to or removing domain controllers from your forest
   - Creating or deleting shortcut trusts within your forest
   - Adding attributes to or removing attributes from the set of attributes that replicate to the global catalog (the partial attribute set)

4. Run `rendom.exe/list` to generate a Domainlist.xml file, which contains a description of the forest.

5. Edit the Domainlist.xml file to specify details about the new forest. You can change either the Domain Name System (DNS) name (the field bounded by the `<DNSname>` `</DNSname>` tags), the NetBIOS name (the field bounded by the `<NetBiosName>` `</NetBiosName>` tags), or both names for any particular domain in the forest. You cannot, however, change the globally unique identifier (GUID) in the field bounded by the `<Guid></Guid>` tags.

6. Run `domren.exe/upload` to generate domain rename instructions in a Dclist.xml file.

7. Push domain rename instructions by executing the following command:

   `repadmin /syncall /d /e /P /q <domain master>`

   where `<domain master>` is the primary server responsible for the domain.

8. Run `rendom/prepare` to verify that the domain controllers are ready.

9. Run `rendom/execute` to rename the domains.

10. Look through the Dclist.xml file for the Done state or an Error state for the domain controllers involved in the renaming process.

11. If necessary, update Microsoft Exchange Server.

12. Run `rendom/end` to unfreeze the forest configuration.

After the domain is renamed, you must reestablish any external trusts. You also need to fix Group Policy Objects (GPOs) and the GPO references in each renamed domain by running the GPO and link fix-up tool, Gpfixup.exe, once in each renamed domain:

```
gpfixup
/olddns:OldDomainDnsName/newdns:NewDomainDNSName
/oldnb:OldDomainNetBIOSName
/newnb:NewDomainNetBIOSName  /dc:DcDnsName
2>&1>gpfixup.log
```

After running the `gpfixup` command, you must use the following command to force replication of the Group Policy fix changes:

```
repadmin /syncall /d /e /P /q DcDnsName NewDomainDN
```

Configuring Forest and Domain Trusts

THE BOTTOM LINE

To create a trust between a forest or domain, use the Active Directory Domains and Trusts New Trust Wizard. With this wizard, you can choose the trust type, specify whether the trust is one way or two way, and/or designate whether it is transitive.

If you are creating a forest trust, you can specify the scope of authentication:

- *Forest-wide authentication:* Windows automatically authenticates users from the specified forest for all resources in the local forest. This option is preferred when both forests belong to the same organization.

- *Selective authentication:* Windows does not automatically authenticate users from the specified forest for any resources in the local forest. After you finish this wizard, grant individual access to each domain and server that you want to make available to users in this specified forests. This option is preferred if the forests belongs to different organizations.

 CREATE A TWO-WAY FOREST TRUST

GET READY. To create a two-way forest trust, perform the following steps:

1. In *Server Manager* or *Administrative Tools*, open Active Directory Domains and Trusts.

2. In the console tree, right-click the domain node for the forest root domain for which you want to establish a trust and choose click Properties.

3. On the *Trusts* tab (see Figure 15-1), click the New Trust button.

Figure 15-1

Managing trusts

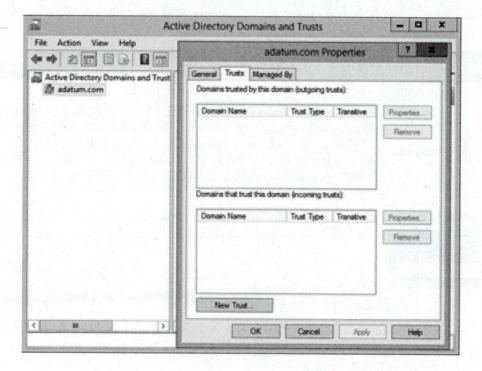

4. In the *New Trust* Wizard, on the *Welcome to the New Trust Wizard* page, click Next.

5. On the *Trust Name* page, type the DNS name of the forest root domain of the other forest, and then click Next.

6. On the *Trust Type* page, click Forest trust, and then click Next.

7. On the *Direction of Trust* page, click Two-way, and then click Next.

8. On the *Sides of Trust* page, click Both this domain and the specified domain, and then click Next.

9. On the *User Name and Password* page, type the user name and password for the appropriate administrator in the specified domain.

10. On the *Outgoing Trust Authentication Level-Local Forest* page, select Forest-wide authentication. Click Next.

11. On the *Trust Selections Complete* page, review the results, and then click Next.

12. On the *Trust Creation Complete* page, review the results, and then click Next.

13. On the *Confirm Outgoing Trust* page, if you want to confirm this trust, click Yes, confirm the outgoing trust, and then supply the appropriate administrative credentials from the specified domain. Click Next.

14. On the *Confirm Incoming Trust* page, if you want to confirm this trust, click Yes, confirm the incoming trust, and then supply the appropriate administrative credentials from the specified domain. Click Next.

15. On the *Completing the New Trust Wizard* page, click Finish.

If you select the trust, and click Properties, to change the following:

- Validate the trust
- The name suffixes, which is used for authentication
- The scope of authentication
- If the other domain supports Kerberos AES Encryption option.

■ Configuring Kerberos Realm Trusts

THE BOTTOM LINE

As explained in Lesson 14, "Designing a Forest and Domain Infrastructure," you can use Windows to create a trust between a Windows domain and a non-Windows Kerberos v5 realm. The trusts allow cross-platform interoperability with security services based on other Kerberos v5 versions, such as UNIX and Linux. Realm trusts can be nontransitive or transitive, and they can be one way or two way.

CERTIFICATION READY
Configure Kerberos
realm trusts
Objective 4.2

To establish a realm trust, use the Active Directory Domains and Trusts console. You then right-click the domain and select Properties. The trust is created via the Trusts tab.

 CREATE A KERBEROS REALM TRUST

GET READY. To create a Kerberos Realm trust, perform the following steps:

1. In *Server Manager* or *Administrative Tools*, open Active Directory Domains and Trusts.
2. When the *Active Directory Domains and Trusts* opens, in the console tree, right-click the domain node for the domain you want to administer and choose Properties.
4. On the *Trusts* tab, click New Trust.
5. In the *New Trust* Wizard, on *the Welcome* page, click Next.
6. On the *Trust Name* page, type the realm name for the target realm, and then click Next.
7. On the *Trust Type* page, select the Realm trust option, and then click Next.
8. On the *Transitivity of Trust* page, do one of the following:
   - To form a trust relationship with the domain and the specified realm, click Nontransitive, and then click Next.
   - To form a trust relationship with the domain and the specified realm and all trusted realms, click Transitive, and then click Next.
9. On the *Direction of Trust* page, do one of the following:
   - To create a two-way, realm trust, click Two-way.
   - To create a one-way, incoming realm trust, click One-way:incoming.
   - To create a one-way, outgoing realm trust, click One-way:outgoing.
10. On the *Trust Password* page, in the *Trust password* and *Confirm trust password* text boxes, type a password. Click Next.
11. On the *Trust Selections Complete* page, click Next.
12. On the *Completing the New Trust Wizard* page, click Finish.
13. Click OK to close the domain *Properties* dialog box.

▪ Implementing a Domain Upgrade

↓
THE BOTTOM LINE

Assuming that you are following good practices or at least want some fault tolerance, your domain should have at least two domain controllers. To get to a Windows Server 2012 or Windows Server 2012 R2 domain, you can either upgrade or migrate to Windows Server 2012 or Windows Server 2012 R2.

CERTIFICATION READY
Implement a domain upgrade
Objective 4.2

To upgrade to a Windows Server 2012 or Windows Server 2012 R2 domain, the domain and forest functional level must be Window Server 2003 or higher. You also have to run adprep to update the forest and domain schema so that the schema can handle Windows Server 2012 or Windows Server 2012 R2. You need to upgrade each domain controller to Windows Server 2012 or Windows Server 2012 R2. After all servers are upgraded, you can then change the forest and domain functional level to Windows Server 2012 or Windows Server 2012 R2.

 UPGRADE A DOMAIN CONTROLLER

GET READY. To upgrade a domain controller to Windows Server 2012 R2, perform the following steps:

1. In a *Command Prompt* window, switch to the support\adprep folder.
2. Type adprep /forestprep and press Enter.
3. When the *ADPREP Warning* appears, type C and press Enter.
4. Type adprep /domainprep /gpprep and press Enter.
5. From the Windows Server 2012 R2 DVD, run setup.exe.
6. On the Windows Server 2012 R2 splash screen, click Install Now.
7. When prompted for important updates for Windows Setup, click Go online to install updates now (recommended).
8. On the *Enter the product key to activate Windows* page, type the product key and click Next.
9. On the *Select the operating system you want to install* page, select Windows Server 2012 R2 Standard (Server with a GUI), and then click Next.
10. On the *License terms* page, select I accept the license terms and click Next.
11. On the *Which type of installation do you want?* page, click Upgrade: Install Windows and keep files, settings, and applications.
12. When the *Compatibility* report opens, click Next. Windows will restart several times.

▪ Implementing a Domain Migration

↓
THE BOTTOM LINE

When migrating from one domain to another, you are essentially moving objects from one domain to another. To perform this type of migration, you must use special Microsoft tools such as the Active Directory Migration Tool (ADMT) and Password Export Server (PES), or you must use third-party software.

If you do not want to use the older domain controllers because the hardware is insufficient for current or upcoming needs, you can migrate to a new set of servers by installing new servers running Windows Server 2012 or Windows Server 2012 R2, promote the servers to domain controllers, and then retire the old servers by removing them as domain controllers. When all the older servers are gone, you can then change the forest and domain functional level to Windows Server 2012 or Windows Server 2012 R2.

Migrating from one domain to another involves the following general steps:

1. Create a new Windows Server 2012 R2 Active Directory Domain Services (AD DS) forest that is independent from the forest and install domain controllers as needed.

2. Deploy new servers that are running the Windows Server 2012 R2 operating system.

3. In the new AD DS forest, deploy the necessary applications, including Microsoft Exchange Server, Microsoft SQL Server, and Microsoft SharePoint Server.

4. Migrate application data and settings for Microsoft applications, corporate custom applications, and third-party applications.

5. Configure DNS infrastructure in both forests.

6. Establish an AD DS trust between the current and the new AD DS forests.

7. Migrate AD DS objects, such as users, computers, groups, and mailboxes.

8. Ensure that users can connect to corporate IT resources in the new AD DS forest.

9. Decommission and remove the environment based on previous operating system's AD DS forest.

Performing an interforest migration to migrate objects involves the following general steps:

1. Enable the File and Printer Sharing exception in Windows Firewall between the domain controllers responsible for the forest.

2. Establish trusts between the source and target domains.

3. In ADMT, transition service accounts by using the Service Account Migration Wizard.

4. In ADMT, migrate global groups by using the Group Account Migration Wizard.

5. In ADMT, migrate other accounts, such as managed service, user, and workstation accounts, with their SID histories by using the Managed Service Account Migration Wizard, User Account Migration Wizard, and Computer Migration Wizard.

6. In ADMT, migrate resources such as member servers and domain local groups by using the Computer Migration Wizard and the Group Account Migration Wizard.

7. In ADMT, add SIDs to access control lists (ACLs) in the target domain so that the security on servers translates and adds the user and groups accounts to the ACLs by using the Security Translation Wizard.

8. In ADMT, perform a remigration of user accounts, workstation computers, and member servers. Remigrate global groups after each batch.

9. In ADMT, migrate domain local groups by using the Group Account Migration Wizard.

10. Migrate domain controllers by removing AD DS from the domain controller, migrate the domain controller as a member server to the target domain, and reinstall AD DS.

11. In ADMT, translate security on member servers by using the Security Translation Wizard.

12. Decommission the source domain.

You can see that each step needs to be planned out and tested before the actual migration.

➕ MORE INFORMATION

For more information on each step during an interforest migration, search for "Checklist: Performing an interforest migration" in Microsoft TechNet.

INSTALL THE ACTIVE DIRECTORY MIGRATION TOOL

GET READY. Before you can install the Active Directory Migration Tool (ADMT) on a server running Windows Server 2008 R2, you must have Microsoft SQL Express or the full version of Microsoft SQL Server. You then can perform the following steps:

1. From the Microsoft SQL Server installation files, double-click admtsetup 32.exe.

2. In the *Welcome to the Active Directory Migration Tool Installation* Wizard, on the *Welcome* page, click Next.

3. On the *License Agreement* page, select I Agree. Click Next.

4. On the *Customer Experience Improvement Program* page, click Next.

5. On the *Database Selection* page, in the *Database (Server\Instance)* text box, type the name of server and instance and click Next.

6. On the *Database Import* page, click Next.

7. After the *Active Directory Migration Tool* is successfully installed, click Finish.

To use ADMT to perform the migration steps, you open the Action menu to start the appropriate wizard, as shown in Figure 15-2. You can also perform the migration steps by using admt.exe or scripts.

Figure 15-2

Accessing the migration wizards

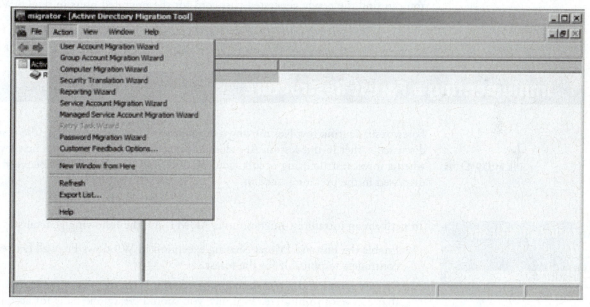

 MIGRATE A USER

GET READY. To migrate a user from contoso.com to adatum.com, you must have a trust established between the two domains. Then perform the following steps:

1. Click the Start button and select All Programs > Administrative Tools > Active Directory Migration Tool.

2. In the *Active Directory Migration Tool* window, open the Action menu and select User Account Migration Wizard.

3. In the *User Account Migration* Wizard, on the *Welcome* page, click Next.

4. On the *Domain Selection* page, in the *Source* section, in the *Domain* text box, type contoso.com. In the *Target* section, in the *Domain* text box, type adatum.com. Click Next.

5. On the *User Selection Option* page, leave *Select users from domain* selected. Click Next.

6. On the *User Selection* page, click Add.

7. In the *Select Users* dialog box, in the *Enter the object names to select* text box, type John Smith and click OK.

8. Back on the *User Selection* page, click Next.

9. On the *Organizational Unit Selection* page, in the *Target OU*, click Browse.

10. In the *Browse for Container* dialog box, select the Users OU and click OK.

11. Back on the *Organizational Unit Select* page, click Next.

12. On the *Password Options* page, select the Generate complex passwords option and click Next.

13. On the *Account Transition Options* page, click Next.

14. On the *User Options* page, click Next.

15. On the *Object Property Exclusion* page, click Next.

16. On the *Conflict Management* page, click Next.

17. On the *Completing the user Account Migration Wizard* page, click Finish.

18. After the migration is complete, click Close.

You can find the newly generated password for the migrated users in the C:\Windows\ADMT\Logs\passwords.txt file.

Implementing a Forest Restructure

THE BOTTOM LINE

Forest restructuring involves moving a domain within a forest by using the rendom tool discussed earlier in this lesson. Any domain, except the forest root, can be moved. Often when a forest restructuring occurs, you can also need to move objects between domains, as discussed in the preceding section.

To perform an intraforest migration via ADMT, use the following general steps:

1. Enable the File and Printer Sharing exception in Windows Firewall between the domain controllers responsible for the forest.

2. Prepare source and target domains by creating a list of roles and locations for all objects that you want to migrate. Typically, you should create one table for account objects (users, groups, and service accounts), and another table including resource objects (workstations, profiles, and domain controllers).

3. Install ADMT in the target.

4. To migrate accounts and resources within a forest, create an account migration group and a resource migration group with the appropriate credentials. You must then add the accounts that will perform the ADMT migrations to the account migration and resource migration groups, as needed.

5. Migrate universal and global groups by using the ADMT Group Account Migration Wizard.

6. Migrate service accounts by using the ADMT Service Account Migration Wizard.

7. Migrate managed service accounts by using the ADMT Managed Service Account Migration Wizard.

8. Migrate user accounts by using the ADMT User Account Migration Wizard.

9. Translate local user profiles by using the ADMT Security Translation Wizard

10. Migrate workstation computers and member servers by using the ADMT Computer Translation Wizard.

11. Migrate domain local groups by using the ADMT Group Account Migration Wizard.

12. Translate security on member servers by using the ADMT Security Translation Wizard.

13. Decommission the source domain.

■ Deploying and Managing a Test Forest

THE BOTTOM LINE

As has been mentioned several times during this lesson as well as in other lessons, you should have a test environment consisting of a test forest, domain, and other primary servers that is isolated from the production network. To test domain renaming, interforest migration, and intraforest migration, you need a test environment that resembles your production environment. You also need the test environment for software upgrades and any other significant changes to the network.

CERTIFICATION READY
Deploy and manage a test forest including synchronization with production forests
Objective 4.2

Deploying a test forest means adding the AD DS role and then running the AD DS Configuration Wizard to create a new forest. With the new forest created, you can synchronize things like Group Policy by using Group Policy Management. However, when you move GPOs from one domain to another, you must use the Migration Table Editor to change the old domain references to the new domain references.

To migrate the GPO settings from one domain to another, use the following general steps:

1. Install the new forest domain controller by using the Active Directory Domain Services Configuration Wizard.

2. Establish a trust between the two forests by using Active Directory Domains and Trusts.

3. In *Group Policy Management*, from the *Group Policy Management Actions* list, add the test forest by selecting Add Forest.

4. Copy objects as necessary for synchronization.

 USE A MIGRATION TABLE

GET READY. To use a migration table while importing GPO settings, perform the following steps:

1. In *Server Manager*, click Tools > Group Policy Management. The *Group Policy Management* Console opens.

2. Navigate to and click the Group Policy Objects container.

3. Right-click a GPO and choose Import.

4. In the *Import Settings* Wizard, On the *Welcome* page, click Next.

5. On the *Backup GPO* page, click Next.

6. On the *Backup location* page, in the *Backup folder* text box, specify the location of the backups and then click Next.

7. On the Source GPO page, click the GPO that you want to import and click Next.

8. On the *Scanning Backup* page, click Next.

9. On the *Migrating References* page, click Using this migration table to map them in the destination GPO.

10. To create a new migration table, click New. The *Migration Table Editor – New* window opens.

11. Click Tools > Populate from Backup. Alternatively, you can also choose Populate from GPO.

12. In the *Select Backup* dialog box, click the GPO that you want to populate the migration table with and click OK. The migration table will populate.

13. Review the *Source Name*. If you want the values to change for the target, in the *Destination Name* column type the new name.

14. Click File > Save. Specify a name in the *File name* text box and click Save.

15. Close the migration table.

16. On the *Migrating References* page, click Next.

17. When the wizard is complete, click Finish.

18. After the import is succeeds, click OK.

19. Close the *Group Policy Management* Console.

You can synchronize a test domain with the forest domain in several ways while keeping the two environments separated. With virtual machines, you can easily make a copy of the domain controller virtual machine and then deploy the copy to the test network. To keep the domain controller with recent accounts and settings, do one of the following:

- Back up the system state and restore to the test domain controller by using an authoritative restore.

- Back up the entire domain controller and restore to the test domain controller.

- Use the LDIFDE commands to export information from Active Directory on the production network and import the information to the test network.

Of course, with virtual machines, copying a production domain controller to the test network is easy. However, if you restore or copy a domain controller or system state, you might need to do some metadata cleanup and seize operations masters by using the ntdsutil.exe.

After the forest is created, you synchronize Group Policy by using Group Policy Management and the following general steps:

1. Establish a trust between the two forests by using Active Directory Domains and Trusts.

2. In *Group Policy Management*, from the *Group Policy Management Actions* list, add the test forest by selecting Add Forest.

3. Copy objects as necessary for synchronization.

WARNING Remember, the test network must be isolated from the production environment and the test domain controllers should never be connected to the production domain.

SKILL SUMMARY

IN THIS LESSON YOU LEARNED:

- Because users, computers, and applications use Active Directory for authentication and authorization, when you rename a domain, you are changing the entire networking environment. Therefore, you must plan out the renaming of a domain and then implement the change during the off hours.

- To create a trust between a forest or domain, use the Active Directory Domains and Trusts New Trust Wizard. With this wizard, you can choose the trust type, specify whether the trust is one way or two way, and/or designate whether it is transitive.

- You can use Windows to create a trust between a Windows domain and a non-Windows Kerberos v5 realm. The trusts allow cross-platform interoperability with security services based on other Kerberos v5 versions, such as UNIX and Linux. Realm trusts can be nontransitive or transitive, and they can be one way or two way.

- When migrating from one domain to another, you are essentially moving objects from one domain to another. To perform this type of migration, you must use special Microsoft tools such as the Active Directory Migration Tool (ADMT) and Password Export Server (PES), or you must use third-party software.

- Forest restructuring involves moving a domain within a forest by using the `rendom` tool. Any domain, except the forest root, can be moved.

- To test domain renaming, interforest migration, and intraforest migration, you need a test environment that resembles your production environment. You also need the test environment for software upgrades and any other significant changes to the network.

■ Knowledge Assessment

Multiple Choice

1. You are an administrator of the `Contoso.com` domain. You want to create a Sales subdomain and move the sales people to the `sales.contoso.com` domain. Which tool is used to migrate the users?
   a. Group Policy Management Console
   b. Server Migration Tool
   c. Active Directory Users and Computers
   d. Active Directory Migration Tool

2. You are an administrator of the `Contoso.com` forest. You have a second forest called `adatum.com`. You want the GPO admins to manage the GPOs in every domain in the `adatum.com` forest. What do you need to do first?
   a. Create a one-way forest trust.
   b. Create a two-way forest trust.
   c. Create a one-way external trust.
   d. Create a two-way external trust.

3. Your corporate office has 2,000 users. You have a branch office with 600 users and three IP subnets. You need to make sure that all users are authenticated by a domain controller in their respective location. You also want to minimize the Active Directory replication traffic between the offices. What do you recommend?
   a. Create one domain with two sites.
   b. Create one domain with four sites.
   c. Create two domains and two sites.
   d. Create two domains with four sites.

4. What must you do before you add a domain controller running the first Windows Server 2012 R2 to a domain that only has Windows Server 2008 R2 domain controllers?
   a. Prepare the domain and forest.
   b. Lock down all domain controllers.
   c. Freeze the schema.
   d. Upgrade the domain functional level to Windows Server 2012.

5. You want to rename a domain. Which command is used to get a description of the forest?
   a. `rendom.exe /prepare`
   b. `rendom.exe /showall`
   c. `rendom.exe /list`
   d. `rendom.exe /domain`

6. Which command is used to fix GPOs after you rename a domain?
   a. `gpfixup`
   b. `repadmin`
   c. `adprep`
   d. `gpupdate`

7. Before you rename a domain, what is the first thing you should do?
   a. Run the `repadmin /syncall` command.
   b. Run the `rendom /prepare` command.
   c. Back up all domain controllers, including the domain controller system state.
   d. Delete all shortcut trusts.

8. Which utility is used to create a Kerberos realm trust?
   a. Active Directory Domains and Trusts
   b. Active Directory Users and Computers
   c. Active Directory Sites and Services
   d. Active Directory Trust Manager

9. Which command prepares a domain so that it can install a Windows Server 2012 R2 domain controller?
   a. `adprep /forestprep`
   b. `adprep /domainprep /gpprep`
   c. `gpofix /domain:<domainname>`
   d. `serverman domainlist`

10. Which of following steps is required to install the Active Directory Migration Tool?
   a. Install the most recent Windows updates.
   b. Run the `gpupdate /force` command.
   c. Within the current forest, establish trusts between the current domain and all other domains.
   d. Have a Microsoft SQL Server installation available.

Best Answer

Choose the letter that corresponds to the best answer. More than one answer choice can achieve the goal. Select the BEST answer.

1. You are establishing a realm trust to the domain of a company that your organization just purchased. Where do you enable support for Kerberos AES Encryption?
   a. In the New Trust Wizard on the Password and Encryption page
   b. In the Properties dialog box of the trust
   c. In the Domain's Properties dialog box
   d. In the Active Directory Users and Computers Domain Properties

2. Which command restructures a forest?
   a. adprep.exe
   b. Active Directory Users and Computers
   c. rendom.exe
   d. Active Directory Domains and Services

3. Which tool is used to migrate service accounts from one domain to another domain?
   a. Active Directory Users and Computers
   b. Active Directory Domains and Services
   c. Server Manager
   d. Active Directory Migration Tool

4. Your organization just purchased a new company. You need to establish a trust between the two forests. Which scope of authentication should you use?
   a. Forest-wide authentication
   b. Selective authentication
   c. Bypass authentication
   d. Domain-wide authentication

5. You just migrated the manage service, users, domain local groups, and servers. Which of the following is used to add SIDs to the access control lists in the target domain?
   a. Resource Properties dialog box
   b. Active Directory Domains and Services
   c. Server Manager
   d. Active Directory Migration Tool

Build a List

1. In order of first to last, specify the steps used to migrate from one domain to another domain.
   _____ Migrate applications data and settings for applications.
   _____ Deploy new servers in new forest.
   _____ Decommission old servers.
   _____ Configure DNS infrastructure in both forest.
   _____ Create the new server Windows Server 2012 R2 forest.
   _____ Migrate objects between domains.
   _____ Deploy necessary applications such as Microsoft SQL Server.
   _____ Establish trusts between forests.
   _____ Users test applications and data access.

2. In order of first to last, specify the steps to migrate objects from one domain to another within the same forest.

_____ Migrate global groups.
_____ Install the Active Directory Migration Tool.
_____ Add SIDs to access control lists.
_____ Migrate service accounts.
_____ Create trusts between domains.
_____ Migrate domain local groups.
_____ Migrate member servers and domain local groups.
_____ Install SQL Server.
_____ Migrate domain controllers.
_____ Migrate service account, user accounts, and workstation accounts.

3. In order of first to last, specify the steps to rename a domain.

_____ Freeze the forest configuration.
_____ Create DNS zones of the new domain.
_____ Execute the `rendom /execute` command.
_____ Relocate folder redirection and roaming user profiles.
_____ Run the `rendom /prepare` command.
_____ Perform a full backup of domain controllers.
_____ Configure an administrative computer that is not a domain controller with Remote Server Administrative Tools.
_____ Generate domain rename instructions.
_____ Generate a file called domainlist.xml.
_____ Run the `rendom /end` command.

■ Business Case Scenarios

Scenario 15-1: Combining Two Domains

You are an administrator for the Contoso Corporation. Your corporation just purchased the Adatum Corporation. Both domains are running at the Windows Server 2012 R2 functional level. You want to combine the two domains into one. How would you proceed?

Scenario 15-2: Renaming a Domain

You are an administrator for the Contoso Corporation. You own a company called Adatum Corp., which has its own domain. Adatum. Corp is changing its name to LitWare. What do you need to do to rename the domain to Litware?

Designing a Group Policy Strategy

70-413 EXAM OBJECTIVE

Objective 4.3 – Design a Group Policy strategy. This objective may include but is not limited to the following: Design considerations including inheritance blocking, enforced policies, loopback processing, security, WMI filtering, site-linked Group Policy Objects (GPOs), slow-link processing, group strategies, organizational unit (OU) hierarchy, Advanced Group Policy Management (AGPM), and Group Policy caching.

LESSON HEADING	EXAM OBJECTIVE
Understanding Group Policy	
Planning Group Policy • Planning Organizational Unit (OU) Hierarchy • Identifying Group Policy Goals • Meeting Organizational Requirements • Planning Delegated Administration	Design an organizational unit (OU) hierarchy Design for group strategies
Group Policy Design • Designing for Group Policy Object Placement • Designing for Inheritance Blocking • Designing for Policy Enforcement • Designing for Security Filters • Designing for WMI Filtering	 Design for inheritance blocking Design for enforced policies Design for security Design for WMI filtering
Deploying Group Policy • Deploying Group Policy Objects • Staging Group Policy Objects for Deployment • Deploying Group Policy for Slow Links • Deploying Site-Linked Group Policy Objects • Deploying Delegated Administration • Understanding Group Policy Caching	 Design for loopback processing Design for slow-link processing Design for site-linked Group Policy Objects (GPOs) Design for Group Policy caching
Managing Group Policy • Performing Maintenance on Group Policy • Configuring Advanced Group Policy Management • Managing Group Policy through Windows PowerShell	 Advanced Group Policy Management (AGPM)

■ Understanding Group Policy

THE BOTTOM LINE

Group Policy is a technology used to configure user and computer settings from a centralized location—Active Directory Domain Services (AD DS). Administrators can control domain-joined computers and users, forcing the computers and clients to meet specific policies.

If you take a step back and analyze any environment, you will see a need for consistency, security, application, and configuration management at a user level and at a computer level. Users need to be prevented from performing certain actions, and computers need to be protected from users. However, users need to perform certain actions and computers need to have the availability to allow users to perform their jobs. Computers must be secured from the users but also need to be usable. You need to define a fine line as you begin creating **Group Policy Objects (GPOs)** with a full understanding of what policies are available, what does what to whom, and where you can manage your environment securely.

Using Group Policy comes with a few requirements. First, you must be in an AD DS environment. GPOs, when created or imported, are stored on the domain controller and replicated between domain controllers within the domain in which they were created. Replicating across domain controllers verifies that all clients requesting services from the domain controller are getting the most up-to-date policies and settings to apply to the computer and user at startup and logon.

At the user level, you want to manage what users can do to their computers and the network environment—for instance, if you want to prevent users from changing desktop backgrounds, screensavers, and themes. You can universally control these features through Group Policy.

At a computer level, the same reasoning applies. In an education setting, for example, you must have restrictions from confidential data in place. Is the data secured if students can log on to their computers with their credentials applied? You can block students from logging on to administrative, faculty, or staff computers based on user account. So if a student attempts to log on to a faculty machine, she will be denied log on. If you are worried a user will leave his computer unlocked, you can configure Group Policy to force screens to lock after a certain amount of time.

These examples are just a few of the more than 3,000 settings available for configuration in Group Policy. As you continue through this lesson, you will learn how to plan, design, deploy and manage Group Policy.

■ Planning Group Policy

↓
THE BOTTOM LINE

A well-thought-out plan is the basis of a successful deployment of Group Policy. Having a solid backbone and well-designed AD DS structure will make configuring and troubleshooting end users and computers easier as the domain grows.

CERTIFICATION READY
Design an organizational
unit (OU) hierarchy
Objective 4.3

CERTIFICATION READY
Design for group
strategies
Objective 4.3

Before you put a Group Policy infrastructure in place, you must carefully plan to ensure it is deployed efficiently. A poorly planned design will cause frustration and headache for administrators and end users as an environment grows.

Group Policy planning starts with knowing what exists in your environment. What users do you have, what do they do, and where are they located? How many computers does the enterprise have? Do those computers exist in the same office? Do users move from computer to computer? What restrictions are required?

Planning Organizational Unit (OU) Hierarchy

A well-planned and well-designed organizational unit (OU) hierarchy enables a more granular, yet well-defined, Group Policy layout. OUs are intended for organizing and securing Active Directory objects in the environment.

TAKE NOTE*

As a best practice, plan OU design appropriately by separating user OUs from computer OUs. This simplifies the GPO creation and management process.

The backbone of Group Policy is the OU hierarchy. Designed from the top down, you can organize your users, computers, servers, service accounts, and so on in a nested manner.

Consider an educational environment with several hundred faculty and staff members. You could also have several hundred to several thousand students in a system. Now break that down. Do you think faculty and staff user and computer accounts should be treated the same? Do some faculty members require different software than staff members? Do some staff members require different restrictions on their computers because of the confidential information held on them? Do some faculty and staff members reside in different AD DS sites? Do students need to access all computers? Could students be grouped by graduation years or by year of admission? Do some students need to have access to certain shares or computers based on their education specialization?

By looking at that basic information, you can see that it can continue to branch off in different directions through the OU hierarchy as the need for requirements are realized. The recommended practice is to create separate user OUs and separate computer OUs, because the default Users and Computers containers cannot have policies applied to them.

GPOs apply in the following order from the top down: local, site, domain, and OU. In an AD DS environment, the focus is primarily on the site, domain, and OU policies as the computers' default local policies typically are not configured.

- *Local policies:* Policies configured locally on the computer are first applied to the user. Site policies are applied next.
- *Site policies:* In a domain environment that has more than one defined AD DS site, any policies applied at the site level are applied after local policies. In some environments, a single site can hold domain controllers for multiple domains that are part of the same

forest. Site policies apply to all domains (within the same forest) found in that site. This is discussed later in this lesson.

- **Domain policies:** After they are applied locally and then at the site level, policies are applied at the domain level. Each domain, when created, has a couple of default GPOs: Default Domain Policy and Default Domain Controllers Policy. Typically, modifying Default Domain Policy or the Default Domain Controller Policy is not recommended, nor is placing domain-affecting policies at the domain level. Any mis-configuration will affect and disrupt all domain users and domain controllers. Ensure that any changes made at the domain level are thoroughly staged and tested before deployment.

- **Organizational unit policies:** After the local, site, and domain policies are set, next come the OU policies. The OU level is where most of the GPOs are linked to meet organizational requirements. This is where having an OU hierarchy in place and segregated is critical to meet planned Group Policy requirements. If multiple GPOs are within an OU, they are then applied based on link order, where a GPO with a link order of 1 has highest precedence in the OU.

As the computer applies the configured policies at each level, the policy closest to the computer object or the user object in Active Directory "wins." This means that if a policy is configured at the site level to apply a specific desktop background, but at the OU level a different policy is configured to apply another background, the settings of the GPO at the OU level are applied.

AD DS has three types of collection objects: Users and Computers, Containers and Organizational Units, and Sites. GPOs can be applied only to OUs. For instance, by default, the domain has two containers: the Users container and the Computers container. Any users or computers found in those two containers or any other default containers cannot have GPOs applied to them.

Remember, Group Policy has two configuration types: **computer configuration** and **user configuration**. As the names suggest, computer configuration applies only to computers and user configuration applies only to users.

As you design the OU structure, you should separate computers from users, keeping them in their own separate OUs, as best practice (see Figure 16-1). This allows for more granular configuration when policies are applied. In some cases, such as kiosks and specialty computers, both computer and user accounts will reside in the same OU. At that point, policies using both user and computer settings will need to be placed in the same OU.

Figure 16-1

Separating users and
computers

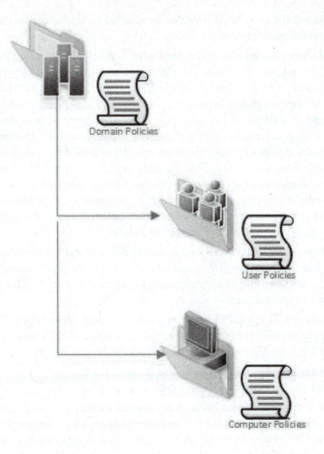

Identifying Group Policy Goals

Every AD DS domain environment has its own Group Policy goals as they are developed. Whether the goal is to offload a multitude of configurations done when a computer is loaded or to map a network drive, Group Policy can meet several goals.

Identifying the goals all comes down to the following questions:

- What policies do I want to apply?
- Who should get these policies?
- What should get these policies?"

If you are starting a new domain or are reorganizing an OU structure, work collectively with other administrators or colleagues to ensure that you have an end goal in sight. For instance, in working with a team of desktop support, server administrators, and help-desk staff, answering these questions collectively is important. If you work outside of a team and are the single administrator for the organization, take additional time to plan and make a goal. Throughout the goal-making process, make it a point to think from beginning to end. Ask yourself, "If I do this, what will happen? Does that meet the defined goal?"

- **What will each Group Policy Object do?** After reviewing the policies and understanding what they do, you can begin to create GPOs to meet your goals. Whether you are on a large team or working solo, go through all available policies to see what they do and what they will affect. Also actively reflect back on your environment when reviewing these policies to see if they can be applied to your situation or requirement in the environment.

- **Who requested the policy and who will administrate it?** A well-documented plan will leave out any questions when it comes to a configured GPO and what it is used for. For example, if a chief security officer (CSO) performs an audit on your environment and requires that computers be locked after three minutes of inactivity, ensure that this request is documented well. If another administrator sees that GPO configured and thinks is useless, believes it is poorly implemented, or removes it to meet his or her own needs, that person just removed a policy required by administration. Now, when the CSO comes in for a follow-up audit and finds it not being applied, whose fault is it? As you document GPOs, define who requested it, what was created, what it will do, and where it was placed. By documenting answers to these simple questions and ensuring that others review the documentation before making changes, you can ensure that the goals of you and others remain to be met.

- **How many GPOs will be required?** Keeping GPOs to a minimum will help keep computer logon processing resources to a minimum. The more GPOs are applied to a user or computer, the more processing is required at log on. This means slower logon times and frustrated users.

- **Where will the GPO link?** You need to know where the policy will link and what it will apply to. Will it be linked at the site, domain, or OU level? How far into the OU levels will it link? Can it be at an OU's root?

- **What settings will be included in each GPO?** Again, know the policy settings available and the benefits they will provide the environment.

- **Will the settings be for a computer or a user?** This will help define the link location within the OU structure. Computer policies will apply only to computers located within the OUs they are linked to. User policies will apply only to users located within the OUs it is linked to.

- **Will this policy need to apply before another policy or after?** GPOs are cumulative and applied in the local, site, domain, and OU processes. After they get to the OU structure, the closest policy is applied last. If multiple GPOs are located within the OU that will overwrite another OU's policies, it might be beneficial to order the GPOs allowing one to apply before the other.

- **Will the policy need to be blocked at a certain OU, or is it required in all OUs?** You can configure organizational units to disable inheritance. Doing so will ensure that an unenforced policy will not be applied to the contents of the OU, or sub-OUs. If it is required in all OUs, a GPO can be configured to be enforced; this will bypass any blocked inheritance on an OU and enforce the policy to apply to its contents and sub-OUs.

- **What type of filtering will be required?** Security filters can be configured to restrict GPOs to apply only to a defined security group—for insta`nce, if a large group of users is located within a single OU. You can configure a security group to include only the users required to have the policy, leaving out all other users unaffected by the policy. Windows Management Instrumentation (WMI) filters allow policies to affect only computers that meet certain hardware and software configurations. For example, you can configure policies to apply a GPO constrained to computers running Windows 8.1 with more than 8GB of free space.

- **Do you need to install and manage software installations? If so, to whom and what?** You can install software applications at the user and computer level. As software is updated by vendors, new applications can also be applied to update an existing application that has been pushed out.

- **Are network shares being used? Are they accessible to all required users?**
  Environments with several network shares with different mapped drive names can become cumbersome to manage. Using Group Policy helps you manage the configuration of network shares and mapped network drives on user computers without their intervention. As policies are created for network shares, ensure that the users within the OU to who the policy will be applied have access to the network share. This might also be a perfect opportunity to create a security group, apply a policy to those users, and grant them the required access to the network drive.

- **Is a location accessible for logon, logoff, startup, and shutdown scripts to be run from?** Some environments run scripts at logon, logoff, startup, and shutdown across the entire enterprise. To avoid storing these scripts on all local machines, you should store them on a network share that all users requiring access to the scripts will have access to. Many enterprise-created scripts used with AD DS are stored within the NETLOGON folder located on the domain controllers. This share provides access to all authenticated users, is an ideal location for multiple connections as it is replicated, and can be pointed to the domain name, such as \\adatum.local\ NETLOGON\.

> **TAKE NOTE** *
>
> Deploying software before deploying scripts ensure that users and computers have the appropriate permissions to access the required files.

Meeting Organizational Requirements

> Organizational requirements are strong drivers for Group Policy configurations. Requirements to meet lower costs, security needs, restrict access to applications, prevent users from modifying settings, and having consistent environments are becoming more prevalent.

Organizations are looking for easier ways to do perform routine and repetitive tasks, cut down computer configuration time, install software, prevent changes, have identical computer layouts, and secure their environment. Group Policy can meet all these requirements.

Think about installing an operating system on 10 computers, from scratch, in a domain environment without the use of imaging software. Setting up each computer to be identical in look, feel, and configuration as all the other computers in the domain without the use of imaging software will be cumbersome and time consuming.

Now, integrate Group Policy settings into that scenario. Many configuration settings found within Group Policy can eliminate the need to perform the repetitive tasks of desktop icon size, Internet Explorer favorites, screensavers, desktop backgrounds, installed software, and so on.

Installing and upgrading software can also take up a considerable amount of time, especially for several users and computers. If you do not have a software management application such as Microsoft System Center Configuration Manager in your toolbox, consider using Group Policy to deploy applications within the environment for applications that are installed using a single .msi file. This cuts down on the legwork, remote access, and instructions sent out to end-users in attempts to have them install the software.

Organizations might also require minimum configuration abilities by end users. You can configure several settings to prevent users from doing pretty much everything. You can even go so far as to make a computer completely unusable for a user. On a simpler scale, you can hide icons, prevent changes, prevent personalization, prevent log off, and prevent changes to the Start Menu.

As a tool to enforce security within the environment, GPOs can be configured to influence and overwrite any user-configured settings that might violate security concerns. By using Group Policy, you can restrict access to computers from unwanted users or user groups. You can prevent applications from being installed or run from any location other than the approved locations, such as program files, Windows, and WINNT. You can configure DNS settings to be assigned statically and not modified. You can even change the default Administrator and Guest account names. If a WSUS server is in place, you can configure settings to enable client-side targeting, forcing the domain computers to check into the WSUS server for updates.

Planning Delegated Administration

Separate from the Delegation of Control Wizard in Active Directory Users and Computers (ADUC), delegating administration within the Group Policy Management Console grants users strict access to OUs and GPOs for linking, modification, analysis, creation, and deletion.

Now that you have all the pieces planned out and have the OU hierarchy all prepared and segregated by departments, users, computers, servers, and specialized equipment, you are ready to plan for administration.

Considering the number of policies and OUs that some companies have, delegating administration to certain OUs so that the management can be offloaded to another administrator is beneficial. *Delegated administration* allows you to take any trusted user account or group and make them administrators to an OU or sub-OU of the hierarchy.

Consider the following items as you plan delegated administration:

- **Team members:** Who on the team can be trusted, has the knowledge, can be trained, and will thoroughly test GPOs before they are applied? Having team members who follow policy and procedures ensures that delegating them administrative tasks for OUs and GPOs will result in a positive outcome.

- **Branch office sites:** When you consider that many enterprises have branch offices with their own IT teams, the primary domain administrator might not want to grant them with greatly elevated rights just to manage GPOs specifically required by the site. Granting them access to the GPOs that affect only the users and computers at the remote site will offload much of the testing and implementation of GPOs. Also, because they work daily with their end users and computer configuration, they know what is and what is not required at the site.

- **Administrative workload:** No matter what area you are in with information technology, always have a backup, whether it is of hardware, software, or personnel. In small to large environments, having a colleague who knows the particulars of GPO administration just as well as you do is extremely beneficial. If you are in a scenario where you are overloaded with work orders, server installations, and problems in the environment, you can share the workload with others. Plan for other personnel to help.

■ Group Policy Design

THE BOTTOM LINE

Group Policy design involves the application of how the Group Policy plan will be implemented. At this stage, you begin to answer and design the details of planned Group Policy Objects. After you answer these questions, you can begin the deployment process.

Earlier in this lesson you learned that GPOs are applied to organizational units, which in turn apply them to users and computers within the OU. Remember that the default Users container and the default Computers container in AD DS cannot have GPOs applied to them. Keep in mind that if you do use the default containers, as new users and computers are added to active directory, they are placed in their respective default container unless you have changed the default location to be an OU or created them manually in an OU. You cannot link GPOs to the default containers, however, objects within the default containers do receive domain-linked GPOs through inheritance.

As you design your Group Policy infrastructure, you need to plan for GPO placement, inheritance blocking, policy enforcement, security filter implementation, and configuration of WMI filtering for the targeted users and computers.

Designing for Group Policy Object Placement

Group Policy placement has its positives and negatives. When GPOs are placed in their proper locations and applied to the correct targets, the intended outcome will meet the organization's needs. If a GPO is placed in the wrong location, or if too many GPOs need to be processed or must be processed over slow links, users can quickly become unhappy.

When the OU hierarchy is in place, you can now assess where GPOs must be linked. As described earlier, you need to design GPOs to target their intended group. For instance, you can create a GPO with user configuration settings and apply it only to OUs that contain users. The same goes for computer configuration settings—apply them to OUs that contain only computers.

You will have plans for multiple GPOs, including the two default GPOs. For instance, you will need a GPO for user configuration settings and a GPO for computer configuration settings. You need to design user configuration GPOs to be placed where the users reside in the OU structure and computer configuration GPOs to be placed where the computers reside in the OU structure. User configuration settings will not apply to computers, and vice-versa, so if you try to apply user settings to the wrong container, nothing will be applied. You can configure and assign user and configuration GPOs to an OU, but for both configuration settings to apply, Loopback Policy processing must be enabled and configured in Merge mode.

TAKE NOTE✳

Design Group Policy placement to enhance GPO processing times across the enterprise.

After settings are configured, disable the other configuration settings on the GPO. For example, if you create a GPO that will contain only computer settings, disable the user settings. This will improve Group Policy processing time. Use loopback processing in instances where the computer and the user must reside in the same OU.

Designing for Inheritance Blocking

By blocking inheritance for an organizational unit, Group Policy Objects outside the OU are prevented from applying to the underlying computers, users, and sub-OUs (child objects). In other words, the OU that is set up to block will not inherit any GPOs higher in the OU design.

Sometimes you might need to create an OU that has a specialized group of computers or users found within it. Because of organizational requirements and/or constraints, the OU and its child objects must stay nested within the OU structure that has been designed. Based on its location, its logical design for administration, or GPO processing order, you might want to allow policies to apply only to the objects. Some policies are required to be applied to the OU, but those outside the OU must not be. As you design your environment, blocking inheritance should be done only as needed. You can design a GPO to use security filtering or WMI filtering to meet the same result.

Benefits of inheritance blocking include the following:

- **Maintain OU structure in large environments:** In a large environment that has a well-defined structure and hierarchy with a small number of OUs, you should block inheritance.

- **Prevent application of unneeded GPOs:** If you have several GPOs that do not relate to the OU you have created and cannot create an OU in an area outside of the hierarchy, block inheritance.

- **Configuring a test OU:** By blocking inheritance on an OU, you can create a Group Policy environment to stage and test computers and users for GPO processing.

Disadvantages of blocking inheritance include the following:

- Administrators might overuse inheritance blocking to make up for a poorly designed Active Directory OU structure.

- Important GPOs might not be enforced, exposing possible security risks to objects within the blocked OU.

- Administrators can use inheritance blocking to troubleshoot a GPO problem. This complicates GPO troubleshooting, however and it may be a bad habit of troubleshooters to not undo what they did to test to see whether it does not resolve a problem.

- Creating multiple enforced OUs, rather than relinking OUs to bypass inheritance blocking, can cause problems.

- Relinking OUs rather than enforcing them can cause problems.

- When an OU blocks inheritance, only unenforced GPOs will be blocked. Any GPOs that are enforced outside the OU will be inherited by the child objects, as shown in Figure 16-2.

Figure 16-2

Blocking inheritance

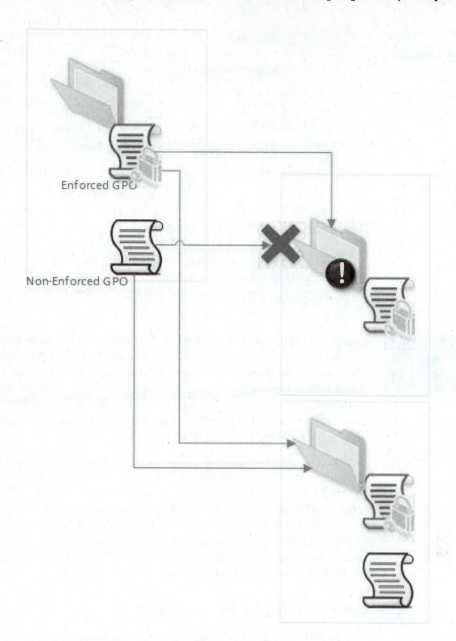

Enforced GPO

Non-Enforced GPO

 BLOCK INHERITANCE ON AN ORGANIZATIONAL UNIT

GET READY. To block inheritance on an organizational unit, perform the following steps.

1. In the *Group Policy Management* console, expand Domains and then expand the domain name to view the OU hierarchy.

2. Right-click your domain name and choose New Organizational Unit.

3. In the *New Organizational Unit* dialog box, in the *Name* text box, type Test Block Inheritance and then click OK.

   The Test Block Inheritance OU has been created and is listed under one level from the domain name.

4. Right-click the Test Block Inheritance OU and choose Block Inheritance.

   The *Test Block Inheritance* OU will now block the inheritance of any non-enforced GPOs, as indicated by the blue icon with the exclamation point (see Figure 16-3).

5. Close the *Group Policy Management* console.

Figure 16-3

Viewing the Block Inheritance icon

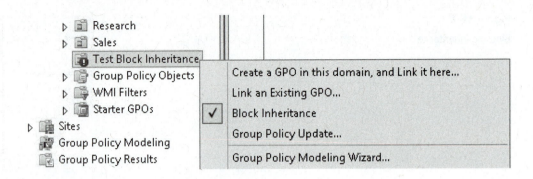

Designing for Policy Enforcement

Policy enforcement ensures that an important policy will not be blocked by any OU that has blocked inheritance configured. If an organizational unit is configured for block inheritance, an enforced policy will still apply to that OU.

Critical GPOs that *must* be applied to all users and/or all computers within an OU or sub-OU can be configured to be enforced. Some environments place critical settings needed by all computers in the domain at the same level as the Default Domain Policy. If a computer does not or cannot retrieve the settings defined in the policy, it might not be able to access the network, resources, domain controllers, or critical services. To fix that problem, you can enforce those environments. Enforcing the policy will ensure that all computers, even those behind an inheritance-blocking OU, will receive the OU.

Enforced GPOs have the final verdict on what settings are applied. If a GPO is enforced at the domain level and is processed down four or five levels where other GPOs are linked, the enforced GPO will take precedence, even if those GPOs in the sub OUs have the same settings. Keep in mind that if a GPO is configured in a sub-OU that has a setting configured that is different from the enforced GPO, the enforced GPO will win. For example, if you configure an enforced OU at the domain level that forces the web page to be *www.microsoft. com*, and then in the sub-OU configure a GPO that is not enforced to be *www.outlook.com*, the result will apply the *www.microsoft.com* setting.

 ENFORCE A GROUP POLICY OBJECT

GET READY. To enforce a Group Policy Object to apply to all organizational units, perform the following steps:

1. In the *Group Policy Management* console, expand Domains and then expand the domain name to view the OU hierarchy.

2. Right-click Default Domain Policy and choose Enforced. The GPO will change to show a padlock, as shown in Figure 16-4. The *Default Domain Policy* is now configured to apply to all OUs, whether or not they are configured for block inheritance.

3. Close the *Group Policy Management* console.

Figure 16-4

Enforcing the Group Policy Objects

Designing for Security Filters

Security filters provide a way to filter GPOs based on user, computer, or security group. When you apply a GPO with security filters configured, the policy will apply only to the user, computer, or security group specified.

Another level of restriction on GPOs is security filtering. Linking takes GPO configuration to the OU level, security filtering then takes it a step further by restricting it to apply to only users or computers found within a security group. Complicating the OU structure to specifically apply GPOs to a limited group of child objects can become an unfortunate habit. If you are planning to create an OU beneath an OU of computers just to apply a single GPO, consider security filtering before adding another OU for GPOs and computer processing to traverse.

If you have a group of users that you want to prevent from using InPrivate filtering but want others within the same OU to be able to use it, you can configure the policy to Turn Off InPrivate Browsing, and then add the security group to the Security Filtering to apply to the group that must have the setting.

Security filters can filter based on users, user groups, computers, or computer groups. Security filters can also be applied at higher levels to reach child objects within each OU beneath. This prevents multiple OUs from being created to meet a GPO need.

If blocking inheritance on an OU becomes necessary, check to see whether you can meet the end goal of blocking inheritance by implementing a security filter. Implementing a security filter on a GPO rather than blocking the inheritance will help maintain the integrity of the overall design and remove the need to have several enforced GPOs.

 ADD A SECURITY FILTER

GET READY. To add a security filter on a Group Policy Object, perform the following steps.

1. Use *Active Directory Users and Computers* to create a domain local security group called Kiosk Computers. Close *Active Directory Users and Computers*.

2. In the *Group Policy Management* console, expand Domains and then expand the domain name to view the OU hierarchy.

3. Right-click Group Policy Objects and choose New.

4. In the *New GPO* dialog box, in the *Name* text box, type Kiosk Restrictions, do not select a starter GPO, and then click OK. The *Kiosk Restrictions* GPO is now listed under *Group Policy Objects*.

5. Select the Kiosk Restrictions GPO. The GPO's configuration settings are presented in the right pane. On the *Scope* tab, find and review the current *Security Filtering* settings.

6. Select Authenticated Users from within the *Security Filtering* area and click Remove.

7. In the *Group Policy Management* dialog box, click OK to remove the delegation privilege.

8. In the *Security Filtering* settings area, click Add.

9. In the *Select User, Computer or Group* dialog box, in the *Enter the object name to select* text box, type Kiosk Computers and then click OK.

10. Look for the Kiosk Computers group listed under *Security Filtering*, as shown in Figure 16-5. When this policy is applied to an OU that contains computers that are member of the group, only those group members will receive the Kiosk Computers policy.

11. Close the *Group Policy Management* console.

Figure 16-5

Configuring security filters

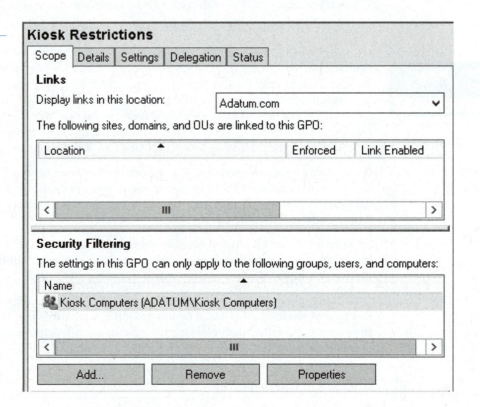

Designing for WMI Filtering

By using the **WMI Query Language**, you can filter based on several hardware and software criteria. When it is added to Group Policy Objects, **WMI filters** will filter the targeted systems based on the specified criteria.

Windows Management Instrumentation (WMI) filters allow you to granularly and dynamically filter and apply GPOs to computers meeting the configured attributes. If you are not familiar with WMI Query Language (WQL), multiple online resources are available for reference.

WMI filters are often used to filter based on computer operating system, disk space, memory, available memory, and CPU. For instance, if you are planning to implement a certain software application that can be applied only on Windows 8.1 computers, you can configure a

WMI filter to do so. After the WMI filter is created, it can be tied to a GPO and applied to the OU. WMI filtering eliminates the need to segregate devices based on operating system.

Table 16-1 lists the WQL query statements for past and current Microsoft Windows operating systems.

Table 16-1

Query Statements per Windows Operating System

OPERATING SYSTEM	WQL QUERY STATEMENT
Windows XP	select * from Win32_OperatingSystem where (Version like "5.1%" or Version like "5.2%") and ProductType = "1"
Windows Server 2003	select * from Win32_OperatingSystem where Version like "5.2%" and ProductType = "3"
Windows Vista	select * from Win32_OperatingSystem where Version like "6.0%" and ProductType = "1"
Windows Server 2008	select * from Win32_OperatingSystem where Version like "6.0%" and ProductType = "3"
Windows 7	select * from Win32_OperatingSystem where Version like "6.1%" and ProductType = "1"
Windows Server 2008 R2	select * from Win32_OperatingSystem where Version like "6.1%" and ProductType = "3"
Windows 8	select * from Win32_OperatingSystem where Version like "6.2%" and ProductType = "1"
Windows Server 2012	select * from Win32_OperatingSystem where Version like "6.2%" and ProductType = "3"
Windows 8.1	select * from Win32_OperatingSystem where Version like "6.3%" and ProductType = "1"
Windows Server 2012 R2	select * from Win32_OperatingSystem where Version like "6.3%" and ProductType = "3"

Just like with blocking inheritance and enforcing policies, you can use WMI filters to your advantage, but do not overuse them because doing so will complicate the troubleshooting process.

 CREATE A WMI FILTER

GET READY. To create and add a WMI filter to a Group Policy Object, perform the following steps.

TAKE NOTE

You can also apply WMI filters to users. This can narrow the scope of a hardware WMI filter by scoping it down to a sAMAccountName or domain\username parameter.

1. In the *Group Policy Management* console, expand Domains and the domain name to view the OU hierarchy.
2. Right-click WMI Filters and choose New.
3. In the *New WMI Filter* dialog box, in the *Name* text box, type Windows 8.1. For the description, type Filters only Windows 8.1 devices. Click Add.
4. In the *WMI Query* dialog box, in the *Query* text box, type select * from Win32_ OperatingSystem where Version like "6.3%" and ProductType = "1"

5. Click OK to close the *WMI Query* dialog box. Click OK to close the *Warning* dialog box asking if you would like to use this namespace. Click Save to close the *New WMI Filter* dialog box.

6. Right-click Group Policy Objects and choose New.

7. In the *New GPO* dialog box, in the *Name* text box, type Windows 8.1 Settings. Do not select a *Starter GPO*. Click OK. The *Windows 8.1 Settings* GPO is now listed under *Group Policy Objects*.

8. If it is not already expanded, expand Group Policy Objects in the OU hierarchy, and then select the Windows 8.1 Settings GPO. The *Windows 8.1 Settings* configuration settings appear in the right pane. Select the Scope tab. Find and review the current *WMI Filtering* settings. From the *WMI Filtering* drop-down list, select Windows 8.1.

9. In the *Group Policy Management* dialog box, click Yes to change the WMI filter to Windows 8.1, as shown in Figure 16-6.

   You can apply the Windows 8.1 WMI filter to any Group Policy Object. When applied to a GPO, the defined WMI filter is applied to only those devices meeting the filter scope.

10. Close the *Group Policy Management* console.

Figure 16-6

Linking a WMI filter

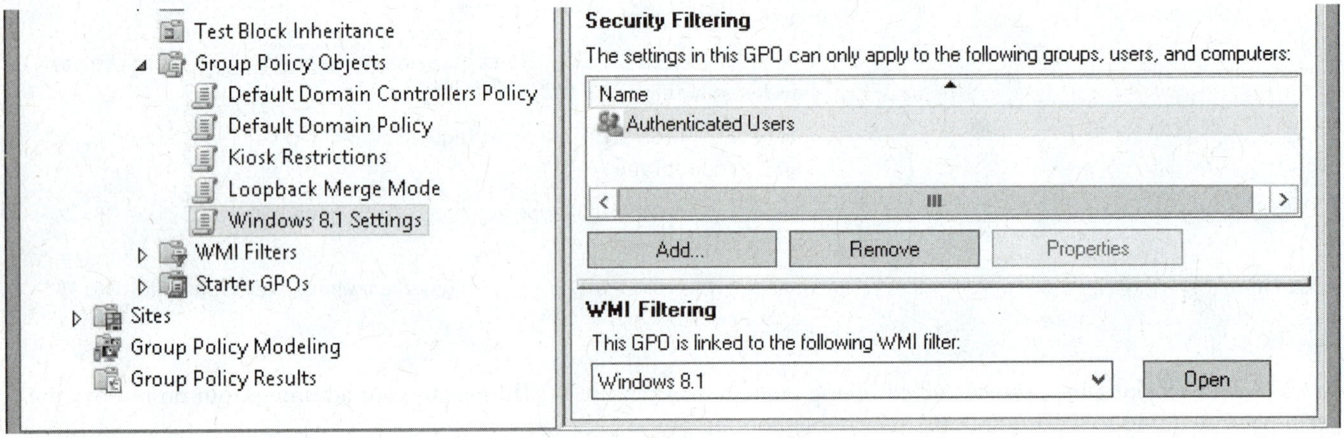

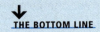

Deploying Group Policy

THE BOTTOM LINE

GPOs must be thoroughly tested before they are deployed into a production environment. Any slow links between sites, domain controllers, and users must be taken into consideration.

Do not take deploying GPOs lightly. Also, do not implement GPOs quickly. Creating GPOs and applying them wherever you see fit is very easy. Do not get ahead of yourself and start linking them everywhere.

You still must take into account several considerations before you do a full out deployment. If you create and link a policy without having it thoroughly tested, it could be a mess to clean up, especially in a large environment. You must also consider what the policies are being applied to. Are they being applied to computers across slow links or in a multi-domain site? Anytime during the deployment process you can also delegate administrative permissions to the OU or to the GPOs themselves.

Continue to document throughout the deployment stage, because the GPO design can quickly change.

Deploying Group Policy Objects

> Even before you create GPOs, you must understand all the design considerations. You must plan for ease of administration, security, management, and inheritance, as well as plan how they will be applied before you create the first GPO.

Designing GPOs is critical for domain operation. If you create a GPO, fully test it, and then begin linking it, you need to decide whether to link it in multiple places or in just one location. Do you want only enterprise administrators, domain administrators, or Group Policy Object creators to be able to manage the GPOs? Or would you require another individual with more restrictive rights? How many GPOs do you want to be processed at startup and logon?

You should link GPOs at the highest level possible. The term *highest level possible* does not mean that you link all GPOs at the site level or domain level if you do not need to. Generally, users and computers are segregated into a well-designed OU hierarchy. Objects intended only to apply to computers can be applied to the OU that contains the computers. Because every domain will have servers in its environment, applying a restrictive computer GPO to the domain level could potentially cause outages and connectivity issues if the policy is applied too high. So, again, as you design the creation and placement of the OU, think of what it is being created for and where it will be linked.

If possible, you should consolidate GPOs. Creating GPOs that contain multiple settings for what requires the policy is best practice. You do not want to create a separate GPO for changing the home page, a separate one for modifying proxy settings, and a separate one for setting the background if they are all intended to be applied to the same targets. If you can consolidate GPOs, do so. The more GPOs that need to be applied to a user or computer, the longer processing will take for the user and computer.

As described earlier in this lesson, enforce OUs that have strict security settings or that absolutely have to be applied to all objects within the OU structure (Default Domain Policy).

Apply Security Filters and WMI filters when they can work to your benefit.

PERFORMING A GROUP POLICY UPDATE

After creating a new GPO or modifying an existing one, and after it is placed within the intended OU, you might prefer a forced update. Group Policy uses the following update defaults:

- **Users:** Updates at user logon. Updates are performed only against the user configuration settings.
- **Computers:** Updates every 90 minutes with a random offset of 0 to 30 minutes. Updates at a computer startup or restart. Updates are performed only against the computer configuration settings.
- **Domain controllers:** Updates every five minutes.

MODIFYING GROUP POLICY REFRESH INTERVAL

If you want to change the default schedule of when Group Policy is applied, you can change the Group Policy Refresh Interval within the following Group Policy location: Computer Configuration > Policies > Administrative Templates > System > Group Policy.

To update the refresh interval for computers, modify the Set Group Policy refresh interval for computers setting. To update the refresh interval for domain controllers, modify the Set Group Policy refresh interval for domain controllers setting.

FORCING AN UPDATE THROUGH GROUP POLICY MANAGEMENT CONSOLE

New in Windows Server 2012, you can perform a Group Policy Update against an OU from within the Group Policy Management Console (GPMC).

To force an update from the client computer, run gpupdate.exe or Invoke-GPUpdate in Windows PowerShell.

To force an update from the GPMC, right click on the OU and select Group Policy Update.

DEPLOYING A LOOPBACK POLICY

Loopback policies are configured when the users that log on to specific computers require different or stricter user policies than those they have when they log on to other computers. Loopback policies are typically used in specific configurations that require OU segregation for stricter and unique policy enforcement, including kiosks, remote desktop sessions, public-use computers, libraries, laboratories, and special-event devices.

User settings are configured on Group Policy Objects and applied to the OU that contains the specialized computers. For example, if you have an OU with kiosk computers, you can configure the user configuration settings to force any users logging on to those computers to have different policies than what are usually applied to that user.

The following loopback processing modes can be selected.

- **Merge mode:** The users' typical configuration settings are applied, followed by the computer configuration settings. Any user settings that are configured in the OU where loopback processing is enabled are merged with those the user already has. Any conflicts are won by the policy closest to the computer. All computer configuration settings have higher precedence when applied in Merge mode.

- **Replace mode:** The users' typical user configuration settings do not follow the user and are not applied when logging on to computers located in the OU where loopback processing is enabled. Only the computer and user configuration settings configured in the OU with loopback processing enabled are applied.

CERTIFICATION READY
Design for loopback processing
Objective 4.3

TAKE NOTE

Use loopback policies in instances where you want user settings to follow them to the OU enabled by loopback policy.

 ENABLE THE LOOPBACK POLICY

GET READY. To create a GPO to enable the loopback policy, perform the following steps:

1. In the *Group Policy Management* console, expand Domains, and then expand the domain name to view the OU hierarchy.

2. Right-click Group Policy Objects and choose New.

3. In the *New GPO* dialog box, in the *Name* text box, type Loopback Merge Mode. Do not select a starter GPO. Click OK.

    The *Loopback Merge Mode* GPO is now listed under *Group Policy Objects*.

4. Right-click Loopback Merge Mode and choose Edit.

5. In the *Group Policy Management Editor* window, navigate to Computer Configuration > Policies > Administrative Templates > System > Group Policy. Double-click Configure

user Group Policy loopback processing mode. The Configure user Group Policy loopback processing mode window displays.

6. In the *Configure user Group Policy loopback processing mode* window, click Enabled. Under *Options*, the *Mode* drop-down menu becomes active.

7. From the *Mode* drop-down list box, select Merge (see Figure 16-7). Click OK.

8. Close the remaining open windows.

Figure 16-7

Configuring loopback policy
Merge mode

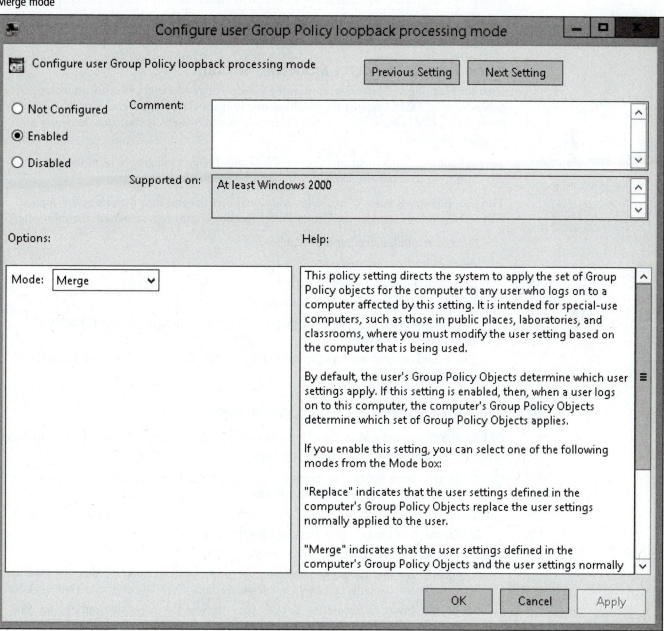

Staging Group Policy Objects for Deployment

Test, test, test! Most importantly, always test your policies by using the Group Policy Modeling Wizard or in an isolated OU that will not affect or force updates on unintended users or machines. Consider it best practice to always test a GPO before it is applied in a production environment.

Imagine installing your entire printer fleet's queues but accidentally changing the default printer throughout your environment to a printer that is not accessible or in a different location or site. That will be disastrous on a large-scale scope, especially if all users print heavily. Think of the inconvenience of having to reach out to every single end user and computer that was on, and had applied the update, when the misconfiguration happened.

You must know what each policy's end result is, who and what it will affect, and whether this configuration meets the end goal.

USING THE GROUP POLICY MODELING WIZARD

Used for planning and testing purposes, the Group Policy Modeling Wizard simulates deployment of a GPO against the specified site, domain controller, users, computers, security groups, and WMI filters. The wizard also simulates deployment against slow networks and loopback processing.

Throughout the deployment process, use the Group Policy Modeling Wizard to your advantage. You want to avoid any user interruption in a production environment.

The Group Policy Results Wizard adds additional benefits and information of the applied GPOs. New information in the Group Policy Results Wizard report include the following:

- Slow or fast link detection is available.
- Block inheritance is configured.
- Loopback processing is configured.
- Processing time is measured for each policy.
- GPO Name is included with the policy and setting to aide in the identification of applied policy or setting.
- The wizard analyzes settings for users and computers and returns the policies and settings applied to the object.

 USE THE GROUP POLICY MODELING WIZARD

GET READY. To model and review GPO results before deployment by using the Group Policy Modeling Wizard, perform the following steps:

1. In the *Group Policy Management* console, expand Domains, and then expand the domain name to view the OU hierarchy.
2. Right-click the domain name and choose Group Policy Modeling Wizard.
3. On the first *Group Policy Modeling Wizard* page, click Next.
3. On the *Domain Controller Selection* page, click Next.
4. On the *User and Computer Selection* page, under *User information*, choose Container or User. Under *Computer information*, choose Container or Computer, and then click Next.
5. On the *Advanced Simulation Options* page, review the selectable options for *Slow network connections*, *Loopback processing*, and *Site testing*. Click Next.
6. On the *Alternate Active Directory Paths* page, select the target user location from which to simulate the settings. Click Next.

7. On the *User Security Groups* page, add or remove security groups for the user to test security-filtering results. Click Next.

8. On the *Computer Security Groups* page, add or remove security groups for the computer to test security-filtering results. Click Next.

9. On the *WMI Filters for Users* page, review the filters options to test WMI filtering. Click Next.

10. On the *WMI Filters for Computers* page, review the filter options. Click Next.

11. On the *Summary of Selections* page, review your selections. If you need to make any changes, you must back up through the wizard. Otherwise, click Next.

    The simulation process will run and, when completed, the *Completing the Group Policy Modeling Wizard* page appears. Click Finish to close the wizard.

12. Review the results as shown in Figure 16-8.

13. Close the remaining open windows.

Figure 16-8

Viewing the Group Policy Modeling Wizard results

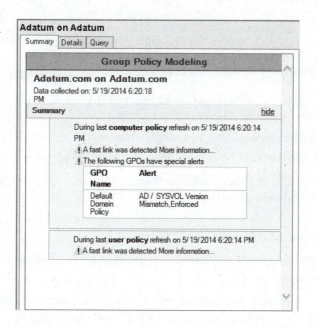

CREATING AN OU FOR TESTING

Before deploying a GPO, you need to create a test user OU and a test computer OU. Whether it is within an existing OU structure or at a base level, the test OU can help you apply policies and their application to users and computers.

If you do not know how computers and users will react to a certain GPO, you can create a temporary user and set up a test computer. If you are creating a new computer policy, you can place the test computer within the OU with the new policy and test its reaction.

Use both the Group Policy Modeling Wizard and the test OU to test a GPO before deployment. Unlike with the Group Policy Modeling Wizard, a test OU cannot simulate a slow network connection unless the test computer is across a slow link.

Deploying Group Policy for Slow Links

Links between a client and the nearest domain controller are measured in kilobytes per second (Kbps). A link slower than 500 KBps is considered slow.

When a domain controller and a client initiate a connection with each other, the domain controller checks the link speed between itself and the client. If it recognizes a slow link (slower than 500 Kbps), it will not allow the client to process all GPOs that are assigned to the client. If you design Group Policy to process over slow links, processing GPOs will increase the logon and startup times for user and computer across the slow link. The default configuration for what happens over slow links can be changed from the following location: Computer Configuration > Policies > Administrative Templates\System\Group Policy.

When a slow link is detected, the following policy settings apply by default:

- Registry Settings (Administrative Templates): Required and cannot be changed
- Security Policies: Required and cannot be changed.
- Encrypted File System (EFS) Recovery Policy: Can be changed from default
- IP Security: Can be changed from default

The following policy settings are not applied by default, because additional processing of these items over slow links will be detrimental:

- Application Deployment: Can be changed from default
- User logon/logoff Scripts: Can be changed from default, but computer startup/shutdown scripts will not be processed
- Folder Redirection: Can be changed from default
- Disk Quotas: Can be changed from default

By using the Group Policy Modeling Wizard, you can model GPOs against a slow link connection to analyze the result of a policy.

 CONFIGURE SLOW-LINK DETECTION

GET READY. To create a GPO to change the default slow-link detection speed, perform the following steps:

1. In the *Group Policy Management* console, expand Domains, and then expand the domain name to view the OU hierarchy.
2. Right-click Group Policy Objects and choose New.
3. In the *New GPO* dialog box, in the Name text box, type SlowLink1000Kbps. Do not select a starter GPO. Click OK.

   The *SlowLink1000Kbps* GPO is now listed under *Group Policy Objects*.
4. Right-click SlowLink1000Kbps and choose Edit.
5. In the *Group Policy Management Editor* window, navigate to Computer Configuration > Policies > Administrative Templates > System > Group Policy.
6. Double-click Configure Group Policy slow link detection.
7. In the *Configure Group Policy slow link detection* dialog box, click Enabled. Under Options, the *Connection Speed (Kbps)* box becomes active.
8. In the *Connection Speed (Kbps)* box, type 1000, as shown in Figure 16-9. Click OK.
9. Close the remaining open windows.

Figure 16-9

Modifying Group Policy slow link detection

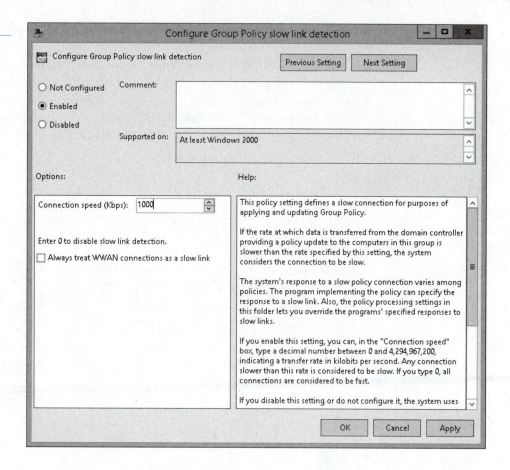

Deploying Site-Linked Group Policy Objects

Site-linked Group Policy Objects are stored in the domain where they are created, and only the location of the site-linked GPO is replicated to other domains in the forest. Site-linked GPOs can be configured incorrectly if they are poorly designed. Careful planning and design will prevent site-linked GPOs from causing unneeded latency and slow logon times for users and computers in multi-domain sites.

GPOs linked at the site level apply first to all users and computers located within that site. Site-linked GPOs will, in turn, affect all users and computers of all domains within the forest located in that site. This means that if three domains have objects located within one site, a GPO linked to the site will apply to every user and computer in that site.

You must understand how site-linked Group Policy processing works before linking GPOs to sites, especially if sites contain multiple domains. Logistically, here is what happens in a poorly designed environment (see Figure 16-10):

1. A domain administrator creates a GPO on a domain controller and links it to a site.

2. The domain controllers in the domain where the GPO was created replicates the GPO with each other. Each domain controller within the domain the site-linked GPO was created has a copy of the GPO.

3. Domain controllers within the forest replicate the GPO's location with each other. The GPO itself is not replicated across the forest; only its location is replicated.

CERTIFICATION READY
Design for site-linked Group Policy Objects (GPOs)
Objective 4.3

4. A computer starts up and/or a user logs on at the site where the GPO is linked. It pulls the assigned GPOs from its closest domain controller.

5. If the site-linked GPO was not created in the client machine's domain, its domain controller will send it to the closest domain controller of the domain that has the copy.

6. If the closest domain controller is not found within the same site and lies across a slow wide area network (WAN) link, the GPO will need to be processed over the WAN link. This will result in slow GPO processing, logons, and startup times for end users.

Figure 16-10

Understanding site-linked processing

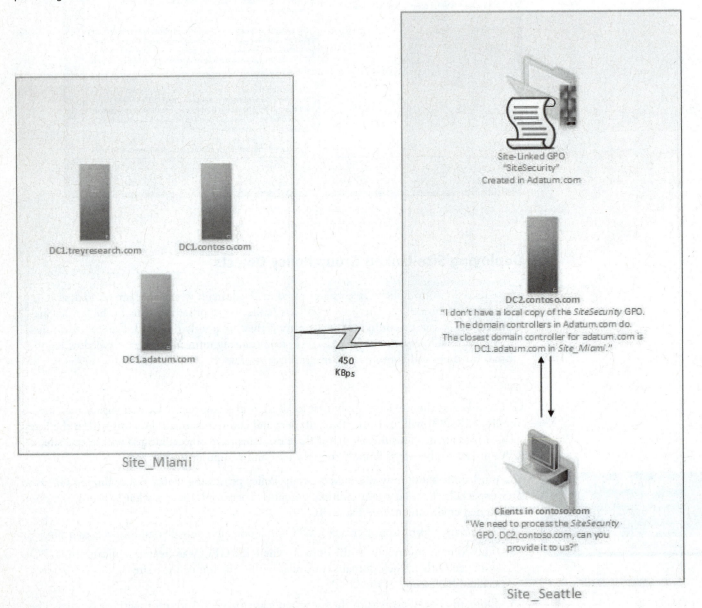

As you can see, if proper domain controller placement, GPO placement, and overall design does not take into consideration GPO processing, then issues will likely happen.

To prevent these issues, be proactive by reviewing the following recommendations.

- Copy the GPO from the domain on which it was created and place it on and link it to each domain. Implement additional filtering options to allow the GPO to affect only computers and/or users within the intended site.

- Place a domain controller for each domain within each site where the clients exist. When a client from another domain attempts to pull the site-linked GPO from another domain controller, it will not need to travel across the WAN link to retrieve the settings.

- Do not create site links. Copy the GPO and link it to the other domains, eliminating any need for site GPO processing. All processing will be done from the local domain controller.

Deploying Delegated Administration

By default, only enterprise administrators, domain administrators, and Group Policy creator owners can create new Group Policy Objects. When you delegate administration to GPOs, you can delegate the creation, modification, and linking to users that do not have the default permissions.

As soon as you start Active Directory OU and GPO design, you should keep delegated administration in the front of your mind. This is to ensure that the security design of Active Directory flows correctly. Just as you would delegate control to add, remove, and modify users and computers in Active Directory Users and Computers (ADUC), you can do the same for GPOs in the Group Policy Management Console (GPMC). Each GPO has its own security settings to allow for delegated control.

Suppose that your company, with more than 25,000 users and computers domain-wide, has headquarters in Seattle and a branch office in Miami. Each office has its own set of policies, restrictions, and security needs in addition to those already required by the company. With the amount of Active Directory objects between both locations, having a group of administrators from the headquarters manage the GPOs at the Miami office will not be feasible. This is where delegation comes in. The system administrators at the headquarters can delegate the Miami office's OUs, objects, and GPOs to the on-site administrators, yet maintain ultimate control, ensuring that the end goal is met. If the placement of OUs, GPOs, and objects is designed correctly, the Miami system administrators can make changes only to the Miami office; they cannot make changes to the headquarters. Delegating these routine tasks not only improves workflow and response times, but also allows for a more secure environment in a large enterprise.

You configure Group Policy delegation within the GPMC. Each site, domain, OU, and GPO has its own separate Delegation tab and settings in the GPMC. Remember that configuring delegation is designed to manage the administration of GPOs.

You must be a domain administrator or enterprise administrator, or your user account must have been delegated Modify permissions on the object you will be delegating permissions to. In a fresh domain, where no delegation has taken place, only the domain administrator or enterprise administrator can delegate permissions.

To view the current Group Policy delegation permissions of a site, domain, or OU, open GPMC, expand to the domain view and select the site, domain, or OU from the tree. When the settings appear in the right pane, click the Delegation tab to view the current permissions.

You can delegate three types of permissions to each site, domain, or OU, as shown in Figure 16-11:

- **Link GPOs:** Users or groups can be delegated permissions to link existing GPOs into the site, domain, and/or OU. Delegation can be restricted to allow GPO links only to that site, domain, or OU, or to the less restrictive linking to that OU and any sub-OUs within. Users granted this permission can link GPOs, change link processing order, and block inheritance on the site, domain, or OU.

- **Perform Group Policy Modeling Analyses:** Users or groups can be delegated permission to run a Group Policy Modeling Analysis against the domain or OU for testing and troubleshooting.

- **Read Group Policy Results Data:** Users or groups can be delegated permission to run Group Policy results data against the domain or OU to view the Resultant Set of Policy as determined by Active Directory.

Figure 16-11

Viewing the Delegation tab

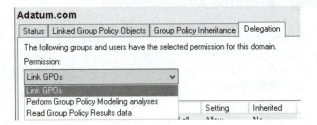

The following are the default specified permissions for the link GPOs, Perform Group Policy Modeling analyses, and Read Group Policy Results Data:

- **Administrators:** Allow permissions to this container and all child containers. It is inherited.

- **Domain Admins:** Allow permissions to this container only. It is not inherited.

- **Enterprise Admins:** Allow permissions to this container and all child containers. It is inherited.

- **SYSTEM:** Allow permissions to this container only. It is not inherited.

As you add group and users to the delegation of the site, domain, or OU, be cautious if you intend to use inheritance. Inheritance placed at the root of an OU cannot be removed from sub-OUs. So, if you delegate permissions at the domain level and then realize that you want to remove those delegated permissions from one or two OUs within the domain, you cannot until inheritance is removed at the top level.

You can delegate three types of permissions to each GPO, as shown in Figure 16-12:

- **Read:** This permission allows the delegated user or group to view the GPO and its settings.

- **Edit settings:** This permission allows the delegated user or group to view and modify the GPO and settings. The delegated user cannot delete the GPO or change its security settings.

- **Edit settings, delete, and modify security:** This permission allows the delegated user or group to view, change, delete, and modify the GPO and its settings.

Figure 16-12

Reviewing delegated
permission types

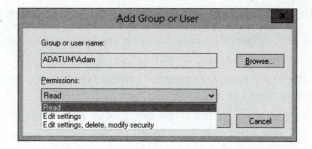

To view the current Group Policy Delegation permissions of a GPO, open the GPMC,
expand the Group Policy Objects container, and select a GPO. With the GPO displayed in
the right pane, click the Delegation tab (see Figure 16-13). The Default Domain Policy uses
the following default security settings:

- **Authenticated Users:** Read (from security filtering)
- **Domain Admins:** Edit settings, delete, and modify security
- **Enterprise Admins:** Edit settings, delete, and modify security
- **ENTERPRISE DOMAIN CONTROLLERS:** Read
- **SYSTEM:** Edit settings, delete, and modify security

Figure 16-13

Reviewing default delegation
security settings

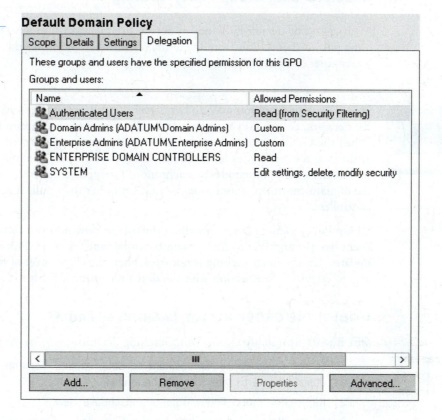

CONFIGURE DELEGATED USERS ON AN ORGANIZATIONAL UNIT

GET READY. To configure a delegated user on an organizational unit, perform the following steps:

1. In the *Group Policy Management* console, expand Domains and expand the domain name to view the OU hierarchy.

2. Right-click your domain name and choose New Organizational Unit.

3. In the *New Organizational Unit* dialog box, in the Name text box, type Miami Users, and then click OK.

   The *Miami Users* OU is created and is listed one level from the domain name.

4. Select the Miami Users OU. The right pane will reflect its current Group Policy configuration.

5. On the *Delegation* tab, from the *Permission* drop-down menu, select Link GPOs. Click the Add button.

6. In the *Select User, Computer, or Group* dialog box, enter the username of the user you want to add and click OK.

7. In the *Add Group or User* dialog box, from the *Permissions* drop-down menu, select This container and all child containers. Click OK.

   The user will be listed within Groups and users on the *Delegation* tab.

8. Close the *Group Policy Management* console.

Understanding Group Policy Caching

> Turned on by default in Windows Server 2012 R2 and Windows 8.1, Group Policy caching pulls certain GPOs from the domain controller and stores them locally on the client computer for faster load times at the next network logon.

CERTIFICATION READY
Design for Group Policy caching
Objective 4.3

When a computer running Windows Server 2012 R2 or Windows 8.1 and later logs on to the network, certain GPOs are cached locally after every background Group Policy update. When the GPOs are cached on the machine, they are used to speed up network logon times at the next startup or user logon. When Group Policy runs at computer startup/shutdown or user logon/logoff and requires a synchronous foreground update, when the client connects to the domain controller it uses its cached GPOs rather than pulls it across the from the domain controllers.

Group Policy caching has its benefits primarily in slow network connections, in which the client has a connection to the domain controller and has the GPOs that require synchronous updates. Group Policy caching is not used when the client is off of the network; it must be able to establish a connection with the domain controller for it to use the cache.

 MODIFY THE GROUP POLICY CACHING DEFAULTS

GET READY. To modify Group Policy caching defaults, perform the following steps:

1. In the *Group Policy Management* console, expand Domains and then expand the domain name to view the OU hierarchy.

2. Right-click Group Policy Objects and choose New.

3. In the *New GPO* dialog box, in the Name text box, type GPOPolicyCaching. Do not select a starter GPO. Click OK.

   The *GPOPolicyCaching* GPO is now listed under *Group Policy Objects*.

4. Right-click GPOPolicyCaching and choose Edit.

5. In the *Group Policy Management Editor* window, navigate to Computer Configuration > Policies > Administrative Templates > System > Group Policy. Double-click Configure Group Policy Caching.

6. In the *Configure Group Policy Caching* window, select *Enabled* (as shown in Figure 16-14) and then click OK.

7. Close any remaining open windows.

Figure 16-14

Enabling a Group Policy caching GPO

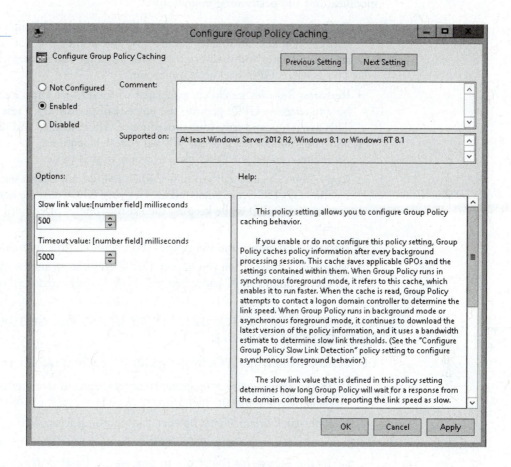

Managing Group Policy

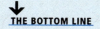
THE BOTTOM LINE
Group Policy management is an ongoing process and must be performed and analyzed frequently. The requirement to back up, restore, and implement additional security measures is critical to operations.

Even when the Group Policy infrastructure is put in place and is operational, you are not done with it. Now you can manage it to ensure optimal operability. You must perform routine maintenance on Group Policy, including performing backups, verifying replication, adding/removing permissions, and modifying GPOs as new technologies are released.

Performing Maintenance on Group Policy

When you need to perform routine backups and test restores, you should make copies of GPOs when planning for new or modified GPOs. If migrations are planned, use the Import and Migration Table tools available in Group Policy.

Maintaining Group Policy is another critical aspect of Group Policy design. Familiarize yourself with the following maintenance tasks to keep Group Policy protected from unintended modifications and performing migrations:

- **Backups:** A routine backup plan for GPOs is critical. Although GPOs are replicated between domain controllers, that does not mean they will not become corrupted or that an administrator will inadvertently make a change and not remember what was changed. This is why a GPO backup is important.

- **Restores:** Restores are closely associated with GPO backups. Because you need to know how to restore a GPO, get into the practice of performing a test restore at least quarterly. This way, you can verify your procedure of GPO backups and restores as well as remain knowledgeable of the process. When a restore is required, you will be ready—and not panicking—to get the GPO back to where it used to be.

- **Copy:** You can copy a group policy when you do not have a starter GPO but need a baseline GPO to create a new GPO. Copying GPOs also are beneficial when you want to test a new GPO while keeping the existing one in place until the new GPO is thoroughly tested.

- **Import:** This allows you to import GPOs from another domain or a forest.

- **Migration tables:** When you import a set of GPOs from another domain or forest, the GPOs can link to UNC paths, network drives, or other resources in the old domain or forest.

BACK UP GROUP POLICY OBJECTS BY USING THE GROUP POLICY MANAGEMENT CONSOLE

GET READY. To back up GPOs by using GPMC, perform the following steps:

1. In the *Group Policy Management* console, expand Domains and then the domain name to view the OU hierarchy.

2. Right-click Group Policy Objects and choose Backup All.

3. In the *Back Up Group Policy Object* dialog box, click Browse.

4. In the *Browse for Folder* dialog box, select Desktop from the list, click Make New Folder, and for the backup location type Backup GPOs. Click OK.

5. Verify that the location path is correct, and then click Back Up.

   The *Backup* window appears, indicating the backup's progress.

6. Verify that all GPOs have succeeded and click OK.

7. Open the file location where the GPO backups have been saved. You should see a list of folders sorted by GUID.

8. Close the *Group Policy Management* console.

BACK UP ALL GROUP POLICY OBJECTS BY USING WINDOWS POWERSHELL

GET READY. To back up all GPOs by using Windows PowerShell, perform the following steps:

1. Open Windows PowerShell.

2. Create a target folder on the user desktop by running the following command:

```
New-Item .\Desktop\BackupGPOPS -Type Directory
```
Verify that the new directory was created.

3. Back up all GPOs by running the following command:
```
Backup-GPO -All -Path .\Desktop\BackupGPOPS
```
Verify that the backups have been created.

4. Close Windows PowerShell by running the Exit command.

Configuring Advanced Group Policy Management

Advanced Group Policy Management (AGPM) is available to Microsoft customers with Software Assurance. With access to the Microsoft Desktop Optimization Pack (MDOP), administrators can install and powerfully manage Group Policy.

Large and complex environments in which multiple changes to Group Policy occur have a need to improve management over all aspects of Group Policy. You also need to improve testing capabilities, roll back any inadvertent changes, restrict policy changes without approval before review, and search for GPOs. AGPM is a powerful tool to manage all these requirements, all from within the GPMC. Available only to Software Assurance customers, AGPM is a key component available in the MDOP for Software Assurance.

AGPM offers the following capabilities for managing Group Policy:

CERTIFICATION READY
Configure Advanced
Group Policy
Management (AGPM)
Objective 4.3

- **Offline editing:** You can create and test GPOs in offline mode before deployment, audit the changes, and compare GPO versions. Offline editing allows you to deploy the GPO in a safe environment before they are deployed into production.

- **Group Policy Management Console integration:** AGPM integrates fully in the GPMC, allowing you to control Group Policy from a single window.

- **Change control:** AGPM provides version tracking, history capture, and rollback of GPO changes. You can configure the email alerting you to any GPO changes.

- **Role-based delegation:** Four roles are involved with an AGPM deployment: Administrator, Approver, Editor, and Reviewer. The Administrator role has full control over AGPM. The Approver role approves the created and deployment of the GPO and can view and compare GPOs. The Editor role can check out a GPO from the archives, modify it, and check it back into the archive. Editors can also view and compare GPOs. The Reviewer role can only view and compare GPOs.

- **Search and filter:** AGPM allows you to search and filter against all GPOs. You can search and filter against the name, status, or comment. You can also filter by users who made changes or by change dates.

- **Cross-forest management:** You can export GPOs from a forest and implement them to another forest. This can be useful if you have an identical testing environment or if you are performing a domain or forest migration.

Managing Group Policy through Windows PowerShell

After the GPMC is installed, you can perform overall Group Policy management—from creation to removal—through Windows PowerShell.

With Windows PowerShell, you can manage basic tasks such as updating Group Policy on clients and remote clients, backing up, generating a Resultant Set of Policy, and more. This means that Windows PowerShell can be used to schedule backups, manage links, block inheritance, and even enforce GPOs. Table 16-2 lists the cmdlets available in the Group Policy Windows PowerShell Module.

Table 16-2

Group Policy Windows
PowerShell Module Cmdlets

CMDLET	DESCRIPTION
Backup-GPO	Performs a backup of all GPOs within a domain or a single GPO. This cmdlet backs up a specified GPO or all the GPOs in a domain to a backup directory. The backup directory and GPO must already exist.
Copy-GPO	Copies specified GPO. This cmdlet creates a (destination) GPO and copies the settings from the source GPO to the new GPO. You can use the cmdlet to copy a GPO from one domain to another domain within the same forest. You can specify a migration table to map security principals and paths when copying across domains. You can also specify whether to copy the access control list (ACL) from the source GPO to the destination GPO.
Get-GPInheritance	Gets Group Policy inheritance information for a domain or a single OU. This cmdlet returns the following information about Group Policy inheritance for a specified domain or OU: A list of GPOs that are linked directly to the location (the GpoLinks property) A list of GPOs that are applied to the location when Group Policy is processed on a client (the InheritedGpoLinks property) Whether inheritance is blocked for the location (the GpoInheritanceBlocked property).
Get-GPO	Gets all GPOs within a domain or a single GPO. This cmdlet gets one GPO or all the GPOs in a domain. You can specify a GPO by its display name or by its globally unique identifier (GUID) to get a single GPO, or you can get all the GPOs in the domain by specifying the All parameter. The cmdlet returns one or more objects that represent the requested GPOs. By default, properties of the requested GPOs are printed to the display; however, you can also pipe the output of this cmdlet to other Group Policy cmdlets.
Get-GPOReport	Generates a report in either XML or HTML format that describes properties and policy settings for a specified GPO or for all GPOs in a domain. The information reported for each GPO includes: details, links, security filtering, WMI filtering, delegation, and computer and user configurations. You can specify the All parameter to generate a report for every GPO in the domain, or you can specify either the Name or Guid parameter to generate a report for a single GPO. You can also pipe GPO objects into this cmdlet. If you specify a file by using the Path parameter, the report is written to a file; otherwise, it is printed to the display.
Get-GPPermission or Get-GPPermissions	Gets the permission level for one or more security principals on the specified GPO. You can use the TargetName and TargetType parameters to specify a user, security group, or computer for which to retrieve the permission level. You can use the All parameter to retrieve the permission level for each security principal (user, security group, or computer) that has permissions on the GPO. You can specify the GPO by its display name or by its GUID.

CMDLET	DESCRIPTION
Get-GPPrefRegistryValue	Retrieves one or more registry preference items under either computer configuration or user configuration in a GPO. Specify the Context parameter (user or computer) to indicate whether to retrieve the registry preference item from computer configuration or user configuration. You can specify the GPO by its display name or by its GUID. You can retrieve registry preference items for a specific registry value or for a key and any of its first-level registry values:
	To retrieve any registry preference items that configure a specific registry value, specify the Key and ValueName parameters.
	To retrieve all registry preference items that configure a registry key and any (first-level) registry values directly under the key, specify the Key parameter but not the ValueName parameter.
	If you specify only a key, the cmdlet also returns its first-level subkeys for which the registry preference items configure the subkey, its values, or any of its subkeys (at any level) or their values. You can use this information to browse for registry preference items.
Get-GPRegistryValue	Retrieves one or more registry-based policy settings under either computer configuration or user configuration in a GPO. You can retrieve registry-based policy settings for a specific registry value or for all the registry values under a key:
	To retrieve the registry-based policy setting that configures a specific registry value, specify the Key and the ValueName parameters.
	To retrieve all the registry-based policy settings that configure values directly under a registry key, specify the Key parameter but not the ValueName parameter.
	If you specify only a key, in addition to the policy settings that configure values under the key, the following first-level subkeys of the key are returned: first-level subkeys that have a policy setting that configures a value. First-level subkeys that have a subkey (at any level) with a policy setting that configures a value. You can use this information to browse for registry-based policy settings.
Get-GPResultantSetOfPolicy	Outputs the RSoP information for a user, a computer, or both to a file.
Get-GPStarterGPO	Gets one starter GPO or all starter GPOs in a domain. You can specify the starter GPO to retrieve either by display name or by GUID, or you can specify the All parameter to get all the starter GPOs in the domain. You can use this cmdlet to get information about a starter GPO, or you can create a new GPO from a specified starter GPO by piping the output of this cmdlet into the New-GPO cmdlet.
Import-GPO	Imports the settings from a GPO backup into a specified target GPO. The target GPO can be in a different domain or forest than that from which the backup was made, and it does not have to exist before the operation. Use the Path parameter to specify the location of the backup, the BackupGpoName parameter to specify the GPO name of the backup to use, or the BackupId parameter to specify the backup ID (GUID) of the backup to use.
	If you specify a GPO name, the cmdlet imports the most recent backup. To import an earlier version of a GPO backup, you must use the BackupID parameter to specify the unique backup ID for the particular version. This is the GUID that uniquely identifies the backup within its backup directory. Use the TargetName parameter or the TargetGuid parameter to specify the target GPO into which the settings should be imported. Use the optional MigrationTable parameter to map security principals and UNC paths across domains. Use the CreateIfNeeded parameter to create a new GPO if the specified target GPO does not exist.

(continued)

Table 16-2

(continued)

Cmdlet	Description
Invoke-GPUpdate	Refreshes Group Policy settings, including security settings that are set on remote computers, by scheduling the running of this cmdlet on a remote computer. You can combine this cmdlet in a scripted fashion to schedule the **Gpupdate** command on a group of computers. You can schedule the refresh immediately to start a refresh of policy settings, or wait for a specified period of time, up to a maximum of 31 days. To avoid putting a load on the network, the refresh times will be offset by a random delay.
New-GPLink	Links a GPO to a site, domain, or OU. By default, the link is enabled, which means that the settings of the GPO are applied at the level of the target Active Directory container (site, domain, or OU) according to the rules of inheritance and precedence when Group Policy is processed. You can specify the GPO by either its display name or its GUID; or the GPO can be piped into the cmdlet. You specify the site, domain, or OU to link to by its LDAP distinguished name. You can use other parameters to specify whether the link is enabled, whether the link is enforced, and the order in which it is applied at the site, domain, or OU.
New-GPO	Creates a new GPO with a specified name. By default, the newly created GPO is not linked to a site, domain, or organizational unit (OU). You can use this cmdlet to create a GPO that is based on a starter GPO by specifying the GUID or the display name of the Starter GPO, or by piping a **StarterGpo** object into the cmdlet. The cmdlet returns a GPO that represents the newly created GPO that you can pipe to other Group Policy cmdlets.
New-GPStarterGPO	Creates a starter GPO with the specified name. If the starter GPOs folder does not exist in SYSVOL when this cmdlet is called, it is created and populated with the eight starter GPOs that ship with Group Policy.
Remove-GPLink	Deletes the link between a GPO and a specified site, domain, or OU. This cmdlet does not delete the actual GPO or any other links between the specified GPO and other sites, domains, or OUs.
Remove-GPO	Removes the GPO container and data from the directory service and the system volume folder (SysVol).
Remove-GPPrefRegistryValue	Removes one or more registry preference items from either computer configuration or user configuration in a GPO. You must specify the **Context** parameter (user or computer) to indicate whether to remove the registry preference item from computer configuration or user configuration. You can specify the GPO by its display name or by its GUID. You can specify either a key or a value: If you specify a key, all registry preference items that configure that registry key or any of its (first-level) values are removed from the specified configuration in the GPO. Registry preference items that configure subkeys of that key (or their values) are not affected. For a key, specify the **Key** parameter without the **ValueName** parameter. If you specify a value, all registry preference items that configure that registry value are removed from the specified configuration in the GPO. For a value, specify the **Key** parameter without the **ValueName** parameter. This cmdlet can take input from the pipeline: You can pipe GPO objects to this cmdlet to remove a specified registry preference item from one or more GPOs. You can pipe **PreferenceRegistrySetting** objects to this cmdlet to remove one or more registry preference items from a specified GPO.

CMDLET	DESCRIPTION
Remove-GPRegistryValue	Removes one or more registry-based policy settings from either computer configuration or user configuration in a GPO. You can specify the GPO by its display name or by its GUID. You can specify either a key or a value: If you specify a key, registry-based policy settings that configure any of its (first-level) values are removed. However, if any registry-based policy settings configure any subkeys or their values, an error occurs and no policy settings are removed (including those for first-level values of the key). For a key, specify the `Key` parameter without the `ValueName` parameter. If you specify a value, the registry-based policy setting that configures that registry value is removed. For a value, specify the `Key` parameter without the `ValueName` parameter. This cmdlet can take input from the pipeline: You can pipe GPO objects to this cmdlet to remove a specified registry-based policy setting from one or more GPOs. You can pipe `PolicyRegistrySetting` objects to this cmdlet to remove one or more registry-based policy settings from a specified GPO.
Rename-GPO	Assigns a different, non-null display name to a GPO. This cmdlet has no effect on the GUID of the GPO.
Restore-GPO	Restores one GPO or all GPOs in a domain from one or more GPO backup files.
Set-GPInheritance	Blocks or unblocks inheritance for a specified domain or OU. GPOs are applied according to the Group Policy hierarchy in the following order: local GPO, GPOs linked to the site, GPOs linked to the domain, and GPOs linked to OUs. By default, an Active Directory container inherits settings from GPOs that are applied at the next higher level in the hierarchy. Blocking inheritance prevents the settings in GPOs that are linked to higher-level sites, domains, or OUs from being automatically inherited by the specified domain or OU, unless the link (at the higher-level container) for a GPO is enforced. Use the `Target` parameter to specify the LDAP distinguished name of the domain or OU, and use the `IsBlocked` parameter to specify whether to block or unblock inheritance.
Set-GPLink	Sets the properties of a GPO link. You can set the following properties: `Enabled:` If the GPO link is enabled, the settings of the GPO are applied when Group Policy is processed for the site, domain or OU. `Enforced:` If the GPO link is enforced, it cannot be blocked at a lower-level (in the Group Policy processing hierarchy) container. `Order:` The order specifies the precedence that the settings of the GPO take over conflicting settings in other GPOs that are linked (and enabled) to the same site, domain, or OU.
Set-GPPermission or Set-GPPermissions	Grants a level of permissions to a security principal (user, security group, or computer) for one GPO or all GPOs in a domain. Use the `TargetName` and `TargetType` parameters to specify a user, security group, or computer for which to set the permission level. You can use the `Name` or the `Guid` parameter to set the permission level for the security principal on a single GPO, or you can use the `All` parameter to set the permission level for the security principal on all GPOs in the domain. By default, if the security principal already has a higher permission level than the specified permission level, the change is not applied. You can specify the `Replace` parameter to remove the existing permission level from the GPO before the new permission level is set. This ensures that the existing permission level is replaced by the new permission level.

(continued)

Table 16-2

(continued)

CMDLET	DESCRIPTION
Set-GPPrefRegistryValue	Configures a registry preference item under either computer configuration or user configuration in a GPO. You can configure the registry preference item for either a registry key or a registry value: For a registry key, specify the Key parameter, but do not specify the ValueName, Type, or Value parameters. For a registry value, specify the Key parameter along with the ValueName, Type, and Value parameters. (All these parameters must be specified.) You must specify the Context parameter (user or computer) to indicate whether to configure the registry preference item in computer configuration or user configuration. You must also specify the Action parameter to set the action that should be applied on the client. You can specify the GPO by its display name or its GUID. You can specify the Disable parameter to create a registry preference item that is disabled. Note: This cmdlet configures new registry preference items. It does not modify existing registry preference items. This cmdlet can take input from the pipeline: You can pipe GPO objects to this cmdlet to set a specified registry preference item on one or more GPOs. You can pipe PreferenceRegistrySetting objects to this cmdlet to set one or more registry preference items on a specified GPO.
Set-GPRegistryValue	Configures a registry-based policy setting under either computer configuration or user configuration in a GPO. The policy setting configures keys or values in the registry on the client computer when the GPO is applied. You can specify the GPO by name or by its GUID, or you can pipe a GPO object to the cmdlet. You can also pipe a PolicyRegistrySetting object (for example, one returned by Get-GPRegistryValue) to the cmdlet. You can configure registry-based policy settings for one or more registry values by passing the Key, ValueName, Value, and Type parameters. For multiple registry values, pass a comma-separated list for both the ValueName and Value parameters. When you specify multiple registry values, only the String and ExpandString data types are supported. One or more registry values share the same name prefix by passing the Key and Type parameters, and a single value or a comma-separated list for the Value parameter. You can optionally specify the value name prefix by using the ValuePrefix parameter. Only the String and ExpandString data types are supported for lists. You can use the Additive parameter to ensure that existing registry values for the key are not overwritten by the new policy setting when the GPO is applied. You can also delete registry values on a client when the GPO is applied by disabling a policy setting with the Disable parameter. You can disable all the registry values under a specified registry key by passing the Key parameter. No subkeys (or their values) will be deleted on the client. A single registry value by passing the Key parameter and the ValueName parameter. Multiple registry values by passing the Key parameter and a comma-separated list for the ValueName parameter.

CREATE AN HTML REPORT OF ALL GPOS BY USING WINDOWS POWERSHELL

GET READY. To create an HTML report of all GPOs in a domain, perform the following steps on a computer that has the GPMC installed:

1. Open Windows PowerShell.
2. Type Get-GPOReport –ReportType Html –All –Path .\Desktop\GPOReport.html and then press Enter.

   The report is saved as GPOreport.html and is now located on you user desktop.
3. Close Windows PowerShell.
4. Navigate to your user desktop and double-click GPOReport.html. The report displays in your default web browser.
5. View the reports and capabilities of the embedded links.
6. Close your browser.

SKILL SUMMARY

IN THIS LESSON YOU LEARNED:

- A well-designed OU hierarchy is critical for both delegated control and Group Policy design.
- Before Group Policy Objects (GPOs) are implemented, you must consider business objectives, goals, centralized management, and administrative requirements.
- You can configure organizational units (OUs) to block the inheritance of any unforced GPOs that would apply to the OU. Block inheritance should be used only when absolutely required.
- You can enforce GPOs to bypass any block inheritance restrictions put in place. This enables administrators to force mission-critical GPOs to apply to all objects throughout the inheritance. Enforcing GPOs should be used only when absolutely required.
- Using block inheritance and policy enforcement together can meet specific goals set by the organization.
- GPOs can specifically target computers, users, groups, hardware, operating systems, and resources by using security filtering and WMI filtering.
- You must test GPOs before applying any policy into a production environment. By using the Group Policy Modeling Wizard, Advanced Group Policy Management (AGPM), and test OUs, a GPO are all tools that can be used to test.
- Slow links must be taken into consideration as you design Group Policy. Some GPOs will not be pulled by the user or computer if a slow link is detected between the domain controller and the client.
- You can design Active Directory sites with Group Policy administration in mind. GPOs linked at the site level are stored in the domain they were created in. Other domains within the same site might require processing over WAN links to apply a site-linked GPO.
- Delegated control can be assigned through the Group Policy Management Console (GPMC). This allows administrators to assign limited rights to users at the OU and GPO levels.
- Group Policy caching improves log on time of network-connected devices by storing GPOs processed during synchronous foreground mode locally to the device.
- The Advanced Group Policy Management (AGPM) tool is available to Software Assurance customers and is packaged with the Microsoft Desktop Optimization Pack (MDOP). AGPM provides change control, role based access control, offline editing and GPMC integration.
- Several Windows PowerShell cmdlets promote the management, automation and scripting of Group Policy tasks such as scheduling backups, testing restores, and overall administration and linking of GPOs.

■ Knowledge Assessment

Multiple Choice

1. Which Windows PowerShell command performs a Group Policy update on a client PC?
   a. Update-GroupPolicy
   b. Invoke-GroupPolicy
   c. Invoke-GPUpdate
   d. GPUPDATE/Force

2. Which of the following tools can be used to test a GPO over slow links before implementation?
   a. Group Policy Modeling Wizard
   b. Group Policy Slow Link Modeler
   c. Group Policy Results Wizard
   d. Enterprise Admins

3. Which of the following delegation permissions—and at which level—would you assign a trusted user permissions allowing them to only link a Group Policy Object to an organizational unit?
   a. Link GPOs; GPO level
   b. Edit settings, delete, modify security; GPO level
   c. Link GPOs; OU level
   d. Edit settings, delete modify security; OU level

4. Your organization's Group Policy design requires a Group Policy Object that must apply to only Windows 8.1 devices. Which of the following tools allows you to apply GPOs to all devices running Windows 8.1?
   a. security filtering
   b. administrative templates
   c. Windows components
   d. WMI filtering

5. You must design your Group Policy to perform routine backups to a remote location. You are not a Software Assurance customer. Which of the following tools are used to meet this requirement? (Choose two.)
   a. Group Policy Management Console (GPMC)
   b. Task Scheduler
   c. Advanced Group Policy Management (AGPM)
   d. Windows PowerShell

6. You have a Group Policy Object that must be applied to all computers, domain controllers, and servers in the domain. Which of the following should be configured in order to meet this requirement?
   a. block inheritance
   b. policy enforcement
   c. site-linked Group Policy Objects
   d. security filtering

7. You are the administrator in a large environment with more than 50 system administrators, all with a mix of domain administrator and enterprise administrator permissions. Recently, you have had issues with unknown administrators implementing GPOs without testing. You need to ensure that a select group of administrators can monitor and approve GPOs before they are applied. Which of the following tools should be used to resolve this issue?
   a. Security filtering
   b. Delegation of Control Wizard
   c. Advanced Group Policy Management (AGPM)
   d. Windows PowerShell

8. You are required to create a GPO to change and prevent the theme from changing on 10 of the 15 computers in the Human Resources department. None of the computers are 100 percent alike in operating system, hardware, or resources. The other five computers must not be restricted. You have access only to create and link new GPOs for that OU, you can also add users to Domain Local groups in ADUC. You cannot create an additional sub-OU to meet this requirement. Which of the following methods should be used to meet the requirement?
   a. Security filtering
   b. WMI filtering
   c. Block inheritance
   d. Policy enforcement

9. You must prevent group policies from being inherited and applying to an OU. Which of the following Group Policy configuration methods should be used?
   a. Enforcement
   b. Loopback Policies
   c. WMI Filtering
   d. Block Inheritance

10. Which of the following can be used from within the GPMC to view the current Resultant Set of Policy (RSoP) for a computer and user on a computer that is already in production and the user has logged on to?
   a. Group Policy Reporting Wizard
   b. Group Policy Inheritance Wizard
   c. Group Policy Results Wizard
   d. Group Policy Modeling Wizard

Best Answer

Choose the letter that corresponds to the best answer. More than one answer choice may achieve the goal. Select the BEST answer.

1. You are required to find a tool to roll back GPOs when changes are unsuccessful after they are applied to an OU. Which of the following tools should be used to roll back to a previous version of a Group GPO?
   a. Volume Shadow Copy
   b. Group Policy Object editor
   c. Windows PowerShell
   d. Advanced Group Policy Management (AGPM)

2. While you are troubleshooting GPO processing against a client, you measure that the connection between the domain controller and the client is less than 500 Kbps. Which of the following should be your next primary concern?
   a. site-linked GPOs
   b. DirectAccess
   c. Group Policy caching
   d. slow link processing

3. Which of the following tools should be used to perform remote commands from an administrative computer to a domain controller to manage Group Policy?
   a. Group Policy Management Console
   b. Windows PowerShell
   c. Command Prompt
   d. Active Directory Users and Computers

4. Which of the following Group Policy methods should you configure to maintain user settings on a computer?
   a. Link Order
   b. Loopback Policy
   c. Security Filtering
   d. WMI Filtering

5. A helpdesk administrator requires access to create and link GPOs in the domain. Through which of the following methods should you grant them access?
   a. Delegate permissions to the user
   b. Grant user domain admin rights
   c. Grant user enterprise admin rights
   d. Provide them your username and password

Matching and Identification

1. Match the Windows PowerShell command to the correct task:
   _____ a) Get-GPOReport
   _____ b) Set-GPPermissions
   _____ c) New-GPLink
   _____ d) Set-GPInheritance
   _____ e) Restore-GPO

   1. Block or unblock inheritance on an OU
   2. Delegate permissions to a security principle on a GPO
   3. Generate an XML or HTML file with details of a specified GPO
   4. Link a GPO to a Site, Domain or OU.
   5. Restores a GPO or set of GPOs from a backup file.

2. Write the command for the specified function or scenario:
   _____ Generate Group Policy results for a user, computer or both.
   _____ Back up a GPO or all GPOs in a domain.
   _____ Create a new GPO.
   _____ Delete a GPO.

Build a List

1. Specify the correct order of how local computer policies and Group Policy Objects are applied to a user or computer.
   _____ Domain
   _____ Local
   _____ OU
   _____ Link order = 2
   _____ Link order = 1
   _____ Site

2. Specify the correct order of how often policies are applied from startup to shutdown.
   _____ computer startup
   _____ computer shutdown
   _____ user logoff
   _____ user logon
   _____ background refresh

Business Case Scenarios

Scenario 16-1: Planning for Active Directory Hierarchy Reorganization

You recently were hired as the IT manager by a corporation with one domain, 4,500 computers, 300 servers, and 4,000 users. Your IT team consists of 10 employees, all with enterprise administrator rights. One of your first tasks is to figure out why logon times are so lengthy, and why some computers have the correct settings applied and some do not. It is a mess and users are upset. You start to dig into Active Directory Users and Computers and Group Policy but notice that users and computers are spread across several different OUs at the same level. Some users and some computers are still in the default containers, and hundreds of GPOs are linked everywhere. All the GPOs are enforced, and block inheritance is on a majority of the OUs.

What considerations will you take into account as you troubleshoot this issue? How will you begin the restructure?

Scenario 16-2: Troubleshooting Sites in a Multi-Domain, Multisite Forest

You are the administrator of a three-domain, two-site, Active Directory Domain Services forest. Users are reporting extremely slow logon times at a site that does not have a domain controller. Users in the other domains have the same problem at the same site. Initial testing shows that the link speeds are not slow between the client and their domain. Users in the other two sites are not having the same problem. Some users who encountered the issues traveled to one of the other sites but did not experience the problem there. However, the issue recurs when they return to their home site. You again verified that the link speeds were adequate. What other considerations should you take into account?

17 **LESSON**

Designing an Active Directory Permission Model

Objective 4.4 – Design an Active Directory permission model. This objective may include but is not limited to: Design considerations including Active Directory object security and Active Directory quotas; customize tasks to delegate in Delegation of Control Wizard; deploy administrative tools on the client devices; delegate permissions on administrative users (AdminSDHolder); configure a plan for Kerberos delegation.

LESSON HEADING	EXAM OBJECTIVE
Designing an Active Directory Permission Model	
• Designing Active Directory Object Security	Design Active Directory object security
• Customizing Tasks Using the Delegation of Control Wizard	Customize tasks to delegate in the Delegation of Control Wizard
• Designing Active Directory Quotas	Design Active Directory quotas
• Deploying Administrative Tools on the Client Computer	Deploy administrative tools on the client devices
• Delegating Permissions on Administration Users	Delegate permissions on administrative users (AdminSDHolder)
• Configuring a Plan for Kerberos Delegation	Configure a plan for Kerberos delegation

KEY TERMS

access control list (ACL)

Active Directory Administrative Task Delegation Model

Active Directory quotas

AdminSDHolder

constrained delegation

Kerberos

Kerberos delegation

Key Distribution Center (KDC)

permissions

Remote Server Administration Tools (RSAT)

rights

security descriptor

service principal name (SPN)

■ Designing an Active Directory Permission Model

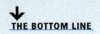

THE BOTTOM LINE
Active Directory consists of objects. Similar to NTFS permissions, Active Directory uses permissions to specify which users can work with a specified Active Directory object.

Precisely what a user can or cannot do on a system or to a resource is determined by two things:

- Rights
- Permissions

Rights authorize a user to perform certain actions on a computer, such as logging on to a system interactively or backing up files and directories on a system. User rights are assigned through local policies or Active Directory Group Policy.

Permissions defines the type of access granted to an object (an object can be identified with a security identifier) or object attribute. The most common objects assigned permissions are NT File System (NTFS) files and folders, printers, and Active Directory objects. Which users can access an object and what actions those users are authorized to perform are recorded in the *access control list (ACL)*, which lists all users and groups that have access to the object.

Designing Active Directory Object Security

As you recall from Lesson 16, "Designing a Group Policy Strategy," organizational units (OUs) are used to organize and manage domain resources such as users, computers, and printers. When you design the OUs, you must look at how these items will be managed and by whom. When objects are organized by OU, you can delegate administrators to an OU to manage those objects. If you organize OUs based on administrative task, you are also designing based on OU permissions, which allow you to delegate administrators to fulfill administrative tasks.

CERTIFICATION READY
Design Active Directory
object security
Objective 4.4

When a user logs on, he receives a token that lists security identifiers for the individual account, historical accounts if the account has been migrated, and every group (directly or recursively) the user belongs to. The token will be used like a set of keys when accessing an object such as an Active Directory object or a NTFS file or folder.

These objects have a *security descriptor* or ACL that lists which group or users can access the object, as well as permissions each group or user has on the object. When the user accesses an object, he and groups stored in the token are compared to the user and groups listed in the security descriptor to see whether the user has access. If you add a user to a group or give him access directly to an object while he is logged on, he must log off and log back on to get an updated token to access the object.

Similar to NTFS folders and files, security settings assigned to the domain are inherited hierarchically in the OU structure. You can overwrite or prevent security settings from inheriting from the container above or below it.

A security descriptor of an Active Directory object contains the following parts:

- **Owner:** The owner can manage the object and has full permissions to the object. She can also reset security settings if she accidentally configures no permissions on the object.
- **Primary group:** This is the owner's group. The default primary group is Domain Users.
- **Control field:** This specifies whether the discretionary access control list (DACL) or system access control list (SACL) are present and whether inheritance is blocked.
- **Optional DACL:** This lists permissions for granting or denying access.
- **Optional SACL:** This lists the auditing permissions when you enable Success or Failure auditing.

The DACL and SACL containers contain one or more access control entries (ACEs), which include the following information:

- The security principal, such as a user or group that is allowed or denied access
- The permission or type of access to the object or object attribute
- Sublevels: on the OU level only, on objects only in the OU, or objects in any sub-OU

Figure 17-1 shows many of the security descriptor on the Security tab of the OU's Properties dialog box and Advanced Security Settings dialog box. To stop inheritance from above, click the *Disable inheritance* button in Advanced Security Settings. The Auditing tab shows the who or what you are auditing for the Active Directory object, assuming that auditing is enabled with Group Policy. To see what permissions a user has on specific object, use the Effective Access tab.

Figure 17-1

Security settings of an organizational unit

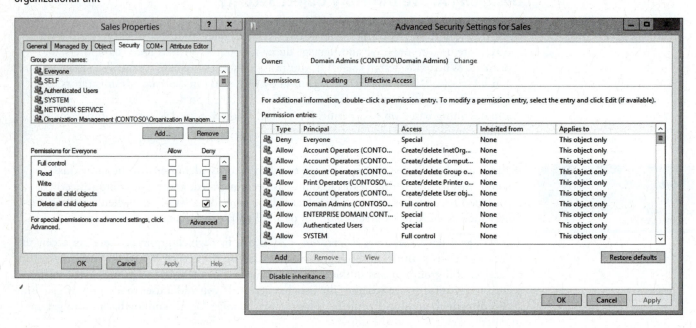

Customizing Tasks Using the Delegation of Control Wizard

> The easiest and most efficient way to assign permissions to an organizational unit so that the user or group can manage it or perform some administrative function is to use the Delegation of Control Wizard. With this wizard, you can assign the minimum permission that a user or group of users needs to complete their authorized tasks.

CERTIFICATION READY
Customize Tasks to delegate in the Delegation of Control Wizard
Objective 4.4

The *Active Directory Administrative Task Delegation Model* defines which groups can perform which tasks at which level. It is based on the principle of least privilege, which specifies that you grant only the rights and permissions to the administrator to do his job—no more, no less. For example, if you want to enable an office manager to reset passwords, you assign just the permission to reset passwords. You do not have to give her the ability to create or delete objects or to modify objects.

With the Active Directory Administrative Tasks Delegation Model, you can divide administrative tasks into two types of groups:

- **Service administration** is responsible for managing network applications and services, including domain controllers, Microsoft Exchange servers, and Microsoft SQL servers.
- **Data administration** is the management of objects such as mailboxes and user accounts.

By organizing the OU structure, you can separate administration responsibility within the domain. For example, you can configure administrative groups based on the following:

- Separate the administration of objects, such as users, groups, and computers, from the infrastructure administration, such as Active Directory Domain Services (AD DS) and Domain Name System (DNS).
- Provide service accounts with the minimum required rights.
- Allow multi-tenancy in a single Active Directory domain.
- Allow application administrators to self-maintain group memberships for their applications.
- Allow owners of distribution lists to self-maintain their members.
- Delegate location information or phone numbers to local administrative staff in the branch office.
- Allow branch office administrators to reinstall clients and rejoin them to the domain.

Whereas Active Directory supports granular control by assigning permissions at OUs, you must also understand that some functions cannot be delegated. That is why Active Directory has domain administrators and enterprise administrators. However, to manage OUs, you do not have to add a user to a built-in high-privileged security group such as the Domain Admins or the Server Operators group. Instead, you have to use the Delegation of Control Wizard to assign permissions to an organizational unit.

The Tasks to Delegate page (see Figure 17-2) provides the security principals with the ability to perform tasks common to branch office administrators, such as creating and managing user accounts, groups, and passwords.

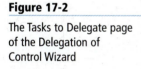

Figure 17-2

The Tasks to Delegate page of the Delegation of Control Wizard

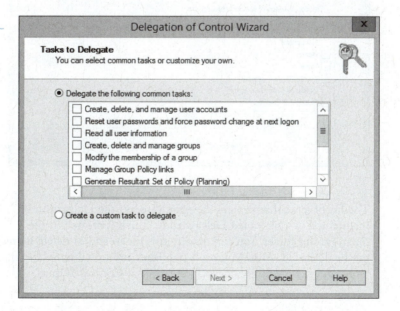

On the Active Directory Object Type page (see Figure 17-3), you can create customized tasks for selected object types by assigning them specific Active Directory permissions.

Figure 17-3

The Active Directory Object Type page of the Delegation of Control Wizard

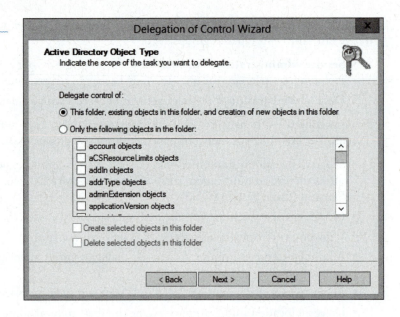

The Permissions page enables you to select permissions for the entire object or for specific object properties (see Figure 17-4). This provides enterprise administrators with a highly granular degree of access control.

Figure 17-4

The Permissions page of the Delegation of Control Wizard

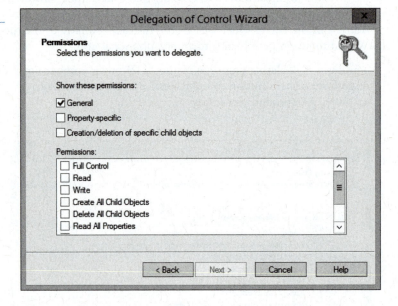

The list of tasks that you can delegate through the Delegation of Control Wizard is maintained in a file called Delegwiz.inf, which is created in the <*Windows installation directory*>\Inf folder. You can modify this file to add or delete items from the list of tasks that can be delegated. Also, Microsoft publishes additional templates that you can add to this file to expand the capability of the Delegation of Control Wizard.

Designing Active Directory Quotas

Active Directory quotas are limits on the number of objects that a security principal can own or create. These quotas help mitigate the risk of denial-of-service attacks against a directory service such as a compromised account, thus creating millions of Active Directory objects, causing a heavy load on the server, and filling up the hard drive as the NTDS.dit file grows.

CERTIFICATION READY
Design Active Directory quotas
Objective 4.4

To manage Active Directory quotas, you can use the `dsadd`, `dsmod`, and `dsquery` commands with the `quota` switch. For example, to add a limit of 10 objects for John Smith on the `contoso.com` domain, use the following command:

```
dsadd quota -part dc=contoso,dc=com -qlimit 10 -acct "cn=John
Smith,OU=Sales,dc=contoso,dc=com"
```

Tombstone objects count toward the quota until the tombstone expires (60 days, by default). Also, the Domain Admins and Enterprise Admins groups are exempt from quota limitations.

Quotas are stored in the NTDS Quotas node in Active Directory Users and Computers (see Figure 17-5). If you cannot see the NT Directory Service (NTDS) quotas, from the View menu select Advanced Features.

Figure 17-5

Viewing the configured quotas

Deploying Administrative Tools on the Client Computer

The *Remote Server Administration Tools (RSAT)* allow you to manage roles and features installed on Windows Server 2012 R2 from a PC running Windows 8.1.

CERTIFICATION READY
Deploy administrative tools on the client computer
Objective 4.4

The tools included with RSAT include the following:

• Server Manager
• Microsoft Management Console (MMC) snap-in

- Windows PowerShell cmdlets and providers
- Command-line tools for managing roles and features running on Windows Server 2012 R2

The tools are designed to remotely manage Windows Server 2012 R2 all installations of Windows Server 2012 including the Server Core installation option and the minimal server graphical interface configuration. In some limited cases, RSAT works with Windows Server 2008 R2, Windows Server 2008, Windows Server 2003 R2, and Windows Server 2003.

> ✚ **MORE INFORMATION**
>
> RSAT can be installed only on computers running Windows 8.1. It provides package files that run on both x86 and x64-based editions of Windows 8.1. You can download RSAT from the Microsoft Download Center by searching for *Remote Server Administration Tools for Windows 8.1*.

INSTALL RSAT ON A WINDOWS 8.1 CLIENT AND CONNECT TO SERVER

 GET READY. To install RSAT and connect to a server, perform the following steps:

1. Log in with administrative credentials.
2. Download the Remote Server Administration Tools for Windows 8.1 64-bit package from the Microsoft Download Center and double-click the Windows6.2-KB2693643-x64.msu installation file.
3. If you see an *Open File-Security Warning* dialog box, click Open.
4. When prompted by the *Windows Update Standalone Installer* dialog box to install the update, click Yes.
5. Read and click I accept to accept the license terms.
6. Press the Windows logo key + Q and use the *Settings* context to search for and select Administrative Tools.
7. In *Server Manager*, select Dashboard.
8. Select Add other Servers to manage.
9. Confirm that location is set to your domain and then click Find Now.
10. Select the server you want to manage and then click the right arrow.
11. Select OK.
12. Review the roles now handled by the server you are connected to.

In earlier RSAT releases, you had to use Control Panel > Programs to turn on the tools you wanted to use. In Windows 8.1, the tools are enabled by default. You can still turn off tools you do not want to use from Control Panel > Programs and Features > Turn Windows features on or off and then selecting the tools. You can also use the Tools menu to access the GUI-based tools from within the Server Manager console.

Delegating Permissions on Administrative Users

> The *AdminSDHolder* object is used to secure privileged users and groups (such as Administrators, Domain Admins, Enterprise Admins, Schema Admins, Domain Controllers, and Server Operators) from unintentional modification. Every hour, security permissions of the privileged group are compared to the permissions listed in the AdminSDHolder object and are reset if they are different.

CERTIFICATION READY
Delegate permissions on administrative users (AdminSDHolder)
Objective 4.4

To access the AdminSDHolder object, open Active Directory Users and Computers under System. Similar to the NTDS Quotas node, if the node is not available, you can use the View menu and select Advanced Features.

The groups protected by AdminSDHolder include the following:

- Account Operators
- Administrator
- Administrators
- Backup Operators
- Domain Admins
- Domain Controllers
- Enterprise Admins
- Krbtgt
- Print Operators
- Read-only Domain Controllers
- Replicator
- Schema Admins
- Server Operators

You can get the list of all protected groups in an Active Directory domain by running the following Windows PowerShell command:

```
Get-ADGroup -LDAPFilter "(admincount=1)"
```

The following groups can be excluded from AdminSDHolder by updating the dsHeuristic flag:

- Account Operators
- Server Operators
- Print Operators
- Backup Operators

You can access the dsHeuristic flag from ADSI Edit under the Configuration partition, CN=Directory Services, CN=Windows NT, CN=Services, CN=Configuration, DC=domain, DC=com.

The hexadecimal dsHeuristic value can be calculated by combining the binary values of each group to exclude and converting the sum to hexadecimal:

Account Operators	0001
Server Operators	0010
Print Operators	0100
Backup Operators	1000

So if you want to exclude Print Operators and Backup Operators, add (in binary) 0100 + 1000 = 1100, and then convert it to a hexadecimal number (12).

By default, the AdminSDHolder SDProp process runs every 60 minutes. To change the frequency, you can create or modify the AdminSDProtectFrequency entry in the HKEY_LOCAL_MACHINE\SYSTEM\CurrentControlSet\Services\NTDS\Parameters subkey. If this key does not exist, the default frequency (60 minutes) is used. Because the AdminSDHolder SDProp task is resource intensive, the recommendation is that you do not change the value. To determine which accounts and groups have been changed back by the AdminSDHolder task, look for Event ID 684 account-management audit entries in the Security event log on the primary domain controller (PDC) emulator.

Following best practices, you should not use administrative accounts to perform everyday tasks. In fact, as an administrator, you should have two accounts: one to perform administrative tasks and a standard account for everyday tasks such as reading or sending email, surfing the Internet, or creating documents. Do not add the standard user account to any account that is protected by the AdminSDHolder object.

To give a certain group the ability to make changes to the accounts protected by AdminSDHolder, you need to delegate permissions to the AdminSDHolder node. After the permissions are added, when the SDProp process executes again, the permissions are applied and the group or user will be able to make changes to the protected object.

TAKE NOTE It is not recommended to change permissions on a protected object. Therefore, you would not typically have to assign permissions to the AdminSDHolder node.

DELEGATE PERMISSIONS TO ADMINSDHOLDER

 GET READY. To delegate permissions to AdminSDHolder, perform the following steps:

1. In *Server Manager* or *Administrative Tools*, open Active Directory Users and Computers.
2. Expand the Contoso.com node.
3. If you cannot see the *System* node, open the View menu, click Advanced Features, and then expand the System node.
5. Right-click AdminSDHolder and choose Properties.
6. In the *AdminSDHolder Properties* dialog box, on the *Security* tab, click the Advanced button.
7. When the *Advanced Security Settings* dialog box opens, on the Permissions tab, click the Enable Inheritance button and then click Apply. When you are prompted to continue, click Yes.
8. Click Add.
9. In the *Permission Entry for AdminSDHolder* dialog box, click the Select a principal link.
10. In the *Select User, Computer, Service Account, or Group* dialog box, in the *Enter the object name to select* text box, type the name of the user or group that you want to add. Click OK.
11. Under *Permissions*, select Full control (see Figure 17-6). Click OK.

Figure 17-6

Viewing server roles/features
via the Server Manager console

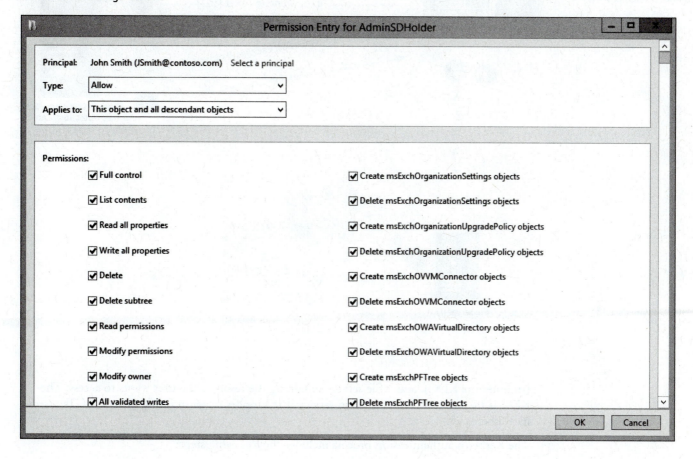

12. Click OK to close the *Advanced Security Settings for AdminSDHolder* dialog box.
13. Click OK to close the *AdminSDHolder Properties* dialog box.

Configuring a Plan for Kerberos Delegation

Kerberos is a computer network authentication protocol that allows hosts to prove their identities securely over a non-secure network. It can also provide mutual authentication so that both the user and server verify each other's identity. For security reasons, Kerberos protocol messages are protected against eavesdropping and replay attacks.

The secure Kerberos protocol supports ticketing authentication. With Kerberos, security and authentication are based on secret key technology, and every host on the network has its own secret key. The *Key Distribution Center (KDC)* maintains a database of these secret keys. Although Kerberos is more secure than NT LAN Manager (NTLM), it is also more complicated than NTLM and requires additional configuration (such as requiring a service principal name for the domain account).

Authenticating and using resources in a domain requires the use of Kerberos v5, a protocol that defines how clients interact with a network authentication service. Figure 17-7 depicts a simplified explanation of what happens between a user/computer, a domain controller

Figure 17-7

The Kerberos
authentication process

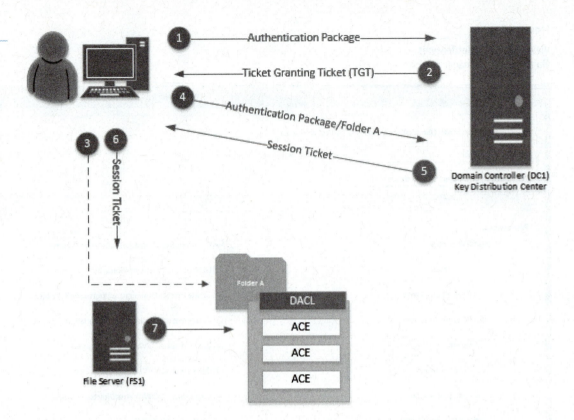

(running the KDC), and a file server containing the resource the user wants to access. The
KDC is the network authentication service that supplies ticket-granting tickets (TGTs) used
by Kerberos v5.

The Kerberos authentication process includes the following steps:

1. When a user logs on to a computer in a domain with the domain account, the Local
   Security Authority (LSA) takes the information and creates an authentication package.
   This package is sent by the user's computer to the KDC.

2. The KDC validates the authentication package and sends a TGT to the user. The
   TGT contains information about the user's computer as well as a list of security
   identifiers (SIDS) for the user account and any group accounts the user belongs to.

3. Any user attempting to access a resource (such as a folder or file) on a file server
   named FS1 will need a session ticket.

4. To get the session ticket, the client creates another authentication package and sends it
   back to the KDC with a request for that resource.

5. The KDC validates the authentication package and sends the user a session ticket.

6. The session ticket is then used to authenticate to FS1. FS1 decrypts and validates
   the ticket.

7. FS1 compares the ticket to a DACL that is attached to the resource. The DACL
   consists of one or more access control entries (ACEs). Each ACE contains a SID for a
   user account or group and the permissions applied to it for the resource. If the ACE
   contains one or more SIDs that matches those in the user's ticket, that user is granted
   the permissions provided for that SID.

For all of this to work and to ensure security, the domain controllers and clients must have
the same time. Windows operating systems include the Time Service tool (W32Time service).
Kerberos authentication works if the time interval between the relevant computers is within

the maximum enabled time parameters (five minutes by default). You can also turn off the Time Service tool and install a third-party time service. Of course, if you have problems authenticating, make sure that the time is correct for the domain controllers and for the client experiencing the problem.

Kerberos offers several benefits. When the client connects to a server or service, Kerberos uses the current client ticket proving that the client is authenticated. As a result, the service does not have to perform authentication to a domain controller. Kerberos also can perform a double-hop authentication, which forwards Kerberos tickets from one service to a supporting service. Both of these Kerberos benefits improve authentication performance.

To secure the double-hop authentication, you can configure Kerberos constrained delegation. **Constrained delegation** restricts which services are allowed to delegate user credentials by specifying, for each application pool or service, the services to which a Kerberos ticket can be forwarded.

Kerberos settings are configured with Group Policy, specifically \Computer Configuration\ Policies\Windows\Settings\Security Settings\Account Policies\Kerberos Policy. It contains the following GPO entries:

- *Enforce user logon restrictions:* Enforces the KDC to check the validity of a user account every time a ticket request is submitted. If a user does not have the right to log on locally or if her account has been disabled, she will not get a ticket. By default, the setting is on.
- *Maximum lifetime for service ticket:* Defines the maximum lifetime of a service ticket (Kerberos ticket). The default lifetime is 10 hours.
- *Maximum lifetime for user ticket:* Defines the maximum lifetime ticket for a Kerberos TGT ticket (user ticket). The default lifetime is 10 hours.
- *Maximum lifetime for user ticket renewal:* Defines how long a service or user ticket can be renewed. By default, it can be renewed up to seven days.
- *Maximum tolerance for computer clock synchronization:* Defines the maximum time skew that can be tolerated between a ticket's timestamp and the current time at the KDC. As explained earlier, Kerberos uses a timestamp to protect against replay attacks. The default setting is five minutes.

MANAGING SERVICE PRINCIPAL NAMES (SPNS)

A service or application that is secured by Kerberos must have an identity (a user account or computer account) within the realm (in this case, the domain) that the system exists on. Although Active Directory can identify an account by using a simple username, the Kerberos standard includes information such as the service class, host name, and port that the account can use.

A *service principal name (SPN)* is the name by which a client uniquely identifies an instance of a service. The client locates the service based on the SPN, which consists of three components:

- The service class, such as HTTP (which includes both the HTTP and HTTPS protocols) or SQLService
- The host name
- The port (if port 80 is not being used)

To establish an SPN for *https://portal.contoso.com* on port 443, use HTTP/portal.contoso. com:443. Kerberos authentication service then uses the SPN to authenticate a service.

When a domain controller's KDC receives the service ticket request from a client, it looks up the requested SPN. The KDC then creates a session key for the service and encrypts the session key with the password of the account with which the SPN is associated. The KDC issues a service ticket, containing the session key, to the client. The client presents the service ticket to the service. The service, which knows its own password, decrypts the session key to complete authentication.

If a client submits a service ticket request for an SPN that does not exist in the identity store, no service ticket can be established and the client throws an access denied error. For this reason, each application (such as Microsoft SharePoint) that that uses Kerberos authentication requires at least one SPN. For example, the intranet Web application app pool account must have an SPN of HTTP/intranet.contoso.com.

The SPN is associated with the application pool, not the server. For each web application, you should assign two SPNs: one with the service's fully qualified domain name (FQDN) and one with the service's NetBIOS name.

You can use ADSI Edit to add SPNs to an account. To configure an SPN for a service or application pool account, you must have domain administrative permissions or a delegation to modify the `ServicePrincipalName` property. You also must run ADSI Edit from a domain controller or load the Windows Server 2012 Remote Server Administration Tools feature.

CONFIGURE A SERVICE PRINCIPAL NAME

 GET READY. To configure a service principal name, perform the following steps:

1. In *Server Manager*,
   click Tools > ADSI Edit. The *ADSI Edit* console opens.
2. Right-click ADSI Edit in the console tree and choose Connect To.
3. In the *Connection Settings* dialog box, click OK.
4. Expand Default Naming Context in the console tree, expand the domain, and then expand the nodes representing the OUs in which the account exists. Click the OU in which the account exists.
5. In the *Details* pane, right-click the service account and choose Properties.
6. When the *Properties* dialog box opens, in the *Attributes* list, double-click servicePrincipalName to display the *Multi-valued String Editor* dialog box (see Figure 17-8).

Figure 17-8

Managing the SPNs for an object

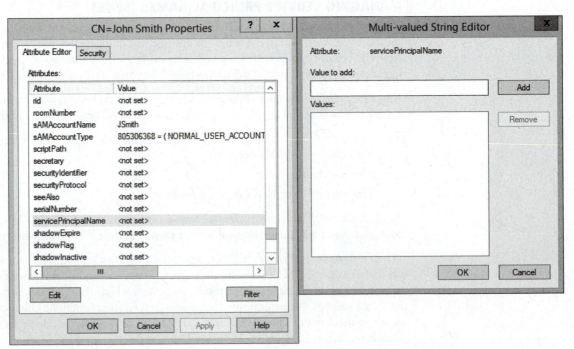

7. In the Value to add field, type the SPN and then click Add.

8. Click OK twice to close the *Multi-valued String Editor* dialog box and the *Properties* dialog box.

Alternatively, you can use the Setspn.exe tool to add SPNs to an account. The syntax is as follows:

```
setspn <domain\user> -s <SPN>
```

In this syntax,

- `<domain\user>` identifies the security principal to which you want to add an SPN.
- `<SPN>` is the service principal name that you want to add.

For example, to add SPNs for the intranet web application to the app pool account used in SharePoint, type the following commands:

```
setspn CONTOSO\SP_WebApps -s
HTTP/portal.contoso.com

setspn CONTOSO\SP_WebApps -s HTTP/portal
```

You must perform separate commands for each SPN.

CONFIGURING KERBEROS DELEGATION

Kerberos delegation allows a Kerberos ticket to be created for another service on the originating user's behalf. This can be done with full delegation or with constrained delegation. As mentioned earlier, constrained delegation is when you specify that the Kerberos delegation can be executed against only a limited set of services.

To configure Kerberos delegation, simply open *Active Directory Users and Computers*, go to the account that has an SPN, open the account's properties, and click *Delegation*. Figure 17-9 shows the Delegation tab.

Figure 17-9

Configuring the Kerberos delegation

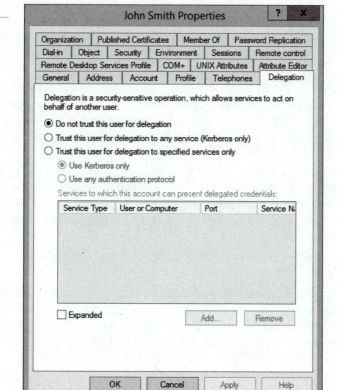

To allow full delegation, select *Trust this user for delegation to any service (Kerberos only)*. To allow for constrained delegation, select the *Trust this user for delegation to specified services only*. You can then select to use only for Kerberos, or you can specify *Use any authentication protocol*, and then click the *Add* button to specify which services to be delegated for a user or computer and to specify the user or computer.

SKILL SUMMARY

IN THIS LESSON YOU LEARNED:

- Active Directory consists of objects. Similar to NTFS permissions, Active Directory uses permissions to specify which users can do with a specified Active Directory object.

- Organizational units (OUs) are used to organize and manage domain resources such as users, computers and printers.

- When you design the OUs, you must look at how these items will be managed and by whom. When objects are organized by OU, you can delegate administrators to an OU to manage those objects. If you organize OUs based on administrative task, you are also designing based on OU permissions, which allow you to delegate administrators to fulfill administrative tasks.

- The easiest and most efficient way to assign permissions to an organizational unit so that the user or group can manage it or perform some administrative function is to use the Delegation of Control Wizard. With this wizard, you can assign the minimum permission that a user or group of users needs to complete their authorized tasks.

- Active Directory quotas are limits on the number of objects that a security principal can own or create. These quotas help mitigate the risk of denial-of-service attacks against a directory service.

- The AdminSDHolder object is used to secure privileged users and groups (such as Administrators, Domain Admins, Enterprise Admins, Schema Admins, Domain Controllers, and Server Operators) from unintentional modification.

- Kerberos is a computer network authentication protocol that allows hosts to prove their identities securely over a non-secure network. It can also provide mutual authentication so that both the user and server verify each other's identity. For security reasons, Kerberos protocol messages are protected against eavesdropping and replay attacks.

- A service or application that is secured by Kerberos must have an identity (a user account or computer account) within the realm (in this case, the domain) that the system exists on. Although Active Directory can identify an account by using a simple username, the Kerberos standard includes information such as the service class, host name, and port that the account can use.

- A service principal name (SPN) is the name by which a client uniquely identifies an instance of a service.

- Kerberos delegation allows a Kerberos ticket to be created for another service on the originating user's behalf. This can be done with full delegation or with constrained delegation. Constrained delegation is when you specify that the Kerberos delegation can be executed against only a limited set of services.

■ Knowledge Assessment

Multiple Choice

1. Which of the following lists every user and group that has access to an Active Directory object?
   a. rights statement
   b. control field
   c. security descriptor
   d. Active Directory quota

2. Which of the following lists the security principals and permissions assigned to an object?
   a. access control list
   b. right list
   c. control field
   d. delegation list

3. Which of the following models describes assigning your resources in organizational units so that you can grant permissions to manage those resources without assigning unneeded permissions?
   a. Active Directory Sizing Model
   b. Active Directory Authorization Model
   c. Active Directory Administrative Task Delegation Model
   d. Active Directory Management Reduction Model

4. Which of the following tools allows you to grant administrative permissions efficiently to an organizational unit?
   a. Rights Management Wizard
   b. Permissions Management Wizard
   c. Permissions Separation Wizard
   d. Delegation of Control Wizard

5. Which of the following are found with the Delegation of Control Wizard? (Choose all that apply.)
   a. Create, delete, and manage user accounts
   b. Manage all objects
   c. Reset user passwords and force password changes at next logon
   d. Manage printers

6. Which of the following is used to limit the number objects a user or group can create in Active Directory?
   a. Active Directory Delegation specifier
   b. Active Directory Permission counter
   c. Active Directory limits
   d. Active Directory quotas

7. How often does the SDProp process run?
   a. Every 30 minutes
   b. Every hour
   c. Every two hours
   d. Every four hours
   e. Every 24 hours

8. Which of the following resets permissions for a secure privileged user or group?
   a. Krbtgt
   b. NTDS quotas
   c. Delegation of Control Wizard
   d. AdminSDHolder

9. Which of the following is the preferred authentication protocol used with Active Directory?
   a. NTFS
   b. NTLM
   c. Kerberos
   d. Basic
   e. MS-CHAPv2

10. What two ways define a service principal name to an account?
    a. Using ADSI Edit
    b. Using the Active Directory Sites and Services console
    c. Using the Key Distribution Center (KDC)
    d. Using the setspn.exe command.

Best Answer

Choose the letter that corresponds to the best answer. More than one answer choice can achieve the goal. Select the BEST answer.

1. Which of the following allows a user to do an activity such as performing a backup of all files on the server?
   a. rights
   b. permission
   c. Delegation of Control
   d. Active Directory quota

2. Which of the following allows an administrator to manage Active Directory from his or her computer? (Choose two answers.)
   a. Remote Assistance
   b. Remote Server Administration Tools (RSAT)
   c. Remote Desktop
   d. Computer Management
   e. Server Manager

3. You have a website hosted by multiple web servers. You want to use Kerberos for authentication. Which of the following statements are true?
   a. You need only an SPN if the application is using port 443.
   b. The `application` pool on each server should get an SPN.
   c. The account that runs the application pool should get an SPN.
   d. Each server should get an SPN.

4. You want to configure Kerberos delegation but also want to make sure that the SPN is used only for the SharePoint portal. What do you do?
   a. Select *Configure single delegation*.
   b. Select *Use any authentication protocol*.
   c. Configure *Trust this user for delegation to any service (Kerberos only)*.
   d. Define constrained delegation for the account used in the application pool.

5. You need to allow a special management team to audit whether the Domain Admin access has modified. What should you do?
   a. Add the management team to the Auditor group.
   b. Delegate permissions to AdminSDHolder for the management team.
   c. Give access to the security logs for the management team.
   d. Add the management team to the Domain Administrators group.

Build a List

1. In order of first to last, specify the steps to delegate permissions to AdminSDHolder.

    _____ Expand System and right-click AdminSDHolder.
    _____ Click the Advanced button.
    _____ Open Active Directory Users and Computers.
    _____ Click Add and specify the user account or group.
    _____ Select Full Control.
    _____ Select the Security tab.

2. In order of first to last, specify the steps to configure Kerberos delegation. Not all steps will be used, and steps can be used more than once.

    _____ Open ASDI Edit and access the Default Naming Context.
    _____ Open Active Directory Users and Computers.
    _____ Click the Add button.
    _____ Set the servicePrincipalName.
    _____ Click Browse and browse to the certificate.
    _____ Select *Trust this user for delegation to any service (Kerberos only)*.
    _____ Right-click the account and choose Properties.
    _____ Click the Delegation tab.

Choose an Option

1. In figure 17-10, which option would you select to configure constrained delegation?

Figure 17-10

Question 1

Business Case Scenarios

Scenario 17-1: Using Kerberos

You have a client application/service placed on Server1. When a user accesses the application/service, you want the server to send a Kerberos request on behalf of the user running the application. How should you approach this?

Scenario 17-2: Planning the Organizational Units

You are an administrator for a large organization, with 10,000 users in a single domain among five large offices and 22 small sales sites. You have a relatively large group of administrators. Some administrators are used to manage the users and computers, two administrators are used to manage the printers, branch managers need to manage the users at their site, and some administrators are used for Microsoft Exchange Server and Microsoft SQL Server. How would you organize your domain so that you can establish the proper rights and permissions?

Designing an Active Directory Sites Topology

70-413 EXAM OBJECTIVE

Objective 5.1 – Design an Active Directory sites topology. This objective may include but is not limited to: Design considerations including proximity of domain controllers, replication optimization, and site link; monitor and resolve Active Directory replication conflicts

LESSON HEADING	EXAM OBJECTIVE
Planning an Active Directory Sites	
• Gathering Network Information	
• Determining Proximity of Domain Controllers	Design proximity of domain controllers
• Designing Sites	
• Optimizing Replication	Design replication optimization
• Determining Site Links	Design site links
• Identifying and Resolving Active Directory Replication Conflicts	Monitor and resolve Active Directory replication conflicts

KEY TERMS

bridgehead server	Inter-site Topology Generator (ISTG)	multimaster replication
change notification	intersite replication	site
Default-First-Site-Name	intrasite replication	site link bridge object
domain controller	Knowledge Consistency Checker (KCC)	site link cost
full mesh topology		site link object
hub and spoke topology	latency period	SYSVOL
hybrid topology		

■ Planning an Active Directory Sites

THE BOTTOM LINE

Active Directory domains, trees, and forests are logical representation of your network organization, which allows you to organize them in the best way to manage. To identify domains, trees, and forests, Active Directory is closely tied to Domain Name System (DNS). Conversely, sites and domain controllers represent the physical structure of your network.

A *site* consists of one or more IP subnets connected by a high-speed link and typically defined by a geographical location. Consider a four-story office building. Although it includes several subnets, all computers within the building use layer-2 and layer-3 switches to communicate with each other. If you have multiple sites, each site is connected to other sites over a much slower wide area network (WAN) link—at least, slower than the local area network (LAN) speeds you find within an individual site. You can then define various network traffic patterns based on how the sites are defined.

When a user logs on, Active Directory clients locate an Active Directory domain server (using the DNS SRV resource records) known as a domain controller in the same site as the user's computer. Each domain has its own set of domain controllers to provide access to the domain resources, such as users and computers.

For fault tolerance, a site should have two or more domain controllers. That way, if one domain controller fails, the other can still service the clients. Whenever an object (such as a username or password) is modified, it is automatically replicated to the other domain controllers within a domain.

A *domain controller* is a Windows server that stores a replica of the account and security information for the domain and defines the domain boundaries. To make a computer running Windows Server 2012 R2 a domain controller, you must install the Active Directory Domain Services (AD DS) role and promote the server to a domain controller.

After you design the logical infrastructure for AD DS by deciding how many forests and domains to create, you can begin to consider the physical aspects of the AD DS infrastructure. The physical topology of AD DS is reflected in its domain controllers and consists of questions like the following:

- How many domain controllers should I use?
- Where should the domain controllers be located?
- How should be domain controllers be connected?

Domain controllers are essential in authentication and authorization. They must first verify your identity. As soon as your identity is determined, it is used to check your access to a wide range of resources based on rights and permissions.

Gathering Network Information

After you gather the information needed to answer these questions, you can begin to design the topology elements, such as sites, site links, replication, and global catalog servers. Much of the same information you gathered when considering your forest and domain hierarchy can also affect the physical topology design. However, you also need to know some other elements.

Replication is one of the most critical aspects of the physical AD DS topology. If your entire enterprise network is located in a single office building, your topology design could not be simpler. All your domain controllers can be located in the same site, and you can let them replicate at will, because they are all connected to the same high-speed network.

This is rarely the case, however. Whether you are constructing a new AD DS infrastructure or upgrading an existing one, most enterprise networks have computers in various different locations, and those locations could well be connected by different technologies, running at different speeds, and operating under different traffic conditions.

Therefore, as in the forest design process, a diagram of the enterprise network is essential and should include the types and speeds of all WAN links connecting remote locations together. A diagram of the link speeds will help you determine whether and how well the connections can handle replication traffic generated by domain controllers. Therefore, the diagram should include not only the raw speeds of the WAN links, but also an indication of their current traffic conditions.

Network traffic levels are a subject that many administrators ignore until a communication problem arises. You might have taken baseline measurements of your WAN links' bandwidth usage at the time they were installed, but if the figures you have are more than a year old, you should repeat those measurements when planning for a major update to your AD DS replication infrastructure.

In addition to the information about the internetwork links, you must also compile information about each individual remote network, including the following:

- Number of domains
- Number of domain controllers per domain
- Number of servers per domain
- Number of workstations per domain
- Number of users per domain
- IP network addresses in use

This information is necessary to help you create a site infrastructure and determine where to locate your domain controllers and global catalog servers. The network addresses are required because when Windows computers authenticate to Active Directory, they discover the nearest domain controller based on their IP subnet addresses.

Determining Proximity of Domain Controllers

> When you determine the Active Directory topology, you need to consider the location of the domain controllers. One of the main factors when determining where to place the domain controllers is to place them near resources that need to use them.

CERTIFICATION READY
Designing proximity of domain controllers
Objective 5.1

User logging on to the network will authenticate with a domain controller. Slow client logon performance can be caused by the following:

- Unavailable domain controller
- Very busy domain controller
- Domain controller overwhelmed by Lightweight Directory Access Protocol (LDAP) traffic
- Client receiving Group Policy Objects (GPOs) from off-site domain controller.
- Heavily congested links to domain controllers
- Large number of GPOs
- Inefficient logon scripts
- Malware
- Applications and services started during startup or logon
- Installation of updates or software
- Use of roaming profiles

While having a domain controller at every site is not necessary, users who log on with a local domain controller will log on more quickly than with a remote domain controller. Therefore, if you often have unavailable or busy domain controllers, congested WAN links, or scripts or programs that run from a remote domain controller, you should install a domain controller locally.

When you add a domain controller to the domain, the domain controller advertises itself with Service (SRV) resource records in DNS. The SRV records are used to locate servers that perform authentication and directory access for Kerberos version 5 (v5) and LDAP. The _tcp folder within a domain zone contains the SRV records for all domain controllers in the domain. The _sites\sitename_tcp folder lists the domain controllers for a specific site.

Not every physical site needs to have an onsite domain controller. If a location has only has a few users, or the location is connected to a high-speed WAN link may still work fine. If a site does not have a domain controller, automatic site coverage enables each domain controller to check all sites in a forest and check the replication cost matrix to determine the lowest-site connection to provide services for a site. Site coverage is determined by looking at site link costs and the domain controllers at each site. If a site has no domain controllers and calculates that two or more sites have the same cost, it breaks the tie by choosing the site with the largest number of domain controllers. If a tie still exists, it then chooses the site that is first alphabetically. After the site is calculated, the domain controller registers the SRV record to the target site for the domain controllers for this domain in the site. Site links and site link costs are discussed in more detail later in the lesson.

You should deploy a domain controller to sites that have services or applications that use AD DS intensively such as Microsoft Exchange Server. For larger sites and sites that have intensive use of AD DS, you should consider placing two domain controllers for each domain in a site. If you have users from multiple domains in a site, you should considering two domain controllers for each domain in a site and you should assign the global catalog server role to at least one of them. Lastly, you should not deploy a domain controller in a location where you cannot guarantee the physical security of the domain controller.

Designing Sites

In Active Directory terminology, a site is a special type of AD DS container object that provides the connection between the logical AD DS infrastructure—forests, domains, and organizational units—and the physical network infrastructure—cables, routers, and WAN links.

The strict definition of a site is an area of an AD DS network in which all the domain controllers are well connected—that is, connected by a fast and reliable network link. The site topology is completely independent of forests and domains; you can have one domain that encompasses many sites or a single site that includes multiple domains.

Unlike the forest and domain design decisions, site divisions are based exclusively on physical network conditions. You do not create a site topology based on business units, contractual requirements, or political decisions. In fact, you do not even necessarily create sites based on geographical divisions. If, sometime in the future, practical needs dictate a global network in which the links between locations are as fast as the links within a location, multiple sites will not be needed.

However, with today's technology, intranetwork connections run at much faster speeds than internetwork links. LANs today typically run at 100 or 1,000 megabits per second (Mbps), whereas the typical WAN connections used by most companies rarely exceed 10 Mbps. This is a vast difference in available bandwidth, and you must also consider that other applications are already using the WAN connections.

The primary reason for creating multiple AD DS sites is to conserve the bandwidth on those relatively slow and expensive WAN connections. They can do this in three ways:

- **Replication:** AD DS domain controllers have two different ways of replicating their data: intrasite and intersite. Intersite replication is compressed and schedulable, so it can use a minimum of bandwidth.

- **Authentication:** Windows client computers always attempt to authenticate themselves through a domain controller on the same site, which prevents the authentication traffic from consuming WAN bandwidth.
- **Applications:** Certain Active Directory–aware applications and services, such as the Distributed File System (DFS) and Microsoft Exchange Server, are conscious of the sites in which their servers reside and make efforts to minimize intersite traffic. DFS clients connect to replicas in their own sites whenever possible, and Exchange servers minimize the message traffic they transmit over intersite WAN links.

USING A SINGLE SITE

When you create a new forest, the Active Directory Domain Services Installation Wizard automatically creates a first site object, which it calls *Default-First-Site-Name*. Until you create additional sites manually, AD DS adds all the computers in the forest to the Default-First-Site-Name site, so distinguishing between the IP subnets on which the computers are located is not necessary.

TAKE NOTE*

You can rename the Default-First-Site-Name site object to reflect the actual location of the site.

In a single site configuration, all domain controllers replicate on demand and do not compress their replication traffic. The goal is to update each domain controller as rapidly as possible, regardless of the amount of bandwidth the replication process consumes.

The single site model assumes that all domain controllers are well connected and that the available bandwidth is not limited. In most cases, a single site requires no configuration and no maintenance.

USING MULTIPLE SITES

In a multiple site model, you must manually create additional sites representing locations that are not well connected or where you want to place domain controllers for performance reasons. You must then create IP Subnet objects for all the subnets on your network and associate them with particular sites.

AD DS uses the term *well connected* to refer to the computers within a single site. However, that term has no strict scientific definition. How enterprise administrators judge what constitutes well connected is up to them and typically depends on the size of the location in question, relative to the size of the entire enterprise.

In many cases, a location with a WAN link that has 512 kilobits per second (Kbps) or more of available bandwidth can be considered well connected and does not require a site of its own. For organizations with large networks, the minimum speed of a well-connected link might be much faster—as fast as 10 Mbps. Of course, the key phrase here is *available bandwidth*. You could have a 100 Mbps link, but if the link is fully saturated, there is no room for AD DS traffic.

You need to consider other issues as well when deciding whether to create a new site. Chief among these is whether you want to install domain controllers at a specific location. If a client computer cannot contact a domain controller, it cannot authenticate to AD DS and, therefore, cannot log on to its domain.

If a remote office does not have a domain controller and its WAN connection should fail, the clients cannot log on and cannot work. Therefore, sometimes you might want to install domain controllers at a remote location, even if it is well connected. Generally, this is because of a large number of users at that location. By making that location a separate site, you keep the authentication traffic local so that clients can log on, even if the connection to the home office is not available.

However, if local authentication is not essential and WAN traffic levels are important, you might want to consider the balance between the replication traffic resulting if you do create a remote site, and the authentication traffic generated if you do not. This balances the size and volatility of the AD DS database with the number of users at the remote site. This again is something that enterprise administrators must measure for themselves.

Finally, consider the matter of applications that are AD DS site-aware. If you plan to deploy servers for applications like those at a remote location, you must create a site at that location as well.

ANOTHER WAY For a small remote location with limited resources, you can reduce the amount of replication traffic and the AD DS administrative requirements by installing a read-only domain controller (RODC).

CREATING A SITE

To create additional sites, you use the Active Directory Sites and Services console, as shown in Figure 18-1. Because the site infrastructure is separate from the forest and domain infrastructure, the only AD DS objects that appear in both the Active Directory Sites and Services console and the Active Directory Users and Computers console are those representing domain controllers.

Figure 18-1

The New Object – Site dialog box

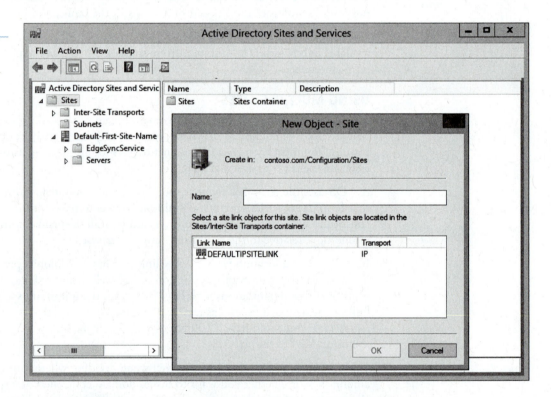

When creating a new site, you must specify the link that it uses to connect to at least one other site. By default, only one site link object, called DEFAULTIPSITELINK, is available, but you likely will create others during the replication topology design process.

After you create a site, you must create subnet objects (see Figure 18-2) and associate them with the sites in which they are located. Assigning subnets to sites ensures that new domain controllers are placed in the correct sites and that clients access the domain controller closest to them.

Figure 18-2

The New Object – Subnet dialog box

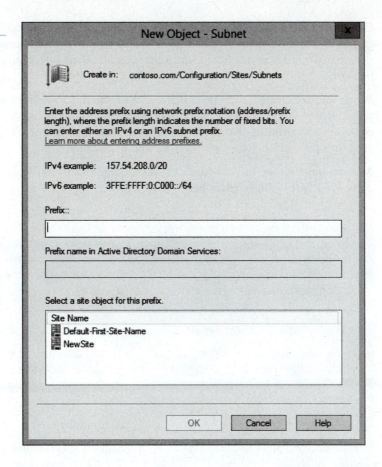

After creating sites and subnets, when you install a new domain controller, the Active Directory Domain Services Installation Wizard automatically places it in the correct site, based on the subnet where its IP address is located. If you have created sites but have not yet created subnets, the wizard enables you to select a site. If you have not yet created additional sites, the wizard automatically adds the domain controller to the Default-First-Site-Name site.

You also should configure one domain controller per site to be a global catalog to speed up AD DS logon and forest searches. Be sure to associate the appropriate IP subnet to each AD DS site. Consider additional sites if a network is separated by a slow WAN link, a network has enough users to justify hosting a domain controller, and heavy directory query traffic slows down a network.

When you create a site, use meaningful names, most likely reflecting the site's location. You should also rename the default site, Default-First-Site-Name, to something more meaningful. Lastly, you should move existing domain controllers to the appropriate sites.

Optimizing Replication

> AD DS uses a ***multimaster replication*** process, which means that you can modify the contents of the AD DS database on any domain controller and have that domain controller automatically propagate the changes to all other domain controllers containing replicas of the modified partition. The exception to this is the Read-only Domain Controller (RODC), which only *receives* replication traffic; it does not send it.

CERTIFICATION READY
Designing replication optimization
Objective 5.1

Creating sites for locations in which a domain controller is placed or in locations where the application requires a site to be created is recommended. An example of such an application is

Distributed File System Namespaces (DFSN). Sites are not necessarily tied to physical or geographical locations. Assuming that the available bandwidth and network latency is adequate (less than 10 milliseconds (ms) latency between locations is recommended), a single site can be used.

When sites are created, they are connected via a site link. Site links provide intersite connectivity for replication. Creating site links means creating a link in the Inter-Site Transports container and ensuring that every site is connected to each other. The same site link can be used for sites with the same connectivity and availability.

As mentioned earlier, the two kinds of AD DS replication traffic are intrasite and intersite. Table 18-1 lists the differences between the two.

Table 18-1

Differences Between Intrasite and Intersite Replication

INTRASITE REPLICATION	INTERSITE REPLICATION
Replication is initiated when an administrator makes a change to the AD DS database.	Replication events occur according to a schedule.
Replication traffic is not compressed.	Replication traffic is compressed.
Domain controllers transmit replication traffic to multiple replication partners.	Domain controllers at each site transmit replication traffic to a bridgehead server, which then transmits to a single bridgehead server at another site.
Rarely needs configuration	Highly configurable
Does not require the configuration of additional AD DS objects.	Requires the creation and configuration of site link objects and possibly site link bridge objects.

Intrasite replication requires no effort from enterprise administrators, whether the network has one site or many. The domain controllers in each site take care of their own interaction. However, administrators must create and configure site link objects to provide the intersite connections.

UNDERSTANDING INTRASITE REPLICATION

Intrasite replication occurs during change notification between domain controllers located within that site. *Change notification* is a notification given by source domain controllers within a site to their replica domain controllers, notifying them that it has new changes that can be replicated. Intrasite replication is considered notify-pull replication, which means that the source domain controller notifies a replica, and then the replica requests the changes.

Taking advantage of localized high-speed local area networks, intrasite replication allows changes to occur as soon as possible. It utilizes Remote Call Procedure over Internet Protocol (RPC over IP) connectivity, Kerberos authentication, and data encryption, allowing efficient and secured data transfer between domain controllers. Unlike intersite replication, in which replication data is compressed, all replication data within a site is not compressed. Intrasite replication topology is generated by the ***Knowledge Consistency Checker (KCC)***.

The KCC on each domain controller creates a bidirectional connection between the source domain controller and the replica domain controller. It ensures that no more than three hops are taken to get directory updates to replica domain controllers. To circumvent more than three hops happening between a source domain controller and a replica domain controller, the KCC creates a shortcut connection with the replica domain controller across the ring to increase replication speed.

When handling the naming contexts (such as directory partitions), the KCC creates a separate replication topology for the schema, configuration, domain, and application partitions to ensure that replica domain controllers have all changes required as soon as possible. The KCC continually checks the topology and dynamically makes needed changes based on the availability of the domain controllers and other factors within the topology.

To further enhance replication within a site, domain controllers use the store-and-forward mechanism to replicate changes to other domain controllers within the site. Store-and-forward replication allows the replica domain controller to store the updates it has received from the source domain controller and issue or forward a change notification to other replica domain controllers. Because this mechanism allows faster replication, the source domain controller does not have to contact every domain controller in the domain to replicate the latest update.

The following process illustrates the intrasite replication process:

1. A directory change occurs on the source domain controller.
2. The source domain controller recognizes that the change has been made and waits 15 seconds before issuing a change notification.
3. The source domain controller contacts the closest replica domain controller, notifying the replica of its latest update.
4. The replica domain controller receives the change notification from the source domain controller.
5. The replica domain controller requests the updates from the source domain controller.
6. The source domain controller initiates the replication operation to the replica domain controller.
7. The replica domain controller pulls the latest replica.

If the site has multiple replica domain controllers, the source domain controller will wait three seconds after issuing the first change notification before sending a change notification to the next domain controller. By waiting three seconds for each change notification, the domain controller can efficiently answer and forward the replication operations to requesting replica domain controllers without being overloaded with replication requests at the same time.

To ensure additional efficiency, after a domain controller receives the directory update, it will not ask or attempt replication back to the source until a new update is required. Urgent replication allows for critical directory information to be delivered to replica domain controllers without waiting on the typical, non-urgent, 15-second and three-second subsequent intervals. For instance, if a user's account locks out on a domain controller, that domain controller urgently replicates the lockout to the primary domain controller (PDC) emulator. The PDC emulator then urgently replicates the lockout to all other domain controllers. Examples of directory updates that are urgently replicated include account lockouts, changes in account lockout policies, changes in the domain password policy, and changes of a domain controller account password.

Non-urgent replication is all other replication that does not include account lockouts, account/password policies, and domain controller accounts. Non-urgent replication occurs through the usual change notification replication operations. For instance, if a computer object is created on a domain controller, replicating it to the next closest domain controller will take about 15 sections through the automatic process.

Password change replication allows domain controllers to reference one domain controller if a password has been changed on one domain controller but the change has not yet replicated throughout the enterprise. Do not confuse password change replication with Password

Replication Policies (PRPs). Although you would think they would be covered by urgent replication, password changes are replicated through the use of non-urgent replication. When a user changes his or her password, that password change is immediately sent to the PDC emulator. The PDC emulator then initiates a non-urgent replication with its replica domain controllers. If a user attempts to log on to a domain controller and the domain controller has not yet received the password change for the user, the domain controller that the user is authenticating against checks with the PDC emulator to see whether it knows the user's latest password. If the PDC emulator has the latest password, it authenticates the user and replicates the new password to the domain controller that the user is attempting authentication against. If a domain controller changes a user's password and cannot contact the PDC emulator, the password change is included in the next non-urgent replication cycle.

Replication conflicts occur when objects are modified by users in an environment. The same object could possibly be modified by two different users at the same time. If this happens, the domain controller receiving the update first compares the version of the change and accepts only the latest version. If both versions are identical, the domain controller accepts the newest update based on the object's version and timestamp. The latest revision always wins in a replication conflict.

UNDERSTANDING INTERSITE REPLICATION

Intersite replication is replication between domain controllers in different sites across a WAN. Intersite replication is considered request-pull replication, meaning that the replica bridgehead server in one site requests the changes from the source bridgehead server.

Intersite replication occurs between domain controllers residing in separate physical locations within the AD DS topology. The KCC and the Intersite Topology Generator create the site topology, and replication occurs between each site's assigned bridgehead servers. Intersite replication is a cost-based replication, allowing replication to occur across the least expensive link. By using scheduling, configured replication intervals, and costs, site links are optimized to provide the fastest and cheapest replication possible between two sites. Intersite replication traffic can occur via RPC over IP or via Simple Mail Transfer Protocol (SMTP).

IP Transports replicates all AD DS partitions synchronously to domain controllers in well-connected sites. Because of its efficiency and reliability, IP Transports is the preferred method of replication between intersite partners. It provides synchronous inbound replication.

SMTP Transports, configured with the SMTP protocol, send replication asynchronously via email messages. SMTP Transports require the implementation of Active Directory Certificate Services (AD CS) and replicate only the schema, configuration, and global catalog partitions. Using SMTP does not replicate the domain partition. SMTP can be used in situations where RPC over TCP/IP is not configured between two sites. Each bridgehead server requires Internet Information Services (IIS) and the domain controller certificate. To use the SMTP links, the SMTP links must have a lower cost than the IP over RPC site links.

Unlike intrasite replication, by default change notification is not used to notify domain controllers in other sites about changes. Replication between sites depends on replication intervals, costs, and schedules. Although change notification between sites is not enabled by default, it can be enabled.

UNDERSTANDING CONNECTION OBJECTS

If you want one domain controller to replicate changes to another domain controller, you must create a connection object (see Figure 18-3). A connection object represents a logical connection between two domain controllers that AD DS replication is using. To create a connection object, use the Active Directory Sites and Services snap-in, the domain controller objects NTDS Settings container. Because AD DS uses pull replication, the connection

Figure 18-3

A connection object connecting
two domain controllers

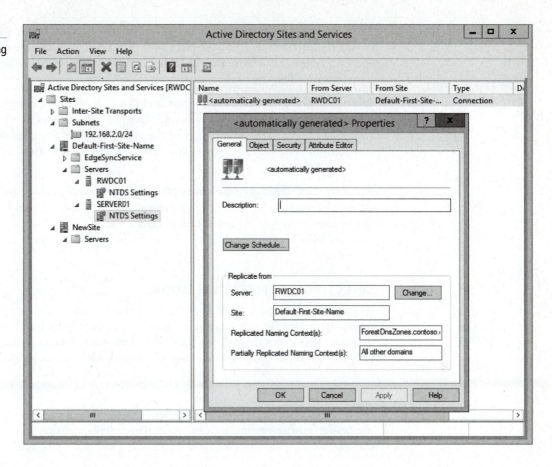

objects are one-way inbound-only replication. To force a replication, just right-click the
connection object and choose Replicate Now. To replicate both domain controllers, you must
replicate the inbound connection object of each domain controller.

The KCC generates and optimizes the replication automatically between domain controllers
within a site to create a two-way, three-hop topology. If you add or remove domain controllers or if a domain controller stops responding, the KCC rearranges the topology dynamically
to form an effective replication topology.

If you have an operations master and want a second domain controller to serve as a standby
operations manager, you should create a connection so that the two domain controllers are
direct replication partners. However, if an operations manager goes down and cannot be recov-
ered quickly, you still have to take the operations masters role from other domain controller.

Notification is the process by which an upstream partner informs its downstream partners
that a change is available and queues the change for replication to its partners. By default, the
domain controller waits 15 seconds to notify its first replication. It then waits three seconds
to notify an additional partner. The notification delay is used to stagger network traffic for
intrasite replication. When the domain controller receives the notification, the directory replication agent (DRA) transfers the changed attributes or objects.

A domain controller might not make any changes for a while. A domain controller will poll
another domain controller to check that it is online and does not have any changes to replicate. By default, the polling interval for intrasite replication is once per hour. Configuring the
polling frequency is possible from the properties of a connection object by clicking Change
Schedule, but it is not recommended. If an upstream partner fails to respond to repeated polling queries, the KCC checks to see whether the upstream server is offline and, if so, rebuilds
the site's replication topology.

Within a site, the connections are arranged in a bidirectional ring, with additional shortcut connections to reduce latency in large sites. The KCC analyzes the replication within a site every 15 minutes to ensure the replication topology is working. When you add or remove a domain controller, the KCC reconfigures the topology.

Intersite topology is based on the spanning tree. As the name implies, a tree structure is created that is redundant and loop-free. One intersite connection exists between any two sites for each directory partition, and the topology generally does not contain any shortcut connections. The KCC automatically creates connection objects, as well as connections between the sites.

The *Inter-site Topology Generator (ISTG)* is responsible for managing the inbound replication connection objects for all bridgehead servers in the site in which it is located. Initially, the first server in a site becomes the ISTG for the site. This role does not change until the current ISTG becomes unavailable. If 60 minutes elapse without a modification, a new ISTG takes over.

SELECTING A REPLICATION MODEL

As part of the site design, enterprise administrators must decide on a topology for the intersite replication traffic. In other words, they must determine which sites will replicate with which. To some extent, this depends on the physical connections connecting the sites. You can create a replication topology that simply uses the entire WAN topology connecting the locations hosting separate sites, or you can designate a subset of the WAN topology to be used for replication.

In an AD DS installation with multiple sites, each site designates one domain controller as the *bridgehead server* for each partition with a replica at that site. The bridgehead servers are the only domain controllers that communicate with the other sites.

Best practice is to allow AD DS to handle the assignment of the bridgehead server tasks to the domain controller it sees best fit. In certain environments, you might need to configure a bridgehead server manually to dedicate it for the additional processing and traffic requirements.

You can designate one or more preferred servers by using the Active Directory Sites and Services snap-in. If you configure multiple preferred bridgehead server for a site, ISTG uses only one of the bridgehead servers. If the designated bridgehead server fails, the ISTG uses one of the other preferred bridgehead servers. However, if you specify one or more bridgehead servers but none of them are available, ISTG does not select another server automatically, and replication will not occur for the site. Therefore, if you manually configure a bridgehead, configure two per site. Also ensure that the domain controller that will be a bridgehead server is a DNS and global catalog server.

SELECTING A REPLICATION MODEL

You can create a replication model at the site level; you do not have to be concerned with selecting which domain controllers participate in intersite replication. For example, in a forest with two domains, the headquarters site might have four domain controllers, two for each domain, as shown in Figure 18-4. A branch office functioning as a separate site also has two domain controllers for each domain. At each of the two sites, one domain controller for each domain is designated as the bridgehead server. The communication between the sites occurs between the two pairs of bridgehead servers.

Figure 18-4

Bridgehead servers for two domains replicating between two sites

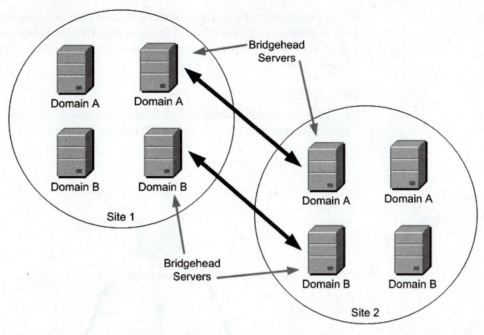

If you expand the example to include two more branch offices, the replication topology becomes more complicated. Assuming that each branch office is a separate site, with at least one domain controller for each of the two domains, you can use several models to build a replication topology, as explained in the following sections.

HUB AND SPOKE

In one model, the ***hub and spoke topology*** (see Figure 18-5), one site—in this case, the headquarters—is designated as the hub and communicates with each of the other sites. The branch office sites do not communicate with each other. Separate links for each domain are still required.

Figure 18-5

The hub and spoke replication topology model

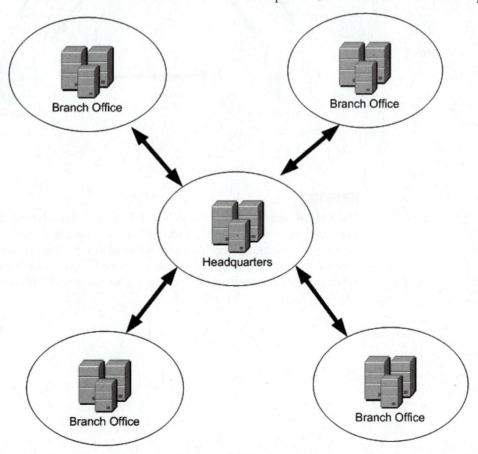

This arrangement is particularly useful if the links to the headquarters site are faster than those between the branch offices. However, the replication *latency period*—that is, the time it takes for changes to propagate to all the domain controllers in the enterprise—can be relatively slow.

FULL MESH

In a *full mesh topology*, each site maintains connections to every other site (see Figure 18-6). This model generates more WAN traffic but generally reduces replication latency.

Figure 18-6

The full mesh replication topology model

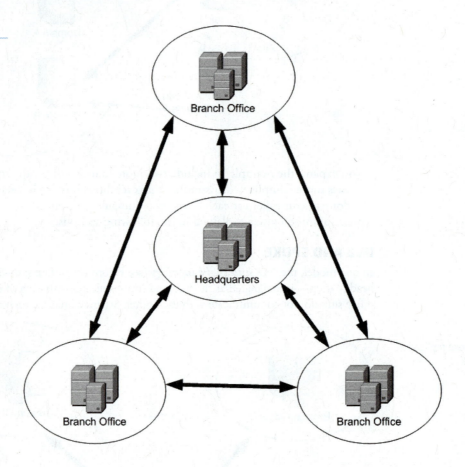

HYBRID

The *hybrid topology* mixes the hub and spoke and the full mesh by using two connected hubs, each of which connects to several branch offices (see Figure 18-7). This arrangement is particularly suitable in larger facilities with fast connections and smaller branch offices with slow connections. For example, you might have hubs in your North American, European, and Asian headquarters, each of which connects to the branch offices on that continent.

Figure 18-7

The hybrid replication topology
model

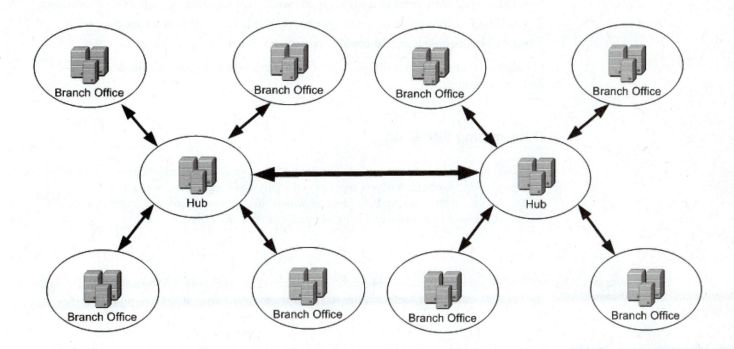

PLANNING GLOBAL CATALOG AND RODC REPLICATION

In addition to the regular replication that occurs with replicating Active Directory objects,
you need to understand how RODC replication and global catalog replication affects the
environment. RODCs replicate domain controllers that run Windows Server 2008 or newer.
Consider using an RODC in an area that needs to look up, search, or access Active Directory
information in an environment that might not be totally secure. Typically, an RODC is near
a writable domain controller that runs Windows Server 2008. The nearest site is defined by
the lowest-cost site link for the site that contains the RODC.

When a user logs on to the domain, she needs to access a global catalog to obtain a list
of universal groups that she belongs to. If you place a domain controller in a site but the
site does not have a global catalog, when the user logs on, she will have to visit another
site to access this information. Also, whereas a domain controller contains copies of
objects and related information for its domain, a global catalog also has read-only copies
of all objects in the forest with commonly accessed attributes that must be replicated
to each global catalog. Lastly, certain applications such as Microsoft Exchange Server
put more load on the global catalogs. As a result, at least one global catalog server is
recommended in each AD DS site, and you should consider placing two global catalog
servers for redundancy.

PLANNING FOR SYSVOL REPLICATION

Domain controllers replicate among themselves a special shared folder called *SYSVOL*. The
SYSVOL stores logon scripts and GPOs. Before Windows Server 2008, File Replication
Service (FRS) was used to perform the replication. Windows Server 2012 and Windows
Server 2012 R2 use DFS Replication service.

DFS Replication has several advantages over FRS:

- An efficient, scalable, and reliable file replication protocol designed for data consistency in a multimaster environment
- Differential replication that increases efficiency by replicating only changed information
- Self-healing for update sequence number (USN) journal wraps and data corruption
- Flexible scheduling and bandwidth-throttling mechanism

In either case, keep in mind the amount of data that needs to be synchronized between domain controllers.

Determining Site Links

To enable replication between two sites, you must have a site link object associated with both of them. A *site link object* represents the physical connection between remote sites. The purpose of the site link is to indicate which sites are connected and to provide details about the cost and availability of the physical connection.

TAKE NOTE A site link represents an available path for replication. A single site link does not control the network routes that replication uses, nor is it aware of routes at the network level.

CERTIFICATION READY
Designing site links
Objective 5.1

By default, the Active Directory Domain Services Installation Wizard creates a site link object called DEFAULTIPSITELINK. If all your sites are connected through WAN links running at the same speed and with the same available bandwidth, you can use this default site link for all your connections. However, if you have WAN connections running at different speeds or with different amounts of bandwidth utilization, you must create additional site link objects and configure them to reflect the physical capabilities of the connections.

TAKE NOTE As with the Default-First-Site-Name site object, you can rename the DEFAULTIPSITELINK object to reflect its actual function.

Each site link object must have at least two site objects associated with it, representing both ends of the connection. When you add sites to a new site link (see Figure 18-8), do not forget to remove them from the DEFAULTIPSITELINK site link, if AD DS has added them to it.

Figure 18-8

A site link's Properties
dialog box

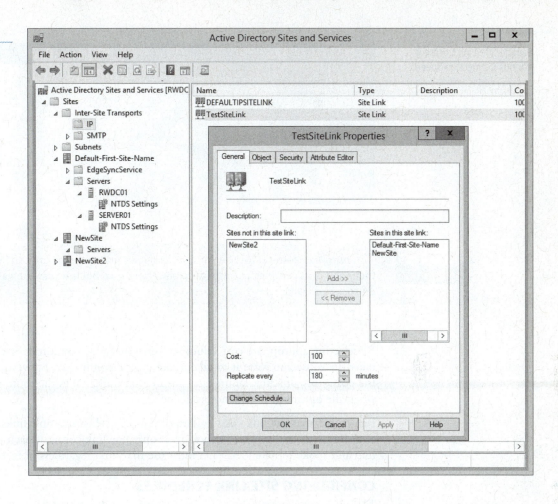

When designing the site links, you also should plan the configuration of the site link attributes. These attributes can greatly influence replication over site links. For each site link, you can configure the site link cost, the replication frequency, and the replication schedule.

CONFIGURING SITE LINK COSTS

When the AD DS replication topology provides a choice between links connecting two sites, it always chooses the link with the lowest cost, as designated by the administrator on the link's Properties dialog box.

The *site link cost* value of a site link does not have to represent an actual monetary value; it is significant only in relation to the costs of the other links. Administrators often calculate site link costs based on the speeds of the links and their available bandwidth. The lower the bandwidth, the higher the cost of the link.

For example, if you decide to create a full mesh topology and your sites are connected by various WAN technologies running at different speeds, you might create a list of designated link costs similar to the one shown in Table 18-2.

Table 18-2

Sample Site Link Costs for
Various Connection Speeds

CONNECTION SPEED	SITE LINK COST
44.7 Mbps	100
10 Mbps	300
3 Mbs	600
1.544	1200
512 Kbps	2400

TAKE NOTE*

The numbers you use for the site link costs are not relevant; only the relationships between them are. You can just as easily drop the trailing zeroes and use the values 1, 3, 6, 12, and 24 for your costs.

By selecting appropriate cost values for your site links, you can ensure that replication traffic takes the route you want it to take under typical conditions. However, be sure also to consider the possibility of a link failure, and ensure that traffic takes the route you want it to take when the optimum path is not available.

Remember that site link costs are important only when multiple links are available between two sites, like in a full mesh topology. If only one link connects each pair of sites, like in a hub and spoke topology, AD DS must use that link, regardless of its cost.

CONFIGURING SITE LINK SCHEDULES

The most efficient way to conserve intersite bandwidth is to specify when AD DS replication should occur. By default, sites replicate every 180 minutes, but you can configure site link objects to replicate more or less frequently as needed. For an AD DS infrastructure that does not change often, you can safely increase the *Replicate every* value on the *General* tab.

By clicking *Change Schedule*, you can also specify the hours of the day and the days of the week that replication should occur, using the interface shown in Figure 18-9. If you have WAN connections that are approaching peak bandwidth utilization during business hours, for example, you can configure replication to occur only when both sites are closed.

Figure 18-9

The Schedule dialog box for a
site link object

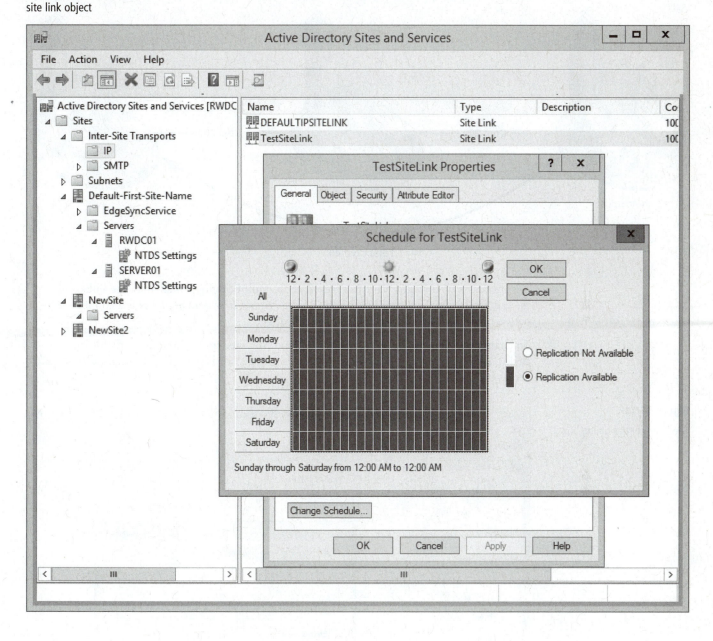

CREATING SITE LINK BRIDGES

By default, site link bridging is enabled for all your site links, rendering all the links transitive.
This means that if a site link connects your North American hub with your European hub,
and another site link connects your European hub to your Asian hub, your North American
site can replicate with your Asian site, as shown in Figure 18-10.

Figure 18-10

Site link bridging in effect

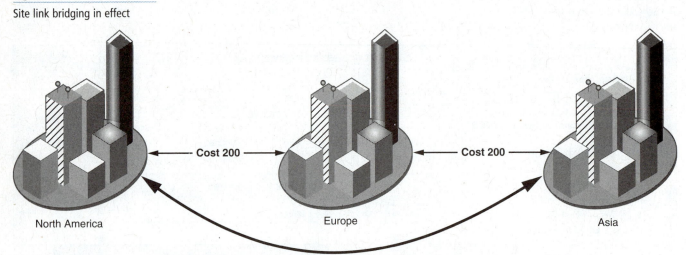

North America   **← Cost 200 →**   Europe   **← Cost 200 →**   Asia

Total Cost 400

In some cases, you might want to turn off the default bridging for all your site links and instead create your own site link bridge objects. A ***site link bridge object*** is a connection between two site links that renders them transitive.

To change the site link bridging default, expand the Sites\Inter-Site Transports folder, right-click IP, and open the IP Properties dialog box (see Figure 18-11). Deselecting the *Bridge all site links* check box disables bridging.

Figure 18-11

The IP Properties dialog box

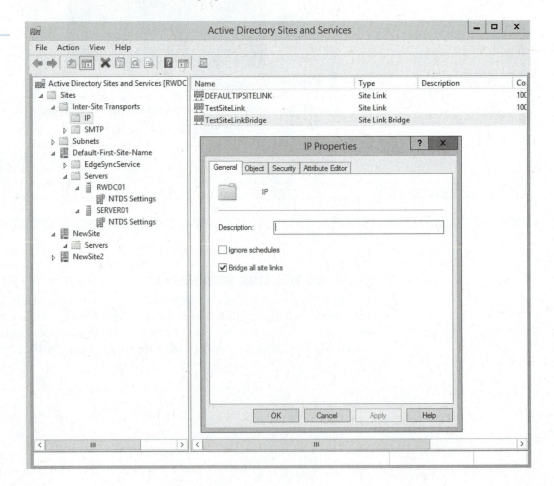

One reason you might want to change the default would be if you have a hybrid replication topology with links between hub sites that are relatively slow or have little available bandwidth. For example, if bridging is enabled for all your sites, the transitive nature of the links means that the branch offices connected to the New York hub not only can replicate with the Paris hub, but also can replicate with all the other three European branch offices. This means that the NY-Paris link must carry multiple copies of the same replication traffic. If the site link between New York and Paris is heavily trafficked already, this could be a problem.

To prevent this behavior, you can disable the default site bridging and then create individual site link bridge objects for each path between a North American branch office and the Paris hub. In the same way, you must create site link bridges from the European branch offices to the New York hub.

For this example, you need to create the following six site link bridges:

- Philadelphia-NY/NY-Paris
- Baltimore-NY/NY-Paris
- Boston-NY/NY-Paris
- NY-Paris/Paris-Brussels
- NY-Paris/Paris-Zurich
- NY-Paris/Paris-Marseille

The result of this arrangement is that the NY-Paris link will have to carry only one copy of the replication traffic for each branch office.

TAKE NOTE *

Each site link bridge must contain at least two site objects, with one common site between them. This enables AD DS to calculate the total cost of the route by adding the costs of the individual site links.

You can also use site link bridge objects to control replication traffic on networks that are not fully routed, such as those using dial-up or demand-dial links, or to control replication traffic routes in a failover situation, such as a malfunction at one of the hub sites.

You should create site link bridges only if you want to specify manually which sites are transitively linked at the network level and which are not. When designing site link bridging, consider the following guidelines:

- If the network is fully routed and you have no need to control the flow of AD DS replication, leave automatic site link bridging enabled for all site links by selecting the *Bridge all site links* option.
- If the network is not fully routed, clear the *Bridge all site links* option for the IP transport, and then configure the site link bridges to map to the physical network connections.
- If you need to control how traffic is routed, you can create and configure site link bridge objects.
- If all site links within the bridge are required to route transitively, you should add site links to a site link bridge.
- If you use manual site link bridges, ensure that the site link in a manual site link bridge has one site in common with another site link in the bridge. That way, the bridge can compute the cost from sites in one link to the sites in other links of the bridge.

Identifying and Resolving Active Directory Replication Conflicts

> Monitoring replication allows you to troubleshoot and narrow down problems between domain controllers when replication is not working properly. Monitoring replication in your enterprise allows you to ensure that all domains within the enterprise are receiving updates to all directory partitions, keeping users and directory data fully accessible.

CERTIFICATION READY
Monitor and resolve
Active Directory
replication conflicts
Objective 5.1

By using Repadmin.exe, Windows PowerShell, and/or the Active Directory Replication Status tool (ADREPLSTATUS), you can monitor your environment for failures and take action to put a resolution in place. Use the commands in Table 18-2 to monitor replication.

Table 18.3

Using Repadmin.exe
Commands to Monitor
Network

COMMAND	DESCRIPTION
REPADMIN.EXE /ReplSummary	Can also be run as REPADMIN /ReplSum. This command examines all inbound and outbound replication between domain controllers and returns a replication summary of the forest or specified domain controllers. After contacting and inventorying the domain controllers, it populates with a summary of failures and deltas (new changes) returned during its examination.
REPADMIN.EXE /ShowRepl	Categorized by directory partitions, this command returns the replication status of all inbound connections from source domain controllers to the domain controller it is run from.
REPADMIN.EXE /ShowRepl /RepsTo	This command displays a summary of all outbound replication connections to replica domain controllers, using the domain controller the command is run from as the source domain controller.
REPADMIN.EXE /Queue	This command displays the current inbound connections that are queued for replication. To view the active inbound replication queue of a domain controller from that domain controller, run REPADMIN /Queue DCName.
REPADMIN.EXE /FailCache	This command displays link and connection failure attempts found by the KCC.

New Windows PowerShell cmdlets in Windows Server 2012 allow for advanced monitoring, troubleshooting, and scripting. You can use Windows PowerShell in place of, or in addition to, the REPADMIN command and ADREPLSTATUS. With the latest releases, these additions make monitoring and troubleshooting from Windows PowerShell more powerful for administrators.

Table 18.4

Using Windows PowerShell Cmdlets for Network Monitoring

Cmdlet	Description
Get-ADReplicationFailure	Using `Get-ADReplicationFailure -target DomainFQDN` returns failure counts, failure types, replica domain controllers, most recent replication failures, and replica domain controllers on which replication failed.
Get-ADReplication PartnerMetadata	Using `Get-ADReplicationPartnerMetadata -target DomainControllerFQDN` returns configuration data and replication state of the domain controller. This way, you can inventory, monitor, and troubleshoot replication between the source and replica domain controller.
Get-ADReplicationUpToD atenessVectorTable	Using `Get-ADReplicationUpToDatenessVector Table -Target "FullyQualifiedDomainName" -Scope Domain*` queries all replication partners' AD DS partitions in the domain returning listings of last replication successes, partitions, replica server, and UsnFilter.

MONITORING REPLICATION WITH THE ACTIVE DIRECTORY REPLICATION STATUS TOOL (ADREPLSTATUS)

Released by Microsoft in 2012, the Active Directory Replication Status Tool (ADREPLSTATUS) allows for much simpler and straightforward monitoring and troubleshooting, taking the results returned and placing them into an easy-to-use application. By using existing tools and commands such as Repadmin.exe, ADREPLSTATUS identifies, prioritizes, and assists in resolving replication errors on specified domain controllers, a domain, or the entire forest. ADREPLSTATUS auto-discovers domain controllers, gathers replication summaries, returns the results in a filterable, sortable list, and provides a links directly to TechNet, providing direct access and faster turnaround time to resolve replication errors.

Compatible with operating systems including Windows Server 2003, Windows XP, and later, you can download the latest version of ADREPLSTATUS from the Microsoft Download Center.

Before installation, ensure that you have installed the required versions of the .NET Framework that ADREPLSTATUS might require: .NET Framework 3.5.1 and .NET Framework 4.0.

MONITOR ACTIVE DIRECTORY REPLICATION WITH ADREPLSTATUS

GET READY. To use ADREPLSTATUS, perform the following steps:

1. If the .NET Framework is not already installed, download and install the versions required for your operating system.
2. Download and install the Active Directory Replication Status Tool from the *Microsoft Download Center*.
3. On the desktop of the client on which the tool is installed, double-click AD Replication Status Tool.
4. Examine the contents of the *Home* tab and the *Configuration/Scope Settings*.
5. From the *Configuration/Scope Settings*, select Forest and then click Refresh Replication Status.
6. When the replication refresh has been completed, if the results are not already displayed, click the Replication Status Viewer tab and review the results (see Figure 18-12).

Figure 18-12

Reviewing the Replication
Status Viewer

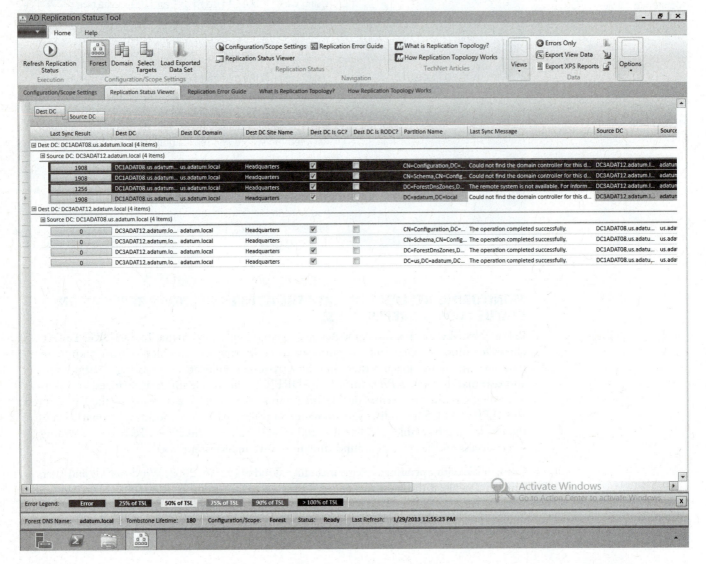

7. Select the Replication Error Guide tab and examine the *Error Code, Message,* and *Technet Article Link* columns (see Figure 18-13).

Figure 18-13

Reviewing the Replication
Error Guide

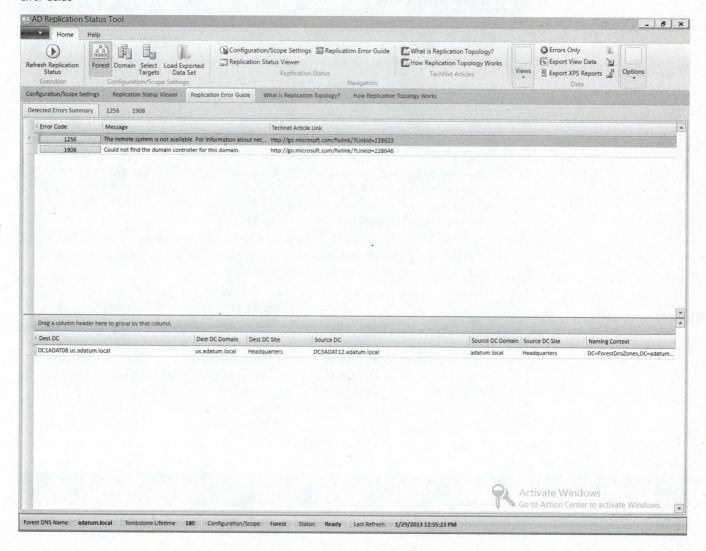

8. If errors are shown, click the error code listed in the *Replication Error Guide*. Follow the directions provided by the displayed TechNet article and make the required changes.

9. Run Refresh Replication Status from the *AD Replication Status Tool*.

10. Continue troubleshooting and resolving errors until errors are no longer reported.

11. Close the *AD Replication Status Tool* when completed.

SKILL SUMMARY

IN THIS LESSON YOU LEARNED:

- Sites and domain controllers represent the physical structure of your network. A site consists of one or more IP subnets connected by a high-speed link and typically defined by a geographical location.

- A domain controller is a Windows server that stores a replica of the account and security information for the domain and defines the domain boundaries.

- When you determine the Active Directory topology, you need to consider the location of the domain controllers. One of the main factors when determining where to place the domain controllers is to place them near resources that need to use them.

- Active Directory Domain Services (AD DS) uses a multimaster replication process, which means that you can modify the contents of the AD DS database on any domain controller and have that domain controller automatically propagate the changes to all other domain controllers containing replicas of the modified partition.

- Intrasite replication occurs during change notification between domain controllers located within that site. Conversely, intersite replication is replication between domain controllers in different sites across a wide area network (WAN).

- To enable replication between two sites, you must have a site link object associated with both of them. A site link object represents the physical connection between remote sites. The purpose of the site link is to indicate which sites are connected and to provide details about the cost and availability of the physical connection.

- Monitoring replication allows you to troubleshoot and narrow down problems between domain controllers when replication is not working properly. Monitoring replication in your enterprise allows you to ensure that all domains within the enterprise are receiving updates to all directory partitions, keeping users and directory data fully accessible.

■ Knowledge Assessment

Multiple Choice

1. Which of the following describes a site?
   a. a campus or building
   b. a city
   c. one or more IP subnets connected by a high-speed link
   d. a building

2. Which of the following stores a replica of the account and security information for a domain?
   a. DNS server
   b. domain controller
   c. DHCP server
   d. content server

3. How do clients find a domain controller?
   a. Refer to the HOSTS file
   b. Do a broadcast looking for domain controllers
   c. Use the IP configuration information received from the DHCP server
   d. Reference the DNS Service (SRV) records

4. Which of the following are reasons to create multiple AD DS sites? (Choose all that apply.)
   a. replication
   b. malware isolation
   c. authentication
   d. applications

5. What is the first site object in an Active Directory?
   a. Default-First-Site-Name
   b. DefaultSite
   c. PrimarySite
   d. BackboneSite

6. Which of the following is recommended when you are defining sites?
   a. Create a site for every switch larger than eight ports.
   b. Create a site for every router or layer-3 switch.
   c. Define one large site to reduce replication.
   d. Rename the Default-First-Site-Name site object to a descriptive name of its current site.

7. Which of the following describe intrasites? (Choose two answers.)
   a. Replication traffic is not compressed.
   b. Replication occurs when changes to the AD DS database occurs.
   c. Traffic to other sites is sent to the bridgehead.
   d. They require the creation and configuration of site link objects.

8. Which is the preferred method to perform Active Directory replication?
   a. IP Transport
   b. SMTP
   c. KCC
   d. DFS

9. Which type of server is designated as the primary domain controller used with replications to domain controllers at other sites?
   a. Knowledge Consistency Checker
   b. PDC emulator
   c. global catalog
   d. bridgehead server

10. If a site does not have a domain controller, how does it determine the nearest site that has a domain controller?
    a. GPO settings
    b. current load of the domain controller
    c. power of the domain controller
    d. site costs

Best Answer

Choose the letter that corresponds to the best answer. More than one answer choice can achieve the goal. Select the BEST answer.

1. Replication is not occurring between sites when a domain controller is not accessible. Each site has five domain controllers. What is configured incorrectly?
   a. site costs
   b. subnets
   c. preferred bridgehead servers
   d. SRV registration

484 | Lesson 18

2. You are an administrator for a large corporation that has seven large sites throughout the United States. You need to ensure that when changes are made in Active Directory, those changes are replicated as quickly as possible. Which replication model would you recommend?
    a. hub and spoke
    b. full mesh
    c. hybrid
    d. volume

3. You are an administrator at a corporation that has 75 small sites spread throughout the western United States. Some of these only have a T-1 connection, whereas others have only a 512 Mbps connection. How would you configure AD DS replication traffic?
    a. Configure DFS replication
    b. Configure the Inter-site Topology Generator
    c. Configure intersite replication
    d. Configure intrasite replication

4. You want to use the SMTP transport for AD DS replication. What mechanism is used to provide the SMTP service?
    a. a third-party STMP software
    b. Microsoft Exchange Server
    c. ISA
    d. IIS

5. You are an administrator for a corporation that has 20 sites with 100 to 200 users and 10 sites with 50 to100 users. Users use Microsoft Exchange and Outlook. What is the minimum number of domain controllers you would install on the smaller sites while keeping cost low?
    a. none
    b. 1
    c. 2
    d. 3

Matching and Identification

1. Identify which of the following describe intrasite replication or intersite replication.
    _____ a) Replication is initiated when AD DS database is changed
    _____ b) Does not require the configuration of additional AD DS objects
    _____ c) Transmits traffic to a bridgehead server
    _____ d) Replication occurs on a schedule
    _____ e) Highly configurable
    _____ f) Replication traffic is compressed
    _____ g) Rarely needs configuration

2. Identify the replication model (hub and spoke, full mesh, hybrid).
    _____ Each site has a connect to every other site.
    _____ All sites are updated through the corporate office.
    _____ Some sites are connected to other sites, whereas other sites are connected only to the corporate office.

Build a List

1. In order of first to last, specify the steps used to determine and configure site links. Not all answers will be used.

   _____ Place the PDC emulator.
   _____ Configure site link schedules
   _____ Create site link bridges
   _____ Create a site bridge.
   _____ Configuring site Link costs.

■ Business Case Scenarios

Scenario 18-1: Designing Sites

You are the administrator for the Contoso Corporation. You have five large sites, each consisting of 500 to 1,000 users, 10 sites with each consisting of 100 to 200 users, and five sites with each consisting 10 to 50 users. The five large sites have a T-3 connection, whereas the medium-sized sites have 10 Mbps links. The five smallest sites have 3 Mbps connections. At times, the small sites' WAN links are saturated. How would you define the sites?

Scenario 18-2: Assigning Site Link Costs

Adatum Corp. has its headquarters in Los Angeles and branch offices in San Francisco, San Diego, and Sacramento, each of which has its own AD DS site. Each branch office has a T-1 connection to the Los Angeles office, running at 1.544 Mbps. The Sacramento connection has an average available bandwidth of 75 percent, the San Diego connection has 60 percent available. and the San Francisco link has 25 percent of its bandwidth available. The company has also just installed new 512 Kbps links between San Diego and San Francisco, San Francisco and Sacramento, and Sacramento and San Diego to create a full mesh replication topology.

You want AD DS replication traffic to use the T-1 connections wherever practical. However, because the Los Angeles to San Francisco link is nearing bandwidth saturation, you want replication traffic to use the other links to connect these two cities. Because of a special arrangement with the company's service provider, Adatum is getting the San Francisco to Sacramento link for half price. By using the following table, assign cost values to the links to provide the most economical connections possible under the current traffic conditions. Explain your answers.

Site Link	Cost
Los Angeles – San Francisco	
Los Angeles – San Diego	
Los Angeles – Sacramento	
Sacramento – San Francisco	
San Diego – San Francisco	
Sacramento – San Diego	

19 LESSON

Designing a Domain Controller Strategy

70-413 EXAM OBJECTIVE

Objective 5.2 – Design a domain controller strategy. This objective may include but is not limited to: Design considerations including global catalog, operations master roles, read-only domain controllers (RODCs), partial attribute set, domain controller cloning, and domain controller placement

LESSON HEADING	EXAM OBJECTIVE
Designing a Domain Controller Strategy	
• Designing Global Catalogs	Design global catalogs
• Designing Partial Attribute Sets	Design partial attribute sets
• Designing Operations Master Roles	Design operations master roles
• Designing Read-Only Domain Controllers (RODC)	Design read-only domain controllers (RODCs)
• Planning Virtualizing Domain Controllers	
• Planning Domain Controller Cloning	Design domain controller cloning
• Planning Domain Controller Placement	Design domain controller placement

KEY TERMS

domain controllers

domain naming master

global catalog

infrastructure master

Ntdsutil.exe

operations masters

partial attribute set

primary domain controller (PDC) emulator

read-only domain controller (RODC)

relative identifier (RID) master

schema master

■ Designing a Domain Controller strategy

THE BOTTOM LINE

Domain controllers are the servers that store and run the Active Directory database. Active Directory is a major component in authentication, authorization, and auditing (AAA). Therefore, you need to understand what the domain controller does, how many domain controllers you need, where to deploy the domain controllers, and how to configure the domain controllers.

A domain partition stores only the information about objects located in that domain. All domain controllers in a domain receive changes and replicate those changes to the domain partition stored on all other domain controllers in the domain. As a result, all domain controllers are peers in the domain and manage replication as a unit.

When a user logs on, Active Directory clients use the DNS Service (SRV) resource records to locate an Active Directory server known as a domain controller. Each domain has its own set of domain controllers to provide access to the domain resources, such as users and computers. Whenever an object (such as a username or password) is modified, it is replicated automatically to the other domain controllers within a domain.

For fault tolerance, a site should have two or more domain controllers. That way, if one domain controller fails, the other domain controller can still service the clients.

A domain controller is a Windows server that stores a replica of the account and security information for the domain and defines the domain boundaries. To make a computer running Windows Server 2012 a domain controller, you must install Active Directory Domain Services (AD DS) and promote the domain controller from Server Manager.

Designing Global Catalogs

Although the global catalog is not one of the five operation masters, it provides a critical functionality for Active Directory. As a domain controller, a *global catalog* stores a full copy of all objects in the domain. It also has a partial copy of all objects for all other domains in the forest. The partial copy of all objects is used for logons, object searches, and universal group membership. The global catalog is required for applications such as Microsoft Exchange Server, Microsoft Office Outlook, and Distributed File System (DFS).

CERTIFICATION READY
Design global catalogs
Objective 5.2

One primary function of a global catalog is to provide search capability of any object in the forest. When a user or an application performs a search in Active Directory, a search request is sent to the global catalog over TCP port 3268, which is used by Active Directory to direct these requests to a global catalog server. The global catalogs are identified by the global catalog SRV records (_gc).

Another function of a global catalog is to resolve User Principal Names (UPNs). All users log on with the domain username (domain_name\username) or the UPN, which uses an email address format (such as username@domainname.ext). The global catalog is used to resolve the UPN name to a username. The global catalog server stores enough information, such as time restrictions, about the user to permit or deny the logon request.

A global catalog is created automatically on the first domain controller in the forest. However, you can optionally configure other domain controllers to serve as global catalogs. When you promote a server to a domain controller by using the Active Directory Domain Services Installation Wizard, you can choose to make the computer a global catalog server. You also can open Active Directory Sites and Services NTDS Settings properties of a domain controller and select the Global Catalog option.

Installing a global catalog server at every site improves performance, but on a large enterprise network with multiple domains, the amount of network traffic resulting from global catalog replication can be significant. Generally speaking, a site with 100 or more users should definitely have one of its domain controllers functioning as a global catalog server.

If every domain controller is a global catalog, you do not have to worry about placement of the infrastructure operations master because the role is no longer necessary. However, every domain controller that is a global catalog partition must be replicated to all other global catalogs. Although a single-domain forest will have a minimal increase in replication traffic, the amount of replication increases significantly for a multiple domain forest because it also must replicate information for all objects within the forest. However, many organizations decide to make every domain controller a global catalog because the benefits of having a domain controller/global catalog outweigh any impact on the network.

You should follow these guidelines from Microsoft:

- Deploy at least one global catalog server in each Active Directory site, especially if you have slow or unreliable connections to the global catalog on another site.
- Have two global catalog servers in each Active Directory site for redundancy.
- If you have more than one domain controller per site, have all of them run as a global catalog server.
- If you have a large number of users, deploying multiple global catalog servers will improve performance.
- Identify all applications such as Microsoft Exchange Server and DFS that require a global catalog in the same Active Directory site.

Designing Partial Attribute Sets

As mentioned earlier, the global catalog contains a partial copy of all objects from other domains in the forest. The partial copy includes attributes *(partial attribute set)* that are commonly used in search and other applications. The reason that only a partial copy is replicated to all domain controllers in other domains is to reduce the amount of replication traffic and to minimize the size of the Active Directory database.

By modifying the schema, you can add attributes to the partial attribute set. To modify the partial attribute set, you must be a member of the Schema Admins group.

 ADD ATTRIBUTES TO THE PARTIAL ATTRIBUTE SET

GET READY. To add an attribute to the partial attribute set, perform the following steps:

1. Right-click the Start button and choose Command Prompt (Admin).
2. In the command prompt window, register the Active Directory schema by executing the regsvr32 schmmgmt.dll command. When the DLL file is registered, click OK.
3. At the command prompt, execute the mmc command.
4. In the console, from the *File* menu, click Add/Remove Snap-in.
5. In the *Add or Remove Snap-ins* dialog box, click Active Directory Schema, then click Add.
6. To close the *Add or Remove Snap-ins* dialog inbox, click OK.
7. In the left pane, expand the Active Directory Schema node and click the Attributes node.
8. In the right pane, scroll down to the desired attribute, right-click it, and then choose Properties.
9. Select the Replicate this attribute to the Global Catalog check box (see Figure 19-1).

Figure 19-1

Replicating an attribute to the global catalog

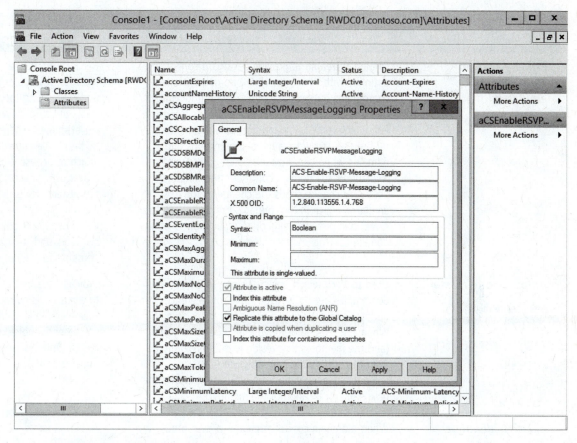

10. Click OK.

For most organizations, you should not have to add attributes to the partial attribute set. However, if you have a special need, such as an application that needs the additional attribute replicated throughout the forest, you can then add the necessary attributes. You should always test in a test environment before deploying the changes to the production environment. A multi-forest environment will require some time for the attribute to be replicated to all global catalogs.

Designing Operations Master Roles

With Active Directory, domain controllers follow a multimaster replication model that ensures copies of all domain objects are found on each domain controller within a domain so that they can be quickly and easily accessed and to provide fault tolerance. To help resolve conflicts and such, all transactions use version IDs and timestamps. However, some critical functions need to have the assurance of little or no risk of error. *Operations masters*, previously referred to as Flexible Single Master Operations (FSMO), are specialized domain controllers that perform certain tasks that can be handled only by a single domain controller in a multimaster environment.

CERTIFICATION READY
Design operations master roles
Objective 5.2

Table 19-1 shows the five operations master roles. When you install a domain, the first domain controller installed for a domain has the primary domain controller (PDC), relative identifier (RID) master, and infrastructure master. Similarly, the first domain controller in the root domain has the Domain Naming and Schema Master roles.

Table 19-1

Operations master roles

OPERATIONS MASTER ROLES	DESCRIPTION	EFFECT OF FAILURE
Primary domain controller (PDC) emulator (one per domain)	Originally created to provide backward compatibility with Windows NT 4.0 domains. It also coordinates password changes, account lockouts, and time synchronization; manages edits to Group Policy Objects (GPOs); and acts as a domain master browser (provides a list of workgroups and domains when you browse). When a password is changed, the domain controller that initiates a password change sends the change to the PDC emulator, which in turn updates the global catalog server and provides immediate replication to other domain controllers in the domain.	Because the PDC emulator is the most heavily operations master used, and considering the tasks it performs, it can affect users when it is down. For example, a changed password might not be immediately replicated, which can cause problems when a user tries to access resources. If the system clocks drift too much, users might not be able to log on as Kerberos fails. Account lockout does not work and you cannot raise the domain's functional level.
Infrastructure master (one per domain)	Used to track which objects belong to which domain, because it is responsible for reference updates from its domain objects to other domains. When you rename or move a member of a group (and the members that reside in different domain from the group), the infrastructure master is responsible for updating the group so it knows the new name or location of the member.	Typically, the loss of the infrastructure master is not be visible to users. However, the loss might be seen if you recently moved or renamed a large number of accounts.
Relative identifier (RID) master (one per domain)	When a domain controller creates a user, group, or computer object, it assigns the object a unique security ID (SID). The SID consists of a domain security ID that identifies the domain to which the object belongs and a relative ID that identifies the object within the domain. The RID master is responsible for assigning relative identifiers to domain controllers in the domain. The RID master assigns a block of 500 identifiers to each domain controller. When 50 percent of the supply of RIDs are used, it contacts the RID to request a new supply.	Although users cannot see the loss of the RID master, it can be seen when administrators are creating objects and the domain runs out of relative IDs to assign. You also cannot move objects between domains.
Schema master (one per forest)	Controls all updates and modifications to the schema. To update the schema of a forest, you must have access to the schema master.	Although the loss of the schema master does not affect the users, you cannot modify the schema or install any applications, such as Microsoft Exchange Server, that would modify the schema. You also cannot raise the functional level of the forest.
Domain naming master (one per forest)	Holds the Domain Naming Master role that controls the addition or removal of domains in the forest.	Although the loss of the domain naming master does not affect users, you cannot add or remove domains from the forests.

According to Microsoft, when you place the operations master roles, you should follow these guidelines:

- Place the domain-level roles on high-performance domain controllers.
- Do not place the infrastructure master on a global catalog server unless you have only one domain or all the domain controllers in your forest are also global catalogs. When all domain controllers are global catalog servers, all domain controllers have up-to-date information about every object in the forest, which eliminates the need for the infrastructure master role. If the infrastructure is not on a domain controller that is not a global catalog, the infrastructure master should have an explicit connection to a domain controller that is a global catalog server. You can place the infrastructure master on the same domain controller that acts as the RID master and PDC emulator. Also, if you enable the Active Directory Recycle Bin, you do not need to worry about placement of the infrastructure master
- The schema master and domain naming master should be on domain controllers in the forest root domain and should be placed on a domain controller that is a global catalog server.
- If possible, the RID master role and PDC emulator role should be on the same domain controller. If you have to separate the roles because of load, you should create explicit connection objects in Active Directory so that they are direct replication partners.
- If the PDC emulator becomes overworked, you should offload non-AD DS roles to other servers, upgrade the emulator, or move the emulator to a more powerful computer.

Lastly, you should create a failover plan in case the domain controller that hosts an operations master fails. Therefore, you should designate which server will be the backup for the operation masters. Of course, because these roles do not transfer automatically, you must transfer or seize the role.

TRANSFERRING THE OPERATIONS MASTERS ROLE

Occasionally, you might need to move the operation master roles to other domain controllers. If you plan to do maintenance in which a domain controller that holds the operations master will be down for an extended period of time, plan to retire a domain controller that holds a role of Operations Master, or need to move the role to a domain controller with more resources, you must transfer the operations master. Transferring an FSMO role requires that the source domain controller and the target domain controller be online.

 TRANSFER THE HOLDERS OF RID MASTER, PDC EMULATOR, OR INFRASTRUCTURE MASTER

GET READY. To transfer the holders of RID Master, PDC emulator, and infrastructure master, perform the following steps:

1. In *Server Manager,* click Tools > Active Directory Sites and Services. The *Active Directory Sites and Services console* opens.
2. I the console tree, right-click the Active Directory Users and Computers node and choose Change Domain Controller.
3. In the *Change Directory Server* dialog box, select the domain controller that you want to transfer the role to and click OK.
4. Right-click the domain and choose Operations Masters.
5. Select the tab that reflects the operations master role you are transferring and click Change.
6. In the *confirmation message* box, click Yes to confirm the change in roles. In the next message box, click OK.
7. When done, click Close to close the *Operations Masters* dialog box.
8. Close the *Active Directory Users and Computers* console.

TRANSFER THE HOLDERS OF THE DOMAIN NAMING OPERATIONS MASTER ROLE

GET READY. To transfer the holder of the Domain Naming Operations Master role holder, perform the following steps:

1. In *Server Manager*, right-click the Active Directory Domains and Trusts node and choose Connect To Domain Controller.
2. In the *Change Directory Server* dialog box, select the domain controller that you want to transfer the role to and click OK.
3. In the console tree, right-click Active Directory Domains and Trusts and choose Operations Master.
4. In the *Change Operations Master* dialog box, click Change.
5. In the confirmation message box, click Yes to confirm the change in roles. In the next message box, click OK.
6. Click Close to close the *Operations Master* dialog box.
7. Close the *Active Directory Domains and Trusts* console.

 TRANSFER THE HOLDERS OF SCHEMA MASTER OPERATIONS MASTER ROLE

GET READY. To transfer the holder of the Schema Master Operations Master role holder, perform the following steps:

1. Right-click the Start button and choose Command Prompt (Admin).
2. At the command prompt, execute the mmc command.
3. In the *MMC* console, from the *File* menu select Add/Remove Snap-in. The *Add or Remove Snap-ins* dialog box opens.
4. Select Active Directory Schema (second option) and click Add. Then click OK to close the *Add/Remove Snap-ins* dialog box.
5. Right-click Active Directory Schema and choose Change Domain Controller.
6. Select the Specify Name option and select the domain controller that you want to switch to. Click OK.
7. In the console tree, right-click Active Directory Schema and choose Operations Master.
8. In the *Change Schema Master* dialog box, click Change.
9. Click OK to close the *Change Schema Master* dialog box.
10. Close the *MMC console* and command prompt.

SEIZING THE OPERATIONS MASTERS ROLE

If a domain controller that holds an Operations Master role has an unrecoverable failure, you cannot transfer roles because the current domain controller is not online. Therefore, you need to size the role. Seizing a FSMO role is a drastic measure that should be performed only in the event of a permanent role holder failure. To seize the role of an operations master, use the ***Ntdsutil.exe*** utility. The ntdsutil.exe is a command-line tool that allows you to manage Active Directory including performing maintenance on the Active Directory database, manage and control single master operations, and remove metadata left behind by domain controllers that were removed from the network without being properly uninstalled.

 SEIZE THE ROLE OF A OPERATIONS MASTER HOLDER

GET READY. To seize the holder of the Schema Master Operations Master role holder, perform the following steps:

1. In Windows Server 2012 R2, right-click the Start button and choose Command Prompt (Admin).

2. From the command prompt, execute the ntdsutil command.

3. At the *ntdsutil* prompt, execute the roles command.

4. At *the fsmo maintenance* prompt, execute the connections command.

5. At the server connections prompt, execute the following command:

   connect to server <FQDN_of_desired_role_holder>

   such as

   connect to server server1.contoso.com

6. At the *server connections* prompt, execute the quit command.

7. At the *fsmo maintenance* prompt, type one of the following commands:

   seize schema master

   seize domain naming master

   seize RID master

   seize PDC

   seize infrastructure master

8. If an *Are you sure?* dialog box appears, click Yes to continue.

9. At the *fsmo maintenance* prompt, execute the quit command.

10. At the *ntdsutil* prompt, execute the quit command.

11. Close the command prompt.

USING WINDOWS POWERSHELL

To enable or disable a global catalog, use the Windows PowerShell `Move-AdDirectoryServerOperation MasterRole` command. For example, to seize the operations master roles, use the following command:

```
Move-ADDirectoryServerOperationMasterRole -Identity Server01
-OperationMasterRole RIDMaster,InfrastructureMaster,DomainNamingMaster-Force
```

Designing Read-Only Domain Controllers (RODCs)

Windows Server 2012 and Windows Server 2012 R2 include the ***read-only domain controller (RODC)***, which contains a full replication of the domain database. It was created to be used in places where a domain controller is needed but the physical security of the domain controller could not be guaranteed. For example, it might be placed in a remote site that is not very secure and has a slower WAN link. Because it has a slow WAN link, a local domain controller would benefit the users at that site.

CERTIFICATION READY
Design read-only domain controllers (RODCs)
Objective 5.2

An RODC does not perform any outbound replication and accepts only inbound replication connections from writable domain controllers. Because the RODC has just a read-only copy of the Active Directory database, the administrator needs to connect to a writable domain controller to make changes to Active Directory.

To deploy an RODC, you need the following:

- Ensure that the forest functional level is Windows Server 2003 or higher.

- Deploy at least one writable domain controller running Windows Server 2008 or higher.

- The RODC must run Windows Server 2008 or Windows Server 2008 R2. Also, the nearest read/write domain controller for the same domain—that is, the domain controller with the lowest link cost—must also run Windows Server 2008 or newer.

If any domain controllers run Windows Server 2003, you need to configure permissions on DNS application directory partitions to allow them to replicate to RODCs by running the **ADPrep** or **RODCPrep** command. The adprep.exe command is located on the \support\adprep folder on the Windows Server 2012 or Windows Server 2012 R2 installation disk.

When you install an RODC, you need to define a delegated administrator who has local administrative permission to the RODC, even though the account is not a member of the Domain Admin or domain built-in Administrators group.

Because RODCs need to be as secure as possible, you can configure each RODC to have its own Password Replication Policy (PRP). On writable domain controllers, Active Directory passwords are stored locally within the ntds.dit file. Because the RODC is put where security cannot be guaranteed, you can specify a particular list of user or group accounts whose password information should be stored (or cached) on a particular RODC.

For example, if you have a Site1 branch, you can configure the RODC to cache only passwords for those users that are members of the Site1 security group. You also can configure specific users or groups whose password information should not be cached on an RODC, such as administrative accounts.

To allow enterprise-wide configuration of the RODC Password Replication Policy, the following security groups are created:

- **Denied RODC Password Replication Group:** By default, members of this group are placed in the Deny list of the Password Replication Policies of all RODCs. Some members include Administrators, Server Operators, Backup Operators, Account Operators, and Denied RODC Password Replication Group.
- **Allowed RODC Password Replication Group:** By default, members of this group are placed in the Allow list of the Password Replication Policies of all RODCs. This group has no members when Windows Server 2008 and above is first installed.

 INSTALL A READ-ONLY DOMAIN CONTROLLER

GET READY. To install an RODC on Windows Server 2012 R2 with the AD DS role installed, perform the following steps:

1. In *Server Manager*, in the left pane, click AD DS. On the right pane, click More in the yellow bar.
2. In the *All Servers Task Details* window, click Promote this server to a domain controller. The *Active Directory Domain Services Configuration Wizard* starts.
3. On the *Deployment Configuration* page, leave *Add a domain controller to an existing domain* selected and then click Next.
4. On the *Domain Controllers Options* page, select Read-only domain controller (RODC) and select the correct site name.
5. Type a *Directory Service Restore Mode (DSRM)* password in the *Password* and *Confirm password* text boxes. Click Next.
6. On the *RODC Options* page, in the *Delegated administrator account* section, click Select. In the *Select User or Group* dialog box, in the *Enter the object names to select* text box, type the name of the account to be used as a delegated administrator and click OK. Click Next.
7. On the *Additional Options* page, click Next.
8. On the *Paths* page, click Next.
9. On the *Review Options* page, click Next.
10. On the *Prerequisites Check* page, click Install.
11. When the installation is complete, restart the domain controller.

To modify the Password Replication policy, after the RODC is installed, just open the Active Directory Users and Computers console, navigate to the Domain Controllers organizational unit (OU), right-click the RODC, and select *Properties*. The Password Replication policy is shown under Password Replication. To add new entries, click the *Add* button. To modify the current entries, click the *Advanced* button.

Planning Virtualizing Domain Controllers

For years, Microsoft did not recommend virtualizing domain controllers. As virtualizing technology has matured, however, Microsoft now supports of virtualized domain controllers. Nevertheless, you must plan the deployment and usage of virtualized domain controllers on a Hyper-V or other non-Microsoft–supported virtualization platform such as VMWare ESXi.

Virtualized domain controllers offer the following advantages:

- Consolidation of multiple controllers with other application servers onto fewer physical servers
- Easy-to-provide a testing environment.
- Ease of deployment
- Minimal performance degradation for a domain controller when virtualized.

Of course, certain risks are involved when using virtualized domain controllers:

- As with any restoration of a domain controller, you could cause data corruption with an improper restore process or the mishandling of .vhd and .vhdx files (such as starting or restoring an older copy or running multiple copies simultaneously).
- Because the .vhd and .vhdx files contain the content of Active Directory, which can be easily copied or hacked, you must ensure that they are secure and accessible only by trusted individuals.

Windows Server 2012 and Windows Server 2012 R2 use a new attribute called *VM-Generation-ID* to safeguard virtual domain controllers from replication issues introduced via snapshots or cloning. When a domain controller starts the virtual machine (VM), the domain controller compares the VM-Generation-ID attribute with the domain controller and the virtual host. Any mismatch assumes that the snapshot was applied or a domain controller was cloned. To protect AD DS, when the mismatch is detected, the domain controller requests a fresh RID pool and USB information.

When deploying virtualized domain controllers, you should follow these guidelines:

- To avoid reverting to a previous version and decreasing performance, do not implement differencing disk virtual hard drives.
- Do not clone an operating system installation without using the System Preparation (Sysprep) tool.
- To help prevent a potential update sequence number (USN) rollback, do not deploy additional domain controllers by using copies of a .vhd or .vhdx file that represents an already deployed domain controller.
- To help avoid potential USN rollbacks, do not use the Hyper-V Export feature to export a virtual machine that is running a domain controller. Also, do not use Hyper-V snapshots on virtual domain controllers, except in lab or testing environments.
- For virtual machines that you configure as domain controllers, disable time synchronization with the host and accept the default Windows Time service (W32time) domain-hierarchy time synchronization.

Planning Domain Controller Cloning

> Starting with Windows Server 2012, you can safely virtualize a domain controller and rapidly deploy virtual domain controllers through cloning. It allows you to quickly restore domain controllers when a failure occurs and to rapidly provision a test environment when you need to deploy and test new features or capabilities before you apply the features or capabilities to production.

CERTIFICATION READY
Design domain controller cloning
Objective 5.2

Before, if you cloned any server, that server would end up with the same domain or forest, which is unsupported with the same domain or forest. You would then have to run Sysprep, which would remove the unique security information before cloning and then promote a domain controller manually. When you clone a domain controller, you perform *safe cloning*, in which a cloned domain controller automatically runs a subset of the Sysprep process and automatically promotes the server to a domain controller.

If you plan to clone virtual domain controllers, your environment must meet the following requirements.

- Use a virtualization product that supports the VM-Generation-ID property, which is supported on Hyper-V in Windows 2012 and Windows Server 2012 R2, and on VMware vSphere 5.0 patch 4 and newer vSphere versions.
- The domain controller must run Windows Server 2012 or Windows Server 2012 R2.
- The PDC emulator must be available on a Windows Server 2012 or Windows Server 2012 R2 domain controller before beginning the domain controller cloning process.
- The forest functional level must be at least Windows Server 2003.
- The schema version must be Windows Server 2012 (version 56) or higher.
- The domain controller to be cloned must be in the Cloneable Domain Controllers group.

The four primary steps to deploy a cloned virtualized domain controller are as follows:

1. Grant the source virtualized domain controller the permission to be cloned by adding the source virtualized domain controller to the Cloneable Domain Controllers group.
2. Run `Get-ADDCCloningExcludedApplicationList` cmdlet in Windows PowerShell to determine which services and applications on the domain controller are not compatible with cloning.
3. Run `New-ADDCCloneConfigFile` to create the clone configuration file, which is stored in the C:\Windows\NTDS.
4. In Hyper-V, export and then import the virtual machine of the source domain controller.

➔ DEPLOY A CLONED VIRTUALIZED DOMAIN CONTROLLER

GET READY. To deploy a cloned virtualized domain controller, perform the following steps:

1. In *Server Manager*, click Tools > Active Directory Users and Computers. The *Active Directory Users and Computers* console opens.
3. Navigate to and click the Domain Controllers OU.
4. Right-click the source virtualized domain controller and choose Properties. The domain controller *Properties* dialog box opens.
5. On the *Member Of* tab, click Add. In the *Select Groups* dialog box, in the *Enter the object names to select* text box, type Cloneable Domain Controllers and click OK.
7. Close the *Active Directory Users and Computers* console.

8. Click the Windows PowerShell icon on the task bar. The Windows *PowerShell* command prompt opens.

9. To display the list of installed services and programs that are not compatible with cloning of the AD server on the source virtualized domain controller, run the following command from Windows PowerShell:

   Get-ADDCCloningExcludedApplicationList

10. Review the list and remove any services and applications that you believe are not safe to clone. The others need to be tested or verified from the vendor.

11. After the list is cleaned up and you still have items that you want to include in the cloning, create a CustomDCCloneAllowList.xml file by running the following command:

    Get-ADDCCloningExcludedApplicationList

    -GenerateXml

12. Run the New-ADDCCloneConfigFile cmdlet on the source virtual domain controller while specifying the configuration settings for the clone domain controller, such as the name, the IP address, and DNS resolver. For example:

    New-ADDCCloneConfigFile –Static -IPv4Address

    "192.168.3.125" -IPv4DNSResolver "192.168.3.120"

    -IPv4SubnetMask "255.255.255.0" -CloneComputerName

    "VServer2" -IPv4DefaultGateway "192.168.3.1"

    -SiteName "Site1"

    Make sure that the site exists. A DCCloneConfig.xml file is created in the C:\Windows\NTDS folder.

13. Back in *Server Manager*, click Tools > Hyper-V Manager. The *Hyper-V Manager console* opens.

14. Right-click the source virtual domain controller and choose Turn Off. If asked whether you are sure, click Turn Off.

15. In *Hyper-V Manager*, right-click the source virtual domain controller and choose Export. In the *Location* text box, specify the folder that you want to export to (such as d:\clone) and click Export. Exporting the image will take several minutes.

16. In *Hyper-V Manager*, right-click the source virtual domain controller and choose Start.

17. In *Hyper-V Manager*, click Action > Import Virtual Machine.

18. When the *Import Virtual Machine Wizard* starts, click Next.

19. On the *Locate Folder* page, specify the exported folder (such as D:\Clone\DC02) in the *Folder* text box and click Next.

20. On the *Select Virtual Machine* page, click Next.

21. On the *Choose Import Type* page, select Copy the virtual machine (create a new unique ID) and click Next.

22. On the *Choose Folders for Virtual Machine Files* page, select Store the virtual machine in a different location, and then specify the following locations:

    Virtual machine configuration folder: D:\Hyper-V\

    Snapshot store: D:\Hyper-V\

    Smart paging folder: D:\Hyper-V\

    Click Next.

23. On the *Choose Folders to Store Virtual Hard Disks* page, in the *Location* text box, type D:\Hyper-V. Click Next.

24. On the *Completing Import Wizard* page, click Finish. Importing will take several minutes.

25. When the import is complete, right-click the new server and click Start.

Planning Domain Controller Placement

To some degree, the designs you have already created for your AD DS infrastructure dictate the basic placement of domain controllers throughout your enterprise. The decisions to create additional forests, domains, and sites all must include the monetary costs and administrative considerations of additional domain controllers in the enterprise administrator's calculations.

CERTIFICATION READY
Design domain controller placement
Objective 5.2

Every forest needs domain controllers for its forest root domain, and every additional domain in a forest needs its own domain controllers. Every site you create also must have domain controllers for the domains with resources at that site. However, you still need to consider further elements of the domain controller deployment process, including the number and type of domain controllers to install at the enterprise's various locations.

HOW MANY DOMAIN CONTROLLERS?

Every domain should have at least two domain controllers for fault-tolerance purposes. Every site should have at least one—and preferably two—domain controllers for each domain with resources at that site. However, under some conditions you might want additional domain controllers.

If you have one domain controller at a remote site but that domain controller fails, users at that site must authenticate through a domain controller at another site. This could be undesirable for several reasons, including the following:

- The link to the other site might be slow or congested.
- The domain controller at the other site might be overburdened with local traffic.
- Business requirements might dictate that all users at the remote site authenticate locally.

In any of these cases, you might want to consider installing multiple domain controllers for each domain at a remote site.

DEPLOYING FOREST ROOT DOMAIN CONTROLLERS

The computer on which you create a forest becomes the first domain controller for the forest root domain. Because anyone who can physically access a forest root domain controller can conceivably damage the entire forest, whether deliberately or not, the physical security of this domain controller is critical. Most forest root domain controllers are deployed in locked server closets or data centers for that reason.

The primary responsibility of the forest root domain is to establish trust paths that enable users in one domain to access resources in other domains. Therefore, if you have a remote site with domain controllers for two domains, a user in one domain accessing the other still has to go through the forest root domain controller in the home office's data center.

Depending on the frequency your users must access other domains and the link speed between the sites, you might need to deploy additional forest root domain controllers at remote sites. If you choose to do this, security of this domain controller is paramount.

ANOTHER WAY * To prevent having to deploy additional forest root domain controllers at remote sites, you can create shortcut trusts between domains lower down in the hierarchy, at the remote site.

SKILL SUMMARY

IN THIS LESSON YOU LEARNED:

- Domain controllers are the servers that store and run the Active Directory database. Active Directory is a major component in authentication, authorization, and auditing (AAA).

- Although the global catalog is not one of the five operation masters, it provides a critical functionality for Active Directory. As a domain controller, a global catalog stores a full copy of all objects in the domain. It also has a partial copy of all objects for all other domains in the forest.

- A partial copy includes attributes (partial attribute set) that are commonly used in search and other applications. The reason that only partial copy is replicated to all domain controllers in other domains is to reduce the amount of replication traffic and to minimize the size of the Active Directory database.

- Operations masters, previously referred to as Flexible Single Master Operations (FMSO), are specialized domain controllers that perform certain tasks that can be handled only by a single domain controller in a multimaster environment.

- Windows Server 2012 and Windows Server 2012 R2 include the read-only domain controller (RODC), which contains a full replication of the domain database. It was created to be used in places where a domain controller is needed but the physical security of the domain controller could not be guaranteed.

- Starting with Windows Server 2012, you can safely virtualize a domain controller and rapidly deploy virtual domain controllers through cloning. It allows you to quickly restore domain controllers when a failure occurs and to rapidly provision a test environment when you need to deploy and test new features or capabilities before you apply the features or capabilities to production.

- Every domain should have at least two domain controllers for fault-tolerance purposes. Every site should have at least one—and preferably two—domain controllers for each domain with resources at that site.

■ Knowledge Assessment

Multiple Choice

1. Which of the following best describes a global catalog? (Choose two answers.)
   a. Has a full copy of objects in the domain.
   b. Has a partial copy of search attributes of all objects in the domain.
   c. Has a full copy of objects in the forest.
   d. Has a partial copy of search attributes of al objects in the forest.

2. Which port does search request use with the global catalog?
   a. 80
   b. 389
   c. 53
   d. 3268

3. Which operations master is the master server for passwords?
   a. naming master
   b. relative identifier (RID) master
   c. infrastructure master
   d. PDC emulator

4. Which role is used to determine the membership of universal groups?
   a. PDC emulator
   b. relative identifier master
   c. infrastructure master
   d. naming master
   e. global catalog

5. If an operations master will be down for an extended period of time, what should you do first?
   a. Transfer the role.
   b. Seize the role.
   c. Make sure that the role is fault tolerant.
   d. You do not have to do anything.

6. In which of the following situations would you not place a domain controller at a remote site?
   a. Where every domain controller is a global catalog.
   b. When you cannot guarantee a domain controller physical security.
   c. When there is too little traffic over the WAN link.
   d. When there is too much WAN bandwidth.

7. Which feature is included with Windows Server 2012 R2 that ensures that a domain controller was not started from a snapshot?
   a. VM clone checking
   b. VM Safe Mode
   c. ntdsutil.exe
   d. VM-Generation-ID

8. How do you add attributes to the partial attribute set that is replicated between global catalogs?
   a. Use Active Directory Users and Computers.
   b. Use Active Directory Sites and Services.
   c. Use Active Directory Domains and Trusts.
   d. Use the Active Directory schema.

9. What is the minimum number of domain controllers recommended for a domain?
   a. 1
   b. 2
   c. 3
   d. 4

10. How many schema masters are there for a domain?
   a. 1
   b. 2
   c. 3
   d. 4

Best Answer

Choose the letter that corresponds to the best answer. More than one answer choice can achieve the goal. Select the BEST answer.

1. You are performing maintenance on the domain controllers, which requires that some of the domain controllers be down for an extended period. Another administrator is having trouble creating a large batch of users. What is the problem?
   a. The RID master is down.
   b. The PDC emulator is down.
   c. The schema master is down.
   d. The domain naming master is down.

2. You need to place a domain controller at a site that will runs a custom kiosk. Because the site is basically a store front, the environment is not as secure as you would like. What should you do?
   a. Remove the global catalog.
   b. Install an RODC.
   c. Remove DNS server.
   d. Remove any operation masters.

3. You do not want the credentials for a service account to be replicated to RODCs. What should you do?
   a. Remove the service account from the Allowed RODC Password Replication Group.
   b. Add the service account to the Denied RODC Password Replication Group.
   c. Select the *Do not replicate to RODC* option via Active Directory Users and Computers.
   d. Add the service account to the GC group

4. How many PDC emulators does a forest have?
   a. one
   b. two
   c. one for each site
   d. one for each domain

5. What is the recommended minimum number of domain controllers recommended for a site?
   a. 1
   b. 2
   c. 3
   d. 4

Matching and Identification

1. Identify the operations master for the following:
   _____ **a)** Coordinates password changes
   _____ **b)** Tracks which objects are part of the domain
   _____ **c)** Controls the addition and removal of domains
   _____ **d)** Controls updates to the schema
   _____ **e)** Acts as the domain master browser
   _____ **f)** Synchronizes time
   _____ **g)** Assigns relative identifiers to domain controllers in the domain
   _____ **h)** Manages edits to GPOs

2. Identify which of the following are guidelines for deploying domain controllers.
   _____ Place global catalog near all application servers
   _____ Deploy one global catalog at each site
   _____ Place schema master placed in most secure domain
   _____ Place schema master in forest-root domain
   _____ Deploy one global catalog per domain
   _____ You should have a minimum of two domain controllers per domain
   _____ Place global catalog near Microsoft Exchange servers

Build a List

1. In order of first to last, specify the steps used to size the PDC emulator using Ntdsutil.

   _____ Execute `roles` command

   _____ Exceute the `seize PDC` command

   _____ Execute `ntdsutil` command

   _____ Open command prompt

   _____ Execute the `connections` command

   _____ Connect to a server by using the `connect to server` command

■ Business Case Scenarios

Scenario 19-1: Designing Domain Controllers

You are an administrator for the Contoso Corporation. You have three large sites each consisting of 500 to 1,000 users. Of these, the corporate office has the majority of application services, such as Microsoft Exchange and SQL servers. You also have 20 smaller sites consisting of 25 to 50 users each. How would you deploy the domain controllers? How would you configure them?

Scenario 19-2: Securing a Remote Site

You have a new site that your company just purchased. When you inspected the site, you realize that the previous server was stored in a closet in a commonly accessed hallway with no locks. You typically install domain controllers at each site. You also need to ensure that if the domain controller is compromised, none of the administrator or service accounts will be accessible. What should you do?

Designing and Implementing a Branch Office Infrastructure

70-413 EXAM OBJECTIVE

Objective 5.3 – Design and implement a branch office infrastructure. This objective may include but is not limited to: Design considerations including RODC, Universal Group Membership Caching (UGMC), global catalog, DNS, DHCP, and BranchCache; implement confidential attributes; delegate administration; modify filtered attributes set; configure Password Replication Policy; configure hash publication.

LESSON HEADING	EXAM OBJECTIVE
Designing a Branch Office Strategy • Using AD DS in the Branch Office • Designing a Branch Office Topology • Evaluating Full Domain Controller and Server Core Domain Controller • Designing Global Catalogs and Universal Group Membership Caching at Branch Offices	Design Universal Group Membership Caching (UGMC) for the branch office Design global catalogs for the branch office
Designing a Read-Only Domain Controller for a Branch Office • Configuring Password Replication Policy • Modifying Filtered Attributes Set and Confidential Attributes	Design RODC for the branch office Configure Password Replication Policy Implement confidential attributes Modify filtered attributes set
Choosing Branch Office Services • Designing DNS for the Branch Office • Designing DHCP for the Branch Office	Design DNS for the branch office Design DHCP for the branch office
Delegating Administration • Using the Delegation of Control Wizard • Using Administrator Role Separation	Delegate administration
Designing BranchCache • Understanding BranchCache Benefits • Understanding Content Servers • Understanding BranchCache Operating Modes • Enabling BranchCache on Content Servers • Configuring a Hosted Cache Mode Server • Configuring Hash Publications	Design BranchCache for the branch office Configure hash publication

■ Designing a Branch Office Strategy

THE BOTTOM LINE

Windows Server 2012, Windows Server 2012 R2, Windows 8, and Windows 8.1 have devoted a great deal of attention to branch office computing and the complications that distance and isolation present to IT administrators. However, before branch office administrators can take charge, enterprise administrators must create the policies that the branch offices will follow.

What constitutes a branch office? This is a question that can have various answers, even within a single enterprise. For a large organization, a branch office can be a headquarters on another continent, with hundreds or thousands of users. Smaller organizations might have branch offices with only a handful of users. Obviously, these offices have vastly different requirements, and enterprise administrators must distinguish between them in their branch office strategies.

For the purposes of this lesson, imagine an organization with branches in three sizes: a large office with 1,000 users, a medium-sized office with 100 users, and a small office with 10 users. Each office has users that must access resources hosted by the corporate headquarters, but they have varying amounts of money, equipment, and administrative expertise with which to do that. Table 20-1 lists the basic resources allotted to each branch size. You will learn about the additional resources needed by each as this lesson progresses.

Table 20-1

Basic Branch Offices Resources

Branch Office Size	Large	Medium	Small
Number of Users	1,000	100	10
Connection to HQ	44.736 Mbps (T-3)	1.544 Mbps (T-1)	512 Kbps (VPN)
IT Support	Full Staf	1 administrator	Branch manager

Long before the branch offices open, enterprise administrators at the corporate headquarters must devise strategies for the design, deployment, and ongoing maintenance of the three branch office types.

Using AD DS in the Branch Office

Lesson 19, "Designing a Domain Controller Strategy," started the discussion on how Active Directory Domain Services (AD DS) design involved remote locations such as branch offices. Creating AD DS design policies for three different sizes of branch office requires you to evaluate the physical and organizational resources available in each branch and integrate them into a companywide AD DS strategy.

The forest and domain structure is the first step in designing the AD DS strategy for the enterprise. For a large remote location, such as a 1,000-user branch office, creating a separate forest or domain might be a logical choice, However, you should not create a domain based on the number of users or based on whether you have management staff at the site. Instead, you should create an organizational unit. Of course, as discussed in Lesson 19, "Designing a Domain Controller Strategy," you should only create a separate forest if the office meets any of the standard requirements, such as a separate identity, specialized schema requirements, or the need for administrative isolation.

A medium-sized location, such as a 100-user branch office, is less likely to have a full IT staff capable of maintaining an entire separate domain. However, an office of this size will likely have one or two dedicated IT staffers to maintain the network. Therefore, a separate organizational unit (OU) is preferable. You can grant the IT staffers at the branch office the permissions needed to administer the OU without giving them complete autonomy.

A small office of 10 users or fewer typically has no dedicated IT staff at all. A branch manager or other employee might be able to perform basic tasks, such as supervising backups and creating user accounts, but even a delegated OU might be too much of a technical responsibility.

Designing a Branch Office Topology

Although you can run a branch office without any AD DS presence, doing so can cause more problems than it resolves in an enterprise that relies on AD DS for authentication and administration. As a result, you should expect to need AD DS in all your branch offices, but how you deploy AD DS depends on the office size and its business requirements.

A large branch office running its own domain must have at least two AD DS domain controllers for fault-tolerance purposes, with one or both also functioning as a Domain Name System (DNS) server. It must also have a global catalog server to provide the branch office users with the ability to search other domains in the forest.

A medium-sized office with 100 users should have at least one domain controller, to provide users with local authentication capabilities, as well as a DNS server and a global catalog server. An office of this size should be equipped with a server closet to physically secure the domain controller and other vital components.

Although it might have its own servers for local data storage, the small branch office should generally not have a domain controller, mainly because no one at the location is qualified to maintain it. Small offices also typically lack the physical security needed to protect a domain controller from unauthorized access or theft. Therefore, users must access a domain controller at another location to authenticate.

TAKE NOTE

When designing a branch office strategy, circumstances could possibly force modifications that counter general design guidelines. For example, a small branch office, despite having only a few users, might house a senior official of the company who demands a certain level of performance. The only way to achieve this performance might be to install a domain controller at the site, despite conditions that would generally rule against it.

The other AD DS–related services and elements you might consider having in a branch office include the following:

- **DNS server:** Despite the lack of a domain controller, however, a small branch office can benefit from having its own DNS server to provide local name resolution services. A DNS server does not require a dedicated computer, consumes few resources, and presents a minimum security risk when configured properly.
- **Operations masters:** Operations masters do not belong in branch offices except in cases where the office has its own domain or forest, as in the large office example. For medium and small offices that represent only part of a larger domain, the operations masters should be located in the headquarters site, where IT staffers perform most of the domain administration tasks.
- **Sites:** The large and medium-sized offices must both be represented in AD DS by their own site objects because they are connected to the headquarters office by relatively slow wide area network (WAN) links. The links all run at different speeds, so the faster site links must have lower costs that reflect these differences.

In addition to the basic resources, Table 20-2 lists the additional topology specifications for the three branch office sizes considered in this lesson.

Table 20-2

Branch Office Topology Specifications

BRANCH OFFICE SIZE	LARGE	MEDIUM	SMALL
Number of Users	1,000	100	10
Connection to HQ	44.736 Mbps (T-3)	1.544 Mbps (T-1)	512 Kbps (VPN)
IT Support	Full Staf	1 administrator	Branch manager
Domain controllers	2	1	0
DNS servers	2	1	1
Global Catalog server	1	1	0
Separate site object	Yes	Yes	No

Evaluating Full Domain Controller and Server Core Domain Controller

Of all the services and components listed in the preceding section, the decision of whether to include a domain controller in a branch office is the most critical and provides the most options.

In addition to the standard, full domain controller, Windows Server 2012 and Windows Server 2012 R2 include the Server Core installation.

USING A FULL DOMAIN CONTROLLER

A full domain controller (or a Server With A GUI) is the result of performing a full installation of Windows Server 2012 or Windows Server 2012 R2 and promoting the server to a domain controller with the default options. It provides all the standard domain controller capabilities. The domain controller replicates the AD DS bidirectionally with the other domain controllers in the domain and includes all the standard AD DS management tools.

A full domain controller also provides the largest attack surface, which is one reason you might hesitate to deploy it in a branch office environment. An attacker might be able to access the AD DS database and modify its contents inappropriately. The domain controller then replicates the content to the other domain controllers, potentially contaminating the entire enterprise. Full domain controllers also have the potential for accidental misuse that can be no less damaging than a deliberate attack.

For these reasons, you should deploy full domain controllers in a branch office only when appropriate personnel are available to maintain them and when the facility has a sufficiently secure location for the servers to prevent unauthorized access.

USING A SERVER CORE DOMAIN CONTROLLER

Server Core is an installation option included with all versions of Windows Server 2012 and Windows Server 2012 R2 that reduces the operating system's footprint by eliminating many of its applications and services, along with the Windows Explorer interface and most of the graphical tools.

To install Server Core, you must choose it from the *Select the operating system you want to install* page of the Install Windows wizard. After you install Server Core, you cannot change the operating system to a full installation, nor can you convert an existing full installation to Server Core. The result of the Server Core installation is a server that starts at the command prompt but is much more secure than a full installation.

Because a Server Core installation runs only a fraction of the operating system code, an attacker has fewer avenues of attack and fewer applications and services through which he might try to obtain elevated privileges. This limited attack surface can be a valuable feature in a branch office that does not have the same physical security as a large headquarters.

Although Server Core does not include all the roles found in a full installation, it does include AD DS and therefore can function as a domain controller. A Server Core domain controller is inherently more secure than one on a fully installed system, but with a trade-off. Server Core lacks most of the graphical administration tools found in a full installation, forcing you to do more work from the command prompt. A Server Core domain controller can therefore require a greater level of administrative expertise than might be found in some branch offices.

Graphical administration is possible by using Microsoft Management Console (MMC) snap-ins from a remote system. However, you can still use command-line tools supplied with Windows Server 20012 R2 or the Windows PowerShell interface.

Designing Global Catalogs and Universal Group Membership Caching at Branch Offices

Lesson 19, "Designing a Domain Controller Strategy," has already covered *global catalogs* thoroughly. When a user logs on, the logon process queries a global catalog to see what universal groups the user is a member of. Without this information, you cannot log on. Therefore, you can install a global catalog at each branch cache, or you can enable *universal group membership caching*.

One way to avoid creating a global catalog server at a particular site is to enable universal group membership caching instead. Universal group membership caching, introduced in Windows Server 2003, enables a domain controller to store users' group memberships in a cache, which it refreshes from a global catalog server every eight hours.

 ENABLE UNIVERSAL GROUP MEMBERSHIP CACHING

GET READY. To enable universal group membership caching, log on as an administrator to a computer running Windows 8 Enterprise edition and then perform the following steps:

1. In *Server Manager* or in *Administrative Tools*, open Active Directory Sites and Services.
2. In the console tree, expand Sites, and then click the site in which you want to enable universal group membership caching.
3. In the details pane, right-click the NTDS Site Settings object and choose Properties.
4. In the *NTDS Site Settings Properties* dialog box (see Figure 20-1), under *Universal Group Membership Caching*, select Enable Universal Group Membership Caching.

Figure 20-1

Configuring site settings

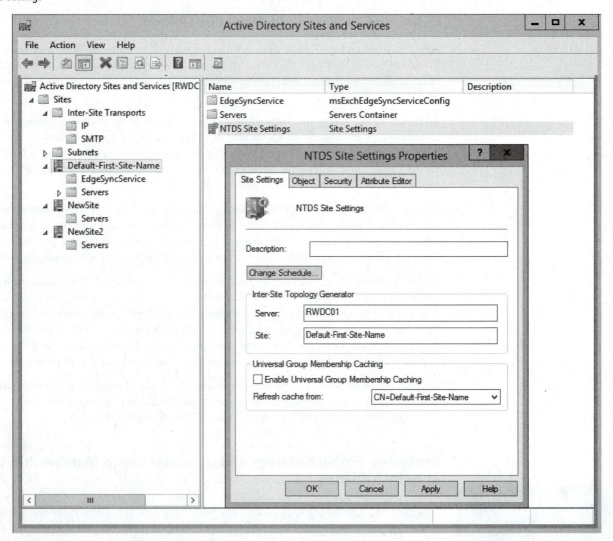

5. From the *Refresh cache from* list, select the site that you want the domain controller to contact when the universal group membership cache must be updated, and then click OK.

■ Designing a Read-Only Domain Controller for a Branch Office

↓
THE BOTTOM LINE

Placing a *read-only domain controller (RODC)* in a branch office increases security by limiting the AD DS replication to incoming traffic only. As a result, the domain controller remains updated with changes administrators make to the read/write replicas on the network, as well as to the schema, configuration partitions, and global catalog, but no outgoing replication traffic leaves the RODC. If attackers manage to gain access to the domain controller—whether remotely or physically—they can damage the local copy of the AD DS database, but those damages cannot contaminate the rest of the domain. Of all the services and components listed in the preceding section, the decision of whether to include a domain controller in a branch office is the most critical and provides the most options.

TAKE NOTE*

Because RODCs cannot write to the AD DS database, they cannot function in any of the operations master roles, nor can they function as bridgehead servers.

CERTIFICATION READY
Designing RODC for the branch office
Objective 5.2

One primary reason for installing an RODC in a branch office is because no administrators at the site have the training to manage the AD DS database. However, if no one in the branch office has administrative credentials for the domain, how do you promote a server to a domain controller, a task that requires Domain Admins privileges?

To address this problem, Windows Server 2012 and Windows Server 2012 R2 include the ability to stage an RODC installation. Staging an installation enables a domain administrator to create the necessary AD DS account for the RODC before the server is actually deployed. (RODC installation was discussed in Lesson 19.)

Configuring Password Replication Policy

As another measure of security, RODCs do not store user credentials like read/write domain controller do. RODCs are designed for locations (such as branch offices) with reduced physical security that are at higher risk for theft or unauthorized access. By not caching credentials, an RODC reduces the information compromised if someone steals the computer.

CERTIFICATION READY
Configure Password Replication Policy
Objective 5.2

Because it does not cache credentials by default, an RODC requires access to a read/write domain controller to authenticate users. The RODC forwards all authentication requests to the read/write domain controller, which in the case of a branch office installation generates WAN traffic and requires a functioning WAN connection for authentication to take place.

However, you can modify the default *Password Replication Policy* so that the RODC caches password for selected users. You can therefore cache passwords for the branch office users on the RODC, eliminating the need to forward authentication requests for those users while still protecting the passwords for the other user accounts in the AD DS database from theft.

To modify the Password Replication Policy, you must open the Properties dialog box for the server in the Active Directory Users and Computers console and select the Password Replication Policy tab, as shown in Figure 20-2.

Figure 20-2

The Password Replication
Policy tab of an RODC's
Properties dialog box

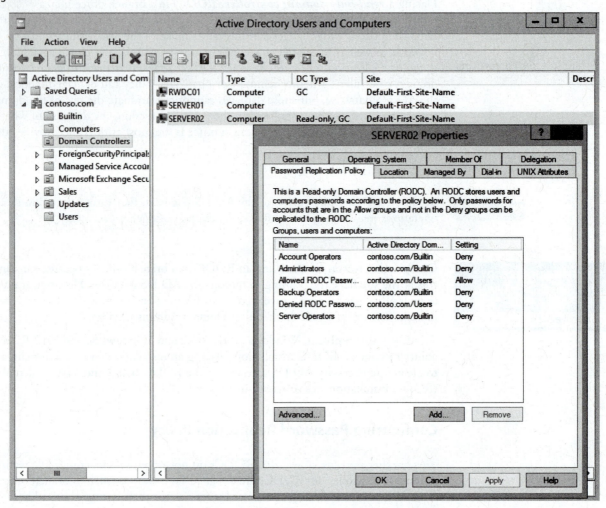

RODCs can function as global catalog servers and as read-only DNS servers, providing the
same protection to your DNS information as to the AD DS database. Finally, the RODC
option is compatible with the Server Core installation option, providing the securest possible
combination for a branch office domain controller.

 CONFIGURE PASSWORD REPLICATION POLICIES ON AN RODC

GET READY. To configure the Password Replication Policy, perform the following steps:

1. On RWDC01, open the Active Directory Users and Computers tool.
2. Expand the domain and click the Domain Controllers OU.
3. Double-click the first read-only server.
4. In the *Properties* dialog box, on the *Password Replication Policy* tab, double-click
   Allowed RODC Password Replication Group.
5. In the *Allowed RODC Password Replication Group Properties* dialog box, on the *Members*
   tab, click Add.

6. In the *Select Users, Contacts Computers, Service Accounts* dialog box , click Object Types. Click to select Computers, and click OK.

7. In the text box, type user01; computer01. Click OK.

8. To close the *Allowed RODC Password Replication Group* dialog box, click OK.

9. In the server *Properties* dialog box, click the Advanced button.

10. In the *Advanced Password Replication Policy* dialog box, click the Prepopulate Passwords button.

11. In the *Select Users or Computers account* dialog box, type user01;computer01 and click OK.

12. When asked if you want to send the current passwords for these accounts to this read-only domain controller now, click Yes.

13. After the passwords are prepopulated, click OK.

14. Close the *Advanced Password Replication* dialog box and the Properties dialog box.

Modifying Filtered Attributes Set and Confidential Attributes

Because the RODC is often placed in a lower security environment, you might not want to replicate certain attributes to it. The ***Filtered Attribute Set (FAS)*** is the set of attributes that are considered sensitive and are not replicated to an RODC. You also can limit users from seeing certain attributes by marking them as confidential.

CERTIFICATION READY
Implement confidential attributes
Objective 5.2

The default FAS contains the following:

- ms-PKI-DPAPIMasterKeys
- ms-PKI-AccountCredentials
- ms-PKI-RoamingTimeStamp
- ms-FVE-KeyPackage
- ms-FVE-RecoveryPassword
- ms-TPM-OwnerInformation

CERTIFICATION READY
Modify filtered attributes set
Objective 5.2

To add an attribute to an RODC FAS, you must first determine the current searchFlags value of the attribute that you want to add, and then set the searchflags 10th bit to 0×200.

To take the security of these attributes one step further, you can mark the attribute as confidential, which removes the ability for the Authenticated Users group, which includes RODCs, to see the attributes. To mark the attribute as confidential, set the 7th bit to 0×080. If you want to add an attribute to the RODC and mark the attribute as confidential, set the searchFlags value to 0×280 (decimal equivalent 640).

 DETERMINE AND MODIFY THE FILTERED ATTRIBUTE SET SEARCHFLAGS

GET READY. To determine and modify the filtered attribute set searchflags for the ms-Exchn-Admins attribute called Contoso-App-Password, perform the following steps:

1. Click the Start button, and then right-click Command Prompt and choose Run as administrator.

2. Type the following command and press Enter:

    ldifde –d CN=ms-Exch-Admins,CN=Schema,CN=Configuration,DC=contoso, DC=com –f en_ldif –l searchflags

3. Verify that the output of the file named en_ldif appears as follows:

```
dn: CN=ms-Exch-Admins,CN=Schema,CN=Configuration,
DC=<domain>
changetype: add
searchFlags: 0
```

where *<domain>* is the distinguished name of your forest root domain.

4. Copy the contents of the output file to a new file named en-fas.ldif.

5. Modify the new file so that it appears as follows, and then save it:

```
dn: CN=ms-Exch-Admins,CN=Schema, CN=Configuration,
DC=contoso,DC=com
changetype: modify
replace: searchFlags
searchFlags: 640
-
```

6. At the command prompt, to import the modified en-fas.ldif file, type the following command and press Enter:

```
ldifde -i -f en-fas.ldif
```

7. To verify that the attribute is added to the RODC FAS, click the Start button, click Administrative Tools, and then click ADSI Edit.

8. Right-click ADSI Edit and choose Connect to.

9. Click Select a well known Naming Context, click Schema, and then click OK.

10. In the console tree, double-click Schema, and then click the CN=Schema,CN=Configuration,DC=Contoso,DC=com container.

11. In the details pane, right-click CN=ms-Exch-Admins and choose Properties.

12. In the list of attributes, verify that the *Confidential* and *RODC_Filtered* flags are set, as shown in Figure 20-3.

Figure 20-3

Verifying the searchFlags

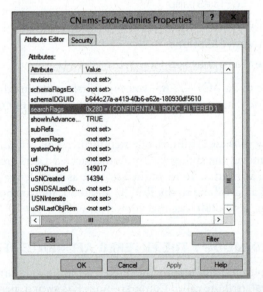

■ Choosing Branch Office Services

THE BOTTOM LINE

As noted earlier in this lesson, branch offices have fewer users than a main office or headquarters, but those users still have needs that administrators must meet apart from Active Directory Domain Services.

In addition to client workstations, and depending on the size of the office, you might want to deploy various other infrastructure and application servers at a branch office. Business and security requirements can compel enterprise administrators to equip a branch office with all the services found in a main office, but in most cases a branch office provides users with a subset of the services they need locally.

Some of the services you might find at a branch office are as follows:

- **DNS:** All offices can benefit from a local DNS server so that DNS queries do not have to be done over a WAN link. If the branch server is also a domain controller, making it a DNS server would make perfect sense because Active Directory information is already being replicated.

- **DHCP server:** All but the smallest branch offices can benefit from Dynamic Host Configuration Protocol (DHCP) servers, to prevent IT staff from having to manually configure workstation TCP/IP settings. DHCP is a service that consumes relatively few resources and is simple to set up, so virtually any branch office with a server can support it.

- **Routing and Remote Access Services (RRAS):** RRAS can provide a branch office with various services, including remote dial-up and virtual private network (VPN) access, DHCP relay, and network address translation (NAT). Generally speaking, only a large branch office would benefit from remote access, because the users could just as easily connect to remote access servers at the headquarters. Having a domain controller at the site also is recommended, to provide local authentication. DHCP relay enables clients to access DHCP servers on other networks, which could conceivably enable branch office workstations to obtain TCP/IP settings from DHCP servers at another site. NAT is built into most of the routers that branch offices use to access the Internet, but an extremely small branch could avoid even that expense by sharing a server's Internet connection using NAT.

- **Windows Server Update Services (WSUS):** Computers in branch offices require the same maintenance as those in main offices or headquarters and extending companywide software update policies to branch offices over WSUS servers is relatively simple. To eliminate the need for WSUS administration at the branch office sites, you can configure WSUS servers to obtain updates from the organization's other WSUS servers at the main office.

- **Distributed File System (DFS) replication:** DFS replication can automatically maintain copies of key files at branch offices, providing remote users with continuous access to essential data. When planning for DFS and similar services at branch offices, enterprise administrators must consider the amount of WAN bandwidth they might consume.

- **Microsoft Cluster Services:** When business requirements call for network applications to be highly available, administrators can deploy cluster nodes in branch offices to provide users with uninterrupted local access to applications, even if the WAN connection should fail.

- **File servers:** Whenever possible, enterprise administrators should implement main-office policies in branch offices as well. If main office users store their data files on servers, branch office users should as well. Even small branches can benefit from a server for local file storage, without the need for a large expenditure or frequent maintenance.

As branch offices get smaller, requirements often diminish, as do budgets, so users are more likely to access network resources from servers at another location using WAN connections. This increases WAN traffic and decreases performance, costs that might eventually be offset by purchasing additional equipment for the branch office.

CERTIFICATION READY
Design DNS for the
branch office
Objective 5.2

Designing DNS for the Branch Office

As you already know, DNS servers are the primary name resolution technology used on networks. As mentioned earlier, if you have a domain controller installed at a branch site, you should install DNS. Servers with read-only domain controllers can still improve client performance by having a local DNS server and can provide availability when the WAN link to a remote DNS server is not available. Installing the DNS server when you install AD DS is best practice.

If you want to have dynamic updates for DNS clients in branch offices that have an RODC, you should have at least one writable Windows Server 2012 or Windows Server 2012 R2 DNS server that hosts the corresponding DNS zone for which client computers in the branch office are attempting to make DNS updates. Of course, the writeable DNS server must register name server (NS) resource records for that zone.

If you have an RODC, the updates are replicated to it quickly. If the writable domain controller is not local but is at a remote site, the RODC will not get the updates until the next scheduled replication cycle. As a result, client computers that use the RODC DNS server for name resolution will be delayed.

Designing DHCP for the Branch Office

DHCP is an essential service that allows clients and some servers to communicate on the network. As clients are turned on, or when a client renews a lease, the DHCP server must be available to assign or renew the lease. So you need to take steps to ensure that DHCP services are available.

CERTIFICATION READY
Design DHCP for the
branch office
Objective 5.2

To make DHCP highly available, you can use split scopes or DHCP failover. In either case, you install a DHCP server at the branch office. Because branch office sites tend to be small, the DHCP server can be installed on the same server as the domain controller. In addition to the local server running DHCP, you will have a central DHCP server. To forward DHCP requests from the branch site to the central DHCP server, you will have an IP helper or DHCP relay agent.

A client requesting a DHCP address will send a broadcast. Because the local server is nearby, it will respond first by offering an IP lease, and the client will finish negotiating with the local server. If the local DHCP server is not available, the centralized server will receive the DHCP requests and lease the address to the client.

USING THE 80/20 SPLIT SCOPES

For years, if you wanted high availability, you would use a split-scope configuration, also known as the 80/20 configuration. Split-scope configuration, uses two DHCP servers, with the same scopes and options. However, the scopes have complementary exclusion ranges so that the addresses that they lease to clients do not overlap. You do not want the two servers to hand out the same address to different clients.

This is known as the 80/20 configuration because the primary server is assigned 80 percent of the available addresses, whereas the secondary server is assigned 20 percent of the available addresses. The secondary server is configured to respond after a delay, giving the primary server the first opportunity to hand out addresses. Because the local server responds first, it leases the address to the clients. If the primary server is not available, the secondary server will respond and lease an address. To simplify the configuring of split-scopes, Windows Server 2012 and Windows Server 2012 R2 includes a Split-Configuration Wizard.

USING DCHP FAILOVER

In the past, DHCP failover was not possible because each DHCP server had its own database. So when a lease was granted to a client, the other DHCP server would not be aware of the other lease. If you assign the same pool of addresses, you would have the same address assigned to two different hosts, causing an IP address conflict. You can use a failover cluster, which requires some manual configuration and monitoring.

With Windows Server 2012 and Windows Server 2012 R2, DHCP can replicate lease information between two DHCP servers for IPv4 scopes and subnets. If one DHCP server fails or becomes overloaded, the other server services the clients for the entire subnet.

DHCP failover establishes a failover relationship between the two DHCP servers. Each relationship has a unique name, which is exchanged during configuration. A single DHCP server can have multiple failover relationships with other DHCP servers as long as each relationship has a unique name.

DHCP failover is time sensitive. The time between partners must be no greater than one minute. If the time is greater, the failover process will halt with a critical error.

■ Delegating Administration

THE BOTTOM LINE

Using security precautions such as Server Core and RODCs in your branch offices can help protect your domains from attack, but equally important to their safety are the privileges you grant to the administrators at the branch office sites.

CERTIFICATION READY
Delegate administration
Objective 5.2

For medium-size or large-sized branch offices with dedicated IT personnel, you can assume that these people have the training and the experience to use administrative credentials responsibly. However, in most cases you will want to restrict their access to the AD DS objects they are responsible for managing.

In smaller branch offices that rely on non-technical people to perform basic administrative tasks, the problem can be even more acute. You might want to grant these people little or no access to the AD DS database, but they might still be responsible for maintaining the servers in the office, including those functioning as domain controllers.

Using the Delegation of Control Wizard

One main reason for dedicating an entire organizational unit to a branch office is so that you can grant the branch office administrators access to the AD DS objects they are responsible for managing without granting them access to anything else. The ***Delegation of Control Wizard*** enables you to select security principals—users or groups—and grant them access to the contents of an OU in various ways.

The Tasks to Delegate page (see Figure 20-4) provides the security principals with the ability to perform tasks common to branch office administrators, such as creating and managing user accounts, groups, and passwords.

Figure 20-4

The Tasks to Delegate page
of the Delegation of Control
Wizard

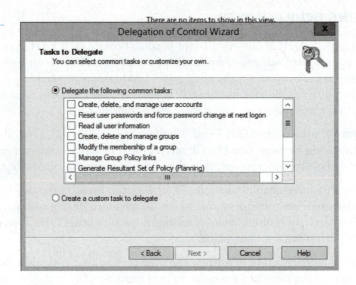

On the Active Directory Object Type page (see Figure 20-5), you can create customized tasks
for selected object types by assigning them specific Active Directory permissions.

Figure 20-5

The Active Directory Object
Type page of the Delegation of
Control Wizard

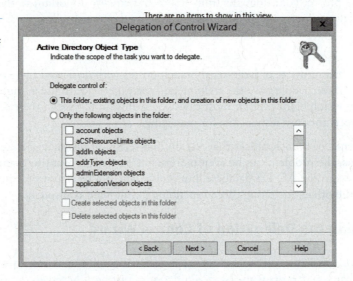

The Permissions page in Figure 20-6 enables you to select permissions for the entire object or
for specific object properties. This provides enterprise administrators with a highly granular
degree of access control.

Figure 20-6

The Permissions page of the Delegation of Control Wizard

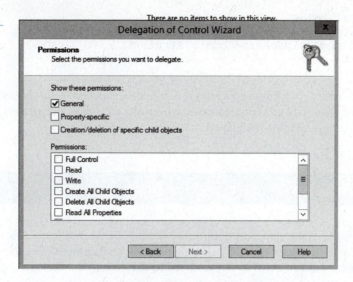

Using Administrator Role Separation

In smaller branch offices with no dedicated IT staff, you might want to grant local users or managers a certain amount of administrative access to an RODC without giving them any privileges in the AD DS domain. This is possible using a feature called *Administrative Role Separation*, which enables you to designate a local administrator for an RODC without granting any domain permissions.

RODC local administrators can log on to the server and perform system maintenance tasks that require administrative access, such as installing software and device drivers, but they cannot perform domain administration tasks, nor can they log on to other domain controllers.

TAKE NOTE

Whereas RODC local administrators do not have permissions to access the domain directly, they do have access to the RODC drives on which a replica of the AD DS database is stored. Access to the drives could therefore enable an individual with these permissions to access the information in the AD DS database. For this reason, administrators to whom you grant these permissions must still be reliable individuals and must take steps to protect their credentials from being shared or stolen.

When you use the Active Directory Domain Services Installation Wizard to promote a computer running Windows Server 2012 or Windows Server 2012 R2 to an RODC, you create the first local administrator on the Delegation of RODC Installation and Administration page. As with all privilege assignments, the best practice is to assign the privilege to a group instead of an individual user, and then add users to the group as needed.

The individuals who receive this privilege can attach the RODC server to the account that the wizard will create in AD DS, even though they lack the Domain Admins or Enterprise Admins rights and permissions that this task would otherwise require. These individuals can also remove the AD DS role from the server.

After the RODC is deployed, you can create additional local administrators by using the Dsmgmt.exe program from the server's command prompt. *Dsmgmt.exe* is an interactive command-line program that administrators can use to manage AD DS partitions and their behavior. The sequence of commands to designate local administrators is as follows:

```
local roles
list roles
add domain\username administrators
quit
quit
```

A successful procedure generates the *Successfully updated local role* message. Issuing the Show role administrators command from the *local roles:* prompt displays a list of the users and groups that are designated as local administrators.

■ Designing Branchcache

THE BOTTOM LINE

BranchCache is designed to optimize the link between branch offices and main offices by caching information from content servers on local computers within the branch. This reduces traffic on the WAN links, reduces response time for opening files, and improves the experience for users connecting over slow links.

CERTIFICATION READY
Designing BranchCache
for the branch office
Objective 5.2

BranchCache is designed to improve the overall experience for companies that have employees working in branch offices. In the past, most companies would set up a dedicated WAN link or a virtual private network (VPN) to provide access to resources located at their main office. In either case, when large files were downloaded by one employee or when multiple employees needed access to resources at the main office concurrently, the available bandwidth would be consumed quickly.

Understanding BranchCache Benefits

BranchCache provides a better approach to managing and optimizing the WAN link. By copying data from content servers and caching it on a server physically located in the branch office, users can access their files over the much faster local area network (LAN) connection. If you do not have a server, you can also configure newer Windows clients to support caching.

BranchCache provides the following additional benefits:
- All data stored in the cache is encrypted.
- By using metadata, you reduce the amount of data traffic traversing the WAN link.
- Users always have access to the current version of the data.

Understanding Content Servers

Content obtained from a *BranchCache-enabled server*, also called a *content server*, can be cached on the client systems at the branch office or on BranchCache servers at the branch office. Future requests for the same content can be delivered from the client system or the BranchCache server without having to cross the slower WAN link.

The following represent the types of BranchCache-enabled servers (content servers) that can be configured. You must deploy at least one or more of these types of servers at your main office:

- **Web servers:** Windows Server 2008 R2, Windows Server 2012, or Windows Server 2012 R2 running Internet Information Services (IIS) with BranchCache enabled. These servers use the Hypertext Transfer Protocol (HTTP) and Hypertext Transfer Protocol Secure (HTTPS) protocols.
- **Application (BITS) servers:** Windows Server 2012 or Windows Server 2012 R2 running the Background Intelligent Transfer Service (BITS) with BranchCache enabled.
- **File servers:** Windows Server 2008 R2, Windows Server 2012, or Windows Server 2012 R2 running the File Service server role and the BranchCache for Network Files role service. These servers use the Server Message Block (SMB) protocol to send content.

Understanding BranchCache Operating Modes

BranchCache has two operating modes: hosted-cache mode and distributed-cache mode. You typically use hosted-cache mode when you have more than 50 systems at the branch office. If you have fewer than 50, distributed-cache mode might be a more viable option.

With *hosted-cache mode* (see Figure 20-7), you deploy a computer running Windows Server 2012 R2 at the branch office. The clients are configured with the server name and can retrieve content from it. If the content is not available in the cache on the local server, the client traverses the WAN link, downloads the data, and makes it available to the hosted cache server for other clients to use. By using the fully qualified domain name (FQDN), the clients can use DNS and thus communicate with the server across subnets.

Figure 20-7

An example of hosted-cache
mode

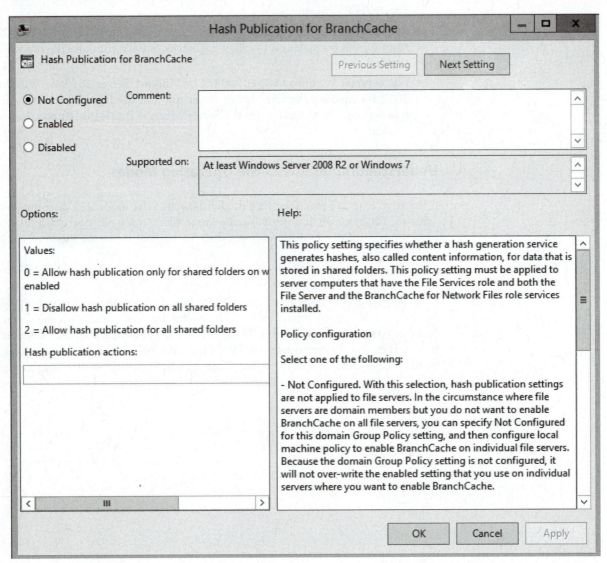

When a Windows 8 or Windows 8.1 client connects to a main office file server and requests
a file, the server first authenticates and authorizes the client. If successful, the server returns
content metadata (identifiers) to the Windows 8.1 client, which then uses the hash information to search for the file on the hosted-cache server. If this is the first time the file has ever
been requested, the Windows 8.1 client contacts the main office file server and retrieves the
file. The Windows 8.1 client then contacts the hosted-cache server located at its branch office
and offers the content to the server. The hosted-cache server then retrieves the content and
caches it. When another Windows 8.1 client at the branch office requests the same file from
the main office file server, the server authenticates and authorizes the client. After the process
is complete, the file server returns metadata, and the Windows 8.1 client obtains the information from the hosted-cache server at its local branch office.

With ***distributed-cache mode*** (see Figure 20-8), Windows 8.1 client computers request data
from the main office and then cache it locally themselves. This content is then made available
to other clients on the same branch office network.

TAKE NOTE*

Windows Server
2012 R2 can support
Windows 7 clients, but
it must have a certifi-
cate compatible with
Transport Layer Security
(TLS). To realize the
best performance and
use the new features
in BranchCache,
use Windows 8 and
Windows 8.1 clients.

Figure 20-8

An example of
distributed-cache mode

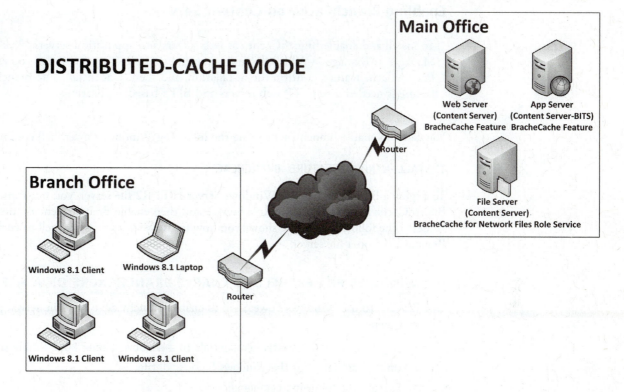

When the first Windows 8.1 client connects and downloads a specific set of files from the main office file server, it becomes the source for that content at the local branch office. When another Windows 8.1 client connects to the main office file server to download the same file, it is authenticated and authorized. The content metadata is then sent from the file server to this client. The Windows 8.1 client uses a special multicast packet to send a request for the segment hashes on the local network to determine whether another computer on the same local network has the data cached. Because the first Windows 8.1 client that connected and downloaded the file already has the content, the second Windows 8.1 client retrieves it directly from that computer.

Distributed-cache mode allows you to take advantage of BranchCache with minimal hardware requirements at the branch office. Although this mode works well in small offices with 50 or fewer computers without a server, it can produce situations in which content has to be retrieved from the main office because the computer that has the data is not currently available on the local network.

You can use a combination of these modes across your branch offices. For example, you can have one branch office that uses distributed-cache mode and another that uses the hosted-cache mode.

In both modes, the client traverses the slower WAN link to communicate with the BranchCache-enabled server located in the main office. After the client is authenticated, content metadata is sent instead of the actual data files. Content metadata is much smaller in size and reduces bandwidth requirements. It also ensures that the clients receive hashes for the most current content. The content itself is broken into blocks (block hashes), each receiving its own hash. The blocks are organized into collections called segments (segment hashes). The content metadata includes both the block and segment hash information. It is the content metadata that the client uses to search for the file in both the hosted-cache and distributed-cache modes.

Enabling BranchCache on Content Servers

To install and enable BranchCache for web servers and application servers, click Server Manager > Manage > Add Roles and Features. After selecting the server, you enable the BranchCache feature, confirm the installation, and then click Install. The BranchCache feature is needed for HTTP web servers and BITS-based applications.

You can also enable BranchCache using the following Windows PowerShell command:

INSTALL-WINDOWSFEATURE BRANCHCACHE

To deploy a BranchCache on a Windows Server 2012 R2 file server, you must install the BranchCache for Network Files Role Service and then enable BranchCache on the Shared Folders. The following exercise shows you how to use Windows PowerShell to enable BranchCache on a file server.

USE WINDOWS POWERSHELL TO ENABLE BRANCHCACHE ON A FILE SERVER

GET READY. To use Windows PowerShell to enable BranchCache on a file server, perform the following steps:

1. Log on with administrative credentials to a Windows Server 2012 R2 file server.
2. On the taskbar, click the Windows Powershell tile.
3. Execute the following command:

   Install-WindowsFeature FS-BranchCache – IncludeManagementTools

   After the install is complete, continue to Step 4. Do not exit Windows PowerShell.
4. Execute the following command:

   Install-WindowsFeature FS-Data-Deduplication-IncludeManagementTools
5. Close the Windows PowerShell window.

After completing the installation of the BranchCache for Network Files Feature, you must create and share a folder.

CREATE AND SHARE A FOLDER

GET READY. To create and share a folder, perform the following steps:

1. On the task bar, click the Server Manager icon to open the *Server Manager* console.
2. Click File and Storage Services > Shares.
3. Click Tasks > New Share.
4. When the New Share Wizard opens, click SMB Share-Quick and then click Next.
5. Select the volume that will be used to store your share and then click Next.
6. Type a share name (such as BranchCacheShare) and click Next.
7. On the *Other Settings* page (see Figure 20-9), select Enable BranchCache on the file share and then click Next.

Figure 20-9

Enabling BranchCache on the
file share

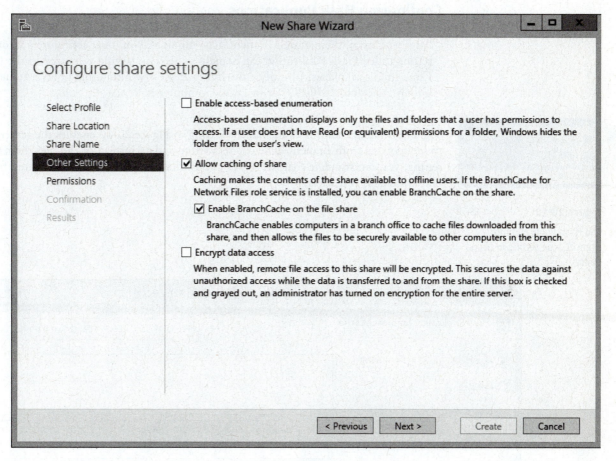

8. On the *Permissions* page, accept the default permissions for the share and then click Next.
9. Review your settings and click Create.
10. Click Close after the share is created.
11. Close Server Manager.

Configuring a Hosted Cache Mode Server

To use hosted cache mode on your branch office network, you must have a server running Windows Server 2008 R2 or higher with the BranchCache feature installed. You must also configure the Turn on BranchCache and Set BranchCache Hosted Cache mode Group Policy settings.

The hosted cache mode server must also have a digital certificate issued by a certification authority (CA) that the BranchCache clients trust. You can install an internal CA on the network and use it to issue the certificate or obtain a certificate from a commercial, third-party CA.

After you obtain the certificate, you must use the Certificates snap-in on the hosted cache server to import it. Finally, you must link the certificate to the BranchCache service by opening an elevated command prompt and typing the following command, replacing the thumbprint variable with the thumbprint value from the certificate you imported.

```
netsh http add sslcert ipport=0.0.0.0:443 certhash=thumbprint
appid={d673f5ee-a714-454d-8de2-492e4c1bd8f8}
```

Configuring Hash Publications

After you install the required BranchCache modules, you must configure a Group Policy setting called Hash Publication for BranchCache. This setting is located in the Computer Configuration\Policies\Administrative Templates\Network\Lanman Server node of a Group Policy object (GPO) or in Local Computer Policy.

CERTIFICATION READY
Configure hash publication
Objective 5.2

The Hash Publication for BranchCache setting in Figure 20-10 enables the server to respond to file requests from BranchCache clients with metadata instead of the files themselves. In this setting, you can stipulate that the server publish hash metadata for all its shared files or for only the shares you select.

Figure 20-10

The Hash Publication for BranchCache setting in Group Policy

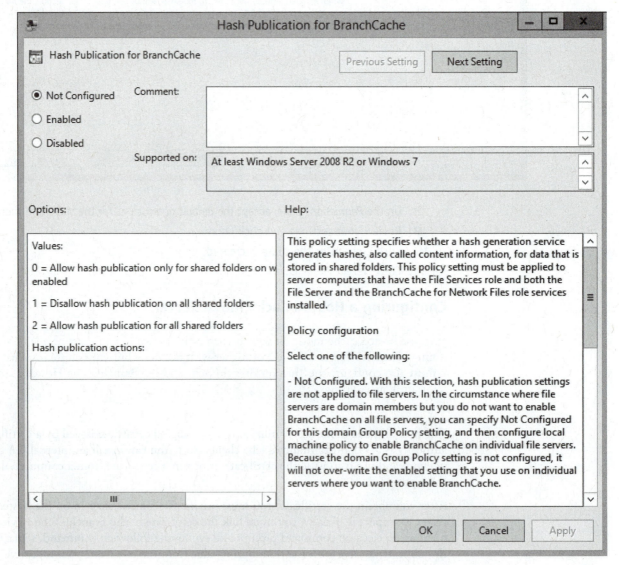

Configuring BranchCache Clients

BranchCache clients must be computers running Windows 7 (Enterprise or Ultimate); Windows 8 or Windows 8.1 (Enterprise); or Windows Server 2008 R2 or higher. BranchCache is enabled by default in Windows 7, Windows 8, and Windows 8.1. To use a computer running Windows Server 2008 R2, Windows Server 2012, or Windows Server 2012 R2 as a BranchCache client, you must install the BranchCache feature.

To configure BranchCache clients, you must configure the appropriate Group Policy settings, found in the Computer Configuration\Policies\Administrative Templates\Network\BranchCache node of a GPO or in Local Computer Policy. The BranchCache Group Policy settings are as follows:

- **Turn on BranchCache** enables BranchCache on the client computer. Enabling this setting along with either *Set BranchCache Distributed Cache mode* or *Set BranchCache Hosted Cache mode* configures the client to use one of those operational modes. Enabling this setting without either one of the mode settings configures the client to cache server data on its local drive only, without accessing caches on other computers.

- **Set BranchCache Distributed Cache mode,** when enabled with the *Turn on BranchCache* setting, configures the client to function in distributed cache mode.

- **Set BranchCache Hosted Cache mode,** when enabled with the *Turn on BranchCache* setting, configures the client to function in hosted cache mode. In the *Enter the location of the hosted cache* field, you must specify the address of the computer that will function as the hosted cache server on the branch office network.

- **Configure BranchCache for network files,** when enabled, controls the round-trip network latency value that BranchCache uses to differentiate local from remote servers. The default setting is 80 ms. When you decrease the value, the client caches more files; increasing the value causes it to cache fewer files.

- **Set percentage of disk space used for client computer cache,** when enabled, specifies the maximum amount of total disk space that the computer should devote to the BranchCache cache. The default value is 5 percent.

SKILL SUMMARY

IN THIS LESSON YOU LEARNED:

- Windows Server 2012, Windows Server 2012 R2, Windows 8, and Windows 8.1 have devoted a great deal of attention to branch office computing and the complications that distance and isolation present to IT administrators. However, before branch office administrators can take charge, enterprise administrators must create the policies that the branch offices will follow

- A large branch office running its own domain must have at least two AD DS domain controllers for fault-tolerance purposes, with one or both also functioning as a Domain Name System (DNS) server. It must also have a global catalog server to provide the branch office users with the ability to search other domains in the forest.

- When a user logs on, the logon process queries a global catalog to see what universal groups the user is a member of. Without this information, you cannot log on. Therefore, you can install a global catalog at each branch cache, or you can enable universal group membership caching.

- Placing a read-only domain controller (RODC) in a branch office increases security by limiting the AD DS replication to incoming traffic only. As a result, the domain controller remains updated with changes administrators make to the read/write replicas on the network, as well as to the schema, configuration partitions, and global catalog, but no outgoing replication traffic leaves the RODC.

- Modifying the default Password Replication Policy allows you to select accounts to cache in the RODC.

- Because the RODC is often placed in a lower security environment, you might not want to replicate certain attributes to it. The Filtered Attribute Set (FAS) is the set of attributes that are considered sensitive and are not replicated to an RODC. You also can limit users from seeing certain attributes by marking the attribute as confidential.

- Using security precautions such as Server Core and RODCs in your branch offices can help protect your domains from attack, but equally important to their safety are the privileges you grant to the administrators at the branch office sites.

- BranchCache is designed to optimize the link between branch offices and main offices by caching information from content servers on local computers within the branch. This reduces traffic on the WAN links, reduces response time for opening files, and improves the experience for users connecting over slow links.

Knowledge Assessment

Multiple Choice

1. What is the minimum number of users for a branch office to be considered a large size?
   a. 10
   b. 100
   c. 250
   d. 500

2. How many domain controllers should you have at large branch office running its own domain?
   a. 1
   b. 2
   c. C
   d. 5

3. What is the disadvantage of using a full domain controller?
   a. It provides the fastest performance possible.
   b. It provides the best chance of corruption.
   c. It requires additional accounts to be configured.
   d. It provides the largest surface attack.

4. Which new Windows Server 2012 R2 feature is a special installation option that creates a minimal environment for running only specific services and roles?
   a. Minimal Installation Option
   b. Server Core
   c. Server Standard
   d. Minimal Server Environment (MSE)

5. How do you manage Active Directory running on a Server Core?
   a. Install the Remote Server Administration Tools for Windows 8.1.
   b. Install the Active Directory Users Tools for Windows 8.1.
   c. Install the Remote Server Administration Tools for Windows Server 2012 R2.
   d. Use Programs and Features on a Windows 8.1 machine to load the Server Administration Tools.

6. What is the minimum forest functional level required by RODC?
   a. Windows Server 2008
   b. Windows Server 2008 R2
   c. Windows Server 2012
   d. Windows Server 2012 R2

7. How do you configure an RODC to cache passwords for selected users?
   a. Add users to the local Password group.
   b. Select the replication password for specified users in the RODC Console.
   c. Enable the Passwords for Users option in the RODC console.
   d. Use the Password Replication Policy.

8. Where do you modify the default Password Replication Policy so that the RODC caches passwords for selected users?
   a. Active Directory RODC console
   b. Active Directory Sites and Services
   c. Active Directory Users and Computers
   d. Active Directory Group Policies Management Console

9. How do you control access to remote administrators so that they can manage only the users at their site?
   a. Use the RODC console.
   b. Use the Computer Management console.
   c. Use the Delegate of Control Wizard.
   d. Use the Server Management console.

10. Which command would you use to create additional local administrators on a RODC?
    a. admin.exe
    b. dsmgmt.exe
    c. usermgt.exe
    d. compuser.exe

Best Answer

Choose the letter that corresponds to the best answer. More than one answer choice can achieve the goal. Select the BEST answer.

1. You have an attribute that you do not want replicated to the RODCs nor seen by typical authenticated users. What can you do?
   a. Hide the attribute.
   b. Mark the attribute as non-transferable.
   c. Configure the permissions for the attribute.
   d. Set the searchflag to 0×280 for the attribute.

2. You have domain controllers running Windows Server 2012 R2. You want to create a fault-tolerant solution for DHCP for a site. What can you do?
   a. Use a DHCP server.
   b. Create two scopes based on the 80/20 split scope.
   c. Establish a DHCP failover.
   d. Create a failover cluster between the branch site and the corporate office.

3. You have a site with 100 users. To make better use of the WAN link that connects to the corporate office, you want to cache web and file content. What would you recommend?
   a. Run Distributed-Cache Mode BranchCache.
   b. Run a Hosted-Cache Mode BranchCache.
   c. Run a Mixed-Cache Mode BranchCache.
   d. Run a Combined-Cache Mode BranchCache.

4. You want to make a web content cache for your HR server. What do you have to do?
   a. Install the BranchCache for Network Files role.
   b. Install the BranchCache feature.
   c. Install the Hash Publication feature.
   d. Install the BranchCache feature on machines running Windows 8.1.

5. You install a domain controller that is a global catalog server at a branch site. You want to make sure that users can log on while keeping costs to a minimum. What should you do?
   a. Enable the always logon option for the users.
   b. Enable universal group membership cashing.
   c. Load the global catalog role on another server.
   d. Install a second domain controller, and configure it as a global catalog.

Matching and Identification

1. Identify which of the following are found with large sites, medium sites, or small sites.
   _____ **a)** 1,200 users
   _____ **b)** T-1 link
   _____ **c)** 2 domain controllers at a site
   _____ **d)** 10 users
   _____ **e)** T-3 link
   _____ **f)** No domain controllers at site
   _____ **g)** 100 users
   _____ **h)** 1 domain controller at a site
   _____ **i)** 512 Kbps link

Build a List

1. In order of first to last, specify how to enable a shared folder so that it can be used with BranchCache. Not all answers will be used.
   _____ Install the BranchCache feature
   _____ Create a shared folder
   _____ Enable BranchCache on the file share using Server Manager
   _____ nstall the BranchCache for Network role service
   _____ Configure the BranchCache clients to enable BranchCache

2. In order of first to last, specify how to enable the universal group membership caching.
   _____ Enable Universal Group Membership Cashing.
   _____ Expand sites and click the desired site.
   _____ Select the domain controller to update the cache from
   _____ Open Active Directory Sites and Services
   _____ Right-click the NTDS Site Settings and choose Properties

■ Business Case Scenarios

Scenario 20-1: Designing a Branch Office

Contoso, Ltd., has recently opened a branch office in Brussels, the company's first in Europe. Although expansion is predicted, the office is currently very small, with five sales associates and a vice president in charge of the European division, none of whom have IT training or experience. The initial plan calls for the office to have seven computers: six workstations and a file server. A 1.5 Mbps WAN connection provides them with access to Active Directory Domain Services domain controllers, email servers, and corporate databases located in the company headquarters in Montreal.

However, two problems have arisen, and the IT director has assigned you to handle them. First, because of trademarking issues, it was recently decided that the European operation must run under another name. As a result, you need to create a new AD DS domain for the Brussels office and any future branches in Europe. Second, the VP in the Brussels office is not satisfied with network performance. She is complaining that logging on to the domain takes too long and that delays occur when establishing access to the North American servers.

How can you redesign the branch office network to address both of these problems without adding any additional computers or personnel to the Brussels office?

Scenario 20-2: Configuring BranchCache

You have 10 computers running Windows 8 at a branch office. After setting up BranchCache in distributed mode, you notice they are still using the slow WAN link to attempt to access files/folders. Is that a typical operation? If not, what could be causing it?

Appendix A
Exam 70-413
Designing and Implementing a Server Infrastructure

EXAM OBJECTIVE	OBJECTIVE NUMBER	LESSON NUMBER
Plan and Deploy a Server Infrastructure		
Design and Plan an Automated Server Installation Strategy	1.1	1
Implement a Server Deployment Infrastructure	1.2	2
Plan and Implement Server Upgrade and Migration	1.3	3
Plan and Deploy Virtual Machine Manager Services	1.4	4
Plan and Implement File and Storage Services	1.5	5
Design and Implement Network Infrastructure Services		
Design and Maintain a Dynamic Host Configuration Protocol (DHCP) Solution	2.1	6
Design a Name Resolution Solution Strategy	2.2	7
Design and Manage an IP Address Management Solution	2.3	8
Design and Implement Network Access Services		
Design a VPN Solution	3.1	9
Design a DirectAccess Solution	3.2	10
Design a Web Application Proxy Solution	3.3	11
Implement a Scalable Remote Access Solution	3.4	12
Design and Implement a Network Protection Solution	3.5	13
Design and Implement an Active Directory Infrastructure (Logical)		
Design a Forest and Domain Infrastructure	4.1	14
Implement a Forest and Domain Infrastructure	4.2	15
Design a Group Policy Strategy	4.3	16
Design an Active Directory Permission Model	4.4	17

(continued)

EXAM OBJECTIVE	OBJECTIVE NUMBER	LESSON NUMBER
Design and Implement an Active Directory Infrastructure (Physical)		
Design an Active Directory Sites Topology	5.1	18
Design a Domain Controller Strategy	5.2	19
Design and Implement a Branch Office Infrastructure	5.3	20

Index